BMA
mims
CONSULTATION
GUIDE

D1434120

mims
CONSULTATION
GUIDE

Written by
Raj Thakkar BSc(Hons)
MBBS MRCGP MRCP(UK)
GP, Buckinghamshire

Reviewed by
Katrina Ford MBChB MRCGP, DRCOG
GP, Worcestershire

Edited by
Paula Hensler MD
and **Hilary Kaube** MBChB

haymarket

Published by Haymarket Medical Media
LONDON

MIMS Consultation Guide
© Haymarket Medical Media, 2011

The publisher and the author have made every effort to ensure the accuracy of this book, but cannot accept responsibility or legal liability for any errors or omissions.

British Library Cataloguing in Publication Data.
A catalogue record for this book is available from the British Library.
ISBN 978-0-9566456-3-0

Published by Haymarket Medical Media
174 Hammersmith Road, London W6 7JP

Printed by Stephens & George Print Group, Merthyr Tydfil, Wales

PEFC
PEFC/16-33-254

PEFC Certified

This product is from sustainably managed forests and controlled sources

www.pefc.co.uk

Disclaimer
This book is not intended to be, nor should be considered, a substitute for professional medical advice. While the content was accurate at the time of writing, medicine evolves continuously; drugs' indications and contraindications, their side-effects and regimens change. Guidelines are published and reviewed. The readers are therefore advised to consult the product information approved for prescribing information, current guidelines and clinical procedures and to make their own enquiries of manufacturers or specialists in relation to drugs, treatments or advice.

CONTENTS

'Dr Thakkar is to be congratulated for compiling such an excellent book. This book will be extremely useful to have as a quick reference guide in consulting rooms.'

Louise Newson, BSc(Hons) MBChB(Hons) MRCP MRCGP, GP in the West Midlands

'A lot of medical information packed into a concise volume'

'A useful pocket reference for medical students and junior doctors'

Ben Riley, MA BM BCh MRCGP
GP in Oxfordshire and Professional Development Board member, Royal College of General Practitioners

'A brilliant and easy-to-use reference tool'

Diana Walters, RGN, D/Cert Independent prescriber, Nurse practitioner in Barley Surgery, Royston and Hertfordshire Urgent Care

'A useful book to invest in for both medical students and junior doctors'

Helga Magnusson, BSc, final year medical student, Warwick Medical School.

'I haven't seen all of this information included in just one book before'

'Breakdown into signs/symptoms, investigations and disease is a good way of categorising the book'

Jodie Apps, MBChB BMedSc, FY1, Heart of England NHS Foundation Trust

FOREWORD

This is the book I wish had been by my side in those early years of general practice. I am a passionate advocate of good communication between doctor and patient, but that communication must be based on sound medical knowledge. The clinical diagnostic process and the understanding of the nature of diseases and illness is still the cornerstone of good medical practice. This compact, well structured aide is comprehensive, accessible and fast. I tried internet searching and using this guide and found the latter quicker, much more accurate and focussed, allowing a deeper perusal of the subject when more time becomes available. Fundamentally, this is a working guide, not for your library, but to be on your desk or in your pocket on the wards. It is designed to help you there and then in the heat of the clinical moment. It begins with a comprehensive guide to the abbreviations now so common in medicine, which can confuse and obfuscate simple conversations and lead to potentially disastrous misunderstandings.

There follow three logical sections: signs and symptoms, investigations and diseases. Each is ordered in an intuitive A to Z format.

Take, as an example, the common general practice symptom 'angular cheilitis', usually caused by a candida infection: what does the guide say? That it might be the sign of a deficiency of iron, folate, vitamin B12 or riboflavin. The investigations section helps further and the disease section will remind you that glucagonoma is an immensely rare cause of angular cheilitis. Many of the lists just jog the memory and help paper over the cracks that all of us have in our working knowledge – using this guide we are less likely to miss that important thought that leads to the deeper clinical understanding of the patient in front of us.

The last few pages are filled with handy information on reference intervals, ECGs, scans and the like, making this a truly useful addition to the armament of any face-to-face healthcare professional and particularly to young doctors and nurses at the coal face.

Peter Tate MBE FRCGP
October 2011
Corfe Castle

About the author
Raj Thakkar BSc(Hons) MBBS MRCGP MRCP(UK) qualified from the University College London School of Medicine in 1999, after intercalating in neuroscience. He went on to train as a GP in the Oxford Deanery during which time he won the first national GP Enterprise Award.
After completing his MRCGP, Raj worked as a senior GP registrar in cardiology and completed his MRCP. He has been a GP partner since 2004. Raj is GP adviser to Haymarket Medical Media and a radio medical presenter.

Acknowledgements from the author
This book is the culmination of hours of planning, meetings and grafting. There are many people I'd like to thank, and here are just some of them. Jenny Gowans without whom this project would not have come into existence; Dr Paula Hensler who painstakingly transformed the book into what it is today; Dr Hilary Kaube, Clara Anderson, Chloe Harman and Lisa Lytle who spent hours upon hours reviewing the manuscript; Stephanie Jackson, Gillian Gould, Sarah Griffiths and Emma Platt who worked on the production; Dr Katrina Ford, whose expertise and insight proved to be priceless; above all, I'd like to thank Charlotte, my wife to be, my best friend, for her unparalleled support and understanding.

Raj Thakkar
November 2011
London

Disclaimer
The author would like to acknowledge that the advice contained in this book is the author's interpretation of current medical knowledge and evidence and represents a snapshot of the clinical guidelines and evidence at the date of publication. Readers should check the latest prescribing information and clinical guidelines to assure themselves that the advice contained herein is still correct.

MIMS Consultation Guide

PREFACE

Medicine has never been so exciting, fast moving or challenging as it is today. The ever-expanding clinical knowledge base requires healthcare professionals to deliver a high quality and evidence-based service to our patients, and we aim to achieve this standard of excellence in an efficient and timely manner. To do this, we typically consider the presenting symptoms and signs and derive a list of plausible diagnoses, organise appropriate investigations, interpret the results, and then formulate a management plan tailored to patients' individual wants and needs.

The *MIMS Consultation Guide* is designed to help you at all of these steps by listing hundreds of differential diagnoses, the salient features and treatments of nearly a thousand diseases and the uses of hundreds of investigations.

The differential diagnoses will help trigger thoughts and give you ideas about a condition that you may not yet have considered. A vast number of diseases are described in the largest chapter of the book, with notes on epidemiology, aetiology and risk factors, clinical features, complications, clinically relevant investigations and treatments. The section on investigations should prove invaluable when interpreting results. At the back of the book, you will find life support algorithms, ECGs, echocardiograms and other important information to help manage your patients.

Of course, not every condition will present with the full repertoire of clinical features or require all the tests described in the book. As with any medical textbook, the text is a guide to help you through a maze, and the clues are usually in the patient in front of you.

Whether you use the book as a learning guide, an aid on the wards or when seeing patients in the surgery and in the community, I hope the *MIMS Consultation Guide* will prove to be a resource you cannot do without.

Raj Thakkar BSc(Hons) MBBS MRCGP MRCP(UK)
November 2011
London

-ve	Negative
+ve	Positive
5-ASA	5-aminosalicylic acid
5FU	5-fluorouracil
5-HIAA	5-hydroxyindoleacetic acid
AA	Aortic aneurysm
AAA	Abdominal aortic aneurysm
ABG	Arterial blood gases
ABPI	Ankle brachial pressure index
ABPM	Ambulatory blood pressure monitoring
AC	Acromioclavicular
ACE	Angiotensin-converting enzyme
Ach	Acetylcholine
ACL	Anterior cruciate ligament
ACR	Urine albumin:creatinine ratio
ACS	Acute coronary syndrome
ACTH	Adrenocorticotrophic hormone
AD/AR	Autosomal dominant/recessive
ADEM	Acute disseminated encephalomyelitis
ADH	Antidiuretic hormone
ADHD	Attention deficit hyperactivity disorder
ADOS	Autism diagnostic observation schedule
AF	Atrial fibrillation
AFB	Acid-fast bacilli
AFP	Alphafetoprotein
AIDS	Acquired immunodeficiency syndrome
ALA	Aminolaevulinic acid
ALL	Acute lymphoblastic leukaemia
ALP	Alkaline phosphatase
Alpha-MPG	Alpha-mercaptopropionylglycine
ALS	Amyotrophic lateral sclerosis
ALT (SPGT)	Alanine aminotransferase

AMD	Age-related macular degeneration
AML	Acute myeloid leukaemia
ANA	Antinuclear antibody
ANCA	Antineutrophil cytoplasmic antibody
Anti-Sm	Anti-Smith antibodies
APKD	Adult polycystic kidney disease
APTT	Activated partial thromboplastin time
AR	Aortic regurgitation
ARB	Angiotensin-receptor blocker
ARC	AIDS-related complex
ARDS	Acute respiratory distress syndrome
ARF	Acute renal failure
ARMD	Age-related macular degeneration
AS	Aortic stenosis
ASD	Atrioseptal defect
ASH	Asymmetric septal hypertrophy
ASM	Acid sphingomyelinase
ASOT	Antistreptolysin O titre
AST	Aspartate aminotransferase
AT	Antithrombin
ATN	Acute tubular necrosis
ATP	Adenosine triphosphate
AV	Atrioventricular
AVM	Arteriovenous malformation
AVR	Aortic valve replacement
AVRT	Atrioventricular re-entry tachycardia
BBB	Bundle branch block
BCC	Basal cell carcinoma
BMD	Bone marrow density
BMI	Body mass index
BODE	BMI, obstruction FEV1, dyspnoea score, exercise performance
BPH	Benign prostatic hyperplasia

BMD	Bone mineral density
BMT	Bone marrow transplant
BP	Blood pressure
BPM	Beats per minute
BPPV	Benign paroxysmal positional vertigo
BSO	Bilateral salpingo-oophorectomy
C1-INH	C1 esterase inhibitor
Ca	Carcinoma
CA 125	Cancer antigen 125
Ca^{2+}	Calcium
CABG	Coronary artery bypass graft
CAH	Congenital adrenal hyperplasia
CAT	Cognitive analytic therapy
C botulinum	*Clostridium botulinum*
CBT	Cognitive behavioural therapy
CBT-BN	CBT for bulimia nervosa
CC	Coracoclavicular
CCB	Calcium-channel blocker
CCF	Congestive cardiac failure
CCK	Cholecystokinin
CCP	Citrullinated peptide
CDC	Centers for Disease Control and Prevention
C difficile	*Clostridium difficile*
CEA	Carcinoembryonic antigen
CF	Cystic fibrosis
CHADS$_2$	Score for stroke risk in AF – congestive heart failure, hypertension, age, diabetes mellitus, stroke symptoms previously or TIA
CHA$_2$DS$_2$-VASc	Score for stroke risk in AF – congestive heart failure, hypertension, age, diabetes mellitus, prior stroke or TIA
CHARGE	Coloboma, heart defects, atresia of choanae, retarded growth, genitourinary defects, ear defects
CHAT	Checklist for autism in toddlers
CHD	Coronary heart disease

CHOP	Cyclophosphamide, doxorubicin (hydroxydaunomycin), vincristine, (originally called oncovin), prednisolone
CIDP	Chronic inflammatory demyelinating polyneuropathy
CIN	Cervical intraepithelial neoplasia
CJD	Creutzfeldt-Jakob disease
CK	Creatine kinase
CKD	Chronic kidney disease
CLL	Chronic lymphocytic leukaemia
CLO	Campylobacter-like organism
CMML	Chronic myelomonocytic leukaemia
CMV	Cytomegalovirus
CNS	Central nervous system
CO$_2$	Carbon dioxide
COC	Combined oral contraceptive pill
COMT	Catechol-O-methyltransferase
COPD	Chronic obstructive pulmonary disease
CPAP	Continuous positive airways pressure
CREST	Calcinosis, Raynaud's phenomenon, oesophageal dysmotility, sclerodactyly and telangiectasia
CRP	C-reactive protein
CSF	Cerebrospinal fluid
CT	Computed tomography
C tetani	*Clostridium tetani*
CTG	Cardiotocograph
CT-KUB	CT scan of kidneys
CTPA	CT pulmonary angiogram
CVA	Cerebrovascular accident
CVD	Cardiovascular disease
CVP	Central venous pressure
CVS	Chorionic villus sampling
DCIS	Ductal carcinoma in situ
DEXA	Dual-emission X-ray absorptiometry
DHEA-S	Dehydroepiandrosterone sulphate

DIC	Disseminated intravascular coagulation
DIDMOAD	Diabetes insipidus, diabetes mellitus, optic atrophy and deafness
DISCO	Diagnostic interview for social and communication disorders
DKA	Diabetic ketoacidosis
D-L	Donath-Landsteiner antibody
DM	Diabetes mellitus
DMARDs	Disease-modifying antirheumatic drugs
DMSA	Dimercaptosuccinic acid
DPP-4	Dipeptidyl peptidase 4
DRE	Digital rectal examination
DU	Duodenal ulcer
DVT	Deep vein thrombosis
E:A	Early:atrial
EBV	Epstein-Barr virus
ECG	Electrocardiogram
ECG-RAD	Right axis deviation in ECG
E coli	*Escherichia coli*
ECT	Electroconvulsive therapy
ED	Erectile dysfunction
EEG	Electroencephalography
EF	Ejection fraction
eGFR	Estimated glomerular filtration rate
EGFR	Epidermal growth factor receptor
ELISA	Enzyme-linked immunosorbent assay
EMDR	Eye movement desensitisation and reprocessing
EMG	Electromyography
ENA	Extractable nuclear antigens
EPP	Extrapleural pneumonectomy
ER	Oestrogen receptor
ERCP	Endoscopic retrograde cholangiopancreatography
ERPC	Evacuation of retained products of conception
ESM	Ejection systolic murmur

ESR	Erythrocyte sedimentation rate
ETT	Endotracheal tube
ETT	Exercise tolerance test
F>M	Females affected more than males
FAP	Familial adenomatous polyposis
FBC	Full blood count
FDP	Fibrin degradation products
Fe^{3+}	Iron
FEV$_1$	Forced expiratory volume in first second
FFP	Fresh frozen plasma
FNA	Fine needle aspiration
FPC	Familial polyposis coli
FRAX®	Fracture risk assessment tool
FSH	Follicle-stimulating hormone
FVC	Forced vital capacity
G6PD	Glucose-6-phosphate dehydrogenase
GALT	Galactose-1-phosphate uridyl transferase
GCS	Glasgow coma scale
GCS	Global clinical score
GDP-1	G-patch domain protein 1
GH	Growth hormone
GHRH	Growth-hormone-releasing hormone
GI	Gastrointestinal
GIST	GI stromal tumour
GLP	Glucagon-like peptide agonist
GnRH	Gonadotropin-releasing hormone
GORD	Gastro-oesophageal reflux disease
GRA	Glucocorticoid-remediable aldosteronism
GT	Glutamyl transferase
GTN	Glyceryl trinitrate
GTT	Glucose tolerance test
GU	Genitourinary

HAART	Highly active antiretroviral treatment
HACEK	*Haemophilus spp, Actinobacillus actinomycetemcomitans, Cardiobacterium hominis, Eikenella corrodens, Kingella kingae*
HAD	Hospital anxiety and depression
HALO	Haemorrhoid artery ligation operation
HAS-BLED	Hypertension, abnormal liver/renal function, stroke history, bleeding predisposition, labile INRs, elderly, drugs/alcohol usage
HAV	Hepatitis A virus
Hb	Haemoglobin
HBcAg	Hepatitis B core antigen
HBeAg	Hepatitis B early antigen
HbM	Hb Milwaukee
HbS	Sickle cell haemoglobin
HBsAg	Hepatitis B surface antigen
HCC	Hepatocellular carcinoma
HCG	Human chorionic gonadotropin
HCM	Hypertrophic cardiomyopathy
HCV	Hepatitis C virus
HDL	High-density lipoprotein
HELLP	Haemolysis, elevated liver enzymes, low platelets
HF-PEF	Heart failure with preserved ejection fraction
HHV	Human herpes virus
HIV	Human immunodeficiency virus
HLA	Human histocompatibility leukocyte antigen
HNPCC	Hereditary non-polyposis colorectal cancer
HOCM	Hypertrophic (obstructive) cardiomyopathy
HONK	Hyperosmolar non-ketotic diabetic coma
HPOA	Hypertrophic pulmonary osteoarthropathy
HPV	Human papillomavirus
H pylori	*Helicobacter pylori*
HRCT	High-resolution computed tomography
HRT	Hormone replacement therapy
HSV	Herpes simplex virus

HUS	Haemolytic uraemic syndrome
HVS	High vaginal swab
IBD	Inflammatory bowel disease
IBS	Irritable bowel syndrome
ICD	Implantable cardioverter-defibrillator
ICP	Intracranial pressure
ICS	Inhaled corticosteroid
IGF-I	Insulin-like growth factor
IGFBP2/3	IGF building protein 2/3
IGT	Impaired glucose tolerance
IHD	Ischaemic heart disease
IM	Intramuscular
IMB	Intermenstrual bleeding
INF	Interferon alpha
INR	International normalised ratio
IOP	Intraocular pressure
ITP	Idiopathic thrombocytopenic purpura
ITU	Intensive therapy unit
IU	International unit
IUD	Intrauterine device
IUGR	Intra-uterine growth retardation
IV	Intravenous
IVC	Inferior vena cava
IVDU	IV drug use
IVI	IV infusion
IVU	IV urogram
JC virus	John Cunningham virus
JVP	Jugular venous pressure
K⁺	Potassium
kPa	Kilopascal
LABA	Long-acting beta-agonist
LAD	Left axis deviation

LAMA	Long-acting anticholinergic
LAMB	Lentigines, atrial myxomas, mucocutaneous myxomas and blue naevi
LARC	Long-acting reversible contraception
LBBB	Left bundle branch block
LCIS	Lobular carcinoma in situ
LDH	Lactate dehydrogenase
LDL	Low-density lipoprotein
LFT	Liver function test
LH	Luteinising hormone
LLETZ	Large loop excision of transformation zone
LMN	Lower motor neuron
LMP	Last menstrual period
LMWH	Low molecular weight heparin
LP	Lumbar puncture
LP-CSF	Cerebrospinal fluid in lumbar puncture
LRTI	Lower respiratory tract infection
LSE	Left sternal edge
LUTS	Lower urinary tract symptoms
LTOT	Long-term oxygen therapy
LV	Left ventricle
LVF	Left ventricular failure
LVH	Left ventricular hypertrophy
LVSD	Left ventricular systolic dysfunction
M>F	Males affected more than females
MAG-3	Mercaptoacetyltriglycine
MAGIC	Mouth and genital ulcers with inflamed cartilage
MALT	Mucosal associated lymphoid tissue
MCA	Middle cerebral artery
MCH	Mean cell haemoglobin
m-CHAT	Modified checklist for autism in toddlers
MCHC	Mean cell haemoglobin concentration
MC&S	Microscopy, culture and sensitivity

MCP	Metacarpophalangeal
MCUG	Micturating cysto-urethrogram
MCV	Mean cell volume
MDT	Multidisciplinary team
ME	Myalgic encephalomyelitis
MELAS	Mitochondrial myopathy, encephalopathy, lactic acidosis and stroke
MEN (1, 2, 2b)	Multiple endocrine neoplasia (1, 2, 2b)
Mg^{2+}	Magnesium
MGUS	Monoclonal gammopathy of undetermined significance
MI	Myocardial infarction
MIBG	Metaiodobenzylguanidine
MMR	Measles, mumps, rubella
MMSE	Mini mental state examination
MND	Motor neuron disease
MODY	Maturity onset diabetes of the young
MPS 1	Mucopolysaccharidosis I
MR	Mitral regurgitation
MR	Magnetic resonance
MRA	Magnetic resonance angiogram
MRCP	Magnetic resonance cholangiopancreatography
MRI	Magnetic resonance imaging
MRSA	Meticillin-resistant *Staphylococcus aureus*
MS	Multiple sclerosis
MSU	Midstream urine
MVP	Mitral valve prolapse
Na$^+$	Sodium
NAD	Nicotinamide adenine dinucleotide
NADH	Nicotinamide adenine dinucleotide hydride
NADPH	NAD phosphate
NAI	Non-accidental injury
NASH	Non-alcoholic steatohepatitis
NBM	Nil by mouth

NIHL	Noise-induced hearing loss
NIV	Non-invasive ventilation
NPA	Nasopharyngeal aspirates
NPV	Negative predictive value
NSAID	Non-steroidal anti-inflammatory drug
NSCLC	Non-small cell lung cancer
NTproBNP	N-terminal pro b-type natriuretic peptide
O_2	Oxygen
OA	Osteoarthritis
OCD	Obsessive compulsive disorder
OCT	Optical coherence tomography
OGD	Oesophagogastroduodenoscopy
OGTT	Oral glucose tolerance test
ORT	Oral rehydration therapy
OT	Occupational therapy
P2	Pulmonary component of second heart sound
PaO_2	Partial pressure of oxygen in arterial blood
PAD	Peripheral artery disease
PAN	Polyarteritis nodosa
PAPP-A	Pregnancy-associated plasma protein A
PARP	Poly (ADP-ribose) polymerase
PBC	Primary biliary cirrhosis
PBG	Porphobilinogen
PCB	Postcoital bleeding
PCI	Percutaneous coronary intervention
PCKD	Polycystic kidney disease
PCL	Posterior cruciate ligament
PCOS	Polycystic ovary syndrome
PCP	*Pneumocystis carinii* pneumonia
PCR	Polymerase chain reaction
PD	Parkinson's disease
PDA	Patent ductus arteriosus

PDE5	Phosphodiesterase type 5
PE	Pulmonary embolism
PEFR	Peak expiratory flow rate
PEG	Percutaneous endoscopic gastrostomy
PET-CT	Positron emission tomography-computed tomography
PFAPA	Periodic fever, aphthous ulceration, pharyngitis, adenitis
PFO	Patent foramen ovale
PGL	Persistent generalised lymphadenopathy
PHQ9	Patient health questionnaire
PID	Pelvic inflammatory disease
PIPJ	Proximal interphalangeal joint
PKU	Phenylketonuria
Plts	Platelets
PMR	Polymyalgia rheumatica
PNET	Primitive neuroectodermal tumour
PO$_4$$^{3-}$	Phosphate
POEMS	Polyneuropathy, organomegaly, endocrinopathy, monoclonal gammopathy and skin changes
PPH	Primary pulmonary hypertension
PPI	Proton pump inhibitor
PPV	Positive predictive value
PR	Per rectum
PRN	Pro re nata (as required)
PSA	Prostate-specific antigen
PT	Prothrombin
PTH	Parathyroid hormone
PTSD	Post traumatic stress disorder
PUO	Pyrexia of unknown origin
PUVA	Psoralen + UVA
PV	Per vaginam
PVD	Peripheral vascular disease
PVH	Pulmonary venous hypertension
RA	Rheumatoid arthritis

RAD	Right access deviation
RAST	Radioallergosorbent test
RBBB	Right bundle branch block
RBC	Red blood cell
RDA	Recommended daily allowance
RF	Rheumatoid factor
RIF	Right iliac fossa
ROM	Range of movement
ROTI	Related organ or tissue impairment
RPR	Rapid plasma reagin test
RR	Relative risk or risk ratio
RSV	Respiratory syncytial virus
RTA	Renal tubular acidosis
RUQ	Right upper quadrant
RV	Right ventricle
RVH	Right ventricular hypertrophy
RWMA	Regional wall motion abnormalities
SABA	Short-acting beta-agonist
SAH	Subarachnoid haemorrhage
SALT	Speech and language therapy
SAMA	Short-acting anticholinergic
SCC	Squamous cell carcinoma
SCID	Severe combined immunodeficiency
SCLC	Small cell lung cancer
sFlt-1	Soluble fms-like tyrosine kinase 1
SHBG	Sex hormone binding globulin
SIADH	Syndrome of inappropriate antidiuretic hormone hypersecretion
SLE	Systemic lupus erythematosus
SMART	Single maintenance and reliever therapy
SNRI	Serotonin noradrenaline reuptake inhibitor
SOB	Shortness of breath
SPD	Symphisis pubis dysfunction

SPECT	Single photon emission computed tomography
SSPE	Subacute sclerosing panencephalitis
SSRI	Selective serotonin reuptake inhibitor
Staph	Staphylococcus
STEMI	ST elevation myocardial infarction
STI	Sexually transmitted infection
Strep	Streptococcus
SVCO	Superior vena cava obstruction
SVT	Supraventricular tachycardia
TAHBSO	Total abdominal hysterectomy and bilateral salpingo-oopherectomy
TB	Tuberculosis
TBG	Thyroxine binding globulin
TCA	Tricyclic antidepressant
TED	Thromboembolus deterrent
TFTs	Thyroid function tests
TG	Triglyceride
TIA	Transient ischaemic attack
TKR	Total knee replacement
TM	Tympanic membrane
TMJ	Temporomandibular joint
TNF	Tumour necrosis factor
TOE	Transoesophageal echocardiography
TPN	Total parenteral nutrition
TR	Tricuspid regurgitation
TSH	Thyroid stimulating hormone
TTE	Trans-thoracic echocardiography
TTG	Tissue transglutaminase
TTP	Thrombotic thrombocytopenic purpura
TURP	Transurethral resection of the prostate
TURBT	Transurethral resection of bladder tumour
TVUSS	Transvaginal ultrasound
U&E	Urea and electrolytes

uE3	Unconjugated oestriol
UKMEC	UK medical eligibility criteria
ULN	Upper limit of normal
UMN	Upper motor neuron
UPSI	Unprotected sexual intercourse
URTI	Upper respiratory tract infection
USS	Ultrasound scan
UTI	Urinary tract infection
VDRL	Venereal Diseases Research Laboratory
VEGF	Vascular endothelial growth factor
VF	Ventricular fibrillation
VLDL	Very low density lipoprotein
VMA	Vanillylmandelic acid
VSD	Ventricular septal defect
VT	Ventricular tachycardia
VTE	Venous thromboembolism
VTEC	Verotoxin-producing *Escherichia coli*
vWF	Von Willebrand factor
VZIG	Varicella zoster immunoglobulin
WBC	White blood cell
WCC	White cell count
WHO	World Health Organization
WPW	Wolff-Parkinson-White syndrome

SIGNS & SYMPTOMS

Abdominal bruising

⚘ DIFFERENTIAL DIAGNOSES
Trauma, haematoma, retroperitoneal haemorrhage (eg pancreatitis, AAA [rupture/dissection], ruptured spleen), clotting disorder

Abdominal bruit

⚘ DIFFERENTIAL DIAGNOSES
Renal artery stenosis, AAA, iliac vessel atheroma, liver disorders (haemangioma/arteriovenous malformation, tumour, hepatitis), chronic bowel ischaemia

Abdominal distension

⚘ DIFFERENTIAL DIAGNOSES
Fat (eg Cushing's syndrome), faeces, flatus (eg IBS, small bowel bacterial overgrowth), bowel obstruction, intussusception, megacolon, fluid (ascites, blood eg ruptured AAA/spleen), fetus, ovarian cyst/carcinoma

Abdominal mass

See also
— *Hepatomegaly*
— *Splenomegaly*
— *Abdominal distension*

⚘ DIFFERENTIAL DIAGNOSES
GI: faeces, appendix mass, Crohn's granuloma, volvulus, diverticular abscess, megacolon, tumour; pancreatic: abscess, pseudocyst, tumour; renal: cyst, polycystic kidney, hydronephrosis, renal transplant (often placed in iliac fossa); bladder: urinary retention, tumour; gynaecological: uterine fibroid, ovarian cyst, tumour, fetus; other: AAA, lymphadenopathy, hernia

Abdominal pain

⚘ DIFFERENTIAL DIAGNOSES
Epigastric: GORD, gastritis, peptic ulcer disease, pancreatitis, biliary colic, gastric carcinoma, hiatus hernia, oesophagitis, pericarditis; right upper quadrant: biliary colic, Budd-Chiari syndrome, cholecystitis, cholangiocarcinoma, cholangitis, hepatitis, liver tumour, liver congestion (eg right heart failure); left upper quadrant: bowel infarction, splenic rupture/infarct; central: leaking/dissecting AAA, bowel obstruction, mesenteric artery occlusion, constipation, intussusception, IBD, gastroenteritis; flank: pyelonephritis, renal mass, renal colic; right iliac fossa: mesenteric adenitis, appendicitis, caecal mass, diverticulitis, ruptured/torted ovarian cyst, ectopic pregnancy, PID; left iliac fossa: diverticulitis, ruptured/torted ovarian cyst, ectopic pregnancy, PID, carcinoma, colitis; suprapubic: cystitis, miscarriage, uteritis, cervical cancer, endometriosis, adenomyosis, PID; other: IBS, pneumonia, MI, shingles, radiculopathy, acute intermittent porphyria,

DKA, lead poisoning, sickle cell crisis, Addisonian crisis, paroxysmal nocturnal haemoglobinuria, paroxysmal cold haemoglobinuria, familial Mediterranean fever, testicular torsion, Meckel's diverticulum, mumps, Henoch-Schönlein purpura, lactose intolerance, parasitic infections, Hirschsprung's disease, pica, hypercalcaemia, altitude sickness, carcinomatosis, Behçet's disease

Abdominal pain (pregnancy)

See also
— *Abdominal pain*

⚘ DIFFERENTIAL DIAGNOSES
Ectopic pregnancy, fetal pressure, labour, Braxton-Hicks contractions, placental abruption, fibroid infarction (red degeneration), amnionitis, ovarian cyst haemorrhage/torsion, round ligament pain, salpingitis, tubo-ovarian abscess, trophoblastic disease, adnexal torsion, uterine torsion/rupture, symphysis pubis dysfunction (SPD), rectus sheath haematoma, polyhydramnios, chorioamnionitis, cholestasis of pregnancy, fatty liver (acute) of pregnancy

Abdominal veins (distended)

⚘ DIFFERENTIAL DIAGNOSES
IVC obstruction (flow in superficial abdominal veins towards the heart), portal hypertension (flow in superficial abdominal veins away from umbilicus – caput medusae)

Absent ankle/knee jerks with upgoing plantars

⚘ DIFFERENTIAL DIAGNOSES
Friedreich's ataxia, tabes dorsalis, subacute combined degeneration of the spinal cord, MND, pellagra, thiamine deficiency, conus medullaris lesion, peripheral neuropathy with cervical myelopathy

Acanthosis nigricans

⚘ DIFFERENTIAL DIAGNOSES
Malignancy (gastric, oesophagus, bladder, colon, lung or kidney cancer), DM, acromegaly, PCOS, Prader-Willi syndrome, iatrogenic (corticosteroids)

Acute confusional state (delirium)

⚘ DIFFERENTIAL DIAGNOSES
Iatrogenic, drug withdrawal, infection, constipation, urinary retention, alcohol intoxication or withdrawal, vitamin deficiency, thyroid disturbance, electrolyte disturbance, head injury, stroke, cerebral tumour/abscess, cardiac failure, MI, hypoxia, seizure, hypo/hyperglycaemia, Addisonian crisis, Cushing's disease, postoperative, poisoning, drug abuse, migraine, SLE/cerebral lupus,

hepatorenal disease, parathyroid disease, methae-moglobinaemia, malignant hypertension, relapsing polychondritis, altitude sickness

Akathisia

⚕ DIFFERENTIAL DIAGNOSES
Parkinsonism, iatrogenic (eg SSRIs, SNRIs, antipsychotics, metoclopramide, prochlorperazine), drug withdrawal (opiates)

Alopecia

⚕ DIFFERENTIAL DIAGNOSES
See *Diseases, alopecia*

Ambiguous genitalia

⚕ DIFFERENTIAL DIAGNOSES
Androgen-secreting tumours, CAH, excess endogenous maternal androgens during pregnancy, androgen insensitivity (testicular feminisation), Leydig cell aplasia, testicular dysplasia, 5 alpha-reductase deficiency (reduced conversion of testosterone to dihydrotestosterone), aromatase deficiency (reduced conversion of androgens to oestrogens), true hermaphrodite (one testicle, one ovary)

Amenorrhoea (primary)

See also
— *Amenorrhoea (secondary)*

⚕ DIFFERENTIAL DIAGNOSES
Imperforate hymen (or other structural defects), ovarian agenesis (Turner's syndrome), testicular feminisation, Kallmann's syndrome

Amenorrhoea (secondary)

⚕ DIFFERENTIAL DIAGNOSES
Pregnancy, breastfeeding, menopause, PCOS, hyperprolactinaemia, premature ovarian failure, hyperthyroidism, anorexia nervosa, stress, hormonal contraception/levonorgestrel intrauterine system, Asherman's syndrome (uterine adhesions), virilisation, autoimmune liver disease, polyendocrine syndrome, coeliac disease, hypothalamic/pituitary dysfunction (eg Sheehan's syndrome), craniopharyngioma

Anal pain

⚕ DIFFERENTIAL DIAGNOSES
Anal fissure, haemorrhoids, abscess, proctitis, IBD, constipation, diarrhoea, foreign body, candida, herpes, trauma, proctalgia fugax (anal sphincter spasm), levator ani syndrome, tumour, prostatitis, coccydynia, endometriosis, PID, fistula

Anal swelling

⚕ DIFFERENTIAL DIAGNOSES
Abscess, fistula, candida, trauma, haemorrhoids, tumour, infection, haematoma, rectal prolapse

Angioedema

⚕ DIFFERENTIAL DIAGNOSES
Idiopathic, iatrogenic (eg ACE inhibitors), allergy, congenital or acquired C1 esterase inhibitor deficiency (or dysfunction), lymphoproliferative disorders

Angioid streaks

⚕ DIFFERENTIAL DIAGNOSES
Pseudoxanthoma elasticum, Paget's disease of the bone, sickle cell anaemia, thalassaemia, DM, haemochromatosis, Ehlers-Danlos syndrome, hypercalcaemia, acromegaly, neurofibromatosis, tuberous sclerosis, Sturge-Weber syndrome, lead poisoning, familial hyperphosphataemia, ITP

Angular cheilitis

⚕ DIFFERENTIAL DIAGNOSES
Deficiency: iron, vitamin B_{12}, folate, riboflavin. Oral candidiasis, glucagonoma

Ankle oedema

⚕ DIFFERENTIAL DIAGNOSES
See *limb swelling*

Anorexia

⚕ DIFFERENTIAL DIAGNOSES
Anorexia and bulimia nervosa, pain, nausea, iatrogenic (eg drugs, radiotherapy), infection (eg TB, Kawasaki disease), cardiac failure, malignancy, hepatorenal disease, thyroid disease, Addison's disease, DKA, gallstone disease, GORD, gastritis, IBD, coeliac disease, pancreatitis, hyponatraemia, Fanconi syndrome, drug or alcohol abuse, stress, bereavement, depression, anxiety

Anorgasmia

⚕ DIFFERENTIAL DIAGNOSES
Advancing age, iatrogenic (eg hysterectomy, prostatectomy, SSRIs, antihistamines, antihypertensives), MS, DM, spinal cord injury, dyspareunia, relationship difficulties, stress, anxiety, depression, embarrassment, difficult past experiences, excess alcohol

Anosmia

⚕ DIFFERENTIAL DIAGNOSES
URTI, rhinitis, sinusitis, deviated nasal septum, nasal

polyp, nasal tumour, smoking, solvent abuse, advancing age, skull fracture, frontal lobe meningioma, Kallmann's syndrome, Foster Kennedy syndrome, Paget's disease of the bone, radiotherapy, DM, sarcoid, Klinefelter's syndrome, Korsakoff's psychosis, sicca syndrome, dementia, Parkinson's disease, Huntington's disease

Anuria

⚕ DIFFERENTIAL DIAGNOSES

Hypovolaemia, renal failure, urinary tract obstruction (eg blocked catheter, stricture, prostatism, stones), UTI

Aphthous ulcers

⚕ DIFFERENTIAL DIAGNOSES

See *Diseases, recurrent aphthous ulceration*

Arthralgia

⚕ DIFFERENTIAL DIAGNOSES

See *joint pain (arthralgia)*

Arthritis

⚕ DIFFERENTIAL DIAGNOSES

OA, RA, SLE, juvenile idiopathic arthritis, gout, pseudogout, seronegative arthritis (Reiter's syndrome, psoriatic, enteropathic, ankylosing spondylitis), septic, traumatic

Ascites

⚕ DIFFERENTIAL DIAGNOSES

Right/congestive cardiac failure, constrictive pericarditis, restrictive cardiomyopathy, tricuspid stenosis, pulmonary hypertension, tumour (eg liver, GI, pancreas, mesothelioma, metastatic, Meig's syndrome), nephrotic syndrome, TB, cirrhosis, portal vein occlusion, Budd-Chiari syndrome, retroperitoneal fibrosis, pancreatitis, ovarian hyperstimulation syndrome, hypothyroidism, galactosaemia, kwashiorkor, wet beriberi

Asterixis (flapping tremor/liver flap)

⚕ DIFFERENTIAL DIAGNOSES

Liver failure, respiratory failure, hypoglycaemia, CKD, barbiturates overdose, brainstem disorders

Ataxia

⚕ DIFFERENTIAL DIAGNOSES

CVA, MS, ADEM, tumour (eg cerebellar pontine angle tumour, including paraneoplastic syndromes), trauma, hypothyroidism, Friedreich's ataxia, ataxia-telangiectasia, Niemann-Pick disease, alcohol intoxication, Wernicke's encephalopathy, Charcot-Marie-Tooth disease, postviral, cerebral palsy, spinocerebellar degeneration, pontine lesion, cerebellar

lesion, multisystem atrophy, Wilson's disease, relapsing polychondritis, abetalipoproteinaemia, Refsum's disease, Angelman syndrome, Kearns-Sayre syndrome, cat-scratch disease, fragile X syndrome, Miller Fisher syndrome, Hartnup disease, altitude sickness

Athetosis (continuous, slow, writhing movements)

⚕ DIFFERENTIAL DIAGNOSES

Cerebral palsy, tumour, stroke, Wilson's disease, metabolic errors (eg PKU, Tay-Sachs disease), Huntington's disease, hepatic encephalopathy, Lesch-Nyhan syndrome

Back pain

⚕ DIFFERENTIAL DIAGNOSES

Muscular/ligamentous damage, disc prolapse, disc degeneration, OA, trauma, osteoporotic crush fracture, radiculopathy, scoliosis, ankylosing spondylitis, spina bifida, Schmorl's nodes, spondylolisthesis, lumbar spine stenosis, tumour (eg myeloma, ALL, pancreatic, metastases), PMR, shingles, pneumonia, abscess, TB, aortic dissection, AAA, meningococcal disease, pancreatitis, peptic ulcer, cholecystitis, biliary colic, renal colic, pyelonephritis, paroxysmal cold haemoglobinuria

Beau's lines (transverse nail depression)

⚕ DIFFERENTIAL DIAGNOSES

Systemic illness, trauma, stress

Behavioural change

See also
— *Acute confusional state (delirium)*

⚕ DIFFERENTIAL DIAGNOSES

Anxiety, agitation, depression, psychosis, personality disorder, iatrogenic, drug withdrawal, constipation, pain, head injury, CVA, hypoxia, epilepsy, cerebral tumour, anaemia, sepsis, metabolic, hormonal and electrolyte disturbance, porphyria

Bilateral hilar lymphadenopathy

⚕ DIFFERENTIAL DIAGNOSES

Sarcoid, TB, carcinoma, lymphoma, silicosis ('egg shell' calcification), histoplasmosis

Bone pain

⚕ DIFFERENTIAL DIAGNOSES

Fracture, Paget's disease of the bone, tumour (osteoid osteoma, primary, myeloma, leukaemia, metastases), iatrogenic (eg bisphosphonates), osteomyelitis, arthritis, sickle cell crisis, osteomalacia, Gaucher's disease

Borborygmi (abdominal gurgling sounds)

⚕ DIFFERENTIAL DIAGNOSES
IBS, excessive wind, bowel obstruction, normal digestion, coeliac disease, lactose intolerance

Bowel habit, altered

See also
— *Constipation*
— *Diarrhoea*

⚕ DIFFERENTIAL DIAGNOSES
Malignancy (eg colorectal carcinoma, carcinoid, lymphoma, metastases), endocrine (eg thyroid or parathyroid disease, Addison's disease), iatrogenic (eg opiates, cholecystectomy), change in diet, gastro- enteritis, pseudomembranous colitis, radiation colitis, IBS, food allergy, IBD, diverticular disease, pancreatic insufficiency, intermittent volvulus, bowel obstruction, electrolyte disturbance, spinal cord lesion, immobility, depression, anxiety

Bowel sounds (overactive)

See also
— *Diseases, small bowel obstruction*
— *Diseases, large bowel obstruction*

⚕ DIFFERENTIAL DIAGNOSES
Bowel obstruction, constipation, infection, GI bleed, food allergy

Bowel sounds (reduced)

⚕ DIFFERENTIAL DIAGNOSES
Sleep, paralytic ileus (potential causes: vascular disease, electrolyte imbalance, sepsis, megacolon, trauma, post-surgery), peritonitis, bowel infarction, iatrogenic (eg anticholinergics, phenothiazines, opiates, radiotherapy)

BP discrepancy (between left and right arm >15mmHg)

⚕ DIFFERENTIAL DIAGNOSES
Congenital anomaly, aortic dissection, arterial thrombosis, coarctation of the aorta, Williams syndrome, subclavian steal syndrome, Takayasu's arteritis, thoracic outlet syndrome

Bradycardia

See also
— *Relative bradycardia*

⚕ DIFFERENTIAL DIAGNOSES
Advancing age, hypertension, iatrogenic (eg beta-blockers, non-dihydropyridine CCBs, digoxin, lithium, cardiac ablation), inferior MI, heart block, sick sinus syndrome, carotid sinus hypersensitivity, congenital heart disease, myocarditis, sleep apnoea, haemochromatosis, athletes, hypothyroidism, cholestatic jaundice, electrolyte disturbance, hypothermia, raised ICP, organophosphate poisoning

Breast lump

⚕ DIFFERENTIAL DIAGNOSES
Benign fibrous mammary dysplasia (cyclical), nodularity, fibrocystic disease, malignancy, duct ectasia, galactocoele, abscess, fat necrosis, fibroadenoma, cyst, lipoma

Breast pain (mastalgia)

⚕ DIFFERENTIAL DIAGNOSES
Cyclical mastalgia, pregnancy, breastfeeding, puberty, abscess, mastitis, malignancy, trauma, duct ectasia

Breath sounds (crackles/crepitations)

⚕ DIFFERENTIAL DIAGNOSES
Secretions, pulmonary oedema, pulmonary fibrosis, COPD, asthma, LRTI, CF, bronchiolitis, bronchiectasis, pulmonary contusion, tumour

Breath sounds (reduced)

⚕ DIFFERENTIAL DIAGNOSES
Poor respiratory effort, obesity, low respiratory rate, upper airway obstruction (foreign body, croup, epiglottitis, angioedema), lower airways obstruction (tumour, foreign body), severe COPD, asthma, pulmonary collapse, pleural effusion, empyema, fibrosis, mesothelioma, bullae, pneumothorax

Breathlessness (acute)

⚕ DIFFERENTIAL DIAGNOSES
Upper airway obstruction (foreign body, croup, epiglottitis, angioedema), pneumothorax, pulmonary embolus, exacerbation of COPD/asthma, influenza, LRTI, sepsis, acute ventricular failure, cardiac tamponade, arrhythmia, methaemoglobinaemia, acidosis (eg uraemia, DKA), altitude sickness, panic attack

Breathlessness (chronic)

⚕ DIFFERENTIAL DIAGNOSES
Poor physical fitness, obesity, anaemia, COPD, asthma, fibrosis, allergic bronchopulmonary aspergillosis, pleural effusion, pulmonary hypertension, chronic pulmonary thromboembolic disease, CHD, ventricular failure, cardiomyopathy, cardiac valve disease, pericardial effusion, arrhythmia, hyperthyroidism, neuromuscular disease, methaemoglobinaemia, relapsing polychondritis

Bronchial breathing

❂ DIFFERENTIAL DIAGNOSES

Lobar pneumonia, massive pleural effusion with atelectasis, complete atelectasis, pulmonary cavitation, tension pneumothorax, tumour. False +ve with auscultation over tracheobronchial tree

Bruising

❂ DIFFERENTIAL DIAGNOSES

Trauma, abuse, clotting disorder/thrombocytopenia (eg ALL, ITP, von Willebrand's disease, DIC), HUS, advancing age, iatrogenic (eg steroids), Cushing's syndrome, vasculitis, collagen disorders, chronic liver disease, scurvy, internal retroperitoneal bleeding (eg pancreatitis, leaking AAA)

Bulbar palsy

❂ DIFFERENTIAL DIAGNOSES

See *Diseases, bulbar palsy*

Bullae

❂ DIFFERENTIAL DIAGNOSES

Insect bite, bullous eczema, photosensitive dermatitis, iatrogenic (eg barbiturates), burn, trauma, pemphigus vulgaris, pemphigoid, dermatitis herpetiformis, bullous impetigo, SLE, psoriasis, epidermolysis bullosa, linear IgA disease, erythema multiforme, toxic epidermal necrolysis, orf, cutaneous porphyria

Cachexia

See also
— *Anorexia*

❂ DIFFERENTIAL DIAGNOSES

Malnutrition, malabsorption, drug or alcohol abuse, cardiac failure, COPD, malignancy, dementia, AIDS, TB, CF, Addison's disease, SLE, IBD, sarcoid, brucellosis, endocarditis, kala-azar, trypanosomiasis, hyperthyroidism, severe burns/trauma

Café au lait spots

❂ DIFFERENTIAL DIAGNOSES

Idiopathic, neurofibromatosis, tuberous sclerosis, McCune Albright syndrome, Fanconi anaemia, Russell-Silver syndrome

Calf swelling

❂ DIFFERENTIAL DIAGNOSES

Ruptured Baker's cyst, cellulitis, DVT, pseudohypertrophy (Duchenne muscular dystrophy), trauma, ruptured gastrocnemius, muscle haematoma, peripheral oedema (eg cardiac failure), venous insufficiency, compartment syndrome

Cardiac apex beat

❂ DIFFERENTIAL DIAGNOSES

Heaving: forceful undisplaced apex causing LVH, seen in pressure overloaded conditions eg, systemic hypertension, aortic stenosis; thrusting: diffuse displaced apex caused by volume overload eg, aortic regurgitation; absent: obesity, COPD, pneumothorax, pericardial effusion, pleural effusion, dextrocardia (apex may be palpable on right chest wall; displaced: left/right ventricular enlargement, pectus excavatum; tapping: represents loud S1 due to mitral stenosis; double impulse: ventricular aneurysm, HOCM; dyskinetic: post MI

Carotid bruit

❂ DIFFERENTIAL DIAGNOSES

Atherosclerosis, arteriovenous malformation, radiation from aortic stenosis, radiotherapy, thoracic outlet syndrome, tumour

Cataract

❂ DIFFERENTIAL DIAGNOSES

See *Diseases, cataract*

Cavitary lung lesion

❂ DIFFERENTIAL DIAGNOSES

Abscess, pneumonia (eg staphylococcal and klebsiella), TB, fungal infections, hydatid cyst, carcinoma, Wegener's granulomatosis, rheumatoid nodules, pulmonary infarction

Chest expansion (reduced)

❂ DIFFERENTIAL DIAGNOSES

Unilateral: pneumothorax, fibrosis, chest wall abnormalities, flail chest, consolidation, malignancy, pleural effusion; bilateral: COPD, asthma, fibrosis, obesity, neuromuscular disease (eg limb girdle dystrophy), Guillain-Barré syndrome, MND, MS, ADEM, myasthenia gravis, iatrogenic (eg suxamethonium), organophosphate poisoning

Chest pain

See also
— *Breast pain (mastalgia)*

❂ DIFFERENTIAL DIAGNOSES

Angina, acute coronary syndrome, aortic dissection, pericarditis, pleurisy, pneumonia, pneumothorax, pneumomediastinum, PE, odynophagia, oesophagitis, GORD, oesophageal spasm, biliary colic, cholecystitis, hepatic congestion, tumour, herpes zoster, cellulitis, skin abscess, rib contusion/fracture, chostochondritis, radiculopathy, trauma, Bornholm disease, familial Mediterranean fever.

Chest wall deformity

⚕ DIFFERENTIAL DIAGNOSES

Trauma, pectus excavatum (funnel chest), pectus carinatum (pigeon chest), Harrison's sulcus (eg asthma, rickets), kyphosis (eg osteoporosis, TB, ankylosing spondylitis), scoliosis, bony malignancy, COPD, asthma

Cheyne-Stokes respiration (oscillating breathing with apnoea and tachypnoea)

⚕ DIFFERENTIAL DIAGNOSES

Terminal illness, opiate abuse, raised ICP, CVA, cardiac failure, altitude sickness, encephalitis

Child with a limp

See also
— *Arthritis*
— *Gait abnormalities*
— *Joint pain (arthralgia)*
— *Groin pain*
— *Limb pain*

⚕ DIFFERENTIAL DIAGNOSES

Trauma, non-accidental injury, plantar foreign body, congenital dislocation of the hip, Perthes' disease, slipped upper femoral epiphysis, transient synovitis, septic arthritis, juvenile idiopathic arthritis, myopathy, neuropathy, cerebral palsy, hypotonia, tumour, hypermobility syndrome, Osgood-Schlatter's disease, osteopetrosis, polio, sickle cell crisis

Chorea

⚕ DIFFERENTIAL DIAGNOSES

Extremes of age, hereditary, Huntington's chorea, Wilson's disease, Friedreich's ataxia, ataxia-telangiectasia, CVA, MS, malignancy, neuroacanthocytosis, chorea gravidarum, SLE, hyperthyroidism, hypoparathyroidism, polycythaemia, acute intermittent porphyria, COC, rheumatic fever (Sydenham's chorea/St Vitus' dance), syphilis, Lyme disease, HIV, CJD, encephalitis, Behçet's disease, alcohol abuse, carbon monoxide poisoning, Lesch-Nyhan disease, phenylketonuria, hepatic encephalopathy, vasculitis, iatrogenic (eg TCA, neuroleptics, levodopa, phenytoin)

Clasp-knife rigidity

⚕ DIFFERENTIAL DIAGNOSES

Corticospinal tract lesion

Claw hand

⚕ DIFFERENTIAL DIAGNOSES

Congenital, genetic, ulnar nerve lesion (distal), C8-T1 spinal cord lesion (eg polio, syringomyelia), brachial plexus lesion (eg trauma, Pancoast tumour), contracture, RA, Charcot-Marie-Tooth disease

Clicking joint

⚕ DIFFERENTIAL DIAGNOSES

Idiopathic, arthritis, loose intraarticular body, meniscal tear, congenital dislocation of the hip

Clonus

⚕ DIFFERENTIAL DIAGNOSES

Suggestive of UMN lesion: CVA, MS, cerebral palsy, cervical myelopathy, spinal cord insult, spastic paraparesis, Brown-Sequard syndrome, meningitis, Huntington's chorea, CJD

Cognitive impairment

See also
— *Acute confusional state (delirium)*

⚕ DIFFERENTIAL DIAGNOSES

Depression, dementia, anaemia, infection, hypothyroidism, malignancy, hypercalcaemia, hypoglycaemia, cerebral palsy, CVA, head injury, liver failure, CKD, drug or alcohol abuse, normal pressure hydrocephalus, vasculitis, malnutrition, genetic disorders, iatrogenic

Colic

⚕ DIFFERENTIAL DIAGNOSES

Obstructed lumen (eg bowel, biliary tree, renal tract), infantile colic

Constipation

⚕ DIFFERENTIAL DIAGNOSES

Low-fibre diet, pregnancy, stool holding (eg behavioural, pain due to anal fissure), iatrogenic (eg TCA, CCBs, opiates, ferrous salts, aluminium salts), dehydration, dementia, Parkinson's disease, CVA, Hirschsprung's disease, diverticulosis, malignancy, hypercalcaemia, hypothyroidism, CF, spinal cord injury, Bartter's syndrome

Cough

⚕ DIFFERENTIAL DIAGNOSES

Smoking, URTI, LRTI, TB, helminthic infection, typhoid fever, typhus, whooping cough, *Pneumocystis carinii* pneumonia, aspergillus, croup, epiglottitis, postnasal drip, pulmonary abscess, postviral cough, foreign body, GORD, asthma/COPD, allergy, allergic bronchopulmonary aspergillosis, extrinsic allergic alveolitis, malignancy (eg bronchogenic carcinoma, eosinophilic leukaemia), pulmonary oedema, CF, vocal cord injury/palsy, interstitial lung disease, pulmonary hamartoma, idiopathic pulmonary fibrosis, bronchiolitis, bronchiectasis, iatrogenic (eg ACE inhibitors), Kartagener's syndrome, mitral stenosis, pericarditis, altitude sickness, psychogenic, Gilles de la Tourette syndrome

Cramp

☺ DIFFERENTIAL DIAGNOSES
Idiopathic, ischaemia, trauma, exercise, prolonged muscle contraction, hypocalcaemia, MND, nerve compression/injury, myopathy, iatrogenic (eg diuretics, CCBs, lithium, beta-agonists), pregnancy, CKD, liver disease

Crying, inconsolable (baby)

☺ DIFFERENTIAL DIAGNOSES
Hunger, thirst, dirty nappy, pain (eg earache, colic, wind, trauma, teething), nappy/clothes too tight, too hot/cold, food allergy, parental separation, child maltreatment, fatigue, sepsis

Cyanosis (central)

☺ DIFFERENTIAL DIAGNOSES
Hypoventilation, hypoxia, high altitude, polycythaemia rubra vera, right to left cardiac shunt, status asthmaticus, exacerbation of COPD, severe chronic lung disease, pulmonary hypertension, pleural effusion, PE, pneumonia, SVCO, status epilepticus, methaemoglobinaemia, choanal atresia

Cyanosis (peripheral)

See also
— Cyanosis (central)

☺ DIFFERENTIAL DIAGNOSES
Arterial thrombosis, Raynaud's phenomenon, shock

Dactylitis

☺ DIFFERENTIAL DIAGNOSES
Sickle cell anaemia, gonorrhoea, seronegative arthritis, sarcoid, TB, leprosy

Deafness

☺ DIFFERENTIAL DIAGNOSES
Conductive: foreign body (eg wax), otitis externa, acute otitis media, glue ear, chronic suppurative otitis media, cholesteatoma, otosclerosis, osteopetrosis, Paget's disease of the bone, ruptured tympanic membrane, Wegener's granulomatosis; sensorineural: noise-induced hearing loss (NIHL), VIIIth cranial nerve palsy, acoustic neuroma, postnasal space tumour, MS, ADEM, CVA, advancing age (presbycusis), head injury, Ménière's disease, iatrogenic,

infection (eg meningitis, encephalitis, mumps), congenital infection (eg rubella, toxoplasmosis), Alport's syndrome, Crigler-Najjar syndrome, DIDMOAD, facioscapulohumeral dystrophy, Jervell and Lange-Nielsen syndrome (see Diseases, long QT syndrome), Kallmann's syndrome, Kearns-Sayre syndrome, Laurence-Moon-Biedl syndrome, Pendred's syndrome, Refsum's disease, relapsing polychondritis, Tay-Sachs disease, Waardenburg syndrome

Delusions

See also
— Acute confusional state (delirium)

☺ DIFFERENTIAL DIAGNOSES
Schizophrenia, severe depression, mania, dementia, alcohol abuse, Othello syndrome (delusional jealousy)

Desquamation (skin)

☺ DIFFERENTIAL DIAGNOSES
Physiological in newborns, Kawasaki disease, ichthyosis, SLE, iatrogenic, mycosis fungoides, erythroderma, burns, infection (eg scarlet fever, measles, echovirus, coxsackie virus, toxic shock syndrome, staphylococcal scalded skin syndrome, fungal), dermatitis, Stevens-Johnson syndrome, toxic epidermal necrolysis

Diarrhoea

See also
— Diseases, gastroenteritis
— Diseases, C difficile

☺ DIFFERENTIAL DIAGNOSES
Viral (eg rotavirus, norovirus, HIV), bacterial (sepsis, C difficile, C perfringens, C botulinum, Vibrio cholerae, Salmonella typhi, typhus, Staphylococcus aureus, Bacillus cereus, V parahaemolyticus, shigella species, Escherichia coli, campylobacter, Q fever), amoebic dysentery, cryptosporidium, microsporidia, helminths, schistosomiasis, toxic shock syndrome, constipation with overflow, ectopic pregnancy, IBD, IBS, malignancy, coeliac disease, Whipple's disease, tropical sprue, scleroderma, toddler diarrhoea, lactose or cow's milk intolerance, Addison's disease, carcinoid, glucagonoma, Zollinger-Ellison syndrome, porphyria, diverticular disease, CF, hyperthyroidism, DM neuropathy, iatrogenic (eg SSRIs, metformin, magnesium salts, antibiotics), anxiety, pellagra, marasmus (protein-energy malnutrition), paroxysmal cold haemoglobinuria

Diplopia

☺ DIFFERENTIAL DIAGNOSES
Orbital fracture, IIIrd, IVth or VIth nerve palsy, malignancy, orbital cellulitis, Graves' ophthalmopathy, myasthenia gravis, sarcoid, DM, MS, internuclear ophthalmoplegia, vitamin A toxicity, corneal scarring, cataract, relapsing polychondritis

Disinhibition

⚕ **DIFFERENTIAL DIAGNOSES**

Drug or alcohol abuse, frontal lobe malignancy, cerebral abscess, CVA, dementia, hypomania, mania, personality disorder, cognitive impairment

Dizziness

See also
— *Vertigo (sensation of acute rotatory movement)*

⚕ **DIFFERENTIAL DIAGNOSES**

Anaemia, aortic stenosis, mitral stenosis, cardiac arrhythmia, hypotension, carotid sinus hypersensitivity, iatrogenic (eg alcohol, benzodiazepines, major tranquillisers, SSRIs, antihypertensives), autonomic neuropathy, peripheral neuropathy, seizures, cerebellar syndrome, brainstem insult, head injury, vertigo, anxiety

Dry eyes

⚕ **DIFFERENTIAL DIAGNOSES**

Idiopathic, allergy, sicca syndrome, vitamin A deficiency, sarcoid, iatrogenic (eg antihistamines, OCP, opiates, ACE inhibitors), facial palsy, blepharitis, rosacea, postmenopause, DM, SLE, scleroderma, RA, laser eye surgery

Dry mouth

⚕ **DIFFERENTIAL DIAGNOSES**

Dehydration, anxiety, sicca syndrome, neuropathy, radiotherapy, Parkinson's disease, HIV, smoking, salivary gland infiltration (eg sarcoid), DM, iatrogenic (eg anticholinergics, chemotherapy)

Dry skin

⚕ **DIFFERENTIAL DIAGNOSES**

Idiopathic, dehydration, low humidity (eg winter, air conditioning), excessive bathing/swimming, detergents, UV exposure, psoriasis, hypothyroidism, eczema, ichthyosis

Dysarthria

⚕ **DIFFERENTIAL DIAGNOSES**

Fatigue, drug and alcohol use, myopathy, myasthenia gravis, bulbar palsy, pseudobulbar palsy, syrinx, MS, ADEM, CVA, PD, cerebellar syndrome, neuropathy, Guillain-Barré syndrome, MND, polio, tumour, cranial nerve palsy, head injury

Dysmenorrhoea

⚕ **DIFFERENTIAL DIAGNOSES**

Idiopathic, endometriosis, adenomyosis, PID, fibroids, polyps, IUD, post-surgical, cervical stenosis

Dyspareunia

⚕ **DIFFERENTIAL DIAGNOSES**

Superficial: vaginismus, vulvitis, atrophic vaginitis, vaginal dryness, candidiasis, vaginal atresia, imperforate hymen, herpes simplex, ulcer, abscess, post-surgical/delivery, vulval malignancy, urethritis, urethral caruncle, vaginal prolapse, tear at introitus. Deep: radiotherapy, PID, endometriosis, endometrial malignancy, cervical malignancy, ovarian malignancy, cervicitis, uterine prolapse. Male: STI, balanitis, candida, prostatitis, phimosis

Dyspepsia

See also
— *Abdominal pain*
— *Chest pain*

⚕ **DIFFERENTIAL DIAGNOSES**

GORD, hiatus hernia, peptic ulcer, gastric malignancy, oesophageal malignancy, oesophagitis, gallstone disease, biliary reflux, pancreatitis, gastritis, infection, food intolerance, NSAIDs

Dysphagia

⚕ **DIFFERENTIAL DIAGNOSES**

Globus, sicca syndrome, pharyngeal pouch, Plummer-Vinson syndrome, oesophageal stricture, foreign body, goitre, achalasia, malignancy (pharyngeal, oesophageal, thyroid, gastric, lymphoma, bronchial, metastases), left atrial enlargement, aortic aneurysm, relapsing polychondritis, scleroderma, bulbar palsy, pseudobulbar palsy, myasthenia gravis, MND

Dysphasia

⚕ **DIFFERENTIAL DIAGNOSES**

Expressive (Broca's area), receptive (Wernicke's area). CVA, tumour, dementia, head injury, MS, ADEM, Parkinson's disease, encephalitis, meningitis, postictal, abscess, vasculitis, hydrocephalus

Dystonia

⚕ **DIFFERENTIAL DIAGNOSES**

Idiopathic, hereditary, Wilson's disease, CVA, birth injury, iatrogenic (eg antipsychotics), spinocerebellar degeneration, mitochondrial disease, carbon monoxide poisoning, encephalitis, tumour

Dysuria

⚕ **DIFFERENTIAL DIAGNOSES**

UTI, STI, interstitial cystitis, radiation cystitis, TB, bladder tumour, bladder stone, prostatitis, dehydration, vaginitis

Ear discharge

⚕ **DIFFERENTIAL DIAGNOSES**

Wax, trauma, otitis externa, foreign body, perforated tympanic membrane with acute otitis media/glue ear/chronic suppurative otitis media, cholesteatoma, head injury (CSF), tympanic tumour, salivary gland tumour

Ear pain (otalgia)

⚕ **DIFFERENTIAL DIAGNOSES**

Trauma, foreign body, wax, otitis externa, otitis media, varicella, impetigo, eczema, furunculosis, bullous myringitis, barotrauma, TMJ dysfunction, mastoiditis, Ramsay-Hunt syndrome, Eustachian tube dysfunction, trigeminal neuralgia, malignancy (eg oral, laryngeal, temporal bone, acoustic neuroma, glomus jugulare) tonsillitis, sinusitis, dental disease, oesophagitis, angina, relapsing polychondritis

Ears (low set)

⚕ **DIFFERENTIAL DIAGNOSES**

Syndromic eg, Down's syndrome, DiGeorge syndrome, Noonan's syndrome

Epistaxis

⚕ **DIFFERENTIAL DIAGNOSES**

Infection, foreign body, allergic rhinitis, clotting disorder, anticoagulation, thrombocytopenia, antiplatelet agents, trauma, relapsing polychondritis, collagen disorders, malignancy

Erythema chronicum migrans

⚕ **DIFFERENTIAL DIAGNOSES**

Lyme disease

Erythema marginatum

⚕ **DIFFERENTIAL DIAGNOSES**

Rheumatic fever

Erythema multiforme

See also
— *Diseases, Stevens-Johnson syndrome*
— *Diseases, toxic epidermal necrolysis (Lyell's syndrome)*

⚕ **DIFFERENTIAL DIAGNOSES**

Idiopathic, iatrogenic (eg penicillin, sulfonamides, sulfonylureas, NSAIDs, salicylates), infection (eg streptococcus, mycoplasma, HIV, HSV, hepatitis, coxsackie virus, enterovirus, echovirus, adenovirus, orf, cat-scratch disease (*Bartonella*), salmonella, proteus, TB, chlamydia,

fungal infections); SLE, malignancy, sarcoid, vasculitis, UV light, radiotherapy

Erythema nodosum

⚕ **DIFFERENTIAL DIAGNOSES**

Sarcoidosis, leukaemia, lymphoma, pregnancy, IBD, Behçet's disease, infections (eg mycoplasma, measles, mumps, streptococcal, TB, leprosy, cat-scratch disease [*Bartonella*]; iatrogenic (eg OCP, sulfonamides)

Exophthalmos

⚕ **DIFFERENTIAL DIAGNOSES**

Retroorbital tumours (optic nerve sheath meningioma, optic nerve glioma, lymphoma, leukaemia, neuroblastoma, lymphangioma, rhabdomyosarcoma, lacrimal gland carcinoma, haemangioma, neurofibroma, metastases), orbital cyst, orbital cellulitis, corticocavernous fistula (pulsatile), cavernous sinus thrombosis, AV malformation, Graves' disease, Wegener's granulomatosis, fungal sinusitis

Eye pain

⚕ **DIFFERENTIAL DIAGNOSES**

Conjunctivitis, foreign body, keratitis (infective, traumatic, autoimmune, UV exposure), corneal ulcer, subconjunctival haemorrhage (although often painless), allergy, dry eye, corneal abrasion, episcleritis, scleritis, acute glaucoma, iritis, periorbital cellulitis, orbital cellulitis, trauma, sinusitis, shingles, optic neuritis, migraine, stye, ectropion, entropion, keratoconus, chalazion, cluster headache

Facial numbness

See also
— *Diseases, Vth cranial nerve palsy*

⚕ **DIFFERENTIAL DIAGNOSES**

Trigeminal nerve palsy, trigeminal neuralgia, trauma, CVA, MS, ADEM, syrinx, trauma, peripheral neuropathy, sarcoid, tumour (sinus, nasopharyngeal, acoustic neuroma, petrous temporal bone lesions), herpes zoster infection, iatrogenic

Facial pain

See also
— *Eye pain*

⚕ **DIFFERENTIAL DIAGNOSES**

Trauma, sinusitis, dental (eg abscess), trigeminal neuralgia, herpes zoster/postherpetic neuralgia, cellulitis, erysipelas, TMJ syndrome, tumour (melanoma, parotid, nasopharyngeal, oral cavity, sinus, nasopharyngeal, cerebral), cervical disc prolapse/degeneration, temporal arteritis, otitis media, otitis externa, mastoiditis, headache (eg migraine), parotitis, osteomyelitis

Faecal incontinence

See also
— *Diarrhoea*

DIFFERENTIAL DIAGNOSES
Dementia, depression, schizophrenia, anxiety, seizures, constipation with overflow, neuropathy, spinal cord disease, CVA, PD, MS, ADEM, postpartum, rectal prolapse, anal tumour, terminal patient

Failure to thrive

DIFFERENTIAL DIAGNOSES
Non-accidental injury, neglect, malnutrition, difficulty in breastfeeding, food allergy (eg cow's milk protein intolerance, lactose intolerance), GORD (infantile), malabsorption (eg coeliac disease, will occur from weaning), posterior urethral valve, sepsis, metabolic (eg cystinuria, medium chain acylcoenzyme A deficiency, PKU, galactosaemia, pyruvate kinase deficiency), CAH, renal tubular acidosis, Bartter's syndrome, osteopetrosis, Fanconi syndrome, congenital heart disease, CF, malignancy, diabetes insipidus, DM, rickets, haemoglobinopathy, immunodeficiency, Niemann-Pick disease, Russell-Silver syndrome, abetalipoproteinaemia, Kearns-Sayre syndrome, Prader-Willi syndrome

Falls

See also
— *Syncope*

DIFFERENTIAL DIAGNOSES
Accidental, neurological/ENT (foot drop, Parkinson's disease, cerebellar syndrome, MS, ADEM, CVA, seizure, dementia, peripheral neuropathy, labyrinthitis, BPPV, cerebral infection), cardiac (arrhythmia, hypotension, aortic or mitral stenosis), shock, myopathy, malignancy

Fasciculation

DIFFERENTIAL DIAGNOSES
Idiopathic, excessive exertion, MND, neuropathy, spinal cord compression, nerve compression, MS, ADEM, myopathy, cervical myelopathy, syrinx, syphilis, polio, hyperthyroidism, Charcot-Marie-Tooth disease, electrolyte disturbance (eg ↓Ca^{2+}/K$^+$), iatrogenic (eg lithium), Lyme disease, organophosphate poisoning

Fatigue

DIFFERENTIAL DIAGNOSES
Idiopathic, stress, anxiety, depression, poor sleep hygiene, sleep apnoea, pregnancy, chronic infection

(eg TB), anaemia, hypothyroidism, DM, Addison's disease, cardiac failure, chronic lung disease, IBD, coeliac disease, malignancy, liver disease, renal failure, Parkinson's disease, ME, iatrogenic (eg antihistamines, beta-blockers), postviral, cataplexy, narcolepsy

Fever

DIFFERENTIAL DIAGNOSES
Infection, post-surgery, tumour, autoimmune disease, connective tissue disease (eg RA, SLE), temporal arteritis, polymyalgia rheumatica, drug fever, granulomatous disease, familial Mediterranean fever, thyroid disease, malignant hyperpyrexia, heat stroke, excessive exercise, MI, sarcoid, IBD, phaeochromocytoma, hypothalamic dysfunction, Fabry disease, vasculitis, PFAPA syndrome (periodic fever, aphthous ulceration, pharyngitis, adenitis), PUO (defined as fever>38.3°C for more than three weeks, may be intermittent, no diagnosis found within one week of investigation/two outpatient visits/three days in hospital)

Finger clubbing

DIFFERENTIAL DIAGNOSES
Cardiac (cyanotic congenital heart disease, subacute infective endocarditis, atrial myxoma), GI (IBD, primary biliary cirrhosis), pulmonary (empyema, abscess, carcinoma, idiopathic fibrosis, bronchiectasis), thyroid acropachy, congenital

Flashing lights (photopsia)

DIFFERENTIAL DIAGNOSES
Migraine, cataract, choroidal tumours, vitreous detachment, retinal detachment, optic neuritis, hypotension, hypoglycaemia, CVA, pre-eclampsia

Flatulence

DIFFERENTIAL DIAGNOSES
Idiopathic, excessive air swallowing, diet (eg carbonated drinks, artificial sweeteners), infection (eg giardiasis), lactose intolerance, coeliac disease, hiatus hernia, IBS

Floaters (entopsia)

DIFFERENTIAL DIAGNOSES
Benign vitreous liquefaction, retinal detachment, vitreous detachment, vitreous haemorrhage, ARMD, toxocara, chorioretinitis, amyloid, tumour, proliferative diabetic retinopathy, iritis, trauma

Flushing

DIFFERENTIAL DIAGNOSES
Anxiety, dietary (eg spicy food), excessive exertion, menopause, rosacea, phaeochromocytoma, carcinoid

syndrome, iatrogenic (eg CCBs, GnRH analogues), alcohol, diet (eg monosodium glutamate), autonomic dysreflexia, PD

Fontanelle (bulging)

⚕ **DIFFERENTIAL DIAGNOSES**

Crying, vomiting, meningitis, encephalitis, hydrocephalus, galactosaemia, tumour, cerebral malaria, cerebral abscess, cerebral haemorrhage, cerebral sinus thrombosis, roseola infantum, polio, hypoparathyroidism, hyperthyroidism, hypothyroidism, DKA, cardiac failure, renal failure, liver failure, leukaemia, vitamin A toxicity, trauma

Foot drop

⚕ **DIFFERENTIAL DIAGNOSES**

L4/L5 root lesion, sciatic nerve palsy, common peroneal nerve palsy (eg traumatic, iatrogenic [post-TKR]), peripheral neuropathy (eg alcoholic, lead poisoning, DM), Guillain-Barré syndrome, myopathy, MND, Charcot-Marie-Tooth disease, compartment syndrome

Frontal bossing

⚕ **DIFFERENTIAL DIAGNOSES**

Extramedullary haemopoiesis (eg thalassaemia), acromegaly, achondroplasia, hydrocephalus, Paget's disease of the bone, rickets, Gorlin's syndrome, congenital syphilis, Crouzon syndrome, Hurler's syndrome, cleidocranial dysostosis, Russell-Silver syndrome

Gait abnormalities (antalgic)

See also
— Child with a limp

⚕ **DIFFERENTIAL DIAGNOSES**

Arthritis, myositis, trauma, tumour, avascular necrosis, DVT

Gait abnormalities (high stepping/ stamping foot)

⚕ **DIFFERENTIAL DIAGNOSES**

See foot drop

Gait abnormalities (scissoring)

⚕ **DIFFERENTIAL DIAGNOSES**

Spasticity, paraplegia, cerebral palsy, spinal cord injury, MS, ADEM, bilateral stroke

Gait abnormalities (waddling)

⚕ **DIFFERENTIAL DIAGNOSES**

Pelvic girdle disease, proximal myopathy, congenital dislocation of the hip, pregnancy

Gait abnormalities (wide-based ataxic)

⚕ **DIFFERENTIAL DIAGNOSES**

Alcohol intoxication, cerebellar syndrome, CVA, posterior column loss, MS, syphilis, cervical myelopathy, peripheral neuropathy

Galactorrhoea

⚕ **DIFFERENTIAL DIAGNOSES**

Idiopathic, pregnancy, lactation, cyclical, PCOS, prolactinoma, pituitary tumour, antidopaminergic agents (eg risperidone, amisulpride, haloperidol, chlorpromazine, SSRIs, metoclopramide, domperidone, opiates, oestrogens), renal failure, hypothyroidism, CKD, excess nipple stimulation, chest/spinal cord injury, newborns (due to circulating maternal oestrogen), male hypogonadism

Genital ulcers

⚕ **DIFFERENTIAL DIAGNOSES**

Herpes simplex, Behçet's syndrome, primary syphilis, chancroid, lymphogranuloma venereum, SLE, donovanosis, post-trauma, malignancy, granuloma inguinale

Geographic tongue

⚕ **DIFFERENTIAL DIAGNOSES**

Idiopathic, familial, vitamin B_2 (riboflavin) deficiency, infancy

GI haemorrhage (fresh rectal bleeding)

⚕ **DIFFERENTIAL DIAGNOSES**

Anal fissure, haemorrhoids, anal infection, trauma, malignancy, IBD, gastroenteritis, large upper GI bleed, Meckel's diverticulum, intussusception, ischaemic colitis, radiation colitis, angiodysplasia, diverticulitis, mesenteric artery infarction, cow's milk protein intolerance, clotting disorders, graft v host disease

GI haemorrhage (haematemesis +/- melaena)

⚕ **DIFFERENTIAL DIAGNOSES**

Mallory-Weiss tear, ruptured oesophageal varices, gastric ulcer, duodenal ulcer, gastritis, oesophagitis, oesophageal carcinoma, gastric carcinoma, clotting disorder, foreign body, trauma, ingestion of corrosive substances, angiodysplasia

GI haemorrhage (melaena)

⚕ **DIFFERENTIAL DIAGNOSES**

Mallory-Weiss tear, oesophageal varices, Meckel's diverticulum, gastric ulcer, duodenal ulcer, gastritis, oesophagitis, oesophageal carcinoma, gastric carcinoma, clotting disorder, foreign body, trauma, ingestion of corrosive substances, angiodysplasia

Gingival hypertrophy

⚕ **DIFFERENTIAL DIAGNOSES**
Acute myeloid leukaemia, iatrogenic (phenytoin, dihydropyridine CCBs, ciclosporin, OCP), pregnancy, tuberous sclerosis, Wegener's granulomatosis

Glossitis

⚕ **DIFFERENTIAL DIAGNOSES**
Idiopathic, infection, allergy, burns, smoking, Stevens-Johnson syndrome, antibiotics, deficiency (iron, vitamin B_{12}, folate, vitamin B_2 (riboflavin), nicotinic acid)

Goitre

See also
— *Thyroid nodule*

⚕ **DIFFERENTIAL DIAGNOSES**
Pregnancy, puberty, stress, infection, infiltration (eg sarcoid), malignancy, hyperthyroid (Graves' disease, De Quervain thyroiditis, subacute lymphocytic thyroiditis [early stages], rarely Hashimoto's); hypothyroid (iodine deficiency, Hashimoto's, subacute lymphocytic thyroiditis [latter stages], Riedel's thyroiditis), euthyroid (simple, Hashimoto's), iatrogenic (eg lithium, carbimazole, iodine)

Groin lump

⚕ **DIFFERENTIAL DIAGNOSES**
Lymphadenopathy (eg infection, tumour), hernia (incisional, femoral, inguinal, strangulated), vascular (femoral artery aneurysm, saphena varix, haematoma), abscess (local, psoas), testicle (undescended, ectopic), lipoma, haemangioma

Groin pain

⚕ **DIFFERENTIAL DIAGNOSES**
Strain, hernia, arthritis, lymphadenopathy, infection, tumour

Guarding

⚕ **DIFFERENTIAL DIAGNOSES**
Peritonism (see *abdominal pain*)

Gynaecomastia

⚕ **DIFFERENTIAL DIAGNOSES**
Physiological (newborn, teenagers, elderly), iatrogenic (spironolactone, chlorpromazine, methyldopa, cimetidine, CCBs, digoxin, oestrogens, antipsychotics, flutamide, finasteride, metronidazole, amiodarone, isoniazid, TCAs, diazepam, diamorphine, antiretrovirals), low testosterone levels (castration, CKD, testosterone resistance, Klinefelter's syndrome), raised oestrogen levels (testicular malignancy, hyperthyroidism, adrenal tumour, chronic liver disease, obesity, hermaphrodite), HIV, spinal cord injury, acromegaly, lymphoma, dialysis, lung malignancy

Haematemesis

⚕ **DIFFERENTIAL DIAGNOSES**
See *GI haemorrhage*

Haematospermia

⚕ **DIFFERENTIAL DIAGNOSES**
Idiopathic, UTI, clotting disorder, trauma, prostatitis, prostatic stones, malignancy, epididymo-orchitis, urethritis, urethral stricture, seminal vesiculitis, TB, syphilis, schistosomiasis

Haematuria

⚕ **DIFFERENTIAL DIAGNOSES**
UTI, calculus, malignancy (renal tract, prostate, metastatic), prostatitis, bladder fistula, PCKD, glomerulonephritis, nephritis, renal papillary necrosis, medullary sponge kidney, trauma, vasculitis, sickle cell anaemia, clotting disorder, infective endocarditis, haemolysis, Alport's syndrome, interstitial cystitis, radiation cystitis, foreign body, malaria, TB, schistosomiasis, phaeochromocytoma

Haemoptysis

⚕ **DIFFERENTIAL DIAGNOSES**
URTI, LRTI (bacterial, lung abscess, aspergilloma, helminthic), nasal polyps, malignancy (laryngeal, nasopharyngeal, pulmonary, metastatic), clotting disorder, trauma, foreign body, severe coughing, CF, PE, bronchiectasis, AV malformation, mitral valve stenosis, pulmonary oedema, hereditary haemorrhagic telangiectasia, Goodpasture's syndrome, mixed connective tissue disease, Wegener's granulomatosis, amyloid, haemosiderosis, polyarteritis nodosa, SLE, endometriosis

Hair discoloration

⚕ **DIFFERENTIAL DIAGNOSES**
Advancing age, drugs, smoking, kwashiorkor, albinism, Waardenburg syndrome, piebaldism

Halitosis

⚕ **DIFFERENTIAL DIAGNOSES**
Poor dentition, smoking, diet, dental abscess, gingivitis,

tonsillitis, appendicitis, gastroenteritis, renal failure, hepatic failure, drugs

Hallucinations

⟁ **DIFFERENTIAL DIAGNOSES**
Hypnogogic/hypnopompic (on falling asleep/waking up), depression, mania, schizophrenia, dementia, hysteria, intercurrent illness, drugs (iatrogenic, illicit drugs, alcohol), electrolyte disturbance, metabolic disturbance, visual impairment, CVA, temporal lobe epilepsy, malignancy

Headache

See also
 — *Facial pain*
 — *Ear pain (otalgia)*
 — *Eye pain*
 — *Diseases, brain tumour*

⟁ **DIFFERENTIAL DIAGNOSES**
Head injury, drugs and analgesia overuse, cervical spondylosis, refractive error, tension headache, chronic daily headache, hypertension, sinusitis, otitis media, cholesteatoma, parotitis, meningitis, encephalitis, influenza, shingles, Lyme disease, syphilis, dental abscess, subarachnoid haemorrhage, intracranial haemorrhage, sinus thrombosis, blocked ventriculoperitoneal shunt, postcoital, temporal arteritis, migraine, cluster headache, raised ICP, benign intracranial hypertension, ADEM, reduced CSF volume (eg after lumbar puncture), antiphospholipid syndrome, carbon monoxide poisoning, vitamin A toxicity, hypercalcaemia, polycythaemia, chronic daily headache, Behçet's disease, paroxysmal cold haemoglobinuria

Heel pain

⟁ **DIFFERENTIAL DIAGNOSES**
Trauma, Achilles tendonitis, Achilles rupture, Achilles apophysitis (Severs disease), plantar fasciitis, calcaneal spur, ulcer, tarsal tunnel syndrome, foreign body, callus, infection, verrucae

Hemiparesis and hemiplegia

⟁ **DIFFERENTIAL DIAGNOSES**
CVA, MS, tumour, cerebral palsy, meningitis, encephalitis, abscess, postictal, head injury, migraine

Hepatomegaly

⟁ **DIFFERENTIAL DIAGNOSES**
Hepatitis (smooth and tender), tumour (primary/metastatic – hard, irregular; lymphoma/leukaemia – smooth, non-tender), tricuspid regurgitation (pulsatile and tender), right heart failure (smooth and tender); cirrhosis, haemochromatosis, amyloid, kwashiorkor, toxocara,

hydatid cyst, myeloproliferative disease, extramedullary haemopoiesis, biliary tree obstruction, Budd-Chiari syndrome, polycystic disease, haemangioma, arteriovenous malformation, Hurler's syndrome, Gaucher's disease

Hepatosplenomegaly

See also
 — *Hepatomegaly*
 — *Splenomegaly*

⟁ **DIFFERENTIAL DIAGNOSES**
Haematological: myeloproliferative disorders, lymphoproliferative disorders, leukaemia, lymphoma, megaloblastic anaemia, extramedullary haemopoiesis (eg thalassaemia). **Infective:** glandular fever, viral hepatitis, Weil's disease, brucellosis, toxoplasmosis, CMV, TB, kala-azar, schistosomiasis, malaria, trypanosomiasis. **Other:** Chronic liver disease with portal hypertension, polycystic disease, amyloid, sarcoid, galactosaemia, SLE, acromegaly, autoimmune hepatitis, paroxysmal cold haemoglobinuria, Hurler's syndrome, Gaucher's syndrome

Hirsutism (female)

⟁ **DIFFERENTIAL DIAGNOSES**
Race, PCOS, androgen-secreting ovarian/adrenal tumour, Cushing's syndrome, CAH, Turner's syndrome, acromegaly, thyroid disease, iatrogenic (eg steroids, ciclosporin, progestogens, phenytoin)

Hoarse voice

⟁ **DIFFERENTIAL DIAGNOSES**
Inhaled corticosteroids, laryngitis, excessive singing, dystonia, GORD, vocal cord cyst/scar, Parkinson's disease, CVA, tumour (laryngeal, thyroid, pharyngeal, pulmonary, oesophageal), recurrent laryngeal nerve palsy (eg left atrial enlargement [Ortner's syndrome], iatrogenic (eg thyroid surgery), MS, polio, syrinx, stress, hypothyroidism, acromegaly, sicca syndrome, granulomatous diseases (eg TB, sarcoid, Wegener's granulomatosis)

Horner's syndrome

See also
 — *Diseases, Horner's syndrome*

⟁ **DIFFERENTIAL DIAGNOSES**
Partial ptosis, miosis, anhydrosis (depending on site of lesion) and apparent enophthalmos

Hydrocoele

⟁ **DIFFERENTIAL DIAGNOSES**
Infancy: usually resolves by one year of age (treat if inguinal hernia present). **Childhood:** idiopathic,

MIMS Consultation Guide

torsion. *Adulthood:* idiopathic, malignancy, torsion, epididymo-orchitis

Hyperacusis

⚕ DIFFERENTIAL DIAGNOSES

VIIth nerve palsy (nerve to stapedius) (see *Diseases, VIIth cranial nerve palsy*). Drug withdrawal (eg benzodiazepine, SSRIs)

Hyperhidrosis

⚕ DIFFERENTIAL DIAGNOSES

Humidity, exertion, cardiac failure, MI, anxiety, hyperthyroidism, phaeochromocytoma, malignancy, infection, hypoglycaemia, active acromegaly, autonomic neuropathy, gustatory sweating, hypotension

Hyperpigmentation

⚕ DIFFERENTIAL DIAGNOSES

Race, postinflammatory, Addison's disease, Peutz-Jeghers syndrome, neurofibromatosis, tuberous sclerosis, acanthosis nigricans, Cushing's disease, carotinaemia, pellagra, eczema, melanoma, naevi, acromegaly, haemochromatosis, pregnancy and OCP (chloasma), jaundice, uraemia

Hypertelorism (orbital)

⚕ DIFFERENTIAL DIAGNOSES

Idiopathic or syndromic eg, DiGeorge syndrome, cri du chat syndrome, Crouzon syndrome, Noonan's syndrome, Job's syndrome (see *Diseases, immunodeficiency [primary]*)

Hypertrichosis (not localised to androgen-dependent areas)

See also
— *Hirsutism (female)*

⚕ DIFFERENTIAL DIAGNOSES

Infancy, congenital, malignancy and paraneoplastic syndrome, iatrogenic, anorexia nervosa (lanugo), malnutrition, Hurler's syndrome, epidermolysis bullosa, porphyria, melanocytic naevus, Becker's naevus, spina bifida, lichen simplex, skin trauma, hypothyroidism, mercury poisoning, pregnancy, SLE, HIV

Hypertrophic pulmonary osteoarthropathy (HPOA)

⚕ DIFFERENTIAL DIAGNOSES

Familial, transient in childhood (Goldbloom's syndrome, rare); **pulmonary causes:** malignancy (90% of cases, especially squamous), mesothelioma, bronchiectasis, fibrosis, CF; **GI:** primary biliary cirrhosis, cirrhosis, IBD, hepatoma; **cardiovascular:** infective endocarditis, cyanotic congenital heart disease; **others:** thymoma, thalassaemia, Graves' disease, POEMS, hereditary haemorrhagic telangiectasia

Hyperventilation

See also
— *Breathlessness*

⚕ DIFFERENTIAL DIAGNOSES

Panic attack, sympathetic overdrive, pain, hypoxia, shock, fever, brainstem lesions, hyperthyroidism, metabolic acidosis (see *Investigations, metabolic acidosis*)

Hypogonadism

⚕ DIFFERENTIAL DIAGNOSES

Hypogonadotropic: hypothalamic/pituitary failure (tumour, apoplexy, Sheehan's syndrome, Kallmann's syndrome, sarcoid, Langerhans' cell histiocytosis, trauma, haemochromatosis, TB, syphilis, encephalitis, autoimmune, radiotherapy, anorexia, empty sella syndrome, trauma, Prader-Willi syndrome, Laurence-Moon-Biedl syndrome, Gaucher's disease); **hypergonadotropic:** gonadal dysgenesis/failure (Turner's syndrome, premature menopause, Noonan's syndrome, Klinefelter's syndrome, iatrogenic, radiotherapy, familial, cryptorchidism, LH/FSH resistance, galactosaemia)

Hypopigmentation

⚕ DIFFERENTIAL DIAGNOSES

Albinism, hypopituitarism, vitiligo, Chediak-Higashi syndrome, PKU, postinflammatory, pityriasis, halo naevus, tuberous sclerosis, morphea, leprosy, piebaldism, topical steroids

Hyposplenism

⚕ DIFFERENTIAL DIAGNOSES

Congenital, surgery, trauma, radiotherapy. Functional hyposplenism: coeliac disease, sickle cell anaemia, thalassaemia major, lymphoma, leukaemia, myeloproliferative diseases, IBD

Hypotension (postural, >20/10mmHg drop)

⚕ DIFFERENTIAL DIAGNOSES

Addison's disease, acute steroid withdrawal, hypopituitarism, iatrogenic (eg antihypertensives, antipsychotic drugs, SSRIs), cardiac failure, aortic valve disease, bradycardia, cardiomyopathy, MI, constrictive pericarditis, pericardial effusion, cardiac tamponade, hypovolaemia, sepsis, Parkinson's disease, MS, autonomic neuropathy (eg DM, multisystem atrophy), subacute combined degeneration of the spinal cord, amyloid, porphyria, Guillain-Barré syndrome, phaeochromocytoma, myelopathy, syrinx, pregnancy, chronic alcoholism

Hypothenar muscle wasting

DIFFERENTIAL DIAGNOSES
Ulnar nerve lesion (see *Diseases, ulnar nerve palsy*), T1 wasting (see *wasting of intrinsic muscles of hand*)

Hypotonia (infant)

DIFFERENTIAL DIAGNOSES
Benign, cerebellar lesion, Down's syndrome, tabes dorsalis, spinal shock, Guillain-Barré syndrome, myopathy, neural tube defect, myasthenia gravis, polio, iatrogenic, Prader-Willi syndrome, sepsis, hypothyroidism, congenital heart disease, cerebral palsy, Pompe disease, cri du chat syndrome

Inco-ordination

DIFFERENTIAL DIAGNOSES
Cerebellar syndrome, proprioceptive abnormality (eg dorsal column lesion), UMN or LMN lesion, primary muscle diseases,iatrogenic (eg sedatives, lithium), Parkinson's disease, MS, MND, myasthenia gravis, meningitis, encephalitis, alcohol abuse, dementia, cerebral tumour, CVA, chorea, hydrocephalus, peripheral neuropathies, HIV, homocystinuria, lead poisoning, altitude sickness, PKU

Infertility

DIFFERENTIAL DIAGNOSES
Male factors account for 30%. Smoking, alcohol, poor diet, ↑age of family planning, endometriosis, ovarian cyst, PCOS, fibroids, previous PID, endometrial polyps, bicornuate uterus, adnexal mass, previous cancer, oligozoospermia, azoospermia, sexual dysfunction, cervical disease, Turner's syndrome. 25% unexplained

Insomnia

DIFFERENTIAL DIAGNOSES
Idiopathic, advanced age, caffeine, light/noise disturbance, frequent flying, hypomania, mania, anxiety, stress, paranoia, bereavement, hyperthyroidism, pain, habitual, nocturia, restless leg syndrome, GORD, orthopnoea, cough/wheeze, drug abuse, sleep apnoea, iatrogenic (eg statins, propranolol, diuretics), dementia, acute confusion, pregnancy

Intermenstrual bleeding

DIFFERENTIAL DIAGNOSES
Trauma, polyps (cervical, endometrial), cervicitis (eg chlamydia, gonorrhoea), ectropion, malignancy (vulval, cervical, endometrial, metastatic), vaginitis (eg severe candidial infection), PID, OCP/LARC/IUD, bleeding disorder

Internuclear ophthalmoplegia

DIFFERENTIAL DIAGNOSES
MS, ADEM, CVA, tumour, encephalitis, Wernicke's encephalopathy, syphilis

Irregular periods

DIFFERENTIAL DIAGNOSES
See *oligomenorrhoea*

Jaccoud's arthropathy

DIFFERENTIAL DIAGNOSES
SLE (50% of cases), recurrent rheumatic fever, IBD, psoriatic arthropathy, malignancy, Sjögren's syndrome

Janeway lesions

DIFFERENTIAL DIAGNOSES
Subacute infective endocarditis

Jaundice

DIFFERENTIAL DIAGNOSES
Prehepatic: haemolysis, Gilbert's syndrome; hepatic: hepatitis-infective, cirrhosis, right heart failure, hepatoma, hepatic failure, drugs, alcoholic liver disease; obstructive: gallstones, lymphoma causing porta hepatis obstruction, cancer head of pancreas, cholangiocarcinoma, primary biliary cirrhosis, sclerosing cholangitis, pregnancy; neonatal: physiological, breastfed babies, galactosaemia, hypothyroidism, infection, haemolysis, inherited bilirubinaemias (unconjugated: Crigler-Nijjar syndrome; conjugated: rotor syndrome, Dubin-Johnson syndrome), biliary atresia

Jaw weakness

DIFFERENTIAL DIAGNOSES
Palsy of motor division of trigeminal nerve (see *Diseases, Vth cranial nerve palsy*); ipsilateral weakness: LMN lesion; contralateral weakness: UMN lesion. Myasthenia gravis, TMJ dysfunction, facioscapulohumeral dystrophy, myotonic dystrophy, Kennedy's disease, MND, syrinx

Joint effusion

DIFFERENTIAL DIAGNOSES
Trauma, post-surgical, overuse, arthritis, infection (eg staphylococcal, TB, gonorrhoea, Lyme disease, brucellosis), haematoma, gout, pseudogout, malignancy, foreign body, familial Mediterranean fever, Behçet's disease

Joint locking

⚕ **DIFFERENTIAL DIAGNOSES**

Arthritis, trauma, foreign body, cartilage tear, large effusion, osteochondritis dissecans

Joint pain (arthralgia)

See also
— *Arthritis*

⚕ **DIFFERENTIAL DIAGNOSES**

Trauma, sprain, tendonitis, gout, pseudogout, cellulitis, osteomyelitis, torn meniscus, rheumatic fever, malignancy, cyst, foreign body, bursitis, fibromyalgia, familial Mediterranean fever, relapsing polychondritis, avascular necrosis, sickle cell crisis, Behçet's disease, thrombosis

Joint swelling

See also
— *Arthritis*

⚕ **DIFFERENTIAL DIAGNOSES**

Gouty tophi, xanthoma, bursitis, lipoma, cyst, malignancy, trauma, infection

Jugular venous pressure (JVP, raised)

⚕ **DIFFERENTIAL DIAGNOSES**

Fluid overload, cardiac failure, pulmonary hypertension (eg PE, COPD), pulmonary stenosis, tricuspid regurgitation/stenosis, complete heart block, ventricular ectopic, pericardial effusion, cardiac tamponade, constrictive pericarditis, restrictive cardiomyopathy, right atrial myxoma, SVCO, jugular venous thrombosis

Kayser-Fleischer rings

⚕ **DIFFERENTIAL DIAGNOSES**

Wilson's disease, cirrhosis (including primary biliary and cryptogenic), primary sclerosing cholangitis

Keratoderma

⚕ **DIFFERENTIAL DIAGNOSES**

Reiter's syndrome, psoriasis, ectodermal dysplasia, tylosis

Koebner phenomenon

⚕ **DIFFERENTIAL DIAGNOSES**

Psoriasis, viral warts, molluscum contagiosum, vitiligo, lichen planus, pityriasis rubra pilaris, keratosis follicularis

Koilonychia

⚕ **DIFFERENTIAL DIAGNOSES**

Iron deficiency, iatrogenic (eg cytotoxic agents), intercurrent idiopathic, systemic illness, hypogonadism, postpartum, trauma (chemical, physical), nail-patella syndrome, polycythaemia, thyroid disease

Kussmaul respiration

⚕ **DIFFERENTIAL DIAGNOSES**

Compensatory breathing for metabolic acidosis

Kyphosis

⚕ **DIFFERENTIAL DIAGNOSES**

Congenital, wedge fracture (eg osteoporosis, TB [Pott's disease]), poor posture, ankylosing spondylitis, spina bifida, neurofibromatosis, malignancy, Scheuermann's disease, muscular dystrophy, Paget's disease, PD

Lead-pipe rigidity

⚕ **DIFFERENTIAL DIAGNOSES**

Parkinsonism

Lens dislocation

⚕ **DIFFERENTIAL DIAGNOSES**

Marfan's syndrome (upward dislocation), Ehlers-Danlos syndrome, homocystinuria (downward dislocation), tumour, trauma, iatrogenic

Leukonychia

⚕ **DIFFERENTIAL DIAGNOSES**

Congenital, malignancy, infection (eg measles), trauma, CKD, liver disease

Leukoplakia

⚕ **DIFFERENTIAL DIAGNOSES**

See *tongue (appearance)*

Lhermitte's sign

⚕ **DIFFERENTIAL DIAGNOSES**

MS, syringomyelia, cervical myelopathy, subacute combined degeneration of the spinal cord, whiplash injury

Libido, loss

⚕ **DIFFERENTIAL DIAGNOSES**

Fatigue, stress, depression, relationship difficulties, low self-esteem, distorted body image, alcohol abuse, illicit drug use, chronic illness, chronic pain, hypothyroidism, anaemia, Parkinson's disease, hyperprolactinaemia, hypogonadism, cirrhosis, iatrogenic (eg SSRIs, sedatives, beta-blockers,

GnRH analogues), dyspareunia, erectile dysfunction, menopause, atrophic vaginitis, vaginal pain, vaginismus, pregnancy

Lid lag

DIFFERENTIAL DIAGNOSES
Sympathetic overdrive, hyperthyroidism, anxiety

Limb pain

See also
— Joint pain (arthralgia)

DIFFERENTIAL DIAGNOSES
Venous insufficiency, varicose veins, phlebitis, peripheral vascular disease, myositis, Paget's disease of the bone, arthritis, DVT, Baker's cyst, cellulitis, ulceration, shingles, bursitis, compartment syndrome, Sudeck's atrophy, prolapsed intervertebral disc, spinal canal stenosis, trauma, paraesthesia, cramp, sickle cell crisis, malignancy

Limb swelling

DIFFERENTIAL DIAGNOSES
Pitting oedema (cardiac failure, low albumin, renal failure, obstructing mass), cellulitis, haematoma, trauma, dermatitis, ruptured Baker's cyst, DVT, varicose veins, compartment syndrome, muscular dystrophy, trypanosomiasis, lymphoma, Milroy's syndrome, iatrogenic (eg CCBs)

Livedo reticularis

DIFFERENTIAL DIAGNOSES
Idiopathic, newborns, congenital, SLE, antiphospholipid syndrome, cold exposure, cryoglobulinaemia, polyarteritis nodosa, hyperviscosity, iatrogenic (eg hydroxyurea)

Loss of consciousness

See also
— Syncope
— Hypotension (postural, >20/10mmHg drop)
— Investigations, ammonia (serum)

DIFFERENTIAL DIAGNOSES
Idiopathic, malingering, psychological, alcohol intoxication, drug overdose, drug withdrawal, poisoning, head injury, shock, meningitis, cerebral abscess, sepsis, intracerebral haemorrhage, brainstem infarction, intracerebral malignancy, Lewy body dementia, epilepsy, narcolepsy, hypoglycaemia, hypoxia, shock, liver failure, renal failure, acid-base disturbance, neuroleptic malignant syndrome

Low mood

DIFFERENTIAL DIAGNOSES
Chronic fatigue, stress, bereavement, depression, anxiety, phobia, dementia, hypothyroidism, hypercalcaemia,

cerebral lesion (eg malignancy), MS, Parkinson's disease, head injury, chronic disease, intercurrent illness, systemic illness, drug and alcohol abuse

Lower urinary tract symptoms in males (hesitancy, poor stream, terminal dribbling, incomplete bladder emptying, nocturia)

See also
— Dysuria
— Polyuria

DIFFERENTIAL DIAGNOSES
Urethral stricture, benign prostatic hypertrophy, prostate cancer, prostatitis, UTI, STI

Lymphadenopathy

DIFFERENTIAL DIAGNOSES
Infection (eg streptococcus, TB, Kawasaki disease, HIV), malignancy, immune (eg SLE, RA), iatrogenic (eg NSAIDs, phenytoin), sarcoid, storage diseases, Langerhans' cell histiocytosis

Macroglossia

DIFFERENTIAL DIAGNOSES
Familial, congenital hypothyroidism, Down's syndrome, acromegaly, amyloid, haemangioma, neurofibroma, Hurler's syndrome

Macular cherry red spots

DIFFERENTIAL DIAGNOSES
Tay-Sachs disease (classic type), retinal artery occlusion, Niemann-Pick disease, GM1 gangliosidosis, Hurler's syndrome, carbon monoxide poisoning, alcohol poisoning

Macule

DIFFERENTIAL DIAGNOSES
<10mm discoloured flat impalpable skin lesion eg, vitiligo, café au lait spots

Malabsorption

DIFFERENTIAL DIAGNOSES
Coeliac disease, tropical sprue, Whipple's disease, blind loop syndrome, previous GI surgery, IBD, post radiation, carcinoma, amyloid, pancreatic malfunction, helminths, Hartnup disease, giardiasis, food intolerance, cystinuria

Marfanoid phenotype

DIFFERENTIAL DIAGNOSES
Marfan's syndrome, MEN2b, homocystinuria

Melaena

⚕ **DIFFERENTIAL DIAGNOSES**

See *GI haemorrhage*

Memory loss

⚕ **DIFFERENTIAL DIAGNOSES**

Advancing age, stress, depression, fugue state, dementia, CVA, head injury, cerebral malignancy, postictal, CJD, Korsakoff's psychosis, hypercalcaemia, hypothyroidism, alcohol abuse, hypoxia, sepsis, iatrogenic, cerebral palsy, transient global amnesia, carbon monoxide poisoning, methaemoglobinaemia, vitamin deficiency (folate and vitamin B$_{12}$)

Menorrhagia

⚕ **DIFFERENTIAL DIAGNOSES**

Fibroids, malignancy (endometrial, ovarian, cervical), PID, uterine polyps, adenomyosis, endometriosis, endometritis, IUD/LARC, OCP, retained products of conception, anovulatory cycles, miscarriage, anticoagulants, bleeding disorder (eg von Willebrand's disease, thrombocytopenia), hepatorenal disease, hypothyroidism

Metallic taste

⚕ **DIFFERENTIAL DIAGNOSES**

Idiopathic, gingivitis, intraoral bleeding, oral infection, contaminated fish poisoning (clupeotoxin), heavy metal poisoning, iatrogenic (eg amiodarone, lithium, antidepressants, metformin, ferrous salts, metronidazole, gold), dehydration, IV contrast media, renal failure, burning mouth syndrome, hypercalcaemia, GORD, sicca syndrome

Microcephaly

⚕ **DIFFERENTIAL DIAGNOSES**

Chromosomal syndromes (eg cri du chat syndrome), fetal alcohol syndrome, malnutrition, maternal PKU, antenatal infection (toxoplasmosis, CMV, rubella), hypoxic brain damage, craniosynostosis

Migratory arthritis

⚕ **DIFFERENTIAL DIAGNOSES**

Rheumatic fever, iatrogenic (eg clopidogrel), malignancy (eg leukaemia, paraneoplastic syndrome), SLE, sarcoid, hepatitis, bacterial endocarditis

Miotic (small) pupil

⚕ **DIFFERENTIAL DIAGNOSES**

Advancing age, excessive ambient light, Horner's syndrome, accommodation, Argyll Robertson pupil, Holmes-Adie pupil, chronic iritis, anisocoria, sarcoid, DM, Lyme disease, encephalitis, pontine lesion, organophosphate poisoning, iatrogenic (eg opiates, phenothiazines, pilocarpine)

Monoarthritis

See also
— *Arthritis*

⚕ **DIFFERENTIAL DIAGNOSES**

OA, gout, septic arthritis, psoriatic arthritis, pseudogout, Reiter's syndrome, trauma, haemarthrosis, leukaemia, reactive arthritis, parvovirus B19, rheumatic fever, enteropathic arthritis, SLE

Mononeuritis multiplex

⚕ **DIFFERENTIAL DIAGNOSES**

RA, DM, malignancy, paraneoplastic syndrome, scleroderma, SLE, PAN, Churg-Strauss syndrome, Wegener's granulomatosis, amyloid, cryoglobulinaemia, Guillain-Barré syndrome, sarcoid, hypereosinophilic syndrome, HIV, Lyme disease, leprosy, nerve compression, alcohol abuse, iatrogenic, Sjögren's syndrome

Motor neuropathy

⚕ **DIFFERENTIAL DIAGNOSES**

Familial, lead poisoning (mainly wrists), Guillain-Barré syndrome, porphyria, acute motor axonal neuropathy, CIDP, Charcot-Marie-Tooth disease, paraneoplastic syndrome, porphyria, DM, Tay-Sachs disease, autoimmune, polio, diphtheria, tetanus, botulism, herpes zoster

Mouth ulcers

⚕ **DIFFERENTIAL DIAGNOSES**

Idiopathic, vitamin deficiency, malabsorption, IBD, malignancy (local, leukaemia, lymphoma), trauma, burns, lichen planus, Behçet's disease, bullous diseases, luteal phase of menstrual cycle, herpes simplex, HIV, RA, SLE, Reiter's disease, stress, Wegener's granulomatosis, eosinophilia, MAGIC syndrome (mouth and genital ulcers with inflamed cartilage), PFAPA syndrome (periodic fever, aphthous ulceration, pharyngitis, adenitis)

Muehrcke's lines (white paired transverse lines in fingernails)

⚕ **DIFFERENTIAL DIAGNOSES**

Severe hypoalbuminaemia, eg, liver disease, nephrotic syndrome, malnutrition

Murmur (diastolic)

⚕ **DIFFERENTIAL DIAGNOSES**

Mitral stenosis, tricuspid stenosis, aortic regurgitation, pulmonary regurgitation, atrial myxoma

Murmur (systolic)

DIFFERENTIAL DIAGNOSES

Hyperdynamic circulation, innocent murmur, aortic sclerosis, aortic stenosis, HCM/HOCM, coarctation of the aorta, pulmonary stenosis, mitral regurgitation, tricuspid regurgitation, VSD

Murmur (systolic and diastolic)

DIFFERENTIAL DIAGNOSES

Mixed aortic valve disease, mixed aortic and mitral valve disease, patent ductus arteriosus (PDA), ASD, anomalous left coronary artery, AV fistula, ruptured sinus of valsalva aneurysm

Murmur, innocent (childhood)

DIFFERENTIAL DIAGNOSES

Still's murmur: Soft, short, midsystolic, heard at left lower sternal edge and apex, varies with posture (louder when supine, quieter on standing or neck hyperextension). *Pulmonary flow murmur:* Upper left sternal edge, may be heard in back, more prominent with fever/anaemia. *Venous hum:* Continuous murmur, inferior to clavicles, especially right side, also heard when standing

Murmur, pathological (childhood)

DIFFERENTIAL DIAGNOSES

Soft murmurs may also be heard in ASD, large VSD, HCM, coarctation of the aorta. Pathological murmur suggested by poor exercise tolerance, failure to thrive, cyanosis, frequent chest infections, feeding difficulties, palpitations, collapse, chest pains, absent femoral pulses, added sounds, arrhythmia, hypertensive, murmur is loud/pansystolic/diastolic/continuous (excluding venous hum)

Muscle stiffness

DIFFERENTIAL DIAGNOSES

Overuse, excessive strain, PMR, haematoma, compartment syndrome, UMN lesion, parkinsonism

Muscle wasting

DIFFERENTIAL DIAGNOSES

Underuse, immobility, dystrophia myotonica, facioscapulohumeral dystrophy, MND, neuropathy, polio, RA, OA, LMN lesion

Muscle weakness

See also
- *Peripheral neuropathy*
- *Mononeuritis multiplex*
- *Motor neuropathy*
- *Muscle wasting*

DIFFERENTIAL DIAGNOSES

CVA, myasthenia gravis, LMN lesion, MND, MS, myopathy, myositis, muscular dystrophy, rhabdomyolysis, corticosteroid, scurvy, hypothyroidism, hyperthyroidism, Cushing's disease, hypercalcaemia, hyperkalaemia, hypokalaemia, DM, malignancy

Myalgia

DIFFERENTIAL DIAGNOSES

Overuse, excessive strain, PMR, haematoma, compartment syndrome, peripheral vascular disease, myositis (eg autoimmune, infection, statins), myopathy, rhabdomyolysis, DVT, scurvy, vitamin D deficiency

Mydriatic (large) pupil

DIFFERENTIAL DIAGNOSES

Fear, IIIrd nerve palsy, Holmes-Adie pupil, trauma, optic nerve lesion, ischaemic iris, trauma, vitreous haemorrhage, brainstem insult, death, iatrogenic (eg SSRIs, atropine, tropicamide, cocaine, amphetamines)

Myoclonus

DIFFERENTIAL DIAGNOSES

Familial, nocturnal, Tay-Sachs disease, Gaucher's disease, encephalitis, epilepsy, dementia, CJD, Parkinson's disease, MS, ADEM, subacute sclerosing panencephalitis, UMN lesion

Myopathy

DIFFERENTIAL DIAGNOSES

Dermatomyositis, polymyositis, muscular dystrophy, mitochondrial myopathies, congenital myopathy, familial periodic paralysis, corticosteroids, Cushing's syndrome, acromegaly, hyperparathyroidism, Addison's syndrome, Conn's syndrome, thyroid disease, electrolyte disturbance, renal failure, liver failure, storage diseases, rhabdomyolysis

Nail (absent)

DIFFERENTIAL DIAGNOSES

Congenital, ichthyosis, sepsis, lichen planus

Nail (longitudinal lines/grooves)

DIFFERENTIAL DIAGNOSES

Age, lichen planus, viral warts, vascular disease

Nail fold infarcts

DIFFERENTIAL DIAGNOSES

Vasculitis, SLE, RA, dermatomyositis, connective tissue disease

Nail fold telangiectasia

𝒸 **DIFFERENTIAL DIAGNOSES**
Dermatomyositis, SLE, systemic sclerosis

Nail lunula (discoloration)

𝒸 **DIFFERENTIAL DIAGNOSES**
Iatrogenic, alcohol, smoking, CKD, psoriasis, nail-patella syndrome, infection, age

Nail lunula (large)

𝒸 **DIFFERENTIAL DIAGNOSES**
Idiopathic, race, hyperthyroidism, nail biting

Nail lunula (small)

𝒸 **DIFFERENTIAL DIAGNOSES**
Idiopathic, Down's syndrome, HIV, iron deficiency anaemia, malnutrition, endocrinopathy, collagen disorders

Nail pitting

𝒸 **DIFFERENTIAL DIAGNOSES**
Psoriasis, traumatic, eczema, alopecia areata

Nail pterygium

𝒸 **DIFFERENTIAL DIAGNOSES**
Lichen planus, peripheral vascular disease, radiotherapy, bullous disease, Stevens-Johnson syndrome, trauma

Nappy (red staining)

See also
— *Haematuria*
— *GI haemorrhage*

𝒸 **DIFFERENTIAL DIAGNOSES**
Urinary: urate (eg Lesch-Nyhan syndrome), UTI; **vaginal:** hormone withdrawal, trauma; **anal:** fissure, infection, dermatitis, cow's milk allergy, galactosaemia

Nasal obstruction

𝒸 **DIFFERENTIAL DIAGNOSES**
Coryza, sinusitis, polyp, rhinitis, enlarged adenoids, foreign body, deviated septum, trauma, malignancy, choanal atresia

Nausea

𝒸 **DIFFERENTIAL DIAGNOSES**
Stress, renal failure, liver disease, drugs, poisoning, gastroenteritis, peritonitis, bowel obstruction, gastritis, vertigo, shock, infection, fever, head injury, pain, pregnancy, MI, cerebral haemorrhage

Neck lump

𝒸 **DIFFERENTIAL DIAGNOSES**
Cyst (dermoid or branchial), thyroid (eg goitre, ectopic thyroid tissue, nodule, thyroglossal cyst, adenoma, malignancy), abscess (acute, TB), lymphadenopathy (infective, malignancy), carotid body tumour, cystic hygroma, pharyngeal pouch, salivary gland (stones, infection, malignancy)

Neck pain

See also
— *Lhermitte's sign*

𝒸 **DIFFERENTIAL DIAGNOSES**
Spondylosis, RA, meningitis, SAH, posterior fossa tumour, whiplash, osteoporosis, torticollis, prolapsed cervical disc, sprain, muscular strain, ankylosing spondylitis, PMR, multiple myeloma, metastatic disease, TB, osteomyelitis, osteomalacia, fibromyalgia

Neck stiffness

𝒸 **DIFFERENTIAL DIAGNOSES**
Spondylosis, RA, meningitis, SAH, posterior fossa tumour, whiplash, PMR, cervical rib, prolapsed cervical disc, polio, influenza, tetanus, pneumonia, abscess

Nerve thickening

𝒸 **DIFFERENTIAL DIAGNOSES**
Idiopathic, leprosy, sarcoid, amyloid, neurofibromatosis, acromegaly, Refsum's disease, DM, Charcot-Marie-Tooth disease

Night sweats

𝒸 **DIFFERENTIAL DIAGNOSES**
Anxiety, stress, malignancy, menopause, hyperthyroidism, fever, TB, brucellosis, typhus, infective endocarditis, typhoid/paratyphoid

Nipple discharge

See also
— *Galactorrhoea*

𝒸 **DIFFERENTIAL DIAGNOSES**
Physiological, pregnancy, lactation, duct ectasia, galactorrhoea, malignancy, mammary dysplasia, ductal papilloma, abscess, fibroadenoma, Paget's disease of the breast, fibrocystic disease, perimenopause, fibroadenosis

Nodule

𝒸 **DIFFERENTIAL DIAGNOSES**
Raised lesion >5mm high/diameter eg, melanoma, bite

Numbness

See also
— *Peripheral neuropathy*

♻ DIFFERENTIAL DIAGNOSES
CVA, cerebral malignancy, spinal cord compression, peripheral neuropathy, MS, ADEM, vasculitis, Raynaud's phenomenon, peripheral vascular disease, DM, thyroid disease, vitamin B$_{12}$ deficiency, lead poisoning, alcohol abuse, inflammatory arthritides, electrolyte disturbance

Nystagmus

♻ DIFFERENTIAL DIAGNOSES
Congenital, labyrinthitis, brainstem lesion (MS, ADEM, CVA, malignancy, syrinx, Arnold-Chiari malformation), cerebellar syndrome (*see Diseases, cerebellar disease*), alcohol intoxication, head injury, optokinetic, Wernicke's encephalopathy, acoustic neuroma, albinism, Noonan's syndrome

Obesity

♻ DIFFERENTIAL DIAGNOSES
Familial, overeating, lack of exercise, Cushing's syndrome, hypothyroidism, leptin deficiency, Prader-Willi syndrome, Laurence-Moon-Biedl syndrome, PCOS, menopause, iatrogenic (eg atypical antipsychotics, steroids)

Odynophagia (painful swallowing)

♻ DIFFERENTIAL DIAGNOSES
Oesophagitis, tonsillitis, malignancy (eg oral, oesophageal), GORD, oesophageal stricture, systemic sclerosis, pharyngitis, glossitis, candidiasis, oral ulceration, achalasia

Oligohydramnios

♻ DIFFERENTIAL DIAGNOSES
Placental dysfunction, posterior urethral valves, bilateral renal agenesis, premature membrane rupture

Oligomenorrhoea

See also
— *Amenorrhoea*

♻ DIFFERENTIAL DIAGNOSES
Dysfunctional uterine bleeding, PCOS, missed miscarriage, stress, anorexia, malnutrition, systemic illness, thyroid disease, prolactinoma, IUD, significant weight change, intercurrent illness, malnutrition, excessive exercise, ovarian tumours, iatrogenic (eg OCP, anabolic steroids, amphetamines)

Onycholysis

♻ DIFFERENTIAL DIAGNOSES
Congenital, infection (fungal, pseudomonas, herpes simplex), psoriasis, trauma, eczema, yellow nail syndrome, DM, scleroderma, sarcoidosis, amyloid, Graves' disease, iatrogenic (eg tetracyclines, chlorpromazine, cytotoxics, OCP)

Onychomadesis (nail–nail bed separation)

♻ DIFFERENTIAL DIAGNOSES
Iatrogenic (eg carbamazepine, tetracyclines), malnutrition, sepsis, hand foot and mouth disease, trauma, hyperthyroidism, fungal infections, tumour, prolonged and repetitive immersion in water, Raynaud's phenomenon

Ophthalmoplegia

See also
— *Internuclear ophthalmoplegia*
— *Diseases, IIIrd, IVth, VIth cranial nerve palsy*

♻ DIFFERENTIAL DIAGNOSES
Kearns-Sayre syndrome, thyroid disease, Wernicke's encephalopathy, brainstem lesion, MS, ADEM, malignancy (brainstem, pineal gland tumour), CVA, circle of Willis aneurysm, meningitis, DM, myasthenia gravis, mitochondrial disease

Opisthotonus

♻ DIFFERENTIAL DIAGNOSES
Behavioural, tetanus, meningitis, encephalitis, kernicterus, neuroleptics, neurosyphilis, cerebral malaria, cerebral palsy, hypoxia, cerebral trauma, CVA, tuberous sclerosis

Optic atrophy

♻ DIFFERENTIAL DIAGNOSES
Glaucoma, retinal artery occlusion, papillitis, retinal ischaemia, optic neuritis, retinitis pigmentosa, glaucoma, orbital abscess, compressive malignancy, radiotherapy, MS, ADEM, DM, vitamin B deficiency, tobacco, alcohol, Paget's disease of the bone, birth asphyxia, Friedreich's ataxia, DIDMOAD, Leber's optic atrophy, sarcoid, trauma, circle of Willis aneurysm

Orogenital ulceration

♻ DIFFERENTIAL DIAGNOSES
Secondary syphilis, pemphigus, herpes simplex, erythema multiforme, Stevens-Johnson syndrome, Behçet's disease, Reiter's disease, Crohn's disease, Strachan's syndrome (neuropathy, ulceration, amblyopia)

Orthopnoea

♻ DIFFERENTIAL DIAGNOSES
Anxiety, left ventricular dysfunction, MI, atrial myxoma, pericardial effusion, COPD, asthma, sleep apnoea, pleural effusion, pneumonia, diaphragmatic paralysis

Pain/temperature sensation loss

⚕ **DIFFERENTIAL DIAGNOSES**
Lateral spinothalamic tract lesion/thalamic lesion: MS, ADEM, syrinx, malignancy, lateral medullary syndrome, abscess, trauma, infarction, Brown-Sequard syndrome, DM

Painful arc (shoulder)

⚕ **DIFFERENTIAL DIAGNOSES**
Supraspinatus tendon lesion: partial rupture, rupture, inflammation

Pale stool

⚕ **DIFFERENTIAL DIAGNOSES**
Steatorrhoea, biliary obstruction (see *jaundice*)

Pallor

⚕ **DIFFERENTIAL DIAGNOSES**
Constitutional, anaemia, vitiligo, albinism, shock, hypopituitarism, hypothyroidism

Palmar erythema

⚕ **DIFFERENTIAL DIAGNOSES**
Idiopathic, chronic liver disease, portal hypertension, eczema, telangiectasia, psoriasis, high oestrogen levels, polycythaemia, RA, pregnancy, hyperthyroidism, chronic leukaemia

Palmoplantar hyperkeratosis

See also
— *Skin (hyperkeratosis)*

⚕ **DIFFERENTIAL DIAGNOSES**
Idiopathic, familial, tylosis, vitamin A toxicity, keratoderma blennorrhagica, secondary syphilis, arsenic poisoning, HPV, epidermolytic palmoplantar keratoderma

Palpitations

⚕ **DIFFERENTIAL DIAGNOSES**
Anxiety, normal sinus rhythm, sinus arrhythmia, sinus tachycardia, atrial ectopics, AF, atrial flutter, SVT, intermittent heart block, ventricular ectopics, ventricular tachycardia, long QT syndromes, accessory bundles and pre-excitation syndromes (eg Wolff-Parkinson-White) electrolyte disturbance, proarrhythmogenic drugs, hyperthyroidism, phaeochromocytoma, sepsis, acid-base disturbance, torsades de pointes

Papilloedema

⚕ **DIFFERENTIAL DIAGNOSES**
↑ICP (tumour, bleed, infarction, venous sinus thrombosis), encephalitis, malignant hypertension, benign intracranial hypertension, Foster Kennedy syndrome, Guillain-Barré syndrome, hypoparathyroidism, lead poisoning, vitamin A toxicity, retinal vein thrombosis, central retinal vein occlusion, hypercapnia, retinoids, altitude sickness, Arnold-Chiari malformation, optic neuritis, leukaemia

Paraesthesia

See also
— *Peripheral neuropathy*

⚕ **DIFFERENTIAL DIAGNOSES**
Thiamine deficiency, spinal cord lesion, phantom limb, subacute combined degeneration of the spinal cord, cerebral malignancy, cerebral abscess, CVA, MS, ADEM, hypocalcaemia, hyperventilation, peripheral vascular disease, SLE, hypothyroidism, alcohol abuse, CKD, amyloid, HIV, leprosy, sarcoid, vasculitis, Charcot-Marie-Tooth disease, paraneoplastic syndrome

Paralysis (flaccid)

See also
— *Peripheral neuropathy*
— *Myopathy*
— *Motor neuropathy*

⚕ **DIFFERENTIAL DIAGNOSES**
LMN lesion, peripheral, transverse myelitis, polio, botulism, mycoplasma, diphtheria, central pontine myelinolysis, encephalitis, spinal cord injury, spinal cord abscess, hypokalaemic periodic paralysis, polio, zoster, Guillain-Barré syndrome, CMV, iatrogenic, *Clostridium botulinum*, Lyme disease

Parkinsonism

⚕ **DIFFERENTIAL DIAGNOSES**
Parkinson's disease, Shy-Drager syndrome (multisystem atrophy), progressive supranuclear palsy, cerebral injury, CVA, iatrogenic (eg metoclopramide, antipsychotics), carbon monoxide poisoning, encephalitis

Parotid lump

⚕ **DIFFERENTIAL DIAGNOSES**
Suppurative parotid infection, mumps, parotid stone obstructing parotid duct, parotid tumour (benign, malignant), sarcoid, Sjögren's syndrome, TB, syphilis, DM, amyloid, HIV, Wegener's granulomatosis, excessive purging (eg bulimia nervosa)

Paroxysmal nocturnal dyspnoea

⚕ **DIFFERENTIAL DIAGNOSES**
See *orthopnoea*

Pectus carinatum

⟲ **DIFFERENTIAL DIAGNOSES**
Idiopathic, familial, genetic (Noonan's syndrome, Marfan's syndrome, Down's syndrome)

Pectus excavatum

⟲ **DIFFERENTIAL DIAGNOSES**
Idiopathic, familial, genetic (Noonan's syndrome, Marfan's syndrome), neuromuscular diseases, rickets

Percussion note, dull (chest examination)

⟲ **DIFFERENTIAL DIAGNOSES**
Consolidation, pleural effusion (stony dull), pulmonary, collapse, elevated hemidiaphragm, pulmonary oedema, pleural thickening

Percussion note, hyper-resonant (chest examination)

⟲ **DIFFERENTIAL DIAGNOSES**
Hyperinflation (COPD, asthma), bullae, pneumothorax

Perianal pain

⟲ **DIFFERENTIAL DIAGNOSES**
Idiopathic, abscess, haemorrhoids, haematoma, IBD, malignancy (eg bladder, prostate), fistula, trauma, PID, endometriosis, adenomyosis, ovarian cyst, pregnancy (including ectopic), UTI, prostatitis, cellulitis, shingles

Peripheral neuropathy

⟲ **DIFFERENTIAL DIAGNOSES**
Idiopathic, DM, alcoholism, thyroid disease, RA, SLE, malignancy, vitamin deficiency, lead poisoning, vasculitis, Guillain-Barré syndrome, amyloid, leprosy, porphyria, acromegaly, sarcoidosis, uraemia, Refsum's disease, POEMS syndrome, Charcot-Marie-Tooth disease (motor neuropathy), iatrogenic (eg metronidazole, amiodarone, phenytoin, nitrofurantoin, cytotoxics, isoniazid), arsenic poisoning, HIV

Pes cavus

⟲ **DIFFERENTIAL DIAGNOSES**
Idiopathic, familial, trauma, burns, polio, Charcot-Marie-Tooth disease, syringomyelia, spina bifida, spasticity eg cerebral palsy, Friedreich's ataxia, spinal tumours (new onset pes cavus), homocystinuria, Becker muscular dystrophy

Pes planus

⟲ **DIFFERENTIAL DIAGNOSES**
Congenital, hypermobility syndrome, collagen disorders, arthritides, neuropathy, tarsal anomalies, ligament

disorders eg torn tibialis posterior/short Achilles, high-heeled shoes, obesity

Petechiae

See also
— *Purpura*

⟲ **DIFFERENTIAL DIAGNOSES**
Excessive coughing (whooping cough) and vomiting, thrombocytopenia/platelet dysfunction, antiplatelet medication, DIC, scurvy, fat embolism, vasculitis, bacterial endocarditis, excess steroids (iatrogenic, Cushing's syndrome), sepsis (eg *Neisseria meningitidis*)

Photophobia

⟲ **DIFFERENTIAL DIAGNOSES**
Iritis, meningitis, migraine, subarachnoid haemorrhage, cataract, corneal ulcer, glaucoma

Photosensitivity

⟲ **DIFFERENTIAL DIAGNOSES**
Iatrogenic (tetracyclines, amiodarone, TCAs, thiazides), dermatitis, cutaneous porphyria (cutanea tarda, variegate, erythropoietic), xeroderma pigmentosum

Pigmentation (brown skin lesions)

⟲ **DIFFERENTIAL DIAGNOSES**
Freckles, melanoma, haemosiderin deposits, post-inflammatory, café au lait spots, acanthosis nigricans, seborrhoeic warts, Addison's disease, haemochromatosis, Peutz-Jeghers syndrome, naevus

Pigmentation (palmar creases and buccal mucosa)

⟲ **DIFFERENTIAL DIAGNOSES**
Addison's disease, ACTH-secreting tumour (Nelson's syndrome, small cell lung cancer)

Pleural effusion

⟲ **DIFFERENTIAL DIAGNOSES**
See *Diseases, pleural effusion*

Pleural rub

⟲ **DIFFERENTIAL DIAGNOSES**
Pleurisy, PE, pleural metastases, mesothelioma, pneumonia

Pleuritic chest pain

⟲ **DIFFERENTIAL DIAGNOSES**
Pleurisy, pneumonia, pneumothorax, PE, rib fracture, tumour, Bornholm disease

Pneumaturia

⚕ **DIFFERENTIAL DIAGNOSES**
Colovesical fistula, gas-forming bacteria

Polyarthritis

⚕ **DIFFERENTIAL DIAGNOSES**
RA, OA, SLE, gout, psoriatic arthritis, enteropathic arthritis, rheumatic fever, Sjögren's syndrome, iatrogenic, viral infection, reactive arthritis, relapsing polychondritis

Polydipsia

⚕ **DIFFERENTIAL DIAGNOSES**
Psychogenic, diabetes insipidus, DM, hypercalcaemia, organophosphate poisoning, Bartter's syndrome

Polyhydramnios

⚕ **DIFFERENTIAL DIAGNOSES**
Multiple pregnancy, neural tube defects (anencephaly, spina bifida), oesophageal atresia, duodenal atresia (eg Down's syndrome), placental tumour, fetal hydrops, gestational diabetes

Polyuria

⚕ **DIFFERENTIAL DIAGNOSES**
High fluid intake, diabetes insipidus, DM, hypercalcaemia, diuretics, organophosphate poisoning, Bartter's syndrome

Postcoital bleeding

⚕ **DIFFERENTIAL DIAGNOSES**
Menstruation, vulvovaginal trauma, vulvovaginitis, PID, STI, candidal infection, poor vaginal lubrication, malignancy, cervical ectropion, polyp, clotting disorder, penile trauma

Postmenopausal bleeding

⚕ **DIFFERENTIAL DIAGNOSES**
Endometrial hyperplasia, malignancy (vulva, cervix, endometrium, ovarian, metastatic), polyp, atrophic vaginitis, HRT, clotting disorder, trauma

Postural hypotension

⚕ **DIFFERENTIAL DIAGNOSES**
See *hypotension (postural, >20/10mmHg drop)*

Pretibial myxoedema

⚕ **DIFFERENTIAL DIAGNOSES**
See *Diseases, Graves' disease*

Priapism

⚕ **DIFFERENTIAL DIAGNOSES**
Polycythaemia, sickle cell anaemia, leukaemia, arterial steal, iatrogenic (eg phosphodiesterase inhibitors)

Proprioception (loss)

See also
— *Peripheral neuropathy*

⚕ **DIFFERENTIAL DIAGNOSES**
Spinocerebellar degeneration (Friedreich's ataxia, ataxia-telangiectasia), syphilis, spinal cord lesion (MS, ADEM, trauma, tumour, abscess, subacute combined degeneration, hemilesion: Brown-Sequard syndrome), CVA

Prostatic enlargement

⚕ **DIFFERENTIAL DIAGNOSES**
Benign prostatic hypertrophy, prostatitis, prostate carcinoma

Protein-losing enteropathy

⚕ **DIFFERENTIAL DIAGNOSES**
Lymphangiectasia (primary, malignancy, lymphoma, TB), coeliac disease, tropical sprue, Whipple's disease, IBD, rectal villous adenoma, colorectal carcinoma

Proximal myopathy

⚕ **DIFFERENTIAL DIAGNOSES**
Corticosteroid, Cushing's syndrome, dystrophia myotonica, facioscapulohumeral dystrophy, malignancy, osteomalacia, polio, DM, polymyositis, hyperthyroidism, PMR, mitochondrial diseases, CKD, McArdle's syndrome

Pruritic rash

⚕ **DIFFERENTIAL DIAGNOSES**
Sweat, eczema (eg atopic, allergic, varicose), scabies, bullous diseases, tinea, lichen planus, urticaria, parasitic

Pruritus (generalised)

⚕ **DIFFERENTIAL DIAGNOSES**
Polycythaemia, iron deficiency, cholestasis, uraemia, thyroid disease, DM, diabetes insipidus, hyperparathyroidism, drug reaction, malignancy (eg lymphoma), parasites

Pruritus (scalp)

See also
— *Pruritic rash*
— *Pruritus (generalised)*

⚕ **DIFFERENTIAL DIAGNOSES**
Psoriasis, head lice, tinea, dermatitis, seborrhoeic dermatitis

Pruritus ani

☿ DIFFERENTIAL DIAGNOSES

Poor hygiene, faecal incontinence, sweat, candida, haemorrhoids, anal fissure, threadworms, lichen sclerosis, malignancy, warts, psoriasis

Pruritus vulvae

See also
— *Pruritus (generalised)*

☿ DIFFERENTIAL DIAGNOSES

Sweat, poor hygiene, VIN, vulval carcinoma, vulval dystrophy, atrophic vaginitis, candidiasis, lichen sclerosus, lichen planus, eczema, psoriasis, pubic lice, genital warts, helminths, scabies, faeces, urinary incontinence, DM, latex allergy, deodorants, pregnancy

Pseudobulbar palsy

☿ DIFFERENTIAL DIAGNOSES

See *Diseases, pseudobulbar palsy*

Psychosis

See also
— *Acute confusional state (delirium)*

☿ DIFFERENTIAL DIAGNOSES

Wilson's disease, drugs, sepsis, cerebral trauma, depression, schizophrenia, mania, borderline personality disorder, dementia, metabolic disturbance, thyroid disease, Cushing's disease, electrolyte disturbance, glucagonoma, Niemann-Pick disease, Wilson's disease

Ptosis

☿ DIFFERENTIAL DIAGNOSES

Unilateral (Horner's syndrome, IIIrd nerve palsy, myasthenia gravis, congenital), bilateral (myasthenia gravis, myotonic dystrophy, bilateral Horner's syndrome, bilateral IIIrd nerve palsies, congenital, Turner's syndrome, Kearns-Sayre syndrome, syphilis, chronic progressive external ophthalmoplegia)

Pulmonary crackles

☿ DIFFERENTIAL DIAGNOSES

See *breath sounds (crackles/crepitations)* and *pulmonary fibrosis*

Pulmonary fibrosis

☿ DIFFERENTIAL DIAGNOSES

Lower lobe (idiopathic pulmonary fibrosis/cryptogenic fibrosing alveolitis, lymphangitis carcinomatosis, iatrogenic, connective tissue disease), apical (ankylosing spondylitis, aspergillosis, extrinsic allergic alveolitis, sarcoid, TB, silicosis),

iatrogenic (radiotherapy, nitrofurantoin, methotrexate, busulfan, amiodarone, bleomycin, sulfasalazine, cyclophosphamide, gold). Other (neurofibromatosis, Langerhans' cell histiocytosis, tuberous sclerosis, lymphangiomyomatosis, systemic sclerosis, SLE, Sjögren's syndrome, polymyositis, RA, asbestosis, chemical exposure)

Pulse (irregular)

☿ DIFFERENTIAL DIAGNOSES

Sinus arrhythmia, sinus tachycardia, atrial ectopics, AF, intermittent/varying heart block, ventricular ectopics, ventricular tachycardia, proarrhythmogenic drugs, hyperthyroidism, phaeochromocytoma, sepsis, acid-base disturbance

Pulse (low volume)

☿ DIFFERENTIAL DIAGNOSES

Hypovolaemia, shock, aortic/mitral stenosis, arterial thrombosis, cardiac failure, cardiac tamponade, restrictive cardiomyopathy, constrictive pericarditis

Pulse (water hammer)

See also
— *Pulse pressure (wide)*

☿ DIFFERENTIAL DIAGNOSES

Aortic regurgitation, PDA, hyperdynamic circulation, anaemia, AVM, bradycardia, pregnancy, thyrotoxicosis

Pulse pressure (narrow)

☿ DIFFERENTIAL DIAGNOSES

Aortic stenosis, hypovolaemia, constrictive pericarditis, cardiac tamponade, pericardial effusion, mitral stenosis, left ventricular systolic failure, HOCM, pulmonary stenosis, tachycardia

Pulse pressure (wide)

☿ DIFFERENTIAL DIAGNOSES

Isolated systolic hypertension, hyperthyroidism, sepsis, pregnancy, PDA, aortic regurgitation, heart block, aortic dissection, raised ICP, anaemia

Pulsus paradoxus

☿ DIFFERENTIAL DIAGNOSES

Cardiac tamponade, pericardial effusion, constrictive pericarditis, restrictive cardiomyopathy, severe asthma/COPD, MI, PE, tension pneumothorax, SVCO, anaphylaxis, obesity, diaphragmatic hernia, gastric volvulus

Purpura

See also
— *Petechiae*

DIFFERENTIAL DIAGNOSES

Advancing age, sepsis, iatrogenic (antiplatelet agents, anticoagulants, steroids), thrombocytopenia (ITP, marrow failure, leukaemia), von Willebrand's disease, SLE, renal failure, hypersplenism, DIC, hereditary haemorrhagic telangiectasia, vasculitis (eg Henoch-Schönlein purpura), scurvy, vitamin K deficiency, amyloid

Pustule

ⓓ DIFFERENTIAL DIAGNOSES

Pus-filled skin lesion <10mm eg acne, rosacea, folliculitis

Pyogenic granuloma

ⓓ DIFFERENTIAL DIAGNOSES

Trauma, foreign body, pregnancy, iatrogenic (eg OCP, indinavir, retinoids, fluorouracil)

Pyrexia of unknown origin

ⓓ DIFFERENTIAL DIAGNOSES

See *fever*

Radiculopathy

ⓓ DIFFERENTIAL DIAGNOSES

Spondylosis, intervertebral disc prolapse, tumour, shingles, trauma, spinal nerve compression

Red eye

ⓓ DIFFERENTIAL DIAGNOSES

Conjunctivitis, subconjunctival haemorrhage, allergy, corneal abrasion, corneal ulcer, keratitis, episcleritis, scleritis, acute glaucoma, iritis, trauma, orbital cellulitis

Red reflex (absent)

ⓓ DIFFERENTIAL DIAGNOSES

Retinoblastoma, retinal detachment, vitreous haemorrhage, glass eye

Reflexes (brisk)

ⓓ DIFFERENTIAL DIAGNOSES

UMN lesion (eg MS, ADEM, CVA, syrinx, myelopathy), pre-eclampsia, magnesium toxicity, MND, hyperthyroidism, alcohol withdrawal, hypocalcaemia

Reflexes (reduced)

See also
— *Peripheral neuropathy*

ⓓ DIFFERENTIAL DIAGNOSES

Advancing age, LMN lesion, cerebellar disease, primary muscle disorder, MND, polio

Reflexes (slow relaxing, Woltman's sign)

ⓓ DIFFERENTIAL DIAGNOSES

Advancing age, hypothyroidism, DM, anorexia nervosa, hypothermia, peripheral artery disease, pregnancy, pernicious anaemia

Relative afferent pupillary defect (Marcus Gunn pupil)

See also
— *Optic atrophy*

ⓓ DIFFERENTIAL DIAGNOSES

Trauma, glaucoma (unilateral), optic neuritis, optic nerve compression, orbital tumour, retinal detachment, macular degeneration, retinal ischaemia, temporal arteritis, retinal infection, central retinal artery occlusion

Relative bradycardia

ⓓ DIFFERENTIAL DIAGNOSES

Typhoid, legionnaires' disease, *Chlamydia pneumoniae*, dengue fever

Renal mass

ⓓ DIFFERENTIAL DIAGNOSES

Simple cyst, carcinoma, hydronephrosis, polycystic kidney disease, amyloid, tuberous sclerosis, von Hippel-Lindau disease

Respiration (low rate)

ⓓ DIFFERENTIAL DIAGNOSES

Sleep, iatrogenic (eg benzodiazepines, opiates), alcohol, carbon dioxide retention, raised ICP, head injury, neuromuscular disease, hypothermia

Retinopathy

ⓓ DIFFERENTIAL DIAGNOSES

Hypertensive (grade 1: silver wiring, grade 2: AV nipping, grade 3: soft exudates, flame haemorrhages, grade 4: papilloedema); diabetic (background: dot/blot haemorrhages, microaneurysms, hard exudates; pre-proliferative: proliferative: new vessel formation, maculopathy); iatrogenic (eg phenothiazines, chloroquine); other (severe anaemia, atherosclerosis, prematurity, retinal vessel occlusion, sickle cell anaemia, SLE, solar retinopathy, trauma, malignancy, HIV, hyperviscosity, radiotherapy)

Rigor

ⓓ DIFFERENTIAL DIAGNOSES

Associated with high fever, usually bacterial infection.

Pneumonia, ARDS, pyelonephritis, UTI, cholecystitis, ascending cholangitis, IBD, septicaemia, malaria, bacterial endocarditis, Dressler's syndrome, septic arthritis, rheumatic fever, paroxysmal cold haemoglobinuria

Romberg's sign (+ve, ataxia worse when eyes shut, proprioceptive loss)

⚕ DIFFERENTIAL DIAGNOSES
Peripheral neuropathy, posterior column loss, MS, ADEM, cervical spondylosis, syphilis, advancing age, alcoholism

Romberg's sign (-ve, ataxia with eyes open or shut)

⚕ DIFFERENTIAL DIAGNOSES
Cerebellar disease, advancing age

Root lesions

⚕ DIFFERENTIAL DIAGNOSES
OA, intervertebral disc prolapse, injury, metastases, bulky nodes

Rose spots

⚕ DIFFERENTIAL DIAGNOSES
Small red macular lesions on trunk and abdomen of patients with typhoid

Roth spots

⚕ DIFFERENTIAL DIAGNOSES
Subacute bacterial endocarditis, PAN, SLE, leukaemia, DM, ischaemia, HIV, pernicious anaemia, carbon monoxide poisoning, prolonged anaesthesia, hypertension, pre-eclampsia, birth trauma, non-accidental injury, AVM, post-ocular surgery

Rubeosis iridis

⚕ DIFFERENTIAL DIAGNOSES
DM, central retinal vein occlusion, ocular ischaemia eg carotid disease, chronic retinal detachment, tumour

S1

⚕ DIFFERENTIAL DIAGNOSES
Closure of mitral/tricuspid valves. Loud in mitral stenosis, tachycardia, quiet in cardiac failure and mitral regurgitation

S2

⚕ DIFFERENTIAL DIAGNOSES
Closure of aortic/pulmonary valves. Loud in hypertension, quiet in valve stenosis. Fixed splitting in ASD.

S3 heart sound (rapid ventricular filling/increased blood volume within ventricle)

⚕ DIFFERENTIAL DIAGNOSES
Normal in young people, athletes, cardiac failure

S4 heart sound (blood forced into a stiff ventricle)

⚕ DIFFERENTIAL DIAGNOSES
Normal in young people, athletes, LVH, LVF, restrictive cardiomyopathy

Sacral dimple/hair

⚕ DIFFERENTIAL DIAGNOSES
Idiopathic, neural tube defect (if draining fluid, swelling, erythematous, sinus present)

Sacroiliac pain

See also
— Back pain

⚕ DIFFERENTIAL DIAGNOSES
OA, spondyloarthritis (eg ankylosing spondylitis, psoriatic arthritis, Reiter's syndrome, enteropathic arthritis), Behçet's syndrome

Saddle-shaped nose

⚕ DIFFERENTIAL DIAGNOSES
Untreated bilateral nasoseptal haematoma, Wegener's granulomatosis, trauma, relapsing polychondritis, congenital syphilis, leprosy, ectodermal dysplasia

Salivary gland enlargement/mass

See also
— Parotid lump

⚕ DIFFERENTIAL DIAGNOSES
Tumour, infection, stone, cyst, Mikulicz's disease, TB, sarcoid, Sjögren's syndrome

Sclera, blue

⚕ DIFFERENTIAL DIAGNOSES
Neonates, Marfan's syndrome, osteogenesis imperfecta, pseudoxanthoma elasticum, Ehlers-Danlos syndrome, scleromalacia, Crouzon syndrome, corticosteroids, scleral blue naevus

Scotoma

⚕ DIFFERENTIAL DIAGNOSES
MS, ADEM, glaucoma, optic nerve tumour, tobacco,

alcohol, vitamin B_{12} deficiency, thiamine deficiency, ischaemia, migraine aura (scintillating scotoma)

Scrotal lump/swelling

⚕ DIFFERENTIAL DIAGNOSES
Testicular (orchitis, tumour – seminoma, teratoma, lymphoma, leukaemia, trauma, torsion), epididymitis, epididymal cyst, hydatid of Morgagni (vestigial remnant), spermatocoele, hydrocoele, haematocoele, varicocoele, hernia

Seizure

⚕ DIFFERENTIAL DIAGNOSES
Febrile convulsion, head injury, iatrogenic (eg TCAs, phenothiazines), drug withdrawal (eg alcohol, benzodiazepines), epilepsy, CVA, cerebral tumour, sepsis, hypoglycaemia, anoxia, severe hypotension, electrolyte/metabolic disturbance, meningitis, encephalitis, ADEM, toxoplasmosis, toxocara, cerebral malaria, Gaucher's disease, pseudoseizure

Shifting dullness

⚕ DIFFERENTIAL DIAGNOSES
See ascites

Short fourth metacarpals

⚕ DIFFERENTIAL DIAGNOSES
Idiopathic, familial, Turner's syndrome, pseudohypoparathyroidism, pseudopseudohypoparathyroidism, Kallmann's syndrome

Short stature

See also
— Diseases, precocious puberty
— Diseases, delayed onset puberty

⚕ DIFFERENTIAL DIAGNOSES
Constitutional, chronic or severe systemic disease, dwarfism, achondroplasia, Turner's syndrome, growth hormone deficiency, osteogenesis imperfecta, congenital hypothyroidism, corticosteroids, hypo-thalamic/pituitary tumour, child abuse, malnutrition, malabsorption, coeliac disease, IBD, neurofibromatosis, pseudohypoparathyroidism type 1a (Albright hereditary osteodystrophy), galactosaemia, Noonan's syndrome, Down's syndrome

Single palmar crease

⚕ DIFFERENTIAL DIAGNOSES
Down's syndrome, cri du chat syndrome, idiopathic

Skin (hyperkeratosis)

See also
— Palmoplantar hyperkeratosis

⚕ DIFFERENTIAL DIAGNOSES
Morphea, connective tissue disease, chemical damage, carcinoid, acromegaly, scar, burns, cutaneous porphyria, acanthosis nigricans

Skin (linear lesions)

See also
— Koebner phenomenon

⚕ DIFFERENTIAL DIAGNOSES
Scratch marks, self harm, scars, scabies, shingles (defined by dermatome)

Skin (ring-shaped lesions)

⚕ DIFFERENTIAL DIAGNOSES
Trauma (eg cigarette burns), eczema, erythema multiforme (target lesions), ringworm, urticaria, bullous diseases, lichen planus, pityriasis rosea, halo naevus, granuloma annulare

Small for gestational age

⚕ DIFFERENTIAL DIAGNOSES
Idiopathic, smoking, alcohol, illicit drug use, chromosomal abnormalities, multiple births, placental anomalies, chronic maternal disease (anaemia, cardiac, endocrine, GI), pre-eclampsia, malnutrition

Soft tissue mass

⚕ DIFFERENTIAL DIAGNOSES
Lipoma, sebaceous cyst, metastases, sarcoma, TB, sarcoid, lymphadenopathy, haematoma, fibrous histiocytoma

Sore mouth

⚕ DIFFERENTIAL DIAGNOSES
Candida, burn, ulcer, tumour, dental abscess, referred pain eg sinusitis, trauma, URTI, foreign body, sicca syndrome, herpes, mucositis, gingivitis, hand foot and mouth disease, burning mouth syndrome, geographic tongue

Sore throat

⚕ DIFFERENTIAL DIAGNOSES
Viral URTI, streptococcal tonsillitis, infectious mononucleosis, quinsy, tumour, allergic rhinitis, sicca syndrome, candidiasis, foreign body, herpes simplex, herpes zoster, GORD, diphtheria, Vincent's angina, burn, TB, dust, smoking, alcohol abuse

Spasticity

⚕ DIFFERENTIAL DIAGNOSES
Spastic hemiparesis: CVA, cerebral malignancy,

ADEM, MS, cerebral palsy, head injury; spastic paraparesis: hereditary, tropical spastic paraparesis, cervical myelopathy, disc prolapse, spinal cord injury (eg traumatic transection), spinal abscess, discitis, transverse/HIV myelitis, spinal tumour, spinal cord compression (malignant infiltration), anterior spinal artery thrombosis, subacute combined degeneration of the spinal cord, MS, ADEM, parasaggital meningioma, mycoplasma TB

Speech disturbance

☿ DIFFERENTIAL DIAGNOSES

Dysphonia, dysphasia, mute, stammer, pressure of speech, fatigue, mania, hypomania, depression, dementia, tongue tie, burns, laryngeal stenosis, laryngeal tumour, laryngeal web, laryngitis, recurrent laryngeal nerve palsy, vocal cord nodules, iatrogenic (eg alcohol, phenytoin), CVA, deafness, XIIth nerve palsy, bulbar palsy, pseudobulbar palsy, cerebellar dysarthria, Parkinson's disease, syrinx, MS, ADEM, MND, myopathy, muscular dystrophy, inhaled corticosteroids

Spider naevi

☿ DIFFERENTIAL DIAGNOSES

Two or more naevi are pathological. Idiopathic, excess oestrogens, pregnancy, chronic liver disease, hyperthyroidism, rosacea

Splenomegaly

See also
— Hepatosplenomegaly

☿ DIFFERENTIAL DIAGNOSES

CML, myelofibrosis, visceral leishmaniasis, leukaemia, lymphoma, portal hypertension, infection (glandular fever, hepatitis, bacterial endocarditis, brucellosis, TB, malaria), haemolytic anaemia, amyloid, Felty's syndrome, Gaucher's disease, sickle cell anaemia (pre-infarction, sequestration crisis, extramedullary haemopoiesis)

Splinter haemorrhages

☿ DIFFERENTIAL DIAGNOSES

Trauma, bacterial endocarditis, mitral stenosis, vasculitis, SLE, scleroderma, RA, anti-phospholipid syndrome, anaemia, leukaemia, lymphoma

Sputum

☿ DIFFERENTIAL DIAGNOSES

Excess: smoking, bronchiectasis, pneumonia; yellow: asthma, allergy; green: infective; brown: may suggest streptococcal infection; pink: pulmonary oedema; bloody (see *haemoptysis*)

Steatorrhoea

☿ DIFFERENTIAL DIAGNOSES

Pancreatic insufficiency, coeliac disease, cholestasis of pregnancy

Strangury

☿ DIFFERENTIAL DIAGNOSES

Calculi, UTI, urethral stricture, urethral tumour, bladder cancer, penile cancer, STI, ureteric stent, prostatism

Striae

☿ DIFFERENTIAL DIAGNOSES

Pregnancy, obesity, glucocorticoid therapy, Cushing's syndrome

Stridor

☿ DIFFERENTIAL DIAGNOSES

Croup, epiglottitis, abscess, anaphylaxis, foreign body, laryngomalacia, laryngeal papillomas/tumour, subglottic haemangioma, Pierre Robin sequence, subglottic stenosis, bacterial tracheitis, diphtheria (inspiratory), vascular rings

Submandibular mass

See also
— Salivary gland enlargement/mass

☿ DIFFERENTIAL DIAGNOSES

Suppurative infection, duct infection, mumps, lymphoma, obstructing stone, submandibular gland malignancy, sarcoidosis, Sjögren's syndrome, lymphadenopathy, ranula, dermoid

Supraclavicular mass

☿ DIFFERENTIAL DIAGNOSES

Lymphadenopathy (reactive, malignant spread eg Virchow's node, gastric cancer, lymphoma), subclavian artery aneurysm

Suprapubic dullness

☿ DIFFERENTIAL DIAGNOSES

Urinary retention, pregnant uterus, massive fibroids, massive ovarian cyst, excessive adipose tissue

Syncope

See also
— Postural hypotension
— Loss of consciousness

☿ DIFFERENTIAL DIAGNOSES

Vasovagal, situational (cough, micturition), carotid sinus

hypersensitivity, postural hypotension (hypovolae-mia, drug-induced, autonomic failure), structural heart disease (aortic stenosis, mitral stenosis, HOCM, atrial myxoma), cardiac arrhythmia (eg Stokes-Adams attack), aortic dissection, PE. Exertional syncope is a sinister symptom

Tachycardia (>100bpm)

⚕ DIFFERENTIAL DIAGNOSES
Exercise, caffeine, pregnancy, anxiety, pain, fever, tach-yarrhythmia (eg AF/atrial flutter, SVT, ventricular tachycardia), cardiac failure, shock, anaemia, metabolic acidosis, respiratory failure, hyperthyroidism, iatrogenic (eg dihydropyridine, CCBs eg amlodipine, beta-agonists, pseudoephedrine), electrolyte disturbance, Guillain-Barré syndrome, McCune Albright syndrome

Tachypnoea

⚕ DIFFERENTIAL DIAGNOSES
See *breathlessness* and *Diseases, anxiety*

Tactile vocal fremitus (increased)

⚕ DIFFERENTIAL DIAGNOSES
Consolidation

Tactile vocal fremitus (reduced)

⚕ DIFFERENTIAL DIAGNOSES
Pneumothorax, pleural effusion, lung collapse

Tardive dyskinesia

⚕ DIFFERENTIAL DIAGNOSES
Prolonged neuroleptic use, anticholinergics, anti-depressants, metoclopramide, prochlorperazine, antiparkinson's drugs, lithium

Taste (loss)

See also
— *Anosmia*

⚕ DIFFERENTIAL DIAGNOSES
Posterior third of tongue – glossopharyngeal nerve palsy; anterior two-thirds of tongue – facial nerve palsy, iatro-genic, Addison's disease, oral infection

Telangiectasia

⚕ DIFFERENTIAL DIAGNOSES
Port wine stain, Sturge-Weber syndrome, ataxia-telangiectasia, pulmonary hypertension, rosacea, hereditary haemorrhagic telangiectasia, chronic liver disease, oestrogen excess, pregnancy, carcinoid syn-drome, scleroderma, radiotherapy

Tenesmus

⚕ DIFFERENTIAL DIAGNOSES
Rectal tumour, rectal polyp, rectal abscess, IBS, IBD, haemorrhoids, proctitis, endometriosis

Terry's nails/lines (white proximal nail with reddened distal nail)

⚕ DIFFERENTIAL DIAGNOSES
Age, cirrhosis, cardiac failure, DM, malignancy, HIV

Testicle (absent)

⚕ DIFFERENTIAL DIAGNOSES
Surgically removed, retractile, undescended, congeni-tally absent

Testicular atrophy

⚕ DIFFERENTIAL DIAGNOSES
Epididymitis, orchitis, torsion, trauma, hernia, tumour, varicocoele

Testicular pain

See also
— *Groin pain*

⚕ DIFFERENTIAL DIAGNOSES
Epididymitis, orchitis, torsion, trauma, hernia, tumour, traumatic haematocoele

Thenar eminence (wasting)

See also
— *Wasting of small muscles of hand*

⚕ DIFFERENTIAL DIAGNOSES
Median nerve lesion, disuse, RA, mononeuritis multi-plex, C8/T1 root lesion, syrinx, trauma

Thyroid nodule

⚕ DIFFERENTIAL DIAGNOSES
Solitary nodule (thyrotoxic: nodule; euthyroid: cyst, carcinoma, adenoma); multinodular goitre (thyro-toxic: toxic multinodular nodule; euthyroid: nontoxic multinodular goitre)

Tibia (bowing)

⚕ DIFFERENTIAL DIAGNOSES
Paget's disease of the bone, rickets, yaws, syphilis, McCune Albright syndrome, trauma, pseudoarthrosis, hemimelia (absence of tibia), fibrous dysplasia, physi-ological, neurofibromatosis

Tics

☾ DIFFERENTIAL DIAGNOSES
Gilles de la Tourette syndrome, head injury, CVA, iatrogenic (eg amphetamines, cocaine, TCAs, opiates)

Tinnitus

☾ DIFFERENTIAL DIAGNOSES
Idiopathic, ear wax, foreign body, trauma, noise- induced tinnitus, barotrauma, tympanic perforation, Eustachian tube dysfunction, Ménière's disease, cochlear damage, iatrogenic (eg salicylates, NSAIDs, loop diuretics) acoustic neuroma, otosclerosis, Paget's disease of the bone, stress, otitis media, otitis externa, presbycusis, meningitis, MS, thyroid disease, pulsatile tinnitus (glomus tumour, AVM), hyperviscosity, TMJ dysfunction

Tongue (appearance)

☾ DIFFERENTIAL DIAGNOSES
Geographic: harmless (idiopathic, riboflavin deficiency); smooth: iron/vitamin B_{12} deficiency; inflamed: candida, burn; persistent ulcer: carcinoma, leukoplakia; pre-malignant: denture trauma, smoking, alcohol, vitamin deficiency, lichen planus, syphilis, HPV, poor dentition, idiopathic. Oral hairy leukoplakia: immunodeficiency, EBV, not premalignant

Trachea (deviated)

☾ DIFFERENTIAL DIAGNOSES
Pulmonary fibrosis, pneumothorax (trachea compressed if under tension), large pleural effusion, chest wall/spinal deformities, thyroid tumour, oesophageal tumour, lymphadenopathy

Tremor

☾ DIFFERENTIAL DIAGNOSES
Fine: anxiety, hyperthyroidism, benign essential tremor (may be coarse); drug withdrawal: eg alcohol, benzodiazepines; sympathomimetic drugs (eg beta-agonists); resting tremor: parkinsonism; intention tremor: cerebellar disease, brainstem disease; flapping tremor: hepatic failure, carbon dioxide retention; choreiform: Huntington's disease, rheumatic fever, hemiballismus

Urinary frequency

See also
   — *Strangury*
   — *Dysuria*

☾ DIFFERENTIAL DIAGNOSES
UTI, cystitis, DM, diabetes insipidus, iatrogenic (eg diuretics, ACE inhibitors, CCBs), hypercalcaemia, bladder/urethral calculus/malignancy, uterine prolapse, prostatic hypertrophy, prostate carcinoma, spastic bladder, overactive bladder, post-radiotherapy, menopause, pregnancy, obesity, fibroids, polydipsia

Urinary retention

☾ DIFFERENTIAL DIAGNOSES
Prostatism, spinal injury/lesion, splanchnic nerve damage, bladder damage, detrusor sphincter dyssynergia, Parkinson's disease, MS, ADEM, UTI, postanaesthetic, iatrogenic (eg TCAs, anticholinergics), urethral obstruction, STI, posterior urethral valve, urethral stricture, psychological

Urine discoloration

☾ DIFFERENTIAL DIAGNOSES
Black on standing: alkaptonuria; red: (see *haematuria*), rifampicin, phenolphthalein, beetroot (acid urine), porphyria (on standing), myoglobin, rhubarb (alkaline urine)

Urticaria

☾ DIFFERENTIAL DIAGNOSES
Parasitic/helminthic infestation, acute allergy (iatrogenic, food), stress, UV exposure, dermographism, cold, heat, vasculitis, hereditary, CMML

Uvula deviation

☾ DIFFERENTIAL DIAGNOSES
Vagus nerve palsy; uvula moves away from side of lesion

Vaginal discharge

See also
   — *Intermenstrual bleeding*
   — *Postcoital bleeding*
   — *Postmenopausal bleeding*

☾ DIFFERENTIAL DIAGNOSES
Physiological, pregnancy, menstruation, retained tampon, chlamydia, gonorrhoea, trichomonas vaginitis, bacterial vaginosis, candidiasis, foreign body, ectropion, polyp, malignancy

Vertigo (sensation of rotatory movement)

☾ DIFFERENTIAL DIAGNOSES
Labyrinthitis, vestibular neuritis, BPPV, otitis media, Ménière's disease, migraine, brainstem ischaemia/stroke, MS, ADEM, iatrogenic (eg alcohol, phenytoin), Wernicke's encephalopathy, lateral medullary syndrome, posterior fossa tumour, Ramsay Hunt syndrome (herpes zoster), temporal lobe epilepsy

Vomiting

See also
— *Nausea*

⚕ DIFFERENTIAL DIAGNOSES
Infection (sepsis, cholecystitis, pyelone-phritis, appendicitis, toxic shock syndrome, pneumonia, PID, HUS, meningitis, malaria, gastritis, gastroenteritis, norovirus, acute otitis media, fever); iatrogenic (side-effect, poisoning including alcohol, vitamin A, lead, chemotherapy); bowel obstruction/carcinoma, achalasia, pharyngeal pouch, peptic ulcer, pyloric stenosis, gastroparesis, pancreatitis, mesenteric adenitis, bowel infarction, pain, pregnancy, anxiety, MI, cardiac failure, DKA, hypercalcaemia, Addison's disease, acute intermittent porphyria, phaeochromocytoma, head injury, migraine, raised ICP, encephalitis, ADEM, CVA, SAH, malignancy, hypertension, acute glaucoma, seizure, labyrinthitis, Ménière's disease, uraemia, Bartter's syndrome, paroxysmal cold haemoglobinuria, Q fever, medium chain acyl-CoA dehydrogenase deficiency

Vulval ulcer

⚕ DIFFERENTIAL DIAGNOSES
HSV, syphilis, chancroid, lymphogranuloma venereum, TB, Behçet's syndrome, granuloma inguinale, Crohn's disease

Vulvovaginal mass

⚕ DIFFERENTIAL DIAGNOSES
Cystocoele, rectocoele, enterocoele, urethrocoele, uterine prolapse, uterine polyp, Bartholin's cyst, sebaceous cyst, abscess, lymphadenopathy, malignancy, warts, urethral caruncle, varicose veins, lipoma

Wasting of intrinsic muscles of hand

⚕ DIFFERENTIAL DIAGNOSES
T1 lesion (brachial plexus lesion, Pancoast tumour, root lesion, cord lesion, cervical rib, syrinx, cervical spondylosis), polio, neurofibroma, RA, MND, disuse, OA, Klumpke's paralysis, primary muscle disease, median/ulnar nerve lesion

Waterbrash

⚕ DIFFERENTIAL DIAGNOSES
Peptic ulcer disease, GORD, scleroderma with oesophageal involvement

Webbed neck

⚕ DIFFERENTIAL DIAGNOSES
Turner's syndrome, Noonan's syndrome, Klippel-Feil syndrome

Weight gain

⚕ DIFFERENTIAL DIAGNOSES
Klinefelter's syndrome, acromegaly, hypopituitarism, insulinoma, hypogonadism, craniopharyngioma, Prader-Willi syndrome, Laurence-Moon-Biedl syndrome, gluttony, lack of exercise, menopause, Cushing's syndrome, hypothyroidism, cardiac failure, PCOS, ascites, nephrotic syndrome, iatrogenic (eg corticosteroids, insulin, sulfonylureas, oestrogen, lithium, sodium valproate, atypical antipsychotics, tamoxifen), smoking cessation

Weight loss

⚕ DIFFERENTIAL DIAGNOSES
Malnutrition, malabsorption, hyperthyroidism, depression, mania, malignancy, alcoholism, poorly controlled/undiagnosed DM, chronic infection (TB, endocarditis, HIV, parasitic infections), Addison's disease, CF, Parkinson's disease, dementia, connective tissue diseases, iatrogenic (eg ACE inhibitors, amiodarone, amphetamines, metformin, levodopa, calcitriol, bicalutamide, clonazepam, clonidine, thyroxine, digoxin, donepezil, SSRIs, leflunomide, NSAIDs, topiramate, zidovudine)

Wheeze (expiratory monophonic)

⚕ DIFFERENTIAL DIAGNOSES
Bronchogenic malignancy, inhaled foreign body, compression by extrinsic mass (mediastinal/oesophageal malignancy, lymphoma), trauma, mucous plug

Wheeze (expiratory polyphonic)

⚕ DIFFERENTIAL DIAGNOSES
Allergic reaction, viral infection, asthma, COPD, pulmonary oedema (cardiac wheeze), iatrogenic (eg beta-blockers), childhood reflux

Wrist drop

See also
— *Diseases, radial nerve lesion*

⚕ DIFFERENTIAL DIAGNOSES
C7 root lesion, radial nerve traction injury

Xanthoma

⚕ DIFFERENTIAL DIAGNOSES
Hypercholesterolaemia, DM, nephrotic syndrome, liver disease, chronic pancreatitis, hypothyroidism, primary biliary cirrhosis

INVESTIGATIONS

Acanthocytes (blood film)

 CLINICAL NOTES

Red blood cells that show many spicules on a wet film. Aetiology/risk factors: Anorexia, hypothyroidism, McLeod syndrome, neuroacanthosis, abetalipoprotein-aemia, alcoholic cirrhosis, uraemia, vitamin E deficiency, hereditary spherocytosis, beta spectrin deficiency.

Acid-fast bacilli culture (eg *Mycobacterium tuberculosis*)

 CLINICAL NOTES

Three early morning sputum samples required on separate days to ensure yield. Consider culture from bronchoscopy samples/gastric washings/CSF/urine.

Acid phosphatase

↑ **RAISED IN/BY**

Prostate cancer (localised and metastatic, used for monitoring and in staging), benign prostatic hypertrophy, prostatitis, urinary catheterisation, Paget's disease of the bone, sepsis, glycogen storage diseases, hyperparathyroidism, MI, renal failure, myeloma.

CLINICAL NOTES

Found in prostate, liver, spleen, semen and bone marrow.

Activated partial thromboplastin time (APTT)

↑ **RAISED IN/BY**

Prolonged APTT: Lab error, insufficient blood sample, abnormal haematocrit, clotting factor (or vitamin K) deficiency or presence of APTT inhibitors: liver disease, DIC, von Willebrand's disease, haemophilia A, Christmas disease, presence of lupus anticoagulant (but APTT may be normal depending on the anticoagulant present. The anticoagulant causes a paradoxical increased risk of thrombosis), replacement clotting factor, heparin, warfarin.

↓ **DECREASED IN/BY**

Acute phase response (may cause ↑factor VIII).

CLINICAL NOTES

Reflects changes in the intrinsic and/or common clotting pathways. Used for heparin monitoring or when patient has symptoms or signs of clotting disorder or recurrent miscarriage. If APTT normal and lupus anticoagulant (LA) suspected, LA-sensitive APTT may be requested.

Adrenocorticotrophic hormone (ACTH)

↑ **RAISED IN/BY**

Cushing's disease (pituitary adenoma). Ectopic ACTH (eg lung tumour), insulin, levodopa, metoclopramide, tetracosactide (synthetic ACTH), Addison's disease, CAH, Nelson's syndrome.

↓ **DECREASED IN/BY**

Iatrogenic (eg steroid treatment), adrenal tumour, hypopituitarism, McCune Albright syndrome.

CLINICAL NOTES

Used in conjunction with cortisol in investigation of pituitary and adrenal disease.

Alanine aminotransferase (ALT, SPGT)

↑ **RAISED IN/BY**

Hepatitis (higher in acute eg 10x ULN than chronic hepatitis eg up to 4x ULN), non-hepatitic infections (eg Weil's disease, glandular fever/EBV, CMV), auto-immune hepatitis, fatty liver, malignancy, obstructive liver disease, alcoholic hepatitis, cirrhosis, glycogen storage diseases, haemochromatosis, Wilson's disease, alpha-1-antitrypsin deficiency, thyroid disease, right/congestive heart failure, iatrogenic (eg methotrexate, paracetamol overdose), liver infarction, trypanosomiasis, abetalipoproteinaemia.

CLINICAL NOTES

Raised ALT more specific for liver disease than AST. ALT>AST suggestive of chronic liver disease, AST> ALT suggestive of alcoholic hepatitis and cirrhosis.

Albumin

↑ **RAISED IN/BY**

Dehydration, insulin, anabolic steroids, growth hormone, androgens.

↓ **DECREASED IN/BY**

Malnutrition, malabsorption, IBD, protein-losing enteropathy, liver disease, nephrotic syndrome, burns, trauma, catabolic states eg malignancy, myeloma (but high total protein/globulins), pregnancy, chronic disease, pancreatitis, bowel obstruction, erythroderma.

CLINICAL NOTES

Prealbumin may be a more useful measure of nutritional state.

Aldosterone

↑ **RAISED IN/BY**

Conn's syndrome (associated with ↓renin: adrenal hyperplasia, adrenal adenoma, adrenal tumour). Iatrogenic, low renal perfusion (eg hypotension, renal artery stenosis), cirrhosis, congestive heart failure, pre-eclampsia, post MI, hyponatraemia, hyperkalaemia, Bartter's syndrome, hard liquorice, diuretics.

↓ DECREASED IN/BY

Addison's disease (autoimmune, TB of the adrenal gland, adrenal infarction eg Waterhouse-Friderichsen syndrome, sarcoidosis, amyloid, HIV, haemochromatosis), hypopituitarism, congenital adrenal hyperplasia, Liddle's syndrome, severe intercurrent illness, abrupt exogenous steroid withdrawal, adrenalectomy, hypokalaemia.

 CLINICAL NOTES

Lying and standing samples and simultaneous renin samples may be required. 24-hour urine collection may be preferred.

Alkaline phosphatase (ALP)

↑ RAISED IN/BY

Placental isoenzyme:
Malignancy: Ovary, testicular seminoma.
Non-malignant: Smokers, pregnancy.
Bone isoenzyme: Normal growth, fracture, Paget's disease of the bone, vitamin D deficiency, primary bone tumour, bony metastases, primary hyperparathyroidism, tertiary hyperparathyroidism, renal osteodystrophy, osteopetrosis.
Liver isoenzyme: Biliary obstruction, obstructive jaundice, PBC, hepatitis (mildly raised), temporal arteritis, polymyalgia rheumatica, cholangitis, sclerosing cholangitis, autoimmune arthritis.

↓ DECREASED IN/BY

Genetic, iatrogenic (COC, fluoxetine), malnutrition, hypothyroidism, zinc deficiency, post blood transfusion.

CLINICAL NOTES

ALP isoenzymes may be requested if the cause of elevated ALP is unknown.

Alpha-fetoprotein (AFP)

↑ RAISED IN/BY

Malignancy: Hepatocellular carcinoma (may be used in diagnosis, screening, prognosis, monitoring), perform six-monthly in high-risk groups eg hepatitis C. Testicular germ cell tumour (teratoma, not for screening, use for diagnosis, prognosis, monitoring, not raised in pure seminoma), unusually – pancreatic, gastric, colonic, nasogastric, breast, lymphoma. Levels correlate with tumour bulk.
Non-malignant: Cirrhosis, hepatitis, liver regeneration, hepatoma, emphysema, ataxia-telangiectasia.

CLINICAL NOTES

Sensitive marker for relapse or treatment response in testicular germ cell tumours, unusual to be raised in healthy people. Used in antenatal screening (eg triple test) where low levels can indicate trisomies (not just Down's syndrome) and high levels can indicate neural tube defects, gastroschisis, omphalocoele and multiple pregnancy.

Ambulatory BP monitoring

CLINICAL NOTES

May be requested to aid diagnosis of white coat hypertension, episodic hypertension (eg phaeochromocytoma), hypotension, assessment of nighttime dipper status (non-dipper status may confer higher CHD risk).

Ammonia (serum)

↑ RAISED IN/BY

Transient (newborn), smoking, Reye's syndrome (associated with hypoglycaemia), hepatic/portosystemic shunt, hepatic encephalopathy, fatty liver of pregnancy, renal failure, renal tubular acidosis, urinary diversion surgery, iatrogenic (eg valproate), haematological malignancies, parenteral nutrition, GI haemorrhage, medium chain acyl-CoA dehydrogenase deficiency, urea cycle defects eg N-acetylglutamate synthetase deficiency, galactosaemia.

↓ DECREASED IN/BY

Hypertension.

CLINICAL NOTES

Ammonia is normally broken down to urea and glutamine. Should be measured in altered consciousness of unknown cause.

Amylase

↑ RAISED IN/BY

P-isoenzyme: Acute pancreatitis (levels increase within 12 hours of onset), chronic pancreatitis (levels not as elevated as in acute disease, levels may decrease as pancreas becomes increasingly damaged), ERCP, pancreatic pseudocyst, pancreatic tumour, iatrogenic (eg OCP, aspirin, NSAIDs, steroids, diuretics both loop and thiazides, alcohol, opiates, methyldopa), mumps.
Non-pancreatic causes: Cholecystitis, cholangitis, bowel obstruction, mesenteric ischaemia, appendicitis, gastroenteritis, perforated peptic ulcer, ovarian or lung cancer, renal failure, liver disease.
S-isoenzyme: Salivary gland insult (eg mumps), liver disease, renal failure, ectopic pregnancy, PID, ovarian cyst, myeloma.

↓ DECREASED IN/BY

Chronic pancreatic damage, pre-eclampsia.

Angiography

CLINICAL NOTES

Used to identify arterial/venous stenosis or blockage. Unstable (intraluminal) coronary plaques may not be identified by conventional angiography.

Angiotensin-converting enzyme (ACE)

↑ RAISED IN/BY

Young age (<20 years), sarcoidosis, TB, leprosy, HIV, fungal infections, asbestosis, silicosis, berylliosis, DM, lymphoma, alcoholic cirrhosis, Gaucher's disease, hyperthyroidism.

↓ DECREASED IN/BY

Hyperlipidaemia, haemolysis, COPD, CF, Ca lung, steroid therapy, severe malnutrition.

📋 CLINICAL NOTES

50-80% sensitive for sarcoid, normal levels may be seen in early or chronic sarcoid. Not specific for sarcoid.

Anisocytes

📋 CLINICAL NOTES

Abnormal variation in RBC size.

Aetiology/risk factors: Iron deficiency, thalassaemia, megaloblastic anaemia, sideroblastic anaemia, post blood transfusion.

Anti-acetylcholine receptor antibodies

↑ RAISED IN/BY

Myasthenia gravis.

📋 CLINICAL NOTES

Used in diagnosis and treatment response of myasthenia gravis. False +ve test seen in MND, small cell lung cancer (SCLC), thymoma, Lambert-Eaton syndrome, increasing age.

Anti-cardiolipin antibodies

↑ RAISED IN/BY

Drug-induced, SLE, anti-phospholipid syndrome, HIV, malignancy.

📋 CLINICAL NOTES

Causes false +ve VDRL test.

Anti-centromere antibodies

↑ RAISED IN/BY

Limited scleroderma (CREST syndrome), systemic sclerosis, SLE, seronegative arthritis, Raynaud's syndrome.

📋 CLINICAL NOTES

Useful to discriminate between limited scleroderma (sensitivity 70%) and diffuse disease (sensitivity for systemic sclerosis 20%). Associated with sclerodactyly and lung involvement.

Anti-double stranded DNA (dsDNA) antibodies

↑ RAISED IN/BY

Active SLE.

📋 CLINICAL NOTES

Specific for SLE, 60% sensitive, associated with SLE nephritis and CNS involvement. Can be negative in quiescent disease. High titre correlates with poor prognosis. May be present in some patients with partial lipodystrophy.

Anti-endomysial antibodies

↑ RAISED IN/BY

Coeliac disease, dermatitis herpetiformis (diagnosis and monitoring).

📋 CLINICAL NOTES

Sensitivity (active coeliac disease) 90%, dermatitis herpetiformis 70%. Very specific. IgA antibodies more specific than IgG. Patient should be checked for IgA deficiency. In IgA deficiency, IgG antibodies should be requested.

Anti-gliadin antibodies

↑ RAISED IN/BY

Coeliac disease.

📋 CLINICAL NOTES

Sensitivity (IgA) 80%, specificity (IgA) 92%. Titres fall if patient on gluten-free diet. Patient should be checked for IgA deficiency. In IgA deficiency, IgG antibodies should be requested.

Anti-hepatitis A antibody

📋 CLINICAL NOTES

IgM positive in current infection. IgG suggests previous infection or successful vaccination.

Anti-hepatitis C (HCV) antibodies

📋 CLINICAL NOTES

Demonstrates exposure to hepatitis C virus, takes months to become positive, unlike PCR, which is usually positive by 7-14 days after infection.

Anti-hep B core antibodies (anti-HBc)

📋 CLINICAL NOTES

IgM type suggests recent or acute infection. IgG type suggests previous infection or chronic infection if in the presence of hep B surface antigen.

Anti-hep B envelope antibodies (anti-HBe)

📋 **CLINICAL NOTES**
Indicates viral elimination and low infectivity.

Anti-hep B surface antibodies (anti-HBs)

📋 **CLINICAL NOTES**
Suggestive of vaccination or recovery from previous infection.

Anti-cyclic citrullinated peptide (CCP) antibodies

📋 **CLINICAL NOTES**
Mainly used in diagnosis of RA. May also be found in a small proportion of patients with Sjögren's syndrome, psoriatic arthritis and children with juvenile idiopathic arthritis. Presence indicates greater risk of destructive joint disease in RA.
Sensitivity for RA: 60-80%, specificity for RA: >90%.

Anti-histone antibodies

↑ **RAISED IN/BY**
Drug-induced lupus, SLE, RA, scleroderma, juvenile RA, PBC, autoimmune hepatitis, dermatomyositis, polymyositis.

📋 **CLINICAL NOTES**
90% sensitive for drug-induced lupus.

Anti-Jo-1 antibodies

↑ **RAISED IN/BY**
Polymyositis, dermatomyositis.

📋 **CLINICAL NOTES**
The presence of anti-Jo-1 antibodies in polymyositis is associated with pulmonary fibrosis.

Anti-La (SSB) antibodies (extractable nuclear antibody)

↑ **RAISED IN/BY**
Sjögren's syndrome, SLE.

Anti-mitochondrial antibodies (AMA)

↑ **RAISED IN/BY**
PBC, sclerosing cholangitis, IBD with liver disease, biliary obstruction. Hepatitis, syphilis, SLE, RA, thyroid disease, Sjögren's syndrome, systemic sclerosis, mycobacterial infection.

📋 **CLINICAL NOTES**
Sensitivity: M2 subtype most specific for PBC (>90%).

Anti-nuclear antibodies (ANA)

↑ **RAISED IN/BY**
SLE, polymyositis, drug-induced lupus, Sjögren's syndrome, RA, juvenile chronic arthritis, scleroderma, autoimmune hepatitis, anti-phospholipid syndrome, myasthenia gravis, polymyositis, dermatomyositis, fibrosing alveolitis, DM, glandular fever, Addison's disease, immune thrombocytopenic purpura (ITP), sclerosing cholangitis, partial lipodystrophy, PBC, myasthenia gravis.

📋 **CLINICAL NOTES**
Sensitivities: Autoimmune hepatitis 100%, SLE 95%, drug-induced lupus 95%, scleroderma 60-90%, Sjögren's syndrome 40-70%, myasthenia gravis 50%, polymyositis/dermatomyositis 40%, RA 30%, idiopathic pulmonary fibrosis 30%, DM 25%, glandular fever/Addison's disease/ITP/normal population 8%. False +ve rate increases with age; -ve ANA makes SLE unlikely.

Anti-parietal cell antibodies

↑ **RAISED IN/BY**
Pernicious anaemia.

📋 **CLINICAL NOTES**
90% sensitive.
False +ve: Relatives, Addison's disease, iron deficiency anaemia, with increasing age.

Anti-phospholipid antibodies (anti-cardiolipin and lupus anticoagulant)

↑ **RAISED IN/BY**
Anti-phospholipid (Hughes) syndrome, SLE, normal population.

📋 **CLINICAL NOTES**
Presence gives false +ve VDRL.

Anti-reticulin antibodies

↑ **RAISED IN/BY**
Coeliac disease, dermatitis herpetiformis, Crohn's disease.

📋 **CLINICAL NOTES**
Titres fall if patient on gluten-free diet.

Anti-RNA polymerase I, II, III antibodies

↑ **RAISED IN/BY**
Systemic sclerosis, particularly with renal involvement.

INVESTIGATIONS

Anti-Ro (SSA) antibodies

↑ RAISED IN/BY

Sjögren's syndrome, SLE, Raynaud's phenomenon.

 CLINICAL NOTES

Presence may cause congenital heart block.

Anti-Scl-70 antibodies (anti-topoisomerase) antibodies

↑ RAISED IN/BY

Diffuse scleroderma, approx 25% patients with SLE.

 CLINICAL NOTES

Systemic sclerosis: Sensitivity 25%, specificity high. Poor prognostic marker, associated with pulmonary fibrosis. Anti-Scl-70 antibodies in patients with SLE confer an increased risk of pulmonary hypertension and renal disease.

Anti-Smith (Sm) antibodies

↑ RAISED IN/BY

SLE.

CLINICAL NOTES

Specific for SLE, 30% sensitivity. Associated with lupus nephritis.

Anti-smooth muscle antibodies

↑ RAISED IN/BY

Autoimmune active hepatitis, PBC, viral infections, autoimmune alopecia, primary pulmonary hypertension, alcoholism.

CLINICAL NOTES

High sensitivity for autoimmune active hepatitis.

Anti-sperm antibodies

CLINICAL NOTES

Antibodies may cause sperm agglutination, immobilisation or death. Males or females may have anti-sperm antibodies.

Antistreptolysin-O-antibodies titre (ASOT)

CLINICAL NOTES

-75% sensitivity for Lancefield group A streptococcus infection.

False +ve: Liver disease, TB, hypercholesterolaemia.

Antithrombin III (AT-III)

↑ RAISED IN/BY

Vitamin K deficiency, hepatitis, cholestasis, renal transplant, may occur with warfarin therapy.

↓ DECREASED IN/BY

Congenital antithrombin deficiency (heterozygous/homozygous), first few days of life, nephrotic syndrome, liver disease, blood loss, malignancy, oestrogens, protein-losing enteropathy, DVT, PE, DIC.

CLINICAL NOTES

Levels should not be checked while on anticoagulants. Only check AT-III when patient clinically stable and if recurrent venous thrombosis or when patient does not respond to heparin. Antithrombin levels *and* activity should be measured. Type 1 deficiency – both levels and activity reduced, type 2 deficiency – reduced activity.

Anti-tissue transglutaminase (TTG) antibodies

↑ RAISED IN/BY

Coeliac disease, dermatitis herpetiformis.

CLINICAL NOTES

Sensitivities: Active coeliac disease 90%, dermatitis herpetiformis 70%. Specificity for coeliac disease >95%. Antibodies used in diagnosis and monitoring. IgA antibodies most specific. Patient should be checked for IgA deficiency. If IgA deficiency, IgG antibodies should be requested.

Anti-U1-RNP antibodies

↑ RAISED IN/BY

Mixed connective tissue disease, SLE, diffuse cutaneous systemic sclerosis.

Apolipoprotein A-I

↑ RAISED IN/BY

Exercise, female gender, change to healthy diet, pregnancy, statins, OCP, carbamazepine, familial.

↓ DECREASED IN/BY

Smoking, CKD, DM, familial, beta-blockers, progestogens, diuretics.

CLINICAL NOTES

Not in routine use by most labs. Reduced levels correlate with CHD risk.

Apolipoprotein E genotype

CLINICAL NOTES

Associated with high cholesterol and triglyceride levels. e2, e3, e4 genotypes exist in combination. e2 associated with reduced lipid clearance and CHD. e2/e2 equates to type 3 hyperlipoproteinaemia. e4 associated with Alzheimer's disease.

Aspartate aminotransferase (AST, SGOT)

↑ RAISED IN/BY
Acute hepatitis (may be 10x ULN), chronic hepatitis (up to 4x ULN), alcoholic liver disease, MI, haemolysis, extreme exercise, muscle injury, pregnancy (including HELLP syndrome), iatrogenic, diphtheria.

📋 **CLINICAL NOTES**
Found in liver, to a lesser extent in heart and muscle.

Atypical lymphocytes (blood film)

📋 **CLINICAL NOTES**
Larger lymphocytes with nucleoli within nuclei.
Aetiology/risk factors: EBV, CMV, varicella, hepatitis A, hepatitis B, parvovirus B19, HIV, rubella, toxoplasmosis, roseola, TB, Q fever, mumps, influenza, mycoplasma infection, pneumonia, sarcoid, stress, lead poisoning, hypopituitarism, thyrotoxicosis, Addison's disease, RA, SLE, immune thrombocytopenic purpura, renal graft rejection, Guillain-Barré syndrome, myasthenia gravis, acute disseminated encephalomyelitis, Hodgkin's lymphoma, agammaglobulinaemia.

Auer rods (blood film)

📋 **CLINICAL NOTES**
Cytoplasmic splinter-like inclusion bodies in blasts.
Aetiology/risk factors: AML but not all subtypes.

Basophilic stippling of erythrocytes (blood film)

📋 **CLINICAL NOTES**
Granular inclusion bodies.
Aetiology/risk factors: Lead poisoning, thalassaemia, sideroblastic anaemia, myelofibrosis.

Basophils

↑ RAISED IN/BY
Urticaria, hypothyroidism, viral infection, myeloproliferative disease, malignancy, haemolytic disease, ulcerative colitis.

Bence-Jones protein (urine)

📋 **CLINICAL NOTES**
Present in multiple myeloma (two-thirds cases). 20% of myeloma cases are Bence-Jones +ve with a normal serum protein electrophoresis. Not detected by standard urinalysis.

Beta 2 microglobulin (blood and urine)

↑ RAISED IN/BY
Malignancy: Multiple myeloma, ALL, CLL, lymphoma, solid tumours. Non-malignant: Renal disease, liver disease, IBD.

📋 **CLINICAL NOTES**
Higher levels correlate with poorer prognosis haematological tumours. Used in treatment monitoring.

Bicarbonate

↑ RAISED IN/BY
Metabolic alkalosis, respiratory acidosis.

↓ DECREASED IN/BY
Metabolic acidosis, respiratory alkalosis.

Bilirubin

See also
— *Signs and symptoms, jaundice*

↑ RAISED IN/BY
Pre-hepatic (unconjugated hyperbilirubinaemia): Haemolysis, iron, folate/vitamin B_{12} deficiencies, haemoglobinopathies, Gilbert's syndrome, Crigler-Najjar syndrome, breast milk jaundice, muscle injury.
Hepatic: Hepatocellular damage/hepatitis, malignancy, cholestasis of pregnancy, right heart failure, Dubin-Johnson syndrome (conjugated hyperbilirubinaemia), Rotor syndrome (conjugated hyperbilirubinaemia), Budd-Chiari syndrome (conjugated hyperbilirubinaemia).
Post-hepatic (will be conjugated hyperbilirubinaemia): Gallstone disease, biliary atresia, cholangiocarcinoma, sclerosing cholangitis, pancreatic tumour (head), obstructive tumours at porta hepatis, parasitic infections.

Bilirubin (urinalysis)

↑ RAISED IN/BY
Seen in conjugated hyperbilirubinaemias.

Bladder tumour antigen (BTA)

↑ RAISED IN/BY
Bladder tumour.

📋 **CLINICAL NOTES**
False +ve in renal stones, UTI, urinary tract surgery.

Blasts (peripheral blood film)

📋 **CLINICAL NOTES**
Nucleated white cell precursors in peripheral film.
Aetiology/risk factors: Leukaemia, myelofibrosis, severe inflammation (leukaemoid reaction).

INVESTIGATIONS

Bone marrow aspirate

📋 **CLINICAL NOTES**

Sample may be required to investigate anaemia, haematological malignancy, myeloproliferative diseases, myelodysplasia, infection (eg TB, typhoid, brucellosis).

Bone marrow core biopsy

📋 **CLINICAL NOTES**

Used to assess marrow structure.

Brain natriuretic peptide (BNP)

↑ **RAISED IN/BY**

LVSD (diagnosis, monitoring and prognosis), LVH, MI, valvular heart disease, hypertension, CKD (reduced clearance of BNP), beta-blockers (at initiation).

↓ **DECREASED IN/BY**

ACE inhibitors, ARBs, beta-blockers, diuretics.

📋 **CLINICAL NOTES**

High -ve predictive value for cardiac failure.

BRCA gene

↑ **RAISED IN/BY**

BRCA1: Increased risk of breast and ovarian cancer.
BRCA2: Increased risk of breast (including male), ovarian, prostate and pancreatic cancers.

📋 **CLINICAL NOTES**

Located on chromosome 17 (*BRCA1*) and 13 (*BRCA2*). Presence confers up to 50-85% chance of developing breast cancer and 15-45% chance of developing ovarian cancer. Higher carriage among Ashkenazi Jews.

Burr cells (blood film)

📋 **CLINICAL NOTES**

Similar to acanthocytes but spurs less pronounced.
Aetiology/risk factors: CKD, gastric carcinoma, blood transfusion.

CA 125

↑ **RAISED IN/BY**

Malignancy: Ovary (levels correlate to clinical course and treatment response, use with imaging for case finding, not currently used for screening), endometrial, cervical, breast, hepatocellular, pancreas, colon, lung, non-Hodgkin's lymphoma.
Non-malignant: Endometriosis, fibroids, menstruation, pregnancy, ovarian hyperstimulation, hepatitis, chronic liver disease, ascites, pancreatitis, IBD, peritonitis, urinary retention, OA, RA, SLE, CKD, cystic fibrosis, DM, diverticulitis, IBS, heart failure, pericarditis, pneumonia.

📋 **CLINICAL NOTES**

Sensitivity: Non-mucinous ovarian carcinomas 80%. Localised ovarian cancer ~50%.

CA 15-3

↑ **RAISED IN/BY**

Malignancy: Breast cancer monitoring. Not used in screening, diagnosis or prognosis. Markedly raised in metastatic breast disease. Ovary, prostate, lung. Raised during treatment due to cell tumour lysis.
Non-malignant: Breastfeeding, PID, pregnancy, endometriosis, hepatitis, chronic liver disease, IBD, CKD, skin diseases.

📋 **CLINICAL NOTES**

Sensitivity: Localised breast cancer 10%, advanced disease 70%.

CA 19-9

↑ **RAISED IN/BY**

Malignancy: Pancreas (not used for screening or early detection, use if disease strongly suspected with other diagnostic tools or for prognosis/monitoring), oesophageal, gastric, colon, biliary, thyroid, ovary.
Non-malignant: Acute cholangitis, cholestasis, jaundice, pancreatitis, IBS, hypothyroidism, DM.

📋 **CLINICAL NOTES**

Sensitivity: Pancreatic cancers 71-93%, gastric cancers 21-42%, colon cancer 20-40%.

CA 27.29

↑ **RAISED IN/BY**

Malignancy: Breast (diagnosis and treatment monitoring), colon, lung, pancreas, prostate, ovary.
Non-malignant: Ovarian cysts, benign liver and renal disease.

📋 **CLINICAL NOTES**

More specific than CA 15-3 for breast cancer.

CA 72-4

↑ **RAISED IN/BY**

Malignancy: Ovarian, pancreas, stomach.

Caeruloplasmin

↑ **RAISED IN/BY**

Acute phase response (eg infection), pregnancy, iatrogenic (eg HRT, OCP, phenobarbital, valproic acid, phenytoin, carbamazepine), tumour.

↓ **DECREASED IN/BY**

Wilson's disease (and gene carriers), low protein states.

CLINICAL NOTES

Associated with reduced blood copper levels and increased urinary copper in Wilson's disease. If reduced blood and urinary copper, consider copper deficiency.

Calcitonin (fasting)

↑ RAISED IN/BY

Malignancy: Medullary cancer of the thyroid (diagnosis and monitoring), MEN, lung, insulinoma, VIPoma, leukaemia.
Non-malignant: C-cell hyperplasia, hypercalcaemia.

CLINICAL NOTES

Sample should be collected on ice.

Calcium

↑ RAISED IN/BY

Primary hyperparathyroidism, malignancy (primary, metastatic, myeloma, paraneoplastic), tertiary hyperparathyroidism, fracture, iatrogenic (eg thiazide-like diuretics), hyperthyroidism, sarcoidosis, vitamin D toxicity, fracture, milk-alkali syndrome, familial hypocalciuric hypercalcaemia, hypoadrenalism, MEN.

↓ DECREASED IN/BY

Hypoparathyroidism, pseudohypoparathyroidism, CKD, vitamin D deficiency, pancreatitis, fluid overload, liver failure, Fanconi syndrome, burns, acute pancreatitis, tumour lysis, salicylate poisoning, DiGeorge syndrome.

CLINICAL NOTES

Calcium should be corrected for albumin status. Corrected calcium = measured calcium + 0.02x (40-albumin).

Carcinoembryonic antigen (CEA)

↑ RAISED IN/BY

Malignancy: Bowel (especially right-sided colonic tumours, useful prognostic marker, used in monitoring, not used in screening or case finding. Levels >5 microgram/L in 3% Dukes A, 25% Dukes B, 45% Dukes C, 65% Dukes D), pancreas, gastric, abdominal lymphoma, oesophageal, mesothelioma, thyroid, lung, breast, ovary.
Non-malignant: 3% population, smokers (up to 19%), cirrhosis, acute pancreatitis, jaundice, IBD, IBS, diverticulitis. Chronic lung diseases, pneumonia.

CLINICAL NOTES

High false +ve rate for malignancy, poor PPV for cancer. Should not be used as a screening tool.

Cardiac catheterisation

CLINICAL NOTES

Indications: Coronary angiography and percutaneous intervention eg stent insertion, measurement of intracardiac pressures, valve pressure gradients, intracardiac oxygen saturation eg shunt assessment, cardiac biopsy, repair of septal defect, assessment of LV function.

Cardiac MRI

CLINICAL NOTES

Indications: In assessment of LVH (gold standard), congenital heart disease, differentiation of cardiomyopathy subtypes, LV function, regional wall motion abnormalities (RWMA), infarcted tissue (gadolinium scan), inducible ischaemia, shunt assessment, cardiac tumours.

Cardiac SPECT/PET

CLINICAL NOTES

Nuclear imaging. Tracer such as thallium. Used to assess myocardial perfusion and viability. Stress images used to measure inducible ischaemia.

CD4 count

↓ DECREASED IN/BY

HIV (CD4 levels and CD4:CD8 decline as HIV progresses) lower levels in the mornings (highest levels seen around midnight), infection, cancer chemotherapy, primary immune deficiencies eg DiGeorge syndrome.

Cerebrospinal fluid (CSF) (red cells)

CLINICAL NOTES

Seen in: Traumatic tap, ADEM, SAH.

CSF (glucose, compared to plasma)

↓ DECREASED IN/BY

Viral, bacterial (glucose lower than viral) and parasitic meningitis, neurosarcoidosis, meningeal metastases, SAH.

CLINICAL NOTES

Normal in encephalitis.

CSF (protein)

↑ RAISED IN/BY

Meningitis, encephalitis, neurosyphilis, SAH, CVA, Guillain-Barré syndrome, ADEM, malignancy, DM.

CLINICAL NOTES

Oligoclonal bands seen in: MS, chronic infection.
Myelin basic protein seen in: ADEM, MS, CVA.

CSF (white cells)

CLINICAL NOTES

Polymorph predominant: Seen in bacterial meningitis.
Eosinophil predominant: Seen in parasitic diseases.

INVESTIGATIONS

Mononuclear cell predominant: Seen in tuberculous and viral meningitis, MS, ADEM, cerebral malignancy, cerebral abscess.

CSF (xanthochromia)

 CLINICAL NOTES

Seen in: SAH, cerebral malignancy, jaundice, haemorrhagic stroke.

Cholinesterase activity

↓ **DECREASED IN/BY**

Organophosphorus pesticide poisoning, pregnancy, shock, malignancy, CKD, chronic liver disease, malnutrition.

 CLINICAL NOTES

Used to assess sensitivity to anaesthetics (suxamethonium) and when managing organophosphate poisoning. Pseudocholinesterase activity raised in acute MI.

Chromogranin A (parathyroid secretory protein 1)

↑ **RAISED IN/BY**

Malignancy: Carcinoid, phaeochromocytoma, neuroblastoma, SCLC, prostate cancer with neuroendocrine features.
Non-malignant: DM, liver disease, IBD, CKD.

 CLINICAL NOTES

Sensitivity: Localised carcinoid ~33%. metastatic carcinoid ~66%. Levels correlate to tumour mass.

C difficile culture (stool)

CLINICAL NOTES

Sensitivity 89-100%.

C difficile toxin (stool)

CLINICAL NOTES

Sensitivity 63-99%.

Computed tomography (CT)

CLINICAL NOTES

High radiation dose (x500 that of chest X-ray).
Indications: Breast cancer (staging), laryngeal cancer (diagnosis, staging), thyroid cancer (staging), lung cancer (diagnosis, staging [PET-CT for NSCLC], oesophageal cancer (staging, PET-CT for distant metastases), stomach cancer (staging), liver primary/metastases (diagnosis, consider if USS -ve and high clinical suspicion of metastases, PET-CT pre-surgical resection), pancreas (diagnosis, staging), colorectal carcinoma

(diagnosis, staging, monitoring ie CT-pneumocolon), renal cancer (diagnosis, staging ie multidetector CT, monitoring), bladder cancer (staging including distant spread unlike MRI, monitoring), ovarian cancer (staging, monitoring), cervical cancer (staging for abdominothoracic disease, PET-CT for nodal metastases), lymphoma (guided biopsy, staging, monitoring), bone/soft tissue tumours (diagnosis, lung metastases, PET-CT for tumour grade, metastases), metastases from tumour of unknown primary, aortic dissection. PE (CTPA), CHD (CT coronary angiography, high negative predictive value, sensitivity for CHD 97.2%, specificity 87.4%, more sensitive and specific than MRI), pericardial disease, aortic valve stenosis gradient/left ventricular function (ECG-gated CT), congenital heart disease, AAA, pleural disease, diffuse lung disease, bronchiectasis, middle ear disease, facial sinuses, oesophageal perforation, lower GI bleed, acute abdomen, abdominal/renal trauma, bowel obstruction, IBD complications, abdominal mass, obstructive jaundice, gallbladder masses, gallbladder wall disease, biliary duct stones (CT cholangiography), pancreatitis (+ complications), insulinoma, atlantoaxial subluxation, guided biopsy, bone sequestra, bone tumour, CVA, subarachnoid haemorrhage, head injury, headache (eg red flags), dementia, seizure, cerebral venous sinus thrombosis, congenital/post-infectious hearing loss, orbital disease, facial trauma, neck injury. Consider in renal failure, renal mass, renal colic, renal calculi, severe renal sepsis, adrenal tumour. Screening for von Hippel-Lindau disease (renal cysts, angiomata, carcinoma, for staging or if MRI cannot be performed).

Coombs' test

CLINICAL NOTES

Direct antiglobulin test: Used to confirm cases of immune haemolysis where RBCs coated in complement or antibodies: Autoimmune, drug-induced, paroxysmal cold haemoglobinuria.
Indirect: Used to detect presence of antibodies against red cell antigens, eg prior to blood transfusion or in pregnancy to assess risk of haemolytic disease of the newborn.

Copper (serum)

↑ **RAISED IN/BY**
Diet.

↓ **DECREASED IN/BY**

Malabsorption, diet, cystic fibrosis, Wilson's disease (associated with low caeruloplasmin and increased urinary copper).

 CLINICAL NOTES

Copper should be requested with caeruloplasmin.

Copper (urine)

↑ RAISED IN/BY
Wilson's disease, diet.

↓ DECREASED IN/BY
Malabsorption, diet.

Cortisol

See also
— *Dexamethasone suppression test*

↑ RAISED IN/BY
Cushing's syndrome, stress, pregnancy, alcohol abuse, depression, iatrogenic.

↓ DECREASED IN/BY
Hypopituitarism, Addison's disease.

📋 **CLINICAL NOTES**
Used in conjunction with ACTH in diagnosis of pituitary and adrenal disease. Urinary cortisol may be used as a screening tool for Cushing's syndrome.

C-peptide

↑ RAISED IN/BY
Insulinoma, insulin resistance, pregnancy, Cushing's disease, renal failure, hypokalaemia.

↓ DECREASED IN/BY
Untreated hypothyroidism and hyperthyroidism, high dietary calcium, exogenous insulin use.

C-reactive protein (CRP)

See also
— *High sensitivity C-reactive protein*

↑ RAISED IN/BY
Infection, inflammation, trauma, latter stages of pregnancy, oestrogen replacement therapy.

↓ DECREASED IN/BY
Unexplained anaemia.

📋 **CLINICAL NOTES**
Poor specificity.

Creatine kinase (CK)

↑ RAISED IN/BY
African-Caribbean origin, large muscle mass, excessive exercise, post-seizure, myositis, polymyositis, dermatomyositis, injection, trauma, haematoma, rhabdomyolysis, neuroleptic malignant syndrome, MI, malignancy, alcoholism, hypothyroidism, muscular dystrophy, renal failure, iatrogenic (eg statins, azathioprine). MELAS syndrome, osteopetrosis, compartment syndrome, Kearns-Sayre syndrome, leptospirosis.

↓ DECREASED IN/BY
Pregnancy.

CK-BB

↑ RAISED IN/BY
Malignancy: GI, breast, prostate, ovarian, lung (SCLC), haematological malignancy.
Non-malignant: MI, cardiac surgery, osteopetrosis.

↓ DECREASED IN/BY
Schizophrenia.

📋 **CLINICAL NOTES**
Derived from number of tissues including brain, prostate gland, ovary, gut, lung.

CK-MB

↑ RAISED IN/BY
MI (4-6 hours after MI, peak at 18-24 hours, falls after 48-72 hours).

📋 **CLINICAL NOTES**
Test superseded by troponin.

CK-MM

↑ RAISED IN/BY
Heart and skeletal muscle disorders.

Creatinine

↑ RAISED IN/BY
Hypovolaemia, renal impairment, dialysis, liver failure, cardiac failure, DM, iatrogenic (eg NSAIDs, trimethoprim, cimetidine, ACE inhibitors/ARBs).

↓ DECREASED IN/BY
Pregnancy, hyperhydration, reduced muscle mass.

Cytoplasmic antineutrophil cytoplasmic antibodies (cANCA)

↑ RAISED IN/BY
Wegener's granulomatosis (diagnosis and monitoring), Churg-Strauss syndrome, microscopic polyangitis, ulcerative colitis, TB, HIV, Hodgkin's disease, monoclonal gammopathies, Goodpasture's syndrome.

📋 **CLINICAL NOTES**
Wegener's granulomatosis: Inactive disease: 63% sensitive, 99.5% specific; active disease: 91% sensitive, 99% specific.

INVESTIGATIONS

D-dimer

↑ RAISED IN/BY

Increasing age, pregnancy, pre-eclampsia, eclampsia, HELLP syndrome, DVT, PE, DIC, recent surgery, trauma, hepatorenal disease, hyperbilirubinaemia, malignancy, sepsis, hyperlipidaemia, haemolysis, cavernous sinus thrombosis.

🗒 CLINICAL NOTES

False +ve if circulating rheumatoid factor, false -ve caused by anticoagulants.

Dexamethasone suppression test (high dose)

🗒 CLINICAL NOTES

Suppression of plasma cortisol suggests Cushing's disease (pituitary adenoma), failure of suppression suggestive of ectopic ACTH or adrenal tumour.

Dexamethasone suppression test (low dose)

🗒 CLINICAL NOTES

Used to confirm diagnosis of Cushing's syndrome, failure to suppress plasma cortisol (abnormal result) consistent with Cushing's syndrome, depression, alcohol abuse, obesity, liver enzyme inducing drugs.

Dehydroepiandrosterone sulphate (DHEAS)

↑ RAISED IN/BY

Newborns, puberty, adrenal hyperplasia, adrenal tumour (DHEAS levels may be normal in non-functioning tumours), PCOS.

↓ DECREASED IN/BY

Hypopituitarism, adrenal failure, infertility, chronic disease, advancing age.

EBV-D early antigen

🗒 CLINICAL NOTES

Used to confirm very recent infection eg within one week. Persistent in one in five people.

EBV-nuclear antigen

🗒 CLINICAL NOTES

Used to confirm previous infection of at least two months. Persists indefinitely.

EBV-viral capsid antigen (immunofluorescence test)

🗒 CLINICAL NOTES

IgM used to confirm current/recent infection. IgG used to confirm previous infection, positive within one week. Persists indefinitely. False -ve rate higher in children.

ECG: left axis deviation (LAD)

🗒 CLINICAL NOTES

Aetiology/risk factors: Wrong lead position, inferior MI, WPW, left anterior fascicular block, LVH, ASD (primum), cardiomyopathy, tricuspid atresia, hyperkalaemia, VSD.

ECG: left bundle branch block (LBBB)

🗒 CLINICAL NOTES

Aetiology/risk factors: MI, CHD, LVH, aortic stenosis, hypertension, cardiomyopathy, myocarditis, pacemaker, post aortic valve replacement, cardiac fibrosis.

ECG: left ventricular hypertrophy

🗒 CLINICAL NOTES

Aetiology/risk factors: False +ve ECG, systemic hypertension (many patients with LVH secondary to hypertension may have a normal ECG), aortic stenosis, coarctation of the aorta, HCM/HOCM, intense exercise, Fabry disease, VSD.

ECG: pathological Q waves

🗒 CLINICAL NOTES

Aetiology/risk factors: Old transmural MI, LBBB, WPW, cardiomyopathy, LVH, myocarditis, myocardial fibrosis, dextrocardia, metastatic disease, muscular dystrophy, sarcoid, amyloid, Friedreich's ataxia, pericardial effusion, pericardial thickening.

ECG: positive R wave in V1

🗒 CLINICAL NOTES

Aetiology/risk factors: Wrong lead position, normal variation, WPW type A, old posterior MI, RVH, RBBB, hypertrophic cardiomyopathy, dextrocardia, Duchenne muscular dystrophy.

ECG: PR interval – prolonged

🗒 CLINICAL NOTES

Aetiology/risk factors: Iatrogenic (beta-blockers, CCBs, flecainide, digoxin, lithium, quinidine, TCAs, methamphetamines), congenital block, CHD, aortic valve disease, aortic valve abscess (evolving PR interval), ASD, PDA, cardiomyopathy, myocarditis, eosinophilic endomyocardial disease, restrictive cardiomyopathy, myotonic dystrophy, rheumatic fever, hypothyroidism, Lyme disease, diphtheria, hypothermia, hypo/hyperkalaemia, hypermagnesaemia, sarcoid, age.

ECG: PR interval - short

Aetiology/risk factors: Pre-excitation syndromes (eg WPW, Low-Ganong-Levine syndrome), hypokaemia, hypocalcaemia, Ebstein's anomaly, AV junctional rhythm, HCM, Duchenne muscular dystrophy, Pompe's disease, SAH.

ECG: QTc interval prolonged

↑ RAISED IN/BY

Prolonged if >450ms in men and >460ms in women.
Note: QTc may only be prolonged during exercise.

See *Diseases, long QT syndrome.*

ECG: right axis deviation (RAD)

CLINICAL NOTES

Aetiology/risk factors: Neonate/infant, RVH, RBBB, MI, ASD (secundum), VSD, left posterior hemi-block, Fallot's tetralogy, pulmonary hypertension, pulmonary stenosis, dextrocardia, PE, children, tall stature, mitral stenosis.

ECG: right bundle branch block (RBBB)

CLINICAL NOTES

Aetiology/risk factors: Partial right bundle block – normal variant affecting 5% population. Neonates/infants, RVH, CHD, cardiomyopathy, ASD, pulmonary stenosis, Fallot's tetrology, Ebstein's anomaly, myocarditis, conduction system fibrosis, PE, pulmonary hypertension, cor pulmonale, Brugada syndrome, mitral stenosis.

ECG: ST elevation

CLINICAL NOTES

Aetiology/risk factors: MI, pericarditis, ventricular aneurysm (persistent), Brugada syndrome, LVH, pacemaker, LBBB, early repolarisation.

ECG: T wave inversion

CLINICAL NOTES

Aetiology/risk factors: Normal (aVR, V1), CHD, cardiomyopathy, strain, LVH, myocarditis, SAH.

Echocardiography (stress)

CLINICAL NOTES

Used to assess inducible ischaemia if patients cannot exercise or ECG not interpretable (eg LBBB).

Echocardiography, transoesophageal (TOE)

CLINICAL NOTES

More sensitive than trans-thoracic echocardiography (TTE) eg in diagnosis of ASDs, vegetations (>90% sensitivity), thrombus within left atrial appendage (these are not demonstrable on TTE), aortic dissection (99% sensitivity), aortic root abscess, high sensitivity for detecting MR in prosthetic valve. Useful in obese patients and those with COPD in whom the quality of TTE images is poor.

Echocardiography, transthoracic (TTE)

CLINICAL NOTES

Used to diagnose and monitor chamber size, cardiac structure, valve disease, ventricular function, ventricular regional wall motion abnormality (RWMA, may be suggestive of ischaemic disease in territory of coronary artery or its branch), congenital heart disease, pulmonary artery pressure, cardiomyopathy, pericardial disease, endocarditis (unreliable for small vegetations <5mm).

Elliptocytes (blood film)

CLINICAL NOTES

Elongated oval-shaped RBCs.
Aetiology/risk factors: Hereditary elliptocytosis or acquired disorders eg iron deficiency anaemia, thalassaemia. Newborns.

Eosinophils

↑ RAISED IN/BY

Asthma, eczema, psoriasis, urticaria, Churg-Strauss syndrome, parasitic infections, cat-scratch disease, allergies, pulmonary eosinophilia, leukaemia, lymphoma, myeloproliferative disease, Addison's disease, Löffler's syndrome, Henoch-Schönlein purpura, acute interstitial nephritis, polyarteritis nodosa, post-splenectomy, penicillins.

Erythrocyte sedimentation rate (ESR)

↑ RAISED IN/BY

Age, idiopathic, macrocytosis, infection, inflammation, vasculitis, autoimmune arthritis, malignancy (eg myeloma), Waldenström's macroglobulinaemia, polymyalgia rheumatica, temporal arteritis, cirrhosis, collagen disease, atrial myxoma, familial Mediterranean fever, menstruation, pregnancy.

↓ DECREASED IN/BY

Sickle cell anaemia, microcytosis, severe leucocytosis, polycythaemia, cardiac failure, hypoalbuminaemia.

CLINICAL NOTES

Ability of RBCs to form rouleaux; it is related to acute

phase proteins/Ig and fibrinogen. Poor specificity. Normal range for men = age/2; women (age+10)/2.

Erythropoietin

↑ RAISED IN/BY

Chronic hypoxia, chronic anaemia, hepatoma, pulmonary tumour, renal tumour, benign renal cyst, PCKD, cerebellar haemangioblastoma, massive fibroids, adrenal tumour (eg phaeochromocytoma), Wilms' tumour, androgens, congenital polycythaemia.

↓ DECREASED IN/BY

Chronic renal failure, anaemia of chronic disease, polycythaemia rubra vera.

▤ CLINICAL NOTES

Raised levels may persist in deficiency anaemia despite replacement with haematinics.

Estimated glomerular filtration rate (eGFR)

↑ RAISED IN/BY

Pregnancy, hyperhydration.

↓ DECREASED IN/BY

Elderly, malnourishment, hypovolaemia, renal failure, liver failure, iatrogenic (eg NSAIDs, trimethoprim, cimetidine, ACE inhibitors/ARBs).

▤ CLINICAL NOTES

eGFR is expressed as $ml/min/1.73m^2$. If African/African-Caribbean, x1.21. Caution if large muscle mass, oedema, muscle wasting conditions, elderly, malnourishment and amputees. Meat should not be eaten for 12 hours before test.

Exercise tolerance test (ETT)

▤ CLINICAL NOTES

Sensitivity 68% for CHD, 77% specificity for CHD. High predictive values in high-risk patients eg >90%. Low predictive values in low-risk people, eg middle-aged women. May also be used to assess exercise-induced arrhythmia eg in cardiomyopathy.

Faecal calprotectin

↑ RAISED IN/BY

IBD, colorectal cancer.

▤ CLINICAL NOTES

Correlates with IBD activity.

Faecal occult blood (FOB)

↑ RAISED IN/BY

GI tract malignancy, peptic ulcer disease, IBD,

diverticulitis, polyps, piles, severe epistaxis, iatrogenic (NSAIDs, anticoagulants, antiplatelet agents, SSRIs, colchicine).

▤ CLINICAL NOTES

Used to screen asymptomatic people for bowel cancer, multiple samples required. False -ve caused by large doses of vitamin C. False +ve with ingestion of red meat, fish, broccoli, horseradish, cauliflower, melon.

Ferritin

↑ RAISED IN/BY

Acute phase response, haemochromatosis, excess dietary iron, multiple transfusions, liver disease, splenic disorders, thalassaemia, marrow disease, myelodysplasia, alcoholism, obesity (normal iron and transferrin), hereditary eg benign hyperferritinaemia.

↓ DECREASED IN/BY

Iron deficiency, malnutrition, malabsorption.

▤ CLINICAL NOTES

70% iron stored as ferritin in men, 80% in women. Correlates to alcohol consumption in men.

Fibrin degradation products (FDPs)

↑ RAISED IN/BY

DIC, pulmonary embolus, liver disease, fibrinolysis.

▤ CLINICAL NOTES

False +ve if circulating rheumatoid factor

Fibrinogen (factor I)

↑ RAISED IN/BY

Acute phase response, sepsis, inflammatory conditions, malignancy (eg Hodgkin's lymphoma), CVA, trauma, chronic DIC, smoking, oestrogen therapy, pregnancy.

↓ DECREASED IN/BY

Familial, large blood transfusion, DIC, liver disease, malnutrition, malignancy, iatrogenic eg fibrinolytics (streptokinase), steroids, valproate.

▤ CLINICAL NOTES

Levels correlate with increased risk of CHD. Dysfibrinogenaemia suggests normal levels of poorly functioning fibrinogen.

5-hydroxyindoleacetic acid (5-HIAA) (urine)

↑ RAISED IN/BY

Carcinoid syndrome (not diagnostic, levels may be intermittently high, may be used for monitoring).

CLINICAL NOTES

5-hydroxyindoleacetic acid (5-HIAA) is a serotonin metabolite. False +ve with drugs and foods (eg paracetamol, caffeine, diazepam, banana, avocado, pineapple, tomato, kiwi). False -ve with drugs (eg aspirin, TCAs, methyldopa).

Fluorescent treponemal antibody absorption test (FTA-ABS)

See also
- *Rapid plasma reagin test*
- *Venereal diseases research laboratory*
- *Treponema pallidum particle agglutination assay*

CLINICAL NOTES

Used to confirm a diagnosis of syphilis after +ve screening tests (VDRL and RPR).

Folate

↑ RAISED IN/BY

Vegetarian diet, bacterial overgrowth, pernicious anaemia, blood transfusion.

↓ DECREASED IN/BY

Pregnancy, iatrogenic (eg OCP, methotrexate, phenytoin, trimethoprim, alcohol), diet, IBD, coeliac disease, myeloproliferative disease, psoriasis, haemolysis, haemodialysis, methylenetetrahydrofolate reductase deficiency.

CLINICAL NOTES

False +ve: Haemolysed blood sample, iron deficiency.

Follicular stimulating hormone (FSH)

↑ RAISED IN/BY

Ovulation, (precocious) puberty, menopause, ovarian agenesis, Turner's syndrome, 17 alpha-hydroxylase deficiency, mumps, chemotherapy, autoimmune disease, PCOS, adrenal disease, ovarian tumour, testicular failure, Klinefelter's syndrome, iatrogenic (eg digoxin, levodopa, clomiphene).

↓ DECREASED IN/BY

Pituitary failure, hypothalamic failure, anorexia nervosa, iatrogenic eg OCP, phenothiazines, GnRH analogues, testosterone antagonists.

Free prostate specific antigen (PSA)

CLINICAL NOTES

Unbound PSA. Value >25% suggestive of lower risk of cancer.

Galactosuria

↑ RAISED IN/BY

Liver disease, galactosaemia.

Gamma glutamyl transpeptidase (gamma GT)

↑ RAISED IN/BY

Men, ageing (women), smoking, obesity, African race, liver disease (especially obstructive, cholestasis, alcoholic), pancreatitis, cardiac failure, MI, DM, renal failure, iatrogenic eg NSAIDs, statins, antifungals, anticonvulsants.

↓ DECREASED IN/BY

Eating (fasting level should be tested). Iatrogenic eg OCP.

CLINICAL NOTES

75% sensitivity for alcohol abuse but low specificity.

Glucose

↑ RAISED IN/BY

DM, DKA (glucose >15, very ketotic, pH <7.2), hyperosmolar non-ketotic diabetic coma (HONK) (glucose often >30, pH >7.2), Cushing's syndrome, iatrogenic (eg corticosteroids, thiazides), Fanconi syndrome, renal glycosuria.

↓ DECREASED IN/BY

Iatrogenic (eg insulin, sulfonylureas, GDP-1 analogues, quinine, trimethoprim, beta-blockers, acute steroid withdrawal), alcohol, cirrhosis, gastric surgery, insulinoma, Addison's disease, CAH, sepsis, hypopituitarism, galactosaemia, medium chain acyl-CoA dehydrogenase deficiency, salicylate poisoning .

Glucose tolerance test (oral, OGTT)

↑ RAISED IN/BY

DM diagnosed if at two hours, venous plasma glucose ≥11.1mmol/L. Impaired glucose tolerance if at two hours venous plasma glucose ≥7.8-≤11.0mmol/L. Failure of suppression of growth hormone suggestive of GH-secreting tumour (pituitary adenoma).

Glycated albumin/fructosamine

CLINICAL NOTES

Used to measure average glucose control over two to three weeks. Consider use when quick measure of glucose control required eg after change in DM treatment or when change in Hb, eg transfusion, haemolysis, haemorrhage. Interpret with care in low protein states, thyroid disease, hypercholesterolaemia.

Growth hormone (GH)

↑ RAISED IN/BY

Gigantism/acromegaly (pituitary adenoma), carcinoid, iatrogenic (eg amphetamines, dopamine, insulin, levodopa, methyldopa), pregnancy, puberty.

↓ DECREASED IN/BY

Pituitary failure, hypothalamic failure, iatrogenic (eg steroids, phenothiazines).

📋 CLINICAL NOTES

Suppression with glucose tolerance test/stimulation with insulin tests required.

Haematocrit

↑ RAISED IN/BY

See *packed cell volume*.

Haemoglobin (Hb)

↑ RAISED IN/BY

Polycythaemia rubra vera, secondary polycythaemia (hypoxia, right to left cardiac shunt, high altitude, smoking, chronic lung disease), excess erythropoietin.

↓ DECREASED IN/BY

Dilutional, infection.
Raised MCV: With megaloblastic change: folate or vitamin B_{12} deficiency. Pregnancy, alcohol misuse, liver disease, hypothyroidism, chronic haemolysis, myelodysplasia, Gaucher's syndrome, paroxysmal cold haemoglobinuria (MCV can be normal).
Normal MCV: Anaemia of chronic disease, renal failure, pregnancy, hypothyroidism, aplastic anaemia.
Reduced MCV: Iron deficiency, thalassaemia, hereditary sideroblastic anaemia, lead poisoning, pyridoxine deficiency, aluminium poisoning. Many infections will reduce Hb.

Haemolysis

📋 CLINICAL NOTES

Aetiology/risk factors: Haemoglobinopathies (sickle cell anaemia, thalassaemia), membrane defects (hereditary spherocytosis, hereditary elliptocytosis), enzyme defects (pyruvate kinase deficiency, G6PD deficiency), infection (sepsis, malaria), haemolytic disease of the newborn, transfusion reaction, iatrogenic (penicillins, cephalosporins, rifampicin, methyldopa, isoniazid, quinine), autoimmune haemolysis (warm: lymphoma, leukaemia, SLE, idiopathic; cold: cold haemaglutinin disease, paroxysmal cold haemoglobinuria, mycoplasma infection, CLL, lymphoma, infectious mononucleosis), metallic heart valves, microangiopathic haemolytic anaemia (HUS), TTP, malignant hypertension, burns, sepsis, pre-eclampsia, paroxysmal nocturnal haemoglobinuria, liver disease, hypersplenism, parasitic infestation.

Hb Barts (gamma$_4$)

📋 CLINICAL NOTES

Occurs in fetus with alpha-thalassaemia.

Hb H (beta$_4$)

📋 CLINICAL NOTES

Hb with four beta chains, occurs in some patients with alpha thalassaemia.

Hb variants

📋 CLINICAL NOTES

Other Hb types exist, including Hb constant spring, D, G, J, M.

HbA (alpha$_2$beta$_2$)

📋 CLINICAL NOTES

Approximately 95-98% normal adult Hb.

HbA1c

↑ RAISED IN/BY

DM.

↓ DECREASED IN/BY

Falsely low in haemolysis, haemorrhage.

📋 CLINICAL NOTES

Reflects blood glucose control (ie diabetic control) over approximately three months. Falsely high in iron deficiency.

HbA$_2$ (alpha$_2$delta$_2$)

↑ RAISED IN/BY

Thalassaemia.

📋 CLINICAL NOTES

2-3% normal adult Hb.

HbC

📋 CLINICAL NOTES

Causes mild haemolytic disease and splenomegaly.

HbE

↑ RAISED IN/BY

Beta chain variant.

📋 CLINICAL NOTES

Causes mild haemolytic disease and microcytosis.

HbF (alpha$_2$gamma$_2$)

📋 CLINICAL NOTES

Fetal Hb, 2% normal adult Hb.

HbS

📋 CLINICAL NOTES

Sickle cell disease.

HbSC

📖 **CLINICAL NOTES**
Sickle cell disease variant, one beta S and one beta C gene.

HCV recombinant immunoblot assay (RIBA)

📖 **CLINICAL NOTES**
Used to exclude false +ve anti-HCV antibody test.

HCV-RNA

📖 **CLINICAL NOTES**
Indicates presence of active infection or if treatment has achieved viral clearance.

HDL (high density lipoprotein) cholesterol

↑ **RAISED IN/BY**
Exercise, weight reduction, healthy diet, nicotinic acid, fibrates, statins.

↓ **DECREASED IN/BY**
Poor diet, smoking.

Heinz bodies (blood film)

📖 **CLINICAL NOTES**
RBCs containing damaged Hb due to oxidation. Aetiology/risk factors: G6PD deficiency, haemolysis, post-splenectomy.

H pylori campylobacter-like organism (CLO) test (rapid urease test)

📖 **CLINICAL NOTES**
Performed during endoscopy to test for presence of H pylori.
False –ve in recent GI bleeding, PPIs, H2 antagonists, antibiotics.

H pylori serology

📖 **CLINICAL NOTES**
Less specific than breath test, antibodies may persist after eradication, lower PPV than breath test/stool antigen test.

H pylori stool antigen test

📖 **CLINICAL NOTES**
Specificity and sensitivity ~95%. PPV >80%.

H pylori urea[13] breath test

📖 **CLINICAL NOTES**
Specificity and sensitivity ≥95%. PPV >80%.

Hepatitis C viral load

📖 **CLINICAL NOTES**
Used to monitor treatment.

Hep B core antigen (HBcAg)

📖 **CLINICAL NOTES**
Disappears early in current infection.

Hep B DNA

📖 **CLINICAL NOTES**
Greater sensitivity than HBeAg to detect viraemia.

Hep B envelope antigen (HBeAg)

📖 **CLINICAL NOTES**
+ve in presence of virus (except certain strains eg Asian), marker of high infectivity whereas clearance and presence of anti-HBe suggests low infectivity. Persistence of HBeAg beyond 10 weeks suggestive of chronic infection; -ve with successful treatment.

Hep B surface antigen (HBsAg)

📖 **CLINICAL NOTES**
+ve early in current infection (from two to four weeks). Subsequent absence implies recovery from infection. Persistence defines chronic carrier status. Not present due to vaccination.

Hepcidin

↑ **RAISED IN/BY**
Chronic inflammation, blood transfusion related iron overload.

↓ **DECREASED IN/BY**
Haemochromatosis, iron deficiency.

📖 **CLINICAL NOTES**
New peptide discovered to be related to iron regulation, inhibits iron release from liver macrophages.

HER2 oncogene

📖 **CLINICAL NOTES**
Present in approximately 25% of breast cancers. May also be present in some ovarian and bladder cancers. HER2-positive cancers have a poorer prognosis. Trastuzumab may be used if HER2-positive (one in three HER-2 positive patients will respond to trastuzumab).

High sensitivity C-reactive protein (hs-CRP)

See also
— *C-reactive protein*

↓ DECREASED IN/BY
Anti-inflammatories, statins.

 CLINICAL NOTES
Used in CHD risk assessment. High levels associated with up to 4x risk of CHD. Poor specificity.

HIV antibodies

 CLINICAL NOTES
Takes up to three to six months to become positive.

HIV viral load

 CLINICAL NOTES
Measure of HIV RNA. Low indicates <500 copies/mL, high suggests >5,000 copies/mL. Used for monitoring.

HLA-B27

↑ RAISED IN/BY
Seronegative spondyloarthropathies (eg ankylosing spondylitis, Reiter's disease, enteropathic arthritis, psoriatic arthritis). May be present in normal population.

Homocysteine (blood)

↑ RAISED IN/BY
Vitamin B$_{12}$ deficiency, folate deficiency, homocystinuria, age, smoking, iatrogenic (eg phenytoin, methotrexate), postmenopause.

CLINICAL NOTES
Raised levels confer higher CVD risk. MI risk x2 in those with highest homocysteine levels compared to those with lowest levels.

Howell-Jolly bodies (blood film)

CLINICAL NOTES
RBCs with visible nuclear remnant.
Aetiology/risk factors: Hyposplenism, haemolysis, sickle cell disease, thalassaemia, vitamin B$_{12}$ deficiency, folate deficiency, leukaemia.

Human chorionic gonadotropin (HCG)

↑ RAISED IN/BY
Malignancy: Gestational trophoblastic tumours (has prognostic value, used also in monitoring molar pregnancy), lung, breast, GI, testicular, lymphoma.

Non-malignant: Early pregnancy.

CLINICAL NOTES
Quantitative tests require serum, not urinary samples. Urinary HCG may take three to five weeks to become negative after a miscarriage. Pregnancy levels peak at about 10 weeks, will fall until 18 weeks, then remain stable. Levels should double every two to three days in early pregnancy – if less than expected doubling rate (or falling), consider ectopic, heterotropic (simultaneous ectopic and intrauterine pregnancy) or pending miscarriage. If excessive increase for gestation, consider twin or molar pregnancy. False +ve urinary HCG (eg anticonvulsants, tranquillisers, hypnotics, cannabis, proteinuria, haematuria). False -ve urinary HCG (too early in pregnancy eg <10 days after conception, phenothiazine, diuretics, dilute urine, antihistamines, HCG antibodies).

Hypochromasia (blood film)

CLINICAL NOTES
Aetiology/risk factors: Reduced haemoglobin.

IgE (total)

↑ RAISED IN/BY
Eczema (atopic), asthma, hayfever, Hodgkin's lymphoma, hyper-IgE syndrome, IgE producing plasma cells in myeloma, parasitic infections, Churg-Strauss syndrome, allergic rhinitis, allergic bronchopulmonary aspergillosis, nephritis.

↓ DECREASED IN/BY
Ataxia-telangiectasia, hereditary, non-IgE secreting myeloma.

CLINICAL NOTES
Normal levels do not exclude allergy.

Immunoreactive trypsin (heel prick test)

CLINICAL NOTES
Used in screening for CF. False -ve if test done beyond first few weeks of life. 90% sensitivity, false +ve rate 0.3%. A +ve test requires subsequent sweat test and genetic testing to confirm CF.

Insulin

↑ RAISED IN/BY
Early DM type 2, insulinoma, insulin resistance, acromegaly, Cushing's syndrome, obesity, steroid therapy, OCP, fructose intolerance, galactose intolerance, exogenous insulin.

↓ DECREASED IN/BY
DM, pancreatic failure, hypopituitarism.

Insulin-like growth factor-1 (IGF-1, somatomedin C)

↑ RAISED IN/BY

Puberty, pregnancy, gigantism, acromegaly.

↓ DECREASED IN/BY

Growth hormone deficiency or resistance, hypopituitarism, age, anorexia nervosa, malnutrition, CKD, chronic liver disease, excess oestrogen.

 CLINICAL NOTES

Used in assessment of pituitary function. May be normal with growth hormone deficiency, in which case, measure IGFBP2 or BP3. Reflects average growth hormone levels. May also be used in monitoring of pituitary tumours.

Insulin tolerance test

 CLINICAL NOTES

Used to assess growth hormone and ACTH/cortisol reserve.

International normalised ratio (INR)-standardised prothrombin time

↑ RAISED IN/BY

Warfarin/phenindione therapy, antibiotics, cimetidine, liver disease, vitamin K deficiency, clotting factor I (fibrinogen), II (prothrombin), V, VII, X deficiency or defects, DIC, von Willebrand's disease.

↓ DECREASED IN/BY

Vitamin K, oestrogens.

 CLINICAL NOTES

Warfarin: target INR: AF/DVT/PE: 2.0-3.0, recurrent DVT/PE: 3.5, metallic prosthetic heart valves: 3.0-4.0. Postoperative: DVT below knee: warfarinise ≥6 weeks, above knee/PE: warfarinise ≥3 months. If no cause found for DVT/PE, warfarinise ≥6 months. If over-warfarinised: INR <6: reduce/stop warfarin and recommence when INR <5. INR 6-8: stop warfarin and recommence when INR <5. If INR >8 (with no or minimal bleeding): oral vitamin K and daily INR. If bleeding: prothrombin complex concentrated factor IX or FFP + IV vitamin K. Simple dental extraction permitted if INR ≤2.5.

Iron (serum)

See also
— *Haemoglobin*

↑ RAISED IN/BY

Excess dietary iron, haemochromatosis (except type 4a), multiple blood transfusions, liver disease, renal disease, oestrogens, alcohol, methyldopa.

↓ DECREASED IN/BY

Poor diet, malabsorption, excess blood loss, testosterone, ACTH, colchicine, desferrioxamine, pregnancy, breastfeeding, growth spurt.

 CLINICAL NOTES

Excess iron may exacerbate porphyria cutanea tarda.

Lactate

↑ RAISED IN/BY

Hypoxia, shock, CCF, MI, exercise, DKA, liver disease, renal disease, G6PD deficiency, pyruvate dehydrogenase deficiency, AIDS, mitochondrial diseases, malignancy, iatrogenic (eg metformin, isoniazid, salicylate poisoning, antifreeze poisoning, antiretrovirals), thiamine deficiency, tissue ischaemia eg small bowel, Kearns-Sayre syndrome, *Clostridium difficile*.

 CLINICAL NOTES

Lactic acidosis causes raised anion gap metabolic acidosis.

Lactate dehydrogenase (LDH)

↑ RAISED IN/BY

CVA, alcohol, haemolysis, myeloproliferative disease, pernicious anaemia, megaloblastic anaemia, thalassaemia, HELLP syndrome, paroxysmal cold haemoglobinuria, PE, pneumonia, bowel ischaemia, renal ischaemia, liver disease, pancreatitis, malignancy, MI, myocarditis, cardiac failure, muscular dystrophy, myxoedema, Hodgkin's disease, CMML, testicular tumours, ALL.

↓ DECREASED IN/BY

Vitamin C toxicity.

 CLINICAL NOTES

Five different isoenzymes exist. LDH 1 (cardiac, renal, RBC, germ cells), LDH 2 (cardiac, RBC, renal), LDH 3 (pulmonary, RBC, heart), LDH 4 (WBC, muscle, hepatic, lymph nodes, placenta, pancreas), LDH 5 (liver, muscle). May also be used in disease monitoring. False +ve in thrombocythaemia. Used as prognostic marker in lymphoma.

LDL cholesterol (low density lipoprotein)

↑ RAISED IN/BY

Familial, pregnancy, dietary, hypothyroidism.

↓ DECREASED IN/BY

Sepsis, thyrotoxicosis, inflammatory conditions, lipoprotein deficiencies, stress, immediately post-MI.

CLINICAL NOTES

Readings may be affected by TG >4.5mmol/L unless measured directly.

Left shift (blood film)

 CLINICAL NOTES

Increased production of immature WBCs.
Aetiology/risk factors: Severe infection, hypoxia, shock.

Leucocytes (urinalysis)

 CLINICAL NOTES

Aetiology/risk factors: UTI, STI, menstruation, vaginal candidiasis, malignancy.

Leucoerythroblastic (blood film)

 CLINICAL NOTES

Immature red and white cells on film.
Aetiology/risk factors: Severe anaemia, bone marrow infiltration, severe hypoxia, myeloproliferative disorders, multiple myeloma, TB of bone marrow, sarcoid, sepsis.

Leukaemoid reaction

 CLINICAL NOTES

Massive increase in WBC.
Aetiology/risk factors: Severe sepsis, burns, malignant marrow infiltration, haemolysis, haemorrhage, TB.

Luteinising hormone (LH)

↑ RAISED IN/BY

Ovarian failure, testicular failure, iatrogenic (eg digoxin, cimetidine, levodopa).

↓ DECREASED IN/BY

Pituitary failure, hypothalamic failure, GnRH analogues, testosterone antagonists.

CLINICAL NOTES

LH<FSH in early part of menstrual cycle, LH>FSH from around day seven to just before menses.

Lipase

↑ RAISED IN/BY

Pancreatitis (up to 5x ULN), pancreatic tumour, gallstone disease, coeliac disease, IBD, peptic ulcer disease, salivary gland disease, CF, iatrogenic eg opiates, indomethacin.

↓ DECREASED IN/BY

Pancreatic failure.

Lipoprotein A

↑ RAISED IN/BY

African-Carribeans, familial, hypothyroidism, DM.

↓ DECREASED IN/BY

Alcoholism, chronic liver disease, malnutrition.

 CLINICAL NOTES

High levels confer increased risk of CVD.

Lupus anticoagulant

↑ RAISED IN/BY

Normal individuals (2-5% population), SLE (30-45% cases), anti-phospholipid syndrome, autoimmune disease, HIV, iatrogenic (eg chlorpromazine, phenothiazines).

CLINICAL NOTES

Paradoxically causes prolonged APTT. Causes false +ve VDRL test.

Lymphocytes

↑ RAISED IN/BY

Viral infections, toxoplasmosis, brucellosis, leukaemia (ALL/CLL), lymphoma, iatrogenic, Addison's disease.

↓ DECREASED IN/BY

Steroid therapy, HIV, marrow failure, pancytopenia, legionnaires' disease, SLE, chemotherapy, uraemia, Bruton's disease, DiGeorge syndrome, reticular dysgenesis, Wiskott-Aldrich syndrome.

Magnesium

↑ RAISED IN/BY

Renal failure, dehydration, rhabdomyolysis, antacid therapy/milk-alkali syndrome, hyperparathyroidism, hypothyroidism, dietary, early, Addison's disease, poorly controlled diabetes, lithium therapy.

↓ DECREASED IN/BY

Post-surgery, severe burns, malabsorption, low dietary Mg^{2+}, diarrhoea/vomiting, IBD, hypoparathyroidism, ethanol, total parenteral nutrition, poorly controlled DM, Conn's syndrome, diuretic therapy, pre-eclampsia.

Magnetic resonance imaging (MRI)

 CLINICAL NOTES

No ionising radiation used. Contraindicated if metallic foreign bodies *in situ*. Indications: Breast cancer (young patients, diagnosis, staging, monitoring), oral/parotid/laryngeal cancers (diagnosis, staging), thyroid tumour (staging), Pancoast tumour staging, better than CT at differentiating atelectasis from tumour, liver primary/secondary, pancreatic cancer (diagnosis/staging), colorectal cancer (staging, monitoring), renal cell carcinoma (diagnosis if CT inadequate/iodine contraindicated, staging), bladder/testicular cancer (staging), ovarian/cervical cancer (diagnosis, staging, monitoring), uterine cancer (diagnosis, staging), lymphoma (staging, monitoring especially with CNS disease), marrow involvement/soft tissue spread of bony tumours, assessment of cardiac function/extent of infarction post-revascularisation, myocardial perfusion, myocardial hibernation, myocarditis, pericardial disease (pericarditis, thickening, effusion), cardiac valve disease (if echocardiography unsuitable), more effective than echocardiogram in measurement of ventricular volume, cardiac amyloid, congenital heart disease, aortic dissection, prosthetic valves (unless severely dehisced), PE (MR angiography if CT contraindicated), acoustic neuroma, parathyroid adenoma, neck mass, sicca syndrome, TMJ dysfunction, Crohn's complications, anorectal sepsis in IBD, cirrhosis, jaundice/biliary disease/biliary leak/chronic pancreatitis (magnetic resonance cholangiopancreatography, MRCP), insulinoma, atlanto-axial subluxation, demyelination, syrinx, spinal disease including metastases, myeloma staging, back pain/spinal cord disease with red flags, slipped disc, oesteomyelitis, distinguishes acute versus chronic osteoporotic fracture and malignant versus oesteoporotic collapse, spina bifida, ligamentous damage, tendon damage, trauma, bone/hip pain (with normal X-ray eg avascular necrosis), knee pain eg meniscal tears, ligamentous damage, heel pain, CVA, space-occupying cerebral lesion, headache (severe sudden onset, acute/abnormal neurology including posterior fossa signs, altered consciousness, recent onset, rapidly increasing in severity, hydrocephalus, nocturnal headaches, dizziness, sensory deficit, altered co-ordination, worse on coughing/sneezing, visual disturbance), dementia, first psychotic episode, seizure, cerebral venous sinus thrombosis/carotid bruits (MR angiography), consider in deafness, fetal abnormalities, endometriosis, intra-abdominal sepsis, dysplastic kidney, MR urogram in pregnant women with renal colic, renal mass, adrenal tumour.

Mammography

📋 **CLINICAL NOTES**
Screening >50 years (UK)/familial breast cancer, breast lump (over 35 years, mammography with clinical assessment and biopsy), breast cancer staging/follow-up, mastalgia.

Mean cell Hb (MCH)

📋 **CLINICAL NOTES**
Average amount of Hb per red cell. MCHC more useful.

Mean cell Hb concentration (MCHC)

↑ **RAISED IN/BY**
Newborns, hereditary spherocytosis, haemolysis.

↓ **DECREASED IN/BY**
Microcytic anaemia, acute leukaemia, leukaemoid reaction.

📋 **CLINICAL NOTES**
(Hb + PCV) x 100. Falsely raised in lipaemia, haemolysis, newborn.

Mean cell volume (MCV)

↑ **RAISED IN/BY**
Pregnancy, iatrogenic (eg methotrexate, azathioprine, phenytoin, antiretrovirals), folate deficiency, vitamin B_{12} deficiency, alcohol misuse, liver disease, hypothyroidism, chronic haemolysis, myelodysplasia, sideroblastic anaemia (some subtypes), haemorrhage, reticulocytosis.

↓ **DECREASED IN/BY**
Iron deficiency, sideroblastic anaemia (some subtypes), lead poisoning, thalassaemia.

Methaemoglobin

↑ **RAISED IN/BY**
Congenital (cytochrome b5 oxidase deficiency/NADH diaphorase deficiency, G6PD deficiency, NADPH-flavin reductase deficiency, HbM), iatrogenic (eg dapsone, quinolones, primaquine, sulfasalazine, nitrates, lidocaine, zopiclone), bacterially contaminated vegetables, water drawn from a well, fertiliser, mothballs, nail polish remover, aniline dyes.

📋 **CLINICAL NOTES**
Levels of methaemoglobin (Fe^{3+}) normally ~3%.

Metabolic acidosis

↑ **RAISED IN/BY**
Anion gap=$[Na^+] + [K^+] - [Cl^-]$
$- [HCO_3^-]$. n=10-18mmol/L.

📋 **CLINICAL NOTES**
Raised anion gap metabolic acidosis: Lactic acidosis, uraemia, ketoacidosis, methanol/methanol/ethylene glycol/salicylate poisoning. Normal anion gap metabolic acidosis: Addison's disease, renal tubular acidosis, acetazolamide, implantation of ureter into colon, diarrhoea, pancreatic fistula, ammonium chloride.

Metabolic alkalosis

📋 **CLINICAL NOTES**
Aetiology/risk factors: Cushing's syndrome, Conn's syndrome, Bartter's syndrome, Liddle's syndrome, beta 2 agonists, antacid/milk-alkali syndrome, abuse, diuretics, rectal villous adenoma, excessive vomiting, pseudo-Bartter's syndrome.

INVESTIGATIONS

Microalbuminuria

↑ RAISED IN/BY

DM, hypertension, smoking, renal artery stenosis, amyloid, glomerulonephritis, CKD.

 CLINICAL NOTES

Microalbuminuria is not detected on dipstick and confers increased risk of CVD and VTE (>30mg/L albumin-2x risk VTE). False +ve in exercise and UTI.

Monocytes

↑ RAISED IN/BY

Infection (eg TB, brucellosis, EBV, CMV), haematological (eg Hodgkin's lymphoma, AML, CMML, myelodysplasia).

Monospot test

 CLINICAL NOTES

Agglutination test for EBV, if negative, consider repeating test after one to two weeks, or perform EBV serology tests.

Myocardial perfusion scan

📋 **CLINICAL NOTES**

Used to assess cardiac perfusion eg flow-limiting coronary lesion, MI, cardiomyopathy, amyloid.

Myoglobin

↑ RAISED IN/BY

MI, trauma, burns, polymyositis/dermatomyositis, rhabdomyolysis, excessive exercise, alcoholism, neuroleptic malignant syndrome, malignant hyperpyrexia, hypokalaemia, hypophosphataemia, myopathy, muscular dystrophy.

📋 **CLINICAL NOTES**

Less specific than troponin I or T for MI (rises 1-3 hours after MI, peak 8-12 hours, falls after 24 hours).

Myositis-specific antibodies

📋 **CLINICAL NOTES**

Highly specific for autoimmune myositis.

Nephrotic range proteinuria

📋 **CLINICAL NOTES**

Aetiology/risk factors: Glomerulonephritis, vasculitides, iatrogenic (eg gold, penicillamine), amyloid, malaria, sickle cell disease, malaria, pre-eclampsia, vesico-ureteric reflux, SLE, malignancy, hepatitis B, DM.

Neuron-specific enolase

↑ RAISED IN/BY

Malignant: SCLC, neuroblastoma, carcinoid, medullary thyroid, melanoma. Non-malignant: Cerebrovascular disease.

Neutrophils

See also
 — *Left shift (blood film)*
 — *Leukaemoid reaction*

↑ RAISED IN/BY

Pregnancy, neonates, varies throughout menstrual cycle, bacterial infection, leukaemia, haemorrhage, inflammation, post-ictal, acidosis, trauma, surgery, burns, PMR, PAN, familial Mediterranean fever, steroid therapy, malignant bone marrow infiltration, leprosy.

↓ DECREASED IN/BY

Viral infection, TB, marrow failure, aplastic anaemia, hypersplenism, severe infection, vitamin B_{12} or folate deficiency, pancytopenia, reticular dysgenesis (an inherited immunodeficiency), iatrogenic (eg chemotherapy, carbimazole, anticonvulsants, chloramphenicol, sulfonamides), Addison's disease.

📋 **CLINICAL NOTES**

Severe infections/inflammation may cause immature white cells to be seen (left shift, or if excessive, leukaemoid reaction).

Nicotine/cotinine (blood/urine/saliva/hair)

📋 **CLINICAL NOTES**

Cotinine, a nicotine metabolite, has a longer half-life than nicotine (up to 40 hours). Quantitative testing is used to monitor tobacco smoke exposure (including passive smoking). It can be used in cessation counselling and establishing nicotine poisoning. It may take 14 days for blood cotinine to be undetectable. Some pesticides contain nicotine.

Nitrites (urinalyisis)

📋 **CLINICAL NOTES**

High specificity for UTI, false -ve rate variable, sensitivity up to 60%.

NTproBNP

↑ RAISED IN/BY

Left ventricular dysfunction (used in diagnosis and assessment of prognosis), CHD, MI, valvular disease, LVH, hypertension, renal failure (reduced clearance), beta-blockers (at initiation).

INVESTIGATIONS

↓ DECREASED IN/BY
ACE inhibitors, ARBs, beta-blockers, diuretics.

📋 CLINICAL NOTES
High NPV for cardiac failure.

Nuclear matrix protein 22 (NMP22) urine test

📋 CLINICAL NOTES
Used to detect bladder cancer in conjunction with cytology and cystoscopy. Sensitivity: 78.1% increasing with stage and grade. Specificity: 66%. PPV 59.5%. NPV 82.5%. False +ve with UTI.

Oestrogen

↑ RAISED IN/BY
PCOS, gonadal tumours, adrenal tumours, HRT, OCP, hyperthyroidism.

↓ DECREASED IN/BY
Pre-puberty, hypopituitarism, ovarian failure (eg menopause, oopherectomy), Turner's syndrome, failing pregnancy, maternal levels relatively lower in Down's syndrome and neural tube defects during pregnancy, eating disorders.

📋 CLINICAL NOTES
Three subtypes: oestradiol, oestriol, oestrone.

Osmolarity (serum)

↑ RAISED IN/BY
Dehydration, diabetes insipidus, hyperosmolar non-ketotic diabetic coma (HONK), DKA, ethanol, ethylene glycol.

↓ DECREASED IN/BY
Water intoxication, SIADH, hyperaldosteronism.

📋 CLINICAL NOTES
Serum osmolality: $2(Na^+ + K^+)$+glucose+urea (mmol/L). Inaccurate if hyperlipidaemic or in high protein states eg myeloma.

p24 antigen

📋 CLINICAL NOTES
Protein +ve 1-4 weeks after HIV infection. Antibodies then develop against p24 antigen. May be used to monitor treatment and progress of disease.

Packed cell volume (PCV)

↑ RAISED IN/BY
Reduced plasma volume/increased red cell mass: polycythaemia rubra vera, secondary polycythaemia

(hypoxia: right to left shunt, chronic exposure to high altitude, smoking, chronic lung disease, Gaisbock's disease. Increased erythropoietin: eg renal tumour, APKD, phaeochromocytoma), dehydration.

↓ DECREASED IN/BY
Increased plasma volume/reduced red cell mass: overhydration, pregnancy, anaemia.

Pancreatic oncofetal antigen (POA)

↑ RAISED IN/BY
Pancreatic cancer.

📋 CLINICAL NOTES
Glycoprotein found in fetal and neoplastic pancreatic tissue. False -ve rate 20%, false +ve rate 10%.

Pancytopaenia

📋 CLINICAL NOTES
Aetiology/risk factors: Malignant marrow infiltration, myelodysplasia, sideroblastic anaemia, myelofibrosis, aplastic anaemia, hypersplenism, SLE, TB, paroxysmal nocturnal haemoglobinuria, iatrogenic (eg chemotherapy, carbimazole, clozapine).

Pappenheimer bodies (blood film)

📋 CLINICAL NOTES
Granules of iron within RBC but separate to haemoglobin.
Aetiology/risk factors: Splenectomy, lead poisoning, malignancy.

Paraproteinaemia

📋 CLINICAL NOTES
Aetiology/risk factors: Heparinised blood sample, multiple myeloma, MGUS, Waldenström's macroglobulinaemia, heavy chain disease, lymphoma, CLL, POEMS syndrome, Schnitzler syndrome, cold agglutinin disease, primary amyloid, paroxysmal cold haemoglobinuria, warm haemolytic anaemia, RA, scleroderma, thyroiditis, pyoderma gangrenosum, chronic liver disease, TB, subacute bacterial endocarditis.

Parathyroid hormone (PTH)

↑ RAISED IN/BY
Primary hyperparathyroidism (hyperplasia, adenoma, carcinoma), secondary hyperparathyroidism (in response to chronic hypocalcaemia, eg secondary to renal failure, vitamin D deficiency), tertiary hyperparathyroidism (autonomous production of PTH after prolonged secondary hyperparathyroidism), para-thyroid-like hormone production (paraneoplastic), lithium (1% hyperparathyroid patients), post radioiodine therapy

(may cause parathyroid adenoma), head and neck radiation, anticonvulsants, steroids, familial, MEN 1 and 2.

↓ DECREASED IN/BY
Post-surgery, familial, autoimmune, radiation, DiGeorge syndrome, haemochromatosis, hypomagnesaemia, vitamin D toxicity, iatrogenic (eg cimetidine, propanolol).

📋 CLINICAL NOTES
Sample should be preserved on ice and taken at a hospital to minimise transport time to lab.

Partial thromboplastin time (PTT)

📋 CLINICAL NOTES
See *activated partial thromboplastin time*.

Peak expiratory flow rate (PEFR)

📋 CLINICAL NOTES
Measure of airway obstruction by assessment of speed of airflow (L/min). May be used in diagnosis and monitoring of asthma and in assessment of acute asthma. Spirometry with reversibility testing is the preferred method of diagnosing asthma.

Perinuclear antineutrophil cytoplasmic antibodies (pANCA)

↑ RAISED IN/BY
Churg-Strauss syndrome, Wegener's granulomatosis, microscopic polyangitis, IBD, idiopathic necrotising glomerulonephritis, primary sclerosing cholangitis, Goodpasture's syndrome.

📋 CLINICAL NOTES
Sensitivity: Wegener's granulomatosis 20%.

pH (urinalysis)

📋 CLINICAL NOTES
Persistent alkaline urine: UTI, pyloric stenosis, vomiting, alkalosis, renal tubular acidosis 1, stale sample, renal failure, iatrogenic (eg bicarbonate, acetazolamide), vegetarians.
Persistent acidic urine: Acidosis, renal tubular acidosis 2 and 4, starvation, DM, uric acid stones, acid diet, diarrhoea.

Phosphate

↑ RAISED IN/BY
Renal failure, diet, hypoparathyroidism, pseudohypoparathyroidsm, tumour lysis, rhabdomyolysis, untreated DKA, acidosis, dietary, excess vitamin D, milk-alkali syndrome, hypomagnesaemia, familial hyperphosphataemia.

↓ DECREASED IN/BY
Hyperparathyroidism, diet, anorexia nervosa, renal dialysis, X-linked hypophosphataemic rickets, vitamin D deficiency, pancreatitis, alcohol abuse, chronic vomiting, Fanconi syndrome, renal tubular disease, DKA treatment (phosphate driven to intracellular compartment), respiratory alkalosis (acute), McCune Albright syndrome, malnutrition.

Plasma protein electrophoresis: beta band

↑ RAISED IN/BY
Myeloma (some cases), MGUS (some cases), hypercholesterolaemia, anaemia (iron deficient).

↓ DECREASED IN/BY
Cirrhosis of the liver, malnutrition, glomerulonephritis, SLE.

📋 CLINICAL NOTES
Beta proteins-LDL, transferrin, fibrinogen, complement C3/C4.

Plasma protein electrophoresis: alpha1 band

↑ RAISED IN/BY
Inflammation.

↓ DECREASED IN/BY
Alpha-1-antitrypsin deficiency, liver disease.

📋 CLINICAL NOTES
Alpha 1 proteins-HDL, TBG, alpha-1-antitrypsin.

Plasma protein electrophoresis: alpha2 band

↑ RAISED IN/BY
Inflamation, nephrotic syndrome.

↓ DECREASED IN/BY
Haemolysis, hyperthyroidism, liver disease.

📋 CLINICAL NOTES
Alpha 2 proteins-VLDL, caeruloplasmin, alpha 2-macroglobulin, haptoglobulin.

Plasma protein electrophoresis: gamma band

See also
— *Paraproteinaemia*

↑ RAISED IN/BY
Polyclonal: Infection, inflammation, autoimmune disease (eg rheumatoid, SLE), immunisation, iatrogenic (eg phenytoin, OCP, methadone). Monoclonal: Multiple

myeloma, Waldenström's macroglobulinaemia, MGUS, CLL, amyloid, heavy chain disease.

↓ DECREASED IN/BY
Marrow failure, aplastic anaemia, immunodeficiency, nephritic syndrome, malnutrition.

📋 **CLINICAL NOTES**
Gamma proteins-immunoglobulins, CRP, factor VIII, alpha-fetoprotein.

Plts

↑ RAISED IN/BY
Essential thrombocytosis, acute phase response, chronic bleeding, polycythaemia rubra vera, post-splenectomy, Kawasaki disease, ADEM, malignancy.

↓ DECREASED IN/BY
Thrombocytopenia: Aplastic anaemia, marrow failure, myelofibrosis, leukaemia, ITP, thrombotic thrombocytopenic purpura, HELLP, DIC, sepsis, bleeding, lymphoma, splenomegaly, SLE, anti-phospholipid syndrome, paroxysmal nocturnal haemoglobinuria, infections (eg viral illness, Weil's disease, diphtheria, Q fever, malaria, typhoid), iatrogenic (eg NSAIDs, heparin, gold, chloramphenicol, co-trimoxazole), Wiskott-Aldrich syndrome, Noonan's syndrome, Fanconi's anaemia. Reduced platelet function: Uraemia, DIC, liver disease, leukaemia, myeloproliferative disorders, Alport's syndrome, Chediak-Higashi syndrome, von Willibrand's disease.

Pleural effusion (amylase)

↑ RAISED IN/BY
Pancreatitis, perforated oesophagus, malignancy, infection.

Pleural effusion (cells)

📋 **CLINICAL NOTES**
Lymphocyte predominant: Infection (TB), malignancy, autoimmune (eg RA, SLE), sarcoidosis. Neutrophil predominant: Pneumonia, PE. Eosinophil predominant: PE, asbestosis, fungal and parasitic infection. Mesothelial cells: PE, malignant mesothelial cells in mesothelioma.

Pleural effusion (glucose)

↑ RAISED IN/BY
<3.3mmol/L: malignancy, autoimmune (eg SLE, RA), infection (TB), perforated oesophagus, empyema.

Pleural effusion (LDH)

↑ RAISED IN/BY
Pleural fluid LDH: Serum LDH >0.6 suggests

exudate: malignancy, autoimmune (RA, SLE), infection (empyema, TB).

Pleural effusion (protein)

See also
— Diseases, pleural effusion

↑ RAISED IN/BY
>35g/L or if protein 25-35g/L but concentration of serum protein is less than 50% than that of pleural sample=exudate.

Pleural effusion (pH)

↑ RAISED IN/BY
pH <7.2: malignancy, autoimmune (eg RA, SLE), infection (eg empyema,TB).

Poikilocytes (blood film)

📋 **CLINICAL NOTES**
Abnormally shaped RBCs. Aetiology/risk factors: Iron deficiency, hereditary elliptocytosis, haemolysis.

Polychromasia (blood film)

📋 **CLINICAL NOTES**
RBCs of varying colour. Aetiology/risk factors: Haemolytic anaemia, bleeding, vitamin B_{12}/folate/iron replacement, malignant marrow infiltration.

Porphyrins (red cell)

↑ RAISED IN/BY
Protoporphyrins: Raised in erythropoietic proto-porphyria. Coproporphyrins: Raised in congenital erythropoietic porphyria.

Porphyrins (stool)

↑ RAISED IN/BY
Coproporphyrins: Raised in hereditary coproporphyria, variegate porphyria, congenital erythropoietic porphyria. Protoporphyrins: Raised in erythropoietic protoporphyria, variegate porphyria.

Porphyrins (urine)

↑ RAISED IN/BY
Porphobilinogen (PBG), delta-aminolaevulinic acid (ALA): acute intermittent porphyria, variegate porphyria (during attacks), hereditary coproporphyria. Uroporphyrins: Raised in porphyria cutanea tarda, congenital erythropoietic porphyria. Coproporphyrins: Raised in variegate porphyria, congenital erythropoietic porphyria, hereditary coproporphyria.

📋 **CLINICAL NOTES**
Collect samples during acute attack and shield from light.

Positron emmision tomography (PET scan)

📋 **CLINICAL NOTES**
Radionuclear scan can define metabolically active cells by radiolabelling glucose. Used in management. May be used to search for primary tumour and is the most sensitive technique for tumour staging and monitoring. Also used in epilepsy, dementia and assessment of cardiac viability.

Potassium

↑ RAISED IN/BY
Iatrogenic (eg ACE inhibitors, spironolactone, amiloride), diet, dehydration, renal failure, blood transfusion, Addison's disease, acute steroid withdrawal, massive haemolysis, rhabdomyolysis, metabolic acidosis, trauma, surgery, burns, tumour lysis syndrome, renal tubular acidosis (type 4).

↓ DECREASED IN/BY
Iatrogenic (eg thiazide type diuretics, loop diuretics, beta-agonists, insulin, steroids), Cushing's syndrome, Conn's syndrome, vomiting, diarrhoea, GI fistula, ileostomy, villous adenoma, alkalosis, renal tubular acidosis (type 1 and 2), Bartter's syndrome, pseudo-Bartter's syndrome, Liddle's syndrome, acute intermittent porphyria.

📋 **CLINICAL NOTES**
May be falsely raised if cells haemolysed *in vitro*.

Progesterone

↑ RAISED IN/BY
Luteal phase of menstruation (levels subsequently fall preceding menstruation), luteal ovarian cyst, rarely ovarian cancer, pregnancy, higher in multiple pregnancies, molar pregnancy, CAH, adrenal tumour.

↓ DECREASED IN/BY
Hypothalamic failure, pituitary failure, ovarian failure, failure of ovulation (day 21 progesterone), failing pregnancy, pre-eclampsia.

Prolactin

↑ RAISED IN/BY
Pituitary adenoma, ectopic production (paraneoplastic), craniopharyngioma (pressure effect on dopamine inhibition), acromegaly, cirrhosis, iatrogenic (eg SSRIs, major tranquillisers, metoclopramide, oestrogen replacement), renal failure, hypothyroidism, renal disease, PCOS, stress, pregnancy, breastfeeding.

📋 **CLINICAL NOTES**
Macroprolactin is inert and bound to IgG.

Prostate specific antigen (PSA)

↑ RAISED IN/BY
Prostate cancer (used to assist diagnosis, prognosis, monitoring). Non-malignant: benign prostatic hypertrophy, age, recent catheterisation, prostatitis, recent ejaculation, statins, recent digital rectal examination, UTI.

↓ DECREASED IN/BY
Prostatectomy, 5 alpha-reductase inhibitors, GnRH analogues.

📋 **CLINICAL NOTES**
Normal PSA may occur in presence of very undifferentiated cancers. 15% of men with prostate cancer will have PSA <4 microgram/L at diagnosis. PSA 4-10 microgram/L: 25% PPV for cancer, PSA >10 microgram/L: 50% PPV for cancer. PSA >100 microgram/L consistent with metastatic disease.

Protein (urine)

↑ RAISED IN/BY
Glomerulonephritis, nephritis, nephrotic syndrome, orthostatic, febrile illness, URTI, haemolytic uraemic syndrome, UTI, pre-eclampsia.

Protein C (levels and function)

↓ DECREASED IN/BY
Sepsis, renal disease, malignancy, pregnancy, liver disease, vitamin K deficiency, DIC, anticoagulants. Familial-heterozygous/homozygous. Type 1 deficiency-reduced protein C levels. Type 2 deficiency-poor protein C function.

📋 **CLINICAL NOTES**
Test should not be carried out for at least 10 days after VTE or while on anticoagulants.

Protein S (levels and function)

↓ DECREASED IN/BY
Sepsis, renal disease, malignancy, pregnancy, liver disease, vitamin K deficiency, DIC, anticoagulants. Familial-heterozygous/homozygous. Type 1 deficiency-reduced protein S levels. Type 2 poor protein S function. Type 3 reduced unbound protein S levels.

📋 **CLINICAL NOTES**
Test should not be carried out for at least 10 days after VTE or while on anticoagulants.

Prothrombin time (PT)

 CLINICAL NOTES

See *international normalised ratio (INR)-standardised prothrombin time.*

Radioallergosorbent test (RAST)

 CLINICAL NOTES

For type 1 hypersensitivity only – allergen specific IgE test. May be requested to test against environmental allergens, specific food allergies, specific drug allergies, urticaria with angioedema, anaphylaxis, insect bite allergies.

Rapid plasma reagin test (RPR)

See also
- *Venereal diseases research laboratory*
- *Fluorescent treponemal antibody absorption test*
- *Treponema pallidum particle agglutination assay*

 CLINICAL NOTES

Used as a screening test for syphilis.

Renin

↑ **RAISED IN/BY**

Hypertension (malignant, renovascular), hypotension, cardiac failure, hyponatraemia, cirrhosis, CKD, renal tumours, sympathetic stimulation, Addison's disease, pre-eclampsia, tumours, spironolactone, vasodilators, diuretics, ACE inhibitors, CCBs.

↓ **DECREASED IN/BY**

Conn's syndrome, Cushing's syndrome, salt-sensitive hypertension (renin resistant), hypernatraemia, beta-blockers, atrial natriuretic peptide.

Reticulocytes (blood film)

 CLINICAL NOTES

Aetiology/risk factors: Haemolytic disease eg sickle cell disease, active bleeding, addition of haematinics.

Rheumatoid factor

↑ **RAISED IN/BY**

Autoimmune diseases (RA, SLE, systemic sclerosis, polymyositis, dermatomyositis, juvenile arthritis, Sjögren's syndrome). Infection (viral hepatitis, glandular fever, TB, leprosy, syphilis, infective endocarditis). Other (normal population, advancing age, family members of RA patients, chronic liver disease, sarcoid).

 CLINICAL NOTES

High titre indicative of poor prognosis in RA

and increases risk of extra-articular disease. Sensitivities: Sjögren's syndrome 90%, RA 70-90%, polymyositis/dermatomyositis 50%, systemic sclerosis 30%, SLE 25%. Not specific for RA. Will give false +ve D-dimer/fibrin degradation product.

Right shift (blood film)

 CLINICAL NOTES

Aetiology/risk factors: Vitamin B_{12} and folate deficiency, hepatorenal diseases.

Ring sideroblasts (blood film)

 CLINICAL NOTES

Aetiology/risk factors: Idiopathic, congenital, myelodysplasia, copper deficiency, zinc poisoning, lead poisoning, coeliac disease, RA, iron overload, trans-fusion, acute myeloid leukaemia, malignancy, alcohol.

Rouleaux (blood film)

See also
- *Erythrocyte sedimentation rate*

 CLINICAL NOTES

Red cell stacking occurring in infection/inflammation causing a raised ESR.

Rubella antibodies

 CLINICAL NOTES

IgM – recent infection. Infant IgM indicates infection contracted *in utero.* IgG – vaccination/past infection. Absence of antibodies confers risk of contracting disease.

S-100 protein

↑ **RAISED IN/BY**

Tumour marker: Malignant melanoma, peripheral nerve schwannoma, clear cell sarcoma, histiocytosis.

Schilling test

 CLINICAL NOTES

Assesses whether vitamin B_{12} deficiency is corrected by vitamin B_{12} replacement, intrinsic factor replacement, correction of bacterial overgrowth with antibiotics or replacement of pancreatic enzymes.

Schistocytes

 CLINICAL NOTES

Fragmented RBCs. Aetiology/risk factors: Microangiopathic haemolytic anaemia, DIC, thrombotic thrombocytopenic purpura, haemolytic uraemic syndrome, renal failure.

Semen pH (semen analysis)

 CLINICAL NOTES

Normal pH 7.2-8.0. Acidic ejaculate suggests seminal vesicle blockage. Alkaline ejaculate may be associated with infection.

Semen volume (semen analysis)

CLINICAL NOTES

High volume dilutes sperm. Normal ejaculate 2-6ml.

Sex hormone binding globulin (SHBG)

↑ RAISED IN/BY

Children and elderly, chronic liver disease, anorexia, oestrogen therapy, hyperthyroidism.

↓ DECREASED IN/BY

Exogenous androgens, postmenopausal women, hypothyroidism, obesity, androgen abuse, Cushing's disease, PCOS.

CLINICAL NOTES

SHBG binds 45% testosterone in men, 70% testosterone in women, dihydrotestosterone and oestradiol. High SHBG indicates lower free testosterone and vice versa.

Short Synacthen® test

CLINICAL NOTES

Assesses adrenal reserve. Poor rise in cortisol suggestive of Addison's disease.

Sodium

↑ RAISED IN/BY

Dehydration, iatrogenic (IV normal saline), diabetes insipidus, adrenal hyperplasia/tumour (eg Conn's syndrome), hyperosmolar non-ketotic diabetic coma (HONK).

↓ DECREASED IN/BY

Hypovolaemia (diarrhoea, vomiting, fistulae, diuretics, renal tubular disease, burns, haemorrhagic shock, bowel obstruction, volvulus, Addison's disease), hypervolaemia (IV fluids, polydipsia, CCF, liver failure, renal failure, renal artery stenosis). Normovolaemia (SIADH, SSRIs, hypothyroidism). CAH, low vol: marasmus, hypopituitarism, pseudo-Bartter's syndrome.

CLINICAL NOTES

Falsely low sodium seen in hyperlipidaema, hyperproteinaemia, hypergylcaemia.

Soluble mesothelin-related peptide (SMRP)

↑ RAISED IN/BY

Malignancy: Mesothelioma, ovary, pulmonary, pancreas, endometrium.

 CLINICAL NOTES

Used for monitoring mesothelioma. Might be useful in screening high-risk patients, although high false +ve rate. Sensitivity: Mesothelioma 72-83%. Specificity: Mesothelioma 72-95%.

Somatomedin C

CLINICAL NOTES

See *insulin-like growth factor-1*.

Specific gravity (urinalysis)

CLINICAL NOTES

Proportional to osmolality, measure of density of urine. Failure to produce dense (concentrated) urine after water deprivation may suggest diabetes insipidus. High specific gravity may also be related to glucose or radio-opaque dyes.

Sperm count/concentration (semen analysis)

See also
— *Diseases, bronchiectasis*

↓ DECREASED IN/BY

Sulfasalazine, varicocoele, trauma, infection, vasectomy, anti-sperm antibodies, hypogonadism eg Klinefelter's syndrome, illicit drug use, smoking, obesity, chemotherapy, retrograde ejaculation, CF, post-radiation, Young's syndrome.

 CLINICAL NOTES

Normal >15 million/mL.

Sperm forms (semen analysis)

CLINICAL NOTES

>4% normal forms acceptable (WHO), although strict criteria used for fertility assessment.

Sperm motility and progression (semen analysis)

↓ DECREASED IN/BY

STI, testicular infection, prostatitis.

CLINICAL NOTES

>40% motility is acceptable. Progression (0-4). 0 implies no motion, 4 is extremely fast with forward motion.

Spherocytes (blood film)

 CLINICAL NOTES

Aetiology/risk factors: Autoimmune haemolysis, hereditary spherocytosis.

Spirometry

 CLINICAL NOTES

FEV_1-forced expiratory volume in one second (volume of air expelled in one second) reduced in restrictive and obstructive lung disease. COPD: Mild: FEV_1 ≥80% predicted; moderate: FEV_1 50-79% predicted; severe: FEV_1 30-49% predicted; very severe: FEV_1 <30% predicted. FVC-forced vital capacity (amount of air expelled in one breath), FEV_1/FVC <0.7 suggestive of obstructive lung disease; normal/>0.7 suggestive of restrictive lung disease. Spirometry used in diagnosis and monitoring of lung disease. Reversibility testing (spirometry pre- and post-bronchodilator used to assess airways reversibility eg asthma. >400ml increase in FEV_1 with bronchodilators/steroids suggestive of asthma. FEV_1 may be normal in predominantly small airways disease asthma.

Sterile pyuria

 CLINICAL NOTES

Aetiology/risk factors: TB, chlamydia, partially treated UTI, recently treated UTI, mixed bacterial growth, <105 colony forming units (CFU) UTI, poor lab conditions to culture bacteria, contamination from vaginal white cells, interstitial nephritis/cystitis, renal tract stones, medullary sponge kidney, papillary necrosis, carcinoma, PCKD, prostatitis, appendicitis, SLE, Kawasaki disease.

Stomatocytes (blood film)

 CLINICAL NOTES

Aetiology/risk factors: Idiopathic, alcohol excess, liver disease.

Stool pH

 CLINICAL NOTES

<5.5 implies carbohydrate malabsorption.

Stool-reducing substances

CLINICAL NOTES

Suggestive of carbohydrate malabsorption eg lactose intolerance.

Sweat test (sweat stimulation)

CLINICAL NOTES

Used to confirm CF if +ve immunoreactive trypsin heel prick test. May be difficult to interpret in newborns, dehydration or skin diseases.

Synovial fluid (appearance)

 CLINICAL NOTES

Clear/straw coloured (normal), cloudy (may indicate presence of inflammatory cells/bacteria), bloody (trauma, clotting disorders, infection), purulent (infection).

Synovial fluid (crystal analysis)

 CLINICAL NOTES

Negatively birefringent suggestive of gout, positively birefringent suggestive of pseudogout.

Synovial fluid (glucose)

↓ DECREASED IN/BY

Infection, inflammation.

Synovial fluid (lactate dehydrogenase)

↑ RAISED IN/BY

Gout, RA, infection.

Synovial fluid (white cells)

↑ RAISED IN/BY

Moderate WCC suggests immune eg RA, rheumatic fever and crystal arthropathy. High WCC suggests infection.

 CLINICAL NOTES

Excess eosinophils may suggest Lyme disease.

Target cells (blood film)

 CLINICAL NOTES

Aetiology/risk factors: Chronic liver disease, iron deficiency anaemia, sickle cell anaemia, thalassaemia, Hb C, splenectomy.

Teardrop cells (blood film)

CLINICAL NOTES

Aetiology/risk factors: Thalassaemia, myelofibrosis.

Testosterone

↑ RAISED IN/BY

Morning (circadian), PCOS, adrenal tumours, ovarian tumours.

↓ DECREASED IN/BY

Elderly males, postmenopausal women, liver disease, alcoholism, hypothalamic failure, pituitary failure, testicular failure, dystrophia myotonica, Klinefelter's syndrome, Prader-Willi syndrome, Kallmann's syndrome, anti-androgenic iatrogenic (eg cimetidine, spironolactone), multiple endocrine deficiencies.

Thick and thin blood films

 CLINICAL NOTES
Used to detect malaria, more sensitive than rapid malaria antigen testing.

Thyroglobulin

↑ **RAISED IN/BY**
Thyroid cancer, goitre, thyroiditis, thyrotoxicosis.

 CLINICAL NOTES
Suppressed TSH may cause 20% false -ve result. Used in thyroid cancer disease monitoring, not used in screening, diagnosis or prognosis. Thyroglobulin antibodies render test unreliable.

Thyroglobulin antibodies

↑ **RAISED IN/BY**
Idiopathic, Graves' disease, Hashimoto's thyroiditis, De Quervain thyroiditis.

 CLINICAL NOTES
May be used as a marker for thyroid cancer.

Thyroid-binding globulin (TBG)

↑ **RAISED IN/BY**
Familial, pregnancy, oestrogen therapy, phenothiazines, viral hepatitis.

↓ **DECREASED IN/BY**
Genetic, hyperthyroidism, steroids (androgens, corticosteroids), chronic liver disease, nephrotic syndrome, severe illness.

Thyroid peroxidase (TPO) antibodies

↑ **RAISED IN/BY**
20% normal population (up to one in five chance of developing hypothyroidism), primary hypothyroidsm, Graves' disease, Hashimoto's thyroiditis, non-thyroid autoimmune disease, De Quervain thyroiditis.

Thyroid-releasing hormone (TRH)

CLINICAL NOTES
Hypothalamic hormone, stimulates release of TSH, not often measured.

Thyroid-stimulating hormone (TSH)

↑ **RAISED IN/BY**
Pituitary tumour, primary hypothyroidism, compensated euthyroidism (subclinical hypothyroidism, free T_4 low/normal), pre-eclampsia, amiodarone.

↓ **DECREASED IN/BY**
Hypopituitarism, thyrotoxicosis, TSH deficiency, sick euthyroid syndrome, overtreatment with levothyroxine.

CLINICAL NOTES
Released by pituitary. Stimulates T_3 and T_4 release from thyroid gland. TSH should be kept suppressed in patients treated for thyroid cancers.

Thyroid-stimulating hormone (TSH) receptor antibodies

↑ **RAISED IN/BY**
Thyroid-stimulating immunoglobulin causing Graves' disease, may be used in monitoring.

Thyroxine (T_4)

↑ **RAISED IN/BY**
Thyrotoxicosis (normal in T_3 thyrotoxicosis), pregnancy, OCP, altitude, amiodarone, intercurrent illness, glucocorticoids. If TSH raised, consider poor compliance with thyroxine, thyroxine resistance, thyroxine-secreting tumours.

↓ **DECREASED IN/BY**
Sick euthyroid syndrome; low/normal: hypothyroidism, TSH deficiency, corticosteroids, protein-losing states, exogenous triiodothyronine, phenytoin.

CLINICAL NOTES
Most T_4 is protein bound. Free T_4 is thought to be the physiologically active component.

Tilt table test

CLINICAL NOTES
Used in assessment of syncope.

Total cholesterol

↑ **RAISED IN/BY**
Diet, familial, DM, obesity, hypothyroidism, pregnancy, nephrotic syndrome, OCP, steroids, beta-blockers, phenytoin.

↓ **DECREASED IN/BY**
Malnutrition, malabsorption, chronic liver disease, malignancy, lipid-lowering therapy.

Total iron-binding capacity (TIBC)

↑ **RAISED IN/BY**
Iron deficiency, OCP, pregnancy.

↓ **DECREASED IN/BY**
Excess iron (not haemochromatosis type 4a), malignancy, chronic inflammation, protein-losing enteropathy, nephrotic syndrome, chloramphenicol.

CLINICAL NOTES
Reflects transferrin which transports iron from gut.

Transferrin

CLINICAL NOTES
See *total iron-binding capacity*.

Triglycerides

↑ RAISED IN/BY

Alcoholism, familial, DM, diet.

↓ DECREASED IN/BY

Malnutrition, malabsorption, chronic liver disease, malignancy, lipid-lowering therapy.

Treponema pallidum particle agglutination assay (TPPA)

See also
- *Rapid plasma reagin test*
- *Venereal diseases research laboratory*
- *Fluorescent treponemal antibody absorption test*

CLINICAL NOTES
Used to confirm a diagnosis of syphilis after positive screening tests (VDRL and RPR).

Triiodothyronine (T$_3$)

↑ RAISED IN/BY

T$_3$ thyrotoxicosis (eg from solitary toxic nodule), pregnancy.

↓ DECREASED IN/BY

Sick euthyroid syndrome, congenital hypothyroidism, CKD, chronic liver disease, MI, infection, iatrogenic eg NSAIDs.

CLINICAL NOTES
Total (not free) T$_3$ raised during pregnancy. T$_3$ used to determine thyrotoxicosis in preference to T$_4$. Reduced conversion to T$_4$ during severe intercurrent illness.

Troponin I, T

↑ RAISED IN/BY

MI, myocarditis, cardiac failure, cardiomyopathy, renal failure, inflammatory conditions.

CLINICAL NOTES
Highly specific for myocardial damage, raised 9-12 hours after MI. Levels correlate with prognosis.

Ultrasound

CLINICAL NOTES
Non-invasive, no ionising radiation. Wide applications including screening/imaging and guided biopsies.

Indications: AAA, suspected gallstones/gallbladder disease, pancreatic disease (tumour/pancreatitis/cyst), liver disease (guided biopsy, jaundice), abdominal pain (perforation, appendicitis), abdominal mass, abdominal abscess, endoluminal USS for GI tumours, renal mass, possibility of renal stones, visible haematuria, persistent non-visible haematuria, screening for APKD (age >20 years), CKD stage 4/5, possible renal tract obstruction, prostatism, urinary incontinence, recurrent/atypical UTI, breast cancer surveillance, oral cancer guided biopsy, thyroid cancer/goitre/mass/nodule/lingual thyroid, neck mass, salivary gland obstruction/mass, sicca syndrome. Testicular mass/suspected tumour, suspected pelvic tumour eg ovarian mass/cyst, endometrial thickness assessment/including endometrial tumour/fibroid, lost IUD, infertility, PCOS, pregnancy monitoring/complications, suspected ectopic pregnancy/miscarriage, postmenopausal bleeding. Guided biopsy for lymphoma, limb mass (extra-osseous), suspected pleural effusion, suspected hydrocephalus in young infants/shunt malfunction, irritable hip/child with a limp.

Urea

↑ RAISED IN/BY

GI haemorrhage, diarrhoea, sepsis, trauma, rhabdomyolysis, hypovolaemia, cardiac failure, renal failure, obstructive uropathy, steroids.

Uric acid

↑ RAISED IN/BY

Excess uric acid: Diet, tumour lysis syndrome, lymphoma, rhabdomyolysis, myeloproliferative diseases, psoriasis, Lesch-Nyhan syndrome. Reduced excretion: CKD, diuretics, hyperparathyroidism, pre-eclampsia, genetic, hypothyroidism.

Urinary casts (microscopy)

CLINICAL NOTES
Red cell casts: Glomerulonephritis, vasculitides, severe hypertension. White cell casts: glomerulonephritis, pyelonephritis. Fine granular /hyaline casts: Normal finding, post-exercise, secondary to loop diuretics, febrile illness. Dense granular casts: Diabetic nephropathy, glomerulonephritis, amyloidosis, interstitial nephritis. Epithelial cell casts: Acute tubular necrosis, glomerulonephritis.

Urinary catecholamines

CLINICAL NOTES
Diagnosis and monitoring of phaeochromocytoma. Catecholamines may be normal in presence of phaeochromocytoma. High false +ve rate: Iatrogenic (eg ACE inhibitors, paracetamol, TCAs, lithium, insulin, aspirin), caffeine, bananas, alcohol, smoking, stress, physical illness. Sample should be stored in a refrigerator.

Urinary crystals (microscopy)

 CLINICAL NOTES

Aetiology/risk factors: Old urine, cold urine, cystine crystals, calcium oxalate/phosphate.

Urinary pus cells (microscopy)

See also
— *Sterile pyuria*

 CLINICAL NOTES

>10/mm³ leucocytes pathological (unspun urine).

Urinary red cells (microscopy)

See also
— *Urinary casts (microscopy)*
— *Signs and symptoms, haematuria*

 CLINICAL NOTES

>2/mm³ on microscopy.

Urine albumin:creatinine (ACR)

See also
— *Urine protein:creatinine*

🗒 **CLINICAL NOTES**

Three positive tests required. More sensitive than PCR for low levels of proteinuria. Should be used in monitoring DM (microalbuminuria if ACR ≥2.5mg/mmol in men or ≥3.5mg/mmol in women or if albumin 30-200mg/L). In non-diabetic patients, ≥30mg/mmol is significant. Repeat early morning sample if ≥30 and <70mg/mmol in non-diabetics. Refer if ACR ≥70mg/mmol or ≥30mg/mmol with haematuria.

Urine protein:creatinine (PCR)

See also
— *Urine albumin:creatinine*

🗒 **CLINICAL NOTES**

Less sensitive than ACR for low levels of proteinuria. Consider specialist referral if ≥100mg/mmol or ≥50mg/mmol with haematuria.

Urobilinogen (urinalysis)

🗒 **CLINICAL NOTES**

+ve in hepatocellular jaundice, absent in obstructive jaundice.

Venereal diseases research laboratory (VDRL)

See also
— *Rapid plasma reagin test*
— *Fluorescent treponemal antibody absorption test*
— *Treponema pallidum particle agglutination assay*

🗒 **CLINICAL NOTES**

Used as a screening test for syphilis. False -ve in if test performed within three months; false +ve VDRL: Lyme disease, HIV, SLE, malaria, anti-cardiolipin antibodies, lupus anticoagulant. FTA-ABS more specific for syphilis than VDRL.

Ventilation/perfusion (V/Q) scan

🗒 **CLINICAL NOTES**

PE: Sensitivity: ~67%. Specificity: 78%.

Very low density lipoprotein (VLDL)

🗒 **CLINICAL NOTES**

Correlates to triglyceride levels.

Water deprivation test

🗒 **CLINICAL NOTES**

If urine osmolarity >600mosmol/kg, diabetes insipidus is excluded, if <400mosmol/kg, consider diabetes insipidus. Increase in urine osmolality in response to desmopressin (>50% in cranial, <45% in nephrogenic diabetes insipidus).

DISEASES

1st cranial nerve palsy

 CLINICAL NOTES

Aetiology/risk factors: Frontal lobe tumour, eg meningioma, leukaemia, head injury, meningitis, encephalitis, DM, MS, syphilis, sarcoid, vasculitis, chronic sinusitis, nasal polyps, nasal tumour. Clinical features: Reduced sense of smell in one or both nostrils.

INVESTIGATIONS

CT/MRI. Investigate according to suspected underlying cause.

MANAGEMENT

Treat underlying cause.

1st-degree heart block

CLINICAL NOTES

Prolonged PR interval (>0.2sec/>5 small squares on ECG). Epidemiology: Overall prevalence 1.13 in 1,000. Aetiology/risk factors: Idiopathic, rheumatic fever, aortic valve disease, endocarditis, diphtheria, IHD, iatrogenic (eg procainamide, digoxin, beta-blockers), electrolyte disturbance, myotonic dystrophy, acute/progressive in aortic root abscess. Clinical features: Usually no associated symptoms and signs.

INVESTIGATIONS

ECG. Investigate according to suspected underlying cause.

MANAGEMENT

Consider treating underlying cause. Monitor if lone 1st-degree block with ECGs performed at regular intervals. Avoid AV node blocking drugs.

2nd-degree heart block (Mobitz I, Wenkebach)

CLINICAL NOTES

Repeating cycles of increasingly prolonged PR interval until no AV conduction. Epidemiology: Nearly 3% of patients with underlying structural heart disease develop some form of 2nd-degree heart block. Aetiology/risk factors: AV nodal disease, increased vagal tone, IHD, electrolyte disturbance, iatrogenic (eg digoxin). Clinical features: Asymptomatic, dizziness, syncope.

INVESTIGATIONS

ECG, consider ambulatory ECG. Investigate according to suspected underlying cause.

MANAGEMENT

Treat underlying causes. Monitor with ECGs performed at regular intervals, usually benign condition with no specific treatment. Avoid AV node blocking drugs.

2nd-degree heart block (Mobitz II)

CLINICAL NOTES

Intermittently non-conducted P waves. Preceding PR interval normal length. P:QRS may occur in eg 2:1, 3:1 or varying ratios. Aetiology/risk factors: MI, IHD, aortic valve disease, myocarditis, iatrogenic (eg CCBs, beta-blockers), electrolyte disturbance, hypothyroidism, hypothermia, trauma, high vagal tone, connective tissue disease, infection (eg endocarditis, Chagas disease, Lyme disease, sarcoid), conduction system fibrosis (eg Lev's disease [older patients], Lenegre's disease [younger patients]), myotonic dystrophy, Duchenne muscular dystrophy, amyloid, haemochromatosis, congenital. Complications: Complete heart block.

INVESTIGATIONS

ECG, consider ambulatory ECG. Echocardiogram. Investigate according to suspected underlying cause.

MANAGEMENT

Treat underlying causes. May require pacemaker. Avoid AV node blocking drugs.

IIIrd cranial nerve palsy

CLINICAL NOTES

Aetiology/risk factors: Posterior communicating artery aneurysm, polyneuropathy (eg diabetes), CVA, Weber's syndrome, MS, Paget's disease of the bone, orbital diseases, eg Graves' disease, cavernous sinus thrombosis, acromegaly, uncal herniation, tumour, lymphoma/leukaemia, TB, HIV, migraine. Clinical features: Diplopia, ptosis (may be complete), eye directed inferiorly and laterally, dilated pupil (unless 'medical third', eg diabetes where pupil is unaffected).

INVESTIGATIONS

CT/MRI. Investigate according to suspected underlying cause.

MANAGEMENT

Treat underlying cause, visual aid.

3rd-degree (complete) heart block

CLINICAL NOTES

No relationship between atrial and ventricular depolarisation. Bundle of His (narrow complex, faster rate) or ventricular (wide complex, worse prognosis, slow escape rhythm ~40bpm). Epidemiology: Prevalence of 0.04%. Aetiology/risk factors: See *2nd-degree heart block (Mobitz II)*; IHD, MI, digoxin poisoning, infection (eg syphilis, diphtheria, viral), aortic valve disease, mitral valve disease, sarcoid. Clinical features: Pre-syncope, syncope, angina, hypotension. Complications: 50% mortality at one year.

INVESTIGATIONS

ECG, echocardiogram, angiography. Investigate according to suspected underlying cause.

MANAGEMENT

May require emergency pacing and atropine, pacemaker; may require ICD device.

IVth cranial nerve palsy

CLINICAL NOTES

Epidemiology: Isolated lesions unlikely. Aetiology/risk factors: Trauma, DM, MS, syphilis, sarcoid, tumour, vasculitis, Paget's disease of the bone, thyroid eye disease. Clinical features: Diplopia worse on looking inferiorly and medially (eg difficulty walking downstairs).

INVESTIGATIONS

CT/MRI. Investigate according to suspected underlying cause.

MANAGEMENT

Treat underlying cause, visual aid.

Vth cranial nerve palsy

CLINICAL NOTES

Aetiology/risk factors: Cavernous sinus thrombosis, trauma, CVA, bulbar palsy, MS, leukaemia, tumour (eg acoustic neuroma, nasopharyngeal cancer), vasculitis, Paget's disease of the bone, herpes zoster. Clinical features: Fasciculation (masseter/ temporalis), altered sensation (ipsilateral), jaw deviation (ipsilateral, LMN). If combined with VIth cranial nerve palsy, consider Gradenigo's syndrome – suggests lesion within petrous temporal bone.

INVESTIGATIONS

CT/MRI. Investigate according to suspected underlying cause.

MANAGEMENT

Treat underlying cause.

VIth cranial nerve palsy

CLINICAL NOTES

Aetiology/risk factors: Polyneuropathy, raised ICP (VIth nerve palsy may be a false localising sign), tumour, abscess, MS, leukaemia, CVA (pontine lesion), aneurysm, cavernous sinus thrombosis, thyroid eye disease, skull fracture, Wernicke's encephalopathy, internuclear ophthalmoplegia, benign intracranial hypertension. Clinical features: Diplopia worse on looking towards affected eye, impairment of lateral movement of affected eye (may be subtle), diplopia disappears when one eye covered. If combined with Vth cranial nerve palsy, consider Gradenigo's syndrome – suggests lesion within petrous temporal bone.

INVESTIGATIONS

CT/MRI. Investigate according to suspected underlying cause.

MANAGEMENT

Treat underlying cause, visual aid.

VIIth cranial nerve palsy

See also
— Bell's palsy

CLINICAL NOTES

Aetiology/risk factors: LMN (Bell's palsy, trauma, surgery, parotid surgery/tumour/infiltration, polio, skull fracture/trauma, acoustic neuroma, Ramsay Hunt syndrome, Lyme disease, sarcoid, cholesteatoma, DM, Guillain-Barré syndrome, Sjögren's syndrome, leukaemia, pre-eclampsia, brainstem insult), UMN (CVA, tumour, brainstem lesions – MS, ADEM). Clinical features: Dribbling, difficulty closing eye, hyperacusis, LMN (forehead also paralysed), UMN (forehead sparing), altered lacrimation and taste (anterior two-thirds of tongue).

INVESTIGATIONS

CT/MRI. Investigate according to suspected underlying cause.

MANAGEMENT

Treat underlying cause. Eye – lubrication, patch, tarsorrhaphy (partial lid-to-lid suture).

VIIIth cranial nerve palsy

CLINICAL NOTES

Aetiology/risk factors: Ménière's disease, Paget's disease of the bone, acoustic neuroma/neurofibroma, trauma, leukaemia, herpes zoster, iatrogenic (gentamicin, furosemide), MS, ADEM, brainstem CVA/ syrinx. Clinical features: Deafness, tinnitus.

INVESTIGATIONS

Rinne's/Weber's test. CT/MRI. Investigate according to suspected underlying cause.

MANAGEMENT

Treat underlying cause, hearing aid, cochlear implant.

IXth cranial nerve palsy

CLINICAL NOTES

Aetiology/risk factors: Paget's disease of the bone, trauma, jugular foramen syndrome, acoustic neuroma, poliomyelitis, MS, ADEM, MND, CVA, Guillain-Barré syndrome, leukaemia. Clinical features: Bilateral nerve defect only – pseudobulbar palsy, altered taste (posterior one-third of tongue), salivary gland dysfunction.

INVESTIGATIONS
CT/MRI. Investigate according to suspected underlying cause.

MANAGEMENT
Treat underlying cause, oral lubricants, SALT assessment.

Xth cranial nerve palsy

CLINICAL NOTES
Aetiology/risk factors: Jugular foramen syndrome, trauma, iatrogenic, acoustic neuroma, neck tumours, poliomyelitis, Guillain-Barré syndrome, MS, CVA, syrinx, Paget's disease of the bone. Clinical features: Nasal regurgitation of food, nasal speech, absent gag reflex.

INVESTIGATIONS
CT/MRI. Investigate according to suspected underlying cause.

MANAGEMENT
Treat underlying cause, SALT.

XIth cranial nerve palsy

CLINICAL NOTES
Aetiology/risk factors: Jugular foramen syndrome, trauma, iatrogenic, acoustic neuroma, neck tumours, polio, Guillain-Barré syndrome, MS, leukaemia, CVA, syrinx. Clinical features: Weakness of sternomastoid (difficulty turning head away from lesion) and trapezius (resulting in shoulder drop).

INVESTIGATIONS
CT/MRI. Investigate according to suspected underlying cause.

MANAGEMENT
Treat underlying cause, physiotherapy.

XIIth cranial nerve palsy

CLINICAL NOTES
Aetiology/risk factors: Syrinx, polio, CVA, jugular foramen syndrome (not always in this syndrome), tumour (chordoma, nasopharyngeal cancer, acoustic neuroma, glioma metastases), trauma, Paget's disease of the bone, MS, internal carotid artery dissection, MND, Kennedy's disease, infectious mononucleosis, amyloid, HIV, SLE. Clinical features: LMN (ipsilateral tongue wasting, tongue moves to side of lesion), UMN (spastic tongue).

INVESTIGATIONS
CT/MRI. Investigate according to suspected underlying cause.

MANAGEMENT
Treat underlying cause, SALT.

Abdominal aortic aneurysm (AAA)

CLINICAL NOTES
Epidemiology: 5% of >60-year-olds; 6,000 deaths per year from rupture (England and Wales). M>F. Aetiology/risk factors: Familial, atherosclerosis, smoking, hypertension, hyperlipidaemia, infections (eg syphilis), Marfan's syndrome, Ehlers-Danlos syndrome. Clinical features: Asymptomatic (incidental finding or found on palpation/imaging), abdominal pain radiating to back, back pain due to erosion of vertebral bodies, pulsatile laterally expansive abdominal mass, bruit. Complications: Emboli, ureteric/bowel/vena caval obstruction, retroperitoneal fibrosis, aortoduodenal fistula, rupture – severe pain and hypotension, high mortality risk, retroperitoneal bleeding (may be suggested by Grey-Turner's sign [flank bruising]), death.

INVESTIGATIONS
USS screening shown to be of benefit in men. CT.

MANAGEMENT
AAA treated surgically/endovascular if >5.5cm (threshold less in women), surgical mortality risk warrants repair or expanding ≥1cm per year or symptomatic. If <5.5cm, regular review required (3.5-4cm: annual USS, 4.0-5.0cm: six-monthly USS, >5cm: three-monthly USS). Control cardiovascular risk factors.

Abetalipoproteinaemia

CLINICAL NOTES
Lipoprotein synthesis disorder. Epidemiology: Rare. Aetiology/risk factors: Autosomal recessive. Clinical features: Failure to thrive, ataxia, retinopathy, steatorrhoea.

INVESTIGATIONS
FBC (acanthocytes). ↑ ALT, ↓ LDL, ↓ VLDL, ↓cholesterol and ↓triglycerides.

MANAGEMENT
Vitamin A and E (fat-soluble) supplements.

Achalasia

CLINICAL NOTES
Oesophageal motility disorder (functional stenosis). Epidemiology: Third to fifth decades. Not familial. Rare (prevalence one in 10^6). Aetiology/risk factors: Rozycki syndrome (infants – deafness, short stature, muscle wasting, vitiligo, achalasia). American trypanosomiasis/DM may cause an achalasia-like picture. Clinical features: Dysphagia (solids and liquids), regurgitation of food, retrosternal chest pain, dyspepsia, cough. Complications: Aspiration, oesophageal malignancy (up to 7%).

INVESTIGATIONS

Chest X-ray: Dilated oesophagus, barium swallow – dilated oesophagus, tapered distally ('bird's beak'), endoscopy (risk of perforation), manometry (if normal, consider pseudoachalasia).

MANAGEMENT

CCB, nitrates, botulinum toxin, balloon dilation (risk of perforation and GORD), Heller myotomy, oesophagectomy, regular follow-up and monitor for malignancy.

Achilles tendon rupture

CLINICAL NOTES

Aetiology/risk factors: Achilles tendonitis, trauma, iatrogenic (eg quinolones, steroids), inflammatory conditions (eg RA, ankylosing spondylitis). Clinical features: Pain, snap may be heard, weakness of plantar flexion, altered gait, palpable tendon defect and failure of slight plantar flexion on squeezing calf (Thompson test, +ve if complete rupture). Complications: Contracture, recurrent rupture, disability.

INVESTIGATIONS

USS/MRI, investigate according to suspected underlying cause.

MANAGEMENT

Treat underlying cause. Analgesia, surgical repair, immobilisation, physiotherapy.

Achilles tendonitis

CLINICAL NOTES

Aetiology/risk factors: Trauma, sport, overuse, inappropriate footwear, flat feet, ankylosing spondylitis, quinolones. Clinical features: Tenderness and crepitus over Achilles tendon. Complications: Rupture.

MANAGEMENT

Treat/address underlying cause, rest, ice, NSAIDs, topical GTN, immobilisation, physiotherapy, steroid injection (increased risk of rupture).

Achondroplasia

CLINICAL NOTES

Form of dwarfism. Aetiology/risk factors: Autosomal dominant/mutation. Homozygous not compatible with life. Clinical features: Short stature (short limbs), ↑lumbar lordosis, frontal bossing, facial hypoplasia, flat nasal bridge. Complications: Psychological, spinal stenosis, hydrocephalus, sleep apnoea, dental complications (crowding of teeth), recurrent otitis media, OA.

INVESTIGATIONS

Prenatal scanning, limb and pelvic X-rays, brain MRI.

MANAGEMENT

Genetic counselling, family therapy, OT, physiotherapy, surgery.

Acne vulgaris

CLINICAL NOTES

Aetiology/risk factors: Puberty, PCOS, hypercornification of pilosebaceous duct, excess sebum production, *Propionibacterium acnes*, genetic component in severe disease, late-onset congenital adrenal hyperplasia (21-hydroxylase deficiency), acromegaly. Clinical features: Chronic pilosebaceous inflammation, multiple comedones (closed [whiteheads], open [blackheads, oxidised sebum turns black]) seborrhoea, papules, pustules, cysts, nodules. Complications: Scarring, postinflammatory hyperpigmentation/ hypopigmentation, depression, low self-esteem.

INVESTIGATIONS

Consider investigation for systemic diseases in resistant or severe cases.

MANAGEMENT

Topical: Benzoyl peroxide, topical antibiotics (erythromycin, clindamycin), topical retinoids (tretinoin, isotretinoin, adapalene [better tolerated]), azelaic acid (good for comedones), nicotinamide (4% has equivalent efficacy to 1% clindamycin), combination topical agents (benzoyl peroxide plus clindamycin, zinc plus topical antibiotics), consider salicylic acid for superficial comedones. Oral: Oral antibiotics – oxytetracycline, lymecycline, give for at least three months before efficacy determined. May also consider dapsone or trimethoprim. For comedonal acne, pustules, papules, inflamed cysts, moderate to severe scarring, consider oral antibiotics with topical non-antimicrobial therapy. Isotretinoin for nodulocystic, conglobate, severe and scarring acne or if causing distress (commenced by specialist). Corticosteroids (systemic or injected), COC (eg co-cyprindiol, drospirenone plus ethinylestradiol). Others: Hyfrecation of comedones, laser therapy.

Acoustic neuroma (schwannoma)

CLINICAL NOTES

Epidemiology: Most common cerebellopontine angle tumour, rare. Aetiology/risk factors: Sporadic, neurofibromatosis (bilateral), radiation. Clinical features: Unilateral deafness, vertigo, Vth and VIIIth cranial nerves most commonly affected; VIth, VIIth, IX-XIth less commonly affected, cerebellar signs. Complications: Raised ICP.

INVESTIGATIONS

Formal audiometry, CT/MRI, investigate according to suspected underlying cause.

DISEASES

MANAGEMENT

Consider watch and wait, radiotherapy, gamma knife or surgery. Microsurgery offers best long-term outcome, but risk of VIIth cranial nerve palsy and brainstem insult.

Acquired immunodeficiency syndrome (AIDS)

CLINICAL NOTES
See *HIV*

Acromegaly

CLINICAL NOTES
Epidemiology: Fourth to sixth decades, rare. Aetiology/risk factors: Hypothalamic tumour (GHRH-secreting), pituitary adenoma (GH-secreting), ectopic GH/GHRH secretion (eg lung, pancreas, thyroid, adrenal, ovarian, carcinoid tumours), McCune-Albright syndrome, MEN1. Clinical features: Fatigue, headaches, change in clothing/shoe size, symptoms of DM, sweating, sleep apnoea, breathlessness, carpal tunnel syndrome, joint pains, coarse features, hirsutism, prominent supraorbital ridge, prognathism, increasing interdental spaces, macroglossia, bitemporal hemianopia (mass effect of pituitary tumour), goitre, doughy hands, greasy skin, acne, acanthosis nigricans, skin tags (associated with large bowel polyps), kyphosis, OA, hypertension, cardiac failure, arrhythmias, hepatomegaly, deep voice, gynaecomastia. Active disease suggested by headache, sweating, soft tissue swelling, hypertension, hyperglycaemia. Complications: Tumour may secrete prolactin, IHD, CVA, DM and diabetes insipidus, colonic polyps, colon cancer, IIIrd nerve palsy, renal stones, ↑mortality.

INVESTIGATIONS
Formal visual field testing, ↑glucose, ↑phosphate, ↑Ca²⁺ (serum – uncommon, urinary – common), ↑triglycerides, GH may be normal, ↑IGF-I (if normal, acromegaly unlikely; if positive, OGTT should be performed), OGTT – failure of GH suppression suggests acromegaly, IGF-binding protein-3, pituitary hormones, TFT, brain MRI, ECG, echocardiogram, may need investigation for sources of ectopic GH/GHRH.

MANAGEMENT
Bromocriptine, cabergoline, octreotide, pegvisomant (GH antagonist), hypophysectomy, radiotherapy, regular monitoring.

Acromioclavicular joint (ACJ) arthritis and injury

CLINICAL NOTES
OA. Clinical features: Shoulder pain, ACJ pain, worse on touching opposing shoulder.
ACJ disruption/ subluxation – trauma, degree measured by Rockwood classification (I-VI). Clinical features: Pain, lateral clavicle, tenderness/swelling/step over ACJ, worse on touching opposing shoulder. Complications: Brachial plexus and proximal vessel injury (neurology and pulses should be assessed), deltoid/trapezius avulsion, clavicular fracture and pneumothorax.

INVESTIGATIONS
ACJ X-ray (taken when ACJ under strain, specialised views), chest X-ray, imaging of scapula may be required.

MANAGEMENT
OA: Analgesia, physiotherapy, steroid injection, surgery.
ACJ trauma: Depends on degree of disruption; if sprain or tear of acromioclavicular (AC) ligaments with intact coracoclavicular (CC) ligaments (Rockwood I, II), conservative treatment; if both AC and CC ligaments disrupted (type III), conservative or surgery. More severe injuries require surgical intervention.

Acute disseminated encephalomyelitis (ADEM)

CLINICAL NOTES
Epidemiology: Rare, children>adults, ↑winter. Aetiology/risk factors: One to 20 days post viral infection, post-vaccination (measles, mumps, rubella). Clinical features: Acute onset CNS inflammation, headache, nausea, vomiting, fatigue, weakness, ataxia, pyramidal signs. Complications: Optic neuritis, deafness, transverse myelitis, Devic's syndrome (optic neuritis and transverse myelitis), hemiparesis, Brown-Séquard syndrome, bowel and bladder involvement, seizure, coma, permanent disability, recurrence (rarely), death (2%).

INVESTIGATIONS
FBC, atypical lymphocytes, ↑plts, CSF (↑RBC, ↑WCC, ↑myelin basic protein), brain MRI, brain biopsy (rarely performed).

MANAGEMENT
IV corticosteroids, 50% have full recovery. Steroid-sparing agents and plasmapheresis may be considered.

Acute intermittent porphyria

CLINICAL NOTES
Epidemiology: Rare, most common porphyria type. F>M (attacks usually during reproductive ages). Aetiology/risk factors: Autosomal dominant/new mutation. Clinical features: Intermittent attacks. Fever, severe abdominal pain, vomiting, constipation/diarrhoea, muscular pain, paralysis, seizures, hypertension, psychosis, confusion. Triggers include stress, smoking, alcohol, tetracyclines, sulfonamides, COC, oral hypoglycaemics. Complications: Respiratory failure, dehydration, renal failure, mistaken for surgical abdomen.

INVESTIGATIONS

During attack – raised urinary porphobilinogen turns red on standing (may not always be present between attacks), ↑WCC, ↓Na⁺, ↓K⁺, proteinuria.

MANAGEMENT

Remove trigger, IV fluids, electrolyte management, analgesia, IV haematin, benzodiazepines if fitting, BP control with beta-blockade.

Acute limb ischaemia

CLINICAL NOTES

Aetiology/risk factors: Atherosclerosis, emboli, thrombophilia, compartment syndrome. Clinical features: Pain, paraesthesia, paralysis, limb pallor, absent pulses, cold limbs, mottled skin. Complications: Gangrene.

INVESTIGATIONS

Conventional or CT/MR angiography.

MANAGEMENT

Thrombolysis, embolectomy, primary angioplasty and stent, consider anticoagulation, amputation. Secondary prevention of cardiovascular disease. Complications: Reperfusion injury.

Acute lymphoblastic leukaemia (ALL)

CLINICAL NOTES

Common ALL: 75% of ALL cases, age at presentation about four years. White race>black race, >85% five-year survival. T-cell ALL: Approximately 50% cure rate. B-cell ALL: 70% cure rate. Clinical features: Pancytopenia, excessive blast cell mass and systemic upset, ie fatigue, bruising, epistaxis, recurrent/resistant infection (viral, bacterial, fungal), fever, weight loss, muscle pain, joint pain, bone pain, mediastinal mass (more common in adults). Complications: Overwhelming infection, haemorrhage, tumour lysis during treatment, leucostasis, testicular infiltration (common recurrence site in children, not adults, recurrence usually bilateral), meningeal involvement (headache, vomiting, cranial nerve palsy, raised ICP), SVCO especially T-cell.

INVESTIGATIONS

FBC (blasts, pancytopenia, 5% cases have no peripheral blasts), ↓MCHC, U&E (↓K⁺, note ↑K⁺ with tumour lysis), glucose, uric acid, LFT (liver infiltration), LDH, beta₂ microglobulin, marrow biopsy. LP-CSF (blast cells suggest meningeal involvement), chest X-ray – thymic enlargement; bone X-ray – metaphyseal anomalies, CT. Testicular biopsy.

MANAGEMENT

Family support, transfusion, antibiotics/antifungals as required, allopurinol for tumour lysis. Common ALL: Children, first-line: Remission induction (eg vincristine, prednisolone, doxorubicin) →intensive consolidation (eg doxorubicin, asparaginase, methotrexate, cytosine arabinoside) →CNS prophylaxis (intrathecal methotrexate, cranial irradiation) →maintenance therapy (eg methotrexate, vincristine, prednisolone, 6-mercaptopurine). Testicular irradiation (some countries advocate prophylactic testicular irradiation). Children, relapse: Bone marrow transplant, total body irradiation, CNS intrathecal methotrexate/irradiation. B-cell diseases require more intense therapy. Adults, first-line: As for children, but more intense consolidation required. Worse prognosis in males and individuals >12 years of age, death.

Acute myeloid leukaemia (AML)

CLINICAL NOTES

Epidemiology: Risk increases with age (two-thirds of cases >60 years), 2,000 per year (UK). Various subtypes. Aetiology/risk factors: t(15:17)-retinoic acid receptor gene translocation in AML M3, Philadelphia chromosome (t(9:22)-ABL/BCR translocation, present in 95% of cases), Down's syndrome, complication of CML, lymphoma, myelodysplasia, chemotherapy. Clinical features: Pancytopenia, excessive blast cell mass and systemic upset, ie fatigue, bruising, epistaxis, recurrent/resistant infection (viral, bacterial, fungal), fever, weight loss, gum hyperplasia, hepatosplenomegaly. Complications: Overwhelming infection, bleeding, cerebral involvement (headache, vomiting, cranial nerve palsy, raised ICP), testicular/skin infiltration, DIC (AML M3), tumour lysis during treatment, leucostasis.

INVESTIGATIONS

WCC (usually ↑), ↓MCHC, U&E, uric acid. Film – blasts (may be absent in peripheral blood), Auer rods (not all subtypes), ring sideroblasts, marrow biopsy, immune typing and cytogenetics.

MANAGEMENT

Family support, transfusion, antibiotics/antifungals as required, allopurinol for tumour lysis. All-trans retinoic acid for AML M3. Chemotherapy (remission induction, eg cytosine and doxorubicin), bone marrow transplant. Consider newer drugs including everolimus, gemtuzumab, CEP-701, arsenic trioxide.

Acute pericarditis

CLINICAL NOTES

Epidemiology: M>F. Aetiology/risk factors: Idiopathic, infection (viral, eg coxsackie/echovirus; bacterial, eg TB, fungal), malignant infiltration, post-MI (20% MI patients, especially ST elevation MI (STEMI)/anterior MI, few days post-MI or two to 10 weeks post-MI (Dressler's syndrome – fever, pericarditis,

DISEASES

↑ESR), thyroid disease, uraemia, autoimmune disease, trauma, iatrogenic, radiotherapy, surgical. Clinical features: Sharp anterior chest pain (↑coughing/lying down), pericardial friction rub (second to fourth intercostal spaces). Complications: Pericardial effusion/tamponade, chronic disease may cause constrictive pericarditis.

INVESTIGATIONS

↑Troponin, ↑ESR, ECG concave 'saddle'-shaped, ST elevation, T waves may then invert before ECG normalises, echocardiogram, chest X-ray, CT, cardiac MRI. Investigate according to suspected underlying cause.

MANAGEMENT

NSAIDs (unless post-MI – ↑myocardial rupture), corticosteroids, pericardiectomy for recurrent/highly symptomatic disease. Colchicine for prevention, treat underlying cause.

Addison's disease

CLINICAL NOTES

Epidemiology: Rare. Aetiology/risk factors: Autoimmune, TB, Waterhouse-Friderichsen syndrome, surgery, amyloid, sarcoid, haemochromatosis, carcinomatosis, autoimmune polyendocrine syndrome, fungal infection, adrenal vein thrombosis, acute steroid withdrawal may cause an Addisonian-like crisis. Clinical features: Non-specific symptoms, fatigue, weight loss, anorexia, weakness, dizziness, postural hypotension, collapse, abdominal pain, nausea, vomiting, diarrhoea, myalgia, cramps, low mood, hyperpigmentation (palmar creases, buccal mucosa, scars), signs of associated autoimmune disease, eg vitiligo. Complications: Benign intracranial hypertension, psychosis, Addisonian crisis (confusion, coma, seizure, tachycardia, severe postural hypotension, hypoglycaemia, death).

INVESTIGATIONS

FBC, ↑eosinophils, ↓neutrophils, ↑lymphocytes, atypical lymphocytes, ↓Na^+, ↑K^+, ↓glucose, uraemia, ↓pH, normal anion gap metabolic acidosis, ↑Ca^{2+}, ↑Mg^{2+} ↑LFT, ↑renin, ↓aldosterone, ↑ACTH, ↓DHEA-S, adrenal auto-antibodies, 21-hydroxylase antibodies (eg polyendocrine syndrome), ANA, short Synacthen® test, abdominal X-ray/CT/MRI, ECG (↑PR, ↑QT).

MANAGEMENT

Steroid replacement therapy. Education: Never stop steroids suddenly, increase steroid dose (x2) with intercurrent illness, steroid bracelet/card.

Adhesive capsulitis (frozen shoulder syndrome)

CLINICAL NOTES

Epidemiology: About 5% orthopaedic referrals. Most common 50-60 years of age. M=F. Aetiology/risk factors: Minor trauma. Associated with DM, Dupuytren's contracture, dyslipidaemia, hyperthyroidism, cardiac disease. Clinical features: Gradual onset and increasing shoulder pain, may lead to stiffness, reduced active and passive shoulder movements, especially external rotation and abduction.

INVESTIGATIONS

Consider X-ray to exclude other pathology, MRI usually normal.

MANAGEMENT

Analgesia, physiotherapy, early use of intra-articular steroids, manipulation under anaesthetic.

African sleeping sickness

CLINICAL NOTES

See trypanosomiasis

Age-related macular degeneration (ARMD)

CLINICAL NOTES

Epidemiology: Increasing prevalence. Aetiology/risk factors: Advancing age, smoking, Caucasians, F>M. Dry type: Slow deterioration of vision, drusen on examination. May progress to wet type. Wet type: Neovascularisation +/–haemorrhage, exudate and fibrosis. Rapid visual loss.

INVESTIGATIONS

Fluoroscein angiography (distinguishes between wet and dry types), ocular coherence tomography.

MANAGEMENT

Vitamins A/C/E and zinc, carotenoids and perhaps folic acid/vitamin B_6/vitamin B_{12} slow progress of dry type, anti-VEGF drugs (ranibizumab, bevacizumab), photodynamic therapy, retinal rotational surgery or radiotherapy for wet type.

Alcoholism

See also
— Wernicke's encephalopathy
— Delirium tremens

CLINICAL NOTES

Epidemiology: Misuse and binge drinking increasing prevalence. About 6% hospital admissions related to alcohol (UK). 2×10^4 premature deaths per year (UK). Consumption: Units (volume drunk (ml)/1,000) x %alcohol, eg a 750ml bottle of 12% wine = 750/1,000 x 12 = 3/4 x 12 = 9 units/bottle. Ask about time of first drink in the day (may drink early), drinking pattern, desire to drink, need to drink daily, other people's views on their drinking. CAGE questionnaire (see page 238), 93%

sensitive, 76% specific. AUDIT (alcohol use disorders identification test, more sensitive and specific than CAGE). Complications: Acute intoxication, withdrawal symptoms – agitation, tremor, sweating, hallucinations, delirium tremens (DTs), seizure – crime, violence, ↓work performance, depression, anxiety, suicide, malnutrition, hypertension, cardiac arrhythmia (eg AF), cardiomyopathy, neuropathy, falls, subdural haemorrhage, Wernicke's encephalopathy (acute thiamine deficiency causing ataxia, VIth nerve palsy, confusion), Korsakoff's psychosis (chronic thiamine deficiency, memory impairment, confabulation), marrow toxicity, oesophagitis, oesophageal varices, haematemesis, peptic ulcer disease, upper GI cancer (eg oesophageal squamous cell cancer), pancreatitis, alcoholic hepatitis, fatty liver, chronic liver disease and cirrhosis (hepatomegaly, unless cirrhotic; jaundice, Dupuytren's contracture, palmar erythema, leuconychia, spider naevi, scratch marks, gynaecomastia, testicular atrophy), portal hypertension (leading to splenomegaly), ascites, erectile dysfunction, fetal alcohol syndrome.

INVESTIGATIONS
Bloods may be normal. ↑MCV, ↑liver transaminases, ↑gamma GT (not specific for alcoholism), ↓albumin, ↑triglycerides, glucose.

MANAGEMENT
Brief intervention for non-dependent drinkers, counselling, social and family support, education, address drinking triggers, eg anxiety, stress, depression. Suicide risk assessment. Detoxification under supervision (may require inpatient care, requires benzodiazepines). Thiamine/vitamin B complex supplements. Refer to local addiction team. Consider disulfiram, beta-blockers. Treat cardiac, neurological, GI complications.

Allergic bronchopulmonary aspergillosis

CLINICAL NOTES
Allergic reaction to *aspergillus spp.* Aetiology/risk factors: Mainly complicates asthmatic and CF patients. Increased risk if coexisting bronchiectasis. Clinical features: Fever, productive cough, wheeze, malaise, headache. Complications: Haemoptysis, proximal bronchiectasis, fungal sinusitis, pulmonary fibrosis, exacerbation asthma/CF.

INVESTIGATIONS
FBC (eosinophilia), serum aspergillus precipitins, elevated total IgE, sputum analysis, +ve immediate skin test, chest X-ray, CT.

MANAGEMENT
Steroids (may become dependent), antifungal agents, regular monitoring including total IgE.

Alopecia

CLINICAL NOTES
Non-scarring alopecia: Epidemiology: Common. *Alopecia areata:* Aetiology/risk factors: Autoimmune Clinical features: Patchy hair loss. May be localised or generalised involving the whole scalp (totalis) or the whole body (universalis). Short tapering hairs at edges of bald patch, 'exclamation mark' hairs indicate active disease. Nails may show pitting/ridging (poor prognostic sign). Others: *Traction alopecia* (due to hair pulling or tight bun/plaits), pattern baldness, iron deficiency, hyperthyroidism, iatrogenic (cytotoxic agents, sodium valproate, heparin, warfarin, methotrexate, beta-blockers), intercurrent illness, hypogonadism (reduced axillary/pubic hair), pregnancy, postpartum, ringworm. *Scarring alopecia:* Aetiology/risk factors: En coup de sabre (morphoea variant), SLE, fungal infection (kerion), folliculitis, burns, lichen planus, radiotherapy. Clinical features: hair follicles destroyed by underlying disease process.

MANAGEMENT
Alopecia areata: Treatment not usually successful long-term. Topical steroids, minoxidil. May require intralesional steroids and topical immune modulation. *Alopecia totalis/universalis:* Oral steroids, steroid sparing agents or biologics may be considered. Wigs, counselling. *Male pattern baldness:* Topical minoxidil, finasteride, trichosurgery. Women – anti-androgens. *Scarring alopecia:* Treat underlying condition.

Alpha-1 antitrypsin deficiency

CLINICAL NOTES
Deficient alpha-1 antitrypsin protease inhibitor. Epidemiology: Thought to be underdiagnosed. Aetiology/risk factors: Genetic – autosomal dominant. Chromosome 14. (MM, normal inhibitor activity. Common phenotypes – heterozygous *PiSS/PiMZ*: about 60% activity; homozygous *PiZZ*: about 10% activity). Smoking accelerates disease. Clinical features: Early COPD/COPD in non-smoker, hepatitis. Complications: See *chronic obstructive pulmonary disease*; liver cirrhosis in homozygous disease, hepatocellular cancer, pneumothorax, bronchiectasis, lung cancer, respiratory failure, bladder cancer. Associated with Wegener's granulomatosis, glomerulonephritis, autoimmune hepatitis, coeliac disease, AAA.

INVESTIGATIONS
LFT (↑transaminases), alpha-1 antitrypsin levels, protein electrophoresis, genetic studies, lung function tests, chest X-ray, pulmonary CT, abdominal imaging, liver biopsy.

MANAGEMENT
Avoid smoking/hepatic insults, eg alcohol abuse. Bronchodilators, ICS if required, monitoring for hepatocellular cancer, liver transplant, alpha-1 antitrypsin infusions. Genetic counselling.

Alport's syndrome

 CLINICAL NOTES

Epidemiology: One in 5,000 births. Aetiology/risk factors: Heterogenous group of diseases, X-linked, autosomal dominant, autosomal recessive. Clinical features: Sensorineural deafness, renal impairment, haematuria. Complications: Maculopathy, cataract, lenticonus, UTI, hypertension, renal failure (accelerated progression to renal disease in some women).

INVESTIGATIONS
Macrothrombocytopenia (large plts, thrombocytopenia), haematuria – may be microscopic, proteinuria (one-third nephrotic range), renal biopsy, regular audiometry.

MANAGEMENT
Manage hypertension, renal support/replacement (transplanted kidneys may be subject to immune attack by Goodpasture's antibody), regular ophthalmology and audiology review. Genetic counselling.

Altitude sickness (acute mountain sickness)

CLINICAL NOTES

Aetiology/risk factors: Reduction in atmospheric pressure, usually seen in unaccustomised climbers. Clinical features: Nausea, vomiting, headache, fatigue, abdominal pain, breathlessness, tachycardia, ataxia. Complications: Pulmonary oedema, cardiac failure, cerebral oedema, seizure, coma, death.

MANAGEMENT
Prevention: Slow ascent, acetazolamide, nifedipine, dexamethasone. Treatment: Rest, decrease altitude, hydration, oxygen, analgesia, acetazolamide, nifedipine, dexamethasone, hyperbaric chamber.

Alzheimer's disease

CLINICAL NOTES

Epidemiology: Most common dementia type. 6% >65-year-olds. Aetiology/risk factors: Advancing age, existing mild memory impairment, family history (first-degree relative up to 40% higher risk), ApoE genotype (chromosome 19), chr 1, 14, 21, Down's syndrome, PSEN1 gene (early onset), HSV infection, cardiovascular risk factors implicated. Clinical features: Progressive, deteriorating memory loss (short-term, semantic, implicit), reduced verbal ability, word-finding difficulties, reduced comprehension and attention, reduced perceptual speed, impaired executive function, depression (may masquerade as dementia), anxiety, social withdrawal, agitation, delusions (including paranoid, Capgras), hallucinations (often visual). Complications: Falls, eventual inability to live independently, environmental danger, aggression, wandering, violence, malnutrition, may be subject to elder abuse, family breakdown.

INVESTIGATIONS
Normal clock test – good NPV for significant disease; MMSE score <25 suggestive of cognitive impairment, investigate for underlying physical cause for presentation; FBC, U&E, TFT, Ca^{2+}, ESR, syphilis serology, ECG, CT/MRI brain, neuropsychology, vitamin B_{12} and folate.

MANAGEMENT
Exclude organic/functional causes for symptoms, eg normal pressure hydrocephalus and other causes of dementia. Risk assessment, eg driving, safety at home. Memory clinics, family support, cholinesterase inhibitors, memantine. Agitation: Assess causes, eg pain, environmental triggers, reduce light therapy, dance, music, pet therapy, multisensory stimulation. Only use antipsychotics at lowest effective dose for psychosis rather than for agitation (increased risk of CVA). Finasteride has been shown to reduce sexual disinhibition.

Amaurosis fugax

CLINICAL NOTES

Aetiology/risk factors: Carotid artery stenosis/thrombosis/dissection, endocarditis, structural cardiac disease, vasculitis, hypotension, severe hypertension, plasma hyperviscosity (eg paraproteinaemia), malaria, compulsive forceful nose blowing, raised ICP, glaucoma. Clinical features: Transient painless acute visual loss (like curtain coming down over eye). Complications: Permanent visual loss, CVA.

INVESTIGATIONS
FBC, glucose, lipids, consider ESR (if concerned about temporal arteritis), carotid artery dopplers, angiography, echocardiogram.

MANAGEMENT
Antiplatelet agents, treat cause, urgent ophthalmological review.

Amyloid

 CLINICAL NOTES

Primary (AL): Produced by clonal plasma cells. Isolated

DISEASES

clone, myeloma, monoclonal gammopathies, lymphoma. Clinical features: Neuropathy, carpal tunnel syndrome, cardiomyopathy (ischaemic, restrictive), cardiac arrhythmia, macroglossia, GI obstruction, malabsorption, purpura (often periorbital), hepatomegaly. *Familial:* Autosomal dominant. Mainly neuronal involvement. *Secondary (AA):* Chronic inflammation/infection (rise in acute phase protein amyloid A), eg bronchiectasis, RA. Clinical features: Hepatosplenomegaly, proteinuria.

⚕ INVESTIGATIONS
Biopsy (Congo red stain), investigate for causes.

Ō MANAGEMENT
Primary: Consider treatment as for myeloma. *Familial:* Liver transplantation. *Secondary:* Treat cause. Treat complications as appropriate.

Anaemia of chronic disease

📋 CLINICAL NOTES
Epidemiology: Common. Aetiology/risk factors: Chronic disease, eg RA, SLE, CKD, malignancy, thyroid disease.

⚕ INVESTIGATIONS
↓Hb, →MCV, →MCH.

Ō MANAGEMENT
Treat underlying cause.

Anal and rectal abscess

See also
— *Perianal abscess*

📋 CLINICAL NOTES
Aetiology/risk factors: Idiopathic, DM, Crohn's disease, trauma, fissure, STI, anal sex, immunodeficiency, diverticulitis. Clinical features: Fever, tachycardia, throbbing anal or rectal pain, pain on defecation, difficulty passing stool, pus per rectum, perianal abscess or painful lump on per rectal examination. Complications: Missed rectal tumour, fistula (high risk, recurrent abscess likely related to fistula).

⚕ INVESTIGATIONS
Investigate according to suspected underlying cause, including HIV and TB, eg FBC, glucose, HIV screen, swabs, USS, MRI, CT, proctosigmoidoscopy.

Ō MANAGEMENT
Analgesia, antibiotics especially if immunoparesis, surgery, high fistulas may require colostomy (defunctioning may be later reversed). High risk of chronic fistula-in-ano.

Anal fissure

📋 CLINICAL NOTES
Aetiology/risk factors: Spontaneous, constipation, anal trauma, Crohn's disease, severe diarrhoea, childbirth, anal infection. Clinical features: Intense anal pain on defecation and chronic burning pain after passage of stool. PR bleeding (usually fresh blood on toilet paper). Fissure most commonly posterior and midline. Complications: Chronicity (more than six weeks), severe anal spasm.

Ō MANAGEMENT
Analgesia, anal hygiene, maximum one week topical anaesthetic, eg 5% lignocaine ointment/steroid. If not healing, 0.4% topical GTN twice daily for a maximum two months/CCBs to reduce anal tone, laxatives, sphincterotomy, avoid constipation.

Angelman syndrome

📋 CLINICAL NOTES
Aetiology/risk factors: Rare (one in 20,000-40,000 births) neurodevelopmental disorder caused by chromosome 15 defects. Clinical features: Microcephaly, developmental delay, ataxia, seizures, quasi-purposeful mouth and tongue movements, unprovoked laughing and clapping.

⚕ INVESTIGATIONS
Characteristic EEG (not associated with seizures), genetic testing.

Ō MANAGEMENT
Seizure control, genetic counselling, family support.

Angina (stable)

📋 CLINICAL NOTES
Epidemiology: >1.4 x 10⁶ prevalence (UK). Aetiology/risk factors: Advancing age, family history, South Asians, low social class, obesity, smoking, hypertension, dyslipidaemia, DM, renal failure, ↑urinary homocysteine, known history of CHD, aortic stenosis (AS), thrombophilia, postmenopause, anaemia, hypoxia, stress, hyperthyroidism. Clinical features: Exertional chest tightness/pain, may present with exertional breathlessness without tightness/pain, obesity, xanthelasma, tar stains. Complications: Unstable angina, MI, arrhythmia, cardiac failure.

⚕ INVESTIGATIONS
FBC, fasting lipids/glucose, U&E, LFT, TFT, ↑high sensitivity CRP, ↑fibrinogen, ECG, ETT (for CHD, sensitivity 68%, specificity 77%). If cannot tolerate ETT, consider stress echocardiogram, cardiac MR, nuclear studies (eg thallium SPECT). Coronary artery CT, sensitivity for disease 97.2%, specificity 87.4%. Coronary

angiogram (gold standard, perform if +ve/equivocal ETT, angiogram good at identifying flow-limiting stable plaques, may not identify unstable [intra-intimal] plaques, which are better identified by intraluminal USS). Consider investigation for associated diseases, eg COPD.

🗓 MANAGEMENT

Treat underlying cause, eg anaemia, AS. Manage risk factors. Education. Aim to keep pulse rate <60bpm (↓risk of CV events). Beta-blockers, CCBs, nitrates (GTN and longer-acting), nicorandil, ivabradine, statins, antiplatelet agents, PCI, CABG.

Angina variants

📖 CLINICAL NOTES

Decubitus: Worse on laying down. Aetiology/risk factors: Left ventricular systolic dysfunction (LVSD), CHD. *Prinzmetal's:* Coronary spasm at rest. F>M. Clinical features: Unpredictable, chest pain, palpitations. ECG – ST elevation, arrhythmia, heart block. *Nocturnal:* During REM sleep. Aetiology/risk factors: Severe CHD. *Syndrome X:* Epidemiology: F>M. Exercise tolerance test (ETT) +ve, normal angiogram.

Angioedema

📖 CLINICAL NOTES

See *urticaria and angioedema*

Ankle sprain

📖 CLINICAL NOTES

Aetiology/risk factors: Commonly inversion injury. Clinical symptoms: Swelling/tender lateral foot, bruising. Complications: Ankle instability, bony injury – malleoli, distal tibia/fibula, base of fifth metatarsal, calcaneus. Tendon injury – Achilles tendon, posterior tibial tendon, peroneal tendons. Chronic pain, chronic ankle instability, OA.

⚕ INVESTIGATIONS

X-ray to exclude fracture (Ottawa rules – X-ray if tender malleoli/within 6cm above malleoli/base of fifth metatarsal/navicular, inability to bear weight immediately and at presentation to A&E. Ottawa rules do not apply if <18 years, pregnant, intoxicated, head injury, sensory loss, multiple trauma), consider bone scan for occult fracture, MRI for occult fracture/soft tissues, eg unstable ankle.

🗓 MANAGEMENT

Analgesia, rest, ice, compression, elevation, physiotherapy. Crutches/non weight bearing may be used in initial phase. Severe sprain – below knee cast for 10 days improves outcome. Surgery if unstable.

Ankylosing spondylitis

📖 CLINICAL NOTES

Epidemiology: 6.9×10^5 per year (UK). M>F. Onset 15-35 years. Aetiology/risk factors: Environmental trigger in susceptible people (HLA-B27 present in >90% of patients with ankylosing spondylitis versus 8% in general population). Clinical features: Insidious onset low back pain/stiffness (worse after period of immobility), bilateral buttock pain (sacroiliitis), neck/spinal/chest pain, loss of lumbar lordosis, exaggerated thoracic kyphosis, cervical hyperextension, reduced spinal range of movement. Perform Schober's test with patient standing upright. Note point between sacral dimples, mark 5cm above and below that point, ask patient to try to touch their toes to full flexion. Marks <15cm apart abnormal. Inability to stand with heels, hips and occiput against a wall. Complications: Depression, chronic pain, fatigue, functional disability, OA hip, Achilles tendonitis, plantar fasciitis, iritis, aortitis, aortic incompetence, apical pulmonary fibrosis, pulmonary cavitation, pericarditis, cardiomyopathy, cardiac conduction defects, atlanto-axial subluxation, amyloid.

⚕ INVESTIGATIONS

↑ESR/CRP, HLA-B27, X-ray (sacroiliitis, vertebral erosions, squaring of vertebral bodies, syndesmophytes between vertebrae, ossification of spinal ligaments, bamboo spine), chest X-ray, pulmonary CT, MRI, lung function studies, echocardiogram.

🗓 MANAGEMENT

Education, regular follow-up, physiotherapy (↓pain/stiffness, ↑function), NSAIDs, analgesia, steroids (joint injections/systemic), bisphosphonates, sulfasalazine, anti-TNF drugs (etanercept, infliximab, adalimumab), cardiovascular risk assessment, hip replacement, spinal surgery, treat complications accordingly.

Anorexia nervosa

📖 CLINICAL NOTES

Epidemiology: F>M. Underdiagnosed in men. Aetiology/risk factors: Affective/anxiety disorder, poor coping strategies, peer/social pressure, parental criticism, genetic predisposition. Clinical features: Low BMI (mild >17.5kg/m², moderate 15-17.5kg/m², severe <15kg/m²), amenorrhoea, over-exercise, laxative abuse (may cause cardiomyopathy), lanugo hair, diuretic/levothyroxine/appetite suppressant abuse, preoccupation with body image, weight and weight gain. *Screening questions:* Do you think you have an eating problem? Do you worry excessively about your weight? *SCOFF screening tool:* See page 240. Complications: High risk of retinopathy (if type-1 diabetes), dental caries with vomiting, malnutrition, osteoporosis, poor growth, electrolyte and cardiac disturbances, eg ↑QTc, relationship difficulties, refeeding syndrome (seizure, reduced GCS, cardiac arrhythmia, rhabdomyolysis, cardiopulmonary failure), death.

INVESTIGATIONS
FBC, U&E, LFT, TFT, Ca²⁺, phosphate, glucose, ↑SHBG, gonadotrophins, prolactin, ECG, DEXA scan.

MANAGEMENT
Risk assessment, treat comorbidities, address physical complications, self-help and support groups, close monitoring, limit acidic foods if vomiting, dental hygiene, family therapy, CBT, CAT, psychotherapy, psychodynamic therapy, may require inpatient care in severe cases, physical monitoring, eg for refeeding syndrome, care with drugs, particularly with cardiac side-effects, aim for 0.5kg per week weight gain (outpatient setting), multivitamins, consider legal powers to enforce feeding.

Anterior cruciate ligament (ACL) injury

CLINICAL NOTES
Aetiology/risk factors: Trauma, eg twisting injury. Clinical features: May be acute or chronic tear. *Acute tear:* Pain, often immediate (less than two hours) effusion (suggests haemarthrosis), difficult to assess in acute setting due to effusion. Exaggerated anterior movement of tibia. Instability when walking downstairs, Lachman's test, pivot shift, anterior draw tests. Complications: Avulsion fracture, OA, medial collateral and meniscus damage (O'Donoghue's triad).

INVESTIGATIONS
X-ray to exclude avulsion fracture of tibial spine, MRI.

MANAGEMENT
Conservative: If patient has sedentary lifestyle or if no history of knee giving way. *Surgical:* High success rate. Physiotherapy.

Antiphospholipid syndrome (Hughes syndrome)

CLINICAL NOTES
Epidemiology: Underdiagnosed. Aetiology/risk factors: Autoimmune. For risk factors for increased thrombosis, see *deep vein thrombosis*. Clinical features: Arterial and venous thromboses, livedo reticularis. Complications: Migraine, recurrent miscarriage, DVT, CVA, MI, limb ulcers, seizure, memory loss, chorea, Budd-Chiari syndrome, fracture.

INVESTIGATIONS
↓plts. +ve for anticardiolipin antibodies, lupus anticoagulant or both, lupus anticoagulant may cause ↑APTT. ANA.

MANAGEMENT
Lifestyle advice. Low-dose aspirin or anticoagulation.

Antisocial personality disorder (sociopathic personality disorder)

CLINICAL NOTES
Epidemiology: M > F. Aetiology/risk factors: Multifactorial – genetic, family history of antisocial personality disorder, subject of child abuse, losses in childhood, eg a parent. Clinical features: Disregard for wrongdoing, forensic and violent behaviour, drug/alcohol abuse, abuse of animals in childhood, school/work/relationship/family difficulties, deceit, manipulative behaviour. Complications: Affective disorder, self-harm, suicide.

MANAGEMENT
Patients should not be excluded from care decisions. Assess past history/coping strategies/social situation/stressors. Encourage patient's autonomy/inclusion in care plan. Trusting therapeutic relationship required with MDT approach. Risk assessment (including forensic/domestic violence/at-risk children). Manage psychiatric comorbidities (eg affective disorder, psychosis, drug/alcohol dependence). Anger therapy, problem-solving skills training, family therapy, parent training, self-talking therapy, crisis management, drug treatment not routinely used.

Antithrombin III deficiency

CLINICAL NOTES
See *thrombophilias*

Anxiety

CLINICAL NOTES
Epidemiology: Common. Aetiology/risk factors: Neuroses (depression, generalised anxiety disorder, phobia, panic disorder, OCD, post traumatic stress disorder), psychoses (paranoia), hyperthyroidism, palpitations, drug/alcohol withdrawal, phaeochromocytoma, menopause, carcinoid, hypoglycaemia, anorexia nervosa, bulimia nervosa, somatisation, dissociative fugue. Clinical features: Apprehension, irritability, sleep disturbance, poor concentration, over-arousal. Pervasive anxiety (generalised anxiety disorder), intermittent panic/anxiety (panic disorder), situational, eg agoraphobia.

MANAGEMENT
Education. Involve carers/family when appropriate. Crisis management. Involve patients in their own management. Regular review. Treat comorbidities (depression, psychosis, drug/alcohol abuse). Consider computerised CBT. Primary care management: *Panic disorder*: Avoid benzodiazepines when possible. Self-help strategies. CBT, SSRI, SNRI or consider imipramine/clomipramine.

Generalised anxiety disorder: Short courses benzodi- azepines maximum two to four weeks. CBT, SSRI, SNRI, self-help groups. *Phobias:* Flooding or graded exposure. Refer if treatment failure, complex or severe.

Aortic dissection

🗒 CLINICAL NOTES
Type A involves ascending aorta. Type B involves descending aorta, not ascending aorta. Epidemiology: M>F, one in 500. Aetiology/risk factors: Hypertension, trauma, atherosclerosis, col- lagen disorders, eg Marfan's syndrome, Ehlers-Danlos syndrome, relapsing polychondritis, vasculitis, aortic aneurysm. Clinical features: Tearing chest pain radiating to back, shock, absent/reduced peripheral pulses, dif- fering right and left upper limb BP. Complications: MI, tamponade, acute aortic regurgitation (AR), cerebral/ spinal cord/renal/limb/organ ischaemia leading to CVA, paralysis, renal failure and death.

☊ INVESTIGATIONS
Cross-match blood, ECG, chest X-ray (widened medias- tinum), CT, TOE to determine type/exclude AR/aortic root involvement.

🗋 MANAGEMENT
Manage systolic BP between 100mmHg and 120mmHg. Type A – surgical management, type B – conservative management, consider surgery.

Aortic regurgitation (AR)

🗒 CLINICAL NOTES
Epidemiology: M>F except rheumatic. Aetiology/ risk factors: *Acute:* Prosthetic valve failure, trauma, ruptured sinus of valsalva aneurysm, acute rheu- matic fever, infective endocarditis, aortic dissection. *Chronic:* Hypertension, congenital, eg bicuspid/ VSD, chronic rheumatic disease, old age, RA, SLE, ankylosing spondylitis, psoriatic arthritis, Reiter's syndrome, Marfan's syndrome, pseudoxanthoma elasticum, osteogenesis imperfecta, syphilis, Hurler's syndrome, relapsing polychondritis. Clinical features: Breathlessness, fatigue, collapsing water hammer pulse, wide pulse pressure, volume over loaded displaced apex beat, early diastolic murmur left sternal edge (LSE) loudest in held expiration. AR may interfere with anterior mitral valve leaflet (Austin Flint murmur mid-diastolic), De Musset's sign (head nodding), pistol shot sounds on auscultation of femoral arteries. Complications: Cardiac failure, arrhythmia, death.

☊ INVESTIGATIONS
ECG normal, LVH, inverted T waves lateral leads, AV block. Echocardiogram – diseased aortic valve, AR, dilated hyperdynamic LV, LVSD. Cardiac catheterisation. MRI.

🗋 MANAGEMENT
Treat underlying cause, diuretics, valvotomy, valvulo- plasty, AVR, acute causes may require urgent surgery.

Aortic sclerosis

🗒 CLINICAL NOTES
Epidemiology: Common in advancing age. Clinical features: Often incidental finding, no cardiac symptoms, normal pulse character and pressure, short outflow tract systolic murmur, loudest in held expiration, normal S2.

☊ INVESTIGATIONS
Echocardiogram not required except to exclude other conditions/diagnostic difficulties.

🗋 MANAGEMENT
Monitor. No active management required.

Aortic stenosis (AS)

🗒 CLINICAL NOTES
Aetiology/risk factors: Calcific, bicuspid valve, rheu- matic heart disease, HOCM (outflow obstruction due to septal hypertrophy), William's syndrome (supravalvular stenosis), subaortic membrane. Clinical features: SOB/ presyncope/syncope/angina are ominous, slow rising pulse, narrow pulse pressure, heaving apex beat, ejec- tion click (unless calcified), ejection systolic murmur radiating to carotids loudest in held expiration (length of murmur, rather than loudness, correlates with severity), attenuated S2 (normal S2 suggests mild disease or aortic sclerosis), may have reversed splitting S2. S4, signs of cardiac failure. Complications: LVSD due to AS has one to two-year 50% mortality, angina, heart block, embolic disease, acquired von Willebrand's disease, death.

☊ INVESTIGATIONS
ECG: Normal, LVH, strain, right/left anterior bundle branch block, AV block. *Echocardiogram:* LVH, LV dys- function, calcified valve, coexistent AR, valve gradient/ area should be measured. Valve gradient may be under- estimated in presence of LVSD. Severe stenosis peak gradient >65mmHg, maximum velocity >4m/s. *Chest X-ray:* May show post-stenotic dilation. MRI, ECG-gated CT may be used for valve area. Cardiac catheterisation.

🗋 MANAGEMENT
Valvuloplasty or valve replacement if symptomatic/ angina/LVSD/significant AS/deteriorating.

Aplastic anaemia

🗒 CLINICAL NOTES
Epidemiology: Rare. Aetiology/risk factors: Autoimmune, iatrogenic, eg gold; post-viral, eg parvovirus B19; hepatitis, chemotherapy, radiotherapy, Fanconi's anaemia. Clinical features: Fatigue, breathlessness, bleeding, infections.

DISEASES

Complications: High output heart failure, respiratory failure, haemorrhage, sepsis, death.

⚗ INVESTIGATIONS
FBC (pancytopenia), ↓reticulocyte count, marrow biopsy.

⬥ MANAGEMENT
Remove cause, supportive treatment, reverse barrier nursing, ciclosporin, antithymocyte globulins, marrow transplant.

Appendicitis

📋 CLINICAL NOTES
Epidemiology: 7-12% UK incidence. 70,000 operations per year (UK). Peak age 20-40 years and 60s. M>F but more appendicectomies in females (false +ves). Clinical features: Anorexia, nausea, vomiting, +/–diarrhoea/constipation. Vague central abdominal pain shifting to RIF, low-grade pyrexia (increased if perforated), tachycardia (increased if perforated), dry tongue, fetor, peritonism (McBurney's point, may be absent if retrocaecal appendix/during pregnancy), may have appendix mass. Confusion in elderly. Complications: Perforation caused by delay in treatment (leads to x9 risk of fetal death in maternal appendicitis, sepsis, adhesions, infertility). High risk of perforation, peritonitis and abscess in young children. Risk postoperative infection/abscess (may be Gram -ve), 1% appendices contain incidental tumours, eg carcinoid.

⚗ INVESTIGATIONS
↑WCC/CRP. CT sensitive and specific (not routinely recommended in some centres). USS to exclude other causes of RIF pain. Sterile pyuria.

⬥ MANAGEMENT
Appendicectomy. Appendix mass may be treated conservatively. Appendix abscess: Drainage.

Apraxia and dyspraxia

📋 CLINICAL NOTES
Epidemiology: Prevalence up to one in 10. M>F. Often detected in childhood. Associated with dyslexia, dyscalculia, autistic spectrum disorder, ADHD, cerebral palsy. Aetiology/risk factors: Premature birth, CVA, dementia, cerebral trauma, meningitis, encephalitis. Clinical features: ↓Ability to perform complicated voluntary tasks, eg handwriting, planning, copying drawings, construction, dressing, speech.

⬥ MANAGEMENT
Childhood disease requires community paediatric assessment, MDT approach (including teachers, parental education), OT, physiotherapy.

Argyll Robertson pupil

📋 CLINICAL NOTES
Aetiology/risk factors: Neurosyphilis, Parinaud's syndrome. Clinical features: Small irregular pupils, accommodate but poor reaction to light. If associated with vertical gaze palsy, diagnosis is Parinaud's syndrome (midbrain disorder caused by tumour, CVA, MS, ADEM).

⚗ INVESTIGATIONS
CT/MRI. Investigate underlying cause.

⬥ MANAGEMENT
Treat underlying cause.

Arnold Chiari malformation

📋 CLINICAL NOTES
See Chiari malformation

Arrhythmogenic right ventricular cardiomyopathy

📋 CLINICAL NOTES
Right ventricular myocardium infiltration by fatty or fibrofatty material, causing scarring and aneurysm of RV. LV may also be affected. Epidemiology: M>F. ↑Italians. Aetiology/risk factors: Familial (autosomal dominant), Naxos disease (autosomal recessive with palmoplantar keratoderma, woolly hair). Clinical features: Exercise-induced syncope. Complications: RV failure, ventricular arrhythmias, sudden death.

⚗ INVESTIGATIONS
ECG – non-specific, ambulatory ECG, echocardiogram, ETT, MRI.

⬥ MANAGEMENT
Beta-blockade, antiarrhythmics. Consider ICD.

Ascaris lumbricoides infestation

📋 CLINICAL NOTES
Epidemiology: Common. Aetiology/risk factors: Roundworm (may exceed 30.5cm in length). Clinical features: Asymptomatic, urticaria, dry cough, wheeze, fever. Complications: Malabsorption, anaemia, respiratory distress, bowel obstruction, liver and pancreatic duct infestation, jaundice, biliary obstruction, pancreatitis, appendicitis, nephritis, encephalopathy.

⚗ INVESTIGATIONS
Stool microscopy (-ve during pulmonary phase), eosinophilia, ↑IgE.

⬥ MANAGEMENT
Antihelminthics (eg mebendazole, albendazole).

DISEASES

Aspergilloma (pulmonary)

See also
— *Allergic bronchopulmonary aspergillosis*
— *Aspergillosis (invasive)*

 CLINICAL NOTES
Colonisation of lung cavities, eg TB, CF, sarcoid, neoplastic. May complicate immune deficiency. Clinical features: Asymptomatic, cough. Complications: Massive haemoptysis.

INVESTIGATIONS
FBC (eosinophilia), serum aspergillus precipitins, sputum analysis, chest X-ray, CT.

MANAGEMENT
Systemic antifungal agents, intracavity amphotericin, surgical resection, embolisation if significant haemoptysis.

Aspergillosis (invasive)

See also
— *Allergic bronchopulmonary aspergillosis*

CLINICAL NOTES
Epidemiology: Increasing prevalence. Aetiology/risk factors: Immunodeficiency, eg HIV, iatrogenic. Clinical features: Sinusitis, productive cough, haemoptysis, SOB, pleurisy. Complications: Pneumonia, respiratory failure, cardiac/brain/thyroid/eye/renal/liver/spleen involvement, thrombosis, organ failure, high mortality (100% with CNS involvement/endocarditis).

INVESTIGATIONS
Sputum analysis for MC&S, bronchioalveolar lavage, chest X-ray – variable findings, CT.

MANAGEMENT
Commence antifungal medication empirically before confirmatory investigation results.

Asthma (stable)

 CLINICAL NOTES
Epidemiology: Approximately 5×10^6 affected (UK). About 1,200 deaths per year (UK). Aetiology/risk factors: Atopy, family history. Clinical features: Wheeze (polyphonic), cough, diurnal variation (worse in night/early morning), chest tightness, breathlessness, intercostal recession. Triggered by exertion, cold, stress, damp, allergen exposure, infection, NSAIDs, betablockers. Poor asthma control if interfering with sleep, daytime symptoms, interferes with daily activities or requiring short acting bronchodilators. Complications: Exacerbations, pneumothorax, death.

BTS and SIGN Stepwise Management of Asthma guidelines

ADULTS*

STEP 1 Inhaled beta$_2$ agonists.
STEP 2 Addition of ICS, start eg 400 microgram beclometasone or equivalent per day (range 200-800 microgram per day).
STEP 3 Addition of long-acting beta agonist (LABA) – stop if no benefit, not recommended without ICS. If inadequate response to LABA, increase ICS to 800 microgram beclometasone or equivalent per day. If no response to LABA/poor response to ICS, add leukotriene antagonist/theophylline.
STEP 4 Increase ICS to maximum 2,000 microgram beclometasone or equivalent per day, addition of leukotriene antagonists, theophylline, oral beta$_2$ agonists.
Step 5 Addition of oral steroids, steroid-sparing agents, refer for specialist input.
SMART therapy (budesonide/formoterol combination inhaler used as maintenance and reliever) may be considered as an alternative to stepwise approach at Step 2 and 3.

AGE FIVE TO 12 YEARS*

STEP 1 Inhaled beta$_2$ agonists.
STEP 2 Addition of ICS, start eg 200 microgram beclometasone or equivalent per day (range 200-400 microgram per day).
STEP 3 Addition of LABA (stop if no benefit), if inadequate response to LABA, increase ICS to 400 microgram beclometasone or equivalent per day. If no response to LABA/poor response to ICS, add leukotriene antagonist/theophylline.
STEP 4 Increase ICS, maximum 800 microgram beclometasone or equivalent per day.
STEP 5 Add oral steroids, steroid-sparing agents, refer for specialist input.

AGE LESS THAN FIVE YEARS*

STEP 1 Inhaled beta$_2$ agonists.
STEP 2 Addition of ICS 200-400 microgram beclometasone or equivalent per day. Consider leukotriene antagonist if cannot use steroid.
STEP 3 Addition of leukotriene antagonist if already on ICS, if already on leukotriene antagonist, addition of ICS.
Step 4 Refer for specialist input.

* Personal asthma management plans required. Spacer devices should be used where possible, including for mild/moderate exacerbations. Refer if occupational asthma.

Source: British Thoracic Society/Scottish Intercollegiate Guidelines Network (and others). British Guideline on the Management of Asthma (May 2008 – revised May 2011). Available from www.brit-thoracic.org.uk and www.sign.ac.uk

INVESTIGATIONS

IgE, eosinophilia, consider aspergillus precipitins, PEFR (diurnal variation >20% significant, use for at least two weeks for diagnostic purposes, variability not specific to asthma. PEFR <50% of best suggests severe disease, <33% of best suggests life-threatening disease). Spirometry with reversibility testing (adults – beta$_2$ agonist, or 200 microgram beclometasone or equivalent twice daily for 6-8 weeks, or oral prednisolone 30mg once daily for two weeks, +ve if increase in FEV$_1$ of >400ml/15%). ↓FEV$_1$/FVC. An increase in FEV$_1$ of 12% in children >5 years is significant. Note a normal FEV$_1$ may occur in presence of significant small airways disease.

MANAGEMENT

BTS and SIGN guidelines, see page 82): Encourage breastfeeding (reduces risk), smoking cessation advice, control weight, reduce house dust mite burden, Buteyko breathing. *Pharmacological:* Aim to gain initial control (eg no day/night symptoms, no exacerbations/exercise limitation, normal spirometry) by starting treatment at appropriate management step, then step down management to maintain control.

Ataxia telangiectasia

CLINICAL NOTES

See *immunodeficiency (primary)*

Atrial ectopic beats

CLINICAL NOTES

Epidemiology: Common. Clinical features: Asymptomatic, sensation of flutter or missed beat. Complications: May trigger paroxysmal AF.

INVESTIGATIONS

ECG – premature P wave followed by normal QRS, abnormal P wave morphology. Consider ambulatory ECG. Echocardiogram if ECG/clinical evidence of structural heart disease, eg ASD.

MANAGEMENT

Consider beta-blockers.

Atrial fibrillation (AF)[Ref]

CLINICAL NOTES

Epidemiology: 5-10% >65 years. Aetiology/risk factors: Idiopathic (lone), IHD, mitral valve disease, hypertension, cardiac failure, cardiomyopathy, pericarditis, myocarditis, WPW syndrome, ASD, iatrogenic (including digoxin), post cardiac surgery, atrial myxoma, malignant cardiac infiltration, hyperthyroidism, phaeochromocytoma, alcohol abuse, COPD, pneumonia, PE, electrolyte disturbance, exercise, smoking, illicit drugs. Clinical features: May present acutely with hypotension, cardiac failure and rapid ventricular response,

asymptomatic, fatigue, breathlessness, palpitations, chest pain, presyncope, CVA, TIA, irregularly irregular pulse. Complications: ↑x5 risk of CVA, 20% CVAs attributable to AF, cardiac failure.

INVESTIGATIONS

TFT, ECG – narrow complexes, irregular rhythm, no P waves, may see fibrillatory [f] waves. Echocardiogram – atrial size (enlarged size >4.5cm reduces chance of successful cardioversion), mitral valve status, LV function.

MANAGEMENT

Address treatable causes. Hospitalise if cardiovascularly unstable. Cardioversion if clear onset within 24 hours. Anticoagulate according to CHADS$_2$ score. If CHADS2 score is 0-1, use CHA$_2$DS$_2$-VASc score (see page 238). Consider assessing bleeding risk with HAS-BLED score (see page 239). Efficacy of aspirin declines with advancing age, particularly >75 years. Safety profile of aspirin comparable to warfarin. Patients with paroxysmal AF and another risk factor for stroke should be anticoagulated. Dabigatran has been shown to have more favourable outcomes compared to warfarin in non-valvular AF with another risk factor for stroke. Rate control for permanent AF, aim for ventricular rate 70-80bpm using cardioselective beta-blockers/CCBs; consider digoxin monotherapy if sedentary patient or cardiac failure (avoid atrioventricular node-blocking drugs in WPW). Consider rhythm control if LVSD, patient compromised, young patient, significant valve disease, clear precipitant, first episode of persistent AF. Rhythm control performed within 24 hours of onset or once anticoagulated with therapeutic INR for four to six weeks if non-rheumatic patient. Rhythm control for persistent AF with eg sotalol, amiodarone (30-40% chance of successful cardioversion), flecainide if normal angiogram, dronedarone, DC cardioversion. Consider ablation for resistant cases. A recent trial showed higher death rates in rhythm-controlled patients versus rate controlled. Left atrial appendage plugs are available in some centres, preventing thrombus and eliminating need for anticoagulation.

Atrial flutter

CLINICAL NOTES

Atrial rate 250-350bpm due to large atrial re-entrant circuit. Aetiology/risk factors: See *atrial fibrillation*. Clinical features: Palpitations, presyncope, chest pain, often coexisting AF. Complications: Fast ventricular response, syncope, cardiac failure.

INVESTIGATIONS

ECG – sawtooth flutter waves often with block (block may be variable). Echocardiogram.

MANAGEMENT

Anticoagulation, DC or chemical cardioversion (eg amiodarone or sotalol). More resistant to drug therapy than AF. Ablation for recurrent disease is treatment of choice.

DISEASES

Atrial myxoma

CLINICAL NOTES
Epidemiology: Most common cardiac tumour (benign). F>M. 75% left atrium. **Clinical features:** Asymptomatic, fever, breathlessness, mid-diastolic murmur, tumour 'plop'. **Complications:** Syncope if intracardiac obstruction of blood flow, embolic stroke, haemolysis. Carney's syndrome (cardiac, breast, skin myxomas).

INVESTIGATIONS
Very raised ESR, echocardiogram.

MANAGEMENT
Surgery.

Atrial tachycardia

CLINICAL NOTES
Epidemiology: Uncommon. **Aetiology/risk factors:** Idiopathic, structural heart disease, digoxin poisoning (with block). **Clinical features:** Asymptomatic, palpitations, breathless, presyncope, chest pain.

INVESTIGATIONS
ECG, ambulatory ECG, echocardiogram.

MANAGEMENT
Cardioversion, rhythm and rate-controlling agents, ablation.

Atrioseptal defect (ASD)

CLINICAL NOTES
Epidemiology: F>M. *Secundum:* Most common. **Clinical features:** Smaller ASDs asymptomatic, usually present in adulthood with breathlessness and palpitations. Murmur not always present, fixed splitting S2, pulmonary ejection systolic murmur, pulmonary hypertension, pulmonary regurgitation. *Primum:* More serious than secundum. May involve AV valves. **Clinical features:** Presentation in childhood – failure to thrive, breathlessness, cardiac failure. Associated with congenital conditions, eg Down's syndrome, Noonan syndrome, Klinefelter's syndrome, splenic or renal anomalies, murmur not always present, fixed splitting S2, pulmonary ejection systolic murmur, pulmonary hypertension, pulmonary regurgitation. *Others:* Patent foramen ovale (PFO), sinus venosus, coronary sinus and inferior vena cava defects. **Complications:** AF, pulmonary hypertension, Eisenmenger's syndrome, right heart failure, congestive heart failure, systemic emboli.

INVESTIGATIONS
ECG: Prolonged PR interval, RBBB and right axis deviation: secundum. RBBB and left axis deviation: primum. *Echocardiogram:* TOE more sensitive than TTE; may need bubble study. Cardiac catheterisation – determine pressures and step-up in oxygen levels within right atrium.

MANAGEMENT
Treat if increased pulmonary flow x >1.5. Small secundum defects may be left alone. Isolated lesions low risk of infective endocarditis.

Atrioventricular nodal re-entry tachycardia (AVNRT)

CLINICAL NOTES
Intranodal re-entry circuit. **Epidemiology:** F>M, most common regular SVT. **Aetiology/risk factors:** Idiopathic, caffeine, exertion, alcohol, illicit drug use, MI, pre-excitation syndrome. Heart structurally normal. **Clinical features:** Often paroxysmal palpitation, presyncope, syncope, chest pain, SOB.

INVESTIGATIONS
ECG – 140-240bpm, narrow complexes. P waves may not be seen. Atria and ventricles simultaneously depolarised. Ambulatory ECG. Cardiac electrophysiology studies.

MANAGEMENT
Tachycardia control with vagal manoeuvres, IV adenosine, electrical cardioversion. *Long-term:* regular/as required beta-blockers, diltiazem, verapamil, flecainide. Ablation.

Atrioventricular re-entry tachycardia (AVRT)

CLINICAL NOTES
Re-entry circuit that includes AV node in the pathway. **Epidemiology:** M>F. **Aetiology/risk factors:** Accessory pathways, eg WPW, associated with Ebstein's anomaly. **Clinical features:** Palpitations, presyncope, chest pain, polyuria. **Complications:** AF with rapid ventricular response, VF (higher risk of arrhythmia if digoxin/verapamil used, see *Wolff-Parkinson-White syndrome*), syncope, sudden death.

INVESTIGATIONS
ECG – may see features of pre-excitation. Ambulatory ECG. Cardiac electrophysiology studies.

MANAGEMENT
Ablation is treatment of choice. Flecainide, propafenone.

Atrophic vaginitis

CLINICAL NOTES
Epidemiology: 60% prevalence postmenopausal women not on HRT. Usually few years postmenopause. **Clinical features:** Asymptomatic, pruritus, vaginal dryness, infection, bleeding, greenish discharge, dyspareunia, erythematous vagina, loss of vaginal folds, atrophy.

MANAGEMENT
Low-dose topical estradiol/estriol.

Attention deficit hyperactivity disorder (ADHD)

🗒 CLINICAL NOTES

Epidemiology: >1% (UK). Clinical features: Poor attention span, impulsive behaviour, hyperactive, some behaviours more pronounced than others, occur in more than one setting, eg school and home, pervasive, moderate/severe psychological, social, educational and occupational impact. Complications: Dyslexia, reading difficulties, depression, anxiety, conduct disorder, eating disorders, substance misuse.

⟳ INVESTIGATIONS

Social, medical educational assessment (including patient's family).

🗓 MANAGEMENT

Consider watchful waiting for 10 weeks in primary care or referral if at least moderate symptoms. Diagnosis and drug treatment initiated in secondary care only. Support teams made available appropriate for patient's age. Family training/education when appropriate. Teacher/special educational needs co-ordinator involvement. Group therapy. CBT. Social skills training. Balanced diet/exercise. *Drug treatment:* Not advised for preschool children. In school-age children, for moderate disease where non-drug intervention refused or ineffective, or for severe ADHD, drug treatment as part of comprehensive psychological, educational and behavioural approach. Methylphenidate first-line, atomoxetine second-line. Awareness of child consent and protection. *Adult:* Consider, where appropriate, handover to adult psychiatric services and drug treatment first-line if moderate/severe ADHD. Consider CBT.

Autistic spectrum disorders

🗒 CLINICAL NOTES

Include Asperger's syndrome and autism. Epidemiology: 6-10 per 1,000 prevalence. Epilepsy more prevalent. M>F. Clinical features: Autism usually manifests in first three years of life, Asperger's syndrome later. Difficulties in understanding with non-verbal communication, speech and change in routine. Aggression, withdrawal. Patient refers to self in second person. Preoccupation. Collecting. Inability to understand social cues. Poor or intense relationships. Difficulty coping with invasion of personal space. Occasionally possess incredible abilities, eg mathematical/artistic. Delay in speech development. Isolated play. *Asperger's:* Old-fashioned style of speech, excessive honesty, attention to detail. *Autism:* Ignoring other people, poor eye contact, antisocial traits, eg not sharing/ignoring others, loner.

⟳ INVESTIGATIONS

Checklist for Autism in Toddlers (CHAT, specific). M-CHAT (modified CHAT, 97% specific, 95% sensitive). DISCO (Diagnostic Interview for Social and Communication Disorders). ADOS (Autism Diagnostic Observation Schedule).

🗓 MANAGEMENT

Support, eg Lovaas programme, community paediatric support, social services, sleep management, SALT, appropriate education/work placements, consider risperidone for agitation and sleep disturbance.

Autoimmune liver disease

🗒 CLINICAL NOTES

Epidemiology: F>M 4:1. Prevalence: 107 in 10^6. Associated with other autoimmune diseases. Clinical features: Asymptomatic, pruritus, abdominal pain, arthralgia, fatigue, Raynaud's phenomenon, amenorrhoea, jaundice. Complications: Cirrhosis (one in three), chronic liver disease, liver failure, pulmonary involvement, glomerulonephritis, hypersplenism.

⟳ INVESTIGATIONS

↑ALT, AST, IgG, ANA, antismooth muscle antibody (type 1 autoimmune hepatitis), liver-kidney microsome (type 2 autoimmune hepatitis), antihistone antibodies, antimitochondrial antibodies, biopsy.

🗓 MANAGEMENT

Prednisolone, azathioprine, pruritus (cholestyramine, rifampicin, sertraline), albumin dialysis, UV therapy, liver transplant.

Autoimmune polyendocrine syndromes (APS)

🗒 CLINICAL NOTES

Epidemiology: Rare. Clinical features: *APS1*: Two or more of Addison's disease, hypoparathyroidism, candidiasis +/−amenorrhoea; onset infancy. *APS2* (*Schmidt's syndrome*): Addison's disease, autoimmune thyroid disease, +/−type-1 DM. *APS3*: Autoimmune thyroiditis plus another organ-specific autoimmune disease.

⟳ INVESTIGATIONS

Autoantibody assays; screening for other autoimmune diseases, eg coeliac disease.

🗓 MANAGEMENT

Genetic counselling, treat each condition as appropriate, eg lifestyle advice and HRT. Lifelong monitoring.

Autoimmune warm and cold haemolytic anaemia

🗒 CLINICAL NOTES

Warm: Occurring at 37°C. Aetiology/risk factors: Idiopathic, CLL, lymphoma, SLE, iatrogenic. Clinical features: Asymptomatic, jaundice, fatigue.

Cold: Occurring at 4°C or below. Associated with myco-plasma and EBV.

☞ INVESTIGATIONS
Coombs' test +ve, anaemia, reticulocytosis, polychroma-sia. LDH. Investigate for underlying cause.

☗ MANAGEMENT
Warm: Corticosteroids, steroid-sparing immunosup-pressants or biological agents. Consider splenectomy.
Cold: Avoid cold temperatures, steroid sparing immuno-suppressants, plasma exchange. Consider splenectomy.

Autonomic neuropathy

▤ CLINICAL NOTES
Aetiology/risk factors: Advancing age, idiopathic, DM, amyloid, alcohol, Guillain-Barré syndrome, multisystem atrophy, paraneoplastic syndrome, storage diseases, con-nective tissue disease, rheumatological diseases, CKD, liver failure, vitamin deficiency, infection (eg HIV, Lyme disease), iatrogenic (eg chemotherapy, amiodarone), porphyria. Clinical features: Insidious onset (usually), slow progression, urinary symptoms, eg retention, postural hypotension, supine hypertension, palpitations, syncope, sweating disturbances, thermodysregulation, constipation/diarrhoea, lacrimal disturbance, erectile/ejaculatory dysfunction, female sexual dysfunction, pupillary dysfunction, blurred vision, hair loss.

☞ INVESTIGATIONS
Investigate for diagnosis, causes and severity. FBC, U&E, LFT, TFT, glucose, protein electrophoresis, autoim-mune/HIV/porphyria/amyloid screen, ECG (including ambulatory), ambulatory BP monitor, tilt table, LP, USS renal/cystometry, EMG, skin stimulation tests.

☗ MANAGEMENT
Address underlying cause, postural hypotension (general measures, eg stand slowly; mineralocorticoids, eg fludrocortisone), small meals, metoclopramide, laxatives, excessive sweating (propantheline, botuli-num toxin, iontophoresis, sympathectomy), erectile dysfunction (phosphodiesterase inhibitors), hormonal manipulation for female sexual dysfunction, urinary self-catheterisation.

Avascular necrosis (osteonecrosis)

▤ CLINICAL NOTES
Aetiology/risk factors: Idiopathic, iatrogenic, eg steroids, bisphosphonates (jaw), radiotherapy; trauma, DM, SLE, sickle cell anaemia, hypoxia, Perthes' disease, radiotherapy, alcohol abuse, Cushing's syndrome, Caisson disease, renal replacement therapy, pancreatitis, hypertension, thrombosis, vasculitis, Gaucher's disease. Clinical features: Joint pain, limp. Complications: OA, osteochondritis dissecans, disability, chronic pain.

☞ INVESTIGATIONS
X-ray, MRI, bone scan. Investigate for underlying cause.

☗ MANAGEMENT
Treat underlying cause, analgesia, bisphosphonates, physiotherapy, core decompression, graft, osteotomy, joint replacement.

Bacterial vaginosis

See also
— *Genital tract infections (non-STI)*

▤ CLINICAL NOTES
See *sexually transmitted infections and genital infections*

Baker's cyst

▤ CLINICAL NOTES
Epidemiology: Common. Aetiology/risk factors: Associated with OA, RA, septic arthritis, seronegative arthritis, haemophilia, granulomatous diseases, SLE, osteochondritis dissecans, trauma. Clinical features: Cystic popliteal swelling, pain, effusion. Complications: Rupture (may mimic DVT), thrombophlebitis, infection, bleeding (into cyst), calcification, nerve entrapment.

☞ INVESTIGATIONS
X-ray, USS, may require MRI (eg if rapidly growing, to exclude malignant disease).

☗ MANAGEMENT
Reassurance, analgesia, aspiration, sclerotherapy, surgery, eg synovectomy.

Balanitis xerotica obliterans (BXO)

▤ CLINICAL NOTES
See *lichen sclerosus*

Barrett's oesophagus

▤ CLINICAL NOTES
Metaplastic disorder: Squamous to columnar epithelium, occurring at lower oesophagus. Epidemiology: M>F. Aetiology/risk factors: Advancing age, Caucasians, *H pylori*, NSAIDs, GORD, hiatus hernia, smoking, obesity, alcohol. Clinical features: Asymptomatic, dyspepsia. Complications: Stricture, adenocarcinoma.

☞ INVESTIGATIONS
OGD, CLO test and biopsy.

☗ MANAGEMENT
Lifestyle changes, PPI for low-grade dysplasia. *High-grade dysplasia:* Photodynamic therapy, PPI, ablation, oesophagectomy (high risk of malignancy). Regular monitoring.

Bartholin's abscess

📖 CLINICAL NOTES

Clinical features: Erythematous, swollen, tender Bartholin's cyst, fever.

🔍 INVESTIGATIONS

Swabs (to exclude STI, eg gonococcal).

💊 MANAGEMENT

Analgesia, antibiotics, surgery (incision, drainage/ marsupialisation).

Bartter's syndrome

See also
   — Pseudo-Bartter's syndrome

📖 CLINICAL NOTES

Epidemiology: Rare. Aetiology/risk factors: Autosomal recessive. Clinical features: Severe salt wasting, failure to thrive, normo/hypotension, polyuria, polydypsia, constipation.

🔍 INVESTIGATIONS

$\downarrow$K$^+$ $\downarrow$Cl$^-$, metabolic alkalosis, $\uparrow$renin, $\uparrow$aldosterone, and $\uparrow$urinary K$^+$.

💊 MANAGEMENT

NSAIDs, K$^+$ replacement, potassium-sparing diuretics, ACE inhibitors.

Basal cell carcinoma (BCC)

📖 CLINICAL NOTES

Also called rodent ulcer. Epidemiology: Common, M>F. Aetiology/risk factors: White race, UV exposure, genetic, advancing age, immunosuppression, skin types 1 and 2, Gorlin's syndrome. Clinical features: Sun-exposed distribution, usually facial, also on trunk/legs. Pearly rolled edge with telangiectasia and central ulcer, slow-growing lesions. Complications: Deep, bony, orbital or neural invasion, morphoeic subtype aggressive. Some lesions have coexisting SCC.

🔍 INVESTIGATIONS

Biopsy, excision and histology, CT/MRI.

💊 MANAGEMENT

Curettage/cautery/cryotherapy for small low-risk lesions. Imiquimod 5% cream for low-risk lesions, 5FU, photodynamic therapy, avoid high sun exposure. Surgery/radiotherapy for high-risk lesions. Plastic surgery may be required for advanced invasive lesions.

Becker's muscular dystrophy

📖 CLINICAL NOTES

Epidemiology: About five in 10^5 prevalence. Aetiology/ risk factors: X-linked. Clinical features: Developmental delay (motor), walking difficulties late teens, proximal muscle weakness, pseudohypertrophy of calves, Gower sign. Complications: May cause severe disability, scoliosis, cardiomyopathy, cardiac failure, respiratory failure, pneumonia, contractures, dysphagia, myoglobinuria, rhabdomyolysis, malignant hyperpyrexia (under general anaesthetic), cognitive impairment, schizophrenia, premature death (fifth to sixth decade).

🔍 INVESTIGATIONS

$\uparrow$CK, muscle biopsy, genetic studies, EMG, ECG, echocardiogram, lung function.

💊 MANAGEMENT

Genetic counselling, physiotherapy, walking aids, orthopaedic support, vaccinations, MDT approach, monitor cardiac function, treat cardiac and respiratory failure, family support.

Behçet's disease

📖 CLINICAL NOTES

Epidemiology: Rare. Aetiology/risk factors: May be autoimmune, linked to HLA-B51. Clinical features: Painful recurrent orogenital ulcers, may take three weeks to heal, nodules, rash, uveitis, chorioretinitis, joint pain and swelling (often knee), headache, dizziness, abdominal pain. Complications: Scars, vasculitis, thrombosis (including mural and coronary artery), GI bleeding, stroke, aseptic meningitis, encephalitis.

🔍 INVESTIGATIONS

$\downarrow$Hb, $\uparrow$ESR/CRP. Pathergy testing, suggesting skin oversensitivity (small erythematous bump or pustule at needle insertion site one to two days afterwards is +ve). Biopsy, echocardiography, angiography.

💊 MANAGEMENT

Topical steroids, oral steroids, immunomodulators (eg methotrexate, azathioprine, ciclosporin, interferon alfa, anti-TNF therapy.

Bell's palsy

See also
   — VIIth cranial nerve palsy
   — Ramsay-Hunt syndrome
   — Shingles (herpes zoster)

📖 CLINICAL NOTES

Epidemiology: 70% of facial palsies. 11-40 in 10^5 per year. Aetiology/risk factors: Idiopathic, advancing age, viral (herpes simplex/zoster). Clinical features: Rapid onset facial paralysis due to LMN VIIth nerve palsy, no forehead sparing, difficulty closing ipsilateral eye, dribbling, eating/speaking difficulties, hyperacusis, taste disturbance. If herpes zoster in ipsilateral ear, Ramsay

DISEASES

Hunt syndrome. Severity of paralysis may be measured by House-Brackman scale. Complications: Corneal ulceration, partial or no recovery (increased risk if complete palsy at outset, elderly, DM, hypertension, pre-eclampsia, if painful), involvement of adjacent cranial nerves.

☞ INVESTIGATIONS

No specific diagnostic tests are available, nerve conduction studies.

☗ MANAGEMENT

Exclude other causes of VIIth nerve palsy. Most patients recover fully within one month. Steroids (prednisolone 60-80mg per day in an adult five days followed by 10-day taper). Antivirals in isolation not shown to be of benefit in Bell's palsy but should be used with steroids (treat Ramsay Hunt syndrome with antivirals). *Eye:* Lubrication, patch, tarsorrhaphy.

Benign essential tremor

CLINICAL NOTES

Epidemiology: 14% >65 years. Aetiology/risk factors: 50% familial autosomal dominant. Stress, caffeine. Clinical features: Gradual onset, progressive, fine action tremor, mainly hands (approximately 7Hz), may affect speech/head movements. Complications: Difficulty writing/talking/eating, reduced confidence, depression.

☞ INVESTIGATIONS

Investigation to exclude other conditions, TFT, glucose, CT/MRI.

☗ MANAGEMENT

Propranolol, topiramate, phenobarbital, botulinum toxin, thalamotomy.

Benign intracranial hypertension

CLINICAL NOTES

Epidemiology: F>M. Aetiology/risk factors: Idiopathic, obesity, pregnancy, iatrogenic (eg COC, tetracyclines, steroids, nitrofurantoin), head injury, hypervitaminosis A, iron deficiency, polycythaemia rubra vera, myxoedema, Cushing's disease, hypoparathyroidism, Addison's disease, cardiac failure, renal failure, SLE. Clinical features: Headache (worse in morning and evening, worse on coughing/straining), nausea, vomiting, papilloedema. Complications: Visual field defect, VIth nerve palsy (false localising sign).

☞ INVESTIGATIONS

CT/MRI (ventricles not dilated), consider LP.

☗ MANAGEMENT

Treat cause, obesity advice, diuretics, VP shunt/surgery may be required for complications.

Benign paroxysmal positional vertigo (BPPV)

See *vertigo*

Benign prostatic hypertrophy (BPH)

See also
— *Prostate cancer*

CLINICAL NOTES

Epidemiology: 50% of 50-year-olds, 70% of 70-year-olds. Clinical features: Asymptomatic, lower urinary tract symptoms (LUTS – hesitancy, poor stream, terminal dribbling, incomplete bladder emptying, nocturia, straining to pass urine, urinary frequency). Smooth enlarged prostate on digital rectal examination. Complications: ↓quality of life, acute retention, bladder hypertrophy, bladder hyperactivity and urge incontinence, UTI, bladder calculi, hydronephrosis, CKD.

☞ INVESTIGATIONS

International Prostate Symptom score, urinalysis, U&E, eGFR, PSA, ↑acid phosphatase, uroflowmetry, residual volume assessment, urodynamics, renal tract USS.

☗ MANAGEMENT

Watchful waiting if low risk of prostate cancer, medical therapy if no complications (alpha-blockers do not affect disease progression, act on smooth muscle), 5-alpha-reductase inhibitors, eg finasteride, may reduce prostatic volume by 20%, reduce risk of prostate cancer but may increase male breast cancer. Transurethral resection of the prostate (TURP) 70% risk of retrograde ejaculation, 5% risk of erectile dysfunction (ED), <1% risk of incontinence, bleeding. Laser prostatectomy, open prostatectomy.

Benson's syndrome

See also
— *Alzheimer's disease*

CLINICAL NOTES

Posterior cortical atrophy, dementia variant. Clinical features: Progressive, visual agnosias (eyes work but cannot see), apraxias, eg constructional, dressing, ideational, environmental disorientation, left hemineglect. Complications: Progresses to affect short-term memory and cognition.

☞ INVESTIGATIONS

Exclude organic/functional causes for symptoms and other causes of dementia, eg FBC, U&E, TFT, Ca^{2+}, ESR, ECG, CT/MRI brain, neuropsychology, vitamin B_{12}, folate.

MANAGEMENT

Visual aids. Risk assessment (including driving, safety at home), memory clinics, family support. Cholinesterase inhibitors, memantine. Light therapy, dance, music, pet therapy, multisensory stimulation. *Agitation:* Assess causes, eg pain, environment. Only use antipsychotics at lowest effective dose for psychosis rather than for agitation (risk of CVA). Finasteride has been shown to reduce sexual disinhibition.

Bereavement reaction

CLINICAL NOTES

Aetiology/risk factors: Major life changes, eg marriage, divorce, house move, loss of job, death. Clinical features: Shock, denial, numbness, searching, pining, anxiety, guilt, anger, social withdrawal, reduced concentration, final acceptance. Complications: CV events, self-harm/suicide, depression, anxiety, post traumatic stress disorder (PTSD), substance abuse, somatisation, headaches, interference with employment/relationships.

MANAGEMENT

Support groups, counselling, consider antidepressants.

Berry aneurysm

CLINICAL NOTES

Epidemiology: F>M. Anterior communicating artery aneurysm – most common aneurysm of Circle of Willis. 15% of patients have multiple aneurysms. Aetiology/risk factors: Idiopathic, familial, hypertension, smoking. Associated with PCKD, coarctation of aorta, arteriovenous malformation and collagen disorders. Clinical features: Asymptomatic, warning headaches, eg during sexual intercourse, bitemporal visual field defect. Complications: SAH (risk correlates with size of aneurysm).

INVESTIGATIONS

Screening (two or more first-degree relatives with SAH) – CT/MR angiography, cerebral angiography.

MANAGEMENT

Surgery if young patient, aneurysm >7mm, located at junction of internal carotid and posterior communicating artery (high risk of SAH)/basilar artery bifurcation, history of SAH, severe hypertension.

Biliary atresia

CLINICAL NOTES

Epidemiology: Rare. Aetiology/risk factors: Congenital. Clinical features: Progressive neonatal obstructive jaundice, hepatosplenomegaly, pruritus. Complications: Hypercholesterolaemia, cirrhosis, portal hypertension, malabsorption, cholangitis, death (if untreated, by two years).

INVESTIGATIONS

Deranged LFTs, conjugated hyperbilirubinaemia, USS, nuclear medicine (hepatobiliary scintiscanning), liver biopsy, diagnostic laparotomy.

MANAGEMENT

Roux-en-Y or Kasai procedure. Liver transplantation.

Biliary colic

CLINICAL NOTES

See *gallstone disease*

Bipolar affective disorder

See also
— *Depression*

CLINICAL NOTES

Epidemiology: Onset 25-35 years. Aetiology/risk factors: Genetic, environmental. Clinical features: *Bipolar I:* ≥1 episodes of mania, patient may or not have episodes of depression (four or more episodes in one year; rapid-cycling bipolar disorder, F>M). *Bipolar II:* ≥1 depressive episode and ≥1 hypomanic episode. Hypomanic rather than manic features, depression may be severe. Some patients may experience mixed manic/depressive features. Features of hypomania – irritability, elation, pressure of speech, flight of ideas, grandiose ideation, poor concentration, exaggerated optimism, insomnia, hyperactivity, overspending, sexual promiscuity, heightened libido. Complications: Mania (psychosis); grandiose delusions, auditory hallucinations, weight loss, physical exhaustion, dehydration.

INVESTIGATIONS

FBC, U&E, LFT, TFT, Ca^{2+}, MRI brain (if first episode of psychosis).

MANAGEMENT

Consider comorbidities and organic causes, eg infection, thyroid disease, cerebral lesion. Involve family and carers if possible. Self-help groups. Self-monitoring of crisis triggers and signs of relapse. Crisis management plan. Risk assessment. Regular follow-up. General lifestyle advice. Blood and drug monitoring. Refer at-risk patients, newly diagnosed patients, mania, severe depression, decline in functioning, poor medication adherence, drug misuse. Early intervention required for psychosis. *Long-term treatment:* Consider lithium, olanzapine, valproate (care in women of childbearing age); lamotrigine or carbamazepine may be used. Long-term SSRI may be used if no history of hypomania/mania (minimum two years after acute episode). Psychological therapy after acute episode. *Acute:* Hypomania/mania, wean off antidepressants, short-term benzodiazepines/rapid tranquillisation may be used. Consider adding/increasing antipsychotic (olanzapine/quetiapine/risperidone). If not on lithium, consider adding if psychosis not severe and has responded before, otherwise check levels. Consider adding valproate (unless childbearing risk) or increasing dose. *Depression:* Mild, consider antidepressants, mood stabilisers, exercise; moderate/severe, consider SSRI or quetiapine, increase antidepressant dose/change drug if required. Psychological therapy. Exercise. ECT. *Rapid cycling:* Treat acute episode in secondary care. Antimanic drugs. Avoid antidepressants.

Bladder cancer

 CLINICAL NOTES

Epidemiology: Fourth most common cancer in developing world. About 11,000 per year (UK). 90% transitional cell, 6-8% squamous cell, up to 2% adenocarcinoma, small cell (rare). *Aetiology/risk factors:* Smoking (x2-4 risk), advancing age (x15-20 risk >70 years compared with <55 years), genetic (*p53* mutation), chemicals, eg benzene; occupational, eg petroleum, rubber, textile, paint industries; iatrogenic, eg cyclophosphamide, phenacetin; chronic irritation, squamous cell rather than transitional cell cancer; recurrent UTI, bladder stone, long-term catheter, schistosomiasis (schistosomiasis-related cancer usually well differentiated, common in Middle East and Africa). *Clinical features:* Haematuria (nonvisible/visible), non-specific urinary tract symptoms, LUTS, lymphadenopathy. *Complications:* Metastatic disease, spinal cord compression.

INVESTIGATIONS

FBC, U&E, bladder tumour antigen, urinalysis, urine MC&S (sterile pyuria) and cytology. IV urogram (IVU), USS, cystoscopy, MRI pelvis, CT chest and abdomen (distant metastases).

MANAGEMENT

Superficial disease: Cystoscopic resection TURBT and reconstruction and fulguration, intravesical chemotherapy, intravesical BCG (weekly for six weeks, reduces recurrence by up to 60%), monitor for recurrence (88% recur by 15 years). *Muscle-invasive disease*: Radical cystectomy with urinary diversion and/or radiotherapy, chemotherapy. Cisplatin-containing combination chemotherapy, benefits of adjuvant chemotherapy still unconvincing over current regimens). *Metastatic disease*: Chemotherapy, palliative radiotherapy.

Blepharitis

 CLINICAL NOTES

Epidemiology: Common. *Aetiology/risk factors:* Seborrhoeic, staphylococci. *Clinical features:* Eyelid soreness, itching, flaking, grittiness, sticky eyes in morning, swollen eyelids, crusting, may have associated rosacea or seborrhoeic dermatitis. *Complications:* Stye, conjunctivitis, dry eye.

MANAGEMENT

Lid hygiene, avoid eye make-up; eye lubricants, warm eyelid compress twice daily initially, express meibomian glands, cleansing with diluted 50% baby shampoo on cotton bud along lid margin, topical antibiotics if hygiene measures fail/infection, consider oral antibiotics, eg tetracyclines for up to three months.

Body dysmorphic disorder (BDD)

CLINICAL NOTES

Preoccupation with imagined/minor anomaly in appearance. *Epidemiology:* 0.5-0.7% prevalence. *Clinical features:* Excessive use of mirrors, attempts to cover areas of body, comparing to others, excessive seeking of reassurance, patient may seek surgical intervention to 'correct' perceived defect. *Complications:* Depression, anxiety, self-harm, suicide.

MANAGEMENT

Education. Risk management. Regular follow-up. *Mild:* CBT first-line, SSRI, eg fluoxetine. *Moderate:* SSRI/clomipramine or intense CBT. *Children:* CBT, may require SSRI/clomipramine. MDT approach (including child mental health services, social services), family involvement. Support organisations. Manage comorbidities, eg psychosis, depression, anxiety, alcohol and drug abuse, eating disorder, OCD.

Bone tumours (primary)

CLINICAL NOTES

Epidemiology: Rare. *Aetiology/risk factors:* Idiopathic, previous chemotherapy or radiotherapy, familial retinoblastoma, luminous paints (with action of radium on zinc sulphide), Paget's disease of the bone, chronic osteomyelitis, Li-Fraumeni syndrome, translocation 11:22 in Ewing's sarcoma. *Clinical features:* Asymptomatic (incidental finding), pain (often worse at night), warm tender bony swelling, deformity, fever, weight loss. *Complications:* Pathological fracture, metastases, eg local, pulmonary. *Osteosarcoma:* M>F, two peaks, early adulthood and elderly, usually affects metaphysis, mainly lower limb especially around knee. *Ewing's sarcoma:* M>F, peak five to 30 years, diaphyseal. Pelvis and femur commonly affected. Soft tissue equivalent – primitive neuroectodermal tumour (PNET). *Chondrosarcoma:* Fifth to seventh decades, metaphyseal, slow growing. *Others:* Histiocytoma, fibrosarcoma, bone lymphoma, angiosarcoma, giant-cell tumour.

INVESTIGATIONS

FBC, ↑Ca^{2+} and ALP (may rise rapidly), X-ray (Ewing's sarcoma – lamellated or onion skin type periosteal appearance), MRI (marrow and soft tissue involvement), skeletal scintigraphy for multiple lesions, guided biopsy (USS/CT), pulmonary CT, PET-CT.

DISEASES

MANAGEMENT

Surgery, chemotherapy, radiotherapy. Prostheses.

Borderline personality disorder

CLINICAL NOTES

Epidemiology: One in 50 prevalence. F>M. Aetiology/risk factors: Multifactorial. Clinical features: Emotionally unstable, intense volatile relationships, impulsive, anxiety, insecurity, low self-esteem, fear/oversensitive to rejection. Complications: Risk-taking behaviour, drug and alcohol abuse, violence, self-harm, affective disorder, psychosis, suicide (about 15% risk).

MANAGEMENT

MDT approach including carers/family. Effective communication across services. Patients should not be excluded from their own care planning. Encourage autonomy/inclusion in care plan. Trusting therapeutic relationship required, with clear boundaries. Manage change/end of therapeutic relationships carefully. Assess coping strategies, comorbidities, risk assessment of harm to self and others. Plan long-term goals. Crisis anticipation/ prevention/management. Psychological intervention not less than three weeks. Antipsychotics not generally used for medium/long-term treatment. Short-term sedatives in crisis. Manage psychiatric comorbidities, eg affective disorder, psychosis, drug and alcohol dependence.

Bornholm disease (pleurodynia)

CLINICAL NOTES

Epidemiology: Children/young adults. More common in spring and autumn. Aetiology/risk factors: Virus, eg Coxsackie B, causing chest pain. Clinical features: Fever, myalgia, pleuritic chest pain, epigastric pain. Complications: Relapse, myocarditis, viral meningitis.

INVESTIGATIONS

Serology. Investigations to exclude other causes of chest pain.

MANAGEMENT

Analgesia.

Botulism

CLINICAL NOTES

Toxin reduces release of Ach at neuromuscular junction leading to LMN muscle paralysis. Epidemiology: Rare in UK. Aetiology/risk factors: *C botulinum* toxin contracted from food or dirty wounds/shared dirty needles. Clinical features: Food-borne disease preceded by nausea, vomiting, diarrhoea. Neurological symptoms take longer to manifest in wound-borne disease. Neurological symptoms – descending symmetrical flaccid paralysis.

Diplopia, blurred vision, ptosis, dysphagia, facial weakness, dysarthria, dry mouth, paralysis spreads to limbs and muscles of respiration. Complications: Respiratory failure, infantile botulism, death.

INVESTIGATIONS

Wound, stool, serum or contaminated food samples sent for toxin and clostridium.

MANAGEMENT

Prevention with vaccination and immunoglobulin. Antitoxin. Respiratory and general support (may require ventilation). Wound debridement.

Brain tumour

See also
- Gliomas
- Meningioma

CLINICAL NOTES

Epidemiology: Rare, ≤0.01% incidence. Clinical features: Red flags – papilloedema, acute memory/personality change, confusion, seizure, altered consciousness, new onset cluster headache, known primary cancer elsewhere, eg lung, breast, lymphoma; known immunodeficiency, abnormal neurological findings.

INVESTIGATIONS

Brain CT/MRI, lumbar puncture if ICP not raised, biopsy.

MANAGEMENT

Radiotherapy, surgery, chemotherapy, dexamethasone, anticonvulsants.

Branchial cyst

CLINICAL NOTES

Aetiology/risk factors: Embryological defect of second branchial arch. Clinical features: May not present until teens. Cholesterol-filled painless mass at junction of upper and middle thirds of sternocleidomastoid muscle. Complications: Infection, pressure effect, sinus formation.

INVESTIGATIONS

USS, CT, MRI.

MANAGEMENT

Surgery. Treat complications accordingly.

Breast cancer

CLINICAL NOTES

Epidemiology: More than four x 10⁴ cases per year (UK). Most common female cancer (about 13% lifetime risk). May also occur in men. F:M about 100:1. Aetiology/

DISEASES

risk factors: Age, previous history of breast cancer, first child >30 years of age, early menarche (<11 years, x3 risk), late menopause (>54 years, x2 risk), prolonged HRT exposure (especially >10 years, HRT-related breast cancer has a better prognosis than non HRT-related disease), family history (one first-degree relative with breast cancer increases individual risk x2, maternal premenopausal breast cancer increases daughter's risk x3-11), *BRCA1* and *BRCA2* genes confer up to 85% chance of developing breast cancer and 15% chance of ovarian cancer. Ataxia telangiectasia, radiation, lobular and ductal carcinoma in situ (LCIS, DCIS), epitheliosis, benign cellular atypia. *Reduced risk:* Early oophorectomy, breastfeeding (x0.8 risk), high parity. **Clinical features:** Asymptomatic (screening), lump (medial tumours confer adverse prognosis), single duct discharge, bloody discharge, new nipple inversion, skin tethering, peau d'orange, Paget's disease of the breast, lymphadenopathy (supraclavicular nodes confer adverse prognosis). **Complications:** Fungation, local recurrence without metastases (cancer en cuirasse), metastatic disease (ipsiand contralateral breast, mediastinum, bone, liver, brain, skin, ovary causing eg pain, pathological fracture, cord compression, radiculopathy, jaundice, hepatomegaly, ascites, seizures, headaches, focal neurology, pleural effusion), psychological morbidity, death.

INVESTIGATIONS
Ca 15-3, Ca 27.29, screening. Mammogram, USS, MRI, biopsy, oestrogen receptor (ER) status, progestogen receptor (PR) status, HER2 status (15% cancers), BRCA status (*BRCA1* usually -ve for ER, PR; *BRCA2* usually +ve), DEXA scan if given aromatase inhibitor, eg anastrazole.

MANAGEMENT
DCIS: Surgery (conservative or mastectomy) +/– radiotherapy +/–tamoxifen. *LCIS:* Surgery if high risk, tamoxifen. *Surgery:* Wide local excision with adjuvant radiotherapy, or mastectomy and breast reconstruction (immediate/delayed). For sentinel node biopsy unless pregnant, clinical evidence of node involvement, T_3 or T_4 disease, after neoadjuvant chemotherapy or if previous axillary or breast surgery. Axillary dissection if +ve node biopsy. *Radiotherapy:* Adjuvant radiotherapy confers survival benefit after wide local excision and high-risk patients after mastectomy. *Chemotherapy:* ER -ve patients may receive adjuvant systemic chemotherapy. ER +ve patients may also be considered for systemic chemotherapy. ER +ve premenopausal women usually have surgical or chemical oophorectomy as well as tamoxifen. ER +ve postmenopausal women have a regimen of tamoxifen and aromatase inhibitors. Reduced efficacy if tamoxifen is taken with paroxetine. Fluoxetine should also be avoided. Citalopram or venlafaxine may be used. Bisphosphonates recommended for aromatase inhibitor induced bone marrow density (BMD) loss and bone metastases. Emerging evidence that zolidronic acid improves outcome in early disease. HER2 +ve patients may be eligible to receive trastuzumab if normal LV function (continue for one year or until disease progresses). Consider monoclonal antibody bevacizumab for advanced disease.

Breast cyst
CLINICAL NOTES
Epidemiology: Common in pre and perimenopause. **Aetiology/risk factors:** HRT, previous history. **Clinical features:** Tender, smooth, one or more cysts may be present, may be cyclical, may be painful.

INVESTIGATIONS
USS, fine needle aspiration (FNA).

MANAGEMENT
Exclude breast cancer, FNA if painful.

Breast pain (mastalgia)
CLINICAL NOTES
Epidemiology: Common. **Clinical features:** *Cyclical:* Thirties until menopause, luteal phase, commonly upper outer quadrant. *Non-cyclical:* often postmenopausal. *Extramammary:* Non-breast chest pain.

INVESTIGATIONS
No imaging required with normal examination/no features of malignancy in women <40 years unless strong family history of breast cancer.

MANAGEMENT
Appropriate bra size, reduce caffeine and fat intake. Weight reduction. Flaxseed, NSAIDs (including topical), tamoxifen, danazol, bromocriptine.

Bronchiectasis
CLINICAL NOTES
Permanently dilated bronchi have poor secretion clearance, localised or widespread. **Epidemiology:** F>M. **Aetiology/risk factors:** Post-infection, eg pertussis, TB, pneumonia, measles; allergic bronchopulmonary aspergillosis, post bronchial obstruction, post-pneumonitis, bronchiolitis, CF, radiotherapy, Kartagener's syndrome, RA, vasculitis, IBD, immunodeficiency, Young's syndrome (ciliary dyskinesia, azoospermia, sinusitis), yellow nail syndrome. **Clinical features:** Asymptomatic, productive cough, haemoptysis, wheeze, SOB, fatigue, sinusitis, recurrent chest infections, low BMI, finger clubbing in severe cases, coarse pulmonary crepitations (inspiratory and expiratory). **Complications:** Pleurisy, empyema, abscess, massive haemoptysis, amyloid, pulmonary hypertension, cor pulmonale.

DISEASES

INVESTIGATIONS

FBC, CRP, HIV screen, immunoglobulin screen, sputum culture, sweat test for CF, chest X-ray, high-resolution CT, lung function tests.

MANAGEMENT

Treat any underlying cause, smoking cessation, treat infections, chest physiotherapy, bronchodilators if bronchospasm, consider ICS, embolisation, resection of localised diseased lung, lung transplant, long-term oxygen therapy (LTOT).

Bronchiolitis

CLINICAL NOTES

Epidemiology: Common. Aetiology/risk factors: Winter/spring. Infants less than one year of age. Premature and those with congenital diseases at higher risk of admission. Breastfeeding protective. Respiratory syncytial virus (RSV), parainfluenza virus, influenza, adenovirus. Clinical features: Fever, initial coryza, cough, crepitations, wheeze, hyperinflated lungs. Complications: Respiratory distress, reduced feeding, dehydration, irritability, diarrhoea, vomiting, otitis media, apnoea, cardiac failure in those with otherwise undiagnosed cardiac lesions, SIADH, pneumonia, bronchiectasis.

INVESTIGATIONS

Pulse oximetry (may be unreliable if hypothermic/anaemic), nasopharyngeal aspirate (not essential), apnoea monitor.

MANAGEMENT

Barrier nurse; admit if underlying chronic disease, reduced feeding <50% in preceding 24 hours, cyanosis, nasal flaring, grunting, O_2 sats ≤94%, history of apnoea, high RR >70 per min in infants, <12 weeks of age, likely to deteriorate, premature <35 weeks. Supplemental O_2 if sats <94%, pulmonary ventilation if sats <92%, ribavirin if underlying diseases, eg heart disease; studies have shown combination nebulised adrenaline plus oral dexamethasone for six days reduces admission.

Brown-Séquard syndrome

CLINICAL NOTES

Aetiology/risk factors: MS, ADEM, spinal cord tumour, trauma, radiation damage, spinal abscess. Clinical features: Ipsilateral leg: Weakness, hypertonia, ↓joint position sense, ↓vibration sense. Contralateral leg: ↓pain and temperature sensation (to sensory level).

INVESTIGATIONS

MRI, investigate for underlying cause.

MANAGEMENT

Treat underlying cause, OT, physiotherapy.

Brucellosis (Malta/undulant fever)

CLINICAL NOTES

Epidemiology: Rare in UK. Aetiology/risk factors: Bacterial, from untreated cow's/goat's milk, incubation seven to 21 days. Clinical features: Malaise, headache, myalgia, fever (undulant), back pain, sacroiliitis, hepatosplenomegaly. Complications: Chronic infection, osteomyelitis, epididymo-orchitis, meningo-encephalitis, endocarditis.

INVESTIGATIONS

Blood/marrow culture, FBC, lymphocytosis, serology.

MANAGEMENT

Doxycycline and rifampicin.

Brugada syndrome

CLINICAL NOTES

Epidemiology: M>F, south-east Asians. Aetiology/risk factors: Familial, autosomal dominant. Clinical features: Asymptomatic, incidental finding on ECG, palpitations, presyncope, provoked by flecainide, may be associated with other congenital cardiac defects. Complications: Syncope, VF, sudden cardiac death.

INVESTIGATIONS

ECG – coved ST elevation V1, V2, V3. RBBB. Flecainide challenge if resting ECG normal. Electrophysiology studies.

MANAGEMENT

ICD, family screening.

Bruton's disease

CLINICAL NOTES

See immunodeficiency (primary)

Budd-Chiari syndrome

CLINICAL NOTES

Hepatic vein thrombosis. Epidemiology: Rare. Aetiology/risk factors: Idiopathic, hypercoagulable state, thrombophilia, malignancy, radiotherapy, trauma, paroxysmal nocturnal haemoglobinuria. Clinical features: Acute: Abdominal pain, ascites, smooth tender hepatomegaly. Chronic: Signs of chronic liver disease.

INVESTIGATIONS

Abdominal USS/CT, venography, MRI, ascitic tap, liver biopsy.

MANAGEMENT

Ascitic drainage, thrombolysis, venous diversion, liver transplant.

DISEASES

Bulbar palsy

 CLINICAL NOTES

LMN affecting lower cranial nerves. Aetiology/risk factors: CVA, MS, ADEM, tumour, syrinx, MND, polio, diphtheria, muscular dystrophy, Guillain-Barré syndrome, meningitis, neurosyphilis, iatrogenic (surgery, radiotherapy). Clinical features: Dribbling, swallowing difficulties, nasal regurgitation, slurred speech, absent palatal movements, flaccid tongue, tongue fasciculations. Complications: Aspiration pneumonia.

↺ **INVESTIGATIONS**

MRI, investigate according to suspected underlying cause.

◘ **MANAGEMENT**

Treat underlying cause, SALT, dietitian to maintain nutrition and avoid aspiration pneumonia, PEG feeding, communication aids.

Bulimia nervosa

 CLINICAL NOTES

Epidemiology: F>M. Underdiagnosed in men. Aetiology/risk factors: Affective/anxiety disorder, poor coping strategies, peer/social pressure, parental criticism, genetics. Clinical features: Binge eating, purging, laxative abuse, excessive exercise, menstrual disturbance, preoccupation with weight, guilt. Screening questions – Do you think you have an eating problem? Do you worry excessively about your weight? Complications: Dental caries, parotid hypertrophy, malnutrition, osteoporosis, poor growth, cardiomyopathy, electrolyte and ECG anomalies, oesophageal rupture, oedema, death.

↺ **INVESTIGATIONS**

↓K+, LFT, ↓Ca²⁺, ECG, FBC.

◘ **MANAGEMENT**

Risk assessment, treat comorbidities, address physical complications, self-help and support groups, limit acidic food if vomiting/dental hygiene; CBT for bulimia nervosa (CBT-BN), may be offered antidepressants (especially fluoxetine 60mg once daily) as first-line, psychotherapy, family therapy, physical monitoring.

Bullous impetigo

See also
— Impetigo contagiosa

▤ **CLINICAL NOTES**

Aetiology/risk factors: Staphylococcus, streptococci, immunodeficiency, DM, iatrogenic. Clinical features: Painful vesicles/blisters especially trunk, flexures. Complications: Highly contagious, cellulitis.

↺ **INVESTIGATIONS**

Consider FBC, glucose and swab if severe, diagnostic doubt or treatment-resistant.

◘ **MANAGEMENT**

Hygiene, topical or systemic antibiotics.

Bullous diseases

▤ **CLINICAL NOTES**

See pemphigus, pemphigoid and bullous impetigo

Burns

▤ **CLINICAL NOTES**

Epidemiology: Common. Aetiology/risk factors: Hot water, steam, fire, sun, cold, electrical, chemical, frictional. Clinical features: Epidermal burns: First-degree – pain, erythema. Dermal burns: Second-degree, painful or painless, erythema, blistering. Full thickness: Third-degree, underlying tissue may be black or white. Complications: Tracheal oedema, infection, dehydration, electrolyte imbalance, contractures, scarring, haemolysis, rhabdomyolysis, compartment syndrome, cardiac arrhythmia, death.

◘ **MANAGEMENT**

Maintain safe environment, stop burning process, remove loose clothing around burn unless stuck to burned skin, use cool water for at least 10-30 minutes, avoid cooling with ice, avoid creams unless superficial burns, cover burn with cling film, analgesia. Avoid bursting blisters. Specialist help required for burns equivalent to or larger than area of palm; deep dermal and full-thickness burns; burns affecting groin, hands, feet, face, joints, airway; patients with comorbidities; electrical and chemical burns. For large burns: Fluid resuscitation, keep patient warm, plastic surgery. Treat complications accordingly. May require skin grafting. Consider tetanus prophylaxis.

Bursitis

▤ **CLINICAL NOTES**

Epidemiology: Common. Aetiology/risk factors: Repetitive use, eg kneeling for long periods of time, infection, trauma, RA, gout. Clinical features: Red, warm, swollen bursae. Complications: Infection, functional loss.

↺ **INVESTIGATIONS**

Aspiration (send for MC&S, crystals, cholesterol crystals seen in RA).

◘ **MANAGEMENT**

Analgesia, NSAIDs, avoid trigger, intralesional steroids, excision, antibiotics for infection, eg flucloxacillin.

DISEASES

Calcaneal spur (osteophyte)

📖 **CLINICAL NOTES**

Epidemiology: Common. Aetiology/risk factors: Chronic plantar fasciitis. Clinical features: Asymptomatic, heel pain.

🔍 **INVESTIGATIONS**

X-ray.

💊 **MANAGEMENT**

Analgesia, NSAIDs, cushioned footwear, orthotics, physiotherapy, steroid injection, surgery.

Campbell de Morgan spots

📖 **CLINICAL NOTES**

Epidemiology: Common. Aetiology/risk factors: Advancing age. Clinical features: Multiple benign, raised, non-blanching red angiokeratomas. Complications: Bleeding.

💊 **MANAGEMENT**

Cosmetic removal – surgery, laser.

Capgras syndrome

📖 **CLINICAL NOTES**

Epidemiology: Rare. Aetiology/risk factors: Organic disease, eg head injury, CVA; severe illness, eg pneumonia, schizophrenia, affective disorders. Clinical features: Delusion– someone close, eg family member, replaced by impostor, may be partial depending on causation, eg patient sees father as impostor but if speaking to him on telephone, knows it is father. Complications: May consider self as an impostor, violence.

🔍 **INVESTIGATIONS**

Investigate according to suspected underlying cause.

💊 **MANAGEMENT**

Treat underlying cause, psychology, antipsychotics.

Carbon monoxide poisoning

📖 **CLINICAL NOTES**

Epidemiology: About 20 deaths per year (UK). Aetiology/risk factors: Incomplete combustion of fuel, eg faulty boiler. Clinical features: CO has no smell. Headache, fatigue, nausea, vomiting. Complications: Breathlessness, confusion, memory disturbance, visual disturbance, ataxia, MI, cerebral oedema, seizures, death, permanent brain damage, eg Parkinsonism, miscarriage.

🔍 **INVESTIGATIONS**

↑Carboxyhaemoglobin. Investigate to exclude complications and other causes.

💊 **MANAGEMENT**

Remove patient from source, treat other family members, 100% O_2, hyperbaric chamber.

Carbuncle

📖 **CLINICAL NOTES**

Aetiology/risk factors: Staphylococcus, immunodeficiency, DM, iatrogenic. Clinical features: Confluence of multiple infected hair follicles, pain, fever. Complications: Cellulitis, abscess, osteomyelitis, sepsis, scarring, endocarditis.

🔍 **INVESTIGATIONS**

Consider FBC, glucose and swab if severe, diagnostic doubt or treatment-resistant.

💊 **MANAGEMENT**

Antibiotics, incision and drainage.

Carcinoid

📖 **CLINICAL NOTES**

Neuroendocrine tumour. Epidemiology: 1% postmortems. *Carcinoid syndrome*: Occurs when tumour has metastasised to liver; rare as carcinoid usually low grade. Aetiology/risk factors: Sporadic, MEN, neurofibromatosis. Often a pulmonary or abdominal tumour. Clinical features: Upper body flushing, tachycardia, hypotension, wheeze, diarrhoea. Complications: Pulmonary valve stenosis, tricuspid regurgitation, pleural fibrosis, retroperitoneal fibrosis, telangiectasia, bowel obstruction, weight loss, pellagra. Association with horseshoe kidneys.

🔍 **INVESTIGATIONS**

Chromogranin A, 24-hour urine collection (acid bottle) for 5-HIAA, CT, MRI.

💊 **MANAGEMENT**

Surgery, embolisation of hepatic artery. Octreotide (diarrhoea), phenoxybenzamine (flushing), interferon, chemotherapy, radiotherapy (external beam or targeted radionucleotide).

Carney complex (LAMB/NAME syndrome)

📖 **CLINICAL NOTES**

Epidemiology: Rare. Aetiology/risk factors: Autosomal dominant. Clinical features: Cardiac myxoma (may be multiple, may cause cardiac failure and stroke), brain myxomas, breast myxomas, pituitary adenoma, skin tumours, schwannoma, testicular tumours, adrenal hyperplasia (causing Cushing's syndrome), mucosal lentigos, phaeochromocytoma, male subfertility, thyroid disease.

🔍 **INVESTIGATIONS**

FBC, glucose, U&E, ESR, TFT, adrenocorticotropic hormone, growth hormone, echocardiogram.

MANAGEMENT

Medical treatment of endocrine overactivity, surgical resection of myxomas.

Carotid sinus hypersensitivity

CLINICAL NOTES

Epidemiology: M>F. Aetiology/risk factors: Advancing age, more common in those with other cardiovascular risk factors, IHD, digoxin. Clinical features: Presyncope/syncope with head movements, shaving or wearing tight clothes.

INVESTIGATIONS

ECG, ambulatory ECG, echocardiogram, consider ETT. Carotid massage – only perform if no history of CVA/TIA and no carotid bruits, should only be performed in secondary care.

MANAGEMENT

Lifestyle advice, pacemaker if prolonged asystole more than three seconds or more than two syncopal episodes.

Carpal tunnel syndrome

CLINICAL NOTES

See *median nerve palsy*

Cataplexy

CLINICAL NOTES

See *narcolepsy*

Cat-scratch disease

CLINICAL NOTES

Epidemiology: Mainly children, autumn/winter. Aetiology/risk factors: *Bartonella henselae* (flea vector), reservoir – cats (70% are infected), rabbits, dogs, monkeys. Infection by flea bite, animal scratch, bite, licking. Clinical features: Papule one to two days post-inoculation, becomes vesicular before healing. Regional lymph nodes then become enlarged to 2-4cm, takes three months to two years to settle. Fever, malaise. Complications: Suppurative lymphadenopathy, chorioretinitis, endocarditis, hepatitis, pneumonia, encephalitis, ataxia, seizures, arthropathy, thrombocytopenia, erythema multiforme/nodosum, retinitis.

INVESTIGATIONS

FBC (eosinophilia), LFT may be deranged, serology, node biopsy, USS/CT abdomen (liver and spleen lesions), echocardiogram.

MANAGEMENT

Mainly self-limiting without treatment, choice of antibiotic – azithromycin, rifampicin, ciprofloxacin (adults).

Cataract

CLINICAL NOTES

Epidemiology: Common. Aetiology/risk factors: Advancing age, trauma (including iatrogenic), post-infection, DM, smoking, UV exposure, scleritis, iritis, congenital (rubella, toxoplasmosis, influenza, CMV, EBV, measles, herpes zoster/simplex, hypothyroidism), Down's syndrome, Wilson's disease, neurofibromatosis, dystrophia myotonica, Laurence-Moon-Biedl syndrome, Refsum's disease, iatrogenic (steroids, amiodarone, phenothiazines, chloroquine). Clinical features: Gradual visual loss, night glare, difficulty driving, haloes, lens opacities.

MANAGEMENT

Treat underlying cause, watch and wait, phacoemulsification and intraocular lens.

Cauda equina syndrome

See also
— *Spinal cord compression (metastatic)*

CLINICAL NOTES

Epidemiology: Rare. Aetiology/risk factors: Large central lumbar disc herniation, metastases, abscess, trauma. Clinical features: Severe/worsening back pain, sciatica (often bilateral), saddle anaesthesia, bladder/bowel/sexual dysfunction, reduced anal tone, LMN signs in limbs. *Incomplete*: Change in urinary sensation, ↓desire to void, ↓urinary stream, partial saddle/genital sensory loss. *Complete*: Painless urinary retention with overflow, poor outcome. May develop over 24 hours to a few weeks. Complications: Permanent neurological deficit.

INVESTIGATIONS

Prompt MRI, urodynamics.

MANAGEMENT

Refer immediately for consideration of radiotherapy or early surgery, steroids, rehabilitation.

Cavernous sinus thrombosis

CLINICAL NOTES

Epidemiology: Rare. Aetiology/risk factors: Meningitis, head and neck infections, eg cellulitis, erysipelas, sinusitis, mastoiditis, cerebral abscess and dental; trauma, hypercoagulable states, eg thrombophilia, hyperviscosity. Most related to a staphylococcal infection. Clinical features: Fever, severe headache behind ipsilateral eye, periorbital oedema (may spread to contralateral eye), orbital pain, visual disturbance, reduced acuity, diplopia, cranial nerve palsies (III, IV, V [V1,V2 branches], VI; VIth nerve usually affected first), Horner's syndrome. Complications: Meningitis, cerebral abscess, permanent neurological deficit, seizure, coma, death.

INVESTIGATIONS

FBC, D-dimer, blood cultures, LP, CT, MRI, venography.

MANAGEMENT

IV antibiotics (may be required for four weeks), analgesia, anticonvulsants, consider steroids. Anticoagulation controversial. Surgery may be required.

Cellulitis

See also
 — Orbital cellulitis
 — Periorbital cellulitis
 — Erysipelas
 — Necrotising fasciitis

CLINICAL NOTES

Aetiology/risk factors: Most common – *Strep pyogenes*, *Staph aureus* via broken skin, eg trauma, tinea, DM, immunosuppression. Clinical features: Superficial dermal layer infection, tender red skin, lymphatic tracking, oedematous, advancing edge, malaise, fever, tachycardia. Complications: Septicaemia, septic shock, death.

INVESTIGATIONS

FBC, glucose, +/–blood cultures.

MANAGEMENT

If well and no comorbidities, oral antibiotics. If unwell, advanced disease, comorbidities, eg DM, peripheral vascular disease, facial cellulitis, IV antibiotics.

Central retinal vein occlusion

CLINICAL NOTES

Epidemiology: Common. Aetiology/risk factors: Advancing age, hypertension, DM, hyperlipidaemia, hypercoagulable states, eg thrombophilia, hyperviscosity, glaucoma, connective tissue disorders, COC. Clinical features: Painless, visual loss, engorged retinal veins, retinal haemorrhages, soft exudates, papilloedema, relative afferent pupillary defect. Complications: New vessel formation, acute glaucoma, complete visual loss.

INVESTIGATIONS

Fluorescein angiography, electroretinography.

MANAGEMENT

Treat underlying cause. Urgent ophthalmology opinion. Reduction in IOP if raised. Vitreous steroids. Consider vitreous bevacizumab injections. *Non-ischaemic type:* Laser photocoagulation if new vessel formation.

Cerebellar syndrome

CLINICAL NOTES

Aetiology: CVA, malignancy, iatrogenic (eg phenytoin), MS, ADEM, alcoholism, ataxia-telangiectasia,

Friedreich's ataxia, spinocerebellar ataxia, Refsum's disease, Charcot-Marie-Tooth, hypothyroidism, paraneoplastic syndrome. Clinical features: Staccato speech, nystagmus, past pointing, intention tremor, ataxia, dysdiadochokinesia, hypotonia, pendular knee reflex.

INVESTIGATIONS

MRI, investigate according to suspected underlying cause.

MANAGEMENT

Treat underlying cause.

Cerebellopontine angle tumour

CLINICAL NOTES

See *acoustic neuroma (schwannoma)*

Cerebral abscess

CLINICAL NOTES

Epidemiology: Rare, incidence 2-3 x 10^6, more common <40 years of age. Aetiology/risk factors: Haematogenous spread (25%), immunocompromised, infection (otitis media, periorbital cellulitis, mastoiditis, dental/sinus, bacterial endocarditis, pneumonia, bronchiectasis, skin, gut/urinary sepsis), cyanotic congenital heart disease, trauma. Clinical features: Fever, headache, malaise, confusion, mood disturbance, neurological deficit, nausea, vomiting, neck stiffness, altered consciousness, features of raised ICP. Complications: CVA, cavernous sinus thrombosis, epilepsy, permanent neurological deficit, meningitis, death (10%).

INVESTIGATIONS

↑WCC, CRP, CT/MRI, blood cultures, guided biopsy (MC&S for bacteria/virus/fungus).

MANAGEMENT

Analgesia, antibiotics, aspiration/neurosurgery if >2.5cm abscess, treat underlying illness, anticonvulsants.

Cerebral palsy

CLINICAL NOTES

Aetiology/risk factors: Antenatal (most common), perinatal or postnatal cerebral insult, eg infective/anoxic. Clinical features: Non-progressive neurological symptoms, eg spastic paraparesis, hemiparesis, developmental delay, learning disability. Complications: Seizures, contractures, depression, family disharmony, pneumonia, UTI, school difficulties.

MANAGEMENT

Physiotherapy, OT, educational support, family and social support, botulinum toxin, anticonvulsants.

DISEASES

Cerebrovascular accident (CVA)

See also
— *Subarachnoid haemorrhage*

 CLINICAL NOTES

Epidemiology: 11% deaths (UK). **Aetiology/risk factors:** Hypertension, hyperlipidaemia, smoking, diabetes, embolic (carotid artery, mural thrombus, eg post-MI, myocarditis, venous emboli passing through PFO/ASD); haemorrhagic, eg overanticoagulated. **Clinical features:** *Acute:* FAST (Face Arm Speech Test) in community, ROSIER tool in A&E. Slurred speech, dysphasia (expressive, receptive), visual disturbance, cognitive disturbance; parietal lobe syndromes – agnosias (difficulty in recognition), eg astereognosis (patient unable to recognise an object placed in hand when eyes closed), apraxia (difficulty in performing tasks, eg dressing), dyslexia, dyscalculia, altered consciousness, limb weakness/numbness. Hemiplegia – unilateral facial weakness, visual field defect (homonymous hemianopia/quadrantanopia), unilateral arm/leg hypertonia and weakness (flexors overriding extensors in arms, extensors overriding flexors in legs), hyperreflexia, upgoing plantar on affected side of body, sensory loss/inattention. **Complications:** Further cerebral events, permanent neurological damage, depression, DVT, loss of independent living, falls, loss of consciousness (haemorrhagic, brainstem), pneumonia, pressure sores, malnutrition, contractures, disuse atrophy, death.

⅃ **INVESTIGATIONS**

FBC, U&E, LFT, glucose, fasting lipids, ECG, CT, MRI (more sensitive than CT, immediate CT/MRI if considered for thrombolysis/bleeding risk/GCS <13/fluctuating symptoms/papilloedema/fever/neck stiffness/severe headache at time of onset), carotid dopplers (surgery recommended if >70% stenosis), consider echocardiogram (if concern about PFO/ASD). ↑Inflammatory markers especially IL-6, also CRP/fibrinogen, predict poor outcome.

🗔 MANAGEMENT

Admit to stroke unit. Consider imaging within one hour if patient fulfils NICE criteria,[Ref2] ie patient a candidate for thrombolysis, on anticoagulants, has a bleeding tendency, GCS <13, fluctuating symptoms, fever, papilloedema, severe headache at onset of stroke symptoms. If patient does not fulfil these criteria, imaging within 24 hours. *Thrombolysis:* Alteplase given within specialised service. Indicated if acute ischaemic stroke, treatment within three hours of onset of symptoms, able to lower BP to 185/110mmHg. If patient does not fulfil guidelines for thrombolysis and has had acute ischaemic stroke without primary haemorrhage, they should receive clopidogrel as a first-line antiplatelet agent. If in AF (see *atrial fibrillation*), consider anticoagulation after two weeks of clopidogrel or equivalent. O₂ if sats

<95%. Monitor BM. Control BP acutely if hypertensive encephalopathy/nephropathy/aortic dissection/coronary event/cardiac failure/pregnancy complication/cerebral bleed with systolic BP >200mmHg/planning thrombolysis to ≤185/110mmHg. Consider surgery if cerebral haemorrhage and hydrocephalus/MCA infarction and patient <60 years. Commence statins after 48 hours. Secondary prevention. SALT assessment. Nutrition/fluid management. Early mobilisation. Neurophysiotherapy. OT assessment. Counselling. *Carotid artery stenosis:* endarterectomy is associated with higher periprocedural MI but lower incidence of CVA than stent.

Cervical cancer and CIN

 CLINICAL NOTES

Epidemiology: 2,800 cases per year (UK), 1,000 cancer deaths per year (UK). Second most common female cancer under the age of 35 years. Screening (England) – age 25-49 every three years, 50-64 every five years. Invasive disease rare <25 years, borderline smears common <25 years but usually normal at colposcopy, controversial not to smear from 20 years. Screening from 20 years in Scotland, Wales, N Ireland. *Types:* 85% SCC, 15% adenocarcinoma. **Aetiology/risk factors:** Persistent HPV infection (types 16, 18, 31, 33, 35) present in 99% squamous cancers, smoking, young age at first intercourse (if <20 years, x2 risk compared with first intercourse >20 years of age), multiple sexual partners, immunosuppression. **Clinical features:** Most asymptomatic, postcoital bleeding (PCB), intermenstrual bleeding (IMB), dyspareunia, vaginal discharge, pelvic pain, pelvic mass. **Complications:** Vesicovaginal/colovaginal fistulae, metastases, death.

⅃ **INVESTIGATIONS**

Smear: Risk of false negatives – up to 50% for CIN 1. 60% of mild dyskaryosis will return to normal. 1.5% of smears show moderate/severe dyskaryosis, 0.1% suggest invasive disease. Colposcopy/biopsy, staging – MRI, CT (abdomen and chest), PET-CT (early stage/nodal disease.

🗔 MANAGEMENT

Prevention with barrier contraception and vaccination (bivalent HPV vaccine– covers HPV 16, 18; quadrivalent HPV vaccine covers HPV 6, 11, 16, 18). At seven months, antibody titres: bivalent HPV vaccine > quadrivalent HPV vaccine. Bivalent HPV vaccine response: age 15-25 years>26-55 years. Three-dose vaccination programme (0, one month, six months). Vaccinations prevent 90% new HPV infections. *CIN:* Diathermy, cryocautery, laser ablation for lower-grade CIN. Large loop excision of transformation zone (LLETZ), laser, knife cone biopsy for higher grades. More frequent smears post-treatment required before routine recall. *Cancer:* Surgery – hysterectomy +/–node dissection, radial trachelectomy plus node dissection to maintain fertility, pelvic exenteration. Non-surgical – adjuvant chemoradiotherapy, brachytherapy.

Cervical ectropion (erosion)

 CLINICAL NOTES
Endocervical cells present on outer surface of cervix. Aetiology/risk factors: Pregnancy, hormonal contraception. Clinical features: Asymptomatic, PCB, IMB, vaginal discharge.

 INVESTIGATIONS
Cervical smear.

MANAGEMENT
Reassurance. May need cautery if persistent discharge or IMB.

Cervical intraepithelial neoplasia (CIN)

 CLINICAL NOTES
See *cervical cancer and CIN*

Cervical myelopathy

CLINICAL NOTES
Cervical spine canal stenosis. Epidemiology: Middle aged/elderly. Aetiology/risk factors: Cervical spondylosis, cervical disc prolapse, trauma, tumour. Clinical features: Reduced ROM in neck, progressive limb weakness, bowel and bladder disturbance, restricted neck movements. UMN signs lower limbs – spasticity, exaggerated reflexes, upgoing plantars, clonus; sensory deficit, loss of joint position sense. LMN signs upper limbs – wasting, reduced reflexes, inversion of biceps reflex (absent biceps jerk but finger flexion occurs); inversion of supinator reflex (absent supinator jerk but finger flexion occurs), numbness. Lhermitte's sign.

INVESTIGATIONS
MRI, CT, myelogram nerve conduction studies. Investigate according to suspected underlying cause.

MANAGEMENT
Analgesia, muscle relaxants, neck collar, amitriptyline, gabapentin, cervical injection, surgery.

Charcot-Marie-Tooth disease

 CLINICAL NOTES
Hereditary motor and sensory neuropathy. Aetiology/risk factors: Familial. AD/AR and X-linked forms exist. 4 x 10^5 prevalence. Number of type and subtypes. Clinical features: Type 1: Demyelinating, onset <10 years, difficulty mobilising, falls, sensorimotor neuropathy starts distally in lower limbs, slowly progressive, may progress to upper limbs, weakness, altered sensation/numbness, pes cavus, kyphoscoliosis, distal leg wasting causes inverted champagne bottle deformity, ↓reflexes, foot drop, wasting small muscles of hands, palpable peripheral nerves, respiratory muscle weakness, cerebellar ataxia (upper limbs). *Type 2:* Axonal neuropathy, teens/early adulthood, less wasting/weakness than type 1. Other forms: *Type 2D* (affects mainly upper limbs). *Type 3* eg Dejerine-Sottas disease, segmental demyelination. *Type 4* eg Refsum's disease – retinitis pigmentosa, peripheral neuropathy, cerebellar syndrome, X-linked. Complications: Skin injury, perinatal complications, dilated cardiomyopathy, ankle deformity.

 INVESTIGATIONS
Nerve conduction studies, echocardiogram.

MANAGEMENT
Support, education, mobility aids, physiotherapy, osteotomy.

CHARGE syndrome

CLINICAL NOTES
See *choanal atresia*

Chediak-Higashi disease

CLINICAL NOTES
See *immunodeficiency (primary)*

Chiari malformation

CLINICAL NOTES
Cerebellar herniation through foramen magnum. Epidemiology: F>M. At least one in 1,000 births. Aetiology/risk factors: Idiopathic, genetic, tumour, infection, trauma. Clinical features: *Type I:* Often asymptomatic. No brainstem involvement. *Type II:* Arnold-Chiari malformation – some brainstem herniation occurs. Usually in association with neural tube defects, eg myelomeningocoele, may cause paralysis. *Type III:* Most severe form. May be in association with an encephalocoele. Other symptoms: Vertigo, headache, sensory, motor and visual disturbance, altered coordination. Complications: Pain, depression, feeding and swallowing difficulties, hydrocephalus, scoliosis, tethered cord, syringomyelia.

INVESTIGATIONS
CT/MRI.

MANAGEMENT
May not require treatment, pain control, OT, physiotherapy, family support, neurosurgery, VP shunt.

Chickenpox (varicella zoster)

 CLINICAL NOTES
Epidemiology: Peak prevalence age two to 10 years.

Aetiology/risk factors: Varicella zoster primary infection, incubation nine to 23 days. Infectious from two days before vesicles appear to crusting at about five days. **Clinical features:** Fever, malaise, vesicles, pustules, pruritus. Can affect mucous membranes of mouth and genital region. **Complications:** Ocular involvement, eg optic neuritis, secondary bacterial infection, postinflammatory scarring, hypo/hyperpigmentation, meningitis, encephalitis, ADEM, pneumonitis (smokers x15 risk), hepatitis, reactivation as shingles, repeated chickenpox infection (unusual), fatal if immunocompromised, pregnancy (if maternal infection <20 weeks' gestation with no previous exposure to varicella, 2% risk of fetal varicella syndrome – ocular, CNS, limb defects).

INVESTIGATIONS
No specific tests. Diagnosis on history and clinical appearance.

MANAGEMENT
Antipyretics, antihistamines, calamine lotion, consider aciclovir, vaccination for susceptible groups, immunoglobulin (VZIG) post-exposure (within 10 days) for susceptible groups.

Child abuse

CLINICAL NOTES
Epidemiology: Common. Underdetected. **Aetiology/risk factors:** Multifactorial (abusers previously experienced abuse), parental or child mental illness, poverty, children with physical disability, social isolation, parental drug/alcohol abuse. **Clinical features:** Physical non accidental injury (NAI), sexual abuse, emotional abuse, neglect. Frozen watchfulness, unusual pattern of bruising/burn, bite marks, cigarette burns, retinal haemorrhages, unexplained injuries, genital injuries, multiple attendances to doctor, failure to seek medical advice during illness or overprotection, Munchausen by proxy, delayed presentation, inconsistent explanation of injury (eg baby who is too young to roll over), easily attached to strangers, aggression, thin/malnourished, dirty, school non-attendance, failure to thrive, eating disorders, inappropriate sexual language or play, STI/vaginal discharge, UTI, genital injury, rectal bleeding/injury, self-harm, forensic misdemeanours, alcohol/drug abuse.

MANAGEMENT
Any health professional suspecting NAI needs to take responsibility and act accordingly. Early intervention of social services or police, detailed documentation by experienced paediatrician.

Chlamydia

CLINICAL NOTES
See *sexually transmitted infections and genital infections*

Choanal atresia

CLINICAL NOTES
Epidemiology: One in 10^4, F>M. **Aetiology/risk factors:** Idiopathic, twin births, chromosomal diseases, CHARGE syndrome (coloboma, heart defects, atresia of choanae, retarded growth, genitourinary defects, ear defects). **Clinical features:** Unilateral atresia more common and occurs more commonly on right side. May be asymptomatic if unilateral. Bilateral disease – feeding and breathing difficulties after birth, may present with respiratory distress. **Complications:** Cyanosis, death.

INVESTIGATIONS
Fibreoptic endoscope, tympanometer.

MANAGEMENT
Emergency management if required, consider surgery (emergency or elective).

Cholangiocarcinoma

CLINICAL NOTES
Epidemiology: 2 x 10^5 per year. Peak around 65 years. **Aetiology/risk factors:** Japanese, Israelis, southeast Asians, choledochal cysts, primary sclerosing cholangitis (eg in ulcerative colitis), liver flukes (high in Asian countries), chronic biliary irritation, eg intraductal stones; chronic typhoid infection. **Clinical features:** Obstructive jaundice, pruritus, RUQ pain, RUQ mass, hepatomegaly, cachexia, weight loss, fatigue, malaise. **Complications:** Cholangitis, cholecystitis, empyema.

INVESTIGATIONS
FBC, LFT (obstructive picture), ↑PT, ↑Ca 19.9. USS, CT, magnetic resonance cholangiopancreatography (MRCP), ERCP.

MANAGEMENT
Resection +/–hepatic resection/transplant. Chemotherapy. EGFR1 and EGFR1/HER2 inhibitors. Radiotherapy. Palliative stent/drainage. Survival 1-1.5 years.

Cholangitis

CLINICAL NOTES
Aetiology/risk factors: Primary biliary cirrhosis, sclerosing cholangitis, gallstones, ERCP, biliary stricture, malignancy (eg cholangiocarcinoma, pancreas, liver, metastases), common bile duct diverticulum, parasitic infection, AIDS. **Clinical features:** RUQ pain and tenderness, fever, dark stool, pale urine, jaundice. **Complications:** Sepsis, empyema, altered consciousness, respiratory failure, renal failure, DIC.

INVESTIGATIONS
Bilirubinuria, ↑ALP, ↑gamma GT, ↑WCC, clotting,

U&E, ↑amylase (one in three cases), blood cultures, USS, CT, ERCP, MRCP, biliary scintigraphy.

🖊 MANAGEMENT
Antibiotics, eg ciprofloxacin; may require IV antibiotics, fluids, biliary decompression if poor response to antibiotics, remove stones (ERCP), liver resection. Mortality may be as high as 40%.

Cholecystitis
📋 CLINICAL NOTES
See *gallstone disease*

Cholestasis of pregnancy
📋 CLINICAL NOTES
Epidemiology: 1% pregnancies. Usually third trimester. 70% recurrence rate. Clinical features: Pruritus, abdominal pain, malaise. Complications: Steatorrhoea with fat-soluble vitamin deficiency, intrauterine death controversial.

⚕ INVESTIGATIONS
↑LFT, ↑gamma GT, ↑AT-III, ↑bile acids (may be normal), USS.

🖊 MANAGEMENT
Ursodeoxycholic acid, cholestyramine (for pruritus, no improvement in steatorrhoea/LFT), consider parenteral vitamin K, deliver <38 weeks. Avoid COC postpartum.

Chondromalacia patellae
📋 CLINICAL NOTES
Softening of patella cartilage. Epidemiology: F>M. Teenage years and >5th decade. Aetiology/risk factors: Trauma, excessive sports, knee malalignment, flat feet, OA, previous patella dislocation. Clinical features: Anterior knee pain and crepitus when exercising, squatting, using stairs, eg with combined pressure/ movement of patella; tender patella borders, genu valgum. Complications: Effusion, OA in older age groups.

⚕ INVESTIGATIONS
X-ray, MRI, arthroscopy.

🖊 MANAGEMENT
Stop provoking activities, rest, analgesia, physiotherapy, strapping, orthotics, surgery.

Choriocarcinoma
See also
— *Molar pregnancy (hydatidiform mole)*

📋 CLINICAL NOTES
Form of gestational trophoblastic disease.

Epidemiology: Rare. Aetiology/risk factors: History of molar pregnancy (10% malignant), Asians, women <16 years and >40 years. Clinical features: Irregular vaginal bleeding, abdominal mass, weight loss. Complications: Metastases (lung, brain, GI tract), risk of recurrence in subsequent pregnancies.

⚕ INVESTIGATIONS
FBC, ↑HCG (diagnosis, prognosis, monitoring), CT (abdominal, pulmonary, brain), CSF for staging.

🖊 MANAGEMENT
Evacuation of any retained products of conception (ERPC). Chemotherapy – high-dose methotrexate. If methotrexate-resistant or high-risk, etoposide, dactinomycin, cisplatin or other agents may be used, in isolation or combination. In high-risk patients, consider hysterectomy, radiotherapy. Overall cure rate 98% depending on stage. Patients should not attempt to conceive until 12 months after chemotherapy or on advice from specialist. Avoid hormonal contraception until HCG levels normalised. Avoid IUD until periods normalised. Life-long follow-up.

Chorioretinitis
📋 CLINICAL NOTES
Inflammation of uveal eye structures including choroid and retina. Epidemiology: Rare. Aetiology/risk factors: Usually infective, eg acquired or congenital CMV, toxoplasmosis, HIV, rubella, cat-scratch disease, HSV, toxocara, Lyme disease, TB, fungal; sarcoid, Behçet's disease, DM. Clinical features: Squint, photophobia, floaters, visual disturbance, retinal pigmentation and scarring. Complications: Blindness.

⚕ INVESTIGATIONS
Investigate according to suspected underlying cause.

🖊 MANAGEMENT
Treat underlying cause.

Christmas disease
📋 CLINICAL NOTES
Factor IX deficiency. Aetiology/risk factors: X-linked, mutation. Clinical features: Haemarthrosis, haematomas. Complications: Arthropathy, compartment syndrome, nerve compression.

⚕ INVESTIGATIONS
↑APTT, ↓factor IX.

🖊 MANAGEMENT
Vaccinations (hepatitis B), oral hygiene, avoid IM injections when possible, tranexamic acid (for wounds, avoid in internal bleeding), desmopressin, concentrated clotting factor for significant haemorrhage.

Chronic daily headache

📖 **CLINICAL NOTES**

Aetiology/risk factors: Overuse of analgesia or caffeine, poor sleep hygiene, affective disorders, dehydration, number of subtypes including tension headache, new daily persistent headache, chronic migraine/cluster headache and hemicrania continua. **Clinical features:** Headache 15 or more days per month for at least three months in the absence of another underlying condition. Tension headaches cause pain on both sides of head, like a band around head. New daily persistent headaches are like tension headaches, except continuing. Migraine occurs more in women and cluster headaches, in men. **Complications:** Neuroses and affective disorders.

🔎 **INVESTIGATIONS**

Investigate to exclude secondary causes of headache, eg MRI.

💊 **MANAGEMENT**

Lifestyle advice, maintain hydration, stop regular analgesia, consider beta-blockers, antidepressants, antiepileptics, eg topiramate.

Chronic granulomatous disease

📖 **CLINICAL NOTES**

See *immunodeficiency (primary)*

Chronic inflammatory demyelinating polyradiculopathy (CIDP)

See also
— *Guillain-Barré syndrome*

📖 **CLINICAL NOTES**

Epidemiology: About three in 10^6 prevalence. Peak age 60-70 years. **Aetiology/risk factors:** HLA predisposition, idiopathic, SLE, HIV, hepatitis, paraproteinaemias. **Clinical features:** Symmetrical predominantly motor neuropathy. Proximal and distal muscle weakness. Reduced deep tendon reflexes. May be progressive, relapse and remit, or resolve. **Complications:** Cranial nerve involvement, autonomic neuropathy, sensory involvement including proprioceptive loss, ataxia, neuropathic pain.

🔎 **INVESTIGATIONS**

↑CSF protein, MRI with contrast. EMG. Investigate according to suspected underlying cause.

💊 **MANAGEMENT**

Treat underlying cause. OT, physiotherapy, immunosuppression, plasmapheresis. Immunoglobulin. Analgesia, antidepressants, anticonvulsants for neuropathic pain.

Chronic kidney disease (CKD) [Refs3,4]

See also
— *Kidney (renal) failure, acute*

📖 **CLINICAL NOTES**

Aetiology/risk factors: Acute kidney injury, hypertension, DM, infection, renal artery stenosis, renal tubular acidosis, interstitial nephritis, renal papillary necrosis (NSAIDs, sickle cell disease, DM, TB infection, gout), glomerulonephritis, SLE, myeloma, iatrogenic, PCKD, medullary sponge kidney, obstructive kidney disease. **Clinical features:** Asymptomatic, often found on routine screening, nausea, oedema, half and half nails. **Complications:** Renal osteodystrophy, renal anaemia (consider other causes of anaemia if eGFR ≥60), pericarditis, peripheral neuropathy, hyperkalaemia, endstage renal failure. Proteinuria increases risk of cardiovascular disease, progression to renal failure and death, and is an adverse prognostic indicator irrespective of CKD stage.

🔎 **INVESTIGATIONS**

FBC, ↓lymphocytes, burr cells, acanthocytes,U&E, eGFR ml/min/1.73m². If new reduction in eGFR to <60, repeat eGFR within two weeks to exclude acute renal failure (ARF) suggested by >25% drop in eGFR. Correct eGFR x 1.2 if African/African-Carribean. *Stage 1:* eGFR ≥90 and other evidence of renal disease present, eg abnormal examination, structurally abnormal kidneys, known genetic renal disease or proteinuria or haematuria. *Stage 2:* eGFR 60-89 and other evidence of renal disease. *Stage 3a:* eGFR 45-59 irrespective of other evidence of renal disease. *Stage 3b:* eGFR 30-44 irrespective of other evidence of renal disease. *Stage 4:* eGFR 15-29 irrespective of other evidence of renal disease. *Stage 5:* eGFR <15 irrespective of other evidence of renal disease. ACR – first pass urine required; CKDp denotes CKD with proteinuria. Proteinuria abnormal if ACR >30mg/mmol if non-diabetic; diabetic, >2.5 in men, >3.5 in women. Haematuria – use urinalysis sticks in preference to microscopy, blood on two out of three samples implies +ve result (if no proteinuria). Consider uric acid, PSA. If CKD stage 4/5, for Ca^{2+}, PO_4^{3-} and consider PTH and Mg^{2+}. If CKD stage 3B/4/5, for Hb. Renal USS, nuclear medicine for renal functional drainage, MRI, CT.

💊 **MANAGEMENT**

Stages 1 and 2: Check creatinine, eGFR, urinary protein (ACR), BP and cardiovascular risk every 12 months. Seek advice if fall in eGFR 5ml/min/year or 10ml/min in five years. Check BP and ACR; aim for maximum 140/90mmHg or maximum 130/80mmHg for patients with proteinuria (urinary ACR >30mg if not diabetic; seek advice if ACR >70mg). Investigate causes of haematuria if present. Manage cardiovascular risk factors and comorbidities. *Stage 3:* Initial assessment – seek advice if unwell or systemic disease with renal involvement. Assess for causes of reduced eGFR, eg infection, cardiac failure, obstructive nephropathy, NSAIDs, trimethoprim. Assess for haematuria and ACR (suggestive of progressive kidney disease). USS for structural anomalies. Continuing management (reassess six months after initial assessment, then annually); check eGFR, K⁺. Seek advice if fall in eGFR 5ml/min/year or 10ml/min in five years. Check Hb; renal anaemia unlikely unless at least stage 3B. Check BP and ACR; aim for maximum 140/90mmHg or maximum 130/80mmHg for patients with proteinuria (urinary ACR >30mg if not diabetic; seek advice if ACR >70mg). Manage cardiovascular risk factors and comorbidities. Immunisations. *Stages 4 and 5:* Initial assessment, usually discuss case with specialist. Assess for causes of reduced eGFR, eg infection, cardiac failure, obstructive nephropathy, NSAIDs, trimethoprim. Assess for haematuria and ACR (suggestive of progressive kidney disease). USS for structural anomalies. Check Hb, Ca^{2+}, PO_4^{3-}. Continuing management (reassess three-monthly); check Hb, eGFR, K⁺, Ca^{2+}, PO_4^{3-}, ACR and BP. Aim for maximum 140/90mmHg or maximum 130/80mmHg for patients with proteinuria (urinary ACR >30mg if not diabetic; seek advice if ACR >70mg). Manage cardiovascular risk factors and comorbidities. Immunisations. Seek nephrologist advice – stage 4/5, non-diabetics with ACR >70mg, ACR >30mg (and haematuria, declining eGFR 5ml/min/1.73m² per year, >10ml/min/1.73m² in five years, poorly controlled hypertension while on at least four drugs, genetic causes suspected, if diabetic and eGFR <30), Hb <11g/dl, abnormal Ca^{2+}, K+, PO_4^{3-}. Monitor K⁺ and eGFR one to two weeks after introducing/changing dose of ACE inhibitor/ARB. Do not start ACE inhibitor/ARB if K⁺ >5.0mmol/L. Stop ACE inhibitor/ARB if causes K⁺ to exceed 6.0mmol/L and other hyperkalaemic drugs have been stopped. Stop/reduce ACE inhibitor/ARB if eGFR falls ≥25% after excluding other causes, eg NSAIDS. Renal osteodystrophy – consider vitamin D replacement/osteoporosis prophylaxis and phosphate binders. Treat anaemia (adults Hb <11g/dl), maintain Hb 10.5-12.5g/dl with eg darbepoetin. Refer to urology if concerned about malignancy, urinary tract obstruction or stones.

Chronic liver disease

See also
 — *Liver failure*

📖 CLINICAL NOTES
Epidemiology: UK hospital admission rates for liver disease increasing. Aetiology/risk factors: Chronic alcohol abuse, viral hepatitis (hepatitis B, C), PBC, autoimmune liver disease, Wilson's disease, haemochromatosis, alpha-1 antitrypsin deficiency, steatohepatitis, iatrogenic, eg methotrexate, methyldopa, amiodarone, phenytoin, propylthiouracil; cardiac failure, galactosaemia. Clinical features: Finger clubbing, leuconychia, Dupuytren's contracture, palmar erythema, scratch marks (excoriation due to pruritus), spider naevi,

gynaecomastia, ↓secondary sexual hair, testicular atrophy, xanthelasma, hepatomegaly (not in cirrhosis). Complications: Liver failure (fatigue, anorexia, nausea, vomiting, poor memory, encephalopathy, oedema, hypoglycaemia, jaundice, coagulopathy), cirrhosis, portal hypertension (ascites, oesophageal varices, splenomegaly, caput medusae). Bacterial peritonitis, hepatorenal syndrome, hepatopulmonary syndrome, ischaemic bowel, hepatocellular cancer, cardiomyopathy, death.

⚕ INVESTIGATIONS
FBC, target cells, stomatocytes, acanthocytes, ↑MCV, U&E, LFT (↑transaminases in hepatocyte damage, ↓albumin), ↑PT, ↓Na⁺, ↑aldosterone, ↑ACE, USS, CT/MRI, chest X-ray (pleural effusions). Investigate according to suspected underlying cause, eg ferritin, autoimmune screen, hepatitis screen, glucose, ceruloplasmin, alpha-1 antitrypsin assay, liver biopsy.

💊 MANAGEMENT
Treat underlying cause, lifestyle management, monitor for hepatocellular cancer, nutrition, spironolactone, treat liver failure in specialist unit, liver transplantation.

Chronic lymphocytic leukaemia (CLL)

📖 CLINICAL NOTES
Epidemiology: More common >65 years. M>F. Aetiology/risk factors: Trisomy 12, deletion of chromosome 13q14 (prognostically adverse). Clinical features: Asymptomatic (25%), fatigue, painless mobile lymphadenopathy, splenomegaly, recurrent infection, eg shingles. Complications: Immunodeficiency, sepsis, haemorrhage, haemolysis, marrow infiltration, transformation to aggressive undifferentiated form (Richter's syndrome).

⚕ INVESTIGATIONS
↓platelet, →/↓Hb, lymphocytosis usually 10-100 x 10⁹/L but may be considerably higher, or lower; smear cells on film, macroglobulinaemia, beta₂ microglobulin, consider node biopsy.

💊 MANAGEMENT
Watch and wait, monitor for bulky lymphadenopathy, constitutional symptoms. Chemotherapy, eg fludarabine. Radiotherapy, eg for painful splenomegaly; splenectomy, immunoglobulin if recurrent infections, may require prophylactic antibiotics, vaccinations.

Chronic myeloid leukaemia (CML)

📖 CLINICAL NOTES
Myeloproliferative disease. Epidemiology: One to two in 10⁵ per year. Aetiology/risk factors: 95% Philadelphia chromosome (9:22 translocation). Clinical

features: Asymptomatic in early stages (50%), fatigue, weight loss, abdominal distension, excess bleeding. **Complications:** Leucostasis 15% cases, tachycardia, tachypnoea, confusion, visual loss (retinal vein occlusion, papilloedema), priapism, stroke, sideroblastic anaemia, transformation to acute leukaemia/blast crisis, death.

INVESTIGATIONS
Anaemia, WCC 25-1,000 x 10^9/L, ↑plts (may be low in hypersplenism, marrow failure, blast transformation), ↓leucocyte ALP, ↑uric acid, chromosomal analysis.

MANAGEMENT
Imatinib, interferon alfa may be used as alternative, cytarabine. Stem cell transplant. 87% reach remission.

Chronic myelomonocytic leukaemia (CMML)
See also
— *Myelodysplasia*

CLINICAL NOTES
Epidemiology: Rare. M>F. Mean age 65-75 years. **Aetiology/risk factors:** Advancing age, ionising radiation, iatrogenic, chromosome 7 abnormalities/trisomy 8 – poor prognostically. **Clinical features:** Fever, fatigue, weight loss, bruising, bleeding, urticaria, infections, splenomegaly (mild). **Complications:** 20% blast transformation to AML, death.

INVESTIGATIONS
↓Hb (poor prognosis), ↓plts, monocytosis, blasts in film (higher in CMML-2 than CMML-1), cytogenetic studies, LDH (↑confers poor prognosis), beta-2 microglobulin, CT (for organomegaly).

MANAGEMENT
Watch and wait, hydroxyurea, cytarabine, imatinib if PDGFR-beta/TEL translocation. Stem cell transplant.

Chronic necrotising pulmonary aspergillosis
See also
— *Allergic bronchopulmonary aspergillosis*
— *Aspergillosis (invasive)*
— *Aspergilloma (pulmonary)*

CLINICAL NOTES
Epidemiology: Rare. **Aetiology/risk factors:** ↑ in immunodeficiency, alcoholism, silicosis, aspergillus infection. **Clinical features:** Usually presents as resistant pneumonia, cough, fever, night sweats, weight loss. **Complications:** Cavitation, respiratory failure.

INVESTIGATIONS
FBC, sputum culture, chest X-ray, CT, lung biopsy.

MANAGEMENT
Treat underlying cause. Voriconazole superior to IV amphotericin. IV miconazole, ketoconazole less effective. Pulmonary support.

Chronic obstructive pulmonary disease (COPD)

CLINICAL NOTES
Epidemiology: Underdiagnosed, consider in those >35 years who are smokers. Fifth biggest cause of death worldwide. **Aetiology/risk factors:** Smoking, alpha-1 antitrypsin deficiency. **Clinical features:** SOB, chronic cough, wheeze, sputum production, winter exacerbations, pursed lip breathing, use of accessory respiratory muscles, hyperexpanded lungs, tracheal tug. *MRC dyspnoea score:* see page 239. **Complications:** Exacerbations (including infective, frequency correlates to mortality), pneumothorax, AF, cor pulmonale, bronchiectasis, polycythaemia, depression, death.

INVESTIGATIONS
Spirometry: FEV_1/FVC <0.7. Predicted FEV_1 mild: ≥80%, moderate 50-79%, severe 30-49%, very severe <30% (or FEV_1 <50% with respiratory failure). Rate of decline in FEV_1 correlates to mortality. Patient should be assessed for reversibility of airways obstruction with spirometry after beta-agonist or steroids (to exclude asthma). O_2 sats, chest X-ray. BODE (BMI, obstruction [FEV_1], dyspnoea score, exercise performance) is a mortality index.

MANAGEMENT
NICE:[Ref5] Education, self-management plans, regular review, promote good drug adherence and inhaler technique, smoking cessation, dietary advice, pulmonary rehabilitation. *Pharmacological:* First-line, commence short-acting beta-agonist (SABA) and/or anticholinergic (SAMA). Add in long-acting beta-agonist (LABA) or anticholinergic (LAMA) if SABA/SAMA not working or exacerbations and FEV_1 ≥50% predicted. If FEV_1 <50% predicted in patient in whom SABA/SAMA ineffective, or patient continues to have exacerbations, offer combination LABA plus ICS or LAMA. Use combination LABA plus ICS and LAMA in patients who remain symptomatic irrespective of FEV_1. Consider theophylline, non-invasive ventilation (NIV), long-term oxygen therapy (LTOT). Offer influenza (including swine flu) vaccination, consider pneumococcal vaccination. Consider mucolytics. Consider home nebulisers. May need anti-influenza drugs. Palliative care (MDT approach, opiates and benzodiazepines). *Exacerbations:* Prednisolone 30-40mg OD for seven to 14 days, consider reducing regimen of oral steroids, increase bronchodilators +/–via nebuliser, antibiotics if infective. Admit if severe SOB, confusion, cannot manage at home, comorbidities, worsening cor pulmonale, already on LTOT, low O_2 sats/acidosis/PaO_2 <7kPa, abnormal chest X-ray. Follow-up one week after discharge reduces readmission risk.

Chronic suppurative otitis media

CLINICAL NOTES

Epidemiology: Common. Aetiology/risk factors: URTI, recent use of antibiotics/incomplete course of antibiotics, immunodeficiency. Clinical features: More than four-week history of otorrhoea, central pars tensa perforation – benign; pars flaccida perforation may be suggestive of cholesteatoma; foul-smelling discharge, granulation tissue, conductive hearing loss. Complications: Labyrinthitis, mastoiditis, VIIth nerve paralysis, cholesteatoma, dural abscess, cerebral abscess, meningitis, cavernous sinus thrombosis.

INVESTIGATIONS

Swabs not generally recommended, audiometry, imaging to exclude complications.

MANAGEMENT

Keep ear dry. If discharging, consider antibiotics. Referral to ENT if persistent aural discharge or perforation, for aural toilet, tympanoplasty or management of complications, eg surgery for cholesteatoma.

Cirrhosis

CLINICAL NOTES

See *chronic liver disease*

Cleft lip/palate

CLINICAL NOTES

Epidemiology: About one in 1,000 live births. Aetiology/risk factors: Idiopathic, family history, trisomies, Pierre Robin syndrome, maternal drugs (eg antiepileptics), maternal infection (eg rubella). Complications: Bilateral, extensive, otitis media, LRTI, feeding difficulties, maternal bonding difficulties, cosmetic.

INVESTIGATIONS

CT/MRI.

MANAGEMENT

Special teats, dental plate can be fitted early to aid breast-feeding, *Surgery:* Repair lip by six months and palate by 12 months. SALT. Counselling.

Cleidocranial dysostosis

CLINICAL NOTES

Aetiology/risk factors: Autosomal dominant, *RUNX2* gene. Clinical features: Delayed closure of cranial sutures. Clavicle dysplasia, dental abnormalities. Complications: Permanent failure of suture closure, delayed shedding of milk teeth, delayed eruption of adult teeth, scoliosis, recurrent otitis media, recurrent sinus infections, developmental delay.

INVESTIGATIONS

Genetic testing, prenatal diagnosis, X-ray, CT, MRI.

MANAGEMENT

Dental involvement, OT, SALT, physiotherapy, orthopaedic surgery, osteoporosis prophylaxis.

C difficile

CLINICAL NOTES

Epidemiology: Leading healthcare-related cause of death in developed world. >5 x 10^4 cases per year (UK). Aetiology/risk factors: ↑with antibiotic use (especially broad-spectrum cephalosporins), long hospital stay, immunodeficiency, institutions (eg nursing home), PPI, IBD. Clinical features: Asymptomatic, diarrhoea. Complications: Colitis, megacolon, sepsis, shock, death.

INVESTIGATIONS

FBC, ESR, lactate, U&E, LFT, clotting. *C difficile* toxin in stool sample (sensitivity 63-99%), stool culture (sensitivity 89-100%). X-ray, thickened bowel wall, dilation. CT abdomen. Colonoscopy – pseudomembranes.

MANAGEMENT

Assess severity: *Mild:* ≤3 (Bristol stool chart 5-7) stool/day, normal WCC. *Moderate:* three to five stool per day, ↑WCC <20 x 10^9/L. *Severe:* ↑WCC >20 x 10^9/L, fever >38.5°C, acute rise and worsening creatinine, acute colitis. *Complicated:* ↓BP, ileus (partial), severe disease on CT. *Life-threatening:* Toxic megacolon, complete ileus. Assess for severe colitis; high mortality (stool >6/24 hours and one or more of pulse >90, fever >37.8°C, Hb <10.5g/L, ESR >30mm/hour). *Assess for risk of fulminant disease:* WCC >16 x 10^9/L at start of treatment and increasing WCC, and presence of IBD, immunodeficiency, surgery within one month, Ig therapy with one month, malignancy, infection with ribotype 027(NAP1). Fluid resuscitation. Stop causative antibiotic. Oral/IV metronidazole and/or vancomycin depending on severity. Monoclonal antibodies against *C difficile* toxins A and B have been advocated. Consider early colectomy with megacolon or fulminant colitis.

Club foot (talipes equinovarus)

CLINICAL NOTES

Epidemiology: One in 1,000 live births. Aetiology/risk factors: M>F. One in 30 siblings will be affected. Associated with spina bifida and muscular dystrophy. Clinical features: Foot in extension with varus deformity, 50% bilateral compared with talipes calcaneovalgus (foot pointing up with valgus deformity).

INVESTIGATIONS

Detected on routine antenatal screening or neonatal examination.

DISEASES

MANAGEMENT
Current best practice is casting and bracing (Ponseti method), rather than surgical treatment.

Cluster headache

CLINICAL NOTES
Epidemiology: About one in 1,000 prevalence. Aetiology/risk factors: M>F. smoking, exertion, hot weather. Clinical features: Unilateral headaches occur several times a day for weeks at a time. Headaches come on without warning, are very severe and usually last less than an hour. Clusters of headaches may occur every few months to years. Eyes normally water and become red during attacks. Nasal congestion may occur. Complications: Depression, anxiety, self-harm.

INVESTIGATIONS
Consider CT/MRI.

MANAGEMENT
Prevention: Good sleep hygiene, reduce alcohol, smoking cessation advice. Pizotifen, verapamil, lithium, topiramate, occipital nerve and deep brain stimulation. Treatment: Triptans. Octreotide, 100% O_2.

Coarctation of the aorta

CLINICAL NOTES
Epidemiology: 5-10% of congenital heart disease lesions. M>F (non-complex: isolated or associated with VSD, left ventricular outflow tract obstruction or aortopulmonary window), M=F (associated with complex lesions: double outlet right ventricle or truncus arteriosus). ↑ in chromosomal conditions, eg Turner's syndrome (may be multiple coarctations). About 50% of patients have biscupid aortic valve. Associated with Circle of Willis aneurysms. Rarely, aortic arch completely interrupted. Clinical features: Depend on a number of factors, including associated lesions, site, length and severity of coarctation. Asymptomatic, hypertension, cold lower limbs, radiofemoral delay, radioradial delay, systolic murmur upper chest/back, collateral artery bruits (eg thoracic arteries). Symptoms in infants with proximal lesions (proximal to ductus arteriosus) will manifest when ductus closes – poor feeding, tachypnoea, lethargy. Complications: Renal hypoperfusion and hypertension (hypertension can occur after repair), aortic dissection, cardiac failure in proximal lesions, death.

INVESTIGATIONS
ECG – LVH. Chest X-ray – post-stenotic dilation, rib notching. Echocardiogram, CT, magnetic resonance angiogram (MRA). Cardiac catheterisation.

MANAGEMENT
Medical – prostaglandin E1 to maintain patency of ductus in neonates who have a duct-dependent circulation. ACE inhibitors, dilation, surgical (including flaps, end-to-end anastamosis, graft).

Coeliac disease

CLINICAL NOTES
Epidemiology: Thought to be underdiagnosed. 0.1-0.2% UK prevalence. ↑Western Ireland (up to one in 200-300). Aetiology/risk factors: Familial, HLA DQ2 and DQ8. Clinical features: Symptoms present after weaning, chronic/intermittent diarrhoea, steatorrhoea, persistent nausea/vomiting, fatigue, failure to thrive, weight loss, oral aphthous ulcers, angular stomatitis, amenorrhoea. Complications: Anaemia, dermatitis herpetiformis, ulcerative jejunitis, GI lymphoma (in untreated coeliac disease), GI cancer, osteoporosis, osteomalacia, hyposplenism, infertility, cerebellar calcification, neuropathy, atopy. Associated with autoimmune diseases, depression, anxiety.

INVESTIGATIONS
Anaemia (iron/folate/B_{12} deficiency), ring sideroblasts, anti-TTG antibodies, anti-endomysial antibodies, anti-reticulin antibodies (low specificity), IgA quantification, ↑lipase, duodenal/jejunal biopsy.

MANAGEMENT
Education. Avoid gluten, eg wheat, rye, barley. Replace iron, vitamin B_{12}, folate, Ca^{2+} if required. Regular followup. Pneumococcal vaccination. Dapsone for dermatitis herpetiformis.

Colic (infantile)

CLINICAL NOTES
Epidemiology: Common. Aetiology/risk factors: Unknown, may be related to cow's milk protein or lactose intolerance, parental anxiety. Clinical features: Crying (three hours or more per day for three days or more per week, often afternoon/evening, inconsolable), drawing up legs.

MANAGEMENT
Reassurance that most settle by around three months, soya formula, herbal tea and hypo-allergenic diet may be helpful, simethicone not recommended, consider lactase in feeds.

Colorectal cancer

CLINICAL NOTES
Epidemiology: Third most common cancer in UK. Majority adenocarcinoma, rarely squamous cell. Aetiology/risk factors: Advancing age, M>F, affected first-degree relatives, obesity, smoking, reduced circulating 25-hydroxy(OH) vitamin D, IBD, acromegaly, poor diet (eg red meat); genetic – FPC/HNPCC, associated with endometrial cancer. Aspirin protective. Clinical features: Left-sided tumours more common than

right-sided. Colonic tumours more common than rectal tumours. Asymptomatic, fatigue, weight loss, abdominal pain, change in bowel habit, per rectal bleeding, tenesmus, abdominal mass, rectal mass. Complications: Bowel obstruction, anaemia, fistulae, perforation, metastatic disease.

INVESTIGATIONS
Carcinoembryonic antigen (CEA) for prognosis and monitoring (not diagnosis, very undifferentiated tumours may not produce CEA), raised >5 microgram/L in 3% Dukes A, 25% Dukes B, 45% Dukes C, 65% Dukes D, sigmoidoscopy (but 5% of patients have tumours at more than one site, so whole bowel should be evaluated), colonoscopy, double contrast barium enema, CT pneumocolon. *Staging:* Chest X-ray, CT, PET-CT, MRI. *Monitoring:* CT, MRI, PET-CT.

💊 MANAGEMENT
Screening, surgery may be used in all stages, chemotherapy – 5FU, irinotecan, oxaliplatin for locally advanced/metastatic disease. Anti-EGFR cetuximab and anti-VEGF bevacizumab improve survival. Neoadjuvant radiotherapy more effective than adjuvant. Regular review. Palliation.

Common cold

📋 CLINICAL NOTES
Epidemiology: Common. Aetiology/risk factors: Viral, eg rhinovirus. Clinical features: Fever, coryza, sore throat, sneezing, malaise. Complications: Secondary bacterial infection (eg sinusitis, otitis media, LRTI), febrile convulsions.

INVESTIGATIONS
Nil.

💊 MANAGEMENT
Antipyretics for symptom control (note fever can enhance immune system and viral clearance), anti-inflammatories, decongestants.

Common peroneal nerve palsy

📋 CLINICAL NOTES
Aetiology/risk factors: Trauma (knee, fibular fracture), long-term immobility (eg coma), anorexia nervosa, tumour compression, neuropathy, iatrogenic (eg tight plaster cast), vasculitis, DM, leprosy, mono-neuritis multiplex. Clinical features: Trips and falls, difficulty walking upstairs, high-stepping gait, muscle atrophy, weak foot inversion/eversion, weak dorsiflexion (foot drop). If L5 root lesion, foot eversion remains intact and mild sensory loss dorsum of foot.

INVESTIGATIONS
X-ray, MRI, nerve conduction studies.

💊 MANAGEMENT
Treat underlying cause, physiotherapy, caliper/splints, steroid injection, surgery.

Common variable immunodeficiency

📋 CLINICAL NOTES
See *immunodeficiency (primary)*

Compartment syndrome

📋 CLINICAL NOTES
Epidemiology: Most commonly in lower limb. Aetiology/risk factors: Limb trauma, excessive exercise, tight plaster cast, burns, poorly sited IV drip, bites, haematoma/internal haemorrhage (anticoagulated patients at higher risk), nephrotic syndrome. Clinical features: Acute onset (eg less than two days after initial insult), severe pain, pins and needles, altered sensation, cool peripheries, poor/absent distal pulses, pallor. Complications: Necrosis, contractures (Volkmann's), nerve damage, infection, gangrene, amputation, renal failure, death.

INVESTIGATIONS
FBC, U&E (↑K⁺, ↓eGFR), ↑CK, clotting screen, compartment pressures should be measured with tonometer.

💊 MANAGEMENT
Treat underlying cause, fasciotomy, debride necrotic tissue.

Congenital adrenal hyperplasia

📋 CLINICAL NOTES
Epidemiology: Rare. Aetiology/risk factors: Autosomal recessive, enzyme deficiencies (21-hydroxylase most common [90% cases], 11-hydroxylase, 3 beta-hdyroxysteroid dehydrogenase, 17-hydroxylase) causing excess androgens, hypocortisolaemia. Clinical features: Depends on metabolic error. *Males:* Failure to thrive, salt-losing crisis (vomiting, hyponatraemia, hyperkalaemia, dehydration, hypotension), ambiguous genitalia, clitoromegaly, precocious puberty, hypospadias, cryptorchidism, hypertension. *Females:* Ambiguous genitalia, precocious puberty, virilisation, amenorrhoea, infertility, hypertension, salt-losing crisis.

INVESTIGATIONS
↑ACTH, ↓Na⁺, ↑↓K⁺, ↓glucose, 21-hydroxylase deficiency (↑17-hydroxyprogesterone), 11-hydroxylase deficiency (↑11-dehyroxycortisol).

💊 MANAGEMENT
Salt-losing crisis needs hospitalisation, fluid and electrolyte management. Glucocorticoid replacement, mineralocorticoid replacement, GnRH analogues to suppress precocious puberty.

DISEASES

Congenital dislocation of the hip

 CLINICAL NOTES

See *developmental dysplasia of the hip (congenital subluxation/dislocation of the hip)*

Congenital hypothyroidism (cretinism)

See also
— *Pendred's syndrome*

 CLINICAL NOTES

Epidemiology: F>M. One in 3,500 live births (UK). **Aetiology/risk factors:** Thyroid gland agenesis, iatrogenic (eg radioiodine in pregnancy), pituitary failure, metabolic error. **Clinical features:** Presentation depends on severity – oedematous facies, tongue protrusion, low hairline, neonatal jaundice, hypotonia, constipation, excessive sleepiness, short stature, broad hands, large fontanelles, hoarse cry. **Complications:** If untreated – mental retardation, short stature, cardiac anomalies.

 INVESTIGATIONS

Routine neonatal screening: Guthrie test (most cases picked up before clinical features present). TFT, thyroid scintigraphy, long bone X-ray, detailed hearing test.

MANAGEMENT

Early treatment with thyroxine, regular TFT.

Congenital rubella

 CLINICAL NOTES

See *rubella (German measles)*

Conjunctivitis

 CLINICAL NOTES

Epidemiology: Common. **Aetiology/risk factors:** Higher risk with contact lenses; bacterial (*Strep pneumoniae, Staph aureus, Haemophilus influenzae, Moraxella catarrhalis*), ophthalmia neonatorum (chlamydia, gonorrhoea), viral, fungal, parasitic, allergic. **Clinical features:** Soreness (minimal pain), pruritus (especially with contact lenses and allergy), pus (may cause blurring of vision), conjunctival injection, normal acuity, bilateral suggestive of allergic conjunctivitis. **Complications:** Periorbital cellulitis, orbital abscess, otitis media, meningitis.

 INVESTIGATIONS

Swab if resistant or concerned about ophthalmia neonatorum.

MANAGEMENT

Refer if cannot exclude more serious cause of red eye or ophthalmia neonatorum. Most cases self-limiting (about 65%). Delayed topical antibiotics (eg chloramphenicol, fusidic acid, simple conjunctivitis may resolve after seven days irrespective of antibiotics). Avoid contact lenses.

Conn's disease/syndrome

 CLINICAL NOTES

See *hyperaldosteronism*

Constipation in children

 CLINICAL NOTES

Epidemiology: One in three children. **Aetiology/risk factors:** Idiopathic, poor fluid intake, stool holding, breastfeeding, coeliac disease, IBD, endocrinopathies, metabolic diseases, food allergy, CF, Hirschsprung's disease, cerebral palsy, lead poisoning. **Clinical features:** Fewer than three bowel movements per week, soiling, palpable stool, large stool, pain on defecation, overflow incontinence. **Complications:** Anal fissure, dilated rectum, soiling.

 INVESTIGATIONS

No investigations required for simple idiopathic constipation. Consider investigations for specific causes if red flags.

MANAGEMENT

Treat cause, laxatives (disimpaction plus maintenance doses, macrogol +/–stimulant or osmotic laxative), encourage fluid intake, star charts.

Constrictive pericarditis

 CLINICAL NOTES

Fibrous calcified pericardium. **Aetiology/risk factors:** Infections (bacterial, TB), haemopericardium, rheumatic heart disease, radiotherapy, post-traumatic. **Clinical features:** SOB, cough, fatigue, low volume pulse, pulsus paradoxus, tachycardia, Kussmaul's sign, raised JVP, impalpable apex (unlike restrictive cardiomyopathy), diastolic pericardial knock, quiet heart sounds, hepatomegaly, peripheral oedema, ascites. **Complications:** Arrhythmia, tamponade.

 INVESTIGATIONS

ECG – non-specific changes. Chest X-ray – normal cardiac size, venous congestion, pericardial calcification. Echocardiogram – restrictive ventricular filling. MRI, CT, cardiac catheterisation, pericardial biopsy.

MANAGEMENT

Treat underlying cause, pericardiectomy.

Contraception (combined oral contraceptive pill, COC)

 CLINICAL NOTES

COC containing ethinylestradiol. 93-99% efficient, user dependent (↓if eg missed pill, diarrhoea and

DISEASES

vomiting, enzyme-inducing drugs. Recent guidelines do not consider concomitant use of antibiotics as risk for COC failure). Contraindications (UKMEC 4): Less than six weeks postpartum and breastfeeding, history of CVD/VTE/trophoblastic disease, smoker >15 per day if >35 years, BP >160/95mmHg, BMI ≥40kg/m², hypertensive retinopathy, secondary Raynaud's with lupus anticoagulant, thrombophilia, migraine with aura, pulmonary hypertension, AF, cardiac valve disease, liver tumour, viral hepatitis, diabetic microvascular complications, diabetic vascular disease >20 years. Breast cancer. Stop if develops migraine +/–aura. Precautions (risk>benefit, UKMEC 3): Six weeks to six months postpartum and breastfeeding, less than three weeks postpartum, immobile, smoker <15 per day if >35 years. Epidemiology: Smoker if >35 years, BMI 35-39kg/m², BP 140-150/90-94mmHg, migraine if >35 years, if develops migraine <35 years, Ca breast (remission ≥5 years), breast cancer (*BRCA1*/*BRCA2*), risk factors for CVD, history cholestasis/COC induced cirrhosis, diabetic microvascular complications, diabetic vascular disease >20 years, familial hypercholesterolaemia, on enzyme inducers, family history VTE <45 years. Missed pill rules: See page 241. Breakthrough bleeding: Consider other causes of vaginal bleeding/ectopic/miscarriage/iatrogenic/OTC medication and remedies/poor COC absorption, eg bowel disease, cervical neoplasia/STI. Consider progestogen change or increasing ethinylestradiol dose. Tricycling (three-month pack) indications: Lifestyle, menorrhagia, dysmenorrhoea, endometriosis, headaches in pill-free week, poor adherence with monthly pill-free week.

MANAGEMENT

Consider alternative contraception if poor compliance, eg long-acting reversible contraception (LARC). *Breakthrough bleeding:* Change progesterone/ increase ethinylestradiol/use phasic pill. *Nausea/weight gain/breast enlargement:* Increase progesterone/decrease ethinylestradiol. *Vaginal dryness, depression, weight gain, hirsutism, acne, breast tenderness:* Decrease progesterone/increase ethinylestradiol/use COC with norgestimate, gestodene, desogestrel, drospirenone, co-cyprindiol.

Corneal abrasion

CLINICAL NOTES

Epidemiology: Common. Aetiology/risk factors: Trauma, foreign body, sicca syndrome, contact lenses, iatrogenic (eg anaesthetic, laser, tonometry). Clinical features: Pain, excessive tear production, blepharospasm. Complications: Conjunctivitis, keratitis, uveitis, corneal perforation.

INVESTIGATIONS

Fluoroscein examination (ideally with slit lamp).

MANAGEMENT

Heals in one to three days. Topical antibiotics, consider eye patch, refer if concerned about foreign body or failure to heal. Ensure all foreign bodies removed when using local anaesthetics to avoid further corneal damage. Lubrication.

Cortical venous thrombosis

See also
— *Cavernous sinus thrombosis*

CLINICAL NOTES

Aetiology/risk factors: Hypercoagulable states, thrombophilia, dehydration, hyperviscosity syndrome, oestrogens, pregnancy, infection, inflammatory diseases, eg IBD. Clinical features: nausea, vomiting, headache, neurological deficit. *Venous sinus thrombosis: lateral* (VIth/VIIth nerve palsy, field defect), *cavernous* (IIIth, IVth, Vth (1st, 2nd branches), VIth palsy, central retinal vein thrombosis, chemosis), *sigmoid* (cerebellar and lower brain stem syndrome), *inferior petrosal* (Vth, VIth palsy). Complications: Permanent neurological deficit (venous infarction) seizure.

INVESTIGATIONS

Exclude meningitis, CT (if NAD, for LP. Initial CT may be normal, LP may be normal or +ve for RBC/bilirubin), MR angiogram.

MANAGEMENT

Analgesia, consider antibiotics and anticoagulation.

Cow's milk protein intolerance

CLINICAL NOTES

Epidemiology: 2-7.5% prevalence. Aetiology/risk factors: Allergy to cow's milk protein. Can occur post-gastritis. Family history of atopy. Clinical features: Symptoms occur shortly after cow's milk exposure at about one year of age (or earlier through breast milk). Immediate or delayed hypersensitivity reactions. Dermatitis (atopic, contact), urticaria, diarrhoea, vomiting, constipation, rhinitis, wheezing. Complications: Angioedema, haematemesis, bloody diarrhoea/colitis, protein-losing enteropathy, failure to thrive, anaphylaxis.

INVESTIGATIONS

Consider skin test, RAST. If severe, FBC, U&E, LFT, bowel biopsy.

MANAGEMENT

If breastfed, cow's milk elimination diet for mother, (including no eggs), if improvement, slow introduction of cow's milk protein in maternal diet. If after reintroduction, symptoms recur, elimination diet and Ca²⁺ supplements. If no improvement with maternal elimination diet, consider other diagnoses. Extensively hydrolysed formula beyond breastfeeding and cow's milk free diet until about one year of age, continue this diet for six months. If formula fed, elimination diet (if no improvement with extensively hydrolysed formula, trial of amino acid based formula, also exclude peanut or soya).

Craniopharyngioma

 CLINICAL NOTES
Benign juxtapituitary brain tumour. Epidemiology: One in 10^5 incidence. Aetiology/risk factors: Idiopathic. Peaks – childhood and elderly. Clinical features: Tumours mainly arising from Rathke's pouch/craniopharyngeal duct. Most commonly supra or infrasellar. Locally invasive. Headaches, visual field defects (chiasmal pressure effects, bitemporal inferior quadrantanopia or hemianopia), pituitary endocrine dysfunction (eg poor growth in children, pubertal disturbance, hypothyroidism, diabetes insipidus, ↓gonadotrophins – amenorrhoea/impotence), pseudodementia, incontinence. Complications: Raised ICP, hydrocephalus, permanent neurological defect, life-long endocrinopathy.

⚕ **INVESTIGATIONS**
Skull X-ray (calcification up to 90% in children), CT, MRI, endocrine/pituitary function tests, formal visual field testing, psychiatric assessment.

🖰 **MANAGEMENT**
Surgical resection, high recurrence rate/mortality. Radiotherapy. Gamma knife radiosurgery. In situ chemotherapy. Endocrine replacement.

Craniosynostosis

See also
 — *Plagiocephaly (positional)*

📅 **CLINICAL NOTES**
Epidemiology: About one in 2,000 to 3,000. Aetiology/risk factors: M>F. Primary, secondary to underlying cerebral anomaly or syndrome, eg Crouzon syndrome. Clinical features: Premature neonatal skull suture closure (normally fuse by 24 months), skull malformation, eg flattening, microcephaly, premature fontanelle closure (normal – 90% close by seven to 19 months, average, 14 months), palpable ridged sutures. Subtypes: Sagittal synostosis (most common), coronal, metopic, lambdoid. Complications: Raised ICP, learning difficulties, permanent neurological deficit, skull deformity.

⚕ **INVESTIGATIONS**
CT/MRI.

🖰 **MANAGEMENT**
Surgery for significant cases.

CREST syndrome

📅 **CLINICAL NOTES**
See *limited systemic sclerosis (including CREST)*

Creutzfeld-Jakob disease (new variant) (nvCJD)

📅 **CLINICAL NOTES**
Epidemiology: Rare. Aetiology/risk factors: Contaminated beef, iatrogenic (eg contaminated grafts). Caused by prions. Clinical features: Presents with depression, dementia (rapid onset), anxiety, agitation, psychosis, limb pain, myoclonus, death.

⚕ **INVESTIGATIONS**
EEG (biphasic high amplitude sharp waves), tonsillar/brain biopsy, often postmortem diagnosis.

🖰 **MANAGEMENT**
Supportive.

Cri du chat syndrome

📅 **CLINICAL NOTES**
Epidemiology: Rare. Aetiology/risk factors: Partial deletion chromosome 5. Clinical features: High-pitched cat-like cry, mental retardation, hypertelorism, failure to thrive, microcephaly, cardiac abnormalities (ASD).

⚕ **INVESTIGATIONS**
Genetic testing.

🖰 **MANAGEMENT**
Genetic counselling, karyotype of both parents. Supportive.

Crigler-Najjar syndrome

📅 **CLINICAL NOTES**
Uridine-diphosphate glycosyltransferase deficiency. Epidemiology: Rare. Aetiology/risk factors: Congenital, mutation chromosome 2. Type 1 fatal without treatment. Type 2 (Arias syndrome) less severe. Clinical features: Neonatal jaundice (more severe in type 1). Complications: *Type 1:* Kernicterus (jaundice), hypotonia, oculomotor lesions, deafness, death. *Type 2:* 'Crises' during infection or drug-related.

⚕ **INVESTIGATIONS**
Isolated unconjugated hyperbilirubinaemia, enzyme assays, phenobarbital challenge, liver biopsy.

🖰 **MANAGEMENT**
Type 1: Phototherapy, plasma exchange, calcium phosphate, liver transplant. *Type 2:* No treatment, or phenobarbital.

Crohn's disease

See also
- *Ulcerative colitis*

 CLINICAL NOTES
Granulomatous inflammatory bowel disease. Epidemiology: About 40 in 100,000 (UK) prevalence. F>M. Peaks – young adults aged 15-35 years and elderly. Aetiology/risk factors: Multifactorial, genetic susceptibility, smoking, infective. Clinical features: May affect any part of gut from mouth to anus, transmural inflammation, skip lesions. Abdominal pain, diarrhoea, PR bleeding. Anal pain, abscess, tags, fissures. Fatigue, pallor, erythema nodosum, pyoderma gangrenosum, finger clubbing, Crohn's mass, mouth ulcers. Complications: Malabsorption including vitamin B_{12}/Fe^{2+} deficiency, fistulae (enteroenteral, -vaginal, -vesical, -cutaneous, -anal), bowel strictures, bowel obstruction, iritis, arthritis, colorectal cancer, abscesses, gallstones, depression.

 INVESTIGATIONS
$\downarrow$Hb, $\uparrow$ESR/CRP, $\downarrow$albumin, U&E, $\downarrow$$Mg^{2+}$, HLA B27 (associated with arthritis), $\uparrow$lipase, faecal calprotectin (correlates with disease activity), barium studies, colonoscopy, endoscopy and biopsy, video capsule endoscopy (if no stricture), white cell scan, abdominal X-rays if suspected toxic dilation, CT if suspected abscess or perforation, MRI if anorectal sepsis.

MANAGEMENT
Lifestyle advice, dietary advice, loperamide, codeine. Steroids for acute flare, reduce dose once improving, consider steroid maintenance (plus osteoporosis prophylaxis) or steroid-sparing agents eg 5-ASA drugs, azathioprine, methotrexate. Anti-TNF therapy, eg infliximab. Antibiotics for anal/active disease, eg metronidazole/ciprofloxacin. *Surgery:* Resection, pouch procedures. Regular follow-up. Treat complications accordingly. Urgent referral if bowel obstruction, abdominal dilation, severe pain/bleeding, generally unwell, accelerated weight loss, concern about cancer, complications, eg iritis, abscess, fistulae.

Croup (acute laryngotracheobronchitis)

CLINICAL NOTES
Epidemiology: Six months to three years, unusual above six years of age. Aetiology/risk factors: Viral (eg parainfluenza, adenovirus, RSV, rhinovirus, influenza, measles). Clinical features: Barking, seal-like cough, sore throat, runny nose, mild/moderate fever, inspiratory stridor, respiratory distress. Symptoms resolve after three days. Red flags: Stridor, severe intercostal recession, reduced air entry, central cyanosis, agitation or reduced consciousness.

 INVESTIGATIONS
Sats <95% are indicative of respiratory decompensation.

MANAGEMENT
Exclude epiglottitis (examination of oropharynx only by a specialist if epiglottitis suspected)/foreign body. *Symptomatic:* OTC medication, cool air (not steam), cool drinks, consider steroids, eg dexamethasone/ prednisolone. Single dose of oral dexamethasone (0.15mg per kg body weight). Nebulised adrenaline, intubation. Avoid sedative antitussives.

Crouzon syndrome (craniofacial dysostosis)

See also
- *Craniosynostosis*

CLINICAL NOTES
Epidemiology: Rare. Aetiology/risk factors: Autosomal dominant, *FGFR2* and *FGFR3* mutations. Clinical features: Craniosynostosis, exophthalmos, orbital hypertelorism, squint, blue sclera, relative prognathism, short upper lip, high arched palate, nasal obstruction, normal/sometimes reduced mental ability, +/–cleft palate. Complications: Raised ICP.

 INVESTIGATIONS
Skull X-ray, CT. Genetic testing.

MANAGEMENT
May require surgery, genetic counselling.

Cryptogenic fibrosing alveolitis

CLINICAL NOTES
See *idiopathic pulmonary fibrosis*

Cryptorchidism

CLINICAL NOTES
See *undescended testes (cryptorchidism)*

Cushing's syndrome

CLINICAL NOTES
Aetiology/risk factors: Cushing's 'disease' – rare (pituitary/hypothalamic ACTH secretion). Iatrogenic, eg steroids – common. Adrenal adenoma/carcinoma, paraneoplastic ACTH secretion, Carney complex, McCune-Albright syndrome. Clinical features: Fatigue, weight gain, bruising, hirsutism, irregular periods, erectile dysfunction, polyuria, polydypsia, depression, hypertension, centripetal obesity, interscapular fat pad, thin skin, striae, purpura, moon face, proximal myopathy. Complications: Osteoporosis, fractures, hyperglycaemia, benign intracranial hypertension.

DISEASES

INVESTIGATIONS

↑glucose, ↓K⁺, metabolic acidosis. ↑24-hour urinary cortisol and low-dose dexamethasone suppression tests to confirm diagnosis. Subsequent tests to establish cause – ACTH (low in adrenal disease, corticosteroid therapy, high in pituitary/ectopic production of ACTH including Cushing's disease). High-dose dexamethasone suppression test (suppression suggestive of Cushing's disease). Abdominal CT/MRI, nuclear medicine.

MANAGEMENT

Treat any underlying cause. Metyrapone, ketoconazole. Adrenal adenoma – surgery. Adrenal carcinoma – surgery, radiotherapy. Cushing's disease – pituitary surgery, bilateral adrenalectomy (risk of Nelson's syndrome – enlarging ACTH-secreting pituitary tumour, may require pituitary radiotherapy). Cushing's syndrome of unknown aetiology – bilateral adrenalectomy.

Cystic fibrosis (CF)

CLINICAL NOTES

Epidemiology: Prevalence one in 2,500 and one in 25 carrier frequency (Caucasians). Aetiology/risk factors: Autosomal recessive, chromosome 7. Several hundred mutations identified. Clinical features/ complications: Failure to thrive, low BMI, finger clubbing, nasal polyps, thick pulmonary secretions, multiple infections and colonisation, including pseudomonas and aspergillus; allergic bronchopulmonary aspergillosis, cyanosis, use of accessory muscles of respiration, coarse crepitations, bronchiectasis, haemoptysis, pneumothorax, pulmonary hypertension, cor pulmonale. GI – neonatal jaundice, meconium ileus, rectal prolapse, pseudo-Bartter's syndrome, pancreatic failure, malabsorption, bowel obstruction, cirrhosis and portal hypertension, gallstones, male infertility, epididymal cysts, osteoporosis, haemorrhagic disease of the newborn.

INVESTIGATIONS

Prenatal (CVS/amniocentesis) or neonatal screening, immunoreactive trypsin (heel prick test), sweat test, chest X-ray, CT, abdominal USS, sputum culture for infections, aspergillus precipitins, stool fat profile, spirometry, FBC, U&E, LFT, glucose, clotting studies, ↑lipase, growth and weight charts.

MANAGEMENT

MDT approach. Antibiotics may be used for infection or prophylaxis (azithromycin has anti-inflammatory effect and affects the biofilm of pseudomonas. Ciprofloxacin may still be effective against pseudomonas despite in vitro resistance); DNase, bronchodilators, pulmonary physiotherapy, embolisation for haemoptysis, lung/ heart-lung transplant, pancreatic supplements, vitamin supplements, high-calorie diet, ursodeoxycholic acid for poor biliary flow, diabetes treatment, salt replacement

in hot weather, assisted conception techniques, liver transplant, regular review, counselling, genetic counselling. Patients do not tend to live much beyond their forties.

Cystic hygroma (lymphangioma)

CLINICAL NOTES

Epidemiology: Most cases present by age two years. Aetiology/risk factors: Idiopathic, maternal alcoholism, associated with syndromes, including Turner's, Down's, Edward's, Patau. Clinical features: Progressively enlarging painless transluminable lymphatic mass; three out of four cases in head and neck, particularly posterior triangle of neck, one in five cases occur in axilla. Complications: Failure to advance in labour, obstructed labour, recurrence if lesion not completely resected, airways obstruction, infection, bleeding, local invasion.

INVESTIGATIONS

About 60% diagnosed antenatally by USS, ↑AFP and FSH studies. Postnatally, USS, CT, MRI, biopsy.

MANAGEMENT

Surgery, sclerotherapy, radiofrequency ablation, intralesional therapy, anti-VEGF therapy under evaluation.

Cystinosis

CLINICAL NOTES

Cystine transport disorder. Epidemiology: Rare. M>F. Aetiology/risk factors: Autosomal recessive. Clinical features: Presentation depends on subtype and severity. Infantile most severe. Polyuria, failure to thrive, vomiting. Complications: Fanconi syndrome, metabolic acidosis, blindness, DM, chronic liver disease, cerebral involvement, rickets, endocrinopathies. Symptoms may deteriorate during intercurrent illness.

INVESTIGATIONS

↑Leucocyte cystine. ↓pH, ↓eGFR, ↓K⁺, ↓Na⁺, ↓PO_4^{3-}, ↓bicarbonate. TFT, growth profile. Urine – amino aciduria, glucose, PO_4^{3-}. Renal USS. Cerebral CT/MRI. Retinal imaging.

MANAGEMENT

Dietary advice, phosphocysteamine, hydration, electrolyte replacement, vitamin D replacement, indometacin, growth hormone replacement, renal transplant.

Cystinuria

CLINICAL NOTES

Epidemiology: About one in 10^4. Aetiology/risk factors: Autosomal recessive. Clinical features: Renal stones, abdominal pain, haematuria, failure to thrive. Complications: UTI, CKD, malabsorption, growth retardation, blindness, myopathy, DM.

INVESTIGATIONS
Urinalysis (sodium cyanide-nitroprusside test), stone analysis, urine cystine capacity. USS, CT-KUB.

MANAGEMENT
Hyperhydration, urinary alkalinisation, D-penicillamine, alpha-MPG, or captopril, remove stones.

Deep vein thrombosis (DVT)

See also
— *Pulmonary embolus*

CLINICAL NOTES
Aetiology/risk factors: ↑risk with pregnancy/post-partum, COC, HRT, thrombophilia, antiphospholipid syndrome, intercurrent illness, malignant disease, pelvic mass, smoking, flying especially more than four hours, immobility, recent surgery/trauma, nephrotic syndrome (↓AT-III), obesity. A significant number of people with superficial vein thrombosis might also have a DVT. Clinical features: Pain, swelling, erythema, dilated superficial veins, warm and tender on palpation, +/- fever. Complications: Embolic disease (eg PE) especially with proximal DVT eg pelvic/thigh; recurrent DVT, post-thrombotic syndrome (oedema, circulatory insufficiency, poor wound healing, ulceration).

INVESTIGATIONS
AT-III. *D-dimer:* High NPV. Duplex USS (colour flow), venography. Wells score:[Ref6] One point each for active malignancy or within six months, history of DVT, recently bed-bound for more than three days/major surgery in past four weeks, calf swelling discrepancy >3cm, superficial collateral veins dilated (not varicose), whole leg swollen, tender along deep veins, pitting oedema more severe in index leg, paralysis/immobilised by plaster cast. Minus two points if alternative diagnosis plausible or more likely. Three or more points suggest high probability of DVT; one to two points, moderate probability; ≤0 low probability. Perform D-dimer if low probability of DVT. If high probability, +ve D-dimer, pregnant, IVDU, patient requires LMWH and imaging.

MANAGEMENT
Treat underlying risk factors. Treat if high clinical suspicion even if tests inconclusive. LMWH until fully warfarinised. Consider anti-embolic stockings – graduated TEDs for two weeks. Dabigatran (oral thrombin inhibitor) may be as good as warfarin in management of acute venous thromboembolic disease.

Delayed onset puberty

CLINICAL NOTES
Girls: Normal onset around 11 years with breast bud development, if delay >13 years, requires investigation.

Primary amenorrhoea by 15 years requires investigation. Boys: Testicles begin to enlarge by 12 years. Other pubertal characteristics occur at around 14 years. Investigation required if no pubertal signs by 14 years. Aetiology/risk factors: Systemic steroids. *Normal height plus true pubertal delay/primary amenorrhoea:* Reduced gonadotrophins (hypothalamic/pituitary diseases), eating disorders, Kallmann's syndrome (anosmia, colour blindness, midline defects), Klinefelter's syndrome. *Normal height with secondary amenorrhoea:* PCOS. *Normal/short stature plus delayed puberty/pubertal arrest:* Significant systemic disease, eg IBD, brain tumour, Turner's syndrome (requires urgent referral). *Short stature plus pubertal delay:* Constitutional; subtle pathology, eg coeliac disease. Complications: Low self-esteem, depression, anxiety.

INVESTIGATIONS
FBC, CRP, U&E, ALP, TSH, T_4, coeliac screen, FSH, LH, early morning oestradiol and testosterone (low detectable levels imply imminent puberty in girls/boys respectively) prolactin, chromosomal analysis, consider investigation for PCOS.

MANAGEMENT
Early signs of puberty with fast growth in girls/slow growth in boys likely to be normal. If normal history, examination and investigations, initially monitor at three and six months. Refer if growth/puberty mismatch or obvious cause on history, examination or investigation. Treat underlying causes if possible. *Boys:* Three to 12 months testosterone (oral or depot). *Girls:* Consider ethinylestradiol.

Delirium tremens

See also
— *Alcoholism*
— *Wernicke's encephalopathy*

CLINICAL NOTES
Aetiology/risk factors: Alcohol withdrawal in a physically dependent patient. Clinical features: Two to three days post alcohol withdrawal, often associated with trauma or infection. Agitation, insomnia, aggression, sympathetic overdrive, tachycardia, fever, visual hallucinations, tremor, delusions, confusion, pain. Complications: Arrhythmia, seizure, death (5%).

INVESTIGATIONS
FBC, U&E, LFT, glucose, ECG.

MANAGEMENT
Exclude other causes for delirium. IV fluids, benzodiazepines, high-dose B-complex vitamins/parenteral thiamine to prevent Wernicke's encephalopathy. Address alcohol addiction.

DISEASES

Depression

See also
— *Bipolar affective disorder*

 CLINICAL NOTES
Epidemiology: Common, peak age 20s-50s. M=F (F>M in elderly). Aetiology/risk factors: Endogenous, genetic, adverse life event (reactive), chronic disease. Clinical features: One month or more; persistent lowering of mood, loss of interest and enjoyment, poor outlook for future, fatigue, sleep disturbance, guilt, low self-esteem, poor memory and concentration, ideas of self-harm/suicide, poor appetite. Mild, four symptoms; moderate, five to six symptoms; severe, seven or more, or psychosis or act of self-harm. *Seasonal affective disorder:* Low mood/depression over winter months. Complications: Anxiety, phobia, social decline, relationship breakdown/low libido, employment difficulties, lack of self-care, delusions (eg persecutory, paranoid, nihilistic), auditory hallucinations (second person), self-harm, suicide, homicide.

V **INVESTIGATIONS**
Consider investigation to look for physical causes of low mood eg anaemia, hypothyroidism, hypercalcaemia, intracerebral pathology. Patient health questionnaire (PHQ9)/hospital anxiety and depression (HAD) scores.

MANAGEMENT
Screen high-risk groups, eg patients with chronic disease, by asking: 1. Have you been feeling down/depressed/hopeless over the past month? 2. Have you been bothered by having little interest/pleasure over the past month? Risk assessment, quantify severity with PHQ9/HAD/Beck scores. *Mild*: Watchful waiting, lifestyle advice, exercise, sleep hygiene, counselling, CBT. Consider antidepressants if past history of moderate or severe disease, associated with comorbidities, initial therapies have failed. Antidepressants in mild depression may be no more effective than placebo. *Moderate-severe*: Add in antidepressant therapy. *Severe*: Consider admission, antidepressants, psychology, ECT, antipsychotics. Antidepressants should be used for six months after recovery to prevent relapse. Sertraline safe if recent acute coronary syndrome (ACS). Sertraline may be more effective than citalopram in depression. *Seasonal affective disorder:* Light therapy, SSRI first-line.

Dermatitis

See also
— *Eczema (atopic)*

Dermatitis herpetiformis

 CLINICAL NOTES
Epidemiology: Teenage to 40 years. Aetiology/risk factors: Autoimmune, allergy to gliadin. IgA mediated.

Almost all have coeliac disease. Clinical features: Bullous rash, intense pruritus (scalp, elbows, knees, buttocks). Complications: Distress, secondary infection.

V **INVESTIGATIONS**
FBC, haematinics test, anti-TTG antibodies, IgA (false negative anti-TTG if IgA deficiency), TFT (30% abnormal), skin biopsy, immunofluorescence, endoscopy.

MANAGEMENT
Gluten-free diet, dapsone, high-potency topical steroids, oral steroids, regular monitoring for complications of coeliac disease.

Dermatofibroma

CLINICAL NOTES
Epidemiology: Common. Aetiology/risk factors: May be a reaction to trauma. Multiple lesions if immunosuppressed. M>F. Clinical features: Hard and mobile nodule <10mm. Complications: Sometimes difficult to distinguish from malignancy; one in four recur after excision.

V **INVESTIGATIONS**
Consider imaging or biopsy if malignancy cannot be excluded.

MANAGEMENT
Reassurance, consider excision.

Dermatomyositis

See also
— *Polymyositis*

CLINICAL NOTES
Epidemiology: Peak ages five to 15 and 40-70 years. F>M. Aetiology/risk factors: May be associated with malignancy (higher risk with advancing age). Autoimmune. Associated with Raynaud's disease, RA, Sjögren's syndrome, scleroderma. Clinical features: Onset weeks to months, symptoms may be intermittent, proximal myopathy, muscle tenderness, heliotrope rash periorbital, dorsum hands/knuckles (Gottron's papules). Fatigue, weight loss, nail fold telangiectasia, periorbital oedema. Complications: Calcinosis, dysphagia, peptic ulcer disease, pulmonary complications (SOB, aspiration, interstitial lung disease, respiratory failure), infections, cardiac complications (myocarditis, arrhythmias, cardiomyopathy, cardiac failure), pregnancy (deterioration of disease, premature birth, stillbirth).

V **INVESTIGATIONS**
→ ↑ESR, ↑CK, ↑myoglobin, autoantibody screen (myositis-specific antibodies), antihistone antibodies, anti-Jo-1 antibodies, ANA, MRI, EMG, muscle biopsy, chest X-ray/pulmonary CT, lung function tests. Investigate for malignancy if >40 years.

MANAGEMENT

Physiotherapy, corticosteroids (plus bisphosphonates), azathioprine, methotrexate, ciclosporin, hydroxychloroquine, immunoglobulin, tacrolimus, rituximab, infliximab, surgery for Ca^{2+} deposits.

Developmental dysplasia of the hip (congenital subluxation/dislocation of the hip)

CLINICAL NOTES

Epidemiology: F>M. Aetiology/risk factors: Breech presentation, family history, oligohydramnios, primigravida, large birthweight, post-dates babies. Clinical features: May appear normal at birth, left affected more than right, may be bilateral. Barlow's test: Dislocatable hips. Ortolani's test: Reduces dislocated hip (both have poor sensitivity), affected side extra thigh crease, reduced abduction, limp, maldevelopment.

INVESTIGATIONS

USS (screen at-risk babies), X-ray.

MANAGEMENT

Double nappies to abduct hips. May require splint for three months. May require surgery in older age groups. Pavlik harness, hip spica.

DiGeorge syndrome

CLINICAL NOTES

See immunodeficiency (primary)

Diabetes (type-1)[Ref7]

See also
— Diabetic retinopathy

CLINICAL NOTES

Epidemiology: Usually younger onset than type-2 DM, peak age of onset 12 years. Aetiology/risk factors: HLA DR3/4. 30% concordance (twins), viral, auto-immune, CF, DIDMOAD. Clinical features: May present acutely with ketoacidosis (nausea, vomiting, dehydration, tachypnoea, metabolic acidosis) or weight loss (may be profound), fatigue, polyuria, polydipsia, hunger, blurred vision. Complications: Infections, associated with other autoimmune diseases, microvasculopathy (retinopathy, neuropathy, nephropathy), macrovasculopathy (eg CHD), autonomic neuropathy (ED, gastroparesis, nocturnal diarrhoea, bladder dysfunction), necrobiosis lipoidica (may pre-date diabetes), diabetic foot, gallstone disease, osteoporosis, macrosomia, miscarriage, stillbirth, preeclampsia, DKA (glucose >15, very ketotic, pH <7.2), ↑anion gap metabolic acidosis, partial lipodystrophy.

INVESTIGATIONS

Fasting venous glucose ≥7.0mmol/L or random sample ≥11.1mmol/L (one sample required if classic symptoms, otherwise two samples required), U&E, LFT, HbA1c, fasting lipids. ↓pH/bicarbonate and ↑serum osm in acute setting eg ketoacidosis, urinalysis for ketones. Early morning urine for ACR. Islet cell antibodies and glutamic acid decarboxylase antibodies may be +ve but do not affect management.

MANAGEMENT

Lifestyle management: Diet, weight, exercise, smoking cessation, footcare. Regular recall and review, monitor for depression, ensure good adherence, education – including use of insulin and hypoglycaemia (sweating, shaking, malaise, agitation, dizziness, confusion, palpitation, blurred vision, confusion, aggression, convulsion), of which patients may be unaware. Treat hypoglycaemia with oral/IV glucose, glucagon. Self-monitoring (aim preprandial glucose 4.0-7.0mmol/L, postprandial <9.0mmol/L), HbA1c two to six-monthly (aim <7.5% or <6.5% if high arterial risk, tight control may increase hypoglycaemic attacks). Insulin eg basal/long-acting insulin eg glargine, detemir plus short-acting insulins for mealtimes; insulin pump may be required eg if erratic glucose/severe hypoglycaemia, insulin demands increased during intercurrent illness. Injections into deep subcutaneous fat, sites should be rotated and sharps bin provided. CVD risk management. BP (maintain <140/80mmHg or <130/80mmHg if microvascular disease/cerebrovascular disease). Annual first-pass morning urine for ACR abnormal if >2.5mg/mmol (men), >3.5mg/mmol (women). If ACR abnormal – prescribe ACE/ARB and maintain BP <130/80mmHg. Consider non-diabetic renal disease if absence of retinopathy, severe hypertension, acute proteinuria, haematuria, systemic illness. Cholesterol management. Retinal screening by ophthalmologist, refer immediately if rubeosis iridis (iris neovascularisation), preretinal/vitreous haemorrhage, retinal detachment, acute visual loss; refer urgently if new vessel formation. Annual foot review: Skin, sensation, vascular status. Charcot's joint – urgent referral. Ulcers – urgent referral, monitor for infection, special footware if neuropathy/vascular disease. ED: Phosphodiesterase inhibitors. Gastroparesis: Metoclopramide/domperidone. Painful neuropathy: Analgesia, TCAs, gabapentin. DKA: Rehydration, IV insulin, K+ replacement, consider urinary catheterisation, nasogastric tube, heparinisation. Islet cell/pancreatic transplant. Rituximab shown to delay progression.

Diabetes (type-2) [Ref8]

See also
— Diabetic retinopathy

CLINICAL NOTES

Epidemiology: 50% of type-2 diabetic patients are unaware of their illness. M>F. Aetiology/risk

DISEASES

factors: Advancing age, obesity, family history, 80% concordance (twins), insulin resistance, ↑south-east Asians, increasing seen in teenagers – maturity onset diabetes of the young (MODY); Klinefelter's syndrome, Turner's syndrome, statins may increase risk of diabetes. Clinical features: Asymptomatic (identified on screening, -ve screening test might promote adverse health behaviour), weight loss, polyuria, polydipsia, fatigue. Complications: Microvasculopathy (retinopathy, neuropathy, nephropathy), macrovasculopathy eg CHD, autonomic neuropathy (ED, gastroparesis, nocturnal diarrhoea, bladder dysfunction), necrobiosis lipoidica (may pre-date diabetes), painful neuropathy, diabetic foot, gallstone disease, osteoporosis, infection, macrosomia, miscarriage, stillbirth, pre-eclampsia, HONK (↑↑serum osm, glucose often >30, pH >7.2), partial lipodystrophy, death (HbA1c about 7.5% shown by a recent observational study to have lowest mortality, risk of death increased with levels lower or higher than this).

☞ INVESTIGATIONS

QD score® – 10-year risk prediction calculator. Fasting venous glucose ≥7.0mmol/L or random sample ≥11.1mmol/L (one sample required if classic symptoms, otherwise two samples required), U&E, LFT, HbA1c, fasting lipids. Early morning urine for ACR. Recent recommendations by expert committee[Ref9] that diagnosis should be based on HbA1c ≥ 6.5% (48mmol/mol).

☐ MANAGEMENT

Lifestyle management: Diet, weight, exercise, smoking cessation, footcare. Regular recall and review, monitor for depression, ensure good adherence, education. Monitor HbA1c two to six-monthly until stable, then 6 monthly. General HbA1c target 6.5% but target needs to be agreed with patient. Consider glucose self-monitoring if on insulin or oral hypoglycaemics (eg sulfonylureas). If lifestyle measures inadequate (HbA1c ≥6.5%)/overweight, first-line drug therapy metformin (caution if eGFR <45ml/min/1.73m² and stop if eGFR <30). Consider sulfonylurea if metformin not tolerated/ HbA1c response not adequate (≥6.5)/not overweight/ continued hyperglycaemic symptoms. If sulfonylurea not tolerated or contraindicated (eg elderly, those at risk of significant hypoglycaemia, those living alone, renal disease), or sulfonylurea not effective (HbA1c ≥6.5), substitute sulfonylurea/add DPP-4 inhibitor (gliptin, low risk of hypoglycaemia) or thiazolidinedione (glitazone; note glitazones have been linked to heart failure death, rosiglitazone contraindicated in CHD (and its licence withdrawn in UK). Glitazones not recommended for women at risk of fracture. The MHRA advises that pioglitazone should not be used in patients with a history of bladder cancer or in patients with uninvestigated visible blood in the urine. If metformin and sulfonylurea not effective (HbA1c ≥7.5) add insulin or consider adding DPP-4 inhibitor, thiazolidinedione

or GLP-1 agonist. Initiate insulin if HbA1c >7.5% after MI. Insulin may be used with pioglitazone. GLP-1 agonist may be added to metformin and sulfonylurea third-line, particularly if weight concerns. Manage other CV factors (BP to <140/80mmHg or <130/80mmHg if microvascular/cerebrovascular disease), smoking cessation advice, initiate statins if >40 years and risk of CHD >20% at 10 years or <40 years and high CV risk profile – aim cholesterol <4.0mmol/L, LDL 2.0mmol/L, use fibrate if TGs >4.5mmol/L or add fibrate to statin if TGs remain 2.3-4.5mmol/L. Monitor renal function: Annual first-pass urine ACR, abnormal if >2.5 mg/mmol for men, >3.5 mg/mmol for women, and serum for eGFR – treat with ACE inhibitor/ARB. Exclude other causes of renal disease. Refer for retinopathy screening. Monitor for skin disease and neuropathy. ED – phosphodiesterase inhibitors. Gastroparesis – metoclopramide/domperidone. Painful neuropathy – analgesia, TCAs, gabapentin. Tight glucose control in critically ill patients shown to increase mortality.

Diabetes insipidus

🗎 CLINICAL NOTES

Epidemiology: Rare. Aetiology/risk factors: Idiopathic. Cranial (reduced ADH production): Pituitary surgery, infarction (eg Sheehan's syndrome secondary to postpartum haemorrhage, pituitary apoplexy), tumour, sarcoid, histiocytosis X (Langerhan's cell histiocytosis), Friedreich's ataxia, cranial injury, DIDMOAD, meningitis. Nephrogenic (ADH resistance): Lithium, CKD, hypercalcaemia, hypokalaemia, pyelonephritis, pregnancy (including acute fatty liver of pregnancy), X-linked. Clinical features: Thirst, severe polyuria, urinary incontinence, dizziness, dehydration, postural drop in BP. Infants: Crying, excessively wet nappies, diarrhoea and vomiting, fever, failure to thrive. Complications: Shock, cerebral oedema with rapid reduction in Na+, death.

☞ INVESTIGATIONS

↑Na+, Ca²⁺,↑plasma osmolality, ↓urine osmolality (can exclude diabetes insipidus if urine osmolality >600mosmol/kg eg concentrated urine), water deprivation test, MRI (cranial), renal USS, genetic screening, pituitary function tests.

☐ MANAGEMENT

Treat underlying cause. Cranial: Desmopressin, oral fluids when thirsty. Nephrogenic: Low salt/protein diet, bendroflumethiazide, NSAIDs.

Diabetic retinopathy

🗎 CLINICAL NOTES

Epidemiology: Leading cause of blindness <60 years of age in UK. Prevalence: Impaired glucose tolerance, 6.7%; newly diagnosed DM, 6.2%;

established DM, 21.9%. Aetiology/risk factors: Poorly controlled HBA1c, high TGs, hypertension. Clinical features: *Background*: Acuity normal, micro-aneurysms, dot/blot/flame haemorrhages, hard exudates. *Preproliferative*: Cotton wool spots, large haemorrhages, venous beading. *Proliferative*: New vessel formation (iris, retinal). Maculopathy. Complications: Blindness, correlates with increased risk of all-cause mortality and CVD. Other diabetic-related eye disease – papillopathy, ophthalmoplegia, cataract, infection.

INVESTIGATIONS
Screening with dilated pupils and retinal photography, slit lamp (handheld ophthalmoscope not sensitive or specific enough) at diagnosis and annually.

MANAGEMENT
Refer to specialist: Hard exudates within one disc diameter of fovea, at least preproliferative retinopathy, new vessel formation, haemorrhage, rubeosis iridis, macular oedema, visual loss. Aim for good diabetic control, statins, BP control <130/80mmHg (candesartan 32mg shown to lead to regression in type-2 DM), laser, intravitreal triamcinolone, octreotide, protein kinase C-beta inhibitors.

DIDMOAD (Wolfram syndrome)

CLINICAL NOTES
Epidemiology: Rare, presents in childhood. Aetiology/risk factors: Autosomal recessive. Chromosome 4. Clinical features: Diabetes insipidus (cranial), DM (juvenile onset), optic atrophy, deafness (sensorineural). Also renal tract obstruction, respiratory failure, brainstem atrophy, psychiatric disease.

INVESTIGATIONS
Genetic studies, investigate each component of DIDMOAD complex, CT brain/pulmonary/KUB.

MANAGEMENT
Genetic counselling, treat each component of DIDMOAD complex.

Diffuse systemic sclerosis (diffuse scleroderma)

See also
— *Limited systemic sclerosis (including CREST)*

CLINICAL NOTES
Epidemiology: F>M. 20s-50s. Aetiology/risk factors: Autoimmune, familial. Clinical features: May be rapid onset, fatigue, weight loss, muscle and joint pains, cutaneous disease (tight, leathery, thick, hard skin). Raynaud's phenomenon (often presenting symptom, by weeks or months), tendonopathy. Complications: Severe contractures and disability, myositis, oesophageal scarring, Barrett's oesophagus, constipation, diarrhoea,

malabsorption, intestinal bacterial overgrowth, dental caries, sicca, digital ulceration/gangrene, pulmonary fibrosis, pulmonary hypertension, arrhythmias, pericardial disease, myocarditis, hypertension, renal failure, renal crisis, depression.

INVESTIGATIONS
FBC, ESR, CRP, U&E, ANA +ve, extractable nuclear antigens (ENA), anti-SCL-70 (anti-topoisomerase I antibodies); high specificity, 40% sensitivity, associated with pulmonary fibrosis and poor prognosis. Antihistone antibodies, antimitochondrial antibodies, anti-RNA polymerase antibodies (associated with renal involvement) anti-U1 RNP antibodies. Skin biopsy, endoscopy, ECG, echocardiogram, chest X-ray, lung function tests, pulmonary CT.

MANAGEMENT
Physiotherapy and exercise. Currently, no proven drug treatment to slow progress, although cyclophosphamide, penicillamine and mycophenolate mofetil have been used. Treatment aimed at relieving symptoms and early treatment of complications. Aggressive BP control.

Dilated cardiomyopathy

CLINICAL NOTES
Epidemiology: M>F, ↑black race, prevalence six in 10^5. Aetiology/risk factors: Familial, ischaemic, valvular, hypertensive, tachycardia-induced, viral myocarditis, diphtheria, autoimmune myocarditis, genetic, haemochromatosis, acromegaly, thyrotoxicosis, beriberi, mitochondrial disease, Friedreich's ataxia, sickle cell disease, alcohol, cocaine abuse, iatrogenic (eg doxorubicin, trastuzumab). Clinical features: Fatigue, cachexia, SOB, orthopnea, paroxysmal nocturnal dyspnoea, palpitations, arrhythmia, varying volume pulse, variable BP (low in decompensated failure), raised JVP, valve disease eg functional mitral regurgitation in dilated LV, gallop rhythm in advanced disease, displaced apex, pulmonary crackles, sacral/pitting oedema, painful hepatomegaly, ascites. Complications: Depression, acute cardiac failure, mural thrombus and embolic disease, malignant arrhythmias, death.

INVESTIGATIONS
FBC, U&E, TFT, LFT, ferritin, autoimmune screen, viral studies/infection screen including HIV, hepatitis serology, ECG (may be normal), echocardiogram, cardiac biopsy.

MANAGEMENT
Treat underlying cause. See *left ventricular systolic dysfunction*.

Diphtheria

CLINICAL NOTES
Epidemiology: Rare in vaccinated countries. Aetiology/risk factors: *Corynebacterium diphtheriae*.

Spread through respiratory route or touching contaminated items. Incubation three to five days. Clinical features: Asymptomatic but may still infect others, coryza, fever, malaise, sore throat, odynophagia, cutaneous diphtheria (especially in homeless/overcrowded communities), thick grey-coloured film (pseudomembrane) covering tonsils (may be absent in mild disease), cervical lymphadenopathy. Complications: Upper respiratory obstruction, myocarditis, cardiac arrhythmia, nepthritis, renal failure, ocular diphtheria, neurological involvement, weakness, paralysis, death (10% mortality).

ℭ INVESTIGATIONS
↓plts, U&E, ↑AST, cultures, PCR, toxin testing, LP (elevated protein), ECG, echocardiogram.

⎕ MANAGEMENT
Prevention by vaccination, contact tracing. Supportive, barrier nursing, antitoxin (derived from horse serum, give within 48 hours), penicillin or erythromycin, surgery if upper airway obstruction.

Disseminated intravascular coagulation (DIC)

▤ CLINICAL NOTES
Aetiology/risk factors: Severe sepsis (eg meningococcal disease), fat embolism, pre-eclampsia, AML, disseminated malignancy, trauma, malaria, burns, haemorrhage, red cell transfusions. Clinical features: Acute: Bruising, haemorrhage. Chronic: Thrombosis – superficial, leading to skin necrosis; renal artery thrombosis, hepatic. May present with increasing INR without obvious underlying cause. Complications: Renal failure, gangrene, death.

ℭ INVESTIGATIONS
↓plts, ↑PT, ↑APTT, ↓AT-III, ↓fibrinogen, ↑fibrin degradation products (FDP), D-dimer, blood film (schistocytes). Investigate for causes.

⎕ MANAGEMENT
Treat underlying cause. Acute DIC: Fluid management, platelet transfusion, FFP, recombinant human activated protein C, blood transfusions, all-trans-retinoic acid for AML (M3).

Dissociative fugue

▤ CLINICAL NOTES
Epidemiology: Rare. Aetiology/risk factors: Severe stress. Clinical features: Temporary loss of identity and memory, wandering, distress. Complications: Adoption of new identity, impulsive travel away from home, further fugue episodes, affective disorder.

ℭ INVESTIGATIONS
Investigate to exclude organic and other functional disorders.

⎕ MANAGEMENT
Psychotherapy, CBT. Treat underlying/consequential depression.

Diverticulosis

▤ CLINICAL NOTES
Bulging sacs or pouches of inner lining of intestine (usually large bowel). Epidemiology: 30% >60 years in developed countries. Aetiology/risk factors: Advancing age, low-fibre diet. Clinical features: Asymptomatic unless complications. Complications: Diverticulitis (pain, usually LIF, fever), fistulae (eg colovesical and colovaginal), abscess, PR bleeding (usually arterial, may be severe), stricture, bowel obstruction, perforation, peritonitis.

ℭ INVESTIGATIONS
WCC, abdominal X-ray, USS, CT, colonoscopy, barium enema.

⎕ MANAGEMENT
Diverticulosis: Dietary management. Diverticulitis: Antibiotics, bowel rest, fluids, monitor for complications. Elective bowel resection for recurrent diverticulitis. PR bleeding: Usually self-limiting; if arterial, may be life-threatening. Close monitoring. Transfusion if required. High risk of rebleed. May require surgery. Abscess: Antibiotics. If unwell, drainage. Fistulae: Elective surgery. Stricture: Endoscopic dilation/surgery.

Domestic abuse

▤ CLINICAL NOTES
Epidemiology: About 25% women. Women experience about 35 assaults before reporting crime. Complications: Low self-esteem, depression, anxiety, self-harm, agoraphobia, alcohol and substance abuse, suicide.

⎕ MANAGEMENT
Accurate documentation, reinforce confidentiality, risk assessment, crisis management plan, refuge, counselling, social services, refer to police with consent, regular follow-up.

Down's syndrome

▤ CLINICAL NOTES
Epidemiology: One in 700 live births. Aetiology/risk factors: Trisomy 21, 14:21 translocation, mosaicism. ↑with maternal age. Clinical features: Short stature, low-set ears, epicanthic folds, cataracts, Brushfield spots, flat nasal bridge, macroglossia, single palmar crease, inturned little finger, hypotonia, sandal gap toe, hypermobile joints, mental retardation, cardiac lesions – commonly Fallot's tetralogy, septal defects.

Complications: Alzheimer's disease, endocarditis, hypothyroidism, acute leukaemia, duodenal atresia, Hirschsprung's disease, keratoconus, ocular ectropion.

INVESTIGATIONS

Prenatal screening. Pregnancy associated plasma protein-A (PAPP-A), AFP, unconjugated oestriol (uE3), free beta or total HCG, inhibin-A, nuchal scanning, CVS, amniocentesis. *UK screening committee benchmarks:* Detection rate 75%, false +ve rate <3% (since April 2010, UK target is detection rate 90%, false +ve rate <2%).

MANAGEMENT

MDT approach: Family and educational support, physiotherapy, OT, speech therapy, dietitian, GP and hospital specialists, depending on needs.

Drug abuse (illicit)

CLINICAL NOTES

Epidemiology: About 10% adults. Aetiology/risk factors: Social pressure, depression, anxiety, personality disorder, abuse, under duress. Complications: Psychosis, prescription fraud, crime, violence, social decline, sexual promiscuity, hepatitis, HIV, overdose, self-harm, suicide.

INVESTIGATIONS

Toxicology screen (urine).

MANAGEMENT

Manage triggers, addiction counselling (specific drug dependencies), social support, clean needle schemes, contraception, vaccination.

Dubin-Johnson syndrome

CLINICAL NOTES

Epidemiology: Rare. Aetiology/risk factors: Autosomal recessive. Clinical features: Usually asymptomatic, jaundice in teenagers, RUQ pain.

INVESTIGATIONS

Isolated conjugated hyperbilirubinaemia. ↑urine coproporphyrin, ↑urine coproporphyrin I:coproporphyrin III. ↑PT. Liver hyperpigmentation on laparoscopy.

MANAGEMENT

No specific treatment required.

Duchenne muscular dystrophy

CLINICAL NOTES

Epidemiology: Prevalence one in 3,500 (males); female carriers may have mild symptoms. Aetiology/risk factors: X-linked recessive. Clinical features: Presents in childhood, progressive, motor developmental delay, proximal muscle weakness, waddling gait, hypotonia, pseudohypertrophy of calves, Gower's sign.

Complications: Cardiomyopathy, cardiac failure, arrhythmias, contractures, pneumonia, learning difficulties (one in five), osteoporosis, unable to walk before teens, thromboembolic disease, premature death (early 20s).

INVESTIGATIONS

↑↑CK (also ↑in carriers), muscle biopsy, genetic studies, EMG, ECG, echocardiogram, lung function tests.

MANAGEMENT

Genetic counselling, physiotherapy, walking aids, vaccinations, MDT approach, monitor cardiac function, treat cardiac and respiratory failure, family support.

Duct ectasia (breast)

CLINICAL NOTES

Epidemiology: Common, 40s-60s. Clinical features: Multiductal creamy/greenish discharge. Juxta-areola lump. Complications: Infection, pain. May be underlying malignancy.

INVESTIGATIONS

Swab discharge. USS, mammogram.

MANAGEMENT

Exclude malignancy. Consider surgical excision of duct (microdochectomy/total duct excision).

Dupuytren's contracture

CLINICAL NOTES

Epidemiology: M>F. Common. Aetiology/risk factors: Advancing age, familial, idiopathic, chronic liver disease, alcohol abuse, hyperlipidaemia, smoking, DM, manual workers, Peyronie's disease, AIDS, iatrogenic (eg phenytoin). Clinical features: Palmar fascia contractures, thickened rigged nodular fascia, often ring finger affected first. Complications: Progression, bilateral, fixed flexion deformity, foot and penis involvement, functional disability.

INVESTIGATIONS

Investigate according to suspected underlying cause.

MANAGEMENT

Treat underlying cause, watch and wait (may regress or not cause function disturbance), intralesional steroids/gamma interferon (INF)/collagenase, 5FU, radiotherapy. Fasciotomy/fasciectomy once metacarpophalangeal joint (MCPJ) contracture more than about 40° or proximal interphalangeal joint (PIPJ) contracture more than about 20° or if significant functional disability.

Dysfunctional uterine bleeding (DUB)

CLINICAL NOTES

Epidemiology: Most common cause of menorrhagia, around menarche and perimenopause. Aetiology/

risk factors: Anovulatory cycles, no identifiable pelvic disease. Clinical features: Menorrhagia, polymenorrhoea. Complications: Anaemia, dysmenorrhoea.

⚕ INVESTIGATIONS
FBC, TFT, clotting, swabs. Pelvic USS if >40 years or clinical presentation suggestive of pelvic pathology. Endometrial biopsy/hysteroscopy if clinical presentation suggestive of pelvic pathology.

☐ MANAGEMENT
Check smear history. Once treatable/sinister causes excluded, ferrous sulphate if anaemic, tranexamic acid, mefanamic acid, COC, levonorgestrel IUS. Consider GnRH analogues, endometrial ablation, hysterectomy.

Dyslexia

🗏 CLINICAL NOTES
Epidemiology: Common, underdiagnosed. M>F. Aetiology/risk factors: May be familial. Clinical features: Looks at written words but difficulty seeing them, delayed developmental milestones in language, reading, comprehension, spelling; difficulty differentiating similar-looking letters or words eg 'b' and 'd', 'nit' and 'tin'; difficulty appreciating whether words rhyme. Complications: Bullying, embarrassment, poor educational achievement in some, low self-esteem, depression.

⚕ INVESTIGATIONS
Formal assessment, eg by educational psychologist or community paediatrician.

☐ MANAGEMENT
Specialised teaching techniques, eg phonics. Teaching using multiple senses, eg reading, listening and tracing shapes of letters or words, develop awareness of phonemes. Parental support (teaching parents, reading games), computer software, specialised reading books and guides.

Dyspraxia

🗏 CLINICAL NOTES
See apraxia and dyspraxia

Dystonia

🗏 CLINICAL NOTES
Involuntary muscle contraction. Epidemiology: F>M. Aetiology/risk factors: Familial (autosomal dominant) if occurs at young age, idiopathic, trauma, CVA, post-infection, poisoning, iatrogenic. Acute dystonic reaction, eg oculogyric crisis, is a medical emergency often secondary to drugs (eg neuroleptics, metoclopramide). Clinical features: Generalised dystonia (various parts of body), local muscle contractions (eg head, neck causing twisting, painful), tongue (dysarthria), rapid blinking,

arytenoid muscles of vocal cord apparatus. May be triggered by voluntary movements, stress, anxiety. Complications: Depression, social phobia.

⚕ INVESTIGATIONS
EMG, EEG.

☐ MANAGEMENT
Procyclidine, benzodiazepines, baclofen, sensory trick (touching adjacent/affected part), botulinum toxin injection, deep brain stimulation, surgery.

Dystrophia myotonica

🗏 CLINICAL NOTES
Epidemiology: M>F. Aetiology/risk factors: Genetic, autosomal dominant, trinucleotide repeat disorder (shows genetic anticipation), chromosome 19. Clinical features: Myotonia (reduced muscular relaxation), slurred speech, myopathic face, wasting facial muscles, cataracts, bilateral ptosis, frontal balding, absent reflexes, cardiomyopathy, testicular atrophy, goitre. Complications: DM, cardiac failure, functional disability.

⚕ INVESTIGATIONS
Diagnosis usually on clinical grounds, ↓testosterone.

☐ MANAGEMENT
Mexiletine, phenytoin and acetazolamide may help. SALT. Treat complications accordingly. Genetic counselling.

Eaton-Lambert syndrome

See also
— *Myasthenia gravis*

Eclampsia

🗏 CLINICAL NOTES
See *pre-eclampsia*

Ectodermal dysplasia

🗏 CLINICAL NOTES
Epidemiology: Seven in 10^4 births. *Hypohidrotic*: X-linked, alopecia, saddle nose, thickened lips, large ears, dry/thin/sparse hair, dry skin, ridged/brittle nails, incisors/canines poorly developed. *Hidrotic*: Autosomal dominant, sparse/brittle hair, absent eyebrows, hyperkeratotic palms and soles, discoloured/brittle nails, moist skin.

⚕ INVESTIGATIONS
Laboratory studies not useful in diagnosis. Sweat pore counts, pilocarpine iontophoresis, skin biopsy.

☐ MANAGEMENT
No treatment available.

Ectopic pregnancy

Epidemiology: One in 90 pregnancies, increasing incidence. Aetiology/risk factors: Spontaneous, pregnancy with IUD, previous ectopic pregnancy (10%), previous PID, previous tubal surgery, endometriosis, assisted reproduction, smoking, >40 years. Heterotopic pregnancy (if coexistent ectopic and intra-uterine pregnancy). Clinical features: Abdominal pain (90%), vaginal bleeding (50-80%), shoulder tip pain, diarrhoea, pain on passing stool (blood in pouch of Douglas), abdominal tenderness (90%), adnexal tenderness, adnexal mass, cervical excitation, hypotension, dizziness/collapse, tachycardia. Complications: Recurrent ectopic pregnancy, surgery rendering patient infertile, shock, death.

INVESTIGATIONS

FBC, group and save, ↑amylase. Transvaginal ultrasound (TVUSS). Serial serum HCG (normally doubles every 48 hours, falls with miscarriage, monitor until <20IU/L, increases at reduced velocity suggests ectopic. Once HCG 1,000IU/L repeat TVUSS when intrauterine pregnancy would be visible.

MANAGEMENT

May spontaneously resolve. HCG monitored every two to three days until <20IU/L; TVUSS repeated weekly. 25% of women will require intervention. *Medical management:* Methotrexate – expect tubal miscarriage after three to seven days, may need two doses. Should avoid conceiving for three months. *Surgical management:* Salpingostomy, salpingectomy.

Ectropion (cervical)

CLINICAL NOTES

See *cervical ectropion (erosion)*

Ectropion (ocular)

CLINICAL NOTES

Epidemiology: Common. Aetiology/risk factors: Ageing, VIIth nerve palsy, poorly fitted glasses, false eye, tumour, Down's syndrome, microphthalmos, ichthyosis. Clinical features: Lower eyelid eversion, irritation, excess watering, Complications: Infection, corneal ulcer, keratitis.

MANAGEMENT

Lubrication, taping of eyelid, blepharoplasty.

Eczema (atopic)

See also
— *Pompholyx*

Epidemiology: M>F. 17% children. Onset less than two years of age. Aetiology/risk factors: Associated with personal or family history of hayfever, asthma (atopic diseases). May be triggered by heat, teething, dust, pets, food, stress. Other forms of dermatitis may be caused by contact allergy, eg latex/nickel. Clinical features: Pruritus, dry skin (flexures, or if aged less than four years, cheeks, forehead, extensor surfaces), symmetrical, dry, erythematous lesions, papules, vesicles, excoriation, pompholyx, inflammation. Complications: Bacterial infection (often staphylococcal) – weeping, impetigo, pustules, crusts. *Eczema herpeticum:* Blisters, ulceration, painful, rapidly worsening, systemic upset (risk of mortality). Lichenification, molluscum coinfection, stigma, depression, poor sleep, erythroderma.

INVESTIGATIONS

↑eosinophils. Swabs if infection suspected. Allergy testing not usually helpful but consider IgE and specific RASTs.

MANAGEMENT

Education, reduce ambient heating, avoid woollen clothes, pets, soap/bubble bath. Soap substitutes (eg Aqueous Cream BP), bath oils. Emollients (frequent and regular use, greasy if lichenification, creams if exudative). Topical steroids at strength to control inflammation. *Duration of steroids:* Three to five days for face/neck, up to two weeks in axillae/groin, then reduce potency. If topical steroids do not control (in absence of infection), consider tacrolimus/pimecrolimus. Consider occlusive dressings (with specialist advice). Phototherapy for severe disease. *Infection:* May require combination topical steroids and oral or topical antibiotics (fusidic acid, mupirocin, polymyxins). Oral antibiotics for significant bacterial infection (flucloxacillin/erythromycin seven to 14 days). Recurrent infection may require clearance with chlorhexidine washes. *Eczema herpeticum:* Consider same day admission to secondary care, fluids, analgesia, IV antiviral agents, antibiotic cover if added bacterial infection, supportive management. Consider six to eight-week trial of extensively hydrolysed protein formula/amino acid formula (in case cow's milk allergy) if moderate or severe uncontrolled disease and less than six months of age (specialist advice if continuing this for more than two months). Consider soya (after specialist advice) if more than six months of age. Erythroderma requires hospitalisation.

Edward's syndrome

CLINICAL NOTES

Epidemiology: One in 6,000 live births. Aetiology/risk factors: Trisomy 18, translocation, advancing maternal age. Clinical features: IUGR, prominent occiput, microcephaly, cleft lip, cleft palate, micrognathia, ocular

DISEASES

hypertelorism, ptosis, crossed second and fifth fingers, absent radius, webbed toes, rocker bottom feet, cardiac malformations (eg septal defects, PDA), diaphragmatic hernia, hip dislocation, renal anomalies, mental retardation. Complications: Most die in utero or in first few days; 5-10% of children alive at one year.

🔎 INVESTIGATIONS
Cytogenetic testing, fetal anomaly scan, amniocentesis.

💊 MANAGEMENT
Prenatal diagnosis and genetic counselling. Family support. MDT support. Treat complications accordingly.

Ehlers-Danlos syndrome

📋 CLINICAL NOTES
Epidemiology: About one in 5,000 prevalence. Aetiology/risk factors: Genetic. Clinical features: Six types. Purpura, elastic skin, blue sclera (due to scleromalacia), hypermobile joints. Complications: Poor wound healing, subcutaneous nodules, joint pain, herniae, diverticulosis, GI haemorrhage, mitral valve prolapse, aortic dissection, talipes, kyphoscoliosis.

🔎 INVESTIGATIONS
Diagnosis normally made on clinical presentation and skin biopsy. Echocardiography.

💊 MANAGEMENT
No specific treatment – education, support, physiotherapy, OT. Treat complications. Genetic counselling.

Encephalitis and encephalopathy

📋 CLINICAL NOTES
Epidemiology: Rare. Aetiology/risk factors: Encephalitis: viral (herpes simplex/zoster, coxsackie, Japanese B encephalitis, echovirus, mumps, CMV, HIV, rubella, West Nile virus, rabies, arbovirus, measles [subacute pansclerosing encephalitis]), bacterial (eg listeria, staphylococcus, Borrelia burgdorferi). Others, eg cryptococcus, toxoplasmosis. Encephalopathy: Liver failure, renal failure, paraneoplastic, hypoglycaemia, DKA, HONK, autoimmune disease eg SLE, head injury, iatrogenic, thiamine deficiency. Clinical features: Fever, headache, altered consciousness, mood disturbance, change in behaviour/personality, memory disturbance, joint pains, paralysis, sensory disturbance, weakness, inconsolable crying, vomiting, raised ICP, reduced GCS, neurological deficit. Complications: Seizure, permanent neurological deficit, coma, death (70% mortality with herpes encephalitis without treatment, 30% with treatment).

🔎 INVESTIGATIONS
FBC, U&E, glucose, infection screen (swabs, cultures, PCR, serology eg throat, urine, blood, LP), EEG, CT/MRI, brain biopsy.

💊 MANAGEMENT
Consider ITU, empirical treatment including aciclovir, ceftriaxone, thiamine (if concerned about Wernicke's encephalopathy), antiepileptics. Treat underlying cause.

Endometrial carcinoma

📋 CLINICAL NOTES
Epidemiology: Most common female genital tumour. Presents commonly fifth to eighth decades (5% <40 years). 75% in postmenopausal women. Aetiology/risk factors: Type 1 (80% cases): Unopposed oestrogens – endometrial hyperplasia, low parity, late menopause, obesity, HRT, anovulatory cycles, oestrogen-secreting tumours, HNPCC, tamoxifen. Type 2 (20% cases): Not related to unopposed oestrogens – poorer prognosis. Clinical features: Asymptomatic, IMB or postmenopausal bleeding, pyometra, vaginal discharge, pelvic pain, abnormal endometrial cells on smear, lymphadenopathy. Complications: Metastases (local spread, peritoneal, pulmonary, haematogenous spread uncommon), death.

🔎 INVESTIGATIONS
USS (thickened, irregular endometrium; malignancy risk 0.7 in 1,000 with endometrial thickness <5mm, 73 in 1,000 with thickness >5mm), hysteroscopy and biopsy, MRI.

💊 MANAGEMENT
Surgery: Hysterectomy and bilateral salpingo-oophorectomy (BSO) +/– lymph node dissection. Adjuvant radiotherapy (including brachytherapy). Adjuvant chemotherapy. Hormonal therapy, eg progestogens, tamoxifen, GnRH analogues, aromatase inhibitors.

Endometriosis

📋 CLINICAL NOTES
Ectopic endometrial tissue. Epidemiology: Common. Aetiology/risk factors: Early menarche, late menopause. Clinical features: Asymptomatic, pelvic pain, cyclical dysmenorrhoea, ovulatory pain, deep dyspareunia, painful defecation, dysuria, uterosacral ligament nodules, thickened rectovaginal septum, fixed uterus, palpable ovaries, pelvic and uterosacral ligament tenderness, nodules in pouch of Douglas. Complications: Psychosocial and sexual difficulties, work difficulties, infertility (50% of infertile women have endometriosis, 50% of women with endometriosis are infertile), endometriomas (chocolate cysts, endometriotic cysts affecting ovaries), GI haemorrhage. Rarely, haemoptysis, seizures.

🔎 INVESTIGATIONS
TVUSS, MRI, diagnostic laparoscopy.

💊 MANAGEMENT
NSAIDs, COC (tricyclic/postablation), progestogen-only

pill (POP), levonorgestrel IUS (33% effective), gestrinone, GnRH analogue. Ablation at laparoscopy, excision of lesions, excision of ovarian endometriomas, uterine nerve ablation, total abdominal hysterectomy and bilateral salpingo-oophorectomy (TAHBSO), colo-rectal/urological surgery. Fertility may be improved by diathermy and laser.

Entropion (ocular)

See also
— *Ectropion (ocular)*

📖 CLINICAL NOTES
Aetiology/risk factors: Advancing age, infection, trauma. Clinical features: Corneal irritation by inversion of eyelid (lower>upper lids). Complications: Corneal abrasion/ulcer, infection, pain.

🛅 MANAGEMENT
Lubricants, consider surgery.

Eosinophilic leukaemia and hypereosinophilic syndrome

📖 CLINICAL NOTES
Epidemiology: Acute form and chronic form (hypereosinophilic syndrome) rare. Aetiology/risk factors: Idiopathic, genetic mutation. Clinical features: Fever, malaise, cough (pulmonary infiltrates), pruritus, diarrhoea, myalgia. Complications: Non-infective endocarditis, cardiac failure, blast transformation.

𝒞𝒿 INVESTIGATIONS
Eosinophilia (>1.5 x 10^9/L), ↓Hb, ↓WCC, ↓plts, marrow biopsy, immunophenotyping, cytogenetics, CT, echocardiogram.

🛅 MANAGEMENT
Chemotherapy, interferon alpha, imatinib (in myelopro-liferative subtype of hypereosinophilic syndrome), bone marrow transplant (BMT).

Epididymal cyst

📖 CLINICAL NOTES
Epidemiology: Common. Aetiology/risk factors: Idiopathic, CF, PCKD, von Hippel-Lindau syndrome. Clinical features: Asymptomatic, smooth fluctuant lump behind testicle.

𝒞𝒿 INVESTIGATIONS
USS.

🛅 MANAGEMENT
Reassurance, surgery if causing problems due to size or discomfort.

Epididymitis/epididymo-orchitis

📖 CLINICAL NOTES
Epidemiology: Mainly third to fourth decades. Aetiology/risk factors: STI, *E coli*, brucellosis, mumps, fungal (rare). Amiodarone. UTI, prostatitis, promiscu-ity, homosexuality, non-circumcised, trauma, surgery. Clinical features: Fever, unilateral testicular pain, pain of epididymitis relieved on scrotal elevation (unlike torsion, Prehn's sign), testicular lump, inflamed scrotum, penile discharge, haematospermia, dysuria, urinary frequency, sexual dysfunction, lymphadenopathy, abdominal pain. Complications: Associated orchitis, chronicity, abscess, testicular atrophy, infertility.

𝒞𝒿 INVESTIGATIONS
STI screen, scrotal USS. Important to differentiate from testicular torsion. Urinalysis and MSU.

🛅 MANAGEMENT
Antibiotics, consider ciprofloxacin first-line.

Epiglottitis (acute)

📖 CLINICAL NOTES
Epidemiology: Rare. M>F. Incidence increasing in adults. Aetiology/risk factors: *Haemophilus influenzae type B*; (↓with vaccination), pneumococci, streptococci, viral. Clinical features: Rapidly evolving clinical picture, fever, tachycardia, hypotension, drooling, throat/neck pain, voice changes, cough, earache, respiratory dis-tress. Throat should only be examined by experienced paediatrician or ENT surgeon. Complications: Airway obstruction, abscess, sepsis, meningitis, pneumothorax, mediastinitis, cavernous sinus thrombosis, death.

𝒞𝒿 INVESTIGATIONS
Lateral neck X-ray if laryngoscopy unavailable, MRI to exclude abscess, blood culture/throat swab. Diagnosis by laryngoscopy.

🛅 MANAGEMENT
High intubation rate, third-generation cephalosporins, steroids, tracheostomy, surgery for abscess.

Epilepsy

📖 CLINICAL NOTES
Epidemiology: 0.7% prevalence. 60% start in childhood. Aetiology/risk factors: Idiopathic, head trauma, CVA, space-occupying lesion, severe hypertension, vasculitis, tuberous sclerosis, arteriovenous malformation, SLE, neurosarcoid, post cerebral infection/sepsis, meta-bolic disturbance. Associated with autistic spectrum disorders. Clinical features: Epileptic seizures tend to be stereotyped. Posture may be sustained for several seconds; if head is turned to one side, eyes usually turn in same direction. Tongue-biting fairly specific for

epilepsy, urinary continence not very specific. Sudden drop attacks, early cyanosis or pallor suggest cardiac cause. Epilepsy types and syndromes: *Infantile spasms (West syndrome):* Peak about four months of age, spasms especially in flexion. *Benign epilepsy with centrotemporal spikes (rolandic):* Most common childhood epilepsy, peak onset five to eight years, clonic seizures, unilateral paraesthesia, often on waking. *Juvenile myoclonic epilepsy:* 10% epilepsies, morning myoclonic jerks, worse with alcohol, menstruation and sleep deprivation. *Prodrome:* Unusual and often suggestive of partial seizures eg temporal lobe epilepsy. Prodromal symptoms include mood change, gustatory, auditory and visual hallucinations, déjà vu. *Partial seizures:* One cerebral hemisphere. *Simple partial:* No loss of consciousness. *Complex partial:* Altered consciousness eg temporal lobe epilepsy. *Secondary generalised:* Partial seizure with electrical disturbance spread to both cerebral hemispheres. *Generalised seizures:* Not localised to one cerebral hemisphere. *Tonic-clonic:* Grand mal, sudden onset loss of consciousness followed by limb stiffness (tonic) then jerking phase (clonic), postictal confusion and drowsiness. *Absences:* 12% childhood epilepsies, <10-second pause in activity, eg talking, automatisms, eg lip-smacking. *Post seizure paralysis:* Temporary, Todd's paralysis. Complications: Status epilepticus, stigma, poor quality of life, eg driving restrictions, trauma, eg risk of seizure in dangerous situations.

⟲ INVESTIGATIONS

FBC, U&E, LFT, glucose, Ca^{2+}, Mg^{2+}, CRP, toxic screen (including LP if no raised ICP), drug screen, ECG, MRI/CT brain, MR angiogram if CT/MRI normal, EEG (not specific for epilepsy, 60% false -ve rate with first EEG used to determine epilepsy type, eg 3Hz spikes in absences, consider sleep/sleep deprived/ambulatory EEG. *Infantile spasms:* Hypsarrhythmia pattern seen on EEG.

⬚ MANAGEMENT

MDT approach. Education, family involvement, individualised care plan, regular review, counselling, driving advice. Information about contraception (some anticonvulsants are enzyme inducers including carbamazepine, topiramate, phenytoin). COC with oestrogen ≥50 microgram should be used. Depot progesterone should be given every 10, not 12, weeks. *Postcoital contraception:* Levonorgestrel 1.5mg followed by 750 microgram after 12 hours. *Pregnancy:* Counsel about teratogenicity of drugs, change to safer alternatives, risk of maternal fit probably greater to fetus, do not stop antiepileptics suddenly. High-dose folic acid may be required during pregnancy. Consider administration of vitamin K to newborn. Breastfeeding advice. Anticonvulsants, after discussion with patient, usually after second fit, or after first seizure if neurological deficit or abnormal EEG/MRI/CT, patient wishes. First-line drugs: *Tonic-clonic:* Carbamazepine,

lamotrigine, sodium valproate, topiramate. *Absence:* Ethosuximide, lamotrigine, sodium valproate. *Myoclonic:* Sodium valproate. *Tonic:* Lamotrigine, sodium valproate. *Partial:* Carbamazepine, lamotrigine, oxcarbazepine, sodium valproate, topiramate. *Infantile spasms:* Vigabatrin, steroids. *Lennox-Gastaut syndrome:* Lamotrigine, sodium valproate, topiramate. Vagus nerve stimulation.

Episcleritis

🗎 CLINICAL NOTES

Epidemiology: Common. F>M. Aetiology/risk factors: Idiopathic, IBD, herpes simplex/zoster, hepatitis B, vasculitis (Wegener's granulomatosis, polyarteritis nodosa), autoimmune disorders (RA, SLE), rosacea, thyroid disease, adrenal deficiency, allergy, lymphoma/leukaemia. Clinical features: Usually unilateral eye pain, superficial inflammation, red eye (may be localised area). Complications: Iritis (one in 10 cases), recurrent disease.

⟲ INVESTIGATIONS

Investigate for specific causes.

⬚ MANAGEMENT

Treat underlying cause, may spontaneously resolve, lubricants, topical steroids, NSAIDs.

Erb's palsy

🗎 CLINICAL NOTES

Epidemiology: One in 2,000 births. Aetiology/risk factors: Brachial plexus injury (C5-C7) commonly due to birth trauma (shoulder dystocia, clavicular fracture). C5 most common nerve root to be affected in birth injuries. Nerve may be avulsed from spine, torn or stretched. Clinical features: Arm held in 'waiter's tip' position (arm hanging down, elbow extended, forearm pronated with wrist flexed), ↓shoulder abduction/external rotation, ↓elbow flexion, ↓sensation in distribution of C5-C7.

⟲ INVESTIGATIONS

MRI, nerve conduction studies.

⬚ MANAGEMENT

90% brachial plexus injuries heal without treatment. Physiotherapy, abduction splint, surgery in children (if no improvement by age three to four months, consider nerve graft/transfer; age two to 10 years, consider muscle or tendon transfer, or osteotomy.

Erectile dysfunction (ED)

🗎 CLINICAL NOTES

Epidemiology: Common. Aetiology/risk factors: Idiopathic, depression, anxiety, stress, obesity, alcohol, performance anxiety, relationship difficulties, atrophic vaginitis in partner, smoking, iatrogenic (eg antihypertensives, anti-androgens), cardiovascular disease, hypertension, hyperlipidaemia, CCF, MS, spinal cord injury, parkinsonism, DM, hypothyroidism, hyperprolactinaemia, prostate cancer, hypogonadism, venous leak, pelvic trauma, radiotherapy, Peyronie's disease, hypospadius. Clinical features: Some men will be able to sustain an erection during masturbation or spontaneously. Genital and cardiovascular examination recommended. Complications: Relationship difficulties, depression; ED may precede coronary artery disease.

INVESTIGATIONS
Cardiovascular risk assessment – men with ED are assumed to have CVD until proven otherwise (Princeton consensus). Fasting glucose/lipids, morning testosterone and SHBG, PSA, TFT, prolactin. Consider doppler USS, cavernosogram (high false +ve rate), sleep study.

MANAGEMENT
Exercise, weight loss, smoking cessation, alcohol advice, healthy diet, counselling, sleep hygiene, stress/depression/anxiety management, lipid lowering, testosterone normalisation, BP management, replace thiazides/non-cardioselective beta-blockers, eg with ACE inhibitors/ARB which may improve symptoms. PDE5 inhibitors (tadalafil has longer half-life than sildenafil), intracavernous injections, intra-urethral alprostadil, vacuum devices, penile prostheses.

Erysipelas

CLINICAL NOTES
Aetiology/risk factors: Strep pyogenes, Staph aureus via broken skin eg trauma, tinea. DM, immunosuppression. Clinical features: Deep dermal infection (although sometimes used to describe facial cellulitis), red oedematous tender skin, advancing edge, malaise, fever. Complications: Orbital cellulitis, shock, cavernous sinus thrombosis, gangrene.

INVESTIGATIONS
Consider FBC, glucose, blood cultures.

MANAGEMENT
If well and no comorbidities, prescribe oral antibiotics. If unwell, advanced disease, comorbidities, eg DM, peripheral vascular disease, facial cellulitis, prescribe IV antibiotics.

Erythema toxicum

CLINICAL NOTES
Epidemiology: 50% term infants. Clinical features: Neonatal rash, erythematous macules with central white or yellow pustules/papules, often on face and trunk. Usually lasts five to seven days, starting a day or two after birth.

MANAGEMENT
Reassurance, no specific treatment.

Erythroderma

CLINICAL NOTES
Aetiology/risk factors: Infection, dermatitis, erythema multiforme, Stevens-Johnson syndrome, psoriasis, iatrogenic, lymphoma. Clinical features: ≥90% skin surface inflamed. Complications: Altered thermoregulation, electrolyte and fluid disturbance, secondary infection, cardiac failure, renal failure, shock, death.

INVESTIGATIONS
FBC (anaemia), ↑ESR, ↓albumin, hyperglobulinaemia, U&E, clotting studies.

MANAGEMENT
Admit as emergency to secondary care. Treat underlying cause, emollients, fluid management, temperature control, steroids if erythrodermic pustular psoriasis.

Essential hypertension

See also
— Secondary hypertension
— Malignant hypertension

CLINICAL NOTES
Epidemiology: 20% prevalence, 50% >80-year-olds. Diastolic BP best predictor of CVD if <50 years, systolic and diastolic predictive ages 50-60 years, systolic most predictive >60 years. Aetiology/risk factors: Essential hypertension (approx 95% hypertension), consider white coat effect. Risks: Age, family history, obesity, alcohol, excess dietary sodium. Clinical features: Persistent BP >140/90mmHg (systolic, diastolic, or both). Stage 1 hypertension: Clinic ≥140/90mmHg or ABPM >135/85mmHg. Stage 2 hypertension: Clinic ≥160/100mmHg or ABPM >150/95mmHg. Severe hypertension: Clinic systolic ≥180mmHg or diastolic ≥110mmHg. Usually asymptomatic and often found on routine examination. May present with headaches or visual disturbance. Full cardiovascular examination required. Often no clinical signs. Complications: End organ damage (retinopathy, LVH, nephropathy, neuropathy), CVA. CHD, cardiac failure, malignant hypertension. Retinopathy: Grade 1: Attenuated arterioles, silver wiring, arterial tortuosity. Grade 2: Arteriovenous nipping. Grade 3: Cotton wool spots, haemorrhages. Grade 4: Papilloedema.

INVESTIGATIONS
U&E, baseline LFT (pre-statin or in alcohol abuse), fasting glucose/lipid profile, urine dipstick for protein, ECG. Arm with highest reading should be used in future. Use validated and calibrated equipment. Patient should be relaxed. If initial BP ≥140/90mmHg, repeat at end of consultation. If clinical BP ≥140/90mmHg, offer ABPM

(or home reading if patient cannot tolerate it) to confirm hypertension.

MANAGEMENT

Guidance based on NICE guidelines, 2011.[Ref10] Calculate 10-year or lifetime cardiovascular risk, eg QRISK. *Target BP:* <80 years, clinic <140/90mmHg or ABPM <135/85mmHg; >80 years, clinic <150/90mmHg or ABPM <145/85mmHg. If type-2 diabetes, target is 140/80mmHg. If there is evidence of microvascular disease or CVD, target is 130/80mmHg. Lifestyle measures (weight loss, salt reduction, exercise, smoking cessation). Pharmacological measures: *Stage 1 hypertension* plus one or more of target organ damage, DM, renal disease, CVD or 10-year risk of CVD ≥20%. If <40 years with stage 1 hypertension without target organ damage, CVD, DM or renal disease, consider specialist assessment for secondary hypertension. *Stage 2 or severe hypertension:* CCB first line if ≥55 years or black origin. If not controlled, there is cardiac failure or intolerant of CCB, use a thiazide-like diuretic. Aim to use chlortalidone or indapamide rather than bendroflumethiazide as thiazides of choice. If <55 years, ACE inhibitor (or ARB) first line, or ARB. Combine drugs if treatment failure with single therapy by using ACE inhibitor (or ARB) and CCB. If target BP not achieved, combine ACE inhibitor (or ARB) and CCB and thiazide-like diuretic. If target BP not achieved, combine ACE inhibitor (or ARB) and CCB and thiazide-like diuretic and another diuretic, eg spironolactone or alpha- or beta-blockers. Manage other cardiovascular risk factors.

Essential thrombocythaemia

CLINICAL NOTES

Epidemiology: F>M. >50 years. Aetiology/risk factors: Some have *JAK2* gene defect, rarely familial. Clinical features: Headache, bleeding, thrombosis (arterial/venous, eg MI, CVA, miscarriage). Complications: Leukaemic transformation, myelofibrosis, sideroblastic anaemia.

INVESTIGATIONS

↑↑plts, marrow biopsy.

MANAGEMENT

Aspirin, hydroxyurea, interferon alpha (INF), plateletpheresis.

Extradural haemorrhage

CLINICAL NOTES

Aetiology/risk factors: Head trauma eg blow to side of head, rupture of middle meningeal vessels/dural venous sinus. Clinical features: Lucid period (hours/days) followed by ↓GCS, headache, nausea, vomiting. Complications: Hemiparesis, ipsilateral dilated pupil, seizure, raised ICP, death.

INVESTIGATIONS

CT/MRI.

MANAGEMENT

Decompression and clot evacuation.

Extrinsic allergic alveolitis

CLINICAL NOTES

Hypersensitivity pneumonitis. Epidemiology: 600 per year (UK). Aetiology/risk factors: Actinomycetes (ventilation systems, sugar cane workers, mushroom workers), *Micropolyspora faeni* (farmer's lung), avian excretions (bird fancier's lung), aspergillus (malt workers), mycobacteria (hot tubs), bathtub finishers, other chemical exposure. Clinical features: *Acute:* Breathlessness, pulmonary crackles, fever, headache, myalgia few hours after exposure. *Chronic:* Weight loss, fatigue, cough, breathlessness, inspiratory crackles, finger clubbing. Complications: Irreversible fibrosis, pulmonary hypertension, cor pulmonale.

INVESTIGATIONS

↑ESR, serum precipitins (immunoglobulins), spirometry (restrictive or mixed obstructive/restrictive), chest X-ray (ground glass appearance, nodular shadowing, upper lobe fibrosis, ↓lung volume), CT, lavage, histology.

MANAGEMENT

Removal of precipitant, oxygen, steroids for acute attacks.

Fabry disease

CLINICAL NOTES

Epidemiology: M>F. Aetiology/risk factors: X-linked. Clinical features: Dry/lax skin, multiple angiokeratomata (<4mm) especially thighs, periumbilical, groin. Complications: Arthropathy, corneal dystrophy, hypertension, varicose veins, glomerular damage, renal failure, MI, cardiomyopathy, arrhythmia, severe hand pain, CVA, death 40s/50s.

INVESTIGATIONS

Alpha galactosidase activity, DNA analysis. FBC, U&E, fasting lipids/glucose, ECG (12-lead and ambulatory), echocardiogram.

MANAGEMENT

Enzyme replacement for alpha galactosidase A deficiency.

Facioscapulohumeral dystrophy

CLINICAL NOTES

Epidemiology: Five in 10^5 prevalence. Aetiology/risk factors: Autosomal dominant. Clinical features: Muscle pain, facial weakness, wasting of facial muscles (expressionless facies), difficulty whistling, limb girdle wasting/weakness, winged scapulae, foot drop (anterior compartment destruction), falls. Complications: Retinal detachment, retinopathy, sensorineural deafness, epilepsy, LVH, bundle branch block, arrhythmia, hypertension, restrictive lung disease.

INVESTIGATIONS
CK, EMG, muscle biopsy, genetic studies, echocardiogram, spirometry.

MANAGEMENT
Physiotherapy, OT, falls clinic, ophthalmic surgery, hearing aids, anticonvulsants, hypertension/arrhythmia control, pulmonary support.

Factor V Leiden mutation

CLINICAL NOTES
See *thrombophilias*

Fallot's tetralogy

CLINICAL NOTES
Epidemiology: Most common cyanotic congenital heart disease. Aetiology/risk factors: Idiopathic, Down's syndrome, DiGeorge syndrome, maternal alcohol abuse, maternal PKU. Clinical features: VSD with overriding aorta, pulmonary stenosis, right ventricular hypertrophy. Breathlessness, failure to thrive, syncope/seizures, squatting (to reduce right-left shunt and increase pulmonary flow), cyanosis, clubbing, parasternal heave, systolic thrill, ejection systolic murmur (ESM), absent P2. Complications: Cyanotic spells due to septal spasm, thrombotic strokes, endocarditis, ventricular arrhythmia, embolism, cerebral abscess.

INVESTIGATIONS
FBC (secondary polycythaemia), ECG-RAD, RBBB (partial/compete), RVH. FBC – polycythaemia. Chest X-ray – boot-shaped heart. Echocardiogram, cardiac catheterisation.

MANAGEMENT
Cyanotic spells (oxygen, morphine, beta-blockers, keep knees against chest). Blalock shunt, complete surgical correction, consider ICD.

Familial Mediterranean fever

CLINICAL NOTES
Epidemiology: Rare. Aetiology/risk factors: Familial, eg Ashkenazi Jews. Autosomal recessive, *MEFV* mutation. Clinical features: Starts in childhood/teens. Attacks of fever, abdominal pain and bloating, pleuritic chest pain, joint pain and swelling, rash.

Complications: Pleural effusion, amyloid, lactose intolerance.

INVESTIGATIONS
Leucocytosis, ↑ESR/CRP (during attack), haematuria (5%), proteinuria suggests renal amyloid, consider renal biopsy, chest X-ray, abdominal X-ray, CT.

MANAGEMENT
Colchicine.

Fanconi's anaemia

CLINICAL NOTES
Epidemiology: Rare. Aetiology/risk factors: Autosomal recessive. Clinical features: Symptoms of anaemia or pancytopenia, eg fatigue, breathlessness, recurrent/severe infection and bruising/bleeding. Complications: Skeletal abnormalities (triangular shaped head, radius and thumb dysplasia/aplasia), deafness, cardiac, GI and kidney malformations, aplastic anaemia, AML, solid tumours (especially head and neck, and gynaecological), hypogonadism.

INVESTIGATIONS
FBC, bone marrow and genetic studies, echocardiogram, abdomino-renal USS, X-rays.

MANAGEMENT
Genetic counselling, family therapy, antibiotics, transfusions, androgen therapy (to stimulate marrow), granulocyte colonony stimulating factors, chemotherapy, stem cell transplant. Treat complications accordingly.

Fanconi syndrome

See also
— *Cystinosis*

CLINICAL NOTES
Aminoaciduria, phosphaturia, glycosuria. Aetiology/risk factors: Idiopathic, Wilson's disease, cystinosis, galactosaemia, glycogen storage diseases, tyrosinaemia type I, Lowe syndrome, Dent's disease, heavy metal poisoning (eg lead), MGUS. Clinical features: Anorexia, nausea, vomiting, polyuria, polydipsia, dehydration, failure to thrive, vitamin D resistant rickets, osteomalacia, renal tubular acidosis (type 2). Complications: Failure to thrive, renal failure, metabolic acidosis.

INVESTIGATIONS
FBC, Ca^{2+}, ↓uric acid, ↓phosphate. *Urine:* Phosphaturia, proteinuria (aminoaciduria), glycosuria, excess urinary bicarbonate.

MANAGEMENT
Treat underlying cause. Rehydration, electrolyte and vitamin D replacement.

DISEASES

Fatty liver (steatosis) and steatohepatitis

📋 **CLINICAL NOTES**

Epidemiology: Increasing prevalence, including in children. **Aetiology/risk factors:** Alcohol, non-alcoholic, DM, hypertriglyceridaemia, obesity, rapid weight loss, iatrogenic (amiodarone, steroids, tetracyclines, COC, pregnancy, methotrexate, total parenteral nutrition), Wilson's disease, glycogen storage diseases, medium chain acyl-CoA dehydrogenase deficiency, intestinal bypass surgery. **Clinical features:** Steatosis, asymptomatic. **Complications:** Steatohepatitis (liver inflammation secondary to steatosis), non-alcoholic steatohepatitis (NASH). Malaise, fatigue, RUQ pain, hepatomegaly, splenomegaly, signs of chronic liver disease, cirrhosis, fulminant liver failure, hepatocellular cancer, cardiovascular disease.

🔬 **INVESTIGATIONS**

LFT, normal/raised [x10ULN] transaminases. AST:ALT <1 in non-alcoholic disease, >1 in alcoholic steatohepatitis. Normal/mildly [x3ULN] raised ALP, fasting lipids and glucose, ↑ferritin (if ↑↑consider haemochromatosis). Consider autoimmune screen (false +ve if cirrhosis), copper studies. USS (may miss fibrosis), CT, MRI, biopsy.

💊 **MANAGEMENT**

Lifestyle management, weight loss (gradual), high protein diet, alcohol management, cardiovascular risk assessment, optimal DM and lipid management, avoid precipitating drugs, consider bariatric surgery.

Fatty liver (acute) of pregnancy

📋 **CLINICAL NOTES**

Epidemiology: One in 13,000 pregnancies, third trimester or postpartum. **Aetiology/risk factors:** ↑with male fetus, obesity, multiple pregnancy, first pregnancy, pre-eclampsia. **Clinical features:** Nausea, vomiting, abdominal pain, anorexia, headache, jaundice. **Complications:** Liver failure, coagulopathy, encephalopathy, pre-eclampsia, pancreatitis, renal failure, diabetes insipidus, maternal and perinatal mortality 20-30%.

🔬 **INVESTIGATIONS**

FBC, coagulation screen, U&E, LFT, ↑ammonia, amylase, ↓glucose.

💊 **MANAGEMENT**

ITU, delivery.

Febrile convulsion

📋 **CLINICAL NOTES**

Epidemiology: 3% children, most common at six months to five years of age. **Aetiology/risk factors:** Febrile

illness, may be a family history of convulsions. No good evidence for convulsion caused by rapid rise in temperature. **Clinical features:** Tonic-clonic seizure (in absence of CNS disease or electrolyte disturbances). **Complications:** Status epilepticus, 30% recurrence rate, 1% higher risk of epilepsy than normal population (1.4% versus 2.4%).

🔬 **INVESTIGATIONS**

Consider FBC, U&E, LFT, Ca^{2+}, Mg^{2+}, MSU, blood cultures, LP, CT/MRI brain.

💊 **MANAGEMENT**

Emergency treatment, treat underlying cause, exclude serious causes eg meningococcal disease, antipyretics not shown to reduce risk of febrile seizures, parental support and education.

Febrile neutropenia

📋 **CLINICAL NOTES**

Aetiology/risk factors: Marrow failure, pancytopenia, chemotherapy. **Clinical features:** Infection in context of neutrophil count ≤1.0 x 10^9/L + fever ≥38°C or swinging pyrexia ≥37.5°C or septic. May or may not show signs of localised infection. **Complications:** Septic shock, multiorgan failure, death.

🔬 **INVESTIGATIONS**

FBC, U&E, LFT, clotting screen, cultures – blood x3, urine, long-line, sputum, mouth, axilla, perineum, stool (if loose), chest X-ray. Consider LP.

💊 **MANAGEMENT**

Look for focus of infection (eg infected haematoma from IM injection), reverse barrier nursing, avoid flowers (water may contain pseudomonas), chlorhexidine skin washes eg after toileting, antibacterial mouthwashes plus nystatin, regular observation and monitoring (including for DIC). Broad-spectrum antibiotics if no focus of infection found. Consider vancomycin if long-line infection.

Felty's syndrome

See also
— *Rheumatoid arthritis*

📋 **CLINICAL NOTES**

Aetiology/risk factors: Autosomal dominant. **Clinical features:** RA, neutropenia, splenomegaly.

🔬 **INVESTIGATIONS**

FBC, ↓WCC, ↓plts, ↑rheumatoid factor, USS, CT.

💊 **MANAGEMENT**

Splenectomy, DMARDs eg methotrexate, sulfasalazine, leflunomide.

Fetal alcohol syndrome

📋 **CLINICAL NOTES**

Epidemiology: Common. Aetiology/risk factors: Excess alcohol consumption during pregnancy (dose dependent). Clinical features and complications: Miscarriage, acute neonatal alcohol withdrawal, neonatal hypotonia, IUGR, microcephaly, thin superior lip, thin philtrum, narrow palpebral fissures, epicanthic folds, ptosis, learning disabilities, PDA, ASD, VSD, skeletal deformities, urinary tract deformities, seizures, ataxia, learning disabilities.

🩺 **INVESTIGATIONS**

Investigate according to suspected complications eg CT/MRI brain, renal USS, ECG, echocardiography.

💊 **MANAGEMENT**

Prenatal and antenatal counselling, social support, maternal alcohol addiction management, treat complications accordingly.

Fibroadenoma

📋 **CLINICAL NOTES**

Epidemiology: 12% breast lumps, young adults. Large fibroadenomas in pregnancy and lactation. Clinical features: Well circumscribed lump, mobile. Complications: 0.002% risk of malignancy.

🩺 **INVESTIGATIONS**

USS, mammography in women >35 years, consider FNA.

💊 **MANAGEMENT**

Once malignancy excluded, no action required, consider surgical excision if large or diagnosis equivocal.

Fibroids

📋 **CLINICAL NOTES**

Epidemiology: About 25% of women. Aetiology/risk factors: Obesity, familial, African-Caribbean origin. Clinical features: Asymptomatic, menorrhagia, dysmenorrhoea, pelvic pain, abdominal mass, constipation, urinary frequency, dyspareunia. Complications: Infertility, miscarriage, fibroid enlargement, torsion, infarction (red degeneration causes severe pain), fetal defects, obstructed labour, bleeding, DIC. Erythropoietin secretion and polycythaemia.

🩺 **INVESTIGATIONS**

FBC, USS, MRI.

💊 **MANAGEMENT**

Reassurance. Spontaneous resolution eg postmenopausal. Tranexamic acid, levonorgestrel IUS, GnRH analogues (used pre-surgery), endometrial ablation, uterine artery embolisation, laser ablation, ultrasound ablation, myomectomy, hysterectomy.

Fibromyalgia

📋 **CLINICAL NOTES**

Epidemiology: 0.5-5% UK prevalence. 25-55 years of age. F>M. Aetiology/risk factors: Unknown, may be related to low neuronal serotonin and elevated substance P. Clinical features: More than three months, non-progressive, skeletal pains and tenderness ≥11 of a possible 18 sites (left or right – occiput at nuchal ridge, trapezius, supraspinatus, gluteal, low cervical, second rib, lateral epicondyle, greater trochanter, medial knee), fatigue, sleep disturbance, morning stiffness, restless legs. Complications: Depression, employment and relationship difficulties.

🩺 **INVESTIGATIONS**

Investigate to exclude other causes.

💊 **MANAGEMENT**

Analgesia, antidepressants (TCAs and SSRIs), acupuncture, hydrotherapy, exercise, rest, education, stress management, CBT.

Fifth disease

📋 **CLINICAL NOTES**

Also known as erythema infectiosum or slapped cheek syndrome. Epidemiology: Age three to 15 years. Winter/spring. Incubation four to 14 days. Aetiology/risk factors: Parvovirus B19. Clinical features: Infectious before rash presents, infectivity wanes once rash appears. Coryza, low fever, mild headache, sore throat, red cheeks with periorbital sparing, lacy morbilliform rash on limbs. Complications: Adult women may develop joint pains, fetal hydrops if infection during pregnancy (especially under 20 weeks), aplastic anaemia especially in sickle cell disease.

🩺 **INVESTIGATIONS**

Parvovirus serology.

💊 **MANAGEMENT**

Symptomatic treatment, manage complications accordingly.

Folliculitis

📋 **CLINICAL NOTES**

Epidemiology: Common. Aetiology/risk factors: Skin trauma increases risk, infection (Staph aureus including MRSA, enterobacter, klebsiella, E coli, proteus, pseudomonas, HSV, fungal, pityrosporum), eosinophilic. Clinical features: Inflamed hair follicles. Multiple pustules/papules, erythema, pseudomonal infection may cause systemic upset (fever, headache, GI upset). Complications: Scarring, scarring alopecia, sinus formation, cellulitis, abscess.

DISEASES

INVESTIGATIONS

Swab (MC&S), biopsy (eosinophilia), consider FBC, glucose.

MANAGEMENT

Hygiene, antibacterial soaps if superficial, oral antibiotics, pseudomonas may be self-limiting or require ciprofloxacin, daily aluminium chloride hexahydrate 6.25% in folliculitis of unknown origin, topical mupirocin or if fungal, ketoconazole. *Eosinophilic:* Isotretinoin, UVB, itraconazole, phototherapy. *Herpetic:* Aciclovir/famciclovir.

Foster Kennedy syndrome

CLINICAL NOTES

Aetiology/risk factors: Cerebral mass (usually tumour) and raised ICP. Clinical features: Ipsilateral optic atrophy (pressure effect from tumour), contralateral papilloedema (due to raised ICP), central scotoma, anosmia.

INVESTIGATIONS

CT/MRI brain.

MANAGEMENT

Treat underlying tumour.

Fournier's gangrene

CLINICAL NOTES

Epidemiology: Rare. Aetiology/risk factors: Staphylococcus, streptococci, *E coli*, salmonella, anaerobes, fungi. Immunodeficiency (eg HIV, leukaemia), trauma, anal infection eg Crohn's disease, diverticulitis, skin infection eg cellulitis, hidradenitis, urethral injuries eg catheterisation, UTI, DM, malnutrition, alcoholism, cirrhosis, elderly patients, spinal cord injury. Clinical features: Infection and necrosis of male genitalia. Malaise, fatigue, severe genital pain, fever, tachycardia, inflamed genitalia, crepitation, gangrene. Complications: Shock, 45% mortality.

INVESTIGATIONS

FBC, U&E, glucose, LFT, blood cultures, swabs.

MANAGEMENT

Fluid resuscitation, analgesia, IV antibiotics, inotropic support. *Surgery:* Debridement and grafting/reconstruction.

Fragile X (Martin Bell) syndrome

CLINICAL NOTES

Epidemiology: About one in 6,000 prevalence. Males affected more severely than females. Aetiology/risk factors: X chromosome defect. Clinical features: Mental retardation, anxiety, impulsivity, ADHD, autism,

aggression, avoidance of eye contact, developmental delay. *Males:* Large ears, jaw, forehead and testicles. High arched palate. *Female carriers:* One in three mental retardation. Complications: Epilepsy, fragile X ataxia syndrome (presents in sixth decade).

INVESTIGATIONS

Genetic studies, spinal radiograph, echocardiogram.

MANAGEMENT

SALT, physiotherapy, OT, ophthalmology, otolaryngology, audiology. Metabotropic glutamate receptor 5 antagonists under evaluation. Treat complications accordingly.

Friedreich's ataxia

CLINICAL NOTES

Epidemiology: About one in 50,000. Aetiology/risk factors: Autosomal recessive. Chromosome 9. Reduced mitochondrial frataxin. Clinical features: Onset in second/third decades. Ataxia, nystagmus, loss of proprioception, dysarthria, absent knee and ankle reflexes, upgoing plantars, pes cavus, scoliosis. Complications: Sensorineural hearing loss, diabetes insipidus, cardiomyopathy.

INVESTIGATIONS

FBC, U&E, glucose, vitamin E, ECG, echocardiogram. Nerve conduction studies – motor velocities >40m/s in arms and absent sensory action potentials.

MANAGEMENT

Genetic counselling. Coenzyme Q, idebenone, 5-hydroxytryptophan. Treat complications accordingly.

Frozen shoulder

CLINICAL NOTES

See *adhesive capsulitis*

Galactosaemia

CLINICAL NOTES

Epidemiology: One in 70,000 Caucasians (UK). Galactose-1-phosphate uridyl transferase (GALT) deficiency. Aetiology/risk factors: Autosomal recessive, chromosome 9. Clinical features: Inability to break down galactose begins once milk-feeding starts. Vomiting, diarrhoea, lethargy, failure to thrive/develop, neonatal jaundice, hepatosplenomegaly, bulging fontanelle. Complications: Sepsis (*E coli*), haemolysis, ascites, cataracts, mental retardation, short stature, hypergonadotrophic hypogonadism, hypoglycaemia, seizure, liver failure, clotting disorder, death.

INVESTIGATIONS

↓Hb, ↓pH, ↑serum ammonia, ↓glucose, galactosaemia,

↑bilirubin (unconjugated initially), GALT neonatal screening test (false +ve in G6PD deficiency), erythrocyte GALT analysis if screening test +ve, galactosuria (reducing substance on Clinitest), aminoaciduria, ketonuria, genetic testing.

💊 MANAGEMENT
Remove lactose (glucose plus galactose) and other galactose sources from diet for life (including lactulose laxative), milk substitutes (patients unable to tolerate any form of milk eg protein hydrosylate formula), dietitian, hormone replacement, SALT.

Gallstone disease

📖 CLINICAL NOTES
Epidemiology: Up to 15% UK prevalence. Aetiology/risk factors: Age (more common >40 years), obesity, female, fair features, familial, reduced bile salts, haemolysis, DM, rapid weight loss. Clinical features: Asymptomatic, RUQ pain. Complications: Biliary colic (epigastric/RUQ pain, may be severe, not always colicky, vomiting); acute cholecystitis (RUQ pain, fever, rigors, tachycardia, peritonism, Murphy's sign); acute pancreatitis, obstructive jaundice (dark urine, pale stool); cholangitis (fever, rigors, RUQ pain, tachycardia); empyema (fever, rigors, tachycardia, RUQ pain); polyps, gallstone ileus.

⟳ INVESTIGATIONS
FBC (↓Hb in haemolysis, bile stones, ↑WCC in cholecystitis/cholangitis/empyema); blood film (may see haemolysis if bile stones), LFT (↑conjugated bilirubin/↑ALP in obstructive jaundice), ↑lipase. Abdominal X-ray 10-15% sensitivity for gallstones. USS for gallstones, not sensitive for common bile duct stones, shows thickened gallbladder after recurrent cholecystitis, dilated common bile duct in obstructive jaundice. CT cholangiography or MRCP for ductal stones.

💊 MANAGEMENT
Consider watch and wait if asymptomatic. Biliary colic/cholecystitis: Analgesia, IV antibiotics if infective process, laparoscopic cholecystectomy. Cholangitis: IV antibiotics, endoscopic drainage. Empyema: IV antibiotics, decompression, cholecystectomy. Polyps: If <10mm and asymptomatic, may be left alone; larger ones should be removed as small risk of malignancy. Ileus often requires laparotomy.

Ganglion

📖 CLINICAL NOTES
Epidemiology: Common. Aetiology/risk factors: Idiopathic, OA, repetitive movement, trauma. Clinical features: Spontaneous wrist, knee or foot lump, smooth, fixed, cystic, may be painful. Complications: Functional impairment, nerve impingement.

💊 MANAGEMENT
Watch and wait, splint, needle aspiration (high risk of recurrence), surgical excision.

Gastric cancer

📖 CLINICAL NOTES
95% cases adenocarcinoma, others GI stromal tumours (GIST), mucosa associated lymphoma tissue (MALT), squamous cell, small cell, carcinoid. Epidemiology: Seven to 20 in 10^5 per year. Increasing. Second most common cause of cancer death globally. Aetiology/risk factors: M>F, advancing age, H pylori, smoking, alcohol, diet low in fruit and vegetables and high in salt and preserved foods. Pernicious anaemia, atrophic gastritis, blood group A, family history. Clinical features: 80% cases present with evidence of tumour spread. Weight loss, anorexia, dyspepsia, vomiting, dysphagia, epigastric pain, pallor, epigastric mass, Virchow's node, Sister Mary Joseph nodule, hepatomegaly, jaundice, acanthosis nigricans. Complications: Haematemesis, bowel obstruction, metastatic disease, death.

⟳ INVESTIGATIONS
FBC, burr cells, LFT, endoscopy and biopsy (malignancy may be missed with PPI use), CT, MRI, pelvic imaging (ovarian spread ie Krukenberg tumour).

💊 MANAGEMENT
Surgery (spleen should be preserved if possible, plus adjuvant chemotherapy for high-risk adenocarcinoma). Neoadjuvant/palliative chemotherapy. Adjuvant and palliative radiotherapy. Palliative stent. Anti-VEGF and anti-EGFR receptor agents may be considered.

Gastroenteritis

📖 CLINICAL NOTES
Epidemiology: Common. Aetiology/risk factors: Traveller's diarrhoea: Bacterial>parasitic>viral. E coli most common (normally self-limiting less than three days, incubation half to three days, risk of HUS/TTP if verotoxin-producing eg 0157. Other bacteria (may be associated with blood) – shigella, salmonella (incubation half to two days), campylobacter (incubation up to three days, virulent). See C difficile. Prolonged diarrhoea/immunocompromised – consider non-infective causes of diarrhoea (see Signs & Symptoms, diarrhoea), giardiasis, entamoeba, cryptosporidium, cyclospora, rotavirus. Non-traveller's gastroenteritis: Viral up to 40% including norovirus and rotavirus. Bacterial: Campylobacter most common aetiology. Clinical features: Diarrhoea, abdominal pain (crampy), +/- nausea/vomiting, fever. Complications: Shock, renal failure, electrolyte disturbance, HUS, TTP, Guillain-Barré syndrome, toxic megacolon, septic arthritis (caused by salmonella spp particularly in sickle cell patients), lactose intolerance, drug malabsorption.

INVESTIGATIONS

Consider FBC, U&E, LFT, stool culture (may require three samples on three separate occasions), ↑amylase, microscopy, culture, sensitivity, ova, cysts, parasites. Consider *C difficile* toxin in faeces or sigmoidoscopy.

MANAGEMENT

Oral rehydration therapy (ORT), antiemetics. If significant dehydration, comorbidities or unwell, consider admission. Consider empirical ciprofloxacin (or erythromycin if suspect campylobacter). Antibiotics not indicated in HUS/TTP.

Gastrointestinal stromal tumour (GIST)

CLINICAL NOTES

Sarcoma. Epidemiology: <1,000 per year (UK). Aetiology/risk factors: Age, tyrosine kinase mutations, neurofibromatosis I, familial, Carney complex. Clinical features: Asymptomatic, anaemia, GI haemorrhage, bloating, abdominal mass, weight loss, night sweats, fever. Complications: Intra-abdominal spread, liver/lung/bone metastases, GI obstruction.

INVESTIGATIONS

FBC, LFT, CT, MRI, PET, endoscopy, biopsy (risk of tumour seeding), immunohistochemistry.

MANAGEMENT

Surgery, tyrosine kinase inhibitors (imatinib, sunitinib).

Gastro-oesophageal disease (GORD), infantile

CLINICAL NOTES

Epidemiology: Common. 50% babies, about 1% at one year. Aetiology/risk factors: Low birthweight, overfeeding (occurs with bottle-fed babies – normal requirement 100-120ml/kg per day), air swallowing (wrong angle for bottle-feeding), congenital malformations. Clinical features: Failure to thrive, crying, irritability, poor sleep, poor feeding, back arching during/after feeds, possetting, vomiting, wheezing, apnoea, parental anxiety.

INVESTIGATIONS

Only if complications: pH probe, with apnoea monitor, motility studies, exclude cow's milk protein intolerance/allergy, may require small bowel biopsy.

MANAGEMENT

Reassurance if no complications and gaining weight, avoid overfeeding, alter posture, thickeners, infant specific alginates, domperidone, ranitidine, PPI, consider changing cow's milk formula to casein hydrolysate or amino acid based (six weeks to three months), fundoplication, gastrostomy.

Gastro-oesophageal reflux disease (GORD) in adults

CLINICAL NOTES

Epidemiology: Common. Aetiology/risk factors: M>F, hiatus hernia, obesity, smoking, alcohol, hot drinks, spicy food, fatty meals, systemic sclerosis, achalasia, iatrogenic, pregnancy. Clinical features: Retrosternal burning chest pain worse on laying flat, waterbrash, odynophagia, cough, hoarse voice. Complications: Oesophageal stenosis, Barrett's oesophagus, aspiration pneumonia, pulmonary fibrosis.

INVESTIGATIONS

Endoscopy, barium studies, acid probe, *H pylori* breath test/stool antigen.

MANAGEMENT

Lifestyle management, elevated night posture, refer immediately if GI haemorrhage, urgently if red flags (dysphagia/weight loss/anaemia/persistent vomiting/epigastric mass/resistent dyspepsia for more than four weeks and >55 years), PPI, *H pylori* eradication. Consider fundoplication for hiatus hernia.

Gaucher's disease

CLINICAL NOTES

Lipid storage disease. Epidemiology: Rare. Aetiology/risk factors: Glucocerebrosidase deficiency. Autosomal recessive. Clinical features: Three subtypes. Anaemic symptoms (breathlessness, fatigue), thrombocytopenic symptoms (haemorrhage), hepatosplenomegaly, skeletal deformities, bone pain, corneal deposits, mitral/aortic calcification. Complications: Fetal hydrops, portal hypertension, seizures, premature dementia, factor XI deficiency, death (in childhood in some subtypes).

INVESTIGATIONS

Glucocerebrosidase activity , ↓Hb, ↓plts, LFT, clotting screen, gene testing, abdominal USS/CT, echocardiogram, bone marrow biopsy.

MANAGEMENT

Genetic counselling, imiglucerase replacement types 1 and 3.

Genital tract infections (non-STI)

CLINICAL NOTES

Bacterial vaginosis: Epidemiology: Common. Aetiology/risk factors: *Gardnerella spp*, ↑luteal phase, smoking, IUD, douching and bubble baths. Clinical features: Fishy discharge >pH4.5, amine odour with addition of potassium hydroxide on discharge sample, white discharge, clue cells (Gram stain). *Candidiasis:* Epidemiology: Common, Aetiology/risk factors: Post-antibiotics, pregnancy, steroid use, immunodeficiency, atopy, DM, psoriasis.

Clinical features: Asymptomatic, thick white discharge, pruritus, soreness, dyspareunia (balanitis in men).

 INVESTIGATIONS
High vaginal swabs (HVS).

MANAGEMENT
Bacterial vaginosis: Metronidazole 400mg twice daily orally five days/intravaginal metronidazole gel (0.75%) five days/intravaginal clindamycin 2% seven days. *Candidiasis:* Clotrimazole pessary/10% cream (safe in pregnancy), fluconazole 150mg immediately.

Genital warts (condylomata acuminata)

CLINICAL NOTES
Epidemiology: Common. Aetiology/risk factors: ↑promiscuity, immunodeficiency, ↓with circumcision. >90% HPV 6, 11. Clinical features: Painless warty lesions; warts may also be seen on cervix. Do not mistake penile papules for warts (papules are harmless). Complications: Psychological morbidity, coexistent STI including HIV.

 INVESTIGATIONS
Patient requires full STI screen.

MANAGEMENT
Use condoms, advise patient that recurrence does not necessarily imply infidelity. Warts may be left alone, liquid nitrogen, podophyllotoxin (avoid in pregnancy), imiquimod cream (perianal, avoid in pregnancy), surgery (advanced perianal warts), colposcopy (cervical).

German measles

CLINICAL NOTES
See *rubella (German measles)*

Gestational diabetes

CLINICAL NOTES
Epidemiology: One in 400 pregnancies. Aetiology/risk factors: Obesity, previous gestational diabetes or baby >4.5kg, familial DM, origin, eg South Asian. Clinical features: Asymptomatic, fatigue, polyuria, polydipsia. Complications: Increased mortality (mother and baby), permanent DM, pre-eclampsia, polyhydramnios, prematurity, macrosomia, sacral agenesis, femoral hypoplasia, cardiac defects, neural tube defects, fetal microcolon, hairy ears, obstructed labour.

 INVESTIGATIONS
Confirm by OGTT, fetal anomaly scan.

MANAGEMENT
Lifestyle advice (diet and exercise), maintain good glucose control during pregnancy (consider oral agents eg metformin or insulin), deliver by 38 weeks, repeat OGTT six weeks post-partum.

Giardia

CLINICAL NOTES
See *traveller's diarrhoea*

Gilbert's syndrome

CLINICAL NOTES
Epidemiology: Up to 8% prevalence. Aetiology/risk factors: Autosomal recessive. Clinical features: Asymptomatic. Intermittent jaundice (triggered by alcohol, medication, intercurrent illness, iatrogenic), nausea, malaise, altered concentration.

 INVESTIGATIONS
Unconjugated hyperbilirubinaemia. Bilirubin <100micromol/L. Bilirubin ↑if patient is fasted.

MANAGEMENT
Lifestyle advice.

Gilles de la Tourette syndrome

CLINICAL NOTES
Epidemiology: 1% of school-age children. M>F. Aetiology/risk factors: Genetic. Clinical features: Presents in first two decades. Involuntary motor tics (eg grimacing, blinking, clapping, jumping), sounds (eg humming, coughing) and words (eg coprolalia one in 10 cases). Symptoms may be worse with stress. Complications: Distress, social, employment and family difficulties, OCD, bipolar disorder, autism, Asperger's syndrome, substance misuse.

MANAGEMENT
MDT and family support, self-management techniques, counselling, haloperidol, pimozide, SSRI (eg for OCD).

Glandular fever

CLINICAL NOTES
See *infectious mononucleosis*

Glaucoma (acute angle closure)

CLINICAL NOTES
Epidemiology: Less common than open-angle glaucoma. Aetiology/risk factors: F>M, peak seventh decade, family history longsightedness, iatrogenic (pupillary dilators eg TCAs, chlorpheniramine, ranitidine). Clinical features: Acute onset, red eye, severe pain, vomiting, visual haloes, visual loss, poorly reactive irregular pupil, globe firm to touch. Complications: Permanent visual impairment.

INVESTIGATIONS

↑intraocular pressure (IOP), injected iris, shallow anterior chamber.

MANAGEMENT

Acetazolamide, analgesia, antiemetics, topical pilocarpine, laser iridotomy, surgery. Driving advice.

Glaucoma (open angle)

CLINICAL NOTES

Epidemiology: 500,000 UK prevalence. About 50% undiagnosed. **Aetiology/risk factors:** Age, familial (x3 risk in first-degree relatives), DM, myopia, systemic and ocular hypertension, ↑in African-Caribbeans. **Clinical features:** Asymptomatic, peripheral field loss, disc cupping (may be subtle)/notching, retinal nerve layer loss, peridisc retinal atrophy. **Complications:** Permanent visual impairment.

INVESTIGATIONS

IOP may be normal (one in three cases), formal visual field testing. Screening (requires IOP and fields and optic disc assessment).

MANAGEMENT

Topical – prostaglandin analogues, beta-blockers, alpha-2 agonists, carbonic anhydrase inhibitors, sympathomimetics, surgery (trabeculectomy, drainage tube, laser).

Gliomas (including glioblastoma multiforme)

CLINICAL NOTES

Ependymomas, oligodendrogliomas, astrocytomas, glioblastoma multiforme. Glioblastoma multiforme is a high-grade and highly malignant glioma (most common glioma). **Epidemiology:** Most common brain tumour. Presents mid-50s. **Clinical features:** Headache (may cause patient to wake from sleep), nausea, vomiting, CVA, haemorrhage, localising neurological signs. Tend to be locally invasive. Distant metastases rare. **Complications:** Seizures, raised ICP.

INVESTIGATIONS

CT/MRI, histology (biopsy or at resection).

MANAGEMENT

Surgery (resection/debulking). Adjuvant radiotherapy and chemotherapy. Anti-EGFR agents eg cetuximab. Other biologics under investigation. Antiepileptics, dexamethasone.

Glomerulonephritis

See also
— *Kidney (renal) failure, acute*

CLINICAL NOTES

Aetiology/risk factors: Idiopathic, familial, DM, infection (streptococcal, viral including hepatitis B/C, malaria, HIV), iatrogenic (eg penicillamine, gold, NSAIDs, penicillin), autoimmune (eg SLE, Sjögren's syndrome), vasculitis, malignancy (eg lymphoma, lung, GI, CLL, myeloma), hypertension, pre-eclampsia, sickle cell anaemia, amyloid, sarcoid, Alport's syndrome. *Minimal change disease:* Common in children, one in four to one in three cases of nephrotic syndrome in adults, normal eGFR, nephrotic range proteinuria, steroid responsive, 10% relapse. *Membranous glomerulonephritis:* Peak 20s and 60s. Usually proteinuria/nephrotic range proteinuria, occasionally haematuria, one in three respond to immunosuppressants, one in three progress to CKD. Control BP/proteinuria with ACE inhibitors/ARB, one in 20 risk of renal vein thrombosis; if albumin <20, patient requires anticoagulation. *IgA nephropathy (Berger's disease):* Often few days post-URTI, haematuria (non-visible or visible), occasionally deteriorates to ARF, may cause CKD (one in four will have CKD stage 5 at 20 years). May require steroids. Control BP and proteinuria with ACE inhibitors/ARB. *Focal segmental glomerulosclerosis:* Proteinuria, may cause nephritic syndrome/ARF, one in four reach stage 5 CKD. Treat idiopathic causes with immunosuppressants, control BP and proteinuria with ACE inhibitors/ARB. *Diffuse proliferative glomerulonephritis:* Usually nephritic/haematuria. May cause ARF. Low serum C3. *Mesangiocapillary glomerulonephritis:* Variety of presentations – proteinuria/nephrotic range proteinuria/nephritic syndrome/ARF, may progress to stage 5 CKD. *Crescentic glomerulonephritis:* Rapidly progressive, commonly presents with nephritic syndrome/ARF.

INVESTIGATIONS

Urinalysis and microscopy (red cell casts, proteinuria). Investigate for underlying causes eg complement studies, antistreptolysin O titre (ASOT), hepatitis screen, autoimmune screen, HIV screen, malignancy screen.

MANAGEMENT

Treat underlying cause. See under relevant entry for specific treatments.

Glucagonoma

CLINICAL NOTES

Epidemiology: Rare. May be part of multiple endocrine neoplasia (MEN) syndrome. **Clinical features:** Usually malignant (unlike insulinoma which is usually benign), weight loss, diarrhoea. **Complications:** Necrolytic migrating erythema (erythematous blistering and crusting rash), angular cheilitis, DM, depression, psychosis, DVT, anaemia.

INVESTIGATIONS

FBC, ↑glucose, USS, CT, MRI, abdominal angiography, somatostatin receptor scintigraphy (non-specific).

DISEASES

MANAGEMENT

DVT prophylaxis, insulin, octreotide for rash, chemotherapy, embolisation, surgery (if localised, usually metastatic by presentation).

Glucose-6-phosphate dehydrogenase (G6PD) deficiency

CLINICAL NOTES

Epidemiology: M>F. Multiple variants. Protects against malaria. Aetiology/risk factors: X-linked. Triggers: Iatrogenic, eg aspirin, sulfonamides, nitrofurantoin, NSAIDs, antimalaria medication, broad beans (favism – occurs in Mediterranean form), renal failure, DKA. Clinical features: Different degrees of severity. Asymptomatic, jaundice, splenomegaly. Complications: Haemolysis caused by oxidative stress, gallstones, false +ve galactosaemia screen, methaemoglobinaemia.

INVESTIGATIONS

↓Hb, ↑MCV, ↑reticuloctyes, ↑unconjugated bilirubin, ↑lactate. G6PD enzyme activity assay. Film: Heinz bodies, bite cells.

MANAGEMENT

Avoid triggers, oxygen, transfuse if severe anaemia. Genetic counselling.

Glue ear (secretory otitis media with effusion)

CLINICAL NOTES

Epidemiology: Common. Aetiology/risk factors: Two to five years of age, idiopathic, URTI, acute otitis media, allergy, Eustachian tube dysfunction, large adenoids, barotrauma, rhinitis, cleft lip, Down's syndrome, nasopharyngeal tumour. Clinical features: Asymptomatic, conductive hearing loss, serous effusion, pain. Complications: Acute suppurative otitis media, speech, language and educational difficulties.

INVESTIGATIONS

Audiometry, pneumatic otoscopy/tympanometry. Adults: Investigation to exclude nasopharyngeal tumour.

MANAGEMENT

Watch and wait (maximum three months in children), antibiotics, hearing aids, adenoidectomy, grommets (to ventilate middle ear), educational help.

GM1 gangliosidosis

CLINICAL NOTES

Beta-galactosidase-1 deficiency. Epidemiology: Rare. Aetiology/risk factors: GLB1 mutation, autosomal recessive. Clinical features: Most severe forms present in infancy with regression in development,

hepatosplenomegaly and skeletal deformities. Complications: Seizures, deafness, mental retardation, cardiomyopathy, blindness, macular cherry red spot, gingival hypertrophy, childhood death in severe forms.

INVESTIGATIONS

Screening, genetic studies, leucocyte beta-galactosidase-1 activity. Investigate for complications eg X-ray, USS/CT/MRI, echocardiography, retinophotography.

MANAGEMENT

Symptomatic treatment only. Genetic counselling.

Golfer's elbow (medial epicondylitis)

CLINICAL NOTES

Epidemiology: Common. Aetiology/risk factors: Overuse or repetitive use. Clinical features: Tender medial epicondyle, worse on wrist flexion, pronation and gripping. Complications: Ulnar nerve involvement, OA.

INVESTIGATIONS

Nerve conduction studies if suspected ulnar neuropathy.

MANAGEMENT

Avoid trigger; rest, ice, NSAIDs, wrist exercises progressing to resisted, physiotherapy (more effective than steroid injections at one year), steroid injections (short-term benefit but high recurrence rate and risk of ulnar nerve damage).

Gonorrhoea

CLINICAL NOTES

See sexually transmitted infections and genital infections

Goodpasture's syndrome

CLINICAL NOTES

Epidemiology: Rare. M>F. Presents third to fourth decade. Aetiology/risk factors: Genetic, smoking, postviral, occupational (metal dusts). Clinical features: Nausea, vomiting, breathlessness, hypertension, haemoptysis (50%), haematuria, glomerulonephritis. Complications: Acute renal failure, 20% mortality.

INVESTIGATIONS

FBC (anaemia), U&E, →ESR, antiglomerular basement membrane antibodies, p-ANCA and c-ANCA (positive in one in three patients), urine microscopy (suggestive of glomerulonephritis), renal biopsy, chest X-ray.

MANAGEMENT

May require ventilation and renal replacement therapy acutely. Immunosuppressant therapy, plasmapheresis, renal transplant.

DISEASES

Gorlin's syndrome

📋 **CLINICAL NOTES**

Epidemiology: Rare. Aetiology/risk factors: Sporadic, autosomal dominant. Clinical features and complications: Benign jaw tumours, multiple basal cell carcinomas (BCC) around puberty, frontal bossing, palmar-plantar pitting, medulloblastoma, cardiac fibromas, ovarian fibromas, skeletal deformities, fractures, blindness, deafness, epilepsy, hydrocephalus.

⚕ **INVESTIGATIONS**

Genetic studies, biopsy, X-ray, MRI/CT, echocardiography.

🗋 **MANAGEMENT**

Genetic counselling, treat complications accordingly.

Gout

📋 **CLINICAL NOTES**

Epidemiology: M>F. Three in 1,000 per year (M), 0.2 in 1,000 per year (F). Aetiology/risk factors: Age, familial, cardiac failure, psoriasis, renal failure, purine-rich foods (red meat, offal, pulses, shellfish), alcohol (increases serum uric acid x3) and obesity (increased endogenous uric acid and reduced renal uric acid clearance, increases serum uric acid x2.34), iatrogenic (eg loop and thiazide diuretics, low-dose aspirin, ethambutol, pyrazinamide, insulin), Lesch-Nyhan syndrome, tumour lysis syndrome. Protective: Dairy products, iatrogenic (eg probenecid, losartan, high-dose aspirin >4g per day). Clinical features: Often overweight men 30s-40s: Acute onset joint inflammation, monoarticular (frequency 50% MTPJ, followed by midfoot, ankle, knee, in decreasing frequency), intense over few hours. Complications: Chronic tophaceous gout (may be milky discharge), polyarticular gout, OA, CKD.

⚕ **INVESTIGATIONS**

Concentration for uric acid >0.36mmol/L now considered threshold for concern. Nijmegen score may be used for acute gout diagnosis. Score of ≥8 suggestive of acute gout. Serum uric acid (may be 25% lower during acute attack). U&E, joint aspiration (negatively birefringent crystals). X-ray: Punched-out lesions.

🗋 **MANAGEMENT**

Acute: NSAIDs (consider renal and cardiac comorbidities, PPI cover), colchicine, corticosteroids (intra-articular, systemic). Prevention: Lifestyle (weight, diet), allopurinol (renally excreted, may trigger acute attack, recheck U&E and uric acid at four weeks and aim for uric acid ≤0.30mmol/L). Colchicine may also be used. Febuxostat an alternative to allopurinol. Probenecid is uricosuric; avoid uricosuric agents if eGFR <30ml/min/1.73m². Losartan is uricosuric.

Graft versus host disease (GVHD)

📋 **CLINICAL NOTES**

Immune reaction post-allogeneic stem cell or bone marrow transplantation. Epidemiology: Common. About 35% if donor and recipient related, about 70% if not related. Aetiology/risk factors: HLA mismatch causing T-cells from graft to recognise recipient as foreign tissue. Clinical features: Acute disease within three months of transplant – dermatitis, diarrhoea (may be bloody), hepatitis, jaundice. Chronic more than three months post-transplant; may last throughout recipient's life. Dermatitis, skin thickening, dysphagia, obstructive lung disease, muscle pain, weakness, dry eyes, vaginitis. Complications: Sepsis, GI haemorrhage, pleural effusion, pneumonia, haemorrhagic cystitis, death.

⚕ **INVESTIGATIONS**

FBC, U&E, ↑AST, ↑bilirubin, chest X-ray, hepatic USS, barium swallow, endoscopy, colonoscopy, skin biopsy, spirometry.

🗋 **MANAGEMENT**

Prevention: Seek close donor-recipient match, anti-rejection drugs eg methotrexate, ciclosporin, tacrolimus, antithymocyte globulin, mycophenolate mofetil, thalidomide, extracorporeal photophoresis. Treatment: Continue prophylactic drugs plus topical or systemic steroids, PUVA, azathioprine, ciclosporin, mycophenolate mofetil, antithymocyte globulin, daclizumab, imatinib, etanercept, infliximab, visilizumab. Supportive treatment.

Granuloma annulare

📋 **CLINICAL NOTES**

Benign inflammatory skin condition. Epidemiology: F>M. Aetiology/risk factors: Idiopathic, DM, thyroid disease (rarely). Clinical features: Erythematous raised skin lesions, (papules), may expand into plaques. Normally hands and feet, may be generalised in DM. Occasionally pruritic.

⚕ **INVESTIGATIONS**

Diagnosis based on history and physical examination. Glucose, TFT.

🗋 **MANAGEMENT**

Self-limiting (may take two years to resolve), consider topical steroids, cryotherapy, PUVA.

Graves' disease

See also
— Hyperthyroidism

📋 **CLINICAL NOTES**

Epidemiology: Fourth to sixth decades, F>M. Clinical

features: Thyrotoxicosis (may also be hypothyroid/
euthyroid), thyroid bruit, thyroid acropachy (painful
clubbing), pretibial myxoedema, lid lag, Graves'
eye disease (ophthalmoplegia, especially upward
gaze; exophthalmos and proptosis, corneal ulcers,
conjunctival suffusion, ↓ acuity, papilloedema).
Complications: Psychosis, permanent visual impairment, associated autoimmune disease.

⌀ INVESTIGATIONS
Normal or ↑thyroid auto-antibodies (including thyroid-
stimulating antibodies and thyroglobulin antibodies).
Anaemia of chronic disease, →↑ESR, CT/MRI orbit for
eye disease, screen for other autoimmune diseases.

⏧ MANAGEMENT
Graves' eye disease: Acute loss of acuity or colour vision
may need immediate assessment to rule out optic
nerve compression; steroids for ophthalmoplegia or
orbital oedema, smoking cessation advice (smoking
exacerbates eye disease), eye lubrication, tape eyes
shut/lateral tarsorrhaphy to avoid ulceration, surgical orbital decompression, orbital radiotherapy.
Hyperthyroidism: Beta-blockade, carbimazole or propylthiouracil, radioiodine, partial thyroidectomy, risk
of post-treatment/subclinical hypothyroidism.

Guillain-Barré syndrome

⊞ CLINICAL NOTES
Postinfective polyneuropathy. Epidemiology: About
1,500 cases per year (UK). Aetiology/risk
factors: Bacterial eg campylobacter (worse prognosis),
salmonella; viral eg mumps, measles, CMV, EBV;
lymphoma, postpartum, post-vaccination. Clinical
features: Progressive over weeks, ascending symmetrical paralysis (symptoms start distally, progress
proximally), back pain, neuropathic pain especially
lower limbs, reduced tone and power, reduced reflexes.
Complications: Facial weakness, bulbar palsy, may be
sensory signs, respiratory failure, autonomic dysfunction
(eg tachycardia, postural hypotension). Ocular muscle
weakness, areflexia and ataxia (Miller Fisher syndrome),
residual neurological impairment, SIADH, thromboembolic disease, pneumonia, pressure sores, ileus, affective
disorders.

⌀ INVESTIGATIONS
FBC, atypical lymphocytes, U&E, ↑CSF protein,
nerve conduction studies (axonal neuropathy – poor
prognosis), ECG (heart block, arrhythmias, QRS and T
wave anomalies), monitor lung function and vital signs
for involvement of respiratory muscles and autonomic
dysfunction.

⏧ MANAGEMENT
Immunoglobulins, plasma exchange, IV methylprednisolone, DVT prevention, ventilation if ↓FEV$_1$<1.5L.

⊞ CLINICAL NOTES
Epidemiology: Prevalence around one in 300.
Menstruating women less affected. Aetiology/risk
factors: Autosomal recessive, *HFE* gene mutations
(primary, C282Y mutation found in 6.5-9.4% of UK
population),chronic liver disease, thalassaemia, iatrogenic (multiple transfusions, renal dialysis), diet. Clinical
features and complications: Asymptomatic, fatigue,
nausea, abdominal pain, constipation, bronzed skin,
pancreatic involvement (diabetes, pancreatitis), cardiac
involvement (cardiomyopathy, arrhythmia), chronic
liver disease, cirrhosis, hepatocellular cancer (x200
risk), thyroid disease, pituitary involvement (menstrual
disturbance and loss of libido), testicular failure, arthritis
(often MCPs and PIPJs), pseudogout.

⌀ INVESTIGATIONS
Hb, ↑↑ferritin, iron studies, ↓total iron-binding
capacity, ↑transferrin saturation, ↑transaminases, alpha-
fetoprotein, glucose, amylase, TFT, calcium, ↓hepcidin,
anterior pituitary function tests, sex hormones, ECG,
echocardiography, liver biopsy, genetic studies.

⏧ MANAGEMENT
Genetic counselling, lifestyle changes (avoid vitamin C,
avoid excess iron, increase tea and dairy intake), venesection (maintain Hb around 10g/dL), iron chelation may
be required, treat complications accordingly, regular
monitoring.

Haemolytic uraemic syndrome (HUS)

⊞ CLINICAL NOTES
Epidemiology: Mainly children. Occurs in outbreaks. Aetiology/risk factors: Majority caused by
verotoxin-producing *E coli* (VTEC) 0157 from eg farms,
undercooked/raw meat. Clinical features: Afebrile,
bloody diarrhoea, abdominal pain, bruising, haemolysis
(microangiopathic), jaundice. Complications: Renal
failure, death.

⌀ INVESTIGATIONS
↓ plts, ↓ Hb. *Film:* Schistocytes, ↓ eGFR.
Urinalysis: Haematuria, proteinuria.

⏧ MANAGEMENT
Renal replacement therapy if renal failure, plasma
exchange, antibiotics not indicated.

Haemophilia A

⊞ CLINICAL NOTES
Factor VIII deficiency. Epidemiology: One in 10^4 male
prevalence. Aetiology/risk factors: X-linked, mutation. Clinical features: Haemarthrosis, haematomas.

DISEASES

Complications: Arthropathy, compartment syndrome, nerve compression, severe haemorrhage, death.

 INVESTIGATIONS
↑APTT, ↓factor VIII.

 MANAGEMENT
Vaccinations (including hepatitis B), oral hygiene, avoid IM injections when possible, tranexamic acid (for wounds, avoid if internal bleeding), desmopressin (DDAVP), concentrated clotting factor for significant bleeds.

Haemorrhoids

 CLINICAL NOTES
Epidemiology: Common. Aetiology/risk factors: Idiopathic, pregnancy, portal hypertension, straining at stool, high anal tone. Clinical features: Asymptomatic, anal 'lump', pruritus, bleeding (beware malignancy masquerading as haemorrhoids), mucous discharge, pain, tenesmus, incontinence. Complications: Thrombosed/infarcted pile (causes severe pain), prolapse.

 MANAGEMENT
Prevention: High-fibre diet, anal hygiene. Treatment: Conservative – reduction of prolapse, topical anaesthetics/steroids. Surgical – banding, sclerotherapy, coagulation, haemorrhoidectomy, HALO (haemorrhoid artery ligation operation). Thrombosed: Ice and analgesia, may require surgical intervention.

Hallux valgus

 CLINICAL NOTES
Aetiology/risk factors: Idiopathic, familial (autosomal dominant), tight-fitting shoes, arthritis. Clinical features: Valgus deformity of great toe, usually bilateral. Complications: Bunion, corns, ulceration, involvement of other toes, OA, subluxation, embarrassment.

 MANAGEMENT
Appropriate footwear, cushions and orthotics, physiotherapy, surgery.

Hand, foot and mouth disease

 CLINICAL NOTES
Epidemiology: Common Aetiology/risk factors: Predominantly Coxsackie virus, spread by direct contact or vertical transmission. Incubation five to seven days. Clinical features: Mildly painful oral and palmoplantar vesicles.

 INVESTIGATIONS
No specific tests required.

 MANAGEMENT
Analgesia, no specific treatment.

Hartnup disease

See also
— Vitamin deficiencies and excesses

 CLINICAL NOTES
Epidemiology: Rare. Aetiology/risk factors: Autosomal recessive. Clinical features: Pellagra-type disease, cerebellar ataxia, CKD, malabsorption.

 INVESTIGATIONS
Oral tryptophan challenge and urine chromatography.

 MANAGEMENT
B-complex vitamins and nicotinamide.

Head lice (pediculosis capitis)

 CLINICAL NOTES
Epidemiology: 3 x 10⁶ per year (UK), often occur in school outbreaks. Aetiology/risk factors: Not related to personal hygiene. Very contagious through direct contact or sharing hats/hairbrushes. Clinical features: Average person harbours 20 lice. Each louse lays four to five eggs per day. Once hatched, egg shells known as nits. Lice have 30-day lifespan. Eggs last for five days and lice can survive for three days away from the head. Asymptomatic, pruritus may occur 90 days after infestation, rash. Complications: Stigma, secondary bacterial infection.

 MANAGEMENT
Treat patient and family at same time. Malathion, phenothrin or carbaryl, repeat after seven days (70-80% cure rate). Dimeticone (70% cure rate). 'Bug Buster' regimen, good evidence (wash hair, dedicated conditioner, eliminate tangles, head lice comb, repeat every two to four days for minimum two weeks).

Heat stroke

 CLINICAL NOTES
Aetiology/risk factors: Hot weather, dehydration, alcohol abuse, elderly people, young children, chronic disease eg DM, Alzheimer's disease, iatrogenic eg beta-blockers, antipsychotics, amphetamines, exertion ('exertional heat stroke'). Clinical features: Hyperthermia, nausea, vomiting, tachycardia, tachypnoea, cramps. Complications: Agitation, confusion, altered consciousness, ataxia, seizures, hallucinations, multiorgan failure, death.

 INVESTIGATIONS
Check core temperature (37-40°C suggests heat exhaustion, >40°C suggests heat stroke), ↑WCC, ↑Na⁺ (unless

excess losses or hydrated with plain water), LFT, ↑CK, lactic acidosis, ↑LDH.

MANAGEMENT
Controlled cooling (rapid reduction in temperature eg by water immersion may cause hypertensive crisis and should only be done in hospital), fluid and electrolyte balance.

HELLP syndrome
🗒 CLINICAL NOTES
See *pre-eclampsia*

Hemiballismus
🗒 CLINICAL NOTES
Epidemiology: Rare. Aetiology/risk factors: Lesion of subthalamic nucleus of basal ganglia; CVA, tumour, abscess. Clinical features: Violent unilateral involuntary movements. Complications: Embarrassment, exhaustion.

⚕ INVESTIGATIONS
CT/MRI brain.

🗒 MANAGEMENT
Benzodiazepines, haloperidol, olanzapine, stereotactic surgery.

Henoch-Schönlein purpura
🗒 CLINICAL NOTES
Epidemiology: Most common childhood vasculitis. 24 in 10^5 per year UK childhood incidence. Aetiology/risk factors: M>F, ↑winter, may be triggered by infection, vaccination, iatrogenic. Clinical features: Small vessel vasculitis, rash (purpuric, particularly on buttocks and legs), joint swelling and pain, nausea, vomiting, abdominal pain, headache. Complications: Recurrence, GI haemorrhage, intussusception, bowel infarction, hypertension, nephritis, nephrotic syndrome, renal failure, MI, neuropathy, seizure, death.

⚕ INVESTIGATIONS
FBC (eosinophila), U&E, ↑ESR, ↑IgA, urinalysis (blood and protein), abdominotesticular USS, skin biopsy.

🗒 MANAGEMENT
NSAIDs (unless renal failure), systemic steroids, azathioprine, cyclophosphamide, plasmapheresis. Once urinalysis normalised, monitor regularly for six months.

Hepatic encephalopathy
🗒 CLINICAL NOTES
See *liver failure*

Hepatitis A
🗒 CLINICAL NOTES
Aetiology/risk factors: Incubation 15-50 days. Children – mild infection. Transmission via food, water (faeco-oral contamination). Hepatitis A virus (HAV) faecally shed two weeks before to one week after symptoms. Infection confers lifelong future immunity. No chronic phase. Clinical features: Asymptomatic, flu-like illness, RUQ pain, fever, malaise, fatigue, low mood, pruritus, jaundice. Symptoms may recur over six-month period. Complications: Acute liver failure, Stevens-Johnson syndrome, toxic epidermal necrolysis, death (one in 200).

⚕ INVESTIGATIONS
FBC, atypical lymphocytes, ↑liver transaminases. HAV IgM (raised 1-2 to 14 weeks after infection). HAV IgG suggests previous infection or vaccination.

🗒 MANAGEMENT
Supportive treatment, prevention by vaccination and hygiene.

Hepatitis B
🗒 CLINICAL NOTES
Epidemiology: About one in 1,000 UK prevalence. Aetiology/risk factors: Africa, Asia, Pacific Islands. Incubation one to six months. Transmission via body fluids. Infectious two weeks before jaundice. Clinical features: Subclinical illness, fulminant infection, anorexia, nausea, RUQ pain, jaundice 10-50%. Complications: Hepatic failure, chronic infection (more likely if infection during childhood or if coexistent immunodeficiency), cirrhosis (increased risk with HIV), HCC, glomerulonephritis, cryoglobulinaemia, hepatitis D co-infection or superinfection, death.

⚕ INVESTIGATIONS
FBC, atypical lymphocytes, ↑↑liver transaminases, ↑ALP, ↓albumin, ↑PT. *Serology:* HBsAg +ve up to six months post-exposure, persistence related to carrier status. Not infectious if HBsAg status becomes -ve. If +ve HBsAg, presence of HBeAg implies high infectivity risk; if anti-HBe antibodies present, suggests low infectivity. Anti-HBsAg antibodies in isolation suggest previous vaccination (titres should be checked periodically to ensure immune). Anti-HBcAg antibodies suggest past infection. Alpha-fetoprotein six-monthly to monitor for HCC. Check hepatitis D status. STI and HIV screen.

🗒 MANAGEMENT
Education. Avoid spread of virus. Vaccination of partners of infected patients and those at risk eg occupational. Contact tracing. Consider hepatitis B Ig 500IU IM after single exposure eg sexual contact or needlestick injury

within 48 hours plus accelerated vaccine. Hepatitis B Ig 200IU to babies born to hepatitis B +ve mothers, no added risk with breastfeeding. Supportive management in acute infection. *Chronic infection:* Lamivudine/adefovir/tenofovir/alpha interferon/pegylated interferon alpha-2a/2b.

Hepatitis C

🗒 CLINICAL NOTES

Epidemiology: Four in 1,000 UK prevalence. Aetiology/risk factors: Incubation six to nine weeks. Transmission via body fluids including previous blood transfusion and IV drug users. Clinical features: Acute infection often asymptomatic (hence many undiagnosed cases), acute infection 25% jaundice, abdominal pain, fatigue, depression. Complications: Chronic infection (80%), cirrhosis (up to 20%), chronic liver disease (90%), HCC, DM, glomerulonephritis, autoimmune hepatitis, polyarteritis nodosa, porphyria cutanea tarda, ITP, cryoglobulinaemia.

⚕ INVESTIGATIONS

FBC, deranged LFTs, gamma GT, ferritin, clotting. Hepatitis C virus (HCV) serology – may take three months to seroconvert, +ve in acute and previous infection. Viral PCR. Liver biopsy, alpha-fetoprotein six-monthly to monitor for HCC. STI and HIV screen.

🗋 MANAGEMENT

Education, counselling, alcohol abstinence, ribavirin plus pegylated interferon alpha-2a/2b. Liver transplant. Surveillance for HCC. Contact tracing.

Hepatitis D

🗒 CLINICAL NOTES

5% of hepatitis B carriers also hepatitis D +ve (as co-infection or superinfection).

⚕ INVESTIGATIONS

↑liver transaminases, serology.

🗋 MANAGEMENT

See *hepatitis B*

Hepatitis E

🗒 CLINICAL NOTES

Aetiology/risk factors: Transmission via food, water (faeco-oral contamination). Clinical features: Incubation two to nine weeks, asymptomatic, flu-like illness, RUQ pain, fever, malaise, fatigue, low mood, pruritus, jaundice. Complications: High mortality in pregnancy (one in five), stillbirth.

⚕ INVESTIGATIONS

↑liver transaminases, serology.

🗋 MANAGEMENT

Supportive, self-limiting.

Hepatitis G

🗒 CLINICAL NOTES

C subtype affects humans. May be associated with aplastic anaemia.

Hereditary angioedema

🗒 CLINICAL NOTES

Epidemiology: Rare. Aetiology/risk factors: C1 esterase inhibitor (C1-INH) deficiency. May be triggered by infection eg *H pylori*. Clinical features: Recurrent acute angioedema. Complications: Airway obstruction.

⚕ INVESTIGATIONS

Low complement C2 and C4, C1-INH deficiency (or lack of function in 15% cases).

🗋 MANAGEMENT

Avoid triggers and oestrogens. Danazol or stanozolol for prophylaxis. *Acute attack:* C1-INH replacement (including recombinant human C1-INH, not for type 3), kallikrein inhibitors, FFP, bradykinin antagonists.

Hereditary elliptocytosis

🗒 CLINICAL NOTES

Various subtypes. Aetiology/risk factors: Autosomal dominant. Clinical features: Mainly asymptomatic, splenomegaly, jaundice.

⚕ INVESTIGATIONS

FBC (mild anaemia), reticulocytosis, elliptocytes, poikilocytes.

🗋 MANAGEMENT

Folic acid, may require splenectomy.

Hereditary haemorrhagic telangiectasia

🗒 CLINICAL NOTES

See *Osler-Weber-Rendu syndrome*

Hereditary motor and sensory neuropathy (HMSN)

🗒 CLINICAL NOTES

See *Charcot-Marie-Tooth disease*

Hereditary spherocytosis

🗒 CLINICAL NOTES

Aetiology/risk factors: Autosomal dominant. Clinical features: Asymptomatic, fatigue, splenomegaly, jaundice.

Complications: Haemolysis, pigment gallstones, leg ulcers, aplastic crisis. Symptoms worse in pregnancy.

INVESTIGATIONS
FBC (mild anaemia), ↑MCHC, reticulocytosis, spherocytes, acanthocytes, osmotic fragility test.

MANAGEMENT
Folic acid, may require splenectomy.

Hernia (abdominal wall)

CLINICAL NOTES
Incarcerated = irreducible. Strangulation = vascular compromise. Clinical features: Abdominal wall lump, cough impulse, reduces on laying flat. Epigastric: Superior to umbilicus, midline, normally contains omentum/preperitoneal fat. Clinical features: asymptomatic, pain, nausea, vomiting, early satiety. Complications: High risk of incarceration. Femoral: Medial to femoral vein, inferior and lateral to pubic tubercle. Epidemiology: F>M. Complications: High risk of bowel obstruction/40% risk of strangulation. Inguinal: Epidemiology: M>F, ↑ in premature babies (indirect). Aetiology/risk factors: Obesity, straining, lifting. Clinical features: Asymptomatic, groin pain, lump above and medial to pubic tubercle. Complications: Incarceration (higher risk if indirect eg children), strangulation. Incisional: Aetiology/risk factors: Post-surgical, wound infection, dehiscence, collagen disorders, poor surgical technique, post-operative haematoma, hepatorenal disease, poor wound healing (eg DM, corticosteroids, smoking, malnutrition, malignancy). Complications: Few. Paraumbilical: Clinical features: Half of hernia involves umbilicus, other half involves skin directly inferior or superior to umbilicus. Complications: High risk of incarceration and strangulation. Umbilical: Epidemiology: ↑in premature babies. Aetiology/risk factors: Gastroschisis, omphalocele, obesity, multiple pregnancies, coughing, straining. Clinical features: Bulge directly underneath umbilicus. Complications: Low risk of incarceration. Incarcerated hernia: Clinical features: Tender irreducible lump. Complications: Strangulation. Strangulated hernia: Clinical features: Tender erythematous incarcerated hernia, patient toxic.

INVESTIGATIONS
USS, CT, herniography (for investigation of chronic groin pain). If concerned about strangulation also require FBC, U&E, CRP, group and save crossmatch.

MANAGEMENT
Incarceration, bowel obstruction and visceral strangulation require emergency surgery. Epigastric: Surgery in adults, consider expectant policy if <10 years of age. Femoral: Surgery. Inguinal: Congenital – surgery; small – consider conservative; others – elective surgery.

Incisional: Conservative, surgical (20% recurrence rate). Umbilical: Conservative if <1cm in children, watch and wait, 90% disappear by age two years. Surgery if still present by age five years. Adults, manage cause eg obesity, consider conservative unless eg skin very thin over hernia. Paraumbilical: Surgery.

Herpes simplex

CLINICAL NOTES
See sexually transmitted infections and genital infections

Herpes zoster

CLINICAL NOTES
See chickenpox (varicella zoster) and shingles (herpes zoster)

Hiatus hernia

See also
— Gastro-oesophageal reflux disease

CLINICAL NOTES
Epidemiology: M=F. Sliding – most common, rolling. Clinical features: Asymptomatic, dyspepsia, GORD, flatulence. Complications: Barrett's oesophagus, associated with Ca oesophagus.

INVESTIGATIONS
Barium studies superior to endoscopy.

MANAGEMENT
Weight loss, elevated night-time posture, lifestyle management, alginates, PPI, Nissen's fundoplication.

Hidradenitis suppurativa

CLINICAL NOTES
Suppurative disease of sweat glands. Epidemiology: F>M. Third-fourth decades. Aetiology/risk factors: Smoking, white/African-Caribbean origin, lithium. Clinical features: Lesions predominantly in axillae and groin; also perineal, perianal, scrotal. Pain, itchy, nodules, pustules, purulent discharge. Complications: Inflammation heals by fibrosis, infection (eg cellulitis, abscess), fistulae, sinus formation, ulceration, amyloid, renal failure, hypoalbuminaemia, squamous metaplasia/carcinoma, psychological disturbance.

INVESTIGATIONS
FBC (anaemia of chronic disease), glucose, U&E, LFT, swabs, CT (preoperative).

MANAGEMENT
Lifestyle management (smoking, weight, diet), antibiotics (short courses or long term). Long-term

management: Steroids, COC, retinoids, surgery (may require radical surgery with graft).

Hirschsprung's disease

📅 CLINICAL NOTES

Epidemiology: M>F. Aetiology/risk factors: Segment of aganglionic colon. Occasionally associated with MEN2b, Waardenburg syndrome and Down's syndrome. Clinical features: Age of presentation depends on severity, constipation, failure to pass meconium after birth (exclude imperforate anus), bilious vomiting. Complications: Bowel obstruction, malabsorption, enterocolitis, peptic ulcers, megacolon and perforation.

⚕ INVESTIGATIONS
Barium studies, biopsy.

⚕ MANAGEMENT
Bowel resection if significant symptoms.

Hirsutism

📅 CLINICAL NOTES

Epidemiology: Common. Aetiology/risk factors: Idiopathic, PCOS, adrenal hyperplasia/tumour, ovarian (androgen-secreting) tumour, acromegaly, Cushing's syndrome, iatrogenic (eg insulin, danazol, testosterone, anabolic steroids, corticosteroids, phenytoin, ciclosporin, phenothiazines), familial. Clinical features: Excessive hair growth (androgen-dependent distribution). Complications: Psychological morbidity.

⚕ INVESTIGATIONS

LH:FSH. Measure testosterone and sex hormone binding globulin (SHBG), androstenedione if virilisation, dehydroepiandrosterone sulphate (DHEA-S), ↑ ovarian and not adrenal source of androgen. 17-hydroxyprogesterone – late onset CAH, 24-hour urine collection for cortisol, dexamethasone suppression test. Consider abdominal USS/CT.

⚕ MANAGEMENT

Treat underlying cause. Refer severe/rapidly progressive disease, testosterone levels x2 ULN, treatment failure. Encourage weight loss if obese. Topical treatments – threading, waxing, depilatory creams, eflornithine cream, electrolysis, laser, photoepilation. Systemic treatment (may take months to show effect). COC, especially those containing cyproterone acetate (avoid levonorgestrel and norethisterone; may exacerbate condition), metformin (especially if high BMI), finasteride, thiazolidinediones, cyproterone acetate (may need to be added to first 10 days of COC pack or offer COC containing cyproterone acetate), spironolactone. Consider HRT if menopausal. Regular follow-up.

HIV and AIDS

📅 CLINICAL NOTES

Epidemiology: UK prevalence 77,000. Aetiology/risk factors: Mainly HIV-1, contraction by sexual route, vertical transmission, IV drug abuse or contaminated blood products, sub-Saharan Africa. Clinical features: Incubation two to four weeks. Progression from HIV infection to AIDS about 10 years, modern treatment offers favourable prognosis. *Primary infection:* Occurs few weeks after infection, asymptomatic, fever, sore throat, rash, lymphadenopathy, may be persistent – PGL. Subsequently patient experiences ARC – weight loss, myalgia, sweats, fever, diarrhoea, minor infections eg oral candidiasis, molluscum contagiosum, acne, folliculitis, herpes viruses. *Center for Diseases Control and Prevention (CDC) AIDS-defining illnesses:* Invasive candidiasis (bronchi, trachea, pulmonary, oesophageal. Require systemic azoles). Invasive cervical cancer, recurrent/ multiple bacterial infections, extrapulmonary/disseminated coccidioidomycosis, extrapulmonary cryptococcal infection eg cerebral (chronic meningitis, may not have neck stiffness). More than one month intestinal cryptosporidium, CMV (including retinitis, colitis, neuropathy, outside liver/ spleen/nodes), HIV encephalopathy, chronic or extensive HSV, mycobacterium (tuberculosis, avium), *Pneumocystis carinii* pneumonia (PCP), fever, breathlessness, dry cough, desaturation on exertion, fine pulmonary crackles, ground glass appearance on chest X-ray/CT, cerebral toxoplasmosis (seizures, CVA, personality change, headache, ring enhancing lesions on MRI/CT), lymphoma, Kaposi's sarcoma, progressive multifocal leukoencephalopathy (John Cunningham virus, cerebral demyelination). *Other diseases associated with AIDS:* Psoriasis, anaemia, neuropathy, dementia complex, PE, MI, nephropathy, hepatic disease, sclerosing cholangitis, enteropathy, cardiomyopathy, SCC.

⚕ INVESTIGATIONS

FBC, atypical lymphocytes, U&E, LFT, glucose, lipids, ESR. CMV, toxoplasmosis, hepatitis and syphilis serology. STI screen. HIV load/RNA PCR (check three-monthly, peaks at 30 days. Prognostic 'set point' about six months post-seroconversion; if >10^4/ml, x10 risk of progression to AIDS in five years). p24 antigen (acute infection, ↓ by 10 weeks). HIV (gp120) IgG antibody (+ve after seroconversion, persists throughout illness rapid tests taking 20 minutes available in some areas). CD4 count (check three-monthly, normal range 500-1,500 x 10^6/mm^3, opportunistic infections when CD4 <200). Chronic meningitis – India ink stain on CSF.

⚕ MANAGEMENT

Now considered chronic disease. Education and lifestyle advice (safe sex even between two partners both with HIV, due to different HIV strains and STIs), infection prevention (including measures to reduce vertical transmission), ensure cervical smears up-to-date, post-exposure starter kit if required, vaccinations (non-live vaccines). Chemoprophylaxis when CD4 <200, co-trimoxazole (against PCP and toxoplasmosis). When CD4 <50, offer clarithromycin or azithromycin (against *Mycobacterium avium-intracellulare*). Ganciclovir if CMV +ve. CD4 <200-250 or AIDS-defining illness, offer antiretroviral treatment. *Highly active antiretroviral treatment (HAART) plus monitoring:* Combination of nucleoside and non-nucleoside reverse transcriptase inhibitors if CD4 <350. *Chronic meningitis:* Treat with amphotericin B plus flucytosine, repeated LPs, may require VP shunt. *PCP:* Treat with co-trimoxazole or pentamidine, prednisolone. *Cerebral toxoplasmosis:* Treat with sulfadiazine plus pyrimethamine.

Hodgkin's disease

📋 CLINICAL NOTES
Epidemiology: Peak 10-20 years of age and >50 years. One to two x 10^5 per year UK. M>F. ↓in Japan. Aetiology/risk factors: Genetic, EBV. Clinical features: Classification – lymphocyte rich, nodular lymphocyte predominant (best prognosis), nodular sclerosis, mixed cellularity, lymphocyte depleted (worst prognosis). Usually slow-growing painless lymphadenopathy (neck in 70% cases, axilla, groin), nodes may be tender and fluctuate in size if recent infection, fever (may last one to two weeks; Pel Ebstein fever in latter stages), weight loss, night sweats, pruritus, bone pain. Complications: Alcohol-induced pain (sharp, stabbing, soon after drinking, nodular sclerosing mediastinal type), immunodeficiency, haemolysis, thrombocytopenia, superior vena cava obstruction (SVCO), nerve entrapment, cord compression, ureteric compression, pulmonary collapse, pulmonary infiltrates, pleural effusion, marrow infiltration, pathological fracture, ulcerative skin disease, cerebral lymphoma, raised ICP, cerebellar syndrome, progressive multifocal leukoencephalopathy, Guillain-Barré syndrome.

🔍 INVESTIGATIONS
FBC (normal in early disease; ↓Hb, ↑leucocytes and ↓lymphocytes in advanced disease), atypical lymphocytes, ↑ALP (bone or liver involvement, check isoenzyme if unsure), ↑ESR in more advanced disease, U&E, LFT, LDH (prognostic marker), IgE, node biopsy (Reed-Sternberg cell on histology), marrow biopsy, chest X-ray, CT/USS guided biopsy. *Staging:* CT, MRI, USS, bone scan, PET-CT.

🗄 MANAGEMENT
Supportive, staging, high cure rate. Radiotherapy and chemotherapy both used.

Hoffa's fat pad syndrome

📋 CLINICAL NOTES
Aetiology/risk factors: Inflamed/hypertrophic infra-patellar fat pad. Trauma, excessive use, malignancy. Clinical features: Chronic infrapatellar pain, effusion, swelling, tenderness on infrapatellar palpation on knee straightening. Complications: Fibrosis.

🔍 INVESTIGATIONS
MRI.

🗄 MANAGEMENT
Analgesia, treat underlying cause, steroid injection.

Holmes-Adie pupil

📋 CLINICAL NOTES
Epidemiology: Young adults, F>M. Aetiology/risk factors: Idiopathic, viral. Clinical features: unilateral (four in five cases), slow/incomplete pupillary constriction in response to light (direct and consensual), pupil then remains constricted for longer than expected, normal accommodation, may have absent deep tendon jerks (Holmes-Adie syndrome). Considered a variation of normal; rarely due to lesion in efferent parasympathetic pathway.

🗄 MANAGEMENT
Reassurance.

Homocystinuria

See also
— *Marfan's syndrome*

📋 CLINICAL NOTES
Epidemiology: Rare. Aetiology/risk factors: Autosomal recessive. Clinical features: Marfanoid phenotype, downward lens dislocation (Marfan's is upward), aortic disease rarely a feature (unlike in Marfan's syndrome), kyphosis, scoliosis. Complications: CVD, thromboembolic disease, mental retardation, osteoporosis.

🔍 INVESTIGATIONS
↑methionine, ↑homocysteine (plasma and urine), urine cyanide-nitroprusside test.

🗄 MANAGEMENT
Vitamins B_6, B_{12}, folate supplements. May require dietary methionine restriction.

Hookworm

📋 CLINICAL NOTES
Epidemiology: Most common cause of iron deficiency anaemia worldwide, especially tropical and subtropical regions, affects more than 700 million people worldwide. Aetiology/risk factors: Usually acquired through skin eg walking barefoot, larvae migrate to pulmonary vasculature and to throat, and are eventually swallowed. Attach to upper GI mucosa, causing bleeding. Clinical features: Asymptomatic, localised eczema, fever, cough, wheeze, abdominal pain. Complications: Anaemia, ascites.

🔍 INVESTIGATIONS
IgE, eosinophilia, ↓Hb, stool microscopy.

DISEASES

MANAGEMENT

Mebendazole.

Horner's syndrome

CLINICAL NOTES

Aetiology/risk factors: Lesion of sympathetic supply to affected eye: idiopathic, congenital. *Brainstem:* CVA, MS, ADEM, tumour, syrinx, lateral medullary syndrome. *Pre-superior cervical ganglionic lesions:* CVP line, carotid surgery, Pancoast's tumour, lymphoma, thyroid tumour, cervical rib. *Post-ganglionic:* Cavernous sinus thrombosis, internal carotid artery dissection, orbital tumour/abscess/infiltration. Clinical features: Partial ptosis, miosis, apparent enophthalmos, anhydrosis (proximal lesions), heterochromia if congenital.

INVESTIGATIONS

Topical apraclonidine test, CT/MRI, investigate according to suspected underlying cause.

MANAGEMENT

Treat underlying cause.

Horseshoe kidneys

CLINICAL NOTES

Epidemiology: M>F. About one in 600 live births. Aetiology/risk factors: May be caused by a teratogenic developmental process, Turner's syndrome, familial. Aetiology/risk factors: One in three asymptomatic. Complications: Abdominal pain, UTI, vesicoureteric reflux, stones, hydronephrosis, associated congenital anomalies, associated Wilms' tumour and carcinoid.

INVESTIGATIONS

IVU, CT, diuresis renal scanning.

MANAGEMENT

Surgery for complications.

Huntington's disease

CLINICAL NOTES

Epidemiology: Onset middle age, usually 35-44 years, genetic anticipation autosomal dominant (trinucleotide repeat disease). Often kept hidden in families, so prevalence may be higher. Clinical features: Progressive neurodegenerative disorder. Quasi-purposeful choreiform involuntary jerky movements (including face, eyes, limbs), emotional lability, dementia, speech and swallowing difficulties. Complications: Seizures, dementia, feeding difficulties, aspiration, death.

INVESTIGATIONS

MRI/PET. Genetic studies including family screening.

MANAGEMENT

Speech therapy, physiotherapy, co-enzyme Q10, tetrabenazine, clonazepam, haloperidol, SSRI. Stem cell research, genetic counselling.

Hurler syndrome (MPS type I)

CLINICAL NOTES

Mucopolysaccharidosis (MPS) I. Epidemiology: Rare. Aetiology/risk factors: Alpha-L-iduronidase deficiency. Autosomal recessive. Chromosome 4. Clinical features: Milder forms of alpha-L-iduronidase exist (eg Scheie syndrome). Short stature, mental retardation, macroglossia, herniae, hepatomegaly, splenomegaly, skeletal anomalies, corneal infiltration (unlike Hunter's syndrome, MPS II), cardiomyopathy, CHD. Complications: Cardiorespiratory failure, AR, respiratory tract infection, death (in childhood).

INVESTIGATIONS

May be diagnosed antenatally, alpha-L-iduronidase enzyme assays, ECG, echocardiogram, coronary angiography, abdominal USS/CT, radiography.

MANAGEMENT

Genetic counselling, corneal transplant, physiotherapy, OT, orthopaedic surgery, laronidase replacement, treat complications accordingly.

Hydatidiform mole

See *molar pregnancy (hydatidiform mole)*

Hydrocephalus

CLINICAL NOTES

Epidemiology: Congenital (0.5-3.5 per 100 live births), prevalence 1.5%. Aetiology/risk factors: Obstructive (tumour, intraventricular bleeds, aqueduct stenosis, Arnold-Chiari malformation) and communicating (intracranial haemorrhage, head injury, meningitis). Clinical features: Headaches, high-pitched cry, visual/memory disturbance, personality changes, irritability, nausea, vomiting, may be rapidly progressive, bulging fontanelle, sunset sign (late sign). Disproportionate/rapidly growing occipitofrontal head circumference in infants. *Normal pressure hydrocephalus:* Chronic onset, gait disturbance, pseudodementia, urinary incontinence. Complications: Blocked shunt (headache, nausea, vomiting, collapse), seizures, developmental delay, permanent cerebral damage.

INVESTIGATIONS

Serial measurement of occipitofrontal head circumference in infants. Cerebral USS/CT/MRI.

MANAGEMENT

Ventricular drainage (shunt), endoscopic ventriculostomy, treat cause.

Hyperaldosteronism

See also
- *Liddle's syndrome*
- *Renal artery stenosis*

 CLINICAL NOTES

Aetiology/risk factors: *Familial:* Glucocorticoid-remediable aldosteronism (GRA), autosomal dominant. *Conn's disease/primary hyperaldosteronism:* Adrenal adenoma, adrenal hyperplasia (usually bilateral), adrenal carcinoma, McCune-Albright syndrome. *Secondary:* Excess hard liquorice, diuretics, cardiac failure, nephrotic syndrome, renal artery stenosis, liver failure. Clinical features: Asymptomatic, hypertension, weakness, polyuria, paraesthesia.

 INVESTIGATIONS

Na^+ level depends on case and hydration status, → ↓K^+, ↓Mg^{2+}, ↑aldosterone, renin (if normal or ↑, suggests secondary hyperaldosteronism, ↓renin suggests primary hyperaldosteronism), metabolic alkalosis, Conn's/GRA if fall in cortisol and aldosterone on standing. CT/MRI abdomen. Exclude renal artery stenosis.

MANAGEMENT

Conn's disease: Spironolactone preoperatively for four weeks, surgery. *Bilateral adrenal hyperplasia:* Spironolactone or amiloride.

Hypercalcaemia

CLINICAL NOTES

Epidemiology: Common. Aetiology/risk factors: Malignancy (myeloma, paraneoplastic disease, primary bone tumour, metastases), primary hyperparathyroidism, tertiary hyperparathyroidism, sarcoid, thiazide-like diuretics, fracture, vitamin D excess, milk-alkali syndrome, thyrotoxicosis, familial hypocalcuric hypercalcaemia, hypoadrenalism, confusion, hypertension, fever. Clinical features: Depression, fatigue, nausea, vomiting, abdominal pain (eg constipation, renal colic), polyuria, polydipsia, ↓appetite, weight loss. Complications: Corneal deposits, pancreatitis, renal failure, cardiac arrest.

INVESTIGATIONS

Ca^{2+}, phosphate, PTH, vitamin D, FBC, U&E, TFT, LFT. Raised albumin – consider dehydration; normal/low albumin and normal/low phosphate – if normal urea, likely primary/tertiary hyperparathyroidism. Normal/low albumin and normal/raised phosphate and raised ALP – bone secondaries, hyperthyroidism, sarcoid. Normal/low albumin and normal/raised phosphate and normal ALP – myeloma, vitamin D toxicosis, milk-alkali syndrome. Mg^{2+}, myeloma screen. ECG (↓QT interval), chest X-ray, bone scan.

MANAGEMENT

Treat underlying cause, if Ca^{2+} >3.5mmol/L or symptomatic – rehydration, correct electrolyte imbalances, furosemide, bisphosphonate.

Hypercholesterolaemia

CLINICAL NOTES

Epidemiology: Common. Aetiology/risk factors: High-fat diet, alcohol, smoking, sedentary lifestyle, DM, hypothyroidism, familial (heterozygous 1 in 500 prevalence, autosomal dominant, consider if total cholesterol >6.7mmol/L in children and >7.5mmol/L in adults). Clinical features: Xanthelasma, tendon xanthomas. Complications: CVD, pancreatitis.

INVESTIGATIONS

Fasting lipids and glucose, U&E, LFT, TFT.

MANAGEMENT

People with history of CVD, DM, familial hypercholesterolaemia, ≥75 years of age should be considered high risk for CVD. For other patients 40-74 years, assess 10-year and lifetime CVD risk with QRISK scores. For South Asians, x 10-year risk by 1.4. If one first-degree relative has premature CHD, x risk by 1.5. If more than one first-degree relative has premature CHD, x risk by two. If >40 years of age and 10-year risk for CVD ≥20%, or if risk <20% but BMI >40kg/m²/low socioeconomic group/smoker/CKD/other at-risk chronic disease, consider lipid reduction therapy. Lifestyle advice (weight reduction, diet and exercise advice, smoking and alcohol cessation). BP management. Secondary prevention – initiate statins and aim for cholesterol <4mmol/L or LDL <2mmol/L. If statins not tolerated, consider fibrates, anion exchange resins, nicotinic acid (secondary prevention only). *Familial hypercholesterolaemia:* High-intensity statin, aim to reduce LDL to 50% from baseline.

Hyperemesis gravidarum

CLINICAL NOTES

Epidemiology: 0.1-2% pregnancies. Usually <20 weeks' gestation. Aetiology/risk factors: Previous hyperemesis gravidarum, multiple pregnancy, nulliparity, obesity, thyrotoxicosis, molar pregnancy. Clinical features: Emotional distress, nausea, vomiting. Complications: Dehydration, postural hypotension, tachycardia, ketosis, liver enzyme derangement, hyponatraemia, hypokalaemia, alkalosis, renal failure, maternal psychosis, low birthweight.

INVESTIGATIONS

U&E, LFT, glucose, TFT, obstetric USS.

MANAGEMENT

Antiemetics, consider IV fluids and corticosteroids.

Hyperparathyroidism (primary)

See also
— *Hypercalcaemia*

 CLINICAL NOTES

Epidemiology: Underdiagnosed. **Aetiology/risk factors:** Single parathyroid adenoma (80%), parathyroid hyperplasia, multiple parathyroid adenomas, parathyroid malignancy, MEN. **Clinical features:** Asymptomatic, symptoms of hypercalcaemia, peptic ulcer, myopathy, reduced bone density.

INVESTIGATIONS

↑Mg^{2+}, ↑Ca^{2+}, ↑PTH, phosphate (reduced except in renal failure), ↑ALP, ↑acid phosphatase, ↑uric acid, consider 24-hour urine collection for Ca^{2+}. *Neck imaging:* USS, nuclear medicine, CT, MRI. X-ray (pepperpot skull, parathyroid mass, brown tumours), DEXA scan.

MANAGEMENT

Surveillance and encourage adequate hydration if mild hypercalcaemia, acceptable DEXA, normal renal function and asymptomatic. Consider bisphosphonates, surgery (some parathyroid tissue may be left). Six-monthly monitoring.

Hyperparathyroidism (secondary)

 CLINICAL NOTES

Aetiology/risk factors: Chronic hypocalcaemia with appropriate increase in PTH eg renal failure, vitamin D deficiency, osteoporosis. **Clinical features:** See *hypocalcaemia*. **Complications:** Cardiac valve/arterial/anterior thigh calcification, tertiary hyperparathyroidism.

INVESTIGATIONS

↑PTH, ↓Ca^{2+}.

MANAGEMENT

Vitamin D analogues, calcium, surgery.

Hyperparathyroidism (tertiary)

See also
— *Hypercalcaemia*

CLINICAL NOTES

Aetiology/risk factors: Autonomous production of PTH after prolonged period of hypocalcaemia eg in chronic renal failure. **Clinical features:** Symptoms of hypercalcaemia.

INVESTIGATIONS

↑PTH, ↑Ca^{2+}.

MANAGEMENT

Surgery.

Hyperprolactinaemia

CLINICAL NOTES

Aetiology/risk factors: Pregnancy, breastfeeding, prolactinoma, hypothalamic tumour, acromegaly, PCOS, primary hypothyroidism, SSRI, antipsychotics, dopamine antagonists, COC, opiates, cimetidine, cocaine, head injury, renal failure, liver disease, sarcoidosis, postprandial, postictal, fathers (postpartum). **Clinical features:** Asymptomatic, amenorrhoea, galactorrhoea, ED, ↓libido, visual disturbance (bitemporal hemianopia), headache. **Complications:** Infertility, retroperitoneal fibrosis.

INVESTIGATIONS

Prolactin (macroprolactin, inert, bound to IgG). Pituitary function tests, pituitary MRI, visual field testing. Investigate according to suspected underlying cause.

MANAGEMENT

Dopamine agonists: Cabergoline first-line, bromocriptine. Monitor for complications. Trans-sphenoidal surgery for macroadenoma or resistant to medical management.

Hypertension

CLINICAL NOTES

See *essential hypertension*

Hypertensive retinopathy

CLINICAL NOTES

See *essential hypertension*

Hyperthyroidism

See also
— *Graves' disease*

CLINICAL NOTES

Aetiology/risk factors: Graves' disease, toxic multinodular goitre, toxic adenoma, de Quervain's thyroiditis, malignancy (thyroid, ovarian teratoma), MEN, McCune-Albright syndrome. Iatrogenic – excess thyroxine, amiodarone ($t_{1/2}$ amiodarone may be up to 2.5 months), lithium. **Clinical features:** Weight loss, increased appetite, diarrhoea, sweating, heat intolerance, palpitations (eg tachycardia, AF), amenorrhoea, agitation, irritability, fine tremor, palmar erythema, lid lag, goitre, psychosis. **Complications:** Cardiomyopathy, cardiac failure, angina, osteoporosis, thyroid eye disease, thyroid storm.

INVESTIGATIONS

FBC, atypical lymphocytes, ↓TSH, ↑free T_3/T_4, thyroid autoantibodies, ↑ACE, ↑SHBG, thyroid USS, nuclear medicine (differentiates between Grave's disease, toxic nodular goitre, de Quervain's thyroiditis and hot nodule if toxic adenoma). Visual field testing if Graves' disease.

🔲 MANAGEMENT

Beta-blockade, carbimazole or propylthiouracil, radioiodine, partial thyroidectomy, risk of post-treatment hypothyroidism/subclinical hypothyroidism.

Hypertrophic cardiomyopathy (HCM)

📋 CLINICAL NOTES

Disproportionate LVH for afterload. Epidemiology: Affects up to one in 500. Aetiology/risk factors: Genetic. Clinical features: Asymptomatic/found on family screening, angina, SOB, fatigue, presyncope, palpitations, S4, forceful and double apical impulse and ejection systolic. Pansystolic murmur suggests systolic anterior motion of anterior mitral valve leaflet (SAM), may cause left ventricular obstruction. Complications: Syncope, HOCM due to excessive septal thickness or SAM, malignant arrhythmias, ischaemia, sudden cardiac death.

⚕ INVESTIGATIONS

ECG-LVH, LAD, LBBB, T wave inversion, Q waves, arrhythmias. Echocardiogram-LVH, often septal hypertrophy-asymmetric septal hypertrophy (ASH), outflow tract obstruction (HOCM), SAM. ETT. MRI. Ambulatory ECG. Genetic testing.

🔲 MANAGEMENT

Beta-blockers, CCB, antiarrhythmic agents, pacemaker/ ICD, septal ablation, myotomy, myomectomy, transplant. Family screening.

Hypocalcaemia

📋 CLINICAL NOTES

Aetiology/risk factors: Hypoparathyroidism, pseudo-hypoparathyoidism, renal failure, vitamin D deficiency, malabsorption, osteomalacia, pancreatitis, rhabdomyolysis, hyperhydration, liver disease, dietary phytates (eg chapati). Clinical features: Perioral paraesthesia, carpopedal spasm, tetany, Trousseau's sign (carpopedal spasm with BP cuff), Chvostek's sign (facial twitch with tapping over parotid), cataract.

⚕ INVESTIGATIONS

$\downarrow$Ca^{2+}. $\uparrow$PO$_4^{3-}$ – chronic renal failure, hypo/pseudo-hypoparathyoidism, rhabdomyolysis. Normal/low phosphate – osteomalacia, pancreatitis, hyperhydration. ALP (raised in osteomalacia), ECG.

🔲 MANAGEMENT

Treat cause. *Mild:* Oral Ca^{2+}, daily monitoring. *Severe:* Calcium gluconate IV repeated as required.

Hypoparathyroidism

📋 CLINICAL NOTES

Aetiology/risk factors: Idiopathic, surgical removal of parathyroid glands, autoimmune (eg autoimmune polyendocrine syndrome), haemochromatosis, Wilson's disease, DiGeorge syndrome. Transient – $\downarrow$Mg^{2+}, trauma. Clinical features: See *hypocalcaemia*. Complications: Benign intracranial hypertension.

⚕ INVESTIGATIONS

$\downarrow$Mg^{2+}, $\downarrow$PTH, $\downarrow$Ca^{2+}, $\rightarrow$$\uparrow$PO$_4^{3-}$, $\rightarrow$ALP.

🔲 MANAGEMENT

Alfacalcidol.

Hypopituitarism

📋 CLINICAL NOTES

See *pituitary failure*

Hypospadias

📋 CLINICAL NOTES

Epidemiology: One in 300 male births. Clinical features: *Spectrum of severity:* Mild with urethral opening at dorsal aspect of glans; severe (may be associated with intersex) with urethral opening at scrotal base. Complications: Foreskin anomalies, penile chordee (tethering), erectile and psychosexual difficulties, urinary spraying. If combined with cryptorchidism, may be suggestive of female virilisation.

🔲 MANAGEMENT

Consider surgery.

Hypothyroidism

See also
— *Congenital hypothyroidism (cretinism)*

📋 CLINICAL NOTES

Aetiology/risk factors: *Primary atrophic:* Common, F>M, autoimmune, associated with other autoimmune diseases. *Hashimoto's thyroiditis:* Common, F>M, autoimmune, associated with other autoimmune diseases and Turner's syndrome. *Familial:* Including peroxidase deficiency. *Chronic lymphocytic thyroiditis, iodine deficiency (dietary), de Quervain's thyroiditis:* Viral, tender nodular thyroid, initial thyrotoxicosis, subsequent hypothyroid. *Pendred's syndrome:* Genetic, with deafness. *Postsurgical, post-radioiodine, subacute thyroiditis (temporary), POEMS, drugs:* Amiodarone may cause hyperthyroidism or hypothyroidism. T$_{1/2}$ amiodarone may be up to 2.5 months; lithium. *Pituitary/hypothalamic failure, infiltrative (amyloid, haemochromatosis, sarcoid), postpartum:* Usually temporary, although consider Sheehan's syndrome. Clinical features: Insidious onset, fatigue, weight gain, constipation, menorrhagia, cold intolerance, pseudodementia, pseudodepression, myalgia, $\downarrow$libido, delayed puberty, 'peaches and cream' appearance, hoarse voice, $\uparrow$BMI, bradycardia, dry skin/ hair, goitre (iodine deficiency, Hashimoto's), non-pitting oedema, slow-relaxing reflexes. Complications: Pleural effusion, pericardial effusion, cerebellar dysfunction, peripheral neuropathy, benign intracranial hypertension, bowel obstruction, von Willebrand's disease, psychosis, myxoedema coma (high mortality, due to poor adherence to thyroxine/undiagnosed disease/sedative drugs/ respiratory insult/myocardial insult. $\downarrow$GCS, seizure, hypothermia, hypoglycaemia), congenital defects (cretinism-cognitive defects, cardiac and renal defects, cleft lip).

$\mathcal{Q}$ INVESTIGATIONS

FBC, $\uparrow$basophils, $\uparrow$MCV, $\uparrow$TSH (but $\downarrow$if pituitary/ hypothalamic failure), $\downarrow$T$_4$ (may be normal if subclinical), amiodarone ($\downarrow$T$_3$ and/or $\uparrow$T$_4$), thyroid autoantibodies (thyroid peroxidase, thyroglobulin, high titres in Hashimoto's thyroiditis, also atrophic thyroiditis), $\uparrow$triglycerides, $\downarrow$Na$^+$, $\uparrow$Mg^{2+}, $\uparrow$CK, $\uparrow$uric acid, $\uparrow$LDH, $\uparrow$AST, $\downarrow$SHBG. ECG – prolonged PR, bradycardia.

$\mathbf{\bar{0}}$ MANAGEMENT

Levothyroxine (T$_4$) start at low doses (especially in elderly) and increase every four weeks until TSH normalised. If known CHD, protect with beta-blockade. *Coma:* Supportive measures, check glucose, IV levothyroxine, IV mineralocorticoids (because usually associated with adrenal dysfunction), warm patient.

Hypothyroidism (subclinical)

$\boxed{\equiv}$ CLINICAL NOTES

Epidemiology: 4-10% prevalence Aetiology/risk factors: Pre-eclampsia, chronic autoimmune hypothyroidism, iatrogenic (drugs, surgery, radiation). Clinical features: Asymptomatic +/– poor exercise capacity.

$\mathcal{Q}$ INVESTIGATIONS

$\uparrow$TSH, T$_3$/T$_4$ normal; if +ve thyroid autoantibodies, likely to progress to hypothyroidism.

$\mathbf{\bar{0}}$ MANAGEMENT

Consider levothyroxine if +ve thyroid autoantibodies, post-treatment for hyperthyroidism, TSH >10, symptomatic; or monitor TFT six to 12-monthly.

Ichthyosis

$\boxed{\equiv}$ CLINICAL NOTES

Epidemiology: Multiple subtypes. Vulgaris type most common (one in 250 prevalence, Darier's disease one in 10^5 prevalence, Harlequin 0.5 in 10^5 prevalence). Aetiology/risk factors: Idiopathic, genetic, may be associated with syndromes eg Refsum's disease, malignancy eg lymphoma, thyroid disease, sarcoid. Clinical features: Dry, thickened, scaly, rough skin, palmoplantar keratoderma, some types may have blisters. Complications: Cracking, secondary infection, poor temperature control, depression, visual disturbance, limb, facial and chest wall movement may be affected.

$\mathbf{\bar{0}}$ MANAGEMENT

Daily heavy exfoliation and emollients, retinoids. Family and MDT support.

Idiopathic pulmonary fibrosis

$\boxed{\equiv}$ CLINICAL NOTES

Usual interstitial pneumonia, cryptogenic fibrosing alveolitis. Epidemiology: 20-30 in 10^5 prevalence. Aetiology/ risk factors: Advancing age. M>F. Associated with other autoimmune diseases. Clinical features: Cough, progressive SOB, finger clubbing (two in three cases), end inspiratory crackles. Complications: Respiratory failure, pulmonary hypertension, cor pulmonale, associated with pulmonary malignancy.

$\mathcal{Q}$ INVESTIGATIONS

Spirometry – restrictive picture, $\downarrow$lung volume, $\downarrow$gas transfer, ABG – type 1 respiratory failure, chest X-ray – reduced lung volume, interstitial shadowing, honeycomb lung, high-resolution computed tomography (HRCT), biopsy.

$\mathbf{\bar{0}}$ MANAGEMENT

Steroids, steroid-sparing immunosuppressants, pulmonary rehabilitation, LTOT, lung transplant if <60 years. Vaccinations. Median survival five years.

IgA deficiency

$\boxed{\equiv}$ CLINICAL NOTES

See *immunodeficiency (primary)*

IgA nephropathy

$\boxed{\equiv}$ CLINICAL NOTES

See *glomerulonephritis*

Iliotibial band syndrome

$\boxed{\equiv}$ CLINICAL NOTES

Epidemiology: Young athletes (especially long distance runners), adolescents. Aetiology/risk factors: Overactivity, leg length discrepancy. F>M. Clinical features: Pain lateral knee, worse on knee movement eg when crossing legs. May present with pain by greater trochanter. Weak knee extensors/flexors, weak hip abduction.

$\mathcal{Q}$ INVESTIGATIONS

Usually clinical diagnosis, consider imaging MRI.

$\mathbf{\bar{0}}$ MANAGEMENT

Analgesia, rest, physiotherapy, steroid injection, surgery may be required.

Immune thrombocytopenic purpura (ITP)

CLINICAL NOTES
Autoimmune platelet destruction. Epidemiology: About one in 10[5]. Aetiology/risk factors: More common in childhood. F>M (adults). May be triggered by infection in children, may be familial. Clinical features: Bruising, purpura, epistaxis, menorrhagia. Complications: GI haemorrhage, intracerebral haemorrhage.

INVESTIGATIONS
FBC, atypical lymphocytes, ↓plts, ↑bleeding time, +/– platelet autoantibodies, ANA, marrow biopsy (excess megakaryocytes).

MANAGEMENT
90% spontaneous remission in children (5% in adults). Consider prednisolone if symptomatic bleeding/plts ≤20 x 10⁹/L, immunosuppressants, danazol, anti-D therapy, IV immunoglobulin, consider splenectomy.

Immunodeficiency (primary)

CLINICAL NOTES
Neutrophil-related defects: *Mainly recurrent/severe bacterial diseases*: Chronic granulomatous disease (X-linked, normal phagocytosis, intracellular killing defect), myeloperoxidase deficiency (susceptible to candida). Chediak-Higashi syndrome (normal phago-cytosis, intracellular killing defect). Job's syndrome (rare, hyperimmunoglobulin E syndrome, autosomal dominant/recessive/mutations, broad nasal bridge, prominent forehead, hypertelorism, recurrent sta-phylococcal and fungal infections, multiple fractures, cystic lung disease, eczema). Lazy leucocyte syndrome (defective chemotactic response). Complement deficiencies: *Angiodema, neisseria infections, lupus-like syndrome*: Paroxysmal nocturnal haemoglobinuria, C1 esterase deficiency, C3 deficiency (severe encap-sulated organism infections, eg pneumococcus), C5-9 deficiencies (increased susceptibility to *neisseria spp*). Lymphocyte-related defects: *Susceptible to bacterial, fungal, viral infections*: IgA deficiency (about one in 700 people, usually asymptomatic, more susceptible to giardia infection), common variable (B-cell matura-tion defect), agammaglobulinaemia (Bruton's disease, X-linked, no B-cells, increased risk of ulcerative colitis and infections, death about 40 years of age). DiGeorge syndrome (T-cell defect, chromosome 22, thymus mal-development, may present with neonatal seizures due to hypocalcaemia, failure to thrive, low-set ears, orbital hypertelorism, cleft palate, cardiac defects). Purine nucleoside phosphorylase deficiency (T-cell disorder). Severe combined immunodeficiency (SCID, X-linked or chromosome 20, B and T-cell disorder, severe infections, treat with immunoglobulin and marrow transplant). Ataxia-telangiectasia (autosomal recessive, T and B-cell disorder, ataxia, telangiectasia, malignancy eg breast). Wiskott-Aldrich syndrome (B and T-cell disorder, X-linked, eczema, ↓plts).

MANAGEMENT
Treatment will depend on immune deficiency.

Impaired glucose tolerance

CLINICAL NOTES
Increased vascular risk and risk of developing DM.

INVESTIGATIONS
If fasting glucose ≥6.1, <11.1mmol/L, perform OGTT. If impaired glucose tolerance (IGT), OGTT at two hours ≥7.8, <11.1mmol/L; if DM, OGTT at two hours ≥11.1mmol/L.

MANAGEMENT
Cardiovascular risk assessment, weight reduction, lifestyle management, diabetes prevention. Consider eg metformin, acarbose, glitazones.

Impetigo contagiosa

See also
— *Bullous impetigo*

CLINICAL NOTES
Epidemiology: Common. Aetiology/risk factors: Streptococci and/or staphylococci. More likely if eczema, DM, immunodeficiency (eg leukaemia). Clinical features: Localised often unsightly infection, small pustules/vesicles with overlying yellow honeycomb-like crust. Complications: Highly contagious, cellulitis, sepsis.

INVESTIGATIONS
Consider swab, FBC and glucose if severe, recurrent or resistant to treatment.

MANAGEMENT
Hygiene, topical (fucidin 2% first-line, mupirocin if resistance, retapamulin), or systemic antibiotics (flu-cloxacillin, erythromycin).

Infectious mononucleosis

CLINICAL NOTES
Glandular fever. Epidemiology: Common, especially among students. Aetiology/risk factors: EBV. Close contact, respiratory droplets. Clinical features: Incubation up to four to seven weeks. Sore throat, tonsillitis, white tonsillar exudate, fatigue, fever, nausea, cervical lymphadenopathy, mild hepat-osplenomegaly. Complications: Rash with amoxicillin/ampicillin, arthralgia, hepatitis, myocarditis, nephritis, jaundice, encephalitis, meningitis, transverse myelitis, Guillain-Barré syndrome, cranial nerve palsy, optic

DISEASES

neuritis, haemolysis, splenic rupture, postviral fatigue/depression.

INVESTIGATIONS
FBC and blood film (lymphocytosis, atypical monocytes), Paul-Bunnell test (sheep red cell agglutination, good sensitivity and specificity, false -ve if test too early), monospot (horse red cell agglutination), LFT (raised transaminases), EBV serology (IgM), consider abdominal USS.

MANAGEMENT
Education, avoid contact sports for six weeks (increased risk of splenic rupture), fever control with paracetamol, systemic steroids and IV fluids for severe disease.

Infective endocarditis (IE)

CLINICAL NOTES
Epidemiology: About four in 10^6 per year incidence UK. Aetiology/risk factors: Prosthetic heart valves, rheumatic heart disease, IV drug abuse, congenital heart disease, cardiac pacemakers, central lines, postoperative, indwelling foreign bodies, skin/bone infections, poor dentition (recently questioned), 40% cases normal heart valves. Left>right heart valves affected. *Strep viridans, Staph aureus,* HACEK group (*haemophilus spp, Actinobacillus actinomycetemcomitans, Cardiobacterium hominis, Eikenella corrodens, Kingella kingae*). Culture -ve – *Coxiella burnetii,* legionella, *chlamydia spp, bartonella spp* fungi, non-infective-marantic, Libman-Sacks. Clinical features: *Acute or subacute presentations:* Malaise, fatigue, fever, night sweats, arthralgia, stroke, breathlessness, new and/or progressive cardiac murmur, haematuria (non-visible), splenomegaly, finger clubbing, Osler's nodes, Janeway lesions, splinter haemorrhages, petechiae, Roth spots. Complications: Severe cardiac failure, cardiac abscess, embolic disease, CVA, sepsis, renal failure.

INVESTIGATIONS
FBC: Normochromic anaemia, ↑WCC, ↑↓plts, ↓eGFR, U&E, ↑ALP, ↑ESR, ↑CRP, ↓complement. Blood cultures. Urinalysis. ECG – new/progressive prolonged PR suggests cardiac abscess. Chest X-ray – CCF, emboli, abscesses. Echocardiogram – TTE up to 75% sensitive for vegetations, may not detect vegetations <5mm. TOE higher sensitivity/specificity than TTE, able to detect small vegetations. *Duke's criteria:*[Ref1] IE confirmed if two major, one major/three minor, or five minor criteria. *Major:* +ve blood cultures, +ve echocardiogram findings. *Minor:* Fever >38.0°C, suggestive echocardiogram findings, presence of risk factors for IE, immune/vascular phenomona, suggestive microbiology.

MANAGEMENT
Antibiotics, may require cardiac surgery and valve replacement. Currently, prophylaxis against endocarditis not considered effective.

Inferior vena cava obstruction

CLINICAL NOTES
Epidemiology: Rare. Aetiology/risk factors: Malignancy (eg lymphoma, renal cancer), thrombophilia, dehydration, IVC compression (eg AAA, liver abscess, renal cyst), trauma. Clinical features: Dilated abdominal veins – flow in veins below umbilicus is towards heart.

INVESTIGATIONS
CT, MRI, venography.

MANAGEMENT
Treat underlying cause. Anticoagulants, thrombolysis, ligation, thrombectomy, angioplasty, stents, filters, grafting.

Influenza, avian

CLINICAL NOTES
Epidemiology: Rare in humans. Aetiology/risk factors: Poultry farmers and those in contact with birds most at risk. H5N1 type A influenza virus. Clinical features: Fever ≥38°C, malaise, myalgia, joint pains, cough, sore throat, headache, diarrhoea. Complications: More common in at-risk patients, eg extremes of age, chronic disease, immunocompromised – pneumonia eg streptococcal or staphylococcal, may be cavitating, respiratory distress, myocarditis, encephalitis, death.

INVESTIGATIONS
Nasopharyngeal aspirates (NPA), throat swab, lung function tests, echocardiogram.

MANAGEMENT
Isolation, contact tracing, oseltamivir or zanamivir. Refer to secondary care if complications or O_2 sats ≤94%.

Influenza, seasonal

CLINICAL NOTES
Epidemiology: Winter (more common December-March in northern hemisphere). Aetiology/risk factors: Influenza A or B (A more severe), various strains eg H1N2, H3N2. Virus can survive on hard surfaces for 24 hours. Clinical features: Fever ≥38°C, malaise, myalgia, joint pains, cough, sore throat, headache, diarrhoea. Complications: More common in at-risk patients, eg extremes of age, chronic disease, immunocompromised – pneumonia (eg streptococcal or staphylococcal, may be cavitating), respiratory distress, myocarditis, encephalitis, death.

INVESTIGATIONS
Diagnosis usually clinical.

MANAGEMENT
Symptomatic treatment. Vaccination (70-80% effective,

vaccine not live, avoid if hen's egg allergy/pregnant).
Antivirals: Amantadine, oseltamivir or zanamivir if
elderly, chronic cardiac/renal/pulmonary/liver disease/
neurological conditions, immunosuppressed, ≥65 years
of age. Zanamivir within 36 hours of symptoms for at-risk
children aged five to 12 years. Oseltamivir/zanamivir for
at-risk patients in long-term residential care eg nursing
homes in a local outbreak. Refer to secondary care if
complications or O_2 sats ≤94%.

Influenza, swine

 CLINICAL NOTES
Aetiology/risk factors: H1N1 type A influenza virus.
At-risk groups: Chronic illness (renal, hepatic, cardiac,
pulmonary disease, DM), asthmatic patients who have
required drug treatment in past three years, immunocompromised, pregnancy, less than five or >65 years of
age. Prednisolone >1mg/kg per day can cause prolonged
shedding of H1N1 virus. Clinical features: Most cases
mild. Fever ≥38°C plus two or more of – sore throat,
rhinorrhoea, cough, headache, diarrhoea/vomiting,
otitis media, limb or joint pain and/or significantly
unwell. Complications: Respiratory failure, secondary pneumonia, adult respiratory distress syndrome,
invasive staphylococcal, streptococcal and haemophilus
infections, myocarditis, tachycardia, cardiac failure,
dehydration, encephalitis, seizures, haematemesis,
multiorgan failure, death (6% mortality if admitted to
secondary care).

 INVESTIGATIONS
Swab for surveillance or if hospitalised.

MANAGEMENT
Primary care: *Prevention:* Vaccination. Ensure no
other cause of illness eg meningitis, UTI. Symptomatic
treatment. Oseltamivir (drug of choice) or zanamivir.
Consider prophylaxis in a pandemic. Antibiotics for
associated bacterial infection. Refer to secondary care
if complications or O_2 sats ≤94%.

Ingrowing toenail (onychocryptosis)

 CLINICAL NOTES
Epidemiology: Common. Aetiology/risk factors: Tight-
fitting shoes, round trimming of toenails, trauma,
fungal nail infection, family history. Clinical
features: Pain, infection. Complications: Cellulitis,
osteomyelitis.

 INVESTIGATIONS
Consider FBC, glucose, swabs.

MANAGEMENT
Cut toenails square, avoid tight shoes; antibiotics, nail
elevation, partial/total nail removal and nail matrix
obliteration.

Insulinoma

 CLINICAL NOTES
Usually benign tumour. Epidemiology: Rare. Aetiology/
risk factors: Idiopathic, may be part of MEN1 syndrome.
Clinical features: Hypoglycaemia, compensatory weight
gain.

 INVESTIGATIONS
Fasting blood glucose, C-peptide. Arterial stimulation
and venous insulin sampling, CT, nuclear medicine
(somatostatin-receptor scintigraphy, not specific), MRI,
endoscopic USS.

MANAGEMENT
Consider somatostatin analogues, chemotherapy,
surgery.

Intraductal breast papilloma

 CLINICAL NOTES
Epidemiology: Common. Clinical features: Single duct
watery/bloody discharge.

 INVESTIGATIONS
USS, mammogram, MRI.

MANAGEMENT
Exclude malignancy, excision.

Intussusception

 CLINICAL NOTES
Epidemiology: Most commonly presents six to 12
months of age. Aetiology/risk factors: Idiopathic, CF,
tumour, Meckel's diverticulum, Henoch-Schönlein
purpura. Clinical features: Crying (inconsolable),
drawing up legs, abdominal distension, vomiting, PR
bleeding/redcurrant jelly stool (late sign), tachycardia,
dehydration, abdominal mass. Complications: Bowel
obstruction, bowel ischaemia, shock, death.

 INVESTIGATIONS
FBC, U&E, LFT, crossmatch, USS, CT.

MANAGEMENT
Surgical emergency, fluids, analgesia, nasogastric tube,
reduction with air enema, surgery.

Iritis (anterior uveitis)

 CLINICAL NOTES
Epidemiology: 12-15 in 10^5 per year. Peak 20s-40s.
Aetiology/risk factors: Idiopathic, trauma, infection,
sarcoid, seronegative arthritides, IBD, systemic steroids,
immunodeficiency, TB, STI, helminthic infections.
Clinical features: Photophobia, blurred vision, red eye
(especially on periphery of iris), pupil may be irregular.

DISEASES

Complications: Recurrent uveitis, cataract, glaucoma, hypopyon, degenerative corneal changes.

 INVESTIGATIONS

Investigate according to suspected underlying cause.

 MANAGEMENT

Topical steroids (under specialist guidance), cycloplegics eg cyclopentolate, treat underlying cause.

Iron deficiency anaemia

CLINICAL NOTES

See *Investigations, haemoglobin*

Irritable bowel syndrome (IBS)

CLINICAL NOTES

Epidemiology: 10-20% prevalence. **Aetiology/risk factors:** Idiopathic, stress, anxiety, diet (caffeine, fizzy drinks, chewing gum, sweeteners, fatty food, high insoluble fibre eg bran, nuts, cereals; fruit, chocolate. **Clinical features:** More than six months – abdominal pain relieved by defecation and passing flatus. Bloating, straining at stool, urgency, alternating stool form. Symptoms worse with eating. Mucus may be passed. Fatigue, back pain, bladder symptoms, nausea, anxiety. **Complications:** Depression, social isolation, employment difficulties.

INVESTIGATIONS

Investigate to exclude pathological GI or pelvic disease.

MANAGEMENT

Dietary and lifestyle advice, exercise, regular mealtimes, good sleep hygiene, peppermint, mebeverine, laxatives (not lactulose), loperamide, TCAs (SSRI if TCAs ineffective or contraindicated), CBT.

Irritable hip

CLINICAL NOTES

See *transient synovitis of the hip*

Ischaemic bowel (acute)

CLINICAL NOTES

Aetiology/risk factors: Embolus (from eg AF, mural thrombus, endocarditis), atherosclerosis, hypotension, thrombophilia and hypercoagulable states, hyperlipidaemia, smoking, DM, cirrhosis, sepsis, intra-abdominal inflammation, Caisson disease (decompression sickness). **Clinical features:** Severe constant or colicky abdominal pain. **Complications:** Obstruction, ileus, bowel infarction, gangrene, perforation, sepsis, shock, death.

INVESTIGATIONS

Look for embolic sources ie ECG/echocardiogram.

↑WCC, ↓pH, abdominal X-ray (obstruction), CT (intramural/portal vein gas, bowel oedema), angiography.

MANAGEMENT

Fluid resuscitation, analgesia, thrombolysis (arterial), LMWH (venous), angioplasty, embolectomy, vascular bypass, bowel resection, management of risk factors.

Ischaemic bowel (chronic)

CLINICAL NOTES

Aetiology/risk factors: Severe anaemia, atherosclerosis (hypertension, smoking, hyperlipidaemia, DM, obesity, family history), embolus (from eg AF, mural thrombus, endocarditis), thrombophilia, hypotension, hernia, volvulus, pseudoephedrine, COC, surgery, vasculitis, sickle cell disease, colonoscopy, endurance exercise. **Clinical features:** Abdominal pain after eating (intestinal angina), mild abdominal tenderness, abdominal bruit, weight loss. **Complications:** Acute intestinal ischaemia, malnutrition, perforation and sepsis.

INVESTIGATIONS

FBC, U&E, LFT, fasting lipids/glucose, ECG, exclude underlying coronary and carotid artery disease, USS to exclude AAA, mesenteric duplex/angiography.

MANAGEMENT

Address risk factors/lifestyle, statins, anticoagulation, endarterectomy/vascular bypass.

Ischaemic colitis

CLINICAL NOTES

Usually in watershed between superior and inferior mesenterics (splenic flexure). **Aetiology/risk factors:** Severe anaemia, atherosclerosis (hypertension, smoking, hyperlipidaemia, DM, obesity, family history), embolus (from eg AF, mural thrombus, endocarditis), thrombophilia, hypotension, hernia, volvulus, pseudoephedrine, COC, surgery, vasculitis, sickle cell disease, colonoscopy, endurance exercise. **Clinical features:** abdominal pain, nausea, vomiting. **Complications:** Bloody diarrhoea, infarction, gangrene, sepsis, perforation, stricture, death.

INVESTIGATIONS

FBC, arterial blood gases (metabolic acidosis), abdominal X-ray, barium enema, CT, angiography, colonoscopy.

MANAGEMENT

Address risk factors, bowel rest (IV infusion, nasogastric tube), surgery.

Jervell, Lange-Nielsen syndrome

CLINICAL NOTES

See *long QT syndrome*

DISEASES

Job's syndrome

 CLINICAL NOTES

See *immunodeficiency (primary)*

Kala azar

CLINICAL NOTES

See *leishmaniasis*

Kallmann's syndrome

 CLINICAL NOTES

Epidemiology: Rare. Aetiology/risk factors: Autosomal recessive or X-linked. Clinical features: Hypogonadotropic hypogonadism and anosmia, primary amenorrhoea, cryptorchidism. Complications: Cleft lip, colour blindness, sensorineural deafness, infertility.

INVESTIGATIONS

↓LH, ↓FSH, ↓testosterone, ↓oestrogen, CT/MRI.

MANAGEMENT

Hormonal treatment for sexual development and fertility.

Kaposi's sarcoma

See also
— *HIV and AIDS*

 CLINICAL NOTES

Aetiology/risk factors: HHV 8. *Subtypes:* HIV-associated, African, classic (elderly men – Mediterranean, mid-European and sub-Saharan African descent), iatrogenic (immunosuppressant therapy). Clinical features: Red/blue macules/plaques/nodules, often in lower limb. Complications: Visceral Kaposi's (eg pulmonary, gut), lymphatic involvement.

INVESTIGATIONS

Biopsy, HIV screen.

MANAGEMENT

Cryotherapy, laser therapy, radiotherapy, intralesional vinblastine, topical alitretinoin, systemic chemotherapy, interferon alpha, thalidomide, surgery.

Kawasaki disease

CLINICAL NOTES

Epidemiology: 3.7% mortality (UK). Rare in UK, about x20 greater incidence in Japan. Aetiology/risk factors: Children (about 70% under five years). Clinical features: *Acute stages:* Fever more than five days, malaise, irritability, anorexia, lymphadenopathy >15mm (unilateral), non-exudative conjunctivitis, strawberry tongue, fissured lips, pharyngitis, widespread rash, skin desquamation, finger and toe oedema, aseptic meningitis (50%), diarrhoea, vomiting, arthritis, urethritis. Complications: Coronary artery aneurysms (up to 70% cases, persist in 10% cases, aneurysms <4mm regress, may rupture – risk of rupture persists into adulthood), coronary artery thrombosis, myocarditis, MI, cardiac arrhythmias, hepatitis, death.

INVESTIGATIONS

FBC (normocytic normochromic anaemia, ↑plts), ↑ESR, ↑CRP, sterile pyuria, echocardiogram, angiography, cardiac catheterisation.

MANAGEMENT

Aspirin (risk of Reye's syndrome), IV gammaglobulin, CABG, cardiac transplant.

Kearns-Sayre syndrome

 CLINICAL NOTES

Epidemiology: Rare. Onset first two decades. Aetiology/risk factors: Gene mutation mitochondrial DNA. Clinical features: Progressive ophthalmoplegia, retinitis pigmentosa, cataracts, ptosis, proximal muscle weakness, dysphagia, deafness, dementia, encephalopathy, cerebellar ataxia, palpitations, heart block, cardiomyopathy, CCF, short stature, DM, failure to thrive, delayed puberty.

INVESTIGATIONS

Urinalysis, normal/↑ CK, serum ↑ lactate and ↑pyruvate, ↓Ca²⁺, cerebal MRI, ECG, echocardiogram, audiometry, muscle biopsy.

MANAGEMENT

Co-enzyme Q may help. Surgical intervention for eg ptosis, dysphagia and deafness.

Keloid

CLINICAL NOTES

Epidemiology: Common. Aetiology/risk factors: ↑ dark-skinned people, skin trauma. Clinical features: Fibrous overgrowth of scar, grows beyond scar margins (unlike hypertrophic scar). Complications: Recurrence after surgery.

MANAGEMENT

Intralesional/topical steroids, pressure dressings; other possible treatments – cryosurgery, laser, immunosuppressants, radiotherapy, silicone gel, surgery.

Keratitis

 CLINICAL NOTES

Corneal inflammation. Epidemiology: Acanthamoeba infection is rare. Aetiology/risk factors: Trauma, sicca syndrome, infection (often from contact lenses, lenses may be infected with acanthamoeba), immunodeficiency, DM, RA, topical steroids. Clinical features: Pain, redness, photophobia, excess tear production, grittiness, miosis. Complications: Chronic infection/inflammation, corneal ulceration/perforation, blindness.

⚕ INVESTIGATIONS
Swabs for culture and microscopy.

💊 MANAGEMENT
Treat underlying cause. Avoid contact lenses. Scratch –eye patch for 24 hours, lubricants and topical antibiotic ointment. Infectious – antibacterials, antifungals, antivirals. Acanthamoeba infection may require corneal transplant.

Keratoacanthoma

📋 CLINICAL NOTES
Epidemiology: M>F. Aetiology/risk factors: Sun exposure. Clinical features: Rapidly growing (six weeks) skin lesion with central keratinised crater, up to 25mm, may resolve spontaneously after two months with a scar.

⚕ INVESTIGATIONS
Excisional biopsy.

💊 MANAGEMENT
Excision for cosmetic result and in cases where SCC cannot be excluded (excision biopsy).

Keratoconus

📋 CLINICAL NOTES
Epidemiology: Rare. Aetiology/risk factors: Genetic, collagen disorders, Down's syndrome, Turner's syndrome. Clinical features: Progressive, thinned degenerative 'conical' cornea.

⚕ INVESTIGATIONS
Ophthalmological/optometry assessment.

💊 MANAGEMENT
Contact lens, corneal transplant.

Kidney (renal) failure, acute [Ref12]

See also
— Chronic kidney disease

📋 CLINICAL NOTES
Rapid fall in eGFR. Epidemiology: 1-5% hospital admissions. Aetiology/risk factors: Pre-renal: Hypotension, hypovolaemia, shock. Renal: DM, vascular disease, infection, vasculitis, glomerulonephritis, HUS, TTP, autoimmune, urate crystals, myoglobulin, hypercalcaemia, light chains, sarcoid, lymphoma, papillary necrosis, iatrogenic (eg ACE inhibitors, NSAIDs).

Post-renal: Renal tract obstruction eg prostatism. Clinical features: Oliguria/anuria, nausea, vomiting, pruritus, uraemic pigmentation. Complications: CKD, acute tubular necrosis, hyperkalaemia, pulmonary oedema, pericarditis, death.

⚕ INVESTIGATIONS
FBC, schistocytes, U&E. ↑ammonia, ↑amylase, ↑lactate, ↑Mg^{2+}, ↓pH, ↑anion gap metabolic acidosis. If well and unsure if acute deterioration in eGFR, repeat bloods within five days to confirm result/assess for further deterioration; note trimethoprim can cause temporary rise in creatinine. MC&S (red cell casts suggest glomerulonephritis, eosinophils suggest acute interstitial nephritis). ↑urine pH. Renal USS, investigate according to suspected underlying cause.

💊 MANAGEMENT
Stop/treat trigger. Admit. Strict fluid management. Consider renal dose dopamine, renal replacement therapy.

Klinefelter's syndrome

📋 CLINICAL NOTES
Epidemiology: About one in 500 male births. Aetiology/risk factors: One or more extra X chromosomes eg XXY. Clinical features: Poor developmental milestones, tall stature, small testicles, reduced muscle mass, body/facial hair. Gynaecomastia, shyness, osteoporosis, infertility. Complications: Mental retardation correlates with number of extra X chromosomes. Some mosaic cases also have an extra Y chromosome, associated with aggressive behaviour.

⚕ INVESTIGATIONS
↑FSH, ↓testosterone, sperm analysis – azoospermia, genetic testing.

💊 MANAGEMENT
Testosterone replacement therapy, treatment for gynaecomastia, infertility treatment.

Klumpke's paralysis

📋 CLINICAL NOTES
Aetiology/risk factors: Brachial plexus injury (C8-T1), including in childbirth. High risk with large weight babies, gestational diabetes, assisted delivery, breech presentation, shoulder dystocia. Clinical features: Elbow flexed, wrist extended, arm supinated. Complications: Contractures, dislocation of radial head.

⚕ INVESTIGATIONS
Nerve conduction studies, MRI.

💊 MANAGEMENT
Physiotherapy, splinting, neurolysis, nerve graft, tendon transfers, muscle transfer.

Kwashiorkor

📋 **CLINICAL NOTES**

Protein energy malnutrition (predominantly protein). *Epidemiology:* Common in developing countries or elderly/child neglect in developed countries. *Aetiology/ risk factors:* Malnutrition disorder originally thought to be protein deficiency, may be related to free radical damage. *Clinical features:* Lethargy, anorexia, oedema, ascites (often gross), hepatomegaly, hair discolouration (red/yellow), skin ulcers, infection. *Complications:* Poor growth, lactose intolerance, bacterial peritonitis, sepsis, shock, multiorgan failure, coma, death.

🔎 **INVESTIGATIONS**

FBC, $\downarrow$K$^+$, $\downarrow$albumin, $\downarrow$Mg^{2+}, $\downarrow$Ca^{2+}, $\downarrow$PO$_4^{3-}$. HIV screen, glucose, growth chart.

💊 **MANAGEMENT**

Electrolyte correction and fluid management, carbohydrate, fat, then protein supplementation. Vitamin supplement. MDT support.

Lactose intolerance

📋 **CLINICAL NOTES**

Epidemiology: Common. *Aetiology/risk factors:* Triggered by dietary lactose (eg in milk), lactase deficiency (congenital, coeliac disease, IBD, gastroenteritis, malnutrition). *Clinical features:* Abdominal pain, bloating, diarrhoea. *Complications:* Failure to thrive.

🔎 **INVESTIGATIONS**

Normally clinically diagnosed. Consider lactose tolerance test, stool acidity (pH <5.5. is suggestive), stool-reducing substances, hydrogen breath test.

💊 **MANAGEMENT**

Treat underlying cause. May settle if occurred post-gastroenteritis with gradual reintroduction of milk/dairy into diet. Lactose-free products, ensure intake of RDA Ca^{2+}. Lactase supplement.

Langerhans' cell histiocytosis (histiocytosis X)

📋 **CLINICAL NOTES**

Epidemiology: Rare. Spectrum of presentations. *Letterer-Siwe disease:* Highly malignant disease affecting children aged less than two years. Skin manifestations, anaemia, hepatosplenomegaly, pulmonary involvement, cerebral infiltration (may cause diabetes insipidus). Fatal. *Hand-Schuller-Christian disease:* Otitis media, mastoiditis, diabetes insipidus, exophthalmos, hilar lymphadenopathy. *Eosinophilic granuloma:* Cystic lesions in bones, may affect other organs. *Histiocytosis affecting lungs:* Cough, SOB, spares lung bases/cysts, bullae, fibrosis, pneumothoraces.

🔎 **INVESTIGATIONS**

FBC, U&E, LFT, ESR, Coombs' test, immunoglobulins, urine and serum osmolality, urine specific gravity, chest X-ray, pulmonary CT, lung function tests, bronchoscopy, skeletal survey, PET scan, skin biopsy (eg to differentiate from seborrhoeic keratosis).

💊 **MANAGEMENT**

Chemotherapy, steroids (topical, intralesional or systemic), PUVA, surgical excision.

Large bowel obstruction

📋 **CLINICAL NOTES**

Aetiology/risk factors: Colorectal cancer, stricture, constipation, volvulus, adhesions, post-radiation, hernia, paralytic ileus, Hirschsprung's disease, intussusception, retroperitoneal fibrosis, illicit drug trafficking (body packing drugs). Parkinson's disease, dementia, MS. *Clinical features:* Abdominal pain (may be severe with associated ischaemia eg from volvulus/vasculopathy), inability to pass flatus/stool and possibly urine, abdominal distension, nausea, anorexia, vomiting (may progress to feculent), tachycardia, hypotension, septic if gangrene/ perforation, abdominal mass, increased 'tinkling' bowel sounds (unless ileus). *Complications:* Shock, ischaemia, gangrene, sepsis, perforation, peritonitis, death.

🔎 **INVESTIGATIONS**

FBC, U&E, group and save/crossmatch, abdominal X-ray (erect and supine), erect chest X-ray, CT.

💊 **MANAGEMENT**

Nasogastric tube, IV fluids, urinary catheterisation, analgesia, flatus tube. Consider conservative approach if partial obstruction or patient terminally ill. Adhesions and sigmoid volvulus may be treated conservatively. Laparotomy if cause unknown, peritonitis, malignancy (unless advanced), ischaemic aetiology, non-sigmoid volvulus eg caecal.

Laryngeal cancer

📋 **CLINICAL NOTES**

See *naso/oropharyngeal and laryngeal cancers*

Lateral epicondylitis

📋 **CLINICAL NOTES**

See *tennis elbow (lateral epicondylitis)*

Lateral medullary syndrome (Wallenberg's syndrome)

See also
— *Cerebrovascular accident*

📋 **CLINICAL NOTES**

See *Cerebrovascular accident. Aetiology/risk*

DISEASES

factors: Occlusion of posterior inferior cerebellar artery or vertebral artery. Clinical features: Vomiting, vertigo, dysphagia, dysarthria, ipsilateral; VIIth, IXth, Xth, XIth cranial nerve lesions, ipsilateral cerebellar syndrome and Horner's syndrome.

Laurence-Moon-Biedl syndrome

CLINICAL NOTES
Epidemiology: Rare. Aetiology/risk factors: Autosomal recessive. Clinical features: Obesity, mental retardation, retinitis pigmentosa, cataract, deafness, renal cysts, polydactyly, hypogonadism.

ᗯ INVESTIGATIONS
Genetic studies.

ᗢ MANAGEMENT
Genetic counselling. Treat complications accordingly.

Lazy leucocyte syndrome

CLINICAL NOTES
See immunodeficiency (primary)

Leber's optic atrophy

ᗧ CLINICAL NOTES
Optic nerve degeneration. Epidemiology: Rare. M>F. Second-third decade. Aetiology/risk factors: Genetic (mitochondrial). Clinical features: Asymptomatic, variable progressive visual loss, painless. Complications: Bilateral blindness, tremor, cardiac conduction defects.

ᗯ INVESTIGATIONS
Fluorescein angiography, electrophysiology studies, CT/MRI.

ᗢ MANAGEMENT
Genetic counselling, avoid smoking, alcohol, chloramphenicol, ethambutol, antioxidants (eg vitamins C, E, co-enzyme Q10), minocycline, ciclosporin, idebenone (antioxidant under trial).

Left ventricular diastolic failure

ᗧ CLINICAL NOTES
Heart failure with preserved ejection fraction (HF-PEF). Failure of cardiac ventricular relaxation, may explain breathlessness in patients with clinical heart failure but ejection fraction >45%. Epidemiology: F>M. Tend to be older than those with systolic dysfunction. Present in about 50% of patients diagnosed with heart failure. Aetiology/risk factors: Hypertension, CHD, AS, amyloid, HCM, haemochromatosis. Clinical features: Asymptomatic, breathlessness, undisplaced apex beat, S4. Complications: AF, reduced quality of life, depression.

ᗯ INVESTIGATIONS
ECG: Normal, LVH. Echocardiogram: Enlarged atria, early:atrial (E:A) reversal (<0.7), normal or only mildly impaired systolic function, impaired ventricular relaxation/distensibility, tissue doppler, may reveal aetiology eg amyloid. BNP not raised in HF-PEF. Angiography if concerned about ischaemic component to diastolic dysfunction. Investigate according to suspected underlying cause.

ᗢ MANAGEMENT
Treat any underlying cause eg hypertension; rhythm control AF/control rate in permanent AF, beta-blockers, rate-controlling CCBs (eg diltiazem), ACE inhibitors/ARB, loop diuretics if congestion, however, the use of these drugs in HF-PEF not recommended currently.

Left ventricular systolic dysfunction (LVSD), chronic

CLINICAL NOTES
Epidemiology: Common, likely to be underdiagnosed. UK prevalence about 0.8-0.9%. Aetiology/risk factors: Hypertension, CHD, valve disease, cardiomyopathy, arrhythmia, pericardial effusion/pericarditis, congenital heart disease, anaemia, thyrotoxicosis, Paget's disease of the bone, iron overload eg haemochromatosis, beriberi (thiamin, vitamin B_1 deficiency), iatrogenic (eg doxorubicin, trastuzumab). Clinical features: Fatigue, SOB, orthopnea, paroxysmal nocturnal dyspnoea, diaphoresis, palpitations/arrhythmia, peripheral oedema (eg sacral/pedal), varying volume pulse, BP may be high if hypertension or low in decompensated failure, raised JVP, valve disease eg MR in dilated LV, gallop rhythm in advanced disease (S3 high specificity for LVSD), displaced apex, pulmonary crackles. Complications: Cachexia, ascites, painful hepatomegaly, hepatic failure, malignant arrhythmias, acute decompensation, respiratory failure, hyperaldosteronism, shock, death.

ᗯ INVESTIGATIONS
FBC, U&E, ↓Na⁺, ↑aldosterone, ↑lactate, ↑LDH. N-terminal pro b-type natriuretic peptide (NTproBNP) (high NPV for LVSD, also useful in monitoring), ECG (approximately 85% NPV if normal). If ECG and BNP studies normal, cardiac failure unlikely; if abnormal, echocardiogram suggested. Echocardiogram (ejection fraction <45%, may show valve disease/ischaemic damage/hypertensive heart disease/dilated or hypertrophic cardiomyopathy). Consider ETT, cardiac catheterisation, stress echocardiogram, nuclear studies, PET, MRI, biopsy.

ᗢ MANAGEMENT
Treat underlying cause (eg stent, valve repair), lifestyle advice including smoking cessation. Ensure drug adherence – may reduce admissions by about 20%.

ACE inhibitor/ARB (uptitrate to maximum tolerated dose), cardioselective beta-blockers (slowly uptitrate to maximum tolerated dose), spironolactone, loop diuretics (for congestive symptoms). Consider digoxin (reduces hospitalisation rate, may also be used even if in sinus rhythm-positive inotrope), ivabradine shown to reduce cardiovascular death, biventricular pacing, ICD (if malignant arrhythmias eg VT), LV assist device, cardiac transplant. Monitor weight (fluid shift). Replacing iron in deficient individuals (irrespective of anaemia) has been shown to improve functional outcome. Follow CLOUD model for monitoring patients – comorbidity management, lifestyle advice, regular outpatient monitoring, uptitration of drugs, ensure drug adherence.

Leg ulcers

See also
— *Peripheral vascular disease*

CLINICAL NOTES

Epidemiology: Venous most common. *Venous risk factors:* Venous incompetency. Clinical features: Occur by malleoli, associated with venous eczema, haemosiderin deposits, varicose veins, phlebitis, can be painful. Complications: Infection, bleeding. *Arterial risk factors:* Atherosclerosis, DM, sickle cell anaemia. Clinical features: May be painful, intermittent claudication. Complications: Infection, bleeding, gangrene, acute ischaemia. *Others:* Mixed arterial and venous, vasculitis, traumatic, tumour (rolled edges, persistent ulcers), RA, pyoderma gangrenosum.

INVESTIGATIONS

Venous: Doppler required to exclude arterial insufficiency, avoid compression stockings if ankle brachial pressure index (ABPI) <0.8, ABPI may be falsely raised in DM. *Arterial:* ABPI and dopplers required; <0.92 suggests arterial disease.

MANAGEMENT

Venous: Compression bandage to treat ulcer, stockings to prevent recurrence, analgesia, treat infection (remove debris, swab, cleansing, iodine/silver/manuka honey, maggots, antibiotics), venous surgery. *Arterial:* See *peripheral vascular disease.*

Legionnaire's disease

CLINICAL NOTES

See *pneumonia*

Leishmaniasis

CLINICAL NOTES

Epidemiology: Africa, Asia, South America, Europe. Aetiology/risk factors: *Leishmania spp* (protozoa), sandfly vector, animal reservoirs (eg fox, rodents). Incubation one

month to years. Clinical features: Asymptomatic. *Visceral* (Kala azar): low fever, lymphadenopathy, hepatosplenomegaly, roughened skin, immunosuppression, pancytopenia (infection and bleeding lead to death within 12 months). *Cutaneous leishmaniasis:* Painless skin nodules, ulceration, scarring. *Mucocutaneous leishmaniasis:* Skin disease followed by mucous membrane/cartilaginous lesions.

INVESTIGATIONS

FBC, LFT, serology, biopsy.

MANAGEMENT

Pentavalent antimony salts.

Leprosy

CLINICAL NOTES

Epidemiology: One of the most common causes of peripheral neuropathy worldwide. Aetiology/risk factors: *Mycobacterium leprae*, transmitted by prolonged exposure to infectious person (10% of affected people will be infectious). Incubation about five or more years. Clinical features: May take 20 years to manifest, hypopigmented anaesthetic macules, nerve thickening. *Tuberculoid type:* Granulomas with no bacteria but rich in lymphocytes (non-infectious). *Lepromatous type:* Skin lesions contain many bacteria (infectious), erythema nodosum. *Borderline type:* Between tuberculoid and lepromatous. Type dependent on immune response. Complications: Cranial nerve palsy, iritis, scleritis, cataract.

INVESTIGATIONS

↑neutrophils, ↑ESR, skin biopsy.

MANAGEMENT

Tuberculoid: Six months rifampicin and dapsone. *Lepromatous/borderline:* Two years rifampicin, dapsone (may be resistance), clofazimine.

Leptospirosis and Weil's disease

CLINICAL NOTES

Epidemiology: 40 cases per year (UK). Aetiology/risk factors: *Leptospira icterohaemorrhagiae* through contact with water or soil contaminated with infected animal urine. Bacteria enter through broken skin, mucous membranes, placenta or conjunctivae. Incubation one to two weeks. Clinical features: May be asymptomatic. Initial flu-like illness with fever, malaise, muscle aches, lower limb and back pain, diarrhoea and vomiting, headache. >90% recover (mild anicteric leptospirosis) or one to two days later, some may develop Weil's disease – multiorgan vasculitis, jaundice, hepatosplenomegaly, renal failure, liver failure, haemoptysis, haemorrhage, myocarditis, haemolysis, DIC, HUS, TTP.

INVESTIGATIONS

Blood/CSF culture, serology, leucocytosis, U&E, LFT, ↑liver transaminases, ↓plts, ↑CK, clotting, chest X-ray.

MANAGEMENT

Mild disease: Oral doxycycline. *Severe (Weil's) disease:* IV penicillin or erythromycin.

Lewy body dementia

See also
— *Parkinson's disease and Parkinson's plus syndromes*

 CLINICAL NOTES

Epidemiology: Third most common dementia type, associated with Parkinson's disease. Clinical features: Visual hallucinations, daytime sleepiness and fluctuating features common.

Lichen planus

CLINICAL NOTES

Aetiology/risk factors: Autoimmune, may be triggered by hepatitis C and dental amalgam. Associated with other autoimmune disorders. Clinical features: Acute, intensely pruritic rash, resolves spontaneously after months/years. About 65% spontanous resolution at one year. Inflammatory dermatosis, papules, distal limbs, especially forearms (flexor aspect), white lacey hyperkeratosis (Wickham's striae) within flat-topped purplish papules/plaques. Hyperkeratosis in reticular pattern in mouth (often asymptomatic), nail pterygium with longitudinal ridges. May affect genitalia, scalp (scarring alopecia). Bullous lichen planus may be seen. Complications: Distress, recurrence, scarring alopecia, Koebner phenomenon.

INVESTIGATIONS

Can usually be diagnosed from appearance of rash, consider biopsy.

MANAGEMENT

Topical steroids, intralesional steroids if hypertrophic, steroid mouthwashes, oral steroid for widespread disease. Topical tacrolimus (0.1%). Phototherapy. Ciclosporin, mycophenolate mofetil.

Lichen sclerosus

 CLINICAL NOTES

Epidemiology: Infertile ages in females, boys/young men. F>M 10:1. Aetiology/risk factors: May be autoimmune. Clinical features: Foreskin/glans (balanitis xerotica obliterans) or anogenital skin in women. Severe pruritus, pain, constipation, soreness, dyspareunia, dysuria, altered urinary stream, white lesions (may be around vulva and anus, glans, foreskin), scarring, labial shrinkage. Complications: Distress, fissures, labial shrinkage, clitoral adhesions, introital narrowing, phimosis, vulval cancer, may be mistaken for sexual abuse.

INVESTIGATIONS

Biopsy if uncertain/concerned about malignancy.

MANAGEMENT

Female disease: Topical potent steroids (once daily for one month, then alternate days for one month, then biweekly for one month. May need to step up steroid use to get control), follow-up one, three and six months to ensure healing, may require longer-term follow-up/maintenance, monitor for SCC, biopsy if no improvement after four to six weeks. *Male disease:* Topical steroids once daily until settles, then reduce. May require maintenance dose eg weekly. Topical oestrogens not effective. *General advice:* Wash with emollients, biopsy if treatment failure/concerning lesions, laxatives if constipation through anal disease/fissures, monitor for urinary outflow obstruction and sexual dysfunction.

Lichen simplex chronicus

 CLINICAL NOTES

Epidemiology: Common. Aetiology/risk factors: Complication of eczema. Clinical features: Well demarcated scaly plaque, lichenification, pruritus, especially elbow, calf, genitalia, neck. Complications: Distress, secondary bacterial infection.

MANAGEMENT

Occlusive dressings, antihistamines, topical/intralesional steroids, tar preparations.

Liddle's syndrome

See also
— *Hyperaldosteronism*

CLINICAL NOTES

Pseudohyperaldosteronaemia. Epidemiology: Rare. Aetiology/risk factors: Autosomal dominant. Clinical features: Early onset hypertension.

INVESTIGATIONS

Metabolic alkalosis, ↓K⁺, ↓renin, ↓aldosterone.

MANAGEMENT

Triamterene, amiloride, salt restriction.

Limb-girdle dystrophy

CLINICAL NOTES

Epidemiology: Rare. Aetiology/risk factors: Multiple inheritance patterns, mainly autosomal recessive. Clinical features: Dependent on inheritance and may include limb girdle wasting, winged scapula, calf hypertrophy. Complications: Cardiomyopathy, arrhythmia, respiratory failure, neuropathy, dysarthria.

INVESTIGATIONS

↑CK, muscle MRI, EMG, nerve conduction studies, muscle biopsy, ECG, echocardiogram, lung function tests.

DISEASES

MANAGEMENT

Physiotherapy, OT, treat complications accordingly.

Limited systemic sclerosis (including CREST)

See also
— *Diffuse systemic sclerosis (diffuse scleroderma)*

CLINICAL NOTES

Epidemiology: F>M. 20s-50s. Aetiology/ risk factors: Autoimmune, familial. Clinical features: Insidious onset, fatigue, weight loss, limited cutaneous disease (skin is shiny, tight, leathery, thick and hard; limited to face, forearms, lower legs), joint and muscle pains. *CREST:* Calcinosis (tender nodules, fingers, elbows, knees, may be infected), *R*aynaud's phenomenon (often presenting symptom, may precede other symptoms by years), oesophageal dysmotility (reflux, dysphagia), *S*clerodactyly, *T*elangiectasia. Complications: Contractures (skin, tendons), pulmonary fibrosis/hypertension, oesophageal scarring, Barrett's oesophagus, constipation, diarrhoea, malabsorption, intestinal bacterial overgrowth, dental caries, sicca, digital ulceration/gangrene, arrhythmias, myocarditis, hypertension, renal failure/crisis (internal organ complications less likely in limited scleroderma), depression.

INVESTIGATIONS

FBC, ESR, CRP, U&E, ANA +ve, ENA, anticentromere antibodies (high specificity, <60% sensitivity), biopsy (skin), endoscopy, ECG, echocardiogram, chest X-ray, lung function tests, pulmonary CT.

MANAGEMENT

Education and regular follow-up, close BP monitoring (monthly), physiotherapy, OT, analgesia, antacids, metoclopramide. See *Raynaud's phenomenon*. Note CCBs may exacerbate oesophageal reflux. Antibiotics (skin infections and bacterial overgrowth), emollients, penicillamine (skin disease), cyclophosphamide (pulmonary disease), ACE inhibitors (renal disease), steroids not generally effective, surgery (Ca²⁺ deposits, oesophageal dilation, digital amputation, lung transplant), laser for telangiectasia. *Experimental/alternative:* Methotrexate, ciclosporin, gamma interferon, photophoresis, plasmapheresis.

Lipoma

CLINICAL NOTES

Epidemiology: Common. *Isolated:* F>M. *Multiple:* M>F. Aetiology/risk factors: May be hereditary. Multiple lipomatosis (autosomal dominant, M>F), Dercum's disease (painful lipomas, obesity, weakness, headache, memory disturbance, F>M), Gardner's syndrome (autosomal dominant, FPC, osteomas). Clinical features: Adipose tumours, benign. Complications: May be found within muscles, intrathoracic, intra-abdominal, cerebellopontine angle, sarcomatous change (rapid growth, fixed, >5cm, rare).

INVESTIGATIONS

Imaging if concerned about malignant change (USS, MRI).

MANAGEMENT

Remove: Cosmetic/functional disturbance/malignant change.

Listeriosis

CLINICAL NOTES

Epidemiology: Rare in UK. Aetiology/risk factors: *Listeria monocytogenes.* Unpasteurised dairy products eg soft cheese. Paté. Complications: High risk of early labour, miscarriage, stillbirth, meningitis (neonatal and elderly).

INVESTIGATIONS

Cultures (blood, CSF, amniotic fluid, placental and aborted tissue, not vaginal). Serology not clinically useful.

MANAGEMENT

Supportive, ampicillin plus gentamicin.

Liver failure

See also
— *Chronic liver disease*

CLINICAL NOTES

Aetiology/risk factors: Numerous including poisoning, alcohol abuse, drug toxicity, infective hepatitis, decompensated chronic liver disease, tumour, fatty liver, pregnancy, ischaemia, autoimmune disease. Clinical features: Bruising, headache, confusion, depression, disinhibition, fatigue, abdominal distension, may show signs of chronic liver disease, jaundice, ascites, hypo or hypertension (if raised intracranial pressure). Complications: Hepatic encephalopathy (altered mental state/consciousness, confusion, hyperreflexia, difficulty drawing five-pointed star, asterixis), spontaneous bacterial peritonitis, LRTI, haemorrhage, hyperaldosteronism, death.

INVESTIGATIONS

↓plts, clotting derangement, ↑↑transaminases, ↑bilirubin, ↑ammonia, ↑lactate, ↓glucose, U&E, ↓Na⁺, investigate causes, USS (to look for cause, ascites, Budd-Chiari syndrome), CT/MRI.

MANAGEMENT

Treat cause, FFP if DIC, reduce serum ammonia with lactulose, mannitol if raised ICP, dialysis if hepatorenal syndrome, fluid/electrolyte/glucose management, liver transplant.

Liver tumours

CLINICAL NOTES

Hepatocellular cancer (HCC): Epidemiology: Most common primary liver cancer. Increasing incidence. Aetiology/risk factors: Chronic liver disease, high risk – hepatitis B/C, alcohol abuse (men), haemochromatosis, men with primary biliary cirrhosis, foods containing aflatoxins/fungal contaminants, metabolic syndrome, COC (rare). Clinical features: Signs of chronic liver disease, weight loss, RUQ pain, abdominal distension, ascites, jaundice, confusion. Complications: Encephalopathy, upper GI haemorrhage, coagulopathy, metastatic disease (lung, bone, brain), portal vein thrombosis. *Hepatoblastoma:* Epidemiology: Children. Clinical features: Abdominal mass, failure to thrive, vomiting. Complications: Pulmonary metastases. *Hepatic haemangioma:* Benign, within first year of life or in adulthood (eg during pregnancy). May cause abdominal distension in children. Often asymptomatic. Complications: DIC, cardiac failure. *Hepatic adenoma:* F>M (due to COC use), benign. Clinical features: Abdominal pain, intra-abdominal bleeding. Complications: Carcinomatous transformation. *Liver secondaries:* especially GI malignancies, pulmonary, breast (adults).

INVESTIGATIONS

HCC: ↑alpha-fetoprotein (>400ng/ml, 75% sensitivity for HCC, screen high-risk groups for HCC with six-monthly USS and alpha-fetoprotein. Alpha-fetoprotein also ↑in hepatoblastoma). LFT, ↓albumin. *Imaging:* Sensitivity for liver tumours – USS<CT<MRI, PET-CT, chest X-ray (metastases). Biopsy.

MANAGEMENT

HCC: Treat encephalopathy, clotting disorder, infection, varices, ethanol/radiofrequency/microwave ablation, tumour embolisation, systemic chemotherapy, stereotactic radiotherapy, tumour transplant, liver transplantation. Median survival six months. *Hepatoblastoma:* Good response to chemotherapy. Surgery. *Hepatic haemangioma:* Often remain static without symptoms, may be left alone. Some centres follow up radiologically especially over 10cm. Some reports that anti-VEGF antibodies (bevacizumab) cause shrinkage. *Hepatic adenoma:* Stop COC, resection if symptomatic, avoid pregnancy before resection. Regular monthly USS and alpha-fetoprotein.

Long QT syndrome

See also
— *Torsades de pointes*

CLINICAL NOTES

Epidemiology: Underdiagnosed, may be family history of sudden cardiac death. Aetiology/risk factors: *Congenital*: Romano-Ward syndrome, Jervell Lange-Nielsen syndrome (associated with deafness).

Cardiac: Mitral valve prolapse (MVP), MI, bradycardia. *Electrolyte/metabolic/endocrine*: Hypokalaemia, Addison's disease, hypomagnesaemia, hypocalcaemia, hypothyroidism. *Miscellaneous*: Dystrophia myotonica, hypothermia. *Iatrogenic*: Venlafaxine, amiodarone, ciprofloxacin, terfenadine, erythromycin, TCAs, sotalol, organophosphate pesticides. Clinical features: Palpitations, presyncope, syncope (exertional syncope sinister), cardiac examination likely to be normal in inherited causes. Complications: R on T phenomenon, torsades de pointes, ventricular fibrillation, death. Anoxic jerks/seizures may be mistaken for epilepsy.

INVESTIGATIONS

ECG-QT beginning of Q wave to end of T wave, QTc=QT/√RR. Prolonged if >450ms in men and >460ms in women. QTc should be measured manually, may be normal at rest and ambulatory ECG and ETT may be required. Consider genetic testing for inherited syndromes.

MANAGEMENT

Beta-blockers, consider ICD (especially if previous cardiac arrest or QTc >500ms), cardiac sympathectomy.

Lown-Ganong-Levine syndrome

CLINICAL NOTES

Pre-excitation syndrome of heart. Epidemiology: One in 200 prevalence. Aetiology/risk factors: Accessory pathway – James and other fibres. Clinical features: Paroxysmal palpitations (secondary to tachycardia, SVT without atrial flutter/AF, breathlessness, chest pain, presyncope. Complications: Syncope.

INVESTIGATIONS

ECG: short PR (≤0.12s), no delta wave, normal QRS duration, ambulatory ECG (Holter, reveal), electrophysiology.

MANAGEMENT

Acute setting: Resuscitation if required, carotid massage, adenosine. *Stable patients:* Beta-blockade, CCB (non-dihydropyridine), digoxin, ablation.

Lung cancer

CLINICAL NOTES

Epidemiology: Most common cancer worldwide. Aetiology/risk factors: Affects one in five smokers, >90% cancers occur in current and passive smokers. Asbestos, arsenic, idiopathic pulmonary fibrosis (cryptogenic fibrosing alveolitis, may not be a causal relationship), systemic sclerosis, cavitation scars. Clinical features: Nicotine staining, weight loss, PUO, fatigue, malaise, recurrent chest infection, cough, haemoptysis, SOB, chest pain, crepitations, cachexia, pallor. Complications: Pleural effusion, pneumothorax, SVCO, lymphadenopathy, acanthosis nigricans, finger clubbing, hypertrophic pulmonary osteoarthropathy (HPOA), hoarse voice (recurrent

DISEASES

laryngeal nerve palsy), deviated trachea (eg mass effect, fibrosis, effusion), Horner's syndrome and wasting of small muscles of hand (Pancoast tumour). Symptoms suggestive of metastatic disease and paraneoplastic syndromes – bone pain, seizure, headache, visual disturbance, stroke, jaundice, ascites, adrenal infiltration, dysphagia, spinal cord compression, peripheral neuropathy, SIADH, hypercalcaemia, hyperthyroidism, gynaecomastia, Eaton-Lambert syndrome, erythema gyratum repens.

INVESTIGATIONS
FBC, U&E, LFT, Ca²⁺, early chest X-ray, CT, PET-CT, sputum cytology, bronchoscopy, biopsy, chromogranin A (SCLC).

MANAGEMENT
MDT support. Radical surgery (small cell lung cancers usually present too late for radical surgery). Neoadjuvant, adjuvant or radical chemotherapy. Adjuvant or radical radiotherapy. Prophylactic cranial radiation in small cell cancer. VEGF and EGFR inhibitors offer survival benefit in non-small cell cancer and EGFR inhibitors in adenocarcinoma. Palliation.

Lupus vulgaris

See also
— Tuberculosis (pulmonary)

CLINICAL NOTES
Aetiology/risk factors: Cutaneous TB, immunodeficiency. Clinical features: Multiple manifestations, red/purple/brown warty lesions. Some well defined. Complications: Abscesses and ulcers.

INVESTIGATIONS
Tuberculin skin test, biopsy, chest X-ray. Sputum culture.

MANAGEMENT
Combination antituberculous drugs (isoniazid, rifampicin, pyrazinamide, ethambutol).

Lyme disease

CLINICAL NOTES
Epidemiology: High-risk areas – forests/heath of northern hemisphere. UK: New Forest, Exmoor, South Downs, Lake District, Yorkshire, Scottish Highlands. Non-UK endemic areas: France, Germany, Scandinavia, Austria, eastern Europe, North America. Aetiology/risk factors: Borrelia burgdorferi (also B Afzelii), tick vector. Clinical features: Tick has to feed for many hours before infection transmitted. Higher risk of transmission with tick feeding >24 hours. Early stages: Erythema chronicum migrans (75%, up to one month after bite, palpable edge, may contain vesicles), fever, malaise, muscle and joint pains. Complications: Carditis, cardiac arrhythmias, iritis, arthritis, sleep disturbance,

meningo-encephalitis, polyneuropathy, affective disorders, acrodermatitis chronicum atrophicans (B Afzelli).

INVESTIGATIONS
Borrelia serology – IgM, IgG, risk of false -ve in early disease, before seroconversion, repeat serology after two to four weeks if high clinical suspicion, skin culture, joint fluid samples for DNA, ECG (prolonged PR), echocardiogram.

MANAGEMENT
Education and prevention: Check skin regularly for ticks. Early antibiotics (oral: over three to four weeks, doxycycline or amoxicillin. IV: over two to three weeks, ceftriaxone, cefotaxime or penicillin G).

Malaria

CLINICAL NOTES
Epidemiology: About 2,000 per year (UK). Aetiology/risk factors: Endemic areas include sub-Saharan Africa, India, South America. Sickle cell trait, G6PD deficiency and HLA-B53 are protective. Mosquito vector. Clinical features: Malaria may become symptomatic one year after exposure. 10 different types, four particularly relevant to humans. Plasmodium falciparum: Most lethal and most common human malarial infection – fever, malaise, haemolysis, DIC, renal failure, pulmonary oedema, cerebral malaria, acidosis. P vivax, P ovale and P malariae have dormant phases (may be dormant for years); flu-like illness, malaise, arthralgia, cough, headache, diarrhoea, abdominal pain.

INVESTIGATIONS
FBC, U&E, glucose, LFT, thick and thin blood films (repeat on consecutive days if clinical suspicion), malaria antigens (rapid but less sensitive than blood films), blood cultures, urinalysis, chest X-ray, measure G6PD levels if P vivax or P ovale.

MANAGEMENT
Education, mosquito bite avoidance, malaria prophylaxis. Supportive. P falciparum: Admit. Mild disease – quinine plus doxycycline, atovaquone-proguanil, artemether/lumefantrine. Severe disease – IV quinine, followed by doxycycline or clindamycin. Artemisinins for multidrug resistance. Non-falciparum: Chloroquine. Chloroquine-resistant vivax – quinine, artemether/lumefantrine, atovaquone-proguanil. Vivax/ovale should also be treated with primaquine to prevent hepatic disease (care in G6PD deficiency, risk of haemolysis).

Malignant hyperpyrexia

CLINICAL NOTES
Epidemiology: Rare. Aetiology/risk factors: Autosomal dominant, general anaesthetics. Clinical

DISEASES

features: Pyrexia, muscle rigidity. **Complications:** Seizure, rhabdomyolysis, renal failure, death.

INVESTIGATIONS

↑myoglobin, ↑CK, ↓pH, ↓eGFR, ↑K⁺, genetic studies.

MANAGEMENT

Stop offending drug, cooling, fluid/electrolyte management, supportive, dantrolene, genetic counselling.

Malignant hypertension

See also
— *Essential hypertension*

CLINICAL NOTES

Epidemiology: Rare, more common in African-Caribbeans. **Clinical features:** Severe hypertension, headache, nausea, visual disturbance, retinal haemorrhages, papilloedema, confusion. **Complications:** End organ damage, encephalopathy, CVA, seizure, death.

INVESTIGATIONS

U&E, 24-hour urine collection (cortisol, catecholamines), urinalysis, renal USS, ECG, echocardiogram.

MANAGEMENT

Admit to secondary care for rest and controlled BP reduction (rapid reduction may cause stroke).

Marasmus

CLINICAL NOTES

Protein energy malnutrition (predominantly energy). **Epidemiology:** Mainly seen in children in developing countries. High prevalence in Asia, Africa and South America. **Aetiology/risk factors:** Institutionalised children, associated with infection and chronic illness. **Clinical features:** Thin, failure to thrive, severe muscle wasting, absence of body fat, chronic diarrhoea, hair changes (thin, dry). **Complications:** Infection, hypothermia, hypoglycaemia, hypovolaemia, cardiac failure and arrhythmia, infections, death.

INVESTIGATIONS

→/↓Na⁺, ↓K⁺, Ca²⁺ ↓glucose, ↓Hb, ↓albumin. HIV screen, blood parasite screen.

MANAGEMENT

Electrolyte, fluid (including fluid resuscitation/ORT), reduced osmolarity formulation or tailored to electrolyte disturbance; multivitamin and micronutrients. Treat hypothermia, infection. Formula-based milk, peanut-based supplement. Zinc may reduce diarrhoea.

Marble bone disease

See *osteopetrosis*

Marfan's syndrome

See also
— *Homocystinuria*

CLINICAL NOTES

Aetiology/risk factors: Chromosome 15, autosomal dominant. **Clinical features:** Tall stature, long extremities, high arched palate, hypotonia, pectus excavatum, striae, herniae, kyphosis, scoliosis, hypermobile joints, protusio acetabuli, blue sclera, iris tremor, upward lens dislocation, normal IQ, AR, coarctation of the aorta, MVP, cardiac arrhythmia, AAA. **Complications:** Retinal detachment, aortic dissection, infective endocarditis, premature death.

INVESTIGATIONS

Genetic testing, regular ECG/echocardiogram, MRI spine, pelvic X-ray.

MANAGEMENT

Genetic counselling, physiotherapy, ophthalmic surgery, BP control, avoid high-risk sports to reduce dissecting aneurysm, cardiac surgery.

Mastitis

CLINICAL NOTES

Epidemiology: Common in lactating women. **Aetiology/risk factors:** Smoking (non-lactating women), *Staph aureus*. **Clinical features:** Acute onset, breast pain, redness, inflamed breast segment, tachycardia, malaise. **Complications:** Sepsis, abscess, fistula, cellulitis, necrosis.

INVESTIGATIONS

Consider FBC, glucose, swabs, blood cultures.

MANAGEMENT

Antibiotics, continue breastfeeding or expressing from affected side if possible. Discard milk if frank pus. Surgery for abscess.

Mastoiditis

CLINICAL NOTES

Epidemiology: Rare. **Aetiology/risk factors:** Complication of local infection eg otitis media. **Clinical features:** Pain, ear discharge, inflamed tympanic membrane (TM), conductive hearing loss, fever, mastoid tenderness and swelling. **Complications:** Bony necrosis, abscess (superficial, cranial and cerebral), cellulitis, cavernous sinus thrombosis.

INVESTIGATIONS

↑WCC, glucose, blood cultures, X-ray.

MANAGEMENT

Early referral, antibiotics, drainage.

McCune-Albright syndrome

 CLINICAL NOTES

Epidemiology: Rare. *Aetiology/risk factors:* Sporadic mutation. *Clinical features:* Some types present in neonatal period. Café au lait spots, endocrinopathy (eg hyperthyroidism but not immune-mediated, precocious puberty, Conn's syndrome, Cushing's syndrome, gigantism, acromegaly), polycystic fibrous dysplasia. *Complications:* Severe skeletal deformity (eg hemimelia, cranial deformity may cause visual loss and deafness), rickets, variable growth.

⚕ **INVESTIGATIONS**

$\downarrow$TSH, $\uparrow$T$_4$, Ca^{2+}, PO$_4^{3-}$, $\uparrow$oestrogen (intermittent, causing $\downarrow$LH, $\downarrow$FSH), $\uparrow$bilirubin, U&E, $\uparrow$GH, $\uparrow$IGF-1, $\uparrow$cortisol, $\downarrow$ACTH, positive dexamethasone suppression test, pelvic USS, abdominal and brain CT, bone scan, X-ray.

🗄 **MANAGEMENT**

MDT approach. Treat endocrinopathy accordingly. Orthopaedic surgery. Family support.

Measles (rubeola)

 CLINICAL NOTES

Epidemiology: $\downarrow$incidence since MMR vaccination. *Aetiology/risk factors:* Paramyxovirus, highly infectious (respiratory droplet transmission, incubation 10 days. Infectious from prodrome to four days after rash). *Clinical features: Prodrome:* Fever, cough, coryzal symptoms, conjunctivitis, diarrhoea, malaise. Morbilliform rash spreads from postauricular area (maximum intensity after three days). Transient Koplik spots in mouth, +/- hepatomegaly. *Complications:* Febrile convulsion, otitis media, LRTI (including staphylococcal, streptococcal, viral), meningitis, encephalitis (one in 1,000), ADEM (rare), subacute sclerosing panencephalitis (SSPE, rare), croup, bronchiectasis, hepatitis, immunosuppression, pregnancy (risk of fatal pneumonitis, miscarriage, no congenital malformation).

⚕ **INVESTIGATIONS**

Serology: IgM (acute infection, remains positive for up to two months), IgG (from day three to four of rash). Salivary test for acute infection.

🗄 **MANAGEMENT**

Prevention with MMR, supportive treatment.

Meckel's diverticulum

 CLINICAL NOTES

Vestigial remnant located in distal ileum about two feet from caecum. *Epidemiology:* 2% prevalence. May contain gastric, pancreatic or intestinal tissue. *Clinical features:* Asymptomatic or clinical features of complications, more common in males. *Complications:* Haemorrhage

($\uparrow$children aged less than two years), perforation, Meckel's diverticulitis, volvulus, intussusception, fistula, cysts, abscess, carcinoid, leiomyosarcoma, calculi.

⚕ **INVESTIGATIONS**

Abdominal X-ray, barium studies, CT, nuclear medicine.

🗄 **MANAGEMENT**

Surgery if symptomatic/<50 years.

Medial epicondylitis

 CLINICAL NOTES

See *golfer's elbow*

Medial shelf (plica) syndrome

 CLINICAL NOTES

Aetiology/risk factors: Trauma, overuse. Inflamed synovial fold (found above medial meniscus of knee). *Clinical features:* Transient locking, knee pain (inferomedial).

⚕ **INVESTIGATIONS**

Diagnostic arthroscopy.

🗄 **MANAGEMENT**

Rest, physiotherapy, NSAIDs, arthroscopy and plica excision.

Median nerve palsy

 CLINICAL NOTES

Aetiology/risk factors: Carpal tunnel syndrome (idiopathic, familial, obesity, hypothyroidism, fluid overload, post-trauma, lipoma, ganglion, tumour, DM, menopause, amyloid, dialysis, sarcoid, acromegaly, occupational, pregnancy). Pronator teres syndrome, anterior interosseous syndrome, mono-neuritis multiplex, trauma. *Clinical features:* Carpal tunnel syndrome (paraesthesia – radial 3.5 digits, often worse nocturnally, pain may radiate as proximally as shoulder, hand weakness, Phalen's and/or Tinel's signs). Muscle wasting – thenar eminence (abductor pollicis, flexor pollicis brevis, opponens pollicis) and lateral two lumbricals. If nerve damage at elbow or below: $\downarrow$index/middle finger flexion/ flexion distal thumb/thumb opposition/sensory loss radial palm and distal 3.5 fingers dorsally, atrophic skin changes.

⚕ **INVESTIGATIONS**

U&E, LFT (albumin), TFT, consider nerve conduction studies/USS/MRI.

🗄 **MANAGEMENT**

Treat underlying cause, carpal tunnel syndrome (conservative with night splints for six weeks unless motor disturbance, local/systemic steroid therapy, carpal tunnel release). *Other lesions:* Consider surgery.

Medium chain acyl-CoA dehydrogenase deficiency

📋 CLINICAL NOTES
Fatty acid metabolic disorder affecting gluconeogenesis. Epidemiology: About one in 10,000 live births, autosomal recessive. Clinical features: Presents >12 weeks of life (when night feeds are not demanded), vomiting, hypoglycaemia, coma, failure to thrive, steatosis, encephalopathy, seizure, sudden infant death.

🔍 INVESTIGATIONS
Part of UK newborn screening programme (heel prick), ↓glucose, ↓bicarbonate, ↓pH (raised anion gap), ↓carnitine, ↑ammonia, LFT, no ketonuria, genetic studies, liver biopsy (steatosis).

💊 MANAGEMENT
Regular feeding, carnitine, low-fat diet, dietitian, genetic counselling.

Medullary sponge kidney

📋 CLINICAL NOTES
Cysts and ectatic collecting ducts: Epidemiology: F>M. Uncommon. Presents in middle age. Aetiology/risk factors: May be associated with other congenital disorders and Wilms' tumour. Clinical features: Dilated collecting ducts and cysts. One or both kidneys affected. Asymptomatic, nephrocalcinosis (calcium oxalate and phosphate). Complications: Colic, UTIs, haematuria, CKD, renal tubular acidosis (RTA).

🔍 INVESTIGATIONS
Urinalysis, sterile pyuria, U&E, ↑urinary Ca²⁺, USS, CT, IVU.

💊 MANAGEMENT
Regular monitoring, treat complications, bendroflumethiazide.

Meigs syndrome

📋 CLINICAL NOTES
See ovarian germ cell tumours

Melanoma (malignant)

See also
— Naevi

📋 CLINICAL NOTES
Epidemiology: Significant increase in UK incidence over past 20 years. UK prevalence 1:110 (F), 1:150 (M). 9,000 cases per year, 2,000 deaths per year (UK). Australia 1:17 (F), 1:14 (M). Aetiology/risk factors: Sun exposure (especially UVB), fair skin, red hair, blue eyes, >100 benign naevi, sunburn (intermittent), immunosuppression, family history. Clinical features: Superficial spreading: Most common, growth months to years, sun-exposed areas, radial before vertical spread. Nodular: Any site, rapid growth, inflamed/ulcerated, poor prognosis. Lentigo maligna melanoma: Elderly, head/neck, occurs at sites of sun-damaged skin. Acral lentiginous: South-east Asians/ African-Caribbeans, palms, soles, subungual. Melanomas may not be pigmented (amelanotic melanoma). Melanoma can also occur mucosally, orbitally and on vulva. Red flags: Asymmetrical lesion, border irregularity, colour variegation, diameter >6mm, changing/evolving lesion, bleeding, pruritic, inflamed lesion, ulceration. Lymphadenopathy and hepatomegaly suggest metastatic disease.

🔍 INVESTIGATIONS
Biopsy (ulceration, Breslow thickness and Clark levels are prognostic). S100 and LDH markers of disease progression.

💊 MANAGEMENT
Surgery with clear margin. The role of sentinel node dissection in survival not clear currently. Poor response to chemotherapy/radiotherapy, although this may be used for palliation and metastatic disease. Regular follow-up, self-examination, family education (family at increased risk), ipilimumab and vemurafenib for advanced metastatic disease.

MELAS syndrome

📋 CLINICAL NOTES
Epidemiology: Rare. Aetiology/risk factors: Mitochondrial genetic disorder. Clinical features: Symptoms present at four to 15 years old. Mitochondrial myopathy, Encephalopathy, Lactic Acidosis, Stroke. Poor development, attention deficit, muscle weakness, severe mental retardation, sensorineural deafness, diabetes, paralysis, epilepsy.

🔍 INVESTIGATIONS
CK, lactic acid, arterial blood gas, CT/MRI brain, muscle biopsy, genetic studies.

💊 MANAGEMENT
Physiotherapy, family support, cochlear implants, anticonvulsants, hypoglycaemics/insulin, L-arginine, co-enzyme Q10. Genetic counselling.

Ménière's disease

📋 CLINICAL NOTES
Epidemiology: One in 1,000 prevalence. Clinical features: Intermittent attacks, vertigo, tinnitus, nausea, sensation of ear fullness, unilateral sensorineural deafness. Complications: May be debilitating, depression, falls.

🔍 INVESTIGATIONS
MRI (to exclude acoustic neuroma), audiometry.

MANAGEMENT

Antiemetics, betahistine, diuretics, beta-blockers, vestibular physiotherapy, surgery, Cawthorne Cooksey vestibular rehabilitation exercises.

Meningioma

CLINICAL NOTES

Epidemiology: Up to one in four cerebral tumours. F>M. Aetiology/risk factors: Sporadic, genetic, type 2 neurofibromatosis. Clinical features: Depend on site – headache, seizure, frontal lobe symptoms, CVA, cranial nerve dysfunction. Complications: Change in personality, haemorrhage, status epilepticus, raised ICP, recurrence. Higher risk with proliferation markers eg MIB-1. Less likely with progesterone receptors.

INVESTIGATIONS
CT/MRI.

MANAGEMENT
Surgery, radiosurgery, gamma knife stereotactic radiotherapy, embolisation, monitoring for recurrence, antiepileptics. Endocrine manipulation being researched.

Meningitis and septicaemia

CLINICAL NOTES

Epidemiology: Meningococcal disease leading infectious cause of death in children (UK). Aetiology/risk factors: Neisseria meningitidis, Strep pneumoniae, Haemophilus influenzae, Listeria monocytogenes, group B streptococcus, viral, fungal. Clinical features: Meningitis: Headache, nausea, vomiting, malaise, photophobia, neck stiffness (two in three), altered consciousness, confusion, aggression, irritability, seizure, high-pitched crying, poor feeding, fever, bradycardia (due to raised ICP) or tachycardia, apnoea (raised ICP) or tachypnoea, confusion, combative, reduced GCS, vacant expression, bulging fontanelle, Kernig's sign, opisthotonus, focal neurology eg false localising signs of raised ICP. Septicaemia: Early stages may mimic URTI or gastroenteritis. Leg pains, malaise, back pains, tachycardia (early sign), respiratory distress/tachypnoea, peripheral vasoconstriction/cold peripheries, 30% have maculopapular blanching rash, fever, hypotension (late sign), altered GCS (late sign), purpuric rash (late sign). Complications: Meningitis may be complicated by septicaemia. Epilepsy, permanent neurological deficit, limb ischaemia and loss, Waterhouse-Friderichsen syndrome (adrenal haemorrhage), death.

INVESTIGATIONS
FBC, U&E, LFT, glucose, clotting, blood cultures, LP (if part of septic screen or in meningitis if no contraindications, not required in confirmed meningococcal septicaemia), throat swab, chest X-ray, CT brain if raised ICP.

MANAGEMENT
Immediate treatment in community with IM/IV antibiotics (benzylpenicillin [unless severe allergy], infant 300mg, one to nine years 600mg, adult 1,200mg), chloramphenicol or cefotaxime (IM). Then IV ceftriaxone (plus ampicillin if listeria, acyclovir if viral), O_2, fluid resuscitation, inotropic support. Treat contacts. Screen pregnant women for group B streptococcus using enriched culture medium at 35-37 weeks' gestation (if +ve, IV antibiotics required during labour).

Meniscal tear

CLINICAL NOTES

Aetiology/risk factors: Trauma. Clinical features: Delayed swelling (more than two hours after injury), mild knee pain, small effusion, quadriceps wasting, pain on squatting, +ve Thessaly and McMurray tests, tender joint line. Complications: Locking, 'giving way', meniscal cyst.

INVESTIGATIONS
MRI.

MANAGEMENT
Refer if acutely locking. Simple tears, physiotherapy. Large/bucket-handle tears, surgery.

Menopause

CLINICAL NOTES

Perimenopause: Hot flushes, night sweats, irregular periods, palpitations, sleep disturbance, vaginal dryness, dyspareunia, anxiety. Menopause: Average age 52 years (UK), absence of menses for one year (premature if <45 years of age), vaginal atrophy, cystitis, urinary urgency and frequency, weight gain (10% body weight).

INVESTIGATIONS
↑FSH.

MANAGEMENT
CVD risk assessment, osteoporosis risk assessment (eg FRAX® score). Offer topical oestrogens for isolated bladder/vaginal symptoms. HRT if premature menopause (<45 years of age). Risks and benefits: If symptomatic aged 50-60 years, benefits outweigh risks; if >70 years, risks outweigh benefits. ↑VTE especially in first year of use, ↑breast cancer (combined HRT greater risk than oestrogen monotherapy, ↑↑risk after 10 years' use. HRT-related breast cancer has better prognosis than if not on HRT). ↑endometrial cancer (especially with oestrogen monotherapy), possible increase in ovarian cancer, ↓colon cancer, ↓DM, cardiovascular disease – ↑risk of CHD if HRT commenced >20 years postmenopause, ↓risk of CHD if HRT commenced 50-59 years.

DISEASES

↑CVA in older women, ↓menopausal symptoms, ↓osteoporosis, skin ageing, ↓dementia if taken within 10 years of menopause. *HRT contraindications:* CHD, hormone-dependent malignancy, history of VTE, undiagnosed breast mass, PV bleeding of unknown cause. Topical oestrogens can be used. Consider alternatives (clonidine, SSRI, vaginal lubricants).

Menorrhagia

📖 **CLINICAL NOTES**

See *dysfunctional uterine bleeding* and *Signs & Symptoms, menorrhagia*

Meralgia paraesthetica

📖 **CLINICAL NOTES**

Epidemiology: About four in 10,000 per year, M=F, most common middle age. Aetiology/risk factors: Obesity, pregnancy and ascites. Clinical features: Entrapment syndrome (lateral cutaneous nerve of thigh), pain and numbness lateral thigh.

🔬 **INVESTIGATIONS**

Diagnosis based on history and examination.

💊 **MANAGEMENT**

Weight loss, avoid triggers, surgery may rarely be required.

Mesenteric adenitis

📖 **CLINICAL NOTES**

Epidemiology: Children/young adults. Aetiology/risk factors: Likely to be infective. Clinical features: RIF pain and tenderness (may mimic appendicitis), not peritonitic, fever, diarrhoea.

🔬 **INVESTIGATIONS**

Diagnosis based on symptoms and examination.

💊 **MANAGEMENT**

No specific treatment.

Mesothelioma

📖 **CLINICAL NOTES**

Epidemiology: M>F. Sixth to eighth decades. About 2,000 cases per year (UK, expected peak year 2020). Aetiology/risk factors: ↑with asbestos exposure (potency of asbestos types: blue>brown>white). Lag between asbestos exposure and disease up to 50 years. Most commonly pleural, may also affect pericardium and peritoneum. Clinical features: Malaise, weight loss, fatigue, fever, SOB, chest pain, cachexia, finger clubbing, lymphadenopathy, pleural effusion. Complications: Pericardial effusion, ascites, metastatic spread (bone, liver).

🔬 **INVESTIGATIONS**

FBC, U&E, LFT, soluble mesothelin-related peptide. Chest X-ray, CT/MRI, PET, pleural effusion/ascitic fluid for cytology. Biopsy.

💊 **MANAGEMENT**

Cure unlikely unless very localised disease. Most patients not amenable to radical surgery; extrapleural pneumonectomy (EPP). Consider palliative surgery eg pleurectomy. Adjuvant or palliative radiotherapy. Chemotherapy eg pemetrexed, cisplatin, gemcitabine. Median survival less than one year. Compensation for occupational disease may be applied for.

Meticillin resistant *Staph aureus* (MRSA)

📖 **CLINICAL NOTES**

Epidemiology: Community and hospital acquired. ↑infection incidence in UK, ↓Scandinavia/Netherlands (high-cost strategies employed). Aetiology/risk factors: Multidrug resistant *Staph aureus*. Can survive for months on fomites. *Risks for infection:* Overuse of antibiotics, renal dialysis, malignancy, DM, immunodeficiency, post-operative, childhood daycare centres, prisoners, ↑hospital stays (length and frequency). Clinical features: May be asymptomatic colonisation rather than infection. Complications: Abscess, impetigo, folliculitis, cellulitis, UTI, pneumonia, wound infection, septicaemia, graft and joint replacement infection, joint infections, osteomyelitis, empyema, meningitis, toxin-mediated disease: necrotising pneumonia/osteomyelitis, toxic shock syndrome, scalded skin syndrome. Death.

🔬 **INVESTIGATIONS**

Screening: Swabs 25% cases from throat, consider nose, axilla, perineum. *Symptomatic:* Infection site eg wound, blood/sputum/urine cultures.

💊 **MANAGEMENT**

Hand hygiene, 'screen and treat', 'search and destroy'. *Nasal carriage eradication:* Nasal mupirocin plus chlorhexidine body wash +/– oral doxycycline/rifampicin. *Skin infections:* Incision and drainage if abscess. Clindamycin, doxycycline, co-trimoxazole, linezolid. *Systemic/invasive disease:* eg vancomycin, teicoplanin, linezolid.

Microangiopathic haemolytic anaemia (MAHA)

📖 **CLINICAL NOTES**

Red cell destruction secondary to fibrin strands in small vessels. Aetiology/risk factors: TTP, HUS, DIC, pre-eclampsia, malignant hypertension, prosthetic heart valves.

DISEASES

INVESTIGATIONS
FBC (anaemia, reticulocytosis). *Film:* Fragmented red cells (schistocytes/helmet cells), polychromasia.

MANAGEMENT
Treat underlying cause, transfusion/plasma exchange.

Migraine
CLINICAL NOTES
Epidemiology: About 15 in 100 prevalence (UK). One in four women, one in 12 men. 80% occur before 30 years of age. Aetiology/risk factors: F>M. May occur premenstrually or menstrually. Stress, depression, dietary, fatigue, dehydration, alcohol, smoking. Clinical features: Classical migraine (with aura), common migraine (without aura). *Aura:* Warning symptoms eg seeing flashing lights or zigzags, paraesthesia, speech and co-ordination disturbance. *Headache:* Severe, usually unilateral, photophobia, nausea, vomiting. Complications: Abdominal, hemiplegic, basilar migraine. Stroke, depression, anxiety, bipolar.

INVESTIGATIONS
Consider CT/MRI.

MANAGEMENT
Stroke prevention: Avoid COC if migraine with aura or if migraine deteriorates while taking COC. *Migraine prevention:* Ensure well hydrated, good sleep hygiene, avoid triggers eg chocolate, cheese. Beta-blockers, amitriptyline, topiramate, verapamil, lamotrigine, levetiracetam. *Migraine treatment:* Paracetamol, aspirin (adults), NSAIDs, antiemetics, triptans.

Mikulicz's syndrome
CLINICAL NOTES
See *Sjögren's syndrome*

Milia (neonatal)
CLINICAL NOTES
Epidemiology: Common. Clinical features: Small, firm, white papules. Usually on face, especially nose.

MANAGEMENT
Reassurance, settles after few weeks.

Miller Fisher syndrome
CLINICAL NOTES
See *Guillain-Barré syndrome*

Minimal change disease
CLINICAL NOTES
See *glomerulonephritis*

Mitral regurgitation (MR)
CLINICAL NOTES
Epidemiology: Common. Aetiology/risk factors: Functional (eg secondary to dilated LV), LVSD, CHD, papillary muscle dysfunction, hypertension, aortic valve disease, connective tissue disease, acute/chronic rheumatic fever, MVP, chordae rupture, collagen disorders, relapsing polychondritis, endocarditis. Clinical features: Acute MR (eg after MI) may cause flash pulmonary oedema. Asymptomatic, fatigue, SOB, displaced volume – overloaded apex, soft S1, pansystolic murmur radiating to axilla (unless small anteriorly directed jet of MR). Complications: LVSD, AF, endocarditis.

INVESTIGATIONS
ECG – normal, AF, broad p-waves (if in sinus rhythm), LVH. Chest X-ray – left atrial/ventricular enlargement, may see valve calcification. Echocardiogram MR on Doppler, may see a diseased valve, dilated LA, dilated LV, LVSD. Cardiac catheterisation, MRI.

MANAGEMENT
Regular monitoring if asymptomatic, diuretics, treat AF and cardiac failure, surgery (acute, symptomatic or left ventricular end-systolic dimension >4.5cm), endocarditis prophylaxis not routinely recommended.

Mitral stenosis
CLINICAL NOTES
Epidemiology: F>M. Aetiology/risk factors: Congenital (rare), rheumatic fever, calcification, mucopolysaccharidosis, carcinoid, SLE, Lutembacher's syndrome (mitral stenosis with ASD). Clinical features: Breathlessness, palpitations (AF), haemoptysis, hoarse voice and dysphagia (atrial enlargement interfering with recurrent laryngeal nerve – Ortner's syndrome), mitral facies, reduced pulse pressure, low volume pulse, tapping apex beat, opening snap, rumbling low-pitched apical diastolic murmur, loud S1 (attenuated if severe), presystolic (end diastolic) accentuation of murmur if in sinus rhythm. Complications: Pulmonary hypertension – raised JVP, RV heave, loud P2, pulmonary regurgitation – Graham-Steell murmur; tricuspid regurgitation (TR)/right cardiac failure, AF, heart block, CVA, LRTI, endocarditis.

INVESTIGATIONS
ECG: AF, p-mitrale (if in sinus rhythm), RBBB, RAD, tall R waves V1. Chest X-ray – double atrial silhouette, splayed carina, pulmonary venous congestion/hypertension/oedema. *Echocardiogram:* Rheumatic mitral valve, thickened deformed leaflets, restricted leaflet movements, reduced mitral valve area (normal 4-6 cm², symptoms <2.5cm², mild >1.5cm², moderate 1.0-1.5cm², severe <1.0cm²), increased pressure gradient (mild <5mmHg, moderate 5-10mmHg, severe >10mmHg), enlarged LA, increased pulmonary artery pressure,

pulmonary venous hypertension (PVH), cardiac failure. Cardiac catheterisation, MRI.

MANAGEMENT
Treat AF, anticoagulate (high embolic risk), endocarditis prophylaxis not routinely recommended, diuretics, consider operative treatment (repair/replace) if pulmonary hypertension/congestion.

Mitral valve prolapse (MVP)

CLINICAL NOTES
Epidemiology: 2% prevalence. M=F. Aetiology/risk factors: Idiopathic, collagen disorders (Marfan's syndrome, pseudoxanthoma elasticum, osteogenesis imperfecta, Elhers-Danlos syndrome), APKD, myxomatous degeneration. May be associated with AF/arrhythmia. Clinical features: Asymptomatic, atypical chest pain, anxiety (the link is unclear), palpitations, syncope, midsystolic click (occurs earlier with valsalva, later with squatting) may be followed by pansystolic murmur (if associated with MR). Complications: More likely with classic MVP. AF, LVSD, endocarditis, chordal rupture, arrhythmia, MR, embolic disease, pulmonary hypertension, death.

INVESTIGATIONS
ECG may show AF. Echocardiogram, prolapse of one/both mitral valve leaflets ≥2mm beyond annular plane, may show dilated atria and MR. Valve thickness ≥5mm – classic MVP.

MANAGEMENT
Monitor higher-risk patients. Classic MVP (x14 risk embolic disease, endocarditis, death), age >45 years, LVSD, moderate-severe MR. Isolated MVP no treatment required. Beta-blockers for tachyarrhythmias, anticoagulate if AF/previous CVA. Treat associated AF. May require MV surgery (especially men, LVSD, severe MR, hypertension, obesity). Routine prophylaxis for endocarditis not required.

Mixed connective tissue disease (MCTD)

CLINICAL NOTES
Epidemiology: F>M. Peak onset third to fourth decades. Aetiology/risk factors: Autoimmune. Clinical features: Combination of at least two of scleroderma, SLE, polymyositis. Raynaud's is an early feature. SLE may be diagnosed first. Malaise, fatigue, fever, joint pains, muscle pains. Complications: May have features of RA, pulmonary hypertension, cardiac involvement, pericarditis, pregnancy flare, low birthweight, stillbirth.

INVESTIGATIONS
ENA features prominently; anti-U1 ribonucleoprotein (RNP) antibodies.

MANAGEMENT
NSAIDs, prednisolone, immune modulators.

Molar pregnancy (hydatidiform mole)
See also
— Choriocarcinoma

CLINICAL NOTES
Placental cystic disease. Partial or total moles. Epidemiology: Incidence vary, one in 1,000-2,500 pregnancies. Aetiology/risk factors: Previous mole, extremes of fertile age, poor diet (eg low folate), genetic HLA susceptibility, Asian origin. Clinical features: Asymptomatic (found on scan), hyperemesis gravidarum, vaginal bleeding, fetus may be viable in partial mole. Complications: Pre-eclampsia, large for dates fundal height, hypertension, choriocarcinoma.

INVESTIGATIONS
↑HCG , USS, chest X-ray (to look for metastatic disease), clotting screen, crossmatch.

MANAGEMENT
Uterine evacuation, monitor HCG (weekly), conception contraindicated until HCG normalised for six months (may take two years). Contraception may be commenced once HCG normalised. HCG should be monitored six and 10 weeks after subsequent pregnancies.

Molluscum contagiosum

CLINICAL NOTES
Epidemiology: Common, children (especially three to nine years, also teens/early 20s). Aetiology/risk factors: Pox virus, spread by direct contact. Immunosuppression. Clinical features: Pink/skin-coloured umbilicated papules, contains tiny amount of thick sebaceous type material containing virus, may be many, commonly upper limbs, axillae, trunk. Demonstrates Koebner phenomenon. Complications: Secondary bacterial infection, psychological impact.

INVESTIGATIONS
Skin biopsy.

MANAGEMENT
Spontaneous resolution after about two years. Topical treatments eg cryotherapy/curettage painful and may cause scarring.

Monoclonal gammopathy of undetermined significance (MGUS)

CLINICAL NOTES
Monoclonal band on protein electrophoresis in the absence of plasma cell malignancy. Epidemiology: 3%

prevalence age >70 years. Complications: Risk of progression to myeloma.

INVESTIGATIONS
Monoclonal immunoglobulin (Ig) usually <3g/dL (normally IgG), <10% plasma cells in bone marrow, no myeloma-related organ or tissue impairment (ROTI). ↑ESR, →Hb.

MANAGEMENT
Regular Ig quantification and assessment for progression to myeloma.

Morphoea

CLINICAL NOTES
Localised scleroderma. Aetiology/risk factors: Unknown, pregnancy, measles, EBV, ticks, auto-immune. Clinical features: Indurated plaque, poorly defined edge, violaceous in early stages, then ivory-coloured, some have a lilac edge, absence of hair follicles and sweat ducts, atrophied tissues beneath plaque. Other forms: Linear (may cause contractures), en coup de sabre (causes alopecia and may cause skull shrinkage), generalised, pansclerotic (may affect bone growth), atrophoderma of Pasini and Pierini.

INVESTIGATIONS
Biopsy.

MANAGEMENT
Topical: Calcipotriol, intralesional steroids. Systemic: Methotrexate, steroids, ciclosporin, colchicine, penicillamine, phenytoin, tetracycline. Phototherapy.

Morton's neuroma/metatarsalgia

CLINICAL NOTES
Epidemiology: F>M, 40-50 years. Perineural fibrosis, demyelination of common digital nerve in third intermetatarsal space of foot. Aetiology/risk factors: Excessive running, squatting, tight shoes, inflammation. Clinical features: Pain (sharp, neuropathic, worse on weight-bearing and wearing shoes, may be intermittent), tenderness in third intermetatarsal space, reduced sensation, mass may be palpable.

INVESTIGATIONS
Consider MRI.

MANAGEMENT
Avoid tight shoes, shoe pads, NSAIDs, steroid injection under USS guidance, surgery.

Motor neuron disease (MND)

CLINICAL NOTES
Epidemiology: Incidence two in 10^5 per year (England).

Aetiology/risk factors: M>F. Sporadic (90% cases) Peak sixth to seventh decades. Familial form presents earlier than typical forms. Clinical features: Three types. Progressive muscular atrophy: LMN, muscle wasting, weakness, fasciculation. Amyotrophic lateral sclerosis (ALS): UMN and LMN lesions, spasticity, ↑reflexes. Progressive bulbar palsy: Nasal speech, tongue fasciculation. Complications: Painful spasms, aspiration pneumonia, communication and mobility difficulties, mood disturbance, yawning, death often by infection or respiratory failure.

INVESTIGATIONS
Nerve conduction studies, EMG and investigate to exclude other conditions.

MANAGEMENT
MDT approach, physiotherapy, OT, consider riluzole for ALS type, antispasmodics, analgesics, hyoscine or glycopyrrolate for drooling/secretions, PEG feeding, respiratory support.

Multiple endocrine deficiencies

CLINICAL NOTES
Multiple endocrine deficiency syndrome: Schmidt's syndrome, F>M, associated with autoimmune diseases. Hypoadrenalism, hypothyroidism, type-1 DM, sometimes gonadal failure, rarely hypoparathyroidism, hypopituitarism. Polyglandular deficiency with mucocutaneous candidiasis: F>M, associated with auto-immune diseases. Hypoadrenalism, hypoparathyroidism, sometimes gonadal failure, rarely hypothyroidism, type-1 DM, hypopituitarism.

INVESTIGATIONS
Cortisol, ACTH, short Synacthen® test, Ca^{2+}, PTH, glucose, FSH, LH, oestrogen, testosterone, TSH, T_3, T_4, dynamic pituitary testing.

MANAGEMENT
Treat deficiencies accordingly.

Multiple endocrine neoplasia (MEN)

CLINICAL NOTES
Epidemiology: Type 1: Parathyroid adenoma, pituitary adenoma, pancreatic tumours (gastrinoma, VIPoma, islet cell). Type 2a: Medullary thyroid cancer, phaeochromocytoma, parathyroid adenoma. Type 2b: Medullary thyroid cancer, phaeochromocytoma, parathyroid adenoma, delayed puberty, Marfanoid phenotype, mucosal and cutaneous neuromas, may be associated with Hirschsprung's disease.

INVESTIGATIONS
Calcitonin, PTH, Ca^{2+}, TFT, T_3, T_4, thyroglobulin, urinary catecholamines, PTH, nuclear medicine (somatostatin

receptor scintigraphy), CT/MRI (brain, pancreas, adrenals), MIBG scan.

MANAGEMENT
Treat complications accordingly.

Multiple myeloma

CLINICAL NOTES
Epidemiology: 4-6.6 x 10^6 UK incidence. 1-2% of all cancers. Median age at presentation: 70 years. M>F. **Clinical features:** Initially asymptomatic, fatigue, malaise, fever, weight loss, progressively worsening/new thoracic back pain/bone pain, night pain. **Complications:** Immunodeficiency and infection, hypercalcaemia, osteopenia, anaemia, pathological fracture, hyperviscosity syndrome (confusion, headaches, visual disturbance), renal dysfunction (myeloma kidney – dehydration, renal infection, tumour lysis syndrome, gouty nephropathy, hypercalcaemia, Bence-Jones nephropathy, hyperviscosity syndrome, amyloid, drugs (NSAIDS, chemotherapy), spinal cord/nerve compression, neuropathy, pyoderma gangrenosum, missed diagnosis (<5% of cases non-secretory –no paraprotein). 20% cases urinary light chain with no plasma monoclonal immunoglobulin.

INVESTIGATIONS
FBC (Hb <10.0g/dL or >2g/dL lower than lower end of reference range suggests poor prognosis). U&E (creatinine >195mg/L suggests poor prognosis), LFT (high total protein, low albumin, albumin <30g/L poor prognosis), ↑Ca^{2+} (>2.75mmol/L or >0.25mmol/L above upper end of normal reference range suggests poor prognosis), ↑↑ESR (often >100 but may be normal in light chain or non-secretory disease), protein electrophoresis (monoclonal band IgG and IgA para-proteins account for 80%, use immunofixation to distinguish type), paraprotein quantification (IgG >70g/L or IgA >50g/L poor prognosis), uric acid, beta-2 microglobulin (prognostic, adverse if >2mg/L), acid phosphatase, ↑amylase, S100. urine for Bence-Jones protein (failure to test will miss 20% of myeloma cases), urine immunofixation and protein quantification. Skeletal X-ray survey (spine, pelvis, proximal femora, more than three lytic lesions poor prognosis), MRI (staging, treatment planning). Marrow trephine and aspirate (≥10% plasma cells) and cytogenetics.

MANAGEMENT
Supportive therapy: Transfusion/erythropoietin, antibiotics, bisphosphonates, analgesia, hydration, renal support, plasmapheresis for hyperviscosity, vertebroplasty, vaccinations, psychological support. Chemotherapy +/– stem cell transplant, stem cell salvage therapy. Median survival three to five years. Bortezomib (a proteosome inhibitor) and lenalidomide (a thalidomide analogue) being used in US.

Multiple sclerosis (MS)

CLINICAL NOTES
Epidemiology: Prevalence up to 85,000 people (UK). Age 20-40 years at onset. Prevalence increases with greater latitudes. F>M. **Aetiology/risk factors:** Not clear, autoimmune, environmental, familial, infective. **Clinical features:** *Relapsing/remitting*: Most common. Flares followed by recovery (secondary progressive if residual neurological deficit after a relapse). *Primary progressive:* Neurological deterioration from outset. **Complications:** *Acute relapse:* Deterioration over 12-48 hours, optic neuritis (acute reduction in vision, may be painful, may pre-date onset of MS), transverse myelitis (weakness/paralysis lower limbs, sensory level, bowel/bladder dysfunction), Devic's syndrome (optic neuritis and transverse myelitis), spasms, pain, pressure sores, recurrent UTI, depression, LRTI, aspiration, constipation, feeding difficulties, communication difficulties, mobilisation difficulties.

INVESTIGATIONS
MRI (T2 weighted images, periventricular white matter-may be seen in healthy individuals); consider (visual) evoked potential studies, LP (oligoclonal bands, myelin, basic protein). USS if bladder involvement.

MANAGEMENT
Specialist support including neurorehabilitation services (eg physiotherapy, OT, SALT, specialist nurses, social services, psychological and family support, education), crisis/care plan, pain management, ophthalmic services. *Acute episode:* Urgent referral if possible optic neuritis/acute spinal cord lesion (eg possible transverse myelitis), IV methylprednisolone 500mg-1g per day or orally 500mg-2g, three to five days. *Disease modifying drugs:* Consider linoleic acid 17-23g per day, immunosuppressants, immunoglobulin infusions, plasma exchange. Interferon beta/glatiramer acetate for relapsing/remitting MS. Influenza vaccinations. Pregnancy advice (relapse risk reduces during pregnancy/increases temporarily postpartum). LRTI management (see *pneumonia*); aspiration pneumonia – antibiotics, seating adjustments, chest physiotherapy, consider nasogastric tube (short-term), consider PEG. *UTI:* Dipstick/MSU/antibiotics. *Residual volume:* Perform USS to confirm, self-catheterisation. *Urge incontinence:* Anticholinergics. *Nocturia:* Desmopressin (maximum once in 24 hours). Awareness of bowel symptoms. *Constipation:* Fluid and diet advice, laxatives, suppositories, enemas. *Faecal incontinence:* Exclude incontinence with overflow. *Spasticity/spasms:* Exclude pain/infection, neurophysiotherapy, baclofen, gabapentin, tizanidine, diazepam, clonazepam or dantrolene, splints, casts, intrathecal baclofen, phenol injections, botulinum toxin, avoid contractures. *Emotional lability/depression/anxiety:* TCAs, SSRI, psychology. Consider suicide risk assessment.

Nutrition. Communication aids. Help with sexual dysfunction. Mobility aids. Pressure sore avoidance/management. Natalizumab (may be associated with progressive multifocal leucoencephalopathy).

Multisystem atrophy (Shy-Drager syndrome)

📋 CLINICAL NOTES
See *Parkinson's disease and Parkinson's plus syndromes*

Mumps

📋 CLINICAL NOTES
Epidemiology: 3,857 cases in 2010 (UK). Aetiology/risk factors: Paramyxovirus. Often seen in students. Clinical features: Incubation 18-21 days. Infectious from prodrome to four days after beginning of inflammatory phase. *Prodrome:* Fever, headache, malaise, myalgia. *Inflammatory:* Parotitis, orchitis, oophoritis. Complications: Infertility (male), meningitis, encephalitis, pancreatitis, spontaneous miscarriage (slight risk if contracted 12-16 weeks' gestation). No malformation if contracted during pregnancy.

🔍 INVESTIGATIONS
FBC, atypical lymphocytes, mumps serology (IgM, rising IgG), mumps immunoglobulins may be found in saliva. Consider pelvic or scrotal USS for orchitis/oophoritis, abdominal USS for pancreatitis. Salivary test for acute infection.

💊 MANAGEMENT
Prevention with MMR, supportive treatment.

Myasthenia gravis

📋 CLINICAL NOTES
Epidemiology: About one in 2,000 prevalence (UK). Aetiology/risk factors: Autoimmune disease against Ach receptors at neuromuscular junction. Clinical features: Inducible muscle fatigue, often causing ptosis, ophthalmoplegia, dysarthria, dysphagia but may affect any muscle. *Eaton-Lambert syndrome:* Paraneoplastic syndrome, fatigability, hyporeflexia which returns after exercise, autonomic dysfunction, ocular/bulbar muscles seldom affected. Complications: Worse in pregnancy and infection. Drugs eg erythromycin may exacerbate symptoms. May be associated with thymic hyperplasia, thyrotoxicosis (10% cases), impaired quality of life. Aspiration. Myasthenic crisis – vital muscles, eg respiratory, may cause respiratory failure, death.

🔍 INVESTIGATIONS
FBC, atypical lymphocytes, Ach receptor antibodies (90% sensitive, reduced sensitivity if ocular only MG), ANA, TFT, tensilon test, EMG studies, CT (for thymus).

💊 MANAGEMENT
Cholinesterase inhibitors, immunosuppressants, plasmapheresis, immunoglobulin infusions, thymectomy.

Myalgic encephalitis (ME)

📋 CLINICAL NOTES
Chronic fatigue syndrome. Epidemiology: Prevalence four in 1,000 (UK). Aetiology/risk factors: Poorly understood, may have an infectious cause. Clinical features: Fatigue, malaise, headache, poor concentration and memory, sleep disturbance (insomnia, hypersomnia, unrefreshed sleep), muscle pain, joint pains, painful lymph nodes (not enlarged), nausea, benign palpitations, weight stable. Complications: Depression, social/employment difficulties.

🔍 INVESTIGATIONS
Tests to exclude other pathology: Urinalysis, FBC, U&E, LFT, TFT, ESR, CRP, glucose, coeliac screen, CK, ferritin (children/young people), vitamin B_{12}/folate if ↑MCV, consider HIV/hepatitis/chronic bacterial/EBV/toxoplasmosis/CMV screen.

💊 MANAGEMENT
Exclude other causes, education, self-help groups, cautious optimism, community support (OT, nurse, dietitian, physiotherapy, psychology), sleep hygiene, rest periods, education/employment support, CBT, graded exercise. Some authorities suggest vitamin B_{12} injections.

Mycosis fungoides

📋 CLINICAL NOTES
Cutaneous T helper cell (T_H cell) lymphoma. Epidemiology: M=F. Middle age/elderly. Clinical features: Slow-growing pruritic lesions, well-defined patches, scaly plaques and/or papules, may develop ulcerated nodules. Often mistaken for eczema/psoriasis. Complications: Ulceration, Sézary syndrome – erythroderma, node/lung/liver/splenic metastases.

🔍 INVESTIGATIONS
Biopsy.

💊 MANAGEMENT
Topical steroids, nitrogen mustard, psoralens, PUVA, radiotherapy, chemotherapy, interferons, anti-IL2, -CD5 and -CD5 antibodies.

Myelodysplasia

See also
— *Chronic myelomonocytic leukaemia*

📋 CLINICAL NOTES
Stem cell malignancy causing ineffective erythropoiesis. Epidemiology: Increasing incidence with ageing

population. *Aetiology/risk factors:* Genetic, post-chemotherapy or radiotherapy. *Clinical features:* Features of cytopenia (especially ↓Hb). Subtypes include refractory anaemia, refactory anaemia with ring sideroblasts, refractory anaemia with excess blasts in transformation, CMML. *Complications:* Transformation to AML.

ℐ INVESTIGATIONS
FBC, monocytosis, ↓reticulocytes, ring sideroblasts, marrow biopsy, cytogenetics.

⬚ MANAGEMENT
Supportive. Chemotherapy, stem cell transplant.

Myelofibrosis

🗓 CLINICAL NOTES
Fibroblast proliferation (myeloproliferative disease). *Epidemiology:* >50 years. *Clinical features:* Fever, night sweats, weight loss, fatigue, bleeding, infections, extramedullary haemopoiesis, massive splenomegaly, hepatomegaly, abdominal/bone pain. *Complications:* Portal hypertension, splenic infarction, GI haemorrhage, gout, pancytopenia, leukaemic transformation.

ℐ INVESTIGATIONS
FBC, basophilic stippling, leucoerythroblastic film, teardrop cells, uric acid, U&E, marrow biopsy, USS/CT abdomen.

⬚ MANAGEMENT
Ensure vaccinations (eg influenza and pneumococcus) up-to-date, watch and wait, transfusions, steroid therapy, hydroxyurea, thalidomide, radiotherapy, splenectomy, stem cell transplant.

Myeloperoxidase deficiency

🗓 CLINICAL NOTES
See *immunodeficiency (primary)*

Myocardial infarction (STEMI) [Refl3]

See also
  — *Myocardial infarction (nSTEMI)/unstable angina*

🗓 CLINICAL NOTES
Epidemiology.: Mortality falling in UK. CVD remains primary cause of death in UK. *Aetiology/risk factors:* See *stable angina.* *Clinical features:* Silent (about 20%), central crushing chest pain radiating to left arm/jaw, sweating, vomiting, dyspnoea, acute pulmonary oedema, abdominal pain, 'indigestion', confusional, presyncope, syncope, presentation more atypical in women. *Complications:* Further ACS, arrhythmia (eg AF, heart block, VT, VF), thromboembolic disease, acute/chronic cardiac failure/cardiogenic shock,

ventricular aneurysm/rupture/septal defect, papillary muscle rupture and acute MR, may cause crashing heart failure, Dressler's syndrome (see *acute pericarditis*), coronary non-reflow (30-60%, reperfusion failure post-thrombolysis secondary to microvascular obstruction, leads to increased risk of LVSD), hyperglycaemia in DM.

ℐ INVESTIGATIONS
FBC, glucose, U&E, lipids, cardiac troponin (T and I) (↑three hours to 14 days after MI, ↑STEMI/nSTEMI, not raised in unstable angina). ↑LDH, ↑CK-MB. ECG may be normal (ST elevation poor sensitivity for MI). STEMI – ST elevation or new onset LBBB (may see ↓ST in other cardiac territories – indicates multiple vessels affected). *ECG territories:* ↑ST: V3-V4: anterior. V1/2-V4/5: anteroseptal. V1-V6 I, II, aVL: anterolateral. II, III, aVF: inferior. V5-V6 I, aVL, II, III, aVF: inferolateral. II, III, aVF, V1-V3: inferoseptal, V4R: RV infarction. Tall R waves V1/V2, ↓ST V1-V3, T waves remain +ve V1/V2: posterior MI. PR segment elevation – atrial infarction. Persistent ST elevation suggests LV aneurysm. Consider ECG-gated MRI. Chest X-ray. Angiography (and primary angioplasty), echocardiogram (if need to exclude dissection/determine MI if in LBBB or posterior MI/complications of MI/ongoing ischaemia in nSTEMI). CT to exclude other causes of chest pain, perfusion scanning may be used in diagnosis of nSTEMI. Post-MI (if no primary angioplasty) – ETT for risk stratification, angiography if +ve ETT/LVSD, echocardiogram, perfusion scan, electrophysiological studies if non-sustained VT and ejection fraction (EF) <40% or sustained VT/VF (may require ICD). MRI to define myocardial damage.

⬚ MANAGEMENT
Acute: Oxygen (if hypoxia. Note oxygen therapy in non-hypoxic patients may cause vasconstriction and increase infarct size), aspirin 300mg, clopidogrel 300mg, diamorphine, consider IV beta-blockade (unless pulse <60/min, BP <100mmHg systolic or other contraindications), nitrate infusion, caution if low BP, reperfusion therapy, thrombolysis/primary angioplasty/CABG. *Ongoing:* Aspirin 75mg, clopidogrel 75mg (guidelines may vary, UK – for four weeks after STEMI, 12 months after stent/nSTEMI). ACE inhibitors, beta-blockers, statins. Aldosterone antagonist (eplerenone) if associated cardiac failure – initiated day three to 14 post-MI. Consider omega 3 supplements for ventricular electrical stabilisation. May require ICD for malignant arrhythmias. Aim for BP ≤140/90mmHg. Lifestyle advice including smoking cessation counselling/diet/cardiac rehabilitation to build up physical activity, regular monitoring. Sexual activity may be resumed usually after four weeks if well. Consider PDE5 inhibition for ED six months post-MI (if not on nitrate/nicorandil). Ventricular rupture, ventricular septal rupture and acute papillary muscle failure require surgery. Sertraline safe in depression.

Myocardial infarction (nSTEMI)/ unstable angina [Ref14]

See also
— *Myocardial infarction (STEMI)*

📋 CLINICAL NOTES
Non-ST elevation myocardial infarction (nSTEMI). Biochemical markers of myocardial damage eg raised troponin but without ST elevation. If no biochemical myocardial damage, considered to be unstable angina. Aetiology/risk factors: See *stable angina.* Clinical features: Silent, cardiac pain at rest, worsening/severe exertional angina, novel severe angina, nausea, sweating, breathlessness, palpitations, epigastric pain, back pain, confusion. Complications: See *myocardial infarction (STEMI).*

⟳ INVESTIGATIONS
See *myocardial infarction (STEMI).* FBC, glucose, U&E, lipids, cardiac troponin (T and I) (↑three hours to 14 days after MI, ↑STEMI/nSTEMI, not raised in unstable angina). ECG normal, flat or inverted T waves, ST depression.

🔔 MANAGEMENT
See also *myocardial infarction (STEMI).* Aspirin 300mg immediately, clopidogrel 300mg immediately, diamorphine, antiemetic, nitrate infusion, beta-blockers, LMWH, glycoprotein IIb/IIIa inhibitors for high-risk patients. May require anticoagulation for three months, aspirin 75mg, clopidogrel 75mg (length of treatment varies across countries, eg nine to 12 months), beta-blockers, statin, ACE inhibitors, risk-stratify patient (eg ETT), angiogram and treatment of lesion. Address modifiable risk factors.

Myocarditis

📋 CLINICAL NOTES
Aetiology/risk factors: Idiopathic, infective (eg Coxsackie virus, adenovirus, rheumatic, diphtheria, Chagas' disease), iatrogenic, radiation, autoimmune. Clinical features: Asymptomatic, SOB, fatigue, chest pain, palpitations, tachycardia, hypotension, soft heart sounds, gallop (S4), functional valvular regurgitation, pericardial friction rub, peripheral oedema, joint pain. Complications: CVA, MI, severe cardiac failure, malignant arrhythmias, death.

⟳ INVESTIGATIONS
ECG – non-specific ST/T wave changes. Arrhythmias, may see heart-block eg with diphtheria. Chest X-ray – enlarged heart. ↑troponin, viral studies. Echocardiography, MRI, biopsy. Investigate according to suspected underlying cause. ↑LDH.

🔔 MANAGEMENT
Treat underlying cause, rest, treat cardiac failure and arrhythmias. Immunoglobulins.

Myotonic dystrophy

📋 CLINICAL NOTES
See *dystrophia myotonica*

Naevi

📋 CLINICAL NOTES
Epidermal: Hamartoma, various subtypes including sebaceous naevus. Varying pigmentation. Seen in the neonate, growth during childhood. Risk of cancerous (BCC, SCC) change. May be part of epidermal naevus syndrome (associated with epilepsy, spina bifida, nystagmus, ophthalmoplegia, rickets). *Halo:* Benign, due to inflamed melanocytic naevus, more common in Turner's syndrome, mainly truncal, depigmentation around mole itself. *Blue:* Blue/grey colour. Larger (cellular blue) lesions up to 30mm but common blue much smaller (<7mm). Presents in childhood/teens. May be part of Carney complex. Common blue lesions are benign. Cellular blue lesions may undergo malignant change. *Congenital pigmented:* From birth or within first two years (tardive), large (giant hairy/ congenital naevus), risk of melanoma. May have neural involvement eg hydrocephalus. *Strawberry:* F>M. Present from birth/few weeks after birth, grow to maximal size at age four years, then regress. Usually gone by seven to 10 years, mainly head/neck. Multiple lesions associated with internal naevi. Risks of obscuring vision, high output heart failure, consumptive coagulopathy, stridor, spinal cord involvement, bleeding and ulceration. *Compound:* Common, subtype of melanocytic naevus, develop from junctional naevus. Raised, may be hair growth, biopsy required if diagnostic doubt/red flags. *Junctional:* Common, subtype of melanocytic naevus. Flat. Collection of melanocytes at dermoepidermal junction, not as dark as melanomas, risk of malignant transformation (<1%), biopsy required if diagnostic doubt/red flags, otherwise reassure. *Intradermal:* Common, subtype of melanocytic naevus, no pigment (deep melanocytes), <10mm, raised, may have hair growth, biopsy required if diagnostic doubt/ red flags. *Spitz naevus:* >18 months of age. <10mm, raised, red/brown, benign, should be biopsied to rule out melanoma (may be hard to distinguish the two).

Nail-patella syndrome

📋 CLINICAL NOTES
Epidemiology: Rare. Aetiology/risk factors: Genetic-mutation/inherited autosomal dominant. Clinical features: Absent ulnar half of fingernails, especially thumb; lax joints, small patellae, patella dislocation. Complications: CKD, glaucoma, poor dentition, IBS, poor peripheral circulation, neuropathy.

⟳ INVESTIGATIONS
Genetic studies, U&E, renal ultrasound, tonometry and investigate for complications.

DISEASES

MANAGEMENT
Physiotherapy, OT, MDT approach. Treat complications accordingly.

Nappy rash

CLINICAL NOTES
Epidemiology: Common. Clinical features: Candida: Dermatitis with satellite lesions. Ammoniacal: Chemical dermatitis secondary to prolonged urine contact with skin, does not affect skin folds. Seborrhoeic: Often associated with cradle cap, involves skin flexures. Other: Infection, NAI.

MANAGEMENT
Candida: Clotrimazole cream. Ammoniacal: Barrier cream/emollients, frequent nappy changes. Seborrhoeic: Barrier cream/emollients, consider low potency steroids, frequent nappy changes.

Narcolepsy

CLINICAL NOTES
Epidemiology: One in 2,000 (US), one in 600 (Japan). Aetiology/risk factors: Genetic and environmental. HLA susceptibility. Clinical features: Usually begins in early adulthood. Sudden daytime sleep attacks, no warnings, up to 30 minutes, excessive daytime sleepiness, sleep paralysis (up to two minutes when falling asleep/waking), hypnagogic (when falling asleep) and hypnopompic (on waking) hallucinations, sleepwalking. Complications: Cataplexy (sudden loss in muscle tone, 70% of people with narcolepsy).

INVESTIGATIONS
ECG (including ambulatory), CT/MRI brain, sleep studies.

MANAGEMENT
Narcolepsy: CNS stimulants eg modafinil, methylphenidate. Cataplexy: SSRI/SNRI, TCAs, sodium oxybate. Driving advice.

Naso/oropharyngeal and laryngeal cancers
See also
— Oral malignancies

CLINICAL NOTES
Aetiology/risk factors: EBV infection, salty fish, smoking, alcohol, HPV, poor dentition, asbestos exposure, poor diet. Clinical features: Unilateral progressive earache, unilateral serous middle ear effusion, hearing loss, cough, sore throat, hoarse voice, pain and difficulty in swallowing, altered sense of smell, nasal blockage, epistaxis, cervical lymphadenopathy, cranial nerve involvement, fatigue, weight loss.

INVESTIGATIONS
Biopsy. CT/MRI mainly used for staging. PET-CT, local and distant spread.

MANAGEMENT
Radiotherapy including radical, adjuvant and brachytherapy. Chemotherapy including neoadjuvant, Surgery, EGFR inhibitors.

Necrobiosis lipoidica

CLINICAL NOTES
Epidemiology: Peak age 30 years. Aetiology/risk factors: F>M. May pre-date/complicate about 1% cases of DM. True cause unknown. Clinical features: Well demarcated shiny plaque, brown/yellow centre and inflammatory border, telangiectasia, commonly on shins. Complications: Ulceration, scarring.

INVESTIGATIONS
Investigate for DM.

MANAGEMENT
Topical/intralesional steroids (risk of atrophy), plastic surgery. Avoid trauma, aspirin and dipyridamole.

Necrotising fasciitis
See also
— Cellulitis
— Orbital cellulitis
— Periorbital cellulitis
— Erysipelas

CLINICAL NOTES
Epidemiology: Rare. Aetiology/risk factors: Group A streptococci, Staph aureus. Trauma including postoperative, DM, alcohol abuse, malignancy, immunosuppression. Clinical features: Pain, swelling, rapid progression over hours to purplish, blistered skin. Skin comes away with little effort. Fever, malaise, tachycardia, hypotension. Complications: Shock, advancing infection with gangrene, fulminant sepsis and death.

INVESTIGATIONS
FBC, U&E, LFT, glucose, blood cultures.

MANAGEMENT
IV antibiotics, fluids, surgical debridement.

Nelson's syndrome
See also
— Cushing's syndrome

CLINICAL NOTES
Epidemiology: Rare. Aetiology/risk factors: ACTH secreting pituitary tumour caused by surgical bilateral

adrenalectomy. Clinical features: Buccal and palmar pigmentation, bitemporal hemianopia, adrenalectomy scars.

INVESTIGATIONS
↑ACTH, CT, visual field testing.

MANAGEMENT
Pituitary irradiation, hypophysectomy.

Nephritis

CLINICAL NOTES
Acute tubulointerstitial nephritis: Aetiology/risk factors: Idiopathic, infections eg streptococcal, iatrogenic (antibiotics, warfarin, NSAIDs, diuretics, aspirin), sarcoid, autoimmune eg RA, glomerulonephritis. Clinical features: Hypertension, fever, arthralgia, renal impairment, ARF. Complications: ATN. *Chronic tubulointerstitial nephritis:* Aetiology/risk factors: Multiple including autoimmune, granulomatous, electrolyte disturbances, iatrogenic, infection, heavy metals, sickle cell anaemia. Complications: CKD (may progress to stage 5), RTA 1, diabetes insipidus.

INVESTIGATIONS
eGFR, eosinophilia, ↑IgE, urinalysis may be normal/show eosinophils. Sterile pyuria. Renal biopsy. Investigate according to suspected underlying cause.

MANAGEMENT
Treat underlying cause and complications accordingly. Steroids.

Neurofibromatosis

CLINICAL NOTES
Type 1 (von Recklinghausen's disease): Epidemiology: One in 3,000 prevalance. Chromosome 17, autosomal dominant. Clinical features: Six or more café au lait macules >15mm in adults, >5mm if <10 years of age, axillary/inguinal freckling, neurofibromas, Lisch nodules (iris hamartomas), optic nerve gliomas, spinal cord tumours, renal artery stenosis, scoliosis, short stature, phaeochromocytoma, macrocephaly. Complications: Sarcomatous transformation, precocious puberty (hypothalamic glioma). *Type 2:* Epidemiology: One in 25,000 prevalance. Chromosome 22, autosomal dominant. Clinical features: Bilateral acoustic neuromas, meningiomas, gliomas, schwannomas (cranial and spinal), cataracts, neurofibromas. Complications: Sarcomatous transformation.

INVESTIGATIONS
Plain X-rays. CT/MRI, electrophysiology, genetic testing.

MANAGEMENT
MDT approach. Treat complications accordingly. Genetic counselling.

Neuroleptic malignant syndrome

CLINICAL NOTES
Epidemiology: Rare. Aetiology/risk factors: Neuroleptics, levodopa withdrawal, lithium. Clinical features: Hyperpyrexia, altered consciousness, pallor, tachycardia, erratic BP, urinary incontinence, excessive muscle tone, autonomic neuropathy. Complications: Rhabdomyolysis, respiratory failure, acidosis, death.

INVESTIGATIONS
FBC, ↑CK, U&E, LFT, arterial blood gases, ↑urinary myoglobin. ↑CSF protein.

MANAGEMENT
ITU, remove trigger, fluid management, acid-base management, consider dantrolene/bromocriptine. ECT may be helpful.

Niemann-Pick disease

CLINICAL NOTES
Lipid storage disease. Epidemiology: rare. Aetiology/risk factors: Number of subtypes. Clinical features: Age of onset and features depend on subtype. Macular cherry red spot, failure to thrive, feeding problems, hepatosplenomegaly, jaundice. Complications: Seizures, ataxia, gaze palsy, cataplexy, blindness, deafness.

INVESTIGATIONS
Acid sphingomyelinase (ASM) levels, tissue biopsy, investigate for complications.

MANAGEMENT
MDT approach, dietary advice, bone marrow transplant. Treat complications accordingly.

Night terrors

CLINICAL NOTES
Epidemiology: Up to one in 20 children. Aetiology/risk factors: Family history. Clinical features: Waking with screaming, severe anxiety, nocturnal enuresis, no recall of event. Complications: Altered family dynamic, injury.

INVESTIGATIONS
Consider investigations if another diagnosis is more likely or presentation is atypical eg EEG, cerebral MRI.

MANAGEMENT
Reassurance to family, most cases subside. Good sleep hygiene.

Non-Hodgkin's lymphoma

See also
— *Mycosis fungoides*

DISEASES

Epidemiology: 17 in 10⁵ per year (UK). **Aetiology/risk factors:** M>F. 85% B-cell type, 15% T-cell. Many subtypes including hairy cell, plasma cell, mantle cell, Burkitt's lymphoma (aggressive, sub-Saharan Africa, EBV/HIV-related or sporadic), HIV-related (HIV confers a x100 risk of developing lymphoma, may cause primary CNS lymphoma). MALT, enteropathy, eg coeliac disease. Cutaneous – mycosis fungoides, Sézary syndrome. High and low grades. **Clinical features:** Asymptomatic, lymphadenopathy, hepatosplenomegaly. May present with B symptoms – weight loss >10% body weight, night sweats, anorexia. **Complications:** Skin involvement in T-cell disease, hyperviscosity states, mass effects eg spinal cord disease/compression and oesophageal compression from mediastinal node, site-specific, eg pleural effusion and seizures, tumour lysis syndrome.

🔬 **INVESTIGATIONS**

FBC (bone marrow involvement causes pancytopenia), U&E, LFT, uric acid, LDH (prognostic marker), protein electrophoresis (macroglobulinaemia), HIV screen, node biopsy (ideally whole node, microscopy, immuno-histochemistry, cytogenetics), CT/USS-guided biopsy. *Staging:* CT (head/neck/chest/abdomen/pelvis), USS (neck/thyroid/testis), MRI (cerebral/marrow), PET-CT. *Monitoring:* Chest X-ray, CT, PET-CT, MRI (cerebral).

💊 **MANAGEMENT**

Staging (Ann Arbor). Watch and wait with follicular if asymptomatic, may regress spontaneously. Radiotherapy (some subtypes eg Burkitt's require CNS prophylaxis). Chemotherapy (eg CHOP). Anti-CD20 (rituximab) antibodies. Stem cell transplant. Radioimmunotherapy. Surgery.

Noonan's sydrome

📋 **CLINICAL NOTES**

Epidemiology: Turner-like syndrome of males, although can affect females. One in 2,500 children. **Aetiology/risk factors:** Autosomal dominant. **Clinical features:** Mental retardation, orbital hypertelorism, blue/green eyes, nystagmus, thrombocytopenia, clotting factors 8, 11, 12 deficiencies, lymphoedema, delayed puberty, low-set ears, short webbed neck, low hairline, deep groove in upper lip, poor facial expression, pectus excavatum/carinatum, wide-set nipples. Cardiac defects (50% cases) especially right-sided, commonly pulmonary stenosis. Also pulmonary artery stenosis, septal defects, HCM. May have normal or short stature. Normal female fertility.

🔬 **INVESTIGATIONS**

Genetic studies, FBC (↓plts), echocardiography, investigate according to symptoms and complications.

💊 **MANAGEMENT**

MDT approach. Treat complications accordingly. Genetic counselling.

Normal pressure hydrocephalus

📋 **CLINICAL NOTES**

See *hydrocephalus*

Obesity in pregnancy

See also

— *Hyperemesis gravidarum*
— *Fatty liver (acute) of pregnancy*
— *Cholestasis of pregnancy*
— *Gestational diabetes*
— *Molar pregnancy (hydatidiform mole)*

📋 **CLINICAL NOTES**

Complications: ↑BP, pre-eclampsia, gestational diabetes, VTE, caesarean section, congenital abnormalities (small increase, about one in 2,000 live births, including cardiac, neural tube, cleft lip, limb anomalies).

💊 **MANAGEMENT**

Lifestyle advice (diet and exercise), patient education, monitoring.

Obsessive compulsive disorder (OCD)

📋 **CLINICAL NOTES**

Epidemiology: 1-3% prevalence. **Aetiology/risk factors:** Multiple theories – genetic, infective, life event, overprotective parenting. **Clinical features:** May have relapsing/remitting course. Obsessions (repetitive/intrusive thoughts) and/or compulsions (repetitive behaviours patient is driven to perform by anxiety). **Complications:** Interference with daily life, depression, suicide.

💊 **MANAGEMENT**

Education. Risk management. Regular follow-up. CBT (first-line, may require intense CBT if severe), SSRI, clomipramine. Support organisations. Self-help groups. Treat comorbidities – organic disease, psychosis, depression, anxiety, alcohol and drug abuse, eating disorder, body dysmorphic disorder. Neurosurgery may be required for severe treatment-resistant cases.

Occupational lung disease

📋 **CLINICAL NOTES**

See *mesothelioma* and *extrinsic allergic alveolitis*

Oesophageal cancer

📋 **CLINICAL NOTES**

Carcinoma. **Epidemiology:** 13 in 10⁶ per year (UK). Increasing. M>F (except cervical oesophagus in which F>M). High rates in China. **Aetiology/risk factors:** *Squamous cell carcinoma:* High-fat diet,

DISEASES

alcohol, smoking, nitrosamines, Barrett's oesophagus, achalasia, Plummer-Vinson syndrome, tylosis. *Adenocarcinoma*: GORD, Barrett's oesophagus, obesity, achalasia. Clinical features: Often presents late, dysphagia (solids>liquids), odynophagia, vomiting, weight loss, anorexia, pallor, lymphadenopathy, hoarse voice, chest pain, hiccups. Complications: Metastases (eg biliary, causing jaundice; pulmonary, causing effusion), oesophageal occlusion.

INVESTIGATIONS

FBC, LFT, chest X-ray, barium studies (rat's tail), endoscopy, biopsy. *Staging:* CT, endoscopic USS, PET-CT (distant metastases), laparoscopy; bronchoscopy may be required to assess for local metastases preoperatively.

MANAGEMENT

Radical surgery, neoadjuvant chemotherapy, radical chemoradiotherapy, radical radiotherapy, laser ablation. Palliative stenting, radiotherapy and chemotherapy. Photodynamic therapy, PEG tube. EGFR and proteasome inhibitors.

Oesophageal perforation/rupture

CLINICAL NOTES

Aetiology/risk factors: Iatrogenic (eg endoscopy), Boerhaave's syndrome (rupture due to vomiting), oesophageal diverticulum, malignancy, trauma. Clinical features: Very severe retrosternal pain, mediastinitis, epigastric tenderness, surgical emphysema (neck), pneumothorax, pleural effusion, empyema, fistulae, respiratory distress, shock, acidosis, death.

INVESTIGATIONS

Chest X-ray (abnormal 80%, pneumomediastinum 60%), contrast studies (if normal, for CT).

MANAGEMENT

Resuscitation, surgery. High mortality.

Onychogryphosis

MANAGEMENT

Chiropody, nail avulsion.

CLINICAL NOTES

Epidemiology: Common. Aetiology/risk factors: Advancing age, trauma. Clinical features: Grossly dystrophic, thickened toenails, discoloured, ridged, ram's horn like pattern.

Onychomycosis (fungal nail infection)

See also
— *Tinea*

CLINICAL NOTES

Epidemiology: 3% prevalence. Toenails>fingernails. Aetiology/risk factors: Dermatophytes, yeasts, moulds. ↑with age, DM, psoriasis, immunosuppression. Clinical features: Unsightly, brittle, thickened nails, discolouration. Complications: Onycholysis, nail dystrophy, secondary bacterial infection, nail loss, low self-esteem.

INVESTIGATIONS

Microscopy and culture of subungual debris better than clippings.

MANAGEMENT

Minor infections: Topical amorolfine/tioconazole for extended periods. *Extensive infections:* Oral treatment eg terbinafine, itraconazole (griseofulvin is fungistatic, not fungicidal). Terbinafine is fungicidal for dermatophytes but fungistatic for *Candida albicans*).

Optic neuritis

CLINICAL NOTES

May involve orbital or retro-orbital portion. Aetiology/risk factors: Idiopathic, MS, ADEM, iatrogenic, glandular fever, varicella zoster, encephalitis, meningitis, sarcoid, TB, DM, autoimmune. Clinical features: Usually one eye, pain followed by reduced acuity and colour vision, relative afferent pupillary defect, scotoma, flashing lights. Complications: Optic atrophy.

INVESTIGATIONS

Diagnosis is clinical. Visual evoked potentials. MRI brain. Investigate according to suspected underlying cause.

MANAGEMENT

High-dose steroids, interferon.

Oral cancers

See also
— *Naso/oropharyngeal and laryngeal cancers*

CLINICAL NOTES

Epidemiology: 30% of head and neck tumours. Most common is cancer of the lip. 90% SCC. M>F. Aetiology/risk factors: Age, smoking, alcohol (x6 risk), betel nut, sun exposure (lip), HPV. Clinical features: Oral bleeding, speech, masticatory and swallowing difficulties. Sensation of foreign body in throat. White, red or ulcerated lesions. Altered denture position, trismus, pain, lymphadenopathy. Complications: Postsurgical tracheostomy with communication, eating, secretion and infection difficulties, metastases, death.

INVESTIGATIONS

Biopsy. CT/MRI mainly used for staging. PET-CT, local and distant spread.

DISEASES

MANAGEMENT

Radical surgery, radical radiotherapy, systemic/intra-lesional chemotherapy. May require nasogastric/PEG feeding.

Orbital cellulitis

See also
- *Cellulitis*
- *Periorbital cellulitis*
- *Erysipelas*
- *Necrotising fasciitis*

CLINICAL NOTES

Aetiology/risk factors: Sinusitis, stye, trauma, DM, immunosuppression. Clinical features: Orbital pain, pain on eye movement, fever, malaise, lid oedema, eyelid/cheek involvement. Fever, periorbital oedema and erythema, exophthalmos, inflamed sclera. Complications: Blindness, orbital/cerebral abscess, febrile convulsion, cavernous sinus thrombosis.

INVESTIGATIONS

FBC, glucose, blood cultures.

MANAGEMENT

IV antibiotics.

Orf

CLINICAL NOTES

Epidemiology: Underreported. Aetiology/risk factors: Parapox virus, incubation five days, usually transmitted from affected farm animals. Clinical features: Painful, erythematous, non-pruritic papule, pustule or blister, often on finger. Development of central crust with white surround. Not systemically unwell. Complications: Secondary bacterial infection, erythema multiforme, lymphadenitis, fever.

INVESTIGATIONS

Consider PCR but usually a clinical diagnosis.

MANAGEMENT

Heals within six weeks, regular dressing, topical antiseptics, consider prophylactic antibiotics to prevent secondary staphylococcal infection. *Persistent lesions:* Topical imiquimod, curettage, electrodessication.

Osgood-Schlatter's syndrome

CLINICAL NOTES

Epidemiology: Common. Aetiology/risk factors: During puberty, before apophyseal fusion to tibia. M>F. Traction injury of patella tendon into tibial apophysis, particularly teenagers during sport (involving kicking, running, jumping). Clinical features: Tender swollen tibial tuberosity.

INVESTIGATIONS

Clinical diagnosis, consider X-ray if unsure.

MANAGEMENT

Rest, NSAIDs, physiotherapy. Rarely, plaster of Paris immobilisation, surgery.

Osler-Weber-Rendu syndrome

CLINICAL NOTES

Hereditary haemorrhagic telangiectasia. Epidemiology: Prevalence one in 5,000 to one in 8,000 population. Aetiology/risk factors: Autosomal dominant, multiple mutations. Clinical features: Telangiectasia (facial, perioral, tongue, buccal mucosa, lips, nasal mucosa, fingers, GI tract). Complications: GI and pulmonary haemorrhage. Pulmonary arterio-venous malformation, CVA, retinal haemorrhage/detachment, cirrhosis.

INVESTIGATIONS

Capillary microscopy, CT/MRI.

MANAGEMENT

Blood transfusion for acute haemorrhage, surgical or laser ablation, oestrogen.

Osteoarthritis

CLINICAL NOTES

Epidemiology: Common, F>M. Aetiology/risk factors: Age, family history, trauma, septic arthritis, obesity, repetitive joint use, low supporting muscle bulk, neuropathy, RA, haemochromatosis. Clinical features: Pain, joint stiffness after immobility, Heberden's nodes, Bouchard's nodes, z-shaped thumb, joint deformity, joint swelling, fixed flexion deformity, joint effusion (uncommon). Complications: Periarticular muscle wasting, reduced proprioception, functional disability, falls, reduced independence.

INVESTIGATIONS

Consider X-ray. Blood samples when diagnostic difficulty to exclude inflammatory arthritis.

MANAGEMENT

Exercise, analgesia, weight loss, joint injection (corticosteroid), physiotherapy, hydrotherapy, acupuncture, consider glucosamine, joint resurfacing, partial or total joint replacement.

Osteochondritis dissecans

CLINICAL NOTES

Epidemiology: Rare. Children/young adults. Aetiology/risk factors: Cartilage and layer of bone underneath fragment away from rest of bone. Genetic, trauma, excessive use, avascular necrosis. Clinical features: Most commonly affects knee, also elbow, ankle, hip. Pain,

DISEASES

oint locking, sensation of giving way or joint weakness, antalgic gait. Complications: OA, chronic pain, disability.

INVESTIGATIONS

X-ray, CT, MRI, bone scan.

MANAGEMENT

Rest, immobilisation, NSAIDs, physiotherapy, surgery (arthroscopic, removal of foreign bodies, fragment reattachment).

Osteomalacia and rickets

CLINICAL NOTES

Low bone mineralisation (rickets if occurring during bone growth, osteomalacia after growth plate fusion). Epidemiology: Rare in UK. Aetiology/risk factors: Malabsorption, vitamin D deficient diet, breastfed infants of vitamin D deficient mothers, renal failure, liver disease, iatrogenic (anticonvulsants), vitamin D resistant rickets (type I: ↓1 alpha-hydroxylase; type II: 1,25(OH)$_2$ vitamin D resistance). X-linked hypophosphataemic rickets, poor exposure to sunlight, renal tubular acidosis. Vitamin D deficiency commonly seen in adults in UK, particularly Asian and African origin. Clinical features: Rickets: Hypocalcaemia, bow-legged, bone pain, failure to thrive, seizures. Osteomalacia: Proximal myopathy, bone pain, fractures.

INVESTIGATIONS

U&E, ↓Ca²⁺, ↓phosphate, ↓vitamin D (except if resistance), ↑ALP, ↓pH; ↑urinary phosphate (X-linked hypophosphataemic rickets). X-ray: rickets, rickety rosary, bowed lower limb bones, widened ragged metaphyses; osteomalacia, Looser's zones (pseudofractures), bone biopsy.

MANAGEMENT

Calcium and vitamin D supplements. Calciferol (vitamin D₂/D₃) if malabsorption/vitamin D resistance. Alfacalcidol (1 alpha-hydroxylase vitamin D) if renal failure. Calcitriol (1,25(OH)$_2$-vitamin D) for vitamin D resistant rickets. Calcitriol and phosphate in X-linked hypophosphataemic rickets.

Osteomyelitis

CLINICAL NOTES

Aetiology/risk factors: Immunodeficiency, DM, vascular disease, penetrating trauma, sickle cell disease (salmonella spp), post-surgery, spread from other foci (eg skin infections, pneumonia). Staphylococcus, streptococcus, E coli, pseudomonas, salmonella, proteus, TB, fungal infections. Clinical features: Malaise, weight loss, night sweats, pain, localised warmth and erythema. Complications: Sinus and sequestrum formation, chronic infection, fracture, joint destruction, OA, amyloid, SCC in sinuses.

INVESTIGATIONS

FBC (↑WCC, anaemia of chronic disease), ↑ESR, ↑CRP, blood cultures, X-ray, MRI, CT, bone scan, PET, biopsy.

MANAGEMENT

Antibiotics, surgery.

Osteopetrosis

CLINICAL NOTES

Failure of bone resorption. Epidemiology: Rare. Aetiology/risk factors: Autosomal recessive (severe) or autosomal dominant. Clinical features: Failure to thrive, increased risk of fracture, loose teeth. Complications: Marrow failure, growth abnormality, nerve compression (may cause blindness, deafness), hydrocephalus, osteomyelitis.

INVESTIGATIONS

FBC, ↑PTH, ↑CK, ↑acid phosphatase, ↑ALP, X-ray, CT/MRI.

MANAGEMENT

High-dose vitamin D, calcitriol, corticosteroids, interferon gamma, erythropoietin, bone marrow transplant, fracture management.

Osteoporosis

CLINICAL NOTES

Epidemiology: Common, underdiagnosed. Aetiology/risk factors: Poor bone mass development in early adulthood eg 20s, oestrogen deficiency including premature menopause, excess endogenous/exogenous corticosteroids, hyperthyroidism, acromegaly, hyperprolactinaemia, heparin (not studied in LMWH), family history, smoking, alcohol abuse, low physical activity, malabsorption syndromes. Clinical features: Asymptomatic and incidental finding. Complications: Fragility fracture especially hip, spine or wrist. Dowager's hump with spinal disease.

INVESTIGATIONS

FRAX® score or QfractureScore (may be favourable to FRAX®) to assess fracture risk and treatment threshold. DEXA scan to establish bone mass density (BMD). T score: Osteopenia -1.0 to -2.5, osteoporosis ≤2.5. DEXA not required if patient has already had osteoporotic fracture. X-ray (osteoporotic collapse), MRI (distinguish acute from chronic vertebral collapse and osteoporosis from malignant disease). Consider: FBC, calcium, vitamin D, oestrogen, coeliac screen, TFT, FSH.

MANAGEMENT

Lifestyle changes (exercise, smoking/alcohol cessation), falls management, treat cause, calcium/vitamin D, bisphosphonates (treatment/prevention, alendronate first-line). Strontium. Raloxifene.

Othello syndrome

 CLINICAL NOTES

Delusion of morbid jealousy, that partner is being unfaithful. Aetiology/risk factors: Schizophrenia, bipolar disorder, depression, alcoholism. Complications: Violence, stalking behaviour.

MANAGEMENT

See under respective aetiologies.

Ovarian cyst

See also
— *Ovarian cancers (epithelial)*

 CLINICAL NOTES

Epidemiology: One in 25 – symptomatic cyst. Aetiology/risk factors: Follicular cysts, corpus luteum cysts (increased risk with clomiphene), endometrioma (complication of endometriosis), cystadenoma (serous, mucinous, may be very large, risk of malignancy). Clinical features: Asymptomatic, pain, bloating, dyspareunia, pain on passing stool, urinary voiding difficulties, menstrual dysfunction. Complications: Rupture, torsion (more likely in pregnancy, severe pain, shock), bleeding, malignancy, obstruction in labour.

INVESTIGATIONS

CA 125, USS, CT/MRI biopsy.

MANAGEMENT

Follicular and corpus luteum cysts often resolve after a few menstrual cycles, watch and wait, COC. Surgery for large, persistent, complicated, postmenopausal cysts or if malignancy cannot be excluded.

Ovarian fibroma

 CLINICAL NOTES

Clinical features: Solid benign ovarian tumour, may be associated with pleural effusion and ascites (Meigs syndrome). Complications: Ovarian torsion, malignant change.

INVESTIGATIONS

CA125, USS, CT/MRI, biopsy.

MANAGEMENT

Surgical removal.

Ovarian cancers (epithelial)

See also
— *Ovarian cyst*
— *Ovarian fibroma*

 CLINICAL NOTES

Epidemiology: 6,800 cases per year (UK). Peak age 56-60 years. Aetiology/risk factors: Family history *BRCA1/BRCA2*; *BRCA* genes confer 15% chance of developing ovarian cancer and up to 85% chance of breast cancer. Advancing age, low parity, infertility, early menarche, late menopause. PID. COC protective. Clinical features: Late presentation (60%), non-specific, fatigue, fever, weight loss, abdominal mass (40-75%), abdominal pain (10-15%). Increasing abdominal fullness and bloating. Pelvic and back pain. Vaginal bleeding (12%, including postmenopausal bleeding), urinary frequency/urgency. 2% will have a normal examination. Ascites (20-30%), pleural effusion (<10%), DVT, leg oedema, virilisation. *Krukenberg tumour:* Stomach cancer spread to ovary. *Meigs syndrome:* Benign ovarian tumour plus ascites plus pleural effusion. *Pseudo-Meigs:* Malignant ovarian tumour plus ascites plus pleural effusion (ascites and pleural effusion usually do not contain malignant cells).

INVESTIGATIONS

FBC, U&E, LFT, ↑amylase, CA 125 and USS (also consider for multimodal screening, for women >50 years with unexplained/persistent/worsening urinary or abdominal symptoms, USS about 90% sensitive but lower specificity). MRI. *Staging:* CT. *Monitoring:* CA 125 after primary treatment but research questions survival benefit. CT, MRI, PET-CT.

MANAGEMENT

Surgery (pelvic clearance, TAHBSO), omentectomy, nodal clearance, bowel resection, peritoneal stripping, chemotherapy. VGEF and PARP inhibitors.

Ovarian germ cell tumours

 CLINICAL NOTES

See *Ovarian malignancies (epithelial), ovarian cyst* and *ovarian fibroma*

Paget's disease of the bone

CLINICAL NOTES

Epidemiology: 3% >40s, 10% >70s. Aetiology/risk factors: Genetic, 15% familial, viral. Clinical features: Asymptomatic, bone pain, headaches, weakness, bony warmth and deformity. Complications: High output heart failure, bony deformity, nerve compression (eg cranial nerves), brainstem compression, pathological fracture, renal stones, gout, sarcoma.

INVESTIGATIONS

↑ALP (rapid rise with sarcoma), →Ca²⁺ (but ↑immobility, fracture, sarcoma), ↑acid phosphatase, ↑urinary hydroxy-proline, X-ray. CT/MRI to look for nerve compression. Imaging and biopsy if concerned about sarcoma.

MANAGEMENT

Bisphosphonates. Calcitonin. Physiotherapy. Treat complications accordingly.

Pancreatic cancer (exocrine)

📋 CLINICAL NOTES

Epidemiology: 80% cases occur in over-60s. Approximately 8,000 cases a year in the UK. **Aetiology/risk factors:** Smoking, diet (fat, sugar, red meat), obesity, chronic (not acute) pancreatitis, familial (x2 risk), *BRCA* gene, FAP/HNPCC, ataxia telangiectasia, Peutz-Jeghers syndrome. May be reduced risk with statins. **Clinical features:** Often presents late, malaise, fever, fatigue, anorexia, weight loss, cachexia, pruritus, abdominal and/or back pain, steatorrhoea, obstructive jaundice, nausea, gastric ulcer, epigastric tenderness/mass. **Complications:** Acute pancreatitis, metastatic disease (lung, liver, bone), pancreatic pseudocyst, bowel obstruction, pleural effusion.

🔎 INVESTIGATIONS

CA-19-9 tumour marker (if cancer strongly suspected, prognosis, monitoring), ↑carcinoembryonic antigen (CEA), pancreatic oncofetal antigen (false +ve 10%, false -ve 20%), ↑lipase. Clotting. **Diagnosis:** USS (including endoluminal), CT, consider MRI, MRCP, ERCP. Biopsy. ↑amylase in pleural fluid. *Staging:* CT, PET-CT.

💊 MANAGEMENT

Education, support, analgesia, antiemetics, resection (curative/palliative), biliary stent (obstructive jaundice), radiotherapy (neoadjuvant, adjuvant), chemotherapy (neoadjuvant, adjuvant).

Pancreatic pseudocyst

📋 CLINICAL NOTES

Pancreatic fluid collection contained within granulation/fibrous tissue. **Aetiology/risk factors:** Acute/chronic pancreatitis, pancreatic cancer, trauma. **Clinical features:** Abdominal pain and tenderness, bloating, early satiety, nausea, vomiting, abdominal mass. **Complications:** May extend into pelvis/mediastinum/neck, infection, gastrointestinal obstruction, perforation, haemorrhage, venous thrombosis, fistulae.

🔎 INVESTIGATIONS

USS, CT, MRI, ERCP.

💊 MANAGEMENT

Conservative for small cysts, octreotide, drainage, resection.

Pancreatitis (acute)

📋 CLINICAL NOTES

Epidemiology: 3% of hospital admissions for abdominal pain. **Aetiology/risk factors:** Gallstone disease, alcohol misuse, infections (eg mumps, Coxsackie B virus, hepatitis, helminths), trauma, hypercalcaemia, hypertriglyceridaemia, iatrogenic (eg azathioprine,

steroids, thiazides, oestrogens), pancreatic cancer, ERCP, hypothermia, severe hypotension, ischaemia, vasculitis, sclerosing cholangitis. **Clinical features:** Severe epigastric pain radiating to back, vomiting, fever (mild), tachycardia, hypotension, jaundice (if gallstone related), xanthelasma (if lipid disorder), epigastric tenderness, Cullen's sign (umbilical bruising), Grey Turner's sign (flank bruising), ascites. **Complications:** Necrosis (may be infected), haemorrhage, paralytic ileus, shock, ascites, hypoxia, hypocalcaemia, abscess, pseudocyst, pleural effusion, pulmonary oedema, ARDS, DIC, renal failure, fat necrosis, death.

🔎 INVESTIGATIONS

FBC, U&E, LFT, amylase, amylase P (higher specificity), urine amylase (highly specific), glucose, LDH, CRP, Ca^{2+}, ↓PO_4^{3-}, clotting, lipids, ↑lipase, arterial blood gases, erect chest X-ray (to exclude perforated viscus), abdominal X-ray (to exclude obstruction), USS (partly to exclude gallstones, pancreas may look normal), MRCP/ERCP (if gallstones), CT, peritoneal aspiration. ↑amylase in pleural fluid.

💊 MANAGEMENT

Assess prognosis/severity (Glasgow/Ranson's/Apache II[Ref15] scores). Glasgow (≥3 suggests severe disease. Age>55 years, WBC >15x10⁹/L, urea >16mmol/L, glucose >10mmol/L, albumin <32g/L, Ca^{2+} <2mmol/L, LDH >600u/L, AST/ALT >200mmol/L, PO_2 <8kPa). Admit, analgesia, IV fluids, O_2, NBM, urinary catheter, strict fluid balance, treat cause, surgery if infection and necrosis.

Pancreatitis (chronic)

📋 CLINICAL NOTES

Irreversible pancreatic damage through chronic inflammation, necrosis and fibrosis. **Epidemiology:** M>F, prevalence three in 10⁵ (UK). **Aetiology/risk factors:** Familial, autoimmune, tropical, hyperlipidaemia, hypercalcaemia, CF, idiopathic. **Clinical features:** Abdominal pain radiating to back (may be severe), steatorrhoea (in large duct disease), anorexia, nausea. **Complications:** Malaborption, malnutrition, DM, intraductal calculi, pseudocyst, pancreatic cancer (tropical pancreatitis), pleural effusion, pericardial effusion, ascites.

🔎 INVESTIGATIONS

FBC, U&E, LFT, Ca^{2+}, amylase (may be normal to slightly ↑), glucose, pancreatic exocrine function test, faecal elastase (malabsorption), abdominal X-ray (may show calcified ductal stones), abdominal USS (may be normal, consider endoscopic USS), CT. Imaging does not distinguish between inflammatory and malignant mass. ERCP, MRCP (ductal changes).

💊 MANAGEMENT

Lifestyle management, analgesia (watch for opiate

addiction), nutrition, creon, octreotide, cholecystokinin (CCK) antagonists, autoimmune: steroids, monitor for cancer, surgery (resection partial, pancreatoduodenectomy, pseudocyst decompression, nerve transection (coeliac plexus block) for pain, duct decompression, islet cell transplant), awareness of depression/suicide risk as chronic pain.

Paracetamol poisoning

See *poisoning appendices*

Parkinson's disease and Parkinson's plus syndromes

See also
— *Signs & Symptoms, parkinsonism*

📖 CLINICAL NOTES

Epidemiology: About 200 in 10^5 UK prevalence (incidence rises with age). M>F. Aetiology/risk factors: Genetics likely to play a part in cases <50 years of age. Mainly sporadic. Smoking may be protective. Some studies suggest NSAIDs protective. Clinical features: 4-6Hz resting tremor, lead-pipe rigidity (or cogwheeling if tremor superimposed on rigidity), bradykinesia, constipation, hyposmia and sleep disturbance may pre-date classic motor symptoms. Often unilateral symptoms in early stages, insidious onset, gradual decline, pseudodepression, mask-like facies, posturally unstable. Complications: Falls, Lewy body dementia (80%), hallucinations, dyskinesia, social/functional decline, weight loss, malnutrition, drug side-effects, autonomic dysfunction, hypotension, constipation, hyposmia, sleep disturbance, depression.
Multisystem atrophy (Shy-Drager syndrome): A 'Parkinson's plus' syndrome. Epidemiology: Rare. Sixth decade. M>F. Clinical features: Reflect autonomic dysfunction, parkinsonism and cerebellar dysfunction – labile BP, incontinence, ED, tremor, rigidity, bradykinesia, falls, constipation, arrhythmias, swallowing difficulties, salivary dysfunction, breathing difficulties, emotional lability.
Progressive supranuclear palsy (Steele-Richardson-Olszewski syndrome): A 'Parkinson's plus' syndrome. Epidemiology: rare. Onset seventh decade. M>F. Clinical features: falls (often backward), diplopia (especially downward gaze), Parkinsonism, emotional lability, dementia, aspiration pneumonia.

⚕ INVESTIGATIONS

MRI (if basal ganglia imaging required, not usual for Parkinson's disease), nuclear medicine (with dopamine transporter Ioflupane 123I SPECT) to differentiate Parkinson's disease from Parkinson's plus disorders (eg progressive supranuclear palsy, multisystem atrophy) or with diagnostic difficulties.

🔲 MANAGEMENT

Exclude other causes of parkinsonism eg iatrogenic. Consider watch and wait if symptoms not affecting quality of life. Watch for neuropsychiatric drug complications. *Drugs:* Levodopa usually first-line (freezing and chorea will start to occur after around five years – this may be helped by spreading dose throughout day). May be given with peripheral decarboxylase inhibitors eg co-careldopa. Dopamine agonists may be used in younger patients (ropinirole, pergolide, cabergoline, bromocriptine, may be associated with impulse control disorders eg gambling, hypersexualism). Catechol-O-methyltransferase (COMT) inhibitors (entacapone, given with levodopa, may help freezing/chorea side effects), patient controlled apomorphine injections or infusions may be helpful if freezing a problem. Cell transplant (including adrenal and stem cells) and subthalamic nucleus stimulation. Sudden cessation of PD drugs may be fatal. Typical antipsychotics may be fatal in Lewy body dementia. Social and family support, OT.

Parotid tumour

📖 CLINICAL NOTES

80% benign eg pleomorphic adenoma. Aetiology/risk factors: Smoking, radiation, familial, age, secondaries (squamous cell/malignant melanomas). Clinical features: Painful or painless parotid swelling, peritonsillar swelling, lymphadenopathy, facial palsy. Complications: Facial nerve palsy, ulceration, fungation.

⚕ INVESTIGATIONS

Diagnosis: USS, MRI, biopsy. Staging: MRI, PET-CT.

🔲 MANAGEMENT

Refer any salivary gland lump for urgent ENT review/biopsy unless infected, surgery, radiotherapy.

Parotitis (infective)

📖 CLINICAL NOTES

Aetiology/risk factors: Mumps, bacterial (secondary to blocked ducts, poor hygiene), immune deficiency. Clinical features: Acutely painful and tender parotid gland, swelling, erythema, pain on opening mouth, fever. Complications: Cellulitis, abscess, sepsis.

⚕ INVESTIGATIONS

FBC, glucose, USS, CT.

🔲 MANAGEMENT

Analgesia, rehydration, antibiotics (may require IV).

Paroxysmal cold haemoglobinuria

📖 CLINICAL NOTES

Epidemiology: Rare. Aetiology/risk factors: Haemolysis. Occurs after exposure to cold, post-infection, malignancy (eg lung, lymphoma, leukaemia, myeloma). **Clinical features:** Rapid onset, usually self-limiting, fever, urticaria, headache, rigors, diarrhoea, nausea, vomiting, abdominal/back pain, dark urine, oliguria, jaundice, hepatosplenomegaly (25%). **Complications:** Severe anaemia, cardiorespiratory failure, renal failure, death.

⚕ INVESTIGATIONS
Donath-Landsteiner (D-L) antibody test (RBC with P antigen reacting with D-L antibody), ↓Hb, →↑MCV, reticulocytes (low during attack, raised during recovery), monocyte/granulocyte erythrophagocytosis, ↑LDH, ↓C2, ↓C3, ↓C4, Coombs' test, haemoglobinuria.

⛨ MANAGEMENT
Warm patient, blood transfusion, urinary alkalinisation, fluid management, folic acid, treat cause.

Paroxysmal nocturnal haemoglobinuria

▦ CLINICAL NOTES
Epidemiology: Rare. **Clinical features:** Haemolysis, haemoglobinuria, complement deficiency. **Complications:** Venous thrombosis, AML.

⚕ INVESTIGATIONS
↓Hb, ↓WCC, ↓plts, urinary haemosiderin.

⛨ MANAGEMENT
Transfusion, anticoagulate, stem cell transplant.

Partial lipodystrophy

▦ CLINICAL NOTES
Epidemiology: F>M. **Aetiology/risk factors:** Familial, may be triggered by measles. *Variants:* Associated with HIV or total lipodystrophy associated with DM. **Clinical features:** Fat loss upper body and face, fat hypertrophy lower half of body. **Complications:** Retinitis pigmentosa, glomerulonephritis, liver disease, hypocomplementaemia.

⚕ INVESTIGATIONS
Fasting blood glucose, lipid profile, creatinine. ↓C3. ANA, anti double-stranded DNA (may be positive).

⛨ MANAGEMENT
Thiazolidinediones. Cosmetic surgery.

Patella subluxation (recurrent)

▦ CLINICAL NOTES
Epidemiology: F>M. **Aetiology/risk factors:** Tight lateral retinaculum, valgus deformity, trauma, familial, lateral femoral condyle dysplasia, patella alta (high patella). **Clinical features:** Usually lateral subluxation, pressure to lateral patella causes reflex quadriceps contraction.

⛨ MANAGEMENT
Physiotherapy, division of lateral retinaculum.

Patent ductus arteriosus (PDA)

▦ CLINICAL NOTES
Epidemiology: F>M, five to 20 in 100,000 live births. If ductus functional three months after birth, considered PDA. **Aetiology/risk factors:** ↑in premature babies, maternal rubella, babies born at high altitude, maternal antenatal alcohol abuse, maternal phenytoin use. **Clinical features:** Asymptomatic, neonatal oxygen dependance, SOB, failure to thrive, found on screening. Bounding pulse, wide pulse pressure, continuous machinery murmur. **Complications:** Pulmonary hypertension, Eisenmenger's syndrome (with lower limb clubbing), cardiac failure, endocarditis. Ductus may form part of a duct-dependent circulation, where shunting via duct is required to sustain life in more complex congenital cardiac defects .

⚕ INVESTIGATIONS
ECG – LVH, RVH (with Eisenmenger's syndrome). Echocardiogram – flow between aorta and pulmonary artery (ductus), diastolic flow reversal in pulmonary artery (using Doppler, very sensitive and specific).

⛨ MANAGEMENT
Indometacin infusion in neonates to close ductus in absence of duct-dependent circulation. Diuretics until closure. Surgery.

Patent foramen ovale (PFO)

▦ CLINICAL NOTES
Epidemiology: 25% prevalence. **Aetiology/risk factors:** Asymptomatic, may be required for survival in more complex congenital heart disease. **Complications:** CVA (embolic disease), migraine, shunting.

⚕ INVESTIGATIONS
Echocardiogram (with bubble study).

⛨ MANAGEMENT
Consider aspirin/closure if complications, eg CVA.

Pelvic inflammatory disease (PID)

▦ CLINICAL NOTES
Infection of uterus, fallopian tubes, ovaries and adjacent structures. **Epidemiology:** Common. **Aetiology/risk factors:** Chlamydia, gonorrhoea, *Gardnerella vaginalis*, *Mycoplasma genitalium*, haemophilus, enterococci, anaerobes. *Risk factors:* Multiple partners, unprotected

sexual intercourse, young age, urban residence, new partner. Clinical features: Asymptomatic, fever, malaise, tachycardia, pelvic pain, dyspareunia, rectal pain, postcoital/intermenstrual bleeding, vaginal discharge, tender lower abdomen, adnexal tenderness, cervical excitation. Complications: Septicaemia, abscess, recurrent PID, perihepatitis (Fitz-Hugh-Curtis syndrome), chronic pelvic pain, ↑ectopic pregnancy risk, infertility (risk increases x3 with three-day delay in treatment). It is not clear if there might be an increased risk of ovarian cancer.

INVESTIGATIONS
FBC, ↑inflammatory markers, ↑amylase, blood cultures, vaginal and cervical swabs, HCG to exclude pregnancy, USS, laparoscopy may be required.

MANAGEMENT
Rest, analgesia, avoid unprotected sexual intercourse until STI confirmed/treated/contact tracing. Education. Antibiotics – outpatient, eg once daily moxifloxacin 400mg for 14 days, or ofloxacin 400mg twice daily and metronidazole 400mg twice daily (for anaerobic cover) for 14 days. Add cephalosporin if risk of gonorrhoea. If severe pain, septic or pregnant, admit for IV therapy. May require surgery for complcations.

Pemphigoid
CLINICAL NOTES
Epidemiology: Rare. Onset mid-60s (childhood form related to vaccinations). Aetiology/risk factors: Autoimmune (C3 and IgG to basement membrane). Associated with psoriasis, lichen planus. Triggers: Radiotherapy, UV light, iatrogenic (eg loop diuretics, ACE inhibitors, antibiotics). Clinical features: Pruritus, bullous rash, tense bullae. Intermittently flares, burn out less than five years. Complications: Mucosal lesions, erythroderma, secondary infection, mortality up to 40% (due to comorbidities, immunosupression/drug side-effects).

INVESTIGATIONS
FBC, U&E, LFT, glucose, biopsy, immunofluorescence, DEXA (baseline if commencing systemic steroids).

MANAGEMENT
Topical/oral steroids. Tetracyclines and nicotinamide might be considered.

Pemphigus
CLINICAL NOTES
Epidemiology: Rare. Pemphigus vulgaris (most common subtype, fourth to eighth decades). Aetiology/risk factors: Autoimmune (IgG to keratinocytes – epidermal). Paraneoplastic (lymphoproliferative disorders). Associated with myasthenia gravis. Triggers: Stress,

UV light, vaccinations, hormones, iatrogenic (ACE inhibitors, rifampicin). Disease may not resolve after removal of trigger. Clinical features: Vulgaris: Painful, superficial, flaccid, mucosal lesions. Foliaceus: Skin only. Complications: Weight loss (dysphagia due to mucosal lesions), secondary infection, drug side-effects (steroid and immunosuppression), mortality one in 10 cases.

INVESTIGATIONS
FBC, U&E, LFT, glucose, autoimmune screen, urinalysis, chest X-ray, biopsy, immunofluoresence, DEXA (baseline if commencing systemic steroids).

MANAGEMENT
Analgesia, mucosal steroids (asthma inhalers, lozenges, mouthwashes), oral steroids – remission less than two months, NSAIDs, immunoglobulin, plasma exchange.

Pendred's syndrome
CLINICAL NOTES
See hypothyroidism

Penile cancer
CLINICAL NOTES
Epidemiology: More common in Asia/Africa. Rare in developed countries. Aetiology/risk factors: Advancing age (peak seventh decade), viral (HPV), smoking, carcinoma in situ, Bowen's disease, balanitis xerotica obliterans (lichen sclerosis), leucoplakia, Paget's disease of the bone, erythroplasia of Queyrat, melanoma, Kaposi's sarcoma, metastatic disease. Reduced risk with circumcision. Clinical features: Pain, red patches, nodules, ulcers (usually glans/prepuce), haematuria, split urinary stream, ulcer, necrosis, lymphadenopathy. Complications: Metastatic disease (local, skin, lungs, bone).

INVESTIGATIONS
CT/MRI, biopsy.

MANAGEMENT
Laser/cryosurgery, radical surgery, radiotherapy (including brachytherapy). Chemotherapy (including neoadjuvant).

Penile papules
CLINICAL NOTES
Epidemiology: Common. Aetiology/risk factors: Not STI, ↑non-circumcised men. Clinical features: Asymptomatic, pearly papules at rim of glans.

MANAGEMENT
May resolve spontaneously, reassurance, cosmetic surgery (eg laser ablation).

DISEASES

Peptic ulcer (gastric and duodenal ulcer)

📋 **CLINICAL NOTES**

Epidemiology: M>F. Aetiology/risk factors: Aspirin, NSAIDs, steroids, calcium antagonists, bisphosphonates, theophyllines, *H pylori* (95% DU, 80% GU), stress, severe intercurrent illness, smoking, alcohol, bile, Zollinger-Ellison syndrome. Clinical features: Epigastric pain (may be worse after eating, may radiate to back), nausea, belching, dyspepsia, succussion splash (reduced gastric emptying). Red flags: Anaemia, GI haemorrhage, weight loss, persistent vomiting, dysphagia, abdominal swelling/mass. Complications: Anaemia, acute GI bleed, perforation, pyloric stenosis.

⚕️ **INVESTIGATIONS**

FBC, *H pylori* testing (breath/stool antigen), endoscopy (if red flag or >55 years and recent onset/unexplained/persistent symptoms).

💊 **MANAGEMENT**

Refer urgently if red flags. Lifestyle management, avoid triggers eg NSAIDs, empirical PPI treatment (one to two months treatment dose, two months if +ve *H pylori* and NSAID use), *H pylori* eradication if +ve test, post treatment endoscopy with gastric ulcer to exclude malignancy/treatment resistance/ red flags.

Perennial rhinitis

📋 **CLINICAL NOTES**

Epidemiology: Common. Aetiology/risk factors: Allergy to house dust mite faeces, animal dander, fumes, cigarette smoke, no cause found but still have eosinophilia in nasal discharge. Clinical features: Sneezing, rhinorrhoea and congestion.

⚕️ **INVESTIGATIONS**

See *seasonal allergic rhinitis*

💊 **MANAGEMENT**

See *seasonal allergic rhinitis*

Perianal abscess

See also
— *Anal and rectal abscess*

📋 **CLINICAL NOTES**

Epidemiology: Most common anorectal abscess (followed by ischiorectal, intersphincteric and supralevator). M>F. Aetiology/risk factors: Higher risk in Crohn's disease, DM, anal trauma and immunodeficiency. Clinical features: Quickly progressive perianal pain, swelling, pruritus, purulent discharge (ischiorectal/intersphincteric abscesses present with pain, fever and pain/mass on direct rectal examination without localised external signs). Complications: Sepsis, necrosis, fistula.

⚕️ **INVESTIGATIONS**

Consider FBC, glucose, swab (including for TB). MRI and sigmoidoscopy for suspected IBD/ischiorectal/intersphincteric abscesses.

💊 **MANAGEMENT**

Oral antibiotics, surgical (incision and drainage).

Perianal infection of childhood

📋 **CLINICAL NOTES**

Epidemiology: Age three to five years. Aetiology/risk factors: Group A streptococcus. Clinical features: Pain on defecation, pruritus ani, rectal bleeding, perianal erythema, anal fissures. Complications: Local spread, abscess, cellulitis, scarlet fever, glomerulonephritis, avoidance of defecation and constipation.

⚕️ **INVESTIGATIONS**

Perianal swab.

💊 **MANAGEMENT**

Oral co-amoxiclav or clarithromycin.

Pericardial effusion/tamponade

See also
— *Acute pericarditis*

📋 **CLINICAL NOTES**

Aetiology/risk factors: Acute pericarditis, trauma, LRTI, PE, dissecting aortic aneurysm, leukaemia, gout, RA, SLE, hypothyroidism, TB, malignancy. Clinical features: SOB, quiet heart sounds, attenuated apex beat, dullness left lung base (Ewart's sign). Effusion may be large eg 1.5L if chronic. Tamponade – hypotension, pulsus paradoxus, tachycardia, ↑JVP. Complications: Reduced cardiac output, ventricular arrhythmia, death.

⚕️ **INVESTIGATIONS**

ECG – tachycardia, reduced voltages. QRS alternans – large effusion. Total (PQRST) alternans – tamponade. Chest X-ray – globular heart. Echocardiogram – pericardial effusion +/– tamponade. MRI. Cardiac catheterisation. Diagnostic pericardiocentesis. Biopsy.

💊 **MANAGEMENT**

Treat underlying cause (eg antituberculous therapy), pericardiocentesis when compromised, pericardial fenestration for recurrent effusion (eg malignant).

Pericarditis

See
— *Acute pericarditis*
— *Constrictive pericarditis*

Periorbital cellulitis

See also
— *Cellulitis*
— *Orbital cellulitis*
— *Erysipelas*
— *Necrotising fasciitis*

📋 CLINICAL NOTES
Aetiology/risk factors: Sinusitis, meibomianitis, stye, trauma, DM, immunosuppression. Clinical features: Painful eyelids, often afebrile, well, erythematous periorbitally. Complications: Orbital cellulitis and its complications.

🗴 MANAGEMENT
Antibiotics (may only require oral depending on clinical scenario).

Peripheral neuropathy

📋 CLINICAL NOTES
Epidemiology: 0.25% prevalence. Aetiology/risk factors: Age, idiopathic, DM, alcoholism, thyroid disease, RA, SLE, carcinomatosis, vitamin B_{12} deficiency, iatrogenic, vasculitis, amyloid, leprosy, acromegaly, sarcoidosis, uraemia, Refsum's disease, arsenic poisoning, AIDS, POEMS. *Mainly motor*: Charcot-Marie-Tooth disease, lead poisoning, porphyria, Guillain-Barré syndrome. Clinical features: *Sensory*: Feet first usually, pain, paraesthesia, numbness, painless trauma, ↓light touch/pinprick/joint position sense/vibration sense. Signs develop in stocking (+/– glove) distribution. *Autonomic*: Cardiac arrhythmias, sweating, hypotension, bowel and bladder dysfunction. Complications: Loss of quality of life, depression, ulcers, Charcot's joints, falls, reduced independent living.

☾ INVESTIGATIONS
Nerve conduction studies, nerve biopsy, investigate underlying cause.

🗴 MANAGEMENT
Education including safety, checking feet, treat underlying cause, manage ulcers.

Peripheral vascular disease

📋 CLINICAL NOTES
Epidemiology: M>F. Aetiology/risk factors: Hypertension, smoking, hypercholesterolaemia, DM, exacerbated by anaemia, beta-blockers. Clinical features: Exertional buttock or calf pain/cramps, night pain relieved by hanging feet down out of bed, cool feet, loss of limb hair, dry skin, absent/low volume pulses. Complications: Impotence, ulceration, gangrene, critical ischaemia (see *acute limb ischaemia*), associated vascular diseases.

☾ INVESTIGATIONS
FBC, glucose, lipids, U&E, ABPI (0.4-0.9 suggests intermittent claudication, <0.4 critical limb ischaemia), arterial dopplers, angiogram.

🗴 MANAGEMENT
Address risk/exacerbating factors. Angioplasty, stents, bypass graft, limb amputation.

Pernicious anaemia

📋 CLINICAL NOTES
Epidemiology: F>M, most >60 years. Underdiagnosed. Aetiology/risk factors: ↑blood group A, blue eyes, fair hair. ↓vitamin B_{12} (autoimmune, secondary to intrinsic factor deficiency/destruction). Clinical features: Fatigue, glossitis, angular cheilitis. Complications: Angina, cardiac failure, depression, confusion, pseudo-dementia, peripheral neuropathy, subacute combined degeneration of the spinal cord (↓joint position/vibration sense, absent lower limb reflexes, upgoing plantars), associated with other autoimmune diseases.

☾ INVESTIGATIONS
↓ Hb, ↑ MCV, ↓ vitamin B_{12}, ↓ WCC, ↓ plts. *Film:* Megaloblastic picture, parietal cell antibodies (90% sensitive), intrinsic factor antibodies (more specific, less sensitive than parietal cell antibodies), marrow biopsy, Schilling test (assesses whether vitamin B_{12} defiency corrected by vitamin B_{12} replacement, intrinsic factor replacement, correction of bacterial overgrowth with antibiotics or replacement of pancreatic enzymes).

🗴 MANAGEMENT
Treat underlying cause, vitamin B_{12} replacement in malabsorption (initial 1mg alternate days for two weeks/until signs improve, then 1mg every three months).

Perthes' disease

📋 CLINICAL NOTES
Epidemiology: 0.1% children. M>F. Presents at age two to 12 years. Aetiology/risk factors: Bone necrosis of femoral head secondary to vascular compromise. Clinical features: Intermittent limping for weeks-months, pain not severe, reduced hip abduction and adduction, stiffness, limp. Complications: OA, disability.

☾ INVESTIGATIONS
X-ray, arthrogram.

🗴 MANAGEMENT
60% recover with treatment, physiotherapy, brace, surgery (eg osteotomy).

Peutz-Jeghers syndrome

CLINICAL NOTES
Epidemiology: Rare, prevalence around one in 50,000. Aetiology/risk factors: Autosomal dominant. Clinical features: Mucocutaneous pigmentation. Complications: GI malignancy, phaeochromocytoma.

INVESTIGATIONS
FBC, iron studies, endoscopy, colonoscopy, CT, urine catecholamines.

MANAGEMENT
Surgical excision of lesions may be required.

Peyronie's disease

CLINICAL NOTES
Penile angulation secondary to fibrous scarring. Epidemiology: 3% prevalence. Aetiology/risk factors: Post-trauma, familial, age, DM, smoking, associated with Dupuytren's contracture. Clinical features: Painful erections, pain on ejaculation, tenderness, significant progressive penile deviation, palpable penile plaque. Complications: Psychosexual difficulties, anxiety, depression.

INVESTIGATIONS
USS.

MANAGEMENT
Consider tamoxifen, plaque injection (verapamil, interferon, collagenase), surgery.

Phaeochromocytoma

CLINICAL NOTES
Epidemiology: Rare. Aetiology/risk factors: Idiopathic, autosomal dominant, MEN2, neuro-fibromatosis (also associated with somatostatinoma, medullary thyroid cancer), Peutz-Jeghers syndrome, von Hippel Lindau syndrome, Carney complex/LAMB syndrome. Clinical features: Intermittent (minutes to days) hypertension (<1% of hypertension cases), palpitations, chest tightness, sweating, paraesthesia, visual disturbance, SOB, tremor, syncope, flushing, claudication, abdominal pain. Haematuria if bladder involvement. Catecholamine surge may be triggered by cheese, alcohol, sneezing, stress, sex. Complications: Erythropoietin secretion. Malignancy.

INVESTIGATIONS
FBC, chromogranin A, erythropoietin. Urinary glucose (+ve during 30% attacks), 24-hour urine collection (for catecholamines, will need confirmatory samples if raised), abdominal CT/MRI, MIBG scan.

MANAGEMENT
Alpha-blocker followed by beta-blocker. Surgical resection; control BP preoperatively and monitor postoperatively. Lifelong surveillance.

Pharyngeal pouch

CLINICAL NOTES
Pharyngeal diverticulum. Epidemiology: Uncommon. Aetiology/risk factors: F>M. Advancing age. Clinical features: Asymptomatic, gurgling throat noises, neck lump may or may not be palpable. Complications: Dysphagia, halitosis, cough, regurgitation of food on lying flat, aspiration pneumonia, weight loss, tumour (rare).

INVESTIGATIONS
Barium swallow, MRI.

MANAGEMENT
Surgery: Dohlman procedure (endoscopic stapling), cricothyromyotomy.

Pharyngitis

CLINICAL NOTES
Epidemiology: Common. Aetiology/risk factors: Viral eg adenovirus, EBV, primary HIV, HSV, bacterial eg streptococcus, diphtheria. Clinical features: Sore throat, fever, inflamed pharynx/tonsils/soft palate, cervical lymphadenopathy, malaise.

MANAGEMENT
Paracetamol, NSAIDS, consider antibiotics.

Phenylketonuria (PKU)

CLINICAL NOTES
Inability to process phenylalanine. Epidemiology: One in 10,000 live births (UK). ↑ in northern Europe/US. Aetiology/risk factors: Autosomal recessive. Clinical features: If untreated, mental disability, seizures, failure to thrive, eczema, microcephaly, poor pigmentation (blue eyes, light skin).

INVESTIGATIONS
Neonatal screening programme (heelprick test, may be diagnosed antenatally with CVS), genetic testing (false +ve test if galactosaemia).

MANAGEMENT
Lifelong dietary phenylalanine restriction, genetic counselling.

Phimosis

CLINICAL NOTES
Tight non-retractile foreskin. Epidemiology: Common. Aetiology/risk factors: Congenital, scarring, balanitis xerotica obliterans, post-trauma. Clinical features: Pain,

DISEASES

recurrent balanitis, voiding difficulties, foreskin ballooning on passing urine, erectile and ejaculatory difficulties.

🗋 MANAGEMENT
May resolve by four years of age. Gentle daily retraction, consider short-term topical steroids, circumcision.

Pica

📋 CLINICAL NOTES
Epidemiology: Rare. Aetiology/risk factors: Children, malnutrition, malabsorption, mental retardation eg Prader-Willi syndrome, psychiatric illness, pregnancy. Clinical features: Craving for non-foods, eg soil, lasting more than one month. Complications: Poisoning, infection, gut trauma and perforation, dental trauma, malnutrition.

🗋 MANAGEMENT
MDT approach involving physicians, psychologists and social services. Nutritional support. Aversion therapy.

Pick's disease

See also
— *Alzheimer's disease*

📋 CLINICAL NOTES
Clinical features: Frontal lobe dementia. Disinhibition and personality change common.

👂 INVESTIGATIONS
See *Alzheimer's disease*

🗋 MANAGEMENT
See *Alzheimer's disease*

Piebaldism

📋 CLINICAL NOTES
Epidemiology: Rare. Aetiology/risk factors: Autosomal dominant. Clinical features: White forelock, patchy hypopigmentation.

🗋 MANAGEMENT
Depigmented skin is generally considered unresponsive to medical or light treatment.

Pierre-Robin sequence

📋 CLINICAL NOTES
Epidemiology: Rare. Aetiology/risk factors: Idiopathic, genetic, syndromic. Clinical features: Micrognathism (with consequent relatively large tongue), cleft palate (lip usually unaffected). Complications: Feeding difficulties, otitis media, conductive deafness, airway obstruction, laryngomalacia, sleep apnoea, cor pulmonale, failure to thrive, ocular, renal, cardiac and skeletal abnormalities.

👂 INVESTIGATIONS
Antenatal USS, genetic studies, investigate for complications.

🗋 MANAGEMENT
Surgery. Treat complications accordingly.

Pilonidal sinus

📋 CLINICAL NOTES
Epidemiology: Common. Aetiology/risk factors: Familial, obesity, DM, sedentary lifestyle, family history. Clinical features: Obstructed hair follicle causing ingrowing hair, infection, abscess and sinus from skin (commonly on natal cleft) to deeper tissues. Rapid onset localised pain, swelling and fever. Complications: Chronic sinus formation, cellulitis, sepsis.

👂 INVESTIGATIONS
Consider FBC, glucose, swabs, blood cultures.

🗋 MANAGEMENT
Antibiotics, analgesia, surgical (wide excision and healing by secondary intention has lower risk of recurrence). Regular shaving to prevent further episodes.

Pinguecula

See also
— *Pterygium (eye)*

📋 CLINICAL NOTES
Aetiology/risk factors: ↑age, UV exposure, welders, dust, conjunctival collagen degeneration. Clinical features: Usually both eyes, white/yellow conjunctival nodule or patch, mainly nasally, asymptomatic, does not cross limbus or affect cornea (unlike pterygium). Complications: Inflammation, calcification, (may mimic conjunctival intraepithelial neoplasia).

🗋 MANAGEMENT
Avoid triggers, cold compress, lubricants, topical steroids, excision.

Pituitary failure

📋 CLINICAL NOTES
Epidemiology: M>F. Rare. Aetiology/risk factors: *Pituitary:* Tumour, infarction and infiltration eg Sheehan's syndrome, histiocytosis X, sarcoid, TB, syphilis, trauma, radiotherapy. Clinical features: Reflect loss of gonadotrophins, GH, TSH, ACTH, ADH, dependent on whether partial or total loss of pituitary hormones. ↓libido, oligo/amenorrhoea, dyspareunia, ED, central obesity, reduced strength/exercise tolerance, constipation, fatigue, cold intolerance, weight gain, soft dry skin, nausea, vomiting, polyuria (may be masked by ↓cortisol),

DISEASES

dizziness, depigmentation, pallor, breast and testicular atrophy, reduced sexual hair, bitemporal hemianopia if chiasmal compression, slow relaxing reflexes, postural hypotension. Complications: Coma, seizures, death.

INVESTIGATIONS
↓Hb, atypical lymphocytes, ↓LH, ↓FSH, ↓testosterone, ↓oestrogen, ↓DHEA-S, insulin tolerance test (for GH), water deprivation test (for diabetes insipidus), ↓TSH, ↓T$_4$, ↓glucose, ↓Na$^+$, ↑K$^+$, short Synacthen® test, visual field tests, MRI.

MANAGEMENT
Replace hormones as required – growth hormone/somatotropin, oestrogen, testosterone, steroids, thyroxine. Education (eg increase steroids with intercurrent illness).

Pituitary tumours

See also
— *Craniopharyngioma*
— *Pituitary failure*
— *Hyperprolactinaemia*

CLINICAL NOTES
Aetiology/risk factors: *Chromophobe:* 70% of tumours, may cause pressure effects and hypopituitarism, 50% secrete prolactin). *Acidophil:* 15% of tumours, secrete GH/prolactin. *Basophil:* 15% of tumours, secrete ACTH. Clinical features: Related to pressure effects (headache, IIIth, IVth, VIth cranial nerve palsy, bitemporal quadrantanopia/hemianopia, sleep disturbance, appetite changes, CSF rhinorrhoea), excess or deficiency of hormones. Complications: Pituitary apoplexy (adenoma-related pituitary haemorrhage/infarction – sudden onset, headache, visual disturbance, ↓GCS).

INVESTIGATIONS
FBC, U&E, glucose, LH, FSH, testosterone, prolactin, TFT, short Synacthen® test, water deprivation (diabetes insipidus), glucose tolerance test (acromegaly). Visual field studies, MRI brain.

MANAGEMENT
Tumour specific treatment. Surgery, radiotherapy, postoperative hormone replacement.

Pityriasis rosea
CLINICAL NOTES
Epidemiology: 15 in 10^4 prevalence. Second to fifth decades. Sping and autumn. Aetiology/risk factors: Viral (HHV). Clinical features: Asymptomatic, malaise, headache, joint pains followed by herald patch (primary lesion, 10-20mm, round, pale centre, outer scaly darker surround) then truncal rash (smaller lesions similar to herald patch). Rash often described as being in a Christmas tree distribution, found on trunk/neck/proximal limbs. Itchy. Complications: Postinflammatory hyper/hypopigmentation, facial involvement.

INVESTIGATIONS
Diagnosis clinical; usually no investigations required.

MANAGEMENT
Sunlight, calamine, topical steroids, erythromycin. Resolves in two months.

Pityriasis versicolor
CLINICAL NOTES
Epidemiology: Common. Aetiology/risk factors: Yeast infection, excessive sweat, hot weather, DM, immunosuppression. Clinical features: Itchy skin lesions on trunk, proximal limbs. Pigment changes – hyperpigmented lesions in light-skinned people, hypopigmentation in dark-skinned/tanned people. Complications: Postinflammatory hypopigmentation.

INVESTIGATIONS
Skin scrapings for microscopy (often culture negative).

MANAGEMENT
Antifungal (topical or oral), topical selenium sulphide, UV therapy.

Plagiocephaly (positional)
See also
— *Craniosynostosis*

CLINICAL NOTES
Aetiology/risk factors: Related to babies lying on their back. Clinical features: Flattened head.

MANAGEMENT
Exclude craniosynostosis. Reassurance. Resolves within a year.

Plantar fasciitis
CLINICAL NOTES
Epidemiology: 10% prevalence. ↑ages 40-60. Clinical features: Foot pain on walking, tender heel (plantar aspect), pain on extension of first MTPJ and ankle dorsiflexion.

INVESTIGATIONS
X-ray may show incidental calcaneal spur; MRI, although diagnosis should not require MRI.

MANAGEMENT
Most recover within 12 months. Supportive shoes, orthotics, insoles. Avoid triggers eg standing for long periods. Weight loss, NSAIDs, exercises. Physiotherapy

if no improvement after three months. Corticosteroid injection (risk of fat pad degeneration/fascia rupture).

Plantar warts (verrucae)

🗓 CLINICAL NOTES
Epidemiology: Common. Aetiology/risk factors: HPV 1, 2, 4, 63. Eczema, immunodeficiency. Clinical features: May be painful, rough papules, plantar (verruca), plane (may be pigmented), filiform. Often in clusters.

🗓 MANAGEMENT
Watch and wait. Topical salicylic acid (avoid in DM/ peripheral vascular disease), formaldehyde, silver nitrate, liquid nitrogen, laser, regular debridement (twice a week with nail file) podophyllum, occlusion with duct tape (for six days at a time).

Plasmacytoma

See also
— *Multiple myeloma*

🗓 CLINICAL NOTES
Plasma cell malignancy occurring at single site (bone or soft tissue). Epidemiology: M>F. Myeloma x10 greater incidence than plasmacytoma. Clinical features: Bone pain. Complications: Mass effects eg spinal cord compression, may go on to develop myeloma.

🝊 INVESTIGATIONS
See *multiple myeloma*. Electrophoresis (may show monoclonal band – confers increased risk of progression to myeloma).

🗓 MANAGEMENT
Regular monitoring, radiotherapy +/– adjuvant chemotherapy.

Pleural effusion

🗓 CLINICAL NOTES
Aetiology/risk factors: *Transudate*, (eg cardiac failure, superior vena cava obstruction, pericarditis, peritoneal dialysis, hypoalbuminaemia – liver disease/nephrotic syndrome, hypothyroidism), *exudate* (eg pneumonia, TB, empyema, bronchial carcinoma, metastases, mesothelioma, RA, SLE, PE, yellow nail syndrome, vasculitis, Meig's syndrome, pseudo-Meig's syndrome, Dressler's syndrome, toxocara) Clinical features: SOB, chest pain, deviated trachea, cyanosis, stony dull percussion note, reduced breath sounds, reduced vocal fremitus. Complications: Empyema, recurrent effusion, respiratory failure.

🝊 INVESTIGATIONS
Chest X-ray, CT chest, USS (detection of loculation and

pleural metastases), pleural tap – MC+S, protein concentration (transudate protein <25g/L). LDH, raised in exudate. pH <7.1 in exudate, glucose low in RA, infection including TB. Amylase eg pancreatitis-induced effusion, cytology. TFT, D-dimer, autoimmune screen, ANCA, abdominal CT, echocardiogram.

🗓 MANAGEMENT
Treat underlying cause, consider drainage and pleurodesis.

Pneumonia

🗓 CLINICAL NOTES
Epidemiology: Incidence about 1% per year. Aetiology/ risk factors: *Strep pneumoniae* (70% community acquired), *Haemophilus influenzae*, Staph aureus, atypicals (eg mycoplasma, legionella, *chlamydia spp*), Gram-negative bacteria, Q fever, viruses, fungal. Elderly, immobility, chronic cardiorespiratory disease, DM, underlying malignancy may present as recurrent chest infection, immunodeficiency, CVA, muscular disease, bulbar disease, aspiration. Clinical features: Cough, breathlessness, malaise, fever, tachycardia, tachypnoea, chest signs may be absent, reduced pulmonary expansion, dull percussion note, crackles/bronchial breathing. Complications: Sepsis, hypotension, confusion, respiratory failure, pleurisy, pleural effusion, empyema, abscess, cavitation. Mycoplasma – cold agglutinins/ haemolysis, thrombocytopenia, myocarditis, pericarditis, erythema multiforme/nodosum, toxic epidermal necrolysis, meningitis, neuropathy, pancreatitis, hepatitis. Legionella – diarrhoea, hepatitis, pancreatitis, relative bradycardia, SIADH, headache, confusion, renal failure.

🝊 INVESTIGATIONS
FBC, atypical lymphocytosis (mycoplasma), ↓lymphocytes (legionella), U&E, LFT, CRP, O_2 sats/ ABGs, (procalcitonin, under research), blood/sputum cultures, urine for legionella antigen, chest X-ray.

🗓 MANAGEMENT Ref16
Assess mortality risk by CRB65 score taking into account co-morbidities. Confusion, respiratory rate ≥30, BP ≤90mmHg systolic OR ≤60mmHg diastolic, age ≥65 years. Score zero to one, consider home treatment. Score two, consider hospital admission. Score three or more, admit to hospital. Antibiotics (antibiotics might be commenced pre-admission), antipyretics, consider fluids, analgesia, O_2.

Pneumothorax

🗓 CLINICAL NOTES
Epidemiology: M>F. Aetiology/risk factors: ↑tall stature (including Marfan's syndrome), smoking (x22 risk in men, x8 in women), genetic/congenital bullae,

COPD, acute asthma, valsalva manoeuvre (may also cause pneumomediastinum), trauma, CF, sarcoid, TB, iatrogenic, PCP, pulmonary fibrosis, endometriosis, histiocytosis X. Clinical features: Pleuritic chest pain, SOB, reduced chest expansion, hyper-resonant percussion note, reduced breath sounds, tachycardia, pulsus paradoxus in large pneumothoraces. Complications: *Tension pneumothorax:* severe SOB, tracheal/media-stinal shift, hypotension, significant tachycardia >135 BPM. Recurrent pneumothoraces.

INVESTIGATIONS
Chest X-ray, CT, blood gases.

MANAGEMENT
Resuscitation, O$_2$. *Tension pneumothorax*: Insert large bore needle/canula between second and third intercostal spaces on side of pneumothorax, mid-clavicular line for immediate relief plus insert chest drain. *Simple small non-tension pneumothorax (<15% lung affected):* Conservative measures for small lesions. *Compromised bilateral pneumothoraces or known lung disease (>15% lung affected):* Needle aspiration/chest drain. Smoking cessation advice. Pleurodesis for recurrent disease, persistent pneumothoraces, bilateral lesions, and for divers or pilots. Patient should not fly until resolution (usually around 10 days for simple uncomplicated spontaneous pneumothorax).

POEMS syndrome

CLINICAL NOTES
See *hypothyroidism*

Poliomyelitis

CLINICAL NOTES
Epidemiology: Children under three years of age particularly affected. Aetiology/risk factors: Viral. Faeco-oral (can spread rapidly via faeces), respiratory droplet transmission. Incubation one week. Clinical features: Asymptomatic, malaise, fatigue, headache, vomiting, neck stiffness, limb pain. Complications: One in 200 flaccid paralysis – most commonly unilateral lower limb, may occur over a few hours, may affect respiratory muscles causing respiratory failure and death, bulbar muscle disease.

INVESTIGATIONS
Throat swab, stool culture, ↑WCC, CSF studies.

MANAGEMENT
No cure. Vaccination has virtually eradicated polio in developed world. Ventilation (negative pressure ventilator) may be required if respiratory failure. *Limb paralysis:* Mobility aids (physiotherapy, hydrotherapy, orthopaedic surgery, calipers).

Polyarteritis nodosa (PAN)

CLINICAL NOTES
Epidemiology: Rare. M>F. ↑ in 45-65 years age group. Aetiology/risk factors: Associated with hepatitis B infection. Clinical features: Necrotising vasculitis (medium-sized arteries), malaise, fever, weight loss, arthralgia, myalgia, headache, abdominal pain, nausea, vomiting, testicular pain, ovarian pain. Complications: Hypertension, angina, MI, pericarditis, CCF, renal failure, TIA, CVA, visceral artery aneurysms, myelopathy, encephalopathy, cerebral arteritis, mononeuritis multiplex, peripheral neuro-pathy, GI haemorrhage, intestinal, liver and pancreatic infarction, Raynaud's phenomenon, livedo reticularis, purpura, cutaneous ulcers and gangrene.

INVESTIGATIONS
↓eGFR, ↑transaminases, ↑globulins, FBC (neutrophilia +/- eosinophilia), ↑ESR. Renal biopsy. Investigate according to suspected underlying cause eg hepatitis B serology (HBsAg +ve, one in three), pANCA (sometimes +ve, not specific), angiography (microaneurysms), biopsy.

MANAGEMENT
Close monitoring, systemic steroids, cyclophosphamide, methotrexate, treat hepatitis B.

Polycystic kidney disease (PCKD)

CLINICAL NOTES
Epidemiology: *Autosomal dominant type:* One in 400-1,000 Aetiology/risk factors: Autosomal dominant (adult, PCKD1 Chr 16, PCKD2, Chr 4), autosomal recessive (fatal). Clinical features: Asymptomatic, abdominal pain, haematuria. Complications: UTI, epididymal cyst, renal abscess/stones/failure, renal mass and mass effect on other organs, berry aneurysms, liver cysts, polycythaemia (erythropoietin production), mitral valve prolapse.

INVESTIGATIONS
FBC, U&E, urinalysis, sterile pyuria, abdominal USS/CT/MRI.

MANAGEMENT
Family screening, treat hypertension and monitor renal function.

Polycystic ovary syndrome (PCOS)

CLINICAL NOTES
Epidemiology: Up to one in 10 women of childbearing age. Aetiology/risk factors: Genetic, race (south Asians have worse symptoms and higher risk of developing DM), environmental, obesity. *Rotterdam criteria:*[Ref17] two of oligo/anovulation, hyperandrogenism

(clinically and/or biochemically), polycystic ovaries (≥12 immature follicles 2-9mm), volume of ovaries >10ml. Complications: DM, hirsutism, acne, acanthosis nigricans, psychological morbidity, infertility, possible early pregnancy loss/miscarriage.

INVESTIGATIONS
↑LH:FSH, ↑testosterone/androstenidione/DHEA-S/insulin/prolactin. ↓SHBG. USS.

MANAGEMENT
Exclude androgen-secreting tumours, advise weight loss, COC, anti-androgens eg spironolactone/finasteride, fertility treatment. Induce withdrawal bleed with oligomenorrhoea to avoid endometrial hyperplasia.

Polycythaemia rubra vera (PRV)

CLINICAL NOTES
Primary polycythaemia. Epidemiology: Rare. M>F. ↑age. Aetiology/risk factors: >90% have *JAK2 V617F* gene mutation, some cases familial. Clinical features: Asymptomatic, dizziness, headache, pruritus (especially after bath), tinnitus, breathlessness, facial plethora, splenomegaly (60-70%). Complications: CVA, visual disturbance, VTE, arterial thromboembolism, hypertension, gout, peptic ulcer, leukaemic transformation, myelofibrosis, sideroblastic anaemia.

MANAGEMENT
Check FBC every three months, venesection (aim HCT <0.45), antihistamines, hydroxyurea, consider antiplatelet agents/anticoagulation/interferon alpha.

INVESTIGATIONS
↑Hb, ↑RBC, ↑WCC, ↑plts, ↑HCT, ↑neutrophil alkaline phosphatase, ↓MCV, ↓ferritin, ↓erythropoietin, genetic studies, marrow biopsy, USS/CT abdomen.

Polymyalgia rheumatica

CLINICAL NOTES
Epidemiology: F>M. About seven in 1,000 prevalence. Aetiology/risk factors: >50 years, common around 70 years. ↑Northern Europeans. Clinical features: More than two-week history, bilateral pain and stiffness shoulder girdle, lower back pain, bilateral pelvic girdle pain and stiffness, morning stiffness >45 minutes, patient has difficulty raising arms above head and walking downstairs, malaise, depression, weight loss. No muscle weakness. Complications: Temporal arteritis in up to 20%.

INVESTIGATIONS
FBC (normochromic normocytic anaemia), ↑neutrophils, ESR (↑in 80%), ↑ALP (predominantly liver isoenzyme), →CK.

MANAGEMENT
Prednisolone initially 15mg once daily for three weeks, tapering slowly (eg one to two years), steroid counselling, bisphosphonates, monitor glucose and BP.

Polymyositis

See also
— Dermatomyositis

CLINICAL NOTES
Epidemiology: F>M. 30-50 years. African-Caribbean origin>white origin. Aetiology/risk factors: May be associated with malignancy (especially if >40 years of age). Autoimmune. Associated with Raynaud's disease, RA, Sjögren's syndrome, scleroderma. Clinical features: Fatigue, muscle weakness (difficulty standing from sitting/squatting), muscle pain, may have signs of dermatomyositis, proximal myopathy (especially lower limbs), absent reflexes may suggest malignancy. Complications: Bulbar muscle involvement (difficulty speaking/swallowing), respiratory muscle involvement (SOB, aspiration, interstitial lung disease, respiratory failure), cardiac (myocarditis, arrhythmias, cardiomyopathy, cardiac failure), calcinosis, pregnancy (deterioration of disease, premature birth, stillbirth).

INVESTIGATIONS
→↑ESR, ↑CK, ↑myoglobin, autoantibody screen (myositis-specific antibodies), anti-Jo-1 antibodies, antihistone antobodies, ANA, MRI, EMG, muscle biopsy, chest X-ray/pulmonary CT, lung function tests.

MANAGEMENT
Physiotherapy, speech therapy if required, search for malignancy if >40 years, corticosteroids (plus steroid counselling, monitoring, bisphosphonates), azathioprine, methotrexate, ciclosporin, immunoglobulin, tacrolimus, rituximab, infliximab.

Pompholyx

CLINICAL NOTES
Eczema variant. Epidemiology: F>M. Third to fifth decades. Aetiology/risk factors: Stress, contact dermatitis, genetic, sweat. Clinical features: Itchy vesicular lesions lasting three to four weeks on palms and soles. Complications: Distress, secondary infection.

INVESTIGATIONS
Diagnosis on history and skin appearance.

MANAGEMENT
Aluminium subacetate to dry lesions, aluminium chloride for sweating, potent topical steroids until lesions dried out, emollients. Oral steroids, PUVA or methotrexate may also be used. Antibiotics for secondary bacterial infection.

SIGNS & SYMPTOMS

INVESTIGATIONS

DISEASES

Post traumatic stress disorder (PTSD)

📋 CLINICAL NOTES

Epidemiology: 30% of people who experience catastrophic or considerably threatening event. Clinical features: PTSD may be delayed in some cases. Intrusive flashbacks, sleep disturbance, nightmares, anxiety, agitation, poor concentration, emotional numbness, somatisation, avoidance behaviour, children may re-enact event. Complications: Drug and alcohol abuse, depression, phobia, self-harm.

🗓 MANAGEMENT

Screening after a major disaster eg earthquake four weeks after event. Warn patients and families of possible symptoms after an event. Single debriefing not routinely advised. *Mild*: Watchful waiting if symptoms present before four weeks. CBT (all psychological treatments should be trauma/event focused), eye movement desensitisation and reprocessing (EMDR) offered if symptoms more than three months after event. *Severe*: CBT within four weeks. Consider drugs (eg paroxetine, mirtazapine) if patient declines psychological treatment, poor response to psychological treatment, as adjunct to psychological treatment or for sleep disturbance. Risk assessment. Education. Social support. Family support. Self-help/support groups. Regular follow-up. Depression, drug and alcohol abuse may need to be treated before the PTSD.

Posterior cruciate ligament disease (PCL)

📋 CLINICAL NOTES

Stops posterior movement of tibia. Epidemiology: Less common than ACL injury. Aetiology/risk factors: Trauma eg fall on a flexed knee, direct blow to anterior tibia. Clinical features: Popliteal fossa pain, no significant swelling, posterior sag of tibia. Complications: Associated with injury to posteriolateral corner (biceps femoris, popliteus muscle complex, iliotibial tract, arcuate ligament, lateral collateral ligament), peroneal nerve injury, OA.

🔍 INVESTIGATIONS

X-ray, MRI.

🗓 MANAGEMENT

Conservative treatment with physiotherapy may be considered. Surgery.

Posterior urethral valve

📋 CLINICAL NOTES

Epidemiology: Males. One in 8,000 births. Aetiology/risk factors: Sporadic, may be a genetic component. Clinical features: Oligohydramnios (antenatally), poor urinary stream, UTI, nocturnal enuresis, urinary frequency, failure to thrive, palpable bladder. Complications: Retention may present with respiratory distress in babies, hydronephrosis, CKD and renal scarring (if missed).

🔍 INVESTIGATIONS

U&E, MSU, USS (often antenatally), voiding cysto-urethrogram, IVP, dimercaptosuccinic acid (DMSA), mercaptoacetyltriglycine (MAG-3) studies, cystoscopy.

🗓 MANAGEMENT

Self-catheterisation, surgery eg valve ablation or urinary diversion for severe disease. Treat complications accordingly.

Postnatal depression

See also
— *Puerperal psychosis*

📋 CLINICAL NOTES

Epidemiology: Common. About 10% mothers. Aetiology/risk factors: x3 risk compared with non-pregnant women. Increased risk with poor family support, past psychiatric history/depression in pregnancy, adverse life events, premature delivery, maternal death. Clinical features: Depression may take a month to develop postpartum ('baby blues' start around day three postpartum and last few days). Features of depression, feelings of inability to cope with baby, anxiety regarding baby's health. Complications: Puerperal psychosis (may develop acutely), infanticide, homicide.

🔍 INVESTIGATIONS

Screening questions, Edinburgh postnatal depression scale.

🗓 MANAGEMENT

Risk assessment, crisis management plan, support (eg GP, health visitor, family, friends), educate family about postnatal depression, sleep hygiene, good diet, make time for self and partner/friends, self-help, CBT, excercise, social support, SSRI (paroxetine, sertraline), TCAs (imipramine, nortriptyline). Regular close follow-up. May require admission to mother and baby unit and antipsychotics or ECT.

Prader-Willi syndrome

📋 CLINICAL NOTES

Epidemiology: One in 8,000 children, one in 16,000 adults. Aetiology/risk factors: Chromosome 15. Clinical features: Suggest hypothalamic dysfunction, hypotonia, failure to thrive, mental handicap, small genitalia, cryptorchidism, excessive hunger. Complications: Obesity, sleep apnoea, cor pulmonale, short stature, osteoporosis, acanthosis nigricans, DM, hypopituitarism.

DISEASES

INVESTIGATIONS

See *pituitary failure*. Genetic studies. ↓gonadotrophins, ↓IGF-1. ↓testosterone.

MANAGEMENT

MDT approach to control endocrine problems. Growth hormone. Family support. Obesity management.

Precocious puberty

CLINICAL NOTES

Epidemiology: F>M. Below age eight years in females and age nine years in males. **Aetiology/risk factors:** Idiopathic (unlikely in males), hydrocephalus, cerebral tumour (eg craniopharyngioma, hypothalamic, pituitary), ovarian tumours, CAH, adrenal tumours (eg Cushing's syndrome), hepatic tumours, stress, hypothyroidism, familial, LH receptor gene defect (testotoxicosis), McCune-Albright syndrome, neurofibromatosis (hypothalamic glioma), exogenous sex hormones. **Clinical features:** In girls under eight years, following are abnormal – accelerated growth, axillary hair, genital development, menstruation. Pubertal signs may be incongruent and out of sequence, eg excessive pubic hair compared to breast development. Early breast development (larche) or pubic hair (pubarche) usually secondary to mild androgen excess, and in absence of other pubertal signs not neccessarily concerning. Severe androgen excess leads to virilisation and requires investigation. In boys under nine years, following are abnormal – axillary hair, facial hair, development of genitalia, voice deepening, increased muscle mass. **Complications:** Early epiphyseal fusion and short stature, bullying at school.

INVESTIGATIONS

FSH, LH, oestrogen, testosterone, 17-hydroxyprogesterone, AFP, pituitary profile, growth hormone, cerebral CT/MRI. USS – pelvic, adrenal, testicular. Bone age.

MANAGEMENT

GnRH analogues, aromatase inhibitors, tamoxifen, cyproterone acetate, ketoconazole, treat underlying cause (tumour resection).

Pre-eclampsia

CLINICAL NOTES

Epidemiology: 4-8% pregnancies. May occur after delivery. **Aetiology/risk factors:** First baby with a new partner, age <20 or >35 years, black race, nulliparity, mulitiple pregnancy, BMI >35kg/m², molar pregnancy, familial, >10 years after previous pregnancy, history of cardiorenal disease, DM, infertility treatment. **Clinical features:** >20 weeks. BP ≥140/90mmHg (if previously normotensive), ≥30mmHg systolic and/or 15mmHg diastolic above booking if previously hypertensive, asymptomatic, headaches, epigastric pain, vomiting, oedema, unexpected weight gain (fluid retention), flashing lights, proteinuria (≥300mg in 24

hours). **Complications:** *Severe pre-eclampsia:* Resting BP >160/110mmHg on two occasions separated by six hours, 24-hour proteinuria ≥1,000mg (≥2+ on dipstick), reduced urine output <500ml/24 hours, clonus, hyperreflexia, deranged LFT, low plts. *Eclampsia:* Seizures. HELLP syndrome (haemolysis, elevated liver enzymes, low plts). Acute fatty liver of pregnancy, CVA, CVD (in later life), pulmonary oedema, renal tubular necrosis, jaundice, DIC, placental abruption, placental infarction, prematurity, subclinical hypothyroidism, maternal and fetal death.

INVESTIGATIONS

Manual BP (automated may be unreliable in pregnancy), urinalysis (≥1+ protein), ACR, 24-hour urine collection (protein ≥300mg/24 hours), FBC, U&E, ↓Mg²⁺, ↑TSH, LFT (AST >150IU/L suggests HELLP), clotting (perform if HELLP/plts <100 x 10⁹/L), uric acid (correlates with mortality), LDH (↑in HELLP), ↑aldosterone, ↓amylase, +ve D-dimer, ↑soluble fms-like tyrosine kinase 1 (sFlt-1), fetal monitoring eg CTG, biophysical profile on USS.

MANAGEMENT

Calcium (1g per day)/aspirin reduces risk. Treat BP if >160mmHg systolic or >110mmHg diastolic or symptomatic. Aim for 140-155/90-100mmHg. Use methyldopa, CCBs, hydralazine or labetolol, continue antihypertensives after birth, magnesium sulphate reduces risk of eclampsia, corticosteroids (to help fetal lung maturity). May need admission. May need immediate/early delivery (only cure for pre-eclampsia).

Premenstrual syndrome (PMS)

CLINICAL NOTES

Epidemiology: Common. **Clinical features:** Many documented symptoms in the literature. Around one week before menstruation, anxiety, low mood, irritability, low self-esteem/confidence, tearfulness, bloating, breast/muscle pain, sleep disturbance. **Complications:** Violence, relationship breakdown.

MANAGEMENT

Lifestyle advice, reduce alcohol, caffeine and carbo-hydrates. Agnus castus, red clover, bright white light therapy, St John's wort, day 15-28 SSRI, COC (ethinylestradiol 30 microgram, drospirenone 3mg; antimineralocorticoid, anti-adrenergic, non-progestogenic side-effects, mild diuretic), bi/tricyclic COC, oestradiol patches with cyclical progestogen (60% effective), GnRH analogues (with add-back tibolone/HRT, monitor BMD with DEXA), TAHBSO.

Primary biliary cirrhosis

CLINICAL NOTES

Epidemiology: F>M 9:1. **Aetiology/risk factors:** Genetic HLA B8, C4B2. **Clinical features:** Asymptomatic, pruritus, fatigue, xanthelasma, finger clubbing, scratch marks, hepatomegaly, splenomegaly. Complications: Cholangitis, chronic liver disease, portal hypertension and oesophageal varices, malabsorption, liver failure, hepatocellular cancer (especially in men).

⚕ INVESTIGATIONS
↑ALP, ↑gamma GT, antimitochondrial antibodies (95% cases), ANA, antihistone antibodies, bilirubinuria, biopsy if antimitochondrial antibody -ve.

⬛ MANAGEMENT
Ursodeoxycholic acid (response confers good prognosis), pruritus (cholestyramine, phenobarbitone, naloxone, rifampicin), immunosuppressants, fat-soluble vitamins, liver transplant. Farnesoid X-receptor agonists, antiretrovirals and fibrates are currently trialled.

Progressive multifocal leukoencephalopathy

📋 CLINICAL NOTES
Epidemiology: Rare. Aetiology/risk factors: JC virus. Immunodeficiency eg lymphoma, HIV. Clinical features: Features of progressive demyelination eg balance, co-ordination and memory disturbance. Paralysis. Complications: Dementia, coma, death.

⚕ INVESTIGATIONS
MRI/CT, LP, brain biopsy.

⬛ MANAGEMENT
Treat underlying cause. No specific treatment. Patient usually dies within six months.

Progressive supranuclear palsy (Steele-Richardson-Olszewski syndrome)

📋 CLINICAL NOTES
See *Parkinson's disease* and *Parkinson's plus syndromes*

Prostate cancer

See also
— *Benign prostatic hypertrophy*

📋 CLINICAL NOTES
Epidemiology: Most common cancer affecting men. UK incidence about 35,000 per year. 15-30% of men >50 years. 60-70% of men >80 years. 75% of men >85 years but 4% of these die of prostate cancer. Lifetime risk one in 14 men. ↑African-Americans, ↓south Asians. Aetiology/risk factors: Sporadic, genetic component (chr 1 and BRCA). Clinical features: About 50% asymptomatic, hesitancy, poor stream, terminal dribbling, frequency, nocturia, dysuria, impotence, back pain, lymphadenopathy, weight loss, abnormal DRE, irregular/nodular

prostate. Complications: Anaemia, metastases, hypercalcaemia, urinary obstruction, pathological fracture.

⚕ INVESTIGATIONS
FBC, U&E, Ca^{2+} (↑suggests bone metastases), ALP (↑suggests bone metastases), acid phosphatase, chromogranin A, PSA (diagnosis, prognosis, monitoring). PSA correlates with risk of cancer. 15% have normal PSA levels (tumour may be highly undifferentiated – low PSA-secreting). PSA levels and DRE correlate to probability of having cancer. Risk of malignancy related to PSA doubling time. *PSA velocity:* Increase of >0.75ng/ml/year suggests malignancy. Free PSA:total PSA – low free PSA seen in prostate cancer. Transrectal USS and prostate biopsy. Gleason score on biopsy material based on two most predominant cell differentiation populations out of 10. Score ≥8 is a predictor of metastatic potentiial. Urine PCA-3 (trials pending). *If tumour confirmed:* MRI to assess spread/staging, bone scan.

⬛ MANAGEMENT
5alpha-reductase inhibitors shown to be effective primary prevention. *Localised disease:* Consider watchful waiting for older men unsuitable for radical treatment. These patients will receive systemic endocrine therapy eg GnRH analogues if symptoms of tumour progression. Active surveillance adopted in men with well differentiated low stage disease with an acceptable PSA doubling time and velocity who may be suitable for radical surgery if tumour shows signs of progression. Patients reviewed every three months for first two years. Radical prostatectomy +/– adjuvant chemotherapy or neoadjuvant GnRH analogue followed by radical radiotherapy (external beam/brachytherapy) with adjuvant GnRH analogue for about three years. *Localised advanced disease:* GnRH analogues or androgen antagonists or 5alpha-reductase inhibitors. Consider radiotherapy or chemotherapy. *Metastatic disease:* GnRH analogues for 18-24 months followed by addition of androgen antagonists or 5alpha-reductase inhibitors. Chemotherapy eg docetaxel for hormone-refractory disease. *Recurrent disease after radical treatment:* Radiotherapy until PSA climbs to 2ng/ml. Cryotherapy, high frequency ultrasound. *Palliative:* Dexamethasone, bisphosphonate infusions, palliative radiotherapy, radioisotope therapy.

Prostatitis

📋 CLINICAL NOTES
Epidemiology: Common. Aetiology/risk factors: Idiopathic, bacterial. UTI, STI, trauma (including catheterisation) and immunodeficiency (especially HIV) increase risk. May be associated with cancer and benign hyperplasia. Clinical features: Asymptomatic, dysuria, hesitancy, nocturia, perineal pain, pain on defecation, abdominal/pelvic/back pain, pain on orgasm. Systemic features with acute bacterial prostatitis eg fever, flu-like symptoms. Tender swollen prostate on PR examination. Complications: Chronic prostatitis (more than three

DISEASES

months, common, prostate hard on DRE), abscess, epididymitis, infertility, retention of urine.

 INVESTIGATIONS

FBC, blood culture, urinalysis and urine microscopy and culture, , semen culture, note negative cultures in chronic disease, PSA, USS, CT, cystoscopy, urodynamics. Sterile pyuria.

MANAGEMENT

May need admission for IV antibiotics. Antibiotics (prolonged course eg ciprofloxacin, doxycycline, trimethoprim), alpha-blockers, analgesia, treat complications accordingly, consider GUM referral, urological referral suggested.

Protein C deficiency

CLINICAL NOTES

See *thrombophilias*

Protein S deficiency

CLINICAL NOTES

See *thrombophilias*

Prurigo

CLINICAL NOTES

Epidemiology: Common. Aetiology/risk factors: Idiopathic, atopy, advancing age, HIV. Clinical features: Scaly, pruritic papules and nodules, mainly seen on the extensor surfaces of the limbs. Complications: Distress.

INVESTIGATIONS

Consider biopsy and allergy testing.

MANAGEMENT

Reassurance, antihistamines, emollients, topical steroids, calcipotriol, thalidomide, retinoids, PUVA.

Pseudo-Bartter's syndrome

CLINICAL NOTES

Epidemiology: About 12% of patients with CF. Aetiology/risk factors: Complication and often a presentation of CF (most present under six months of age), laxative/diuretic abuse, vomiting eg bulaemia, pyloric stenosis. Clinical features: Dependent on cause, loss of appetite, dehydration.

INVESTIGATIONS

↓Na$^+$, ↓K$^+$, ↓Cl (serum and urine), metabolic alkalosis.

MANAGEMENT

Treat underlying cause, fluid and electrolyte replacement, consider acetazolamide, consider haemodialysis.

Pseudobulbar palsy

CLINICAL NOTES

UMN affecting lower cranial nerves. Aetiology/risk factors: Corticobulbar tract pathology, CVA, MS, MND, tumour, head injury. Clinical features: Duck-like speech, inability to protrude tongue, spastic tongue, absent palatal movement, exaggerated jaw jerk. Complications: Aspiration pneumonia, communication difficulties.

INVESTIGATIONS

MRI brain.

MANAGEMENT

Treat cause, SALT.

Pseudogout

CLINICAL NOTES

Epidemiology: Common. Aetiology/risk factors: Chondrocalcinosis (cartilage calcification) caused by calcium pyrophosphate crystal deposition disease. Idiopathic, advancing age, familial, trauma, hyperparathyroidism, acromegaly, haemochromatosis, DM, hypothyroidism, Wilson's disease, gout. Clinical features: Monoarticular (often knee, may also affect ankles, shoulders, elbows, wrists, hands), acute pain and swelling, lasts days to weeks. Complications: Joint destruction, fractures, falls.

INVESTIGATIONS

FBC, U&E, Ca^{2+}, uric acid, PO$_4$$^{3-}$, joint aspiration (positively birefringent crystals), X-ray (chondrocalcinosis, cysts, spurs, loss of joint space).

MANAGEMENT

Treat underlying cause, NSAIDs, colchicine, intra-articular steroid injection, rest.

Pseudohypoparathyroidism type 1a

See also
— *Pseudopseudohypoparathyroidism*

CLINICAL NOTES

Albright's hereditary osteodystrophy. Resistance to PTH. Epidemiology: F>M. Aetiology/risk factors: Genetic, autosomal dominant. Clinical features: Short stature, obesity, short neck, short fourth and fifth metacarpals/metatarsals, mild mental retardation, hypothyroidism, hypogonadism, tetany, round face, frontal skull bossing, subcutaneous calcification. Complications: Epilepsy, calcification of basal ganglia. Type 1b pseudohypoparathyroidism has normal phenotype.

INVESTIGATIONS

↓Ca^{2+}, ↑PO$_4$$^{3-}$, ↑PTH, TSH, FSH, LH, testosterone, oestrogen, X-ray hands, consider DEXA (especially for type 1b), CT brain. Genetic studies.

MANAGEMENT
Ca²⁺ and vitamin D supplements, may require phosphate binders. Hormone and thyroid replacement. Treat complications accordingly. Genetic counselling.

Pseudo-Meigs syndrome
📖 CLINICAL NOTES
See *ovarian tumours*

Pseudopseudohypoparathyroidism
See also
  — *Pseudohypoparathyroidism*

CLINICAL NOTES
Aetiology/risk factors: Genetic. Clinical features: Phenotypic features of pseudohypoparathyroidism type 1a.

∮ INVESTIGATIONS
Normal biochemistry. Genetic studies.

⎍ MANAGEMENT
Genetic counselling.

Pseudoxanthoma elasticum
📖 CLINICAL NOTES
Elastic fibre disorder. Epidemiology: Rare. F>M. Aetiology/risk factors: Autosomal recessive. Clinical features: Yellow papules and plaques progressing to form loose skin folds, particularly in neck, axillae, antecubital fossae and groins, joint laxity, blue sclera, angioid retinal streaks. Complications: Angina, MI, intermittent claudication, GI bleed, haemoptysis, hypertension, mitral valve prolapse, recurrent miscarriage, hypothyroidism, retinal haemorrhage, macular degeneration.

∮ INVESTIGATIONS
Investigate for complications eg FBC, FOB, urinalysis, CHD risk assessment.

⎍ MANAGEMENT
Vitamins A, C, E; zinc. OT, physiotherapy, plastic surgery. Primary prevention of CHD. Consider intravitreal anti-VEGF. Treat complications accordingly.

Psoriasis
📖 CLINICAL NOTES
Epidemiology: 1-3% prevalence. Aetiology/risk factors: Familial, triggers – infection eg bacterial, HIV, scabies; stress, obesity, smoking, alcohol, iatrogenic

eg lithium, beta-blockers. Clinical features: *Chronic plaque:* 90% cases, large well demarcated plaques, pink with silvery scale, extensor surfaces. *Guttate:* Children/teenagers, post beta-haemolytic streptococcus/viral infection, small plaques over trunk. *Generalised pustular:* Fever, malaise, unwell, pustules. *Palmoplantar pustular:* F>M. Pustules on palms and soles. Complications: Arthropathy, see *psoriatic arthritis*, 10-30%, may resemble OA, RA, oligoarthritis, spondylitis, arthritis mutilans. Nail involvement (50%, pitting, onycholysis, nails may be affected without skin disease), scalp involvement, alopecia, secondary bacterial infection, depression, low self-esteem, suicide, erythroderma (rare, severe pruritus, skin shedding, shock, CCF, renal failure, fluid and electrolyte disturbance, pneumonia, superinfection, pain, death).

∮ INVESTIGATIONS
FBC (eosinophilia), ↑uric acid. Usually diagnosed clinically. Biopsy.

⎍ MANAGEMENT
Chronic plaque psoriasis: Vitamin D analogues (first-line but too irritant for face), emollients, combination vitamin D analogues/betamethasone (not for maintenance), topical steroids (psoriasis may flare once steroids stopped), topical tar agents (cause staining), coal tar bath additives, topical retinoids for very scaly lesions, dithranol (stains skin and clothes, applied for 10-60 minutes then washed off), salicylic acid with steroids or white soft paraffin. *Scalp psoriasis*: vitamin D/betamethasone combination, steroid shampoo/lotion/gel, coconut compounds for scaly disease, tar shampoo (adjunct or for mild scalp disease). *Second-line agents:* Tacrolimus/pimecrolimus, UVB, PUVA, methotrexate, azathioprine, ciclosporin, hydroxyurea. *Third-line:* eg infliximab, etanercept, adalimumab, ustekinumab. *Guttate:* Often resolves spontaneously. *Erythrodermic*: Secondary care, fluids, topical agents, immunosuppressants, infliximab, UVB, PUVA, analgesia. *Generalised pustular*: Urgent referral. *Palmoplantar pustular*: Often requires systemic treatment. Psychodermatology.

Psoriatic arthritis
See also
  — *Psoriasis*

📖 CLINICAL NOTES
Epidemiology: ↑White race. Clinical features: Rash usually precedes arthritis. *Nail disease:* Onycholysis, nail pitting. *Arthritis:* May occur without rash. *Number of presentations:* Dactylitis, monoarthritis, oligoarthritis, RA-like arthritis (F>M), ankylosing spondylitis-like arthritis (M>F). Complications: Arthritis mutilans. Achilles tendonitis, plantar fasciitis, uveitis, aortitis, amyloid.

INVESTIGATIONS

↑ESR, ↑CRP, RF +ve in 5-10%, ↑IgA, ANA -ve, HLA-B27.

 MANAGEMENT

Treat skin lesions, NSAIDs, intra-articular steroids, sulphasalazine, methotrexate. Anti-TNF agents if two or more DMARDs have not worked (etanercept or adalimumab; infliximab if etanercept not tolerated).

Psychosexual disorders

📖 **CLINICAL NOTES**

Epidemiology: About 50% may be affected at some point. Aetiology/risk factors: Relationship difficulties (communication, infidelity, anger, different expectations, cultural differences, dissatisfaction, fear of poor performance, desire for different gender, relationship breakdown, death of previous partner), history of abuse or rape, affective disorder, stress, chronic illness (eg diabetes, CVD, COPD), alcoholism, iatrogenic (eg beta-blockers, SSRI), hypogonadism/postmenopause. Clinical features: Vaginismus, dyspareunia, low sexual drive, lack of sexual arousal, ED, anorgasmia. Complications: Paraphilia (eg public exposure, sexual assault).

 MANAGEMENT

Treat physical cause, general counselling, psychosexual counselling. Short-term trial of non-penetrative intimacy. History of illegal sexual activities requires specialist forensic input and appropriate authorities.

Pterygium (eye)

See also
— *Pinguecula*

📖 **CLINICAL NOTES**

Aetiology/risk factors: Hot climate, dusty/dry environment, UV light. Clinical features: Vascularised growth on nasal side of iris across conjuctiva, painless. Complications: Inflammation, growth across pupil.

 MANAGEMENT

Avoid triggers, excision if interferes with vision.

Puerperal psychosis

See also
— *Postnatal depression*

📖 **CLINICAL NOTES**

Epidemiology: Rare, about 1.2 in 1,000 within three months post-delivery. Aetiology/risk factors: ↑With age, previous history of mental illness or caesarean section. Clinical features: Sleep disturbance, anxiety, agitation, depression, hypomania, mania, hallucinations, delusions, paranoia. Complications: Schizophrenic features, future puerperal psychosis, neglect (self or child), infanticide, suicide.

 MANAGEMENT

Admit to mother and baby unit, atypical antipsychotics, ECT.

Pulmonary artery stenosis

📖 **CLINICAL NOTES**

Aetiology/risk factors: May occur in isolation or with other congenital heart defects or syndromes eg rubella, Williams syndrome. Clinical features: Main artery or branch may be stenosed. Asymptomatic if mild. Breathlessness, fatigue, tachypnoea, tachycardia, difficulty feeding, failure to thrive. Systolic pulmonary murmur. Complications: Disease progression, cyanosis, right ventricular hypertrophy, cardiac failure, syncope, death.

 INVESTIGATIONS

ECG, CT, MRI, cardiac catheterisation, pulmonary angiography and pulmonary perfusion scan.

 MANAGEMENT

Balloon dilation, stent, surgery.

Pulmonary embolus (PE)

See also
— *Deep vein thrombosis*

📖 **CLINICAL NOTES**

Aetiology/risk factors: ↑Risk with pregnancy, postpartum, COC, HRT, thrombophilia, intercurrent illness, smoking, flight especially more than four hours, immobility, recent surgery/trauma, nephrotic syndrome (↓antithrombin-III), obesity, malignancy. Clinical features: SOB, acute onset pleuritic chest pain (peripheral PE), central dull chest pain (larger PEs), haemoptysis, hypotension, syncope, tachycardia, cyanosis. Pleural rub (peripheral PEs), ↑JVP (larger PEs), DVT (proximal DVT more likley to lead to PE than distal). Complications: DIC, circulatory collapse, death.

 INVESTIGATIONS

FBC, D-dimer, blood gases, ↑LDH, clotting screen, AT-III. Chest X-ray, ECG (normal, tachycardia, AF, right heart strain pattern, RBBB, non-specific ST changes, $S_1 Q_3 T_3$ pattern rare), ventilation/perfusion (V/Q) scan, high resolution/spiral CT, CT/MR pulmonary angiography, pulmonary angiogram (gold standard), echocardiogram. *Wells' score for PE:*[Ref18] Clinical diagnosis of DVT, three points. If PE most likely diagnosis, three points. Tachycardia (>100 BPM), 1.5 points. Surgery or immobile for three or more days in past four weeks, 1.5 points. Past history of PE or DVT, one

MIMS Consultation Guide

DISEASES

point. Haemoptysis, one point. Malignancy, one point. *Interpretation*: One to 1.5 points, low risk for PE; two to six points, moderate risk; seven or more points, high risk.

🔆 MANAGEMENT
Resuscitation, O_2, LMWH and warfarinisation (for three to six months, consider lifelong if recurrent PE), thrombolyisis, embolectomy, IVC filter.

Pulmonary hypertension

📖 CLINICAL NOTES
Aetiology/risk factors: Primary pulmonary hypertension (PPH), rare, F>M, may start in childhood. Chronic lung disease (eg COPD, most common cause, chronic thromboembolic disease, fibrosis), cardiac disease (eg congenital heart disease, cardiomyopathy). Clinical features: SOB, fatigue, respiratory distress. Cyanosis, loud P2, peripheral oedema, congested liver and ascites. Complications: Syncope, haemoptysis, cor pulmonale.

𝒸𝒴 INVESTIGATIONS
ECG (RBBB, RAD), RVH, right heart strain. Chest X-ray, O_2 saturation, spirometry, echocardiogram; mean pulmonary artery pressure >25mmHg may require cardiac catheterisation. Pulmonary CT.

🔆 MANAGEMENT
Treat underlying causes, effective contraception, counsel that pregnancy ill-advised, prostaglandin infusion (for PPH), warfarinisation, CCB, diuretics, nitric oxide donors, LTOT, atrial septostomy, transplantation.

Pulmonary regurgitation

📖 CLINICAL NOTES
Epidemiology: More common than pulmonary stenosis. Aetiology/risk factors: Idiopathic, trivial regurgitation often considered normal variant, pulmonary hypertension, endocarditis, rheumatic heart disease, carcinoid. Clinical features: Early diastolic murmur, left sternal edge.

𝒸𝒴 INVESTIGATIONS
ECG, echocardiogram, cardiac catheterisation, MRI.

🔆 MANAGEMENT
Rarely requires treatment.

Pulmonary stenosis

📖 CLINICAL NOTES
Epidemiology: 10% of congenital cardiac conditions. F>M. Aetiology/risk factors: Idiopathic, dysplastic pulmonary valve leaflets, congenital rubella, Turner's syndrome, infective endocarditis, rheumatic fever, carcinoid, cardiac tumour, mass effect from external compression. May be associated with VSD, Fallot's tetralogy (valve

usually biscupid rather than tricuspid), double chambered right ventricle. Clinical features: Valvular, supravalvular or subvalvular. Asymptomatic, exertional breathlessness, fatigue, presyncope. Raised a-wave on JVP, right ventricular heave, ejection systolic murmur (loudest on held inspiration, left sternal edge second intercostal space), wide splitting S2, attenuated P2, S4. Cyanosis if right to left shunt. Complications: Right ventricular hypertrophy, syncope, right heart failure, sudden death (rare).

𝒸𝒴 INVESTIGATIONS
Chest X-ray – post-stenotic pulmonary artery dilation, boot-shaped heart if Fallot's tetralology. ECG – p-pulmonale, RBBB, right axis deviation, RVH. Echocardiogram – right atrial hypertrophy, RVH, increased gradient across valve. Cardiac catheterisation. MRI.

🔆 MANAGEMENT
Valvotomy, balloon valvuloplasty.

Pyloric stenosis

📖 CLINICAL NOTES
Epidemiology: M>F, about three in 1,000 live births per year. Aetiology/risk factors: Usually presents in first four weeks of life. Clinical features: Post-feed projectile vomiting (non-bilious, no diarrhoea), pyloric mass, mass may only be noted after feeds. Complications: Dehydration, malabsorption, metabolic alkalosis, hypokalaemia, pseudo-Bartter's syndrome.

𝒸𝒴 INVESTIGATIONS
USS, electrolytes, arterial blood gases, ↑urine pH.

🔆 MANAGEMENT
Ramsted's pyloromyotomy, open or laparoscopic.

Pyoderma gangrenosum

📖 CLINICAL NOTES
Epidemiology: Rare. Aetiology/risk factors: Idiopathic, associated with RA, IBD (may reflect severity of ulcerative colitis), Wegener's granulomatosis, multiple myeloma, lymphoma, leukaemia, myelofibrosis, seronegative arthritides, HIV, SLE, sarcoid, hepatitis. Clinical features: Necrotic ulcer, irregular blue-red edge to ulcer, pain, arthralgia, malaise, may also occur around stoma sites.

𝒸𝒴 INVESTIGATIONS
Diagnosis is clinical. Investigations needed to exclude other conditions and look for associated disease.

🔆 MANAGEMENT
Colectomy if ulcerative colitis, topical steroids, nitrogen mustard, tacrolimus systemic corticosteroids, thalidomide, ciclosporin, cyclophosphamide, TNF inhibitors, immunoglobulin, minocycline.

Pyogenic granuloma

CLINICAL NOTES

Capillary haemangioma. *Epidemiology:* Often in childhood. F>M. *Aetiology/risk factors:* Triggered by trauma, virus, chemotherapy, oestrogens. *Clinical features:* Rapidly growing painful lesion, fingers, head, neck, external genitalia, oral mucosa in pregnancy. *Complications:* May grow to few centimetres, haemorrhage, ulceration, recurrence.

INVESTIGATIONS

Consider histology to exclude nodular melanoma if diagnostic doubt.

MANAGEMENT

Cautery, cryotherapy, silver nitrate.

Pyruvate kinase deficiency

CLINICAL NOTES

Epidemiology: Four to eight in 10^6 homozygous, 1% prevalence heterozygous. *Aetiology/risk factors:* Autosomal recessive. *Clinical features:* Haemolysis, neonatal jaundice (homozygotes), failure to thrive, gallstones (pigment), splenomegaly. *Complications:* Intrauterine death, leg ulcers, kernicterus.

INVESTIGATIONS

FBC (anaemia, haemolysis, ↑MCV), ↑lactate, blood film (aniso-poikilocytosis), LFT, enzyme assay.

MANAGEMENT

May not require treatment, folate, may require splenectomy, transfusion, bone marrow transplant.

Q fever

CLINICAL NOTES

Epidemiology: About 50 cases per year (UK). *Aetiology/ risk factors: Coxiella burnetii.* Reservoir – farm animals. In milk (especially if unpasteurised) and animal excrement. Airborne transmission to humans. Incubation 14-21 days. Resistant to drying, heat. *Clinical features:* Asymptomatic, high fever, malaise, fatigue, sore throat, chest and abdominal pain, pneumonia, hepatitis, diarrhoea and vomiting, meningitis, encephalitis, dry cough. *Complications:* Chronic Q fever, endocarditis (especially aortic valve), premature labour, miscarriage, IUGR, death.

INVESTIGATIONS

FBC, atypical lymphocytes, ↓plts, U&E, ↑ALT, serology (used in diagnosis of acute and chronic disease, and endocarditis), PCR (low sensitivity), tissue and urine culture. Echocardiogram.

MANAGEMENT

Prevention, vaccine available, doxycycline or tetracycline

(not in pregnancy). Chronic disease doxycylcine plus hydroxychloroquine for at least 18 months. Treat complications accordingly.

Radial nerve palsy

CLINICAL NOTES

Aetiology/risk factors: Trauma eg fracture of humerus, OA, axillary pressure eg crutches, traction injury, neuropathy eg mononeuritis multiplex. *Clinical features: High lesion:* ↓forearm flexion/forearm extension/thumb abduction/extension, wrist/finger drop, ↓sensation radial nerve distribution. *Lower lesion (posterior interosseous branch lesion):* Finger drop, ↓thumb abduction/extension.

INVESTIGATIONS

Consider nerve conduction studies, X-ray, MRI.

MANAGEMENT

Splint, treat cause (may need surgical exploration), physiotherapy, prognosis relates to severity of injury rather than treatment.

Ramsay-Hunt syndrome

CLINICAL NOTES

See *Bell's palsy*

Raynaud's phenomenon

CLINICAL NOTES

Epidemiology: Common. *Aetiology/risk factors:* Primary (Raynaud's disease, F>M, onset in teens, cold-induced peripheral vasospasm), autoimmune Raynaud's phenomenon (isolated Raynaud's and +ve ANA/nailfold capillaries, may go on to develop connective tissue disease). Connective tissue diseases (systemic sclerosis, SLE, polymyositis, dermatomyositis), mixed connective tissue disease, undifferentiated (arthralgia, photosensitivity, do not fulfil criteria for specific connective tissue disease), vasculitis, occupational eg machine operators. *Clinical features:* Attacks of pain, paraesthesia, numbness, colour change (white, blue, red). *Complications:* Ischaemic digital ulceration, infection, gangrene.

INVESTIGATIONS

Consider investigations to identify cause: FBC, ESR, CK, ANA (usually -ve if primary Raynaud's), ENA, anti double-stranded DNA/anti-Ro/antitopoisomerase (anti-SCl 70)/anticentromere antibodies, nailfold capillaroscopy, thermography.

MANAGEMENT

Avoid cold exposure, smoking and beta-blockers. Consider aspirin, antioxidants, CCBs, ARBs, SSRI, topical nitrates, IV prostacyclin, phosphodiesterase inhibitors, endothelin antagonists, digital sympathectomy. Treat underlying cause.

Recurrent aphthous ulceration

📖 **CLINICAL NOTES**

Epidemiology: Common. Aetiology/risk factors: Idiopathic, IBD, folate deficiency, coeliac disease, trauma, Behçet's disease, Reiter's disease, immunodeficiency, infection, food allergy, stress. Clinical features: Recurrent ulceration lasting approximately 10 days that subsequently heals.

🩺 **INVESTIGATIONS**

FBC, vitamin B_{12}, folate, ferritin, ESR, coeliac screen.

💊 **MANAGEMENT**

Refer if red flags (persistent more than three to four weeks, rolled edge, indurated, high-risk patients). Hydrocortisone lozenges, triamcinolone paste, beta-methasone tablets dissolved in water as mouthwash three times a day, asthma steroid inhalers, colchicine, systemic immunosuppressants, benzydamine oral rinse.

Recurrent miscarriage

📖 **CLINICAL NOTES**

Three or more consecutive miscarriages. Epidemiology: 1% women of childbearing age. Aetiology/risk factors: Idiopathic, genetic translocation, infection, chronic disease eg DM, bicornuate/septate uterus, uterine fibroids, smoking, drug and alcohol abuse, excessive caffeine, obesity, PCOS, stress, antiphospholipid syndrome, thrombophilia.

🩺 **INVESTIGATIONS**

Thrombophilia screen, anticardiolipin antibodies, lupus anticoagulant, FSH, TFT, karyotyping, pelvic USS, hysterosalpingogram, cytogenetics of fetal products.

💊 **MANAGEMENT**

Lifestyle management. Psychological support. Treat underlying cause.

Recurrent shoulder dislocation

📖 **CLINICAL NOTES**

Epidemiology: Most commonly dislocated joint. Aetiology/risk factors: Shallow glenoid (M>F), trauma (often anterior dislocation), rotator cuff disease. Posterior dislocations rare. Clinical features: Pain, change in bony contour, reduced ROM, difficulty in touching opposing shoulder. Complications: Recurrent dislocation (initial dislocation causes labrum to tear – Bankart lesion – leading to one in three risk of recurrent dislocation; subluxation, fracture, brachial plexus inury, vascular injury.

🩺 **INVESTIGATIONS**

X-ray, CT, MRI, MR arthrography.

💊 **MANAGEMENT**

Reduction, surgery, physiotherapy.

Refsum's disease

See also
— *Charcot-Marie-Tooth disease*

📖 **CLINICAL NOTES**

Epidemiology: Rare. Aetiology/risk factors: Autosomal recessive. Clinical features: Ataxia, neuropathy, nerve thickening, retinitis pigmentosa, cataract, ichthyosis, deafness, bone defects. Complications: Cardiomyopathy.

🩺 **INVESTIGATIONS**

↑Serum phytanic acid, CSF, echocardiogram, X-ray, audiology.

💊 **MANAGEMENT**

Phytanic acid free diet (exclude animal fat, dairy, leafy green vegetables), emollients, keratolytics, consider cochlear implant, ophthalmic, dermatology, cardiology and neurological review.

Reiter's disease (reactive arthritis)

📖 **CLINICAL NOTES**

Epidemiology: Incidence 5.0 in 100,000 patients, age 20-40 years. Aetiology/risk factors: Cervicitis, urethritis, dysentery, STI. Clinical features: Urethritis, arthritis, conjunctivitis. Complications: Balanitis, buccal ulceration, uveitis, plantar fasciitis, kerato-derma blennorrhagica, sacroiliitis, arthropathy, onycholysis, calcaneal spurs. Complications: Cardiomyopathy, aortic incompetence, cardiac conduction defects. Chronic Reiter's disease (80% have disease activity at five years).

🩺 **INVESTIGATIONS**

→↑ESR/CRP, HLA-B27, STI screen, stool culture, X-ray affected joint.

💊 **MANAGEMENT**

Treat underlying infection, NSAIDs, sulphasalazine, methotrexate, consider infliximab.

Relapsing polychondritis

📖 **CLINICAL NOTES**

Epidemiology: Rare. Aetiology/risk factors: Autoimmune, HLA DR4. Clinical features: Progressive, fever, malaise, inflammation and deformity of cartilage (nose, ear, larnyx, bronchi), saddle nose, joint pains. Complications: Epistaxis, LRTI, cardiovascular (valve regurgitation, aortic dissection, AAA, arrhythmia, MI), polyarthritis (seronegative), CNS (nerve palsy, seizure, ataxia, dementia), eye (episcleritis, scleritis, leading to blindness), deafness, renal involvement, vasculitis, anaemia, infection, premature death.

⚕ INVESTIGATIONS
↓Hb, ↑ESR, ↑CRP, collagen autoantibodies, ECG, echocardiogram, cardiac catheterisation, abdominal USS, chest X-ray, lung function tests, pulmonary CT, cartilage MRI, cartilage biopsy.

▣ MANAGEMENT
Corticosteroids, methotrexate, azathioprine, infliximab.

Renal artery stenosis

See also
— *Kidney (renal) failure, acute*

▣ CLINICAL NOTES
Epidemiology: Underdiagnosed, may affect up to 10% of hypertensive patients. Aetiology/risk factors: Atherosclerosis (M>F, older age groups, 70-90% cases), fibromuscular dysplasia (F>M, younger age groups, bilateral 60% cases). Associated with neurofibromatosis. Clinical features: Asymptomatic, resistant hypertension, revealed by reduction (>20-25%) in eGFR with ACE inhibitors. Pulmonary oedema, audible bruits. Complications: Renal failure, flash pulmonary oedema, hyperaldosteronism.

⚕ INVESTIGATIONS
U&E, ↓Na⁺, ↑aldosterone (secondary), proteinuria (may be only presenting feature – below nephrotic range), MR/CT angiography, USS (shrunken kidneys), Doppler USS (highly sensitive and specific), captopril renography.

▣ MANAGEMENT
Lifestyle measures, cardiovascular risk assessment, percutaneous intervention, open surgery.

Renal cell carcinoma (hypernephroma, adenocarcinoma)

▣ CLINICAL NOTES
Epidemiology: 2% of all cancers, incidence increased over past 30 years, 85% renal tumours of renal cell carcinoma (usually located in upper renal pole). M>F, average age 65 years. Aetiology/risk factors: Smoking, obesity, family history, occupational (oil, steel, cleaning industries, asbestos), phenacetin nephropathy, von Hippel-Lindau syndrome. Clinical features: Asymptomatic, haematuria, renal mass, loin pain, sterile pyuria, malaise, fatigue, weight loss, fever (PUO), varicocoele (2% male patients present like this, especially left-sided varicocoele). Complications: Local invasion/distant spread (lymphatic/haematogenous) common, renal vein/inferior vena caval invasion, pathological fracture, lung and cerebral metastases,

hypertension, polycythaemia (raised erythropoietin), hypercalcaemia.

⚕ INVESTIGATIONS
FBC (anaemia or polycythaemia if erythropoietin-secreting tumour), Ca²⁺, U&E, ↑ESR, urinalysis (sterile pyuria, cytology), chest X-ray (pulmonary metastases), USS (sensitive for renal mass >2cm), CT (sensitive for renal mass 1-1.5cm). *Staging:* Multidetector CT. *Monitoring:* chest X-ray, CT. DMSA, MAG-3 scans.

▣ MANAGEMENT
Surgery: Radical partial/total nephrectomy (plus arterial/venous ligation, +/– lymphatic resection), may require resection of bladder. Rarely secondaries may regress after tumour resection. Metastatic lesions may be surgically removed. *Embolisation/arterial occlusion:* If surgery contraindicated. *Systemic treatments (poor response overall):* Interferon alpha, medroxyprogesterone acetate, flutamide, tamoxifen, tyrosine kinase inhibitor (sunitinib), multikinase inhibitor (sorafenib), Anti-VEGF antibody (bevacizumab). mTOR inhibitors (everolimus/temsirolimus). Five-year survival rate 66% for stage I, 11% for stage IV.

Renal colic and stones

▣ CLINICAL NOTES
Epidemiology: 1-15% lifetime risk of renal stones. Peak age 20-50 years. Aetiology/risk factors: White race, M>F, obesity, dehydration, hypercalcaemia, recurrent infection (especially proteus, klebsiella, urease splitters associated with staghorn and struvite stones). IBD, urinary diversion surgery, medullary sponge kidney. *Stone types:* Calcium oxalate (most common), calcium phosphate, mixed calcium oxalate/phosphate, uric acid, cystine, struvite (infection-related), RTA. Clinical features: Asymptomatic, renal colic (sharp, severe, intermittent, loin to groin), vomiting, voiding difficulties, visible/non-visible haematuria. Complications: Infection, renal tract obstruction, recurrence (20% within one year of treatment, 50% within 10 years), renal failure, bladder cancer.

⚕ INVESTIGATIONS
Urinalysis: Red cells, may suggest infection (nitrites, leucocytes), urinary pH (acidic – uric acid/cystine stones), urinary MC&S. Sterile pyuria. FBC, U&E, Ca²⁺, uric acid. X-ray/CT kidney, ureter bladder (KUB), USS.

▣ MANAGEMENT
No further investigation if oxalate stones found on microscopy if asymptomatic or absence of previous stones/recurrent UTI/haematuria. Treat infection. *Acute renal colic:* Analgesia, NSAIDs, alpha-blockers for distal stones. *Uric acid stones:* Urinary alkalinisation eg sodium bicarbonate/potassium citrate, allopurinol. *Cystine stones:* D-penicillamine. Lithotripsy (ultrasound/

DISEASES

laser/electrohydraulic), ureteroscopy (via urethra), percutaneous nephrolithotomy (if stones >2cm/ staghorn), may require urgent decompression – urinary stenting, nephrostomy. Hydration (drink >2L fluids per day). Balanced diet (low-calcium diet may precipitate oxalate stones). Encourage low dietary oxalate (high oxalate foods – black tea, rhubarb, spinach, cocoa, nuts), high-citrate and low-sodium diet.

Renal cyst (simple)

 CLINICAL NOTES
Epidemiology: One in 50 (<50 years), one in five (elderly). Clinical features: Usually asymptomatic incidental finding, may be multiple, loin pain.

MANAGEMENT
Drain if symptomatic.

Renal tubular acidosis

 CLINICAL NOTES
Type 1 (distal): Common, impaired acidification of urine. Aetiology/risk factors: Idiopathic, genetic, chronic infection, renal tract obstruction, chronic interstitial nephritis, hypercalcaemia, SLE, chronic active hepatitis, Sjögren's syndrome, medullary sponge kidney, iatrogenic (eg lithium, amphotericin), transplant rejection. Complications: Renal stones. Type 2 (proximal): Reduced bicarbonate absorption. Aetiology/ risk factors: Idiopathic, heavy metals, iatrogenic (eg acetazolamide, sulfonamides), interstitial nephritis, multiple myeloma, amyloid, Fanconi syndrome. Clinical features: Failure to thrive, nausea, vomiting, dehydration. Complications: Osteomalacia/rickets. Type 4: Aetiology/risk factors: aldosterone deficiency, DM, ACE inhibitors, NSAIDs.

INVESTIGATIONS
Type 1: Normal eGFR, ↓plasma K⁺, plasma HCO₃ <10mmol/L, urine pH >5.3. Type 2: ↓plasma K⁺, plasma HCO₃ 14-20mmol/L, metabolic acidosis, urine pH normal or mildy acidic. Type 4: Metabolic acidosis, ↑K⁺, eGFR (mildly reduced), urinary pH<5.4.

MANAGEMENT
Type 1: Treat hypokalaemia in acute setting, then acidosis. Bicarbonate supplementation long-term. Type 2: Bicarbonate, vitamin D. Type 4: Fludrocortisone. Treat underlying cause.

Restrictive cardiomyopathy

 CLINICAL NOTES
Epidemiology: Rare. Aetiology/risk factors: Idiopathic, familial, amyloid, sarcoid, endomyocardial fibrosis, Loeffler endocarditis, scleroderma, haemochromatosis, glycogen storage diseases, carcinoid, malignancy,

hypereosinophilic disease. Clinical features: SOB, fatigue, raised JVP, hepatomegaly, peripheral oedema, ascites, Kussmaul's sign, palpable apex (unlike constrictive pericarditis), S4 (early disease), S3 (later disease). Complications: Arrhythmia, embolic disease, hepatic congestion.

INVESTIGATIONS
ECG – non specific ST, T wave changes, p-mitrale, p-pulmonale, prolonged PR, arrhythmia. Chest X-ray – cardiomegaly, atrial enlargement, pulmonary venous congestion. Echocardiogram – normal systolic function (unless advanced), diastolic dysfunction, myocardial thickening, myocardial infiltration, E:A reversal, atrial enlargement. Cardiac catheterisation to determine intracardiac pressures. MRT/CT.

MANAGEMENT
Treat underlying cause and cardiac failure/rhythm disturbance. Consider anticoagulation.

Retinal artery occlusion

 CLINICAL NOTES
Aetiology/risk factors: Plasma hyperviscosity, thrombophilia, atheroma, thromboembolic disease, temporal arteritis, vasculitis, sickle cell anaemia, acute glaucoma. Clinical features: Sudden onset visual loss (complete if central artery occlusion), painless, cherry red macular spots, relative afferent pupillary defect. Complications: Chronic new vessel formation.

INVESTIGATIONS
Investigate according to suspected underlying cause.

MANAGEMENT
Immediate ophthalmic referral. Repeated direct ocular massage (≈10 seconds at a time), reduce IOP (eg with inhaled CO_2/O_2, hyperbaric O_2, anterior chamber paracentesis, timolol, carbonic anhydrase inhibitors eg acetazolamide), thrombolysis.

Retinal detachment

 CLINICAL NOTES
Aetiology/risk factors: Idiopathic, posterior vitreous detachment, uveitis, tumour, advancing age, myopia, trauma, DM, hypertension, sickle cell anaemia, Marfan's syndrome. Clinical features: Asymptomatic, new onset floaters, lines, hazy vision and/or flashing lights. Visual loss, painless, shadow (peripheral→central), examination with ophthalmoscope may be normal, relative afferent pupillary defect, loss of red reflex, retinal folds, vitreous debris. Complications: Macular detachment, proliferative retinopathy.

INVESTIGATIONS
Clinical visualisation, acuity testing.

DISEASES

MANAGEMENT

Refer to ophthalmologist immediately if visual loss, field defect, haemorrhage, detachment on direct fundoscopy, otherwise for review within 24 hours. Laser or cryotherapy for tear, surgery for detachment (vitrectomy, pneumatic retinoplexy, silicone scleral buckling).

Retinitis pigmentosa

CLINICAL NOTES

Epidemiology: One in 4,000. Aetiology/risk factors: Idiopathic, Refsum's disease, Friedreich's ataxia, Kearns-Sayre syndrome, Laurence-Moon-Biedl syndrome, abetalipoproteinaemia. Clinical features: Progressive, begins with peripheral visual loss (tunnel vision), night blindness, black reticular spiculated pattern on fundoscopy. Complications: Eventually results in blindness.

INVESTIGATIONS

Slit-lamp biomicroscopy. USS eye, fluorescein angiography, optical computer tomography (OCT). Investigate according to suspected underlying cause.

MANAGEMENT

Genetic counselling. Vitamin A/betacarotene, acetazolamide.

Retinoblastoma

CLINICAL NOTES

Epidemiology: One in 15-20,000 live births. Aetiology/risk factors: Sporadic, 15% unilateral, all bilateral cases have *RB1* mutation. Clinical features: Usually present at less than two years old, absence of red reflex, squint, poor visual fixation. Complications: Increased risk of other primary cancers if *RB1* mutation (melanoma, SCC, sarcomas eg Ewing's, Wilms' tumour), associated mental retardation if associated with deletion of long arm of chromosome 13, retinal detachment, cerebral seeding, metastases (bone, liver, pulmonary, lymph node), glaucoma.

INVESTIGATIONS

FBC, chest X-ray, bone scan, CT/MRI orbit, consider LP. Genetic studies.

MANAGEMENT

Genetic counselling, staging, if >7mm, cryosurgery/photocoagulation. 3-10mm, brachytherapy. >10mm, radiotherapy. Bilateral/invasive disease/relapse, radio/chemotherapy. Regular monitoring. 90% cure rate. Surgical resection of globe and prosthesis.

Retroperitoneal fibrosis

CLINICAL NOTES

Epidemiology: Rare. M>F. Peak incidence fifth to seventh decade. Aetiology/risk factors: Idiopathic (70%), autoimmune (eg RA, SLE, scleroderma), malignancy (8% cases, eg sarcoma, carcinoma (eg lung, colon, breast), lymphoma, carcinoid), radiotherapy, trauma, immunosuppression, AAA, thyroiditis, sarcoid, vasculitis (eg Wegener's granulomatosis). Iatrogenic (eg methysergide, hydralazine, beta-blockers, bromocriptine, methyldopa). Clinical features: Hypertension, vague abdominal pain, back pain, fever, lower limb oedema, malaise. Complications: Progressive ureteric obstruction, hydronephrosis, renal failure, ascites, bowel obstruction, spinal cord compression, sclerosing cholangitis.

INVESTIGATIONS

↑ESR, U&E, IVU (medially deviated ureters), CT/MRI, biopsy.

MANAGEMENT

Poor prognosis. Treat cause, palliate with steroids, surgery, ureteric stent, nephrostomy.

Reye's syndrome

CLINICAL NOTES

Characterised by acute, life-threatening non-inflammatory encephalopathy and fatty degeneration of liver. Epidemiology: Rare. Children/teens. Aetiology/risk factors: Post-viral, triggered by aspirin, antihistamine, may be underlying metabolic disorder. Clinical features: Predominantly affects brain and liver. Diarrhoea, vomiting, encephalopathy (altered consciousness, irritability, coma), death.

INVESTIGATIONS

↑ammonia, ↓pH, ↑LFT.

MANAGEMENT

No specific treatment.

Rhabdomyolysis

CLINICAL NOTES

Epidemiology: M>F. Aetiology/risk factors: Trauma, compartment syndrome, burns, electrocution, myositis (eg autoimmune, muscle necrosis, infection, iatrogenic), excessive exercise, malignant hyperpyrexia, neuroleptic malignant syndrome, alcoholism, status epilepticus, McArdle's syndrome, prolonged immobility, hypothermia, flu-like illness, sepsis, gangrene, drug misuse, poisoning, DKA, thyroid disease. Clinical features: Muscle pain, dark urine. Complications: Hyperkalaemia, renal failure, metabolic acidosis, DIC, dehydration, death.

INVESTIGATIONS

↑myoglobin, ↑K^+, ↑PO_4^{3-}, ↓Ca^{2+}, ↑↑creatine kinase, ↑creatinine, clotting screen, TFT, glucose, blood gases.

MANAGEMENT
Address cause, IV rehydration, urinary alkalinisation.

Rheumatic fever

CLINICAL NOTES
Epidemiology: Rare in developed countries. **Aetiology/risk factors:** Complication of group A streptococcal throat infection. *Duckett Jones criteria for diagnosis:*[Ref9] Evidence of recent streptococcal infection (eg ↑ASOT, +ve throat swab, recent scarlet fever) plus two major, or one major and two minor, criteria. *Major criteria:* Pancarditis, polyarthritis, Sydenham's chorea (St Vitus' dance), erythema marginatum, subcutaneous nodules. *Minor citieria:* Fever, joint pains, inflammatory markers, prolonged PR interval, previous rheumatic fever. **Complications:** Rheumatic heart disease (carditis, particularly aortic and mitral), cardiac failure.

INVESTIGATIONS
FBC, ESR, CRP, ASOT, throat swab, ECG (prolonged PR), echocardiogram.

MANAGEMENT
Antibiotics (penicillin or macrolide, 10 days), NSAIDs, regular cardiac review, treat cardiac failure, may require cardiac valve replacement, benzodiazepines or haloperidol for chorea.

Rheumatoid arthritis (RA)

CLINICAL NOTES
Epidemiology: About 1% prevalence. Peaks in fifth decade. **Aetiology/risk factors:** F>M. ↑ Smokers. Autoimmune, HLA-DR4. **Clinical features:** Symmetrical progressive deforming polyarthropathy. Pain, swelling, morning stiffness, mainly affecting small joints. May present with monoarthritis. Boggy synovium with active disease. **Complications:** Lack of function, deformity (joint destruction, tendinitis, tendon rupture, Boutonnière and swan neck finger deformities, z-shaped thumb, subluxation and ulnar deviation of fingers and MCPJ), muscle wasting, atlanto-axial subluxation (risk of transecting cervical spinal cord hyperextension). Neuropathy, carpal tunnel syndrome, rheumatoid nodules (commonly extensor surface of elbow, associated with rheumatoid factor [RF] and more extensive disease), pyoderma gangrenosum, anaemia (secondary to nephropathy, gastric haemorrhage, malnutrition, chronic disease, Felty's syndrome, haemolysis, immunosuppressants).Renal failure (drug toxicity, amyloid, vasculitis), eye disease (episcleritis, scleritis, scleromalacia, scleromalacia perforans, sicca syndrome), rheumatoid lung (may cause haemoptysis, SOB, pneumothorax, pulmonary hypertension, cor pulmonale, fibrosis, methotrexate-induced fibrosis, bronchiectasis, bronchiolitis obliterans, pleural effusion, nodules, Caplan's syndrome, pulmonary vasculitis, fibrobullous disease, increased incidence of lung malignancy), pericarditis, CVD, lymphoma, oestoporosis, depression.

INVESTIGATIONS
FBC, atypical lymphocytes, ring sideroblasts, ESR/CRP (monitoring), U&E, LFT, glucose, fasting lipids, RF (RF, not specific, presence confers higher risk of extra-articular disease), anticyclic citrullinated peptide (CCP) antibodies (more specific than RF), autoimmune screen (ANA +ve in 30%), antihistone antibodies, urinalysis, X-ray (joint, chest), DEXA scan, lung function tests, pulmonary CT.

MANAGEMENT
Early referral, education, lifestyle, regular follow up, cardiovascular risk assessment, analgesia, physiotherapy, OT. DMARDs eg methotrexate, sulfasalazine, ciclosporin, gold, penicillamine, azathioprine, hydroxychloroquine, leflunamide. Consider combination methotrexate plus another DMARD plus steroid within three months of persistent symptoms, if combination DMARD therapy fails, for escalating doses of monotherapy. *Steroids:* Short-term use for rheumatoid flares (oral, depot), long-term if DMARDs declined/unsuitable, bisphosphonates required. Surgery. *Biological treatments:* Anakinra (IL-1 antagonist), anti TNF-alpha therapy (eg infliximab, etanercept). Monitoring (drugs, FBC, U&E, LFT, CRP, urinalysis, function and pain scores, BP, CVD risk, depression risk, osteoporosis risk, vasculitis, eye disease.

Rickets

CLINICAL NOTES
See *osteomalacia and rickets*

Right heart failure

See also
— *Pulmonary hypertension*

CLINICAL NOTES
Aetiology/risk factors: Cor pulmonale (right heart failure secondary to pulmonary disease eg COPD, chronic thromboembolic disease), pulmonary stenosis, pulmonary regurgitation, tricuspid stenosis, TR, congenital heart disease, RV MI, LV dysfunction. **Clinical features:** Breathlessness, presyncope, syncope, tachycardia, raised JVP, loud P2 (pulmonary hypertension), TR, PR, hepatomegaly, ascites, peripheral oedema.

INVESTIGATIONS
FBC (secondary polycythaemia), U&E, ↑ALT, ECG-RAD, RBBB, p-pulmonale, right heart strain, RVH. Echocardiogram. Lung function tests, chest X-ray, CT/CTPA.

MANAGEMENT
Treat underlying cause, LTOT, venesection if significant polycythaemia, heart-lung transplantation.

Romano-Ward syndrome

 CLINICAL NOTES

See *long QT syndrome*

Rosacea

 CLINICAL NOTES

Epidemiology: Common. Aetiology/risk factors: Multifactorial, alcohol, caffeine, spicy foods, sunlight exposure, wind, extremes of temperature, menopause, vasodilators, steroids, make-up. Clinical features: Persistent facial erythema, flushing, telangiectasia on convex surfaces, papules, pustules. Complications: Low self-esteem, ocular involvement, blepharitis, recurrent chalazion, keratitis, scleritis, iritis, facial burning, oedema, nodules, phyma – skin thickening, eg rhinophyma (nose), metophyma (forehead), otophyma (ears), gnathophyma (chin), blepharophyma (eyes), neck and trunk lesions.

MANAGEMENT

Avoid triggers, sun protection. *Topical:* Metronidazole (0.75%), erythromycin, clindamycin, tacrolimus (good for steroid-induced rosacea), azelaic gel. *Oral:* Antibiotics (may require courses for six to 12 weeks at a time, tetracyclines, erythromycin), isotretinoin. *Other:* Laser, surgery for phyma.

Roseola infantum (sixth disease)

CLINICAL NOTES

Epidemiology: Children six months to four years. Aetiology/risk factors: HHV 6. Clinical features: High fever (about 72 hours), agitation, sore throat, pink elliptical macular rash (neck and trunk) which begins as fever settles, rash lasts up to 48 hours. Complications: Febrile convulsion; rarely, hepatitis, encephalitis.

INVESTIGATIONS

FBC, atypical lymphocytes.

MANAGEMENT

NSAIDs, paracetamol, fluids.

Rotator cuff disorders

See also
— *Adhesive capsulitis (frozen shoulder syndrome)*

CLINICAL NOTES

Aetiology/risk factors: *Impingement:* Caused by supraspinatus impinged in subacromial space caused by tendonitis, tendon injury, subacromial bursitis, calcification, bony spurs, pain radiating distally. Clinical features: Painful arc on abduction, painless if abducted with shoulder in full external rotation. *Tendonitis:* Shoulder pain. Painful arc (about 60° to 120°) with active abduction in supraspinatus tendonitis/partial supraspinatus tear. Painless if abducted with shoulder in full external rotation. Pain on resisted elbow flexion in bicepital tendonitis. Pain on resisted internal rotation in subscapularis tendonitis. Pain on external rotation in infraspinatus tendonitis. *Partial/complete tear:* Acute or chronic. Often affects supraspinatus. Aetiology/risk factors: Trauma or tendinitis. Clinical features: Pain and weakness on abduction. Positive drop-arm test implies complete tear. Complications: OA, shoulder dislocation, functional disability.

INVESTIGATIONS

X-ray (calcified tendons), MRI.

MANAGEMENT

Analgesia, physiotherapy. *Impingement:* Subacromial steroid, surgery (tendon release, subacromial decompression – can be laparoscopic). *Tears:* Consider surgery.

Rotor syndrome

CLINICAL NOTES

Epidemiology: Rare. Aetiology/risk factors: Autosomal recessive. Benign. Clinical features: Isolated conjugated hyperbilirubinaemia.

INVESTIGATIONS

↑ Urinary bilirubin, urine coproporphyrin I:coproporphyrin III not as high as in Dubin-Johnson syndrome.

MANAGEMENT

No specific treatment required.

Rubella (German measles)

CLINICAL NOTES

Epidemiology: Rare with advent of vaccination. Aetiology/risk factors: Togavirus. Clinical features: Incubation two to three weeks. Infectious seven days before to five days after onset of symptoms. Malaise, fever, loss of appetite, conjunctivitis, coryza, arthralgia, macular rash (starts proximally and travels distally), lymphadenopathy (postauricular, occipital, cervical), soft palate petechiae. Complications: Orchitis, encephalitis, Guillain-Barré syndrome. If contracted during pregnancy, early miscarriage, congenital rubella syndrome (severe mental retardation, microcephaly, sensorineural deafness, cataract, glaucoma, microphthalmia, DM, IUGR, thrombocytopenia, haemolysis, PDA, pulmonary artery stenosis).

INVESTIGATIONS

FBC, atypical lymphocytes, ↓WCC (with relative lymphocytosis), ↓plts, rubella serology (acute infection, IgM, but may persist for 12 months. Rising IgG titres), PCR, swabs (upper respiratory). Blood, urine, CSF cultures and microscopy.

DISEASES

MANAGEMENT
Prevention with MMR vaccination. Treat complications accordingly.

Russell-Silver syndrome

📋 CLINICAL NOTES
Epidemiology: Rare. Aetiology/risk factors: Idiopathic, chromosomes 7,11,17 anomalies. Clinical features: Low birthweight, failure to thrive, right-left body asymmetry eg limb length discrepancy, hemihypertrophy, short stature, short phalanges, micrognathia, triangular-shaped head, café au lait spots, GORD, hydronephrosis, horseshoe kidneys. Complications: Hypoglycaemia, CKD, learning difficulties.

🔍 INVESTIGATIONS
Genetic studies, investigate for complications.

💊 MANAGEMENT
Family support, MDT approach, genetic counselling. Treat complications accordingly.

Salicylate poisoning

📋 CLINICAL NOTES
See *poisoning appendices*

Salivary gland obstruction

📋 CLINICAL NOTES
Epidemiology: Rare <40 years of age. Most commonly affects submandibular gland. Clinical features: Asymptomatic, intermittent salivary gland swelling, exacerbated by mastication.

🔍 INVESTIGATIONS
↑lipase, USS, sialogram, MR sialography, X-ray if stone is in floor of mouth.

💊 MANAGEMENT
Salivary gland massage, surgery.

Sarcoid

📋 CLINICAL NOTES
Granulomatous disease affecting multiple body systems. Epidemiology: Approx 16-19 in 10^5 UK prevalence. Peak presentatons 20s-30s. Aetiology/risk factors: F>M. ↑ African-Americans in rural areas. Unknown, familial, infective. Clinical features: Asymptomatic – bilateral hilar lymphadeno-pathy found on chest X-ray, cough, weight loss, fatigue, fever, SOB, rash. Complications: Hepatic and splenic infiltration, lupus pernio, erythema nodosum, uveitis, sicca syndrome, parotid gland enlargement, myocardial infiltration, arrhythmia, cardiomyopathy, cardiac failure, cranial nerve palsies, cerebral involvement, pituitary infiltration (hypopituitarism), spinal cord granuloma, bone infiltration, renal impairment, nephrocalcinosis, hypercalcaemia.

🔍 INVESTIGATIONS
FBC, atypical lymphocytes, anaemia of chronic disease, ↑ESR, ↑Ca^{2+}, ↑serum ACE (not specific), ↓aldosterone, chest X-ray (normal, bilateral hilar lymphadenopathy, pulmonary infiltration), pulmonary CT. Spirometry (restrictive defect), ↓gas transfer. Granuloma biopsy.

💊 MANAGEMENT
May spontaneously resolve, steroids, steroid-sparing agents eg methotrexate, azathioprine, infliximab, thalidomide; lung transplant.

Scabies

📋 CLINICAL NOTES
Epidemiology: Common. Aetiology/risk factors: Social deprivation, crowded conditions, nursing homes, winter, HIV. Skin contact for significant time. May be contracted from bedlinen, towels, furniture. Clinical features: Asymptomatic for one month unless previously infected. Pruritic skin lesions, papules, vesicles, burrows (≥15mm, flexures and fingerwebs, mite may be seen at one end), may look excoriated and eczematous. Complications: Secondary bacterial infection, super-infestation (Norwegian scabies confers mortality risk), eczema/psoriasis flare, erythroderma.

🔍 INVESTIGATIONS
Skin scraping.

💊 MANAGEMENT
Treat patient, close contacts and family at same time. Whole body permethrin 5% cream and repeat (in one week for classic scabies or twice/three times daily on consecutive days for Norwegian), malathion 0.5% second-line. Wash linen ≥50°C. Contact public health unit if institutional outbreak. Emollients/sedating antihistamines for pruritus. Pruritus may take three weeks to resolve after treatment; if persists for more than six weeks, consider treatment failure.

Scarlet fever (scarlatina)

📋 CLINICAL NOTES
Epidemiology: Peak incidence at age four years, spring and winter. Aetiology/risk factors: Group A streptococci (*Strep pyogenes*). Incubation one to seven days, infective for three weeks. Clinical features: Sore throat, fever (>38.3°C), malaise, headache, nausea, rash (day two to five of illness, starts on neck and face, then spreads), lymphadenopathy, red cheeks, strawberry tongue, red/purulent tonsils, tachycardia. Complications: Otitis media, sinusitis, quinsy, pneumonia, cerebral abscess, meningitis, osteomyelitis, skin desquamation, venous

DISEASES

sinus thrombosis, myocarditis, sepsis, rheumatic fever, glomerulonephritis.

INVESTIGATIONS

Not routinely required. FBC, U&E, throat swab (sensitive but not specific, eg may be commensal), antigen agglutination, ELISA, ASOT.

⬛ MANAGEMENT

Consider paracetamol/NSAIDs, fluids, antibiotics (10 days, penicillins or macrolides).

Scheuermann's disease

📖 CLINICAL NOTES

Osteochondrosis of vertebrae. Epidemiology: Teenagers. Aetiology/risk factors: Autosomal dominant. Clinical features: Kyphosis, back pain, spinal tenderness, tight hamstrings. Complications: Deformity, neurological involvement (rare).

INVESTIGATIONS

X-ray, MRI.

⬛ MANAGEMENT

Controversial. Some think no treatment required because disease usually follows a benign course with few adverse sequelae. Physiotherapy, brace, surgery.

Schistosomiasis (bilharzia)

📖 CLINICAL NOTES

Epidemiology: Common in Africa, India and South America. Aetiology/risk factors: Fluke, various species. Freshwater snail vector. Clinical features: Acute (Katayama fever) local dermatitis at site of entry, urticaria, pruritus, wheeze, cough, hepatosplenomegaly. Depending on subtype, fluke may migrate to bladder/mesenteric veins causing urinary tract disease (Schistosoma haematobium) – symptoms of UTI, haematuria, bladder calcification, risk of bladder SCC; or abdominal disease (S mansoni and S japonicum) – pain, diarrhoea and vomiting, portal hypertension. Complications: CNS involvement.

INVESTIGATIONS

Risk of false negative results with investigation less than three months before exposure. Eosinophilia, serology, urine/faecal microscopy, abdominal X-ray (bladder calcification), CT (abdomen and cerebral), ELISA.

⬛ MANAGEMENT

Predisolone and praziquantel.

Schizophrenia

📖 CLINICAL NOTES

Epidemiology: Lifetime risk about 1%. Aetiology/risk factors: Genetic (concordance in monozygotic twins >>dizygotic twins), environmental, viral infection, postpartum complications, cannabis use (especially potent forms such as skunk). Clinical features: Usually presents <30 years. Schneider's first-rank symptoms: Auditory hallucinations (third person – patient may recognise the voices – running commentry, thought broadcast), delusions of possesion of thought (thought insertion/ withdrawal), passivity (controlled movements, feelings), delusional perception (normal perception attached to delusional interpretation). Other features: Agitation, non-auditory (olfactory, visual, tactile) or second person hallucinations, paranoia, affective disturbance, apparent personality change. Negative symptoms: Lack of self-care, social withdrawal, loss of relationships/ employment. Patients may only present with negative symptoms. Complications: Increased risk of CVD and type-2 diabetes, self-harm, drug and alcohol abuse, harm to others, suicide, murder.

INVESTIGATIONS

Investigate to exclude an organic cause, eg FBC, U&E, LFT, TFT, calcium, glucose, septic screen, autoimmune screen (eg SLE), drug and alcohol screen, MRI (if first episode of psychosis – enlarged ventricles and temporal lobe anomalies are seen).

⬛ MANAGEMENT

Urgent early referral to specialist. Manage physical health needs including cardiovascular risk. Risk assessment including self-harm and harm to others. Consider rapid tranquillisation, admission, detention under mental health laws. CBT. Art therapy if negative symptoms. Family therapy. Insight therapy. Social support. Antipsychotic medication: Atypical antipsychotics first-line, clozapine if two different antipsychotics fail (regular FBC monitoring if on clozapine). Depot preparations if poor compliance. Patient and carers should be made aware of drug side-effects, which include akathisia, parkinsonism, oculogyric crisis, neuroleptic malignant syndrome. Procyclidine for oculogyric crisis, akathisia and tardive dyskinesia. Treat comorbidities including substance abuse. Community/social support/outreach teams. Regular follow-up and monitoring (consider trigger for acute episode, drug adherence, regular risk assessment), formulation of care plan including crisis management.

Sciatica

See also
— Cauda equina syndrome

📖 CLINICAL NOTES

Epidemiology: Common. Aetiology/risk factors: Disc herniation (commonly L5/S1 nerve roots), disc fissure, osteoarthritis, lateral recess stenosis, foraminal stenosis, trauma, seronegative arthritis eg ankylosing spondylitis, infection, Paget's disease of the bone, tumours, vascular anomalies. Clinical features: Unilateral pain, numbness, paraesthesia in distribution of sciatic nerve (buttock, thigh, knee, outer calf and outer foot), mild/no back pain, +ve straight leg raise (>90% sensitivity, low specificity <30%). May have nerve root compression – reduced power in corresponding motor root, reduced reflexes (eg S1 ankle jerk), reduced/absent sensation in corresponding dermatome, often L5/S1. *Red flag features with back pain:* Night pain, age <20 years, >50 years, immunodeficiency, thoracic pain, weight loss, saddle anaesthesia, bowel or bladder dysfunction, bilateral leg involvement, progressive weakness/neurological deficit, ED. Complications: Permanent neurological deficit, depression, chronic pain.

INVESTIGATIONS
Investigate if concerned about sinister cause, complications eg FBC, ESR, U&E, LFT, calcium, protein electrophoresis, PSA, urine (Bence-Jones), X-ray, MRI spine, nuclear medicine .

MANAGEMENT
Exclude sinister causes of back pain (eg infection, malignancy, trauma, cord compression). Immediate referral if cauda equina syndrome. Urgent referral for other red flags. Consider specialist referral/MRI if symptoms for more than six weeks. Analgesia, TCAs, gabapentin, mobilisation, avoid heavy lifting, physiotherapy within two weeks, epidural injection, surgery (for red flag causes and symptoms, severe symptoms). Surgery versus conservative treatment for disc herniation continues to be debated.

Scleritis
CLINICAL NOTES
Epidemiology: Rare. Aetiology/risk factors: Idiopathic, RA, SLE, ankylosing spondylitis, Reiter's syndrome, polyarteritis nodosa, Wegener's granulomatosis, Churg-Strauss syndrome, relapsing polychondritis, infection, trauma, sarcoid, malignancy. Clinical features: Red eye, pain, visual disturbance, photophobia, headache. Complications: Scleromalacia, scleromalacia perforans, iritis, retinal detachment, ischaemia, cataract, glaucoma.

INVESTIGATIONS
Investigate according to suspected underlying cause.

MANAGEMENT
Urgent referral to ophthalmologist, NSAIDS, high-dose oral steroids, steroid injections, treat underlying cause.

Scleroderma
CLINICAL NOTES
See *diffuse systemic sclerosis (diffuse scleroderma)*

Sclerosing cholangitis
CLINICAL NOTES
Epidemiology: M>F 7:3. Fifth decade. Prevalence varies. Aetiology/risk factors: Primary (idiopathic), IBD (75% cases, especially ulcerative colitis), chronic pancreatitis, retroperitoneal fibrosis, HIV, histiocytosis X, Sjögren's syndrome. Clinical features: Asymptomatic, abdominal pain, pruritus, cholestatic jaundice. Complications: Cholangitis, malignancy (cholangiocarcinoma).

INVESTIGATIONS
↑ALP, ↑ESR, ↑gamma GT, ANA, antismooth muscle antibody, antimitochondrial antibodies, bilirubinuria, USS, CT, magnetic resonance cholangiography, ERCP, percutaneous hepatic cholangiogram, biopsy.

MANAGEMENT
Fat-soluble vitamin replacement (A, D, E, K). Cholestyramine, ursodeoxycholic acid. Corticosteroids, ciclosporine, azathioprine. Biliary stents. Liver transplant (with colectomy if colitis).

Scoliosis
CLINICAL NOTES
Epidemiology: Three in 1,000 prevalence. Aetiology/risk factors: Idiopathic (F>M), traumatic, malignancy, osteoporosis, Friedreich's ataxia, polio, syrinx, muscular dystrophy, Marfan's syndrome, osteogenesis imperfecta. Clinical features: Asymptomatic, exclude tumour if pain is present. Complications: Reduced lung function, cardiac compromise, OA, functional disability.

INVESTIGATIONS
X-ray, MRI.

MANAGEMENT
Watch and wait, physiotherapy, cast, brace, surgery.

Seasonal affective disorder
CLINICAL NOTES
See *depression*

Seasonal allergic rhinitis (hayfever)
CLINICAL NOTES
Epidemiology: Up to 30% prevalence in UK. Most affected in June. Aetiology/risk factors: Pollen allergy. Clinical features: Sneezing, nasal discharge, itchy ears/eyes, wheeze. Complications: Reduced performance, eg school examinations.

INVESTIGATIONS
Mainly clinical diagnosis. Skin prick or RAST (specific IgE) may be performed.

MANAGEMENT

Allergen avoidance, antihistamines, nasal sprays (steroid – commence before allergic season, decongestants), oral decongestants (short-term use only due to risks of rhinitis medicamentosa and rebound symptoms), sodium cromoglycate eye drops, consider oral/depot corticosteroids.

Sebaceous cyst (epidermoid)

CLINICAL NOTES

Epidemiology: Common. Aetiology/risk factors: M>F. Idiopathic, associatd with Gardner's syndrome (FPC, osteomas). Clinical features: Firm skin lump, painless, superficial, mobile, central punctum. Complications: Infection, malodorous discharge, malignant change (very rare), rarely congenital scalp cysts communicate intracranially and leak CSF, increasing risk of meningitis.

INVESTIGATIONS

Diagnosis usually clinical.

MANAGEMENT

May resolve spontanously, no action, antibiotics if infected. Consider complete cyst excision with recurrent infections.

Seborrhoeic wart/keratosis

CLINICAL NOTES

Epidemiology: Common, benign. Aetiology/risk factors: Advancing age, light skin, idiopathic, some may be autosomal dominant, sun exposure, immunosuppression, adenocarcinoma (eg stomach). Clinical features: Warty, waxy, pigmented appearance, 'stuck to skin' appearance, well demarcated, 2-30mm. Especially on trunk.

INVESTIGATIONS

Diagnosis usually clinical.

MANAGEMENT

Reassurance, cryotherapy, cauterisation, curettage, excision biopsy when diagnosis in doubt.

Seborrhoeic dermatitis

CLINICAL NOTES

Epidemiology: Common, M>F. Aetiology/risk factors: Yeast, familial, humidity, winter/spring, stress, iatrogenic (eg lithium, gold, chlorpromazine, haloperidol), immunosuppression, Parkinson's disease, CCF. Clinical features: Dandruff, cradle cap, scaling in nasolabial folds. Complications: Exfoliative erythroderma, secondary bacterial infection.

INVESTIGATIONS

Scrapings.

MANAGEMENT

Antifungals (shampoo, creams), topical steroids if inflammatory component. Isotretinoin or keratolytics (salicylic acid, coal tar) if severe. Overnight oil treatment to soften scales in cradle cap.

Secondary hypertension

CLINICAL NOTES

See also

— *Essential hypertension*
— *Cushing's syndrome*
— *Hyperaldosteronism*
— *Liddle's syndrome*
— *Renal artery stenosis*
— *Coarctation of the aorta*

Epidemiology: About 5% hypertensive cases. Aetiology/risk factors: Coarctation of the aorta. Renal disease (chronic UTI, renal artery stenosis, polycystic kidney disease, diabetic nephropathy, hypertensive nephropathy, glomerulonephritis, retroperitoneal fibrosis). Endocrine disease (Conn's disease, Cushing's syndrome, phaeochromocytoma, acromegaly, hyperparathyroidism, hypercalcaemia). Iatrogenic (eg prednisolone). Clinical features: Consider if hypertension in a young patient or resistant hypertension, cushingoid, coarctation (systolic murmur LSE, may be heard at the back, radiofemoral delay), renal mass. Renal artery stenosis may be revealed by excessive fall in eGFR with ACE inhibitor/ARB.

INVESTIGATIONS

See *essential hypertension*. Consider ambulatory 24-hour BP if concerned about white coat effect. 24-hour urine collection for catecholamines/VMA, cortisol. Endocrine suppression tests, eg dexamethasone suppression test. Consider Conn's syndrome if K$^+$<3.5mmol/L (although K$^+$ may be normal), renal ultrasound/MRA/biopsy. Echocardiogram for coarctation and LVH.

MANAGEMENT

Treat underlying cause. See *essential hypertension*.

Septic arthritis

CLINICAL NOTES

Epidemiology: US studies – 20,000 cases suppurative arthritis per year (7.8 per 100,000 person-years) with similar figures for Europe. Aetiology/risk factors: Staphylococci, streptococci, Gram -ve bacteria (eg gonorrhoea), TB, fungal. Trauma, postoperative, DM, sickle cell anaemia (*salmonella spp*), immunosuppression. Clinical features: Acute pain, red and hot swollen joint, effusion, reduced ROM, malaise, fever, tachycardia. Complications: OA, joint destruction, septicaemia.

INVESTIGATIONS

FBC, CRP, blood cultures, X-ray, aspiration (pus, send

for MC&S, if prosthesis, aspiration should be carried out by a specialist).

☐ MANAGEMENT
Analgesia, empirical IV antibiotics until sensitivities known – flucloxacillin, benzylpenicillin, clindamycin, consider gentamicin, cefotaxime in children. Vancomycin if concerned about MRSA. Lavage, debridement (with biopsy for TB).

Sexually transmitted infections (STIs) and genital infections
See also
— *Pelvic inflammatory disease*

📋 CLINICAL NOTES
Chlamydia: Epidemiology: 4-11% female prevalence 15-25 years. Peak 16-19 years (F); 20-24 years (M). Clinical features: Asymptomatic (about 70-90% women, about 50% men, may remain asymptomatic for years), urethritis, epididymo-orchitis, balanitis, cervicitis. Sterile pyuria. Complications: PID, infertility, ectopic pregnancy, ophthalmia neonatorum, Reiter's disease, reactive arthritis. *Gonorrhoea:* Epidemiology: Increasing incidence. Clinical features: 50% asymptomatic carriage (including pharynx and rectum), discharge, dysuria, PID, reactive arthritis, Reiter's syndrome, gonococcal arthritis, disseminated gonorrhoea, ophthalmia neonatorum. *Trichomonas:* Flagellated protozoans. Clinical features: Odorous greenish frothy discharge, itching, pain. *Herpes simplex (HSV 1 and 2):* Either can cause genital sores. Can be spread through oro or genito-genital contact. Clinical features: 25% asymptomatic, painful fluid-filled blisters, episodic episodes or asymptomatic viral shedding. *Syphilis (primary):* Epidemiology: Increasing. HIV a risk factor. Clinical features: Primary syphilitic ulcer (primary chancre) 5-20mm, painless. Complications: x6 increased risk of contracting HIV. Secondary, tertiary and quarternary syphilis. *Warts:* Aetiology/risk factors: Commonly HPV types 6, 11. Clinical features: Vaginal/anal/penile. *Molluscum contagiosum:* Affecting genitals, usually STI. *Pubic lice:* Common. Cause itchy red spots. Complications: Eye infestation.

☾ INVESTIGATIONS
HVS, endocervical swabs, urine PCR for chlamydia, urethral and rectal swabs, viral swabs, HIV screen. Syphilis serology.

☐ MANAGEMENT
Consider referral to GUM clinic for safe sex education, contact tracing and full STI screen. *Chlamydia:* For uncomplicated cases: doxycycline 100mg orally twice a day for seven days or azithromycin 1g orally immediately. *Gonorrhoea:* Ceftriaxone 250mg IM immediately/cefixime 400mg orally immediately.

Trichomonas: Metronidazole 2g immediately/400mg orally twice a day for five days. *Syphilis:* Benzathine penicillin IM, azathioprine (immediate dose) or doxycycline 100mg orally twice a day for 14 days. *HSV:* NSAIDs, antivirals improve healing time. Consider prophylaxis. *Warts:* Podophyllotoxin, imiquimod, cautery, hyfrecation, surgery. *Pubic lice:* Malathion lotion.

Shingles (herpes zoster)

📋 CLINICAL NOTES
Epidemiology: One in five people have shingles at some time in their life. Most common >50 years. Aetiology/risk factors: Varicella zoster, may be triggered by stress, immunosuppression, eg CLL, steroids. Only occurs in those with previous infection with varicella zoster. Clinical features: Localised pain, fever, malaise, rash occurs few days later (dermatomal distribution, may affect more than one dermatome, thoracic and ophthalmic most common). Complications: Post-herpetic neuralgia (33%), secondary bacterial infection, facial palsy (Ramsay Hunt syndrome).

☾ INVESTIGATIONS
Diagnosis usually clinical, based on typical lesions in a single dermatome. Consider investigation according to suspected underlying cause.

☐ MANAGEMENT
Antivirals, analgesia. Post-herpetic. Consider anti-viral agents, eg aciclovir. *Neuralgia:* Simple analgesics, amitriptyline, gabapentin, carbamazepine, phenytoin, topical NSAIDs, topical lidocaine, topical capsaicin, TENS, ganglion ablation. Counsel patient on avoiding spread of virus to vulnerable people, eg pregnant women not exposed to chickenpox before, babies, those on chemotherapy or immunosuppressed, patients with chronic disease.

Sick euthyroid syndrome

📋 CLINICAL NOTES
Abnormal findings on TFT in setting of non-thyroid illness. Aetiology/risk factors: Systemic illness causing deranged TFTs.

☾ INVESTIGATIONS
Often low $TSH/T_3/T_4$ (also seen in pituitary failure).

☐ MANAGEMENT
No action, repeat tests when patient recovered.

Sick sinus syndrome

📋 CLINICAL NOTES
Fibrosis of SA node causing bradycardia and atrial tachyarrhythmia. Aetiology/risk factors: Advancing age (but may affect any age). Clinical

features: Asymptomatic, palpitations, pre-syncope. **Complications:** AF, atrial flutter, embolic disease, sinus arrest and syncope, cardiac failure, cardiac arrest.

INVESTIGATIONS
ECG – 12-lead and ambulatory. TFT, LFT, U&E, calcium. Echocardiogram.

MANAGEMENT
Antiarrhythmics, anticoagulation, ablation, pacemaker.

Sickle cell anaemia (HbS)

CLINICAL NOTES
Epidemiology: Most common haemoglobinopathy. ↑African-Caribbeans. **Aetiology/risk factors:** Genetic, autosomal recessive, (sickle cell trait offers partial protection against falciparum malaria). Amino acid substitution (glutamic acid to valine) on beta chain. **Complications:** Chronic haemolysis and pigment gallstones. *Vaso-occlusive crises:* Severe bone pain, triggered by dehydration, hypoxia, sepsis, cold climates. Avascular necrosis of the hip, dactylitis with resultant shortened fingers and toes. Priapism, CVA, splenic infarction leading to hyposplenism. *Sequestration crises:* Spleen, lung. *Aplastic crisis:* Secondary to parvovirus B19 infection. Invasive bacterial infections (*Strep pneumoniae, Haemophilus influenzae, Neisseria meningitidis*), salmonella spp osteomyelitis, septic arthritis. Renal papillary necrosis, fat embolism.

INVESTIGATIONS
Newborn screening, ↓Hb, Hb electrophoresis (HbS), reticulocytosis, Howell-Jolly bodies, target cells.

MANAGEMENT
Daily antibiotic prophylaxis, pneumococcal vaccine, influenza vaccine, folic acid. Crisis: treat infection, opiate analgesia, hyperhydration, oxygen, warming blanket, consider exchange transfusion (eg for CVA). Consider stem cell transplant.

Sideroblastic anaemia

CLINICAL NOTES
Epidemiology: 5-15% of all myelodysplastic syndromes. 70% of patients >50 years. **Aetiology/risk factors:** Hereditary (X-linked), myelodysplasia, myeloproliferative disorders eg CML, iatrogenic, chemotherapy, radiotherapy, alcoholism, lead poisoning. **Clinical features:** Asymptomatic, fatigue, hepatosplenomegaly. **Complications:** Iron overload (liver, endocrinopathy, cardiomyopathy), leukaemia.

INVESTIGATIONS
X-linked: Pancytopenia, ↓leukocyte ALP score. ↓MCV. ↑MCV if acquired. Film may show ring sideroblasts, anisocytosis, basophilic stippling (eg in lead poisoning).

MANAGEMENT
Treat underlying cause, vitamin B₆, transfusion.

Sinusitis (acute)

CLINICAL NOTES
Epidemiology: Common. **Aetiology/risk factors:** ↑In URTI, smoking, rhinitis, foreign body, dental infection, trauma, atopy, immunodeficiency including DM, Wegener's granulomatosis, Churg-Strauss syndrome, granulomatous diseases, immotile cilia. *Infective: Strep pneumoniae, Haemophilus influenzae, Moraxella catarrhalis.* **Clinical features:** Fever, facial pain (worse on coughing and leaning forward), nasal congestion, bloody purulent discharge, reduced sense of smell, trauma, headache, pain upper teeth, malaise, earache, halitosis. **Complications:** Facial and periorbital cellulitis, meningitis, bleeding, cerebral abscess, osteomyelitis, cavernous sinus thrombosis, sinocutaneous fistula, chronic sinusitis.

INVESTIGATIONS
CT when diagnosis uncertain, eg if suspect cancer. *Red flags:* Unilateral unpleasant or bloody discharge, or when complications.

MANAGEMENT
Address risk factors including smoking. Analgesia, NSAIDs, corticosteroid nasal spray, decongestant nasal spray (short-term only as rebound symptoms – rhinitis medicamentosa), antibiotics (amoxicillin, doxycycline, macrolides) if infection severe, more than five days, complications, comorbidities, elderly.

Sinusitis (chronic)

CLINICAL NOTES
More than 12 weeks. **Epidemiology:** Complication of acute sinusitis. **Aetiology/risk factors:** Gram -ve bacteria, staphylococci, fungi (↑in immunodeficiency, DM, allergic bronchopulmonary aspergillosis). May be associated with nasal polyps. **Clinical features:** Similar to low-grade acute sinusitis. **Complications:** Mucocele, cavernous sinus thrombosis, depression, CNS invasion, invasive fungal disease (*acute:* Fever, headaches, cough, altered mental state, mucosal ulceration or chronic).Mycetoma (cheesy clay-like nasal discharge), granulomatous invasive fungal disease (may present with exophthalmos), death.

INVESTIGATIONS
Swabs, CT, MRI.

MANAGEMENT
Address risk factors including smoking, nasal steroids, dental hygiene, oral steroids. Long-term antibiotics, surgery. Fungal sinusitis requires antifungal agents and surgical intervention.

Sjögren's syndrome

 CLINICAL NOTES

Epidemiology: 0.5-3 % prevalence. F>M (9:1). Peak fourth/fifth decades. Aetiology/risk factors: Primary autoimmune, may be associated with other auto-immune diseases. Clinical features and complications: Dry eyes/mouth/skin, cough, halitosis, dental caries, corneal ulcers, salivary gland enlargement, vaginal dryness, dyspareunia, fatigue, myalgia, Jaccoud's arthropathy, neuropathy, sterile cystitis, lymphoma. Sjögren's syndrome in pregnancy carries a risk of congenital heart block (high risk if anti-Ro antibodies) and neonatal lupus.

CJ **INVESTIGATIONS**

Anti-Ro (60% sensitivity) and anti-La (40% sensitivity) antibodies, Schirmer's tear test, sialometry, salivary gland biopsy.

MANAGEMENT

Lubricants, steroids, cyclophosphamide, azathioprine, hydroxychloroquine. Fetal cardiac complications may respond to antenatal dexamethasone. Regular monitoring.

Slapped cheek syndrome

 CLINICAL NOTES

See *fifth disease*

Sleep apnoea

CLINICAL NOTES

Epidemiology: M>F. About 3% men. Aetiology/risk factors: Smoking, obesity, alcohol, age, iatrogenic (eg benzodiazepines), hypothyroidism, acromegaly, large tonsils and adenoids. Clinical features: Intermittent repeated apnoeas, snoring, daytime sleepiness, headaches. Complications: Pulmonary hypertension, cor pulmonale, hypertension, relationship difficulties, accidents (e.g excess risk of car accidents).

CJ **INVESTIGATIONS**

Epworth Sleepiness Scale. Polysomnography, echocardiogram. Investigate according to suspected underlying cause.

MANAGEMENT

Weight loss, smoke/alcohol cessation, treat other underlying causes, eg thyroid disease. Nasal CPAP, mouth devices, surgery. Advice regarding occupational risk, eg driving.

Slipped upper femoral epiphysis (SUFE)

 CLINICAL NOTES

Epidemiology: M>F, 12-15 years. Two in 10^5 incidence. Aetiology/risk factors: Obesity, poor skeletal maturation.

Clinical features: Leg held in external rotation (worse on hip flexion), affected leg shorter than unaffected side, pain (mild-moderate, worse on movement), limp, may not be able to bear weight (poor prognostic sign), may be bilateral (20%), reduced abduction, reduced internal rotation. Complications: Avascular necrosis, OA, deformity, chondrolysis.

CJ **INVESTIGATIONS**

X-ray (frog-leg view), MRI.

MANAGEMENT

Analgesia, weight control, surgery.

Small bowel bacterial overgrowth

CLINICAL NOTES

Aetiology/risk factors: Post-surgery, diverticulosis, strictures, IBD, fistulae, malignancy, tropical sprue, scleroderma, hypogammaglobulinaemia, immunodeficiency, DM, iatrogenic, age. *E coli* most common cause. Clinical features: Asymptomatic, diarrhoea, abdominal pain, bloating. Complications: Malabsorption (often vitamin B_{12}), osteoporosis, anaemia.

CJ **INVESTIGATIONS**

FBC, ↓vitamin B_{12}, →/↑folate, breath test (glucose/14C-xylose [sensitive and specific]/14C-glycholate), stool-reducing substances, small bowel imaging, culture of aspiration contents.

MANAGEMENT

Treat underlying cause and vitamin deficiency, cholestyramine, broad-spectrum antibiotics.

Small bowel obstruction

CLINICAL NOTES

Epidemiology: 5% acute hospital admissions. About 10% mortality. Aetiology/risk factors: Adhesions, strangulated/incarcerated hernia, malignancy, strictures, gallstone, volvulus, faeces, sepsis, electrolyte disturbance, intussusception, meconium. Clinical features: Colicky abdominal pain, vomiting, inability to pass stool or flatus, abdominal distension, high-pitched bowel sounds (early), absent bowel sounds (late), dehydration, hypotension. Complications: Bowel oedema, ischaemia (fever, tachycardia), gangrene, perforation, peritonitis, death.

CJ **INVESTIGATIONS**

↑WCC/lactate/CRP (bowel ischaemia), ↑amylase, ↓pH, ↓K^+, ↓albumin, ↑eGFR, ↑urea. Supine abdominal X-ray, erect chest X-ray (air under diaphragm), contrast CT.

MANAGEMENT

Urgent surgical referral. Treat cause; 75% adhesion-

DISEASES

related obstruction resolves with conservative management (IV fluids, NBM, analgesia, nasogastric tube, fluid management). Peritonitis, incarcerated hernia, ischaemia, fever, tachycardia, ↑WCC, palpable mass require surgical management.

Solar (actinic) keratosis

 CLINICAL NOTES
Epidemiology: Common. Aetiology/risk factors: ↑Skin types 1 and 2, age, M>F. UV exposure, immunosuppression. Clinical features: Scaly rough brown/red/yellow lesions. May become inflamed. Complications: 10% potential for malignancy (SCC).

🔍 **INVESTIGATIONS**
Biopsy if concerned regarding malignancy.

💊 **MANAGEMENT**
Emollients, sun block, topical diclofenac (3%), 5FU twice a day for three to eight weeks (three to four weeks for face, initially causes inflammatory flare), combination 0.5% fluorouracil and 10% salicylic acid, photodynamic therapy, curettage, cryotherapy. Monitor for complications.

Spina bifida

 CLINICAL NOTES
Vertebral arch dys/agenesis. Epidemiology: Declining in the UK. Aetiology/risk factors: Familial, maternal folic acid deficiency (diet, malabsorption, folate antagonists, eg long-term trimethoprim, methotrexate), Down's syndrome, Edward's syndrome, Patau syndrome, fetal alcohol syndrome, maternal DM. Clinical features: May see tuft of hair, cyst, hypopigmentation, sinus or haemangioma over defect. LMN signs in lower limbs, limb asymmetry, gluteal cleft asymmetry, scoliosis. Occulta: Epidemiology: Very common. Normal skin overlying defect. Cystica (open): Meningocele (meninges mass overlying defect with no neural tissue), myelomeningocele (containing spinal tissue, may be associated with Arnold-Chiari malformation), rachi-schisis (large severe spinal defect), anencephaly (partial agenesis brain and skull). Complications: Bowel and bladder dysfunction, back pain, meningitis, hydrocephalus, pressure sores, UTI, constipation.

🔍 **INVESTIGATIONS**
Maternal alpha-fetoprotein (16-18 weeks), amniotic fluid analysis for acetylcholinesterase, antenatal USS, MRI indicated if neurological abnormality, urodynamics.

💊 **MANAGEMENT**
Prevention: Folic acid supplements (400 microgram once a day in pregnancy, higher doses [5mg] if at risk). Occulta: No treatment. MDT approach. Family support. Physiotherapy, OT, braces (watch for pressure ulcers),

self-catheterisation, bowel regimen. Surgery: defect repair (may offer fetal surgery), ventriculoperitoneal shunt, craniotomy for Arnold-Chiari malformation, spinal fusion, osteotomy.

Spinal canal stenosis

 CLINICAL NOTES
Aetiology/risk factors: Congenital, trauma, spondylolisthesis, ankylosing spondylitis, OA, disc degeneration, achondroplasia, Paget's disease of the bone, malignancy. Clinical features: Spinal claudication (exertional or on standing). Calf pain, paraesthesia or numbness. May be bilateral or unilateral. Complications: Cauda equina compression.

🔍 **INVESTIGATIONS**
X-ray, MRI, CT myelogram.

💊 **MANAGEMENT**
NSAIDs, corticosteroids, amitriptyline, gabapentin, physiotherapy, corset, epidural injections, consider surgery.

Spinal cord compression (metastatic)

See also
 — Cauda equina syndrome
 — Spinal canal stenosis

 CLINICAL NOTES
Clinical features: Spinal pain (may be anywhere in spine), thoracic pain is often a sinister symptom. Pain is progressive and pervasive, may be worse with coughing, sneezing and movement. May waken patient from sleep. Radiculopathy, bladder/bowel dysfunction, limb weakness, sensory level, saddle anaesthesia, new abnormal neurological signs.

🔍 **INVESTIGATIONS**
Full spine MRI unless contraindicated. Myelography. CT may be used in treatment planning.

💊 **MANAGEMENT**
Warn cancer patients (especially high-risk cancers, eg prostate, breast, lung) about risk of spinal cord compression. Immediate referral to secondary care. Analgesia, dexamethasone, radiotherapy, spinal stabilisation, surgery. Monitor cardiorespiratory function for DVT and pressure sores. Consider urinary catheterisation, bowel regimen, bisphosphonates.

Squamous cell carcinoma (skin)

 CLINICAL NOTES
Epidemiology: Common. M>F. Aetiology/risk factors: Age, white race, UV exposure, immunosuppression,

soot, tar, skin types 1 and 2, chronic ulcers (Marjolin's), Bowen's disease, solar/actinic keratosis. Clinical features: Ulcerated crusted lesion that does not heal, sun-exposed distribution. Complications: Metastases, infection.

 INVESTIGATIONS

Excision/punch biopsy, CT/MRI.

 MANAGEMENT

Curettage, cryotherapy, phototherapy, radiotherapy, surgery, avoid sun exposure.

Steatohepatitis

📋 **CLINICAL NOTES**

See *fatty liver (steatosis) and steatohepatitis*

Steatosis

📋 **CLINICAL NOTES**

See *fatty liver (steatosis) and steatohepatitis*

Stevens-Johnson syndrome

📋 **CLINICAL NOTES**

Epidemiology: Rare. F>M. Aetiology/risk factors: Infection (eg streptococcus, mycoplasma, herpes, EBV, HIV, influenza, fungal), iatrogenic (eg penicillins, OCP, sulfonamides, phenytoin, NSAIDs), lymphoma, radiotherapy. Clinical features: Stevens-Johnson syndrome is considered a severe form of erythema multiforme. Fever, sore throat, lesions (mucosa and skin, develop into tense bullae), tachycardia, hypotension, necrosis, sloughing. Complications: Secondary bacterial infection, corneal ulceration, blindness, GI necrosis, pulmonary necrosis, oesophageal stricture, vaginal stenosis, renal failure, seizures, coma, death (5%).

 INVESTIGATIONS

FBC, U&E, LFT, blood cultures, serology, biopsy.

 MANAGEMENT

Treat cause, supportive management (IVI, nasogastric/parenteral feeds, central line), immunoglobulins.

Stokes-Adams attack

📋 **CLINICAL NOTES**

See *Signs & Symptoms, syncope*

Strabismus

📋 **CLINICAL NOTES**

Epidemiology: 2% children, 5% amblyopia. Commonly 18-36 months. Aetiology/risk factors: Idiopathic, familial, prematurity, cerebral palsy, CVA, Guillain-Barré syndrome, chromosomal anomalies (trisomy 21), familial,

severe longsightedness, trauma, tumour (including retinoblastoma), congenital chorioretinitis, toxocara, Graves' eye disease, DM. Clinical features: Four different types. *Inwards*: Esotropia. *Outwards:* Exotropia. *Upwards*: Hypertropia. *Downwards*: Hypotropia. Complications: Altered binocular vision, diplopia, amblyopia.

📿 **INVESTIGATIONS**

Cover test, acuity test, consider CT.

💊 **MANAGEMENT**

Treat underlying cause. Eye patch over good eye to minimise risk of amblyopia in weaker eye. Spectacles, botulinum toxin, surgery.

Strongyloides stercoralis

📋 **CLINICAL NOTES**

Roundworm (soil-dwelling parasitic nematode). Aetiology/risk factors: Infection commonly associated with rural areas, institutions, insanitary conditions. Clinical features: Asymptomatic, weight loss, urticaria, dermatitis, diarrhoea, wheeze, dyspnoea, cough. Complications: Malabsorption, bowel obstruction and perforation, sepsis (especially if immunocompromised), haemoptysis, respiratory failure, meningism, multiorgan failure, anaemia, thrombocytopenia.

📿 **INVESTIGATIONS**

Eosinophilia, Hb, plts, IgE, clotting screen, stool microscopy, serology.

💊 **MANAGEMENT**

Steroids may cause fatality. Anthelminthic therapy. Treat complications accordingly.

Sturge-Weber syndrome

📋 **CLINICAL NOTES**

Epidemiology: Incidence one in 50,000 live births. Aetiology/risk factors: Not known. Clinical features: Port wine stain, intracerebral haemangioma. Complications: Focal neurology, eg hemiparesis. Seizures, glaucoma, learning difficulties.

📿 **INVESTIGATIONS**

Skull X-ray, cerebral calcification, MRI/MRA, IOP.

💊 **MANAGEMENT**

Anticonvulsants, neurosurgical intervention may be required, treat glaucoma, laser for port wine stain.

Stye (hordeolum)

📋 **CLINICAL NOTES**

Epidemiology: Common. Clinical features: *Internal:* Meibomian gland infection. *External:* Lash follicle infection. Painful lid swelling often staphylococcal.

⚕ MANAGEMENT
May resolve spontaneously. *Internal:* Topical antibiotics, incision and curettage. *External:* Compresses, topical antibiotics, lash epilation.

Subarachnoid haemorrhage (SAH)

📖 CLINICAL NOTES
Epidemiology: About 15 in 10^6. F>M. Aetiology/risk factors: Smoking, hypertension, coagulopathy, berry aneurysm (sporadic, familial, associated with PCKD, collagen disorders, coarctation of the aorta), congenital/mycotic aneurysm, arteriovenous malformation. Clinical features: +/– warning headaches, neck stiffness, severe occipital headache, visual disturbance, nausea, vomiting, collapse, seizure, intraocular haemorrhage, papilloedema, false localising signs (third nerve palsy if posterior communicating artery aneurysm), ↓GCS. Complications: Rebleeding (30% risk during initial period), permanent neurological deficit, death (90% deaths occur in first month).

⚕ INVESTIGATIONS
ECG (inverted T waves), CT/MRI, lumbar puncture (if imaging –ve, xanthochromia confirms SAH), CT/MR angiography, cerebral angiography.

⚕ MANAGEMENT
Avoid hypotension as risk of cerebral hypoperfusion, hydration, pain control, vasodilators (nimodipine), clipping or coiling of aneurysm, rest. Screening (if two or more first-degree relatives with SAH).

Subconjunctival haemorrhage

📖 CLINICAL NOTES
Empidemiology: Common. Aetiology/risk factors: Spontaneous, coughing, sneezing, clotting disorder, trauma. Clinical features: Bleeding beneath conjunctiva, normal vision, usually painless.

⚕ INVESTIGATIONS
Consider checking INR/clotting screening and cerebral imaging if recurrent, bilateral or headache.

⚕ MANAGEMENT
No action, consider specialist referral if traumatic or recurrent.

Subdural haemorrhage

📖 CLINICAL NOTES
Aetiology/risk factors: Trauma, coagulopathy, advancing age, chronic alcohol abuse, cerebral tumour. Clinical features: Often slow decline in cognition and

speech, headache, change in personality with chronic haemorrhage, altered balance, focal neurological signs. Complications: Altered conciousness, ↑ICP, false localising neurological signs, seizure, death.

⚕ INVESTIGATIONS
CT/MRI.

⚕ MANAGEMENT
Urgent referral, consider clot evacuation, neuro-rehabilitation.

Superior vena cava obstruction (SVCO)

📖 CLINICAL NOTES
Aetiology/risk factors: Lung malignancy (80% of cases), lymphoma, aortic aneurysm, goitre, thrombophilia. Clinical features: Evolves over a number of weeks, cough, headache, SOB, pre-syncope, oedematous face (periorbital oedema, engorged conjunctivae) and upper body, cyanosis, dilated upper body and neck veins, prominent collateral venous circulation. Symptoms worse on cough/bending forwards. Complications: Syncope, stridor, cerebral oedema.

⚕ INVESTIGATIONS
Chest X-ray, CT, venography.

⚕ MANAGEMENT
Airway resuscitation, oxygen, nurse patient upright, high-dose dexamethasone (eg 16mg once a day), diuretics, thrombolysis, stent (self-expanding endoprosthesis), radiotherapy, chemotherapy.

Syndrome of inappropriate anti-diuretic hormone hypersecretion (SIADH)

📖 CLINICAL NOTES
Epidemiology: Common. F>M. Aetiology/risk factors: Head injury, SAH, cerebral abscess, cerebral sarcoid, ↑ICP, Guillain-Barré syndrome, malignancy (eg brain, lung, pancreas, leukaemia, lymphoma), empyema, pulmonary abscess, pulmonary fibrosis, COPD, artificial ventilation, acute intermittent porphyria, bronchiolitis, iatrogenic (eg thiazide diuretics, NSAIDs, TCAs, nicotine, carbamazepine, phenothiazines, some chemotherapeutic agents), surgery. Clinical features: Should only be diagnosed if euvolaemic and in absence of hypotension, oedema, pain, cardiac failure, liver dysfunction, renal dysfunction or thyroid dysfunction. Often asymptomatic, concentrated urine, agitation, nausea and vomiting, malaise, headache, anorexia, cramps, weakness. Complications: Cerebral oedema, falls, seizure, may cause death (significant mortality risk if serum sodium <130mmol/L).

INVESTIGATIONS

↓Na⁺,plasma cortisol normal, eGFR normal, adrenal function (normal short Synacthen® test). Urine osmolality usually >200mosm/kg, plasma <280mosm/kg, urine sodium usually >30mmol/L.

MANAGEMENT

Treat underlying cause. *Severe:* Hypertonic saline IV, furosemide. *Mild-moderate:* Fluid restriction for a few days. May require demeclocycline (to render kidneys insensitive to ADH). Overzealous correction may cause central pontine myelinolysis.

Syphilis

📅 CLINICAL NOTES

See *sexually transmitted infection and genital infections*

Syringoma

📅 CLINICAL NOTES

Epidemiology: F>M. Starts during teens. *Clinical features:* Benign sweat duct tumours, especially around eyes (may be confused with xanthelasma), smooth yellow/skin-coloured papules.

⌀ INVESTIGATIONS

Clinical diagnosis, biopsy if diagnostic uncertainty.

🗂 MANAGEMENT

Cosmetic surgery.

Syringomyelia/syringobulbia

📅 CLINICAL NOTES

Spinal cord or brainstem cyst. *Aetiology/risk factors:* Idiopathic, associated with Arnold-Chiari malformation, spinal cord tumours, trauma, post-meningitis, tethered spinal cord syndrome. *Clinical features:* Limb weakness, stiffness or pain, facial pain and sensory changes, speech and swallowing difficulties, bowel and bladder dysfunction. *Syringomyelia:* LMN signs and ↓pain and temperature sensation in upper limbs and chest. UMN signs in lower limbs. *Lesions C8/T1:* Horner's syndrome. *Lesions C5 or above:* Nystagmus. Lhermitte's sign. Reduced or excess sweating. Hands swollen, cyanotic, ulcerated. Charcot's joints, kyphoscoliosis, cervical vertebrae fusion, sternal anomalies, cervical ribs. *Syringobulbia:* Nystagmus, Horner's syndrome, bulbar palsy, dissociated facial sensory loss.

⌀ INVESTIGATIONS

MRI.

🗂 MANAGEMENT

Conservative, drainage, surgery (eg treat underlying cause, shunt. Physiotherapy, OT, mobility aids, self-catheterisation.

Systemic lupus erythematosus (SLE)

📅 CLINICAL NOTES

Epidemiology: F>M. Peak onset 14-50 years. *Aetiology/ risk factors:* Autoimmune, genetic, iatrogenic (predilection for lungs). Implicated drugs include hydralazine, isoniazid, procainamide, beta-blockers, phenytoin, COC, tetracyclines, penicillin. Klinefelter's syndrome. *Clinical features:* Fever, malaise, fatigue, skin (photosensitive facial butterfly rash, vasculitis, scarring alopecia, Raynaud's phenomenon, livedo reticularis, subcutaneous nodules, bullae, discoid lupus, telangiectasia), joint pains (non-erosive arthritis [Jaccoud's arthropathy], deformity), muscle pains, oral ulceration. *Complications:* CNS (headaches, psychosis, seizures), pleural effusions, cardiac (pericarditis, pericardial effusions, myocarditis, cardiac failure, Libman-Sacks endocarditis, accelerated CHD, MI), renal (glomerulonephritis, nephrotic syndrome, proteinuria, haematuria), haematological (anaemia of chronic disease, haemolysis, lymphadenopathy, splenomegaly), eyes (sicca syndrome, haemorrhages, papilloedema), three to five times mortality rate of normal population (usual cause of death renal, cardiovascular, infections), miscarriage, VTE.

⌀ INVESTIGATIONS

FBC (anaemia of chronic disease, pancytopenia), atypical lymphocytes, ↓lymphocytes, U&E, LFT, ESR, CRP, ENA, ANA (95%, poor PPV for SLE), anti double-stranded DNA (specific, 60% sensitive, can be used for monitoring, may be positive in quiescent disease, associated with lupus nephritis and CNS disease), anti-Sm (anti-Smith antibodies, an ANA, specific, 30% sensitive for SLE, associated with lupus nephritis). Anticardiolipin antibodies, lupus anti-coagulant, anti-Ro (risk of neonatal lupus and congenital heart block), antihistone antibodies, anti-La antibodies, antimitochondrial antibodies, anti-U1 RNP antibodies. Coombs' test. Urinalysis (non-visible haematuria, protein), ACR, chest X-ray. *Disease monitoring:* Anti double-stranded DNA, low C3, low C4, ESR raised in active disease, CRP often normal (unless infection, arthritis, pericarditis, pleurisy).

🗂 MANAGEMENT

Education, refer urgently if cardiorenal involvement, UV light, sun block, hydroxychloroquine (with annual optician review), systemic steroids for flare, methotrexate, azathioprine, cyclophosphamide, rituximab, mycophenolate mofetil, cardiorenal risk assessment (maintain BP <130/80mmHg), low-dose aspirin for pregnant women.

Tay-Sachs disease (classic type)

📅 CLINICAL NOTES

Lipid storage disease affecting nerve tissue.

DISEASES

Epidemiology: Eastern Europe, Ashkenazi Jews, rare. M=F. Juvenile and late-onset types also occur. Aetiology/ risk factors: Beta-hexosaminidase deficiency. Autosomal recessive. Clinical features: Early childhood (three to six months) – hypotonia (early), deafness, blindness, dysphagia, exaggerated reflexes, seizures, dementia, macular cherry red spots. Complications: Death by about four years.

INVESTIGATIONS
Enzyme assay.

MANAGEMENT
Seizure control, genetic counselling.

Temporomandibular joint dysfunction

CLINICAL NOTES
Epidemiology: F>M. Aetiology/risk factors: Idiopathic, bruxism, trauma, slipped disc, OA, RA, overchewing. Clinical features: Headache, pain, dental malocclusion, jaw clicking, trismus, tinnitus. Complications: Jaw dislocation.

INVESTIGATIONS
ESR if concerned regarding temporal arteritis. X-ray not usually helpful, MRI.

MANAGEMENT
Analgesia, soft diet, low-dose amitriptyline, relaxation, avoid jaw stress, physiotherapy, occlusal splints, intra-articular steroids, botulinum injections (muscles of mastication). Surgery.

Temporal (giant cell) arteritis

CLINICAL NOTES
Epidemiology: Most common vasculitis. Aetiology/ risk factors: More in sixth decade. F>M Clinical features: +/– fever, fatigue, malaise, headache (may be severe, temporal), jaw claudication, scalp tenderness, may have symptoms of polymyalgia rheumatica, tender pulseless temporal arteries. Complications: Visual loss, aortitis, aortic aneurysm.

INVESTIGATIONS
FBC (normochromic normocytic anaemia, ↑plts), ↑ESR (may be normal if recurrent disease), ↑CRP, ↑ALP (predominantly liver isoenzyme), temporal artery biopsy (may be normal especially if on steroids), tendonitis.

MANAGEMENT
Systemic steroids, prednisolone (starting dose 40-60mg once a day, tapering slowly, eg over two years), bisphosphonates, steroid counselling, consider steroid-sparing drugs, monitoring (including glucose and BP).

Tendonitis

CLINICAL NOTES
Epidemiology: Common. Aetiology/risk factors: Idiopathic, repetitive use, overuse, tear, calcific. Clinical features: Pain, tenderness, swelling, crepitus (as tendon moves through sheath). Complications: Disuse atrophy of muscles, tendon rupture, chronic pain.

INVESTIGATIONS
Consider X-ray, USS, MRI.

MANAGEMENT
Rest, ice, physiotherapy, tendon strapping, NSAIDs, ultrasound therapy, steroid injection around tendon, surgery.

Tennis elbow (lateral epicondylitis)

CLINICAL NOTES
Epidemiology: Five to nine times more common than golfer's elbow. Aetiology/risk factors: Over/repetitive use. Clinical features: Pain and tender lateral epicondyle, pain on resisted extension of middle finger or wrist, pain on lifting an object, eg a chair, with outstretched hand. Complications: Distal radiation may imply involvement of posterior interosseous nerve, OA.

INVESTIGATIONS
Diagnosis usually made on clinical grounds.

MANAGEMENT
Avoid trigger. Rest, ice, NSAIDs, passive wrist exercises progressing to resisted movements, physiotherapy (more effective than steroid injections at one year), steroid injections – short-term benefit but high recurrence rate.

Tension pneumothorax

CLINICAL NOTES
See *pneumothorax*

Testicular cancer

CLINICAL NOTES
Epidemiology: Two in 10^5 per year (non-age adjusted). Incidence rising. 95% germ cell – teratomas, peak 20-30 years, seminomas 30-50 years, combined cell type tumours. 5% non-germ cell (Leydig cell, sertoli cell, lymphoma, leukaemia, metastases). Aetiology/risk factors: Cryptorchidism (x10 risk), genetic (chromosome 12), family history, sexual activity at early age, white race, oestrogens, infertility, testicular atrophy, maternal smoking, sedentary lifestyle. Some suggestion these may also be risk factors – vasectomy, torsion, mumps orchitis, early puberty. Clinical features: Testicular swelling, 75% painless, hydrocoele, lymphadenopathy, back/abdominal pain, gynaecomastia, infertility (may present with this).

Complications: Metastases (lymph nodes, retroperitoneal, pulmonary, brain), ureteric obstruction, retrograde ejaculation.

INVESTIGATIONS
HCG (diagnosis, prognosis, monitoring, may be raised in seminoma and 50% teratoma), AFP (case finding, prognosis, monitoring, raised in 70% undifferentiated/intermediate malignant teratomas, not raised in pure seminoma), LDH, placental ALP, USS, CT, MRI, nodal biopsy.

MANAGEMENT
Radical inguinal orchiectomy and adjuvant radiotherapy/chemotherapy depending on stage and tumour type, very high cure rates (90-95%).

Testicular torsion

CLINICAL NOTES
Epidemiology: One in 4,000 <25 years. Two peaks, within first year of life or puberty. Aetiology/risk factors: Idiopathic, trauma, exercise. Clinical features: Acute unilateral scrotal pain, may wake from sleep, lower abdominal pain, vomiting, tender swollen testicle, testicle may be sitting higher and horizontally in scrotum (pain not relieved on elevation – Prehn's sign), inflammation, neonatal (hard enlarged testis, blue scrotum). Complications: Testicular infarction, infertility.

INVESTIGATIONS
Doppler ultrasound (88% sensitive, 90% specific).

MANAGEMENT
Urgent surgical intervention, surgery (both testicles fixed); if testicle non-viable, orchidectomy, prosthesis and contralateral fixation, fertility assistance.

Tetanus

CLINICAL NOTES
Aetiology/risk factors: C tetani toxin (eg found in soil/animal faeces), incubation three to 21 days. Bacteria usually enters through dirty wound. Clinical features: Fever, painful muscle spasms (lockjaw, neck, dysphagia, respiratory muscles, abdominal and back). Complications: Respiratory compromise, death.

INVESTIGATIONS
Diagnosis made clinically.

MANAGEMENT
Clean and treat wound. Penicillin and metronidazole or tetracycline. If tetanus-prone wound, offer tetanus vaccination if not had five throughout life. Tetanus immunoglobulin if wound particularly dirty. Anticonvulsants and muscle relaxants for spasms.

Dantrolene, vecuronium. Infection requires respiratory support and intensive care.

Thalassaemia

CLINICAL NOTES
Alpha thalassaemia: Aetiology/risk factors: South-east Asian, Middle Eastern decent. Major: No alpha chains (Hb Barts), incompatible with life, may present with fetal hydops in utero. Trait: Clinical picture depends on number of missing alpha chains; may be asymptomatic or anaemic with ↓MCV and splenomegaly. Beta thalassaemia: Aetiology/risk factors: Mediterranean and Asian decent. Major: No beta chains (normal fetal Hb as this is 2alpha2gamma). Normal adult Hb is 2alpha2beta hence people become symptomatic when fetal Hb switches to adult Hb – anaemia, failure to thrive, jaundice, hepatosplenomegaly, extramedullary haemopoiesis, frontal bossing, heart failure, death. Trait: Common, mild anaemia, lower MCV than would be expected for iron deficiency anaemia .

INVESTIGATIONS
↓Hb, ↓MCV, film (anisocytosis, teardrop cells, target cells, elliptocytes, basophilic stippling, haemolysis), iron studies, HbA_2. Hb electrophoresis.

MANAGEMENT
Alpha thalassaemia: May require transfusions, folic acid and iron chelation depending on severity.
Beta thalassaemia: Major: Treat with regular folate supplements, lifelong transfusions. Iron chelators to prevent iron overload. Ascorbic acid. Splenectomy, bone marrow transplant. Trait: May require transfusions, folic acid and iron chelation depending on severity.

Thoraco-abdominal aortic aneurysm

CLINICAL NOTES
Aetiology/risk factors: Syphilis, Marfan's syndrome, hypertension, atherosclerosis. Clinical features: Asymptomatic, chest pain radiating to back. Complications: Rupture, dissection, AR, compression of trachaea/oesophagus, fistulae, recurrent laryngeal nerve palsy.

INVESTIGATIONS
Chest X-ray, echocardiogram, CT, aortography.

MANAGEMENT
Monitoring (ultrasound), surgical repair (≥4.5-5cm at aortic sinus or ascending aorta or rapid increase in size).

Threadworms (pinworms)

CLINICAL NOTES
Epidemiology: Most common helminthic infection in UK. 50% childhood risk. Adult worms live about

six weeks. Females lay up to 15,000 eggs in perianal region per night. Aetiology/risk factors: Eggs transfered by faeco-oral route. Eggs may survive for two weeks in bedding/clothes or on toys. Clinical features: Asymptomatic, perianal/vaginal pruritus. Complications: Reinfection, distress, excoriated skin and secondary bacterial infection. Liver, lung, uterine and peritoneal worms – but very rare.

 INVESTIGATIONS

Eosinophilia, IgE. Adhesive tape test for eggs.

MANAGEMENT

Hygiene, wash bedlinen, clothes, toys. Thorough vacuuming including mattresses, damp-dusting, treat household contacts. Mebendazole (only use if aged more than two years) or piperazine (may be used from three months of age) kill worms, not eggs, repeat dose after two weeks.

Thrombophilias

CLINICAL NOTES

Factor V Leiden: Protein C resistance. Epidemiology: about one in 20 prevalence. Aetiology/risk factors: Genetic, autosomal dominant. Clinical features: VTE about x5 risk for heterozygotes, x50-80 risk for homozygotes. Eg recurrent DVT/PE/miscarriage. *Protein S deficiency:* Epidemiology: About one in 50 prevalence. Clinical features: About x10 risk VTE. *Protein C deficiency:* Epidemiology: About one in 300. Clinical features: Up to x15 VTE risk. *Antithrombin III deficiency:* Epidemiology: About one in 500 prevalence. Reduced levels also seen in nephrotic syndrome. Clinical features: Up to x50 VTE risk. *Prothrombin 20210A mutation.* Epidemiology: About one in 50 prevalence. Clinical features: about x3 risk VTE.

INVESTIGATIONS

Thrombophilia screen (should not be performed if anticoagulated, pregnant or on hormonal replacement, during acute event). FBC, clotting screen, protein C (activity and resistance), protein S, lupus anticoagulant, anticardiolipin antibodies, antithrombin, homocysteine, lipoprotein A.

MANAGEMENT

Anticoagulate as directed by specialist. Consider prophylaxis eg for flying.

Thrombophlebitis

CLINICAL NOTES

Epidemiology: Common. Aetiology/risk factors: Venous stasis, varicose veins, trauma eg blood tests, malignancy, thrombophilia, pregnancy. Clinical features: Painful hard superficial veins, erythema, varicose veins. Complications: Clot extension, DVT

(significant number of patients have underlying DVT), cellulitis, recurrent (consider investigating for underlying disease), postinflammatory pigmentation. Thromboplebitis migrans, associated with pancreatic/lung cancer.

 INVESTIGATIONS

Consider investigation to exclude DVT.

MANAGEMENT

NSAIDs, elevation, compression stockings, two to six weeks to heal.

Thrombotic thrombocytopenic purpura (TTP)

CLINICAL NOTES

Epidemiology: F>M. Aetiology/risk factors: Idiopathic, autoimmune (eg SLE), infection (eg *E coli*, HIV), pregnancy, iatrogenic (eg clopidogrel). Clinical features: Seizure, CVA, fluctuating GCS, fever, haemolysis (microangiopathic), bleeding, renal failure.

INVESTIGATIONS

↓plts, ↓Hb. *Film:* schistocytes. U&E, haematuria, proteinuria.

MANAGEMENT

Corticosteroids, plasma exchange, vincristine, splenectomy.

Thyroglossal cyst

CLINICAL NOTES

Epidemiology: Most common congenital neck mass. Aetiology/risk factors: Congenital defect. Clinical features: Midline painless cystic mass in neck that moves superiorly with tongue protrusion. Complications: Infection, rupture, airway obstruction, recurrence.

INVESTIGATIONS

TFT, USS, CT, MRI.

MANAGEMENT

Surgery.

Thyroid cancer

CLINICAL NOTES

Epidemiology: Incidence increasing. Aetiology/risk factors: Most are sporadic. Types: *Papillary:* 60-80% thyroid cancers, may be related to radiation exposure and associated with FAP, nodal and pulmonary spread, fourth to sixth decades. *Follicular:* Second most common thyroid cancer, >50 years, haemato-genous spread. *Medullary:* Third most common thyroid cancer, may be part of MEN2 syndrome. *Anaplastic:* Rare, F>M, more

DISEASES

in seventh decade, very aggressive. *Lymphoma:* More in eighth decade. *Hürthle cell:* Rare, may present with metastases. Clinical features: Neck lump (thyroid/nodes), neck pain, hoarse voice, dysphagia. Complications: Stridor.

INVESTIGATIONS

TSH. *Diagnosis:* ↑calcitonin in medullary cancer. Used in screening, diagnosis, monitoring. USS (specific, not sensitive), FNA cytology/biopsy, nuclear medicine. *Staging:* MRI, nuclear medicine. Thyroglobulin (papillary and follicular, monitor treatment and surveillance, presence of thyroglobulin antibodies may interfere with result). Urinary catecholamines, PTH calcium and genetic analysis in all medullary cancer patients to exclude MEN and for *RET* gene mutations.

MANAGEMENT

Surgical: Total thyroidectomy or lobectomy +/- lymph node resection. More advanced disease requires modified radical neck dissection. Risks of thyroid surgery (bleeding +/- airway compresion, infection, laryngeal nerve palsy, transient hypocalcaemia, hypoparathyroidism, thyroid storm, hypothyroidism). Adjuvant radioiodine ablation therapy for all well-differentiated cancer types except favourable stage patients who received total thyroidectomy. Adjuvant radiotherapy indicated in certain subgroups.
Paclitaxel (anaplastic), tyrosine kinase inhibitors, anti-angiogenesis factors eg CA4P and monoclonal antibodies under research. *Monitoring:* TFT to be kept suppressed by levothyroxine. Thyroglobulin tumour marker should be used for monitoring. Monitor calcitonin in medullary cancer. Family screening if index patient has *RET* gene mutations.

Thyrotoxicosis

CLINICAL NOTES

See *hyperthyroidism* and *Graves' disease*

Tinea

CLINICAL NOTES

Aetiology/risk factors: Excessive sweat, hot environments, poor drying after bathing, closed shoes/trainers, immunosuppression, DM. Clinical features: Tinea capitis (scalp), tinea cruris (groin), tinea corporis (body), tinea pedis (feet). Pruritus, broken erythematous skin and white slough, red scaly lesions that grow outwards leaving central pallor, vesicles and pustules on feet, onycholysis, nail dystrophy. Complications: Secondary bacterial infection, alopecia.

INVESTIGATIONS

FBC, glucose, skin scrapings, nail clippings –microscopy and culture, Wood's light.

MANAGEMENT

Treat underlying cause, education (hygiene), good footwear, topical imidazole treatment, only use topical steroids if marked inflammation (do not use steroids without an imidazole cream); oral antifungals – aggressive disease, onychomycosis.

Toddler diarrhoea

CLINICAL NOTES

Epidemiology: Common. Aetiology/risk factors: Peak one to four years. M>F. Clinical features: Diarrhoea three or more times a day.Undigested food may be seen in stool. Abdominal pain. Normal growth and child is systemically well, abdominal examination normal.

INVESTIGATIONS

Consider investigation to exclude alternative diagnoses.

MANAGEMENT

Reassurance, consider increasing dietary fats and fibre (although may increase diarrhoea). Reduce fruit juices and squashes.

Tonsillitis

CLINICAL NOTES

Epidemiology: Common Aetiology/risk factors: Viral, bacterial eg streptococcus. Atopy, immunodeficiency, family history tonsillitis. Clinical features: Fever, malaise, sore throat, earache, abdominal pain (children), headache, neck pain, cervical lymphadenopathy, foetor, enlarged inflamed tonsils with exudate (exclude glandular fever, blisters indicate Coxsackie virus infection). Complications: Quinsy, scarlet fever, glomerulonephritis, rheumatic fever, guttate psoriasis, otitis media, sinusitis, sepsis, respiratory distress.

INVESTIGATIONS

Swabs not routinely required, consider glandular fever screen.

MANAGEMENT

Consider antibiotics (eg penicillin) if systemically unwell, suspicion of quinsy, history of rheumatic fever, DM, immunodeficiency or if three or more Centor criteria[Ref20] – fever, exudate on tonsils, no cough, tender anterior cervical lymphadenopathy. Symptomatic relief. Refer if systemically unwell/sepsis, respiratory distress, quinsy, guttate psoriasis. Recurrent tonsillitis may warrant tonsillectomy.

Torsades de pointes

See also
— *Long QT interval*

CLINICAL NOTES

Aetiology/risk factors: Long QT interval causing an R

on T phenomenon. May be triggered by stress, exertion, emotion eg increased sympathetic drive, iatrogenic or bradycardia. Clinical features: Pre-syncope, syncope, palpitations. Complications: VF, death.

INVESTIGATIONS

ECG – normally short-lived VT with rotating cardiac axis. May or may not see prolonged QTc on ECG if patient stable.

MANAGEMENT

Acute: Advanced life support, treat causes eg stop precipitating drugs, manage electrolyte imbalance. Mg^{2+}/isoprenaline if acquired long QT. Pacing. *Long-term:* Avoid triggers. Congenital prolonged QTc – beta-blockers, pacing/ICD, cardiac sympathectomy.

Toxic epidermal necrolysis (Lyell's syndrome)

See also
— *Stevens-Johnson syndrome*

CLINICAL NOTES

Life-threatening dermatological condition with cell death and necrosis throughout epidermis. Epidemiology: Rare. Aetiology/risk factors: Toxins, iatrogenic, mycoplasma, hepatitis A, herpes, bone marrow transplant recipients. Clinical features: Life-threatening, fever, malaise, skin sloughing, purpuric macules (widespread, involve mucous membranes), blisters. Complications: Electrolyte disturbance, secondary infection, poor thermoregulation, corneal scarring, mucosal scarring, high mortality.

INVESTIGATIONS

FBC, U&E, LFT glucose, blood cultures, pH, chest X-ray, ECG biopsy. Investigate according to suspected underlying cause.

MANAGEMENT

Immediate transfer hospital facility, ITU/burns unit, consider immunosuppressants, immunoglobulin (toxin neutralisation).

Toxic shock syndrome

CLINICAL NOTES

Epidemiology: Rare. Aetiology/risk factors: Retained tampon, wounds, post-surgery, IV drug abuse. *Staph aureus,* streptococcus. Clinical features: Fever, tachycardia, hypotension, malaise, myalgia, vomiting, diarrhoea, rash, acute confusion, seizure. Complications: Shock, multiorgan failure, death.

INVESTIGATIONS

FBC, U&E, LFT, pH, CRP, cultures (blood, vaginal, skin swabs).

MANAGEMENT

IV fluid resuscitation, IV antibiotics.

Toxocariasis

CLINICAL NOTES

Epidemiology: Asymptomatic disease common. Aetiology/ risk factors: Roundworm, commonly *Toxocara canis* (dogs), occasionally *T catis* (cats), from animal faeces/ vomit or contaminated soil (humans are incidental hosts, not part of worm's lifecycle). Clinical features: *Ocular larva migrans:* Visual disturbance (uveitis, optic neuritis, retinal detachment, abscess, squint). *Visceral larva migrans:* Fever, myalgia, abdominal pain, hepatomegaly, cough, wheeze, pleural effusion. Complications: Blindness, seizure.

INVESTIGATIONS

Eosinophilia (count may be normal in isolated ocular disease), LFT, serology. Chest X-ray/pulmonary CT, abdominal USS/CT, cerebral CT/MRI, biopsy.

MANAGEMENT

Prevention (animal hygiene, deworming), azoles, systemic corticosteroids, ocular surgery.

Toxoplasmosis

CLINICAL NOTES

Epidemiology: 50% UK population exposed (confers lifelong immunity). Endemic in France. Congenital toxoplasmosis rare in UK. Aetiology/risk factors: *Toxoplasma gondii.* Exposure to cat faeces/poor food preparation. Trophozoites travel to brain, eye and muscles. Clinical features: Asymptomatic (80% cases), flu-like illness. If infected during or up to three months before pregnancy, risk of miscarriage or stillbirth (<1%). Congenital toxoplasmosis <40% risk if infected during pregnancy (risks increase the later during pregnancy mother is infected) – uveitis, squint, microphthalmia, choroidoretinitis, cataract, CVA, seizures, myocarditis, jaundice, hepatosplenomegaly, microcephaly, hydrocephalus, cerebral palsy, deafness.

INVESTIGATIONS

FBC, atypical lymphocytes, lymphocytosis. Rising IgM titre (HIV +ve makes test unreliable), tissue biopsy, CT brain, amniocentesis.

MANAGEMENT

Seek expert advice, pyrimethamine, sulfadiazine.

Transient ischaemic attack (TIA)

See also
— *Cerebrovascular accident*

CLINICAL NOTES

Clinical features: Vascular cerebral insult, symptoms resolve completely within 24 hours.

MANAGEMENT

Assess ABCD2 score[Ref21] to risk-stratify those at high risk of stroke. Age ≥60 years, one point. BP at presentation ≥140/90mmHg, one point. Clinical features, unilateral weakness, two points. Speech impairment with no weakness, one point. Duration of symptoms, ≥60 minutes, two points, 10-59 minutes, one point. Add onepoint for DM. Score four or more, or two or more TIAs in one week or high-risk – aspirin 300mg per day, specialist assessment within 24 hours including imaging. If score three or less, specialist assessment within seven days. Daily aspirin 300mg for at least two weeks post-symptoms. Modified release dipyridamole should be used in conjunction with aspirin unless contraindicated. Carotid doppler within one week of TIA and endarterectomy within two weeks of TIA if appropriate. Consider echocardiography. Control risk factors eg hypercholesterolaemia, hypertension – statins. ACE inhibitors. Anticoagulate if in AF. Lifestyle management.

Transient synovitis of the hip
CLINICAL NOTES
Epidemiology: Three to 10 years of age. Aetiology/risk factors: Post-viral, minor trauma. Clinical features: Pain, limping, may refuse to bear weight, global reduction in hip movement.

INVESTIGATIONS
FBC, CRP, USS, aspiration to exclude septic arthritis.

MANAGEMENT
Analgesia.

Transverse myelitis
CLINICAL NOTES
Epidemiology: Peaks 10-19 years and 30-39 years. Rare. Aetiology/risk factors: MS, infection (eg herpes viruses, echovirus), post-vaccination, SLE, Sjögren's syndrome, sarcoid, arteriovenous malformation, vascular insult. Clinical features: Rapid onset (hours to weeks), fever, back pain, sensory disturbance (may include allodynia), sensory level, paraesthesia, limb weakness/spasms, spastic paraparesis, bladder dysfunction (frequency, incontinence, retention), bowel dysfunction (feeling of incomplete evacuation, incontinence, constipation), headache. Complications: Permanent neurological damage, paralysis, sexual dysfunction, osteoporosis, affective disorders, recurrence (uncommon), respiratory failure.

INVESTIGATIONS
MRI, LP. Investigate according to suspected underlying cause.

MANAGEMENT
IV steroids, plasma exchange, analgesia, physiotherapy,

OT, mobility aids, urinary/bladder catheterisation, bowel regimen. Treat underying cause.

Traveller's diarrhoea

See also
— Gastroenteritis

CLINICAL NOTES
Aetiology/risk factors: Infection (bacterial, viral, amoebic, parasitic), may also be floral adjustment. Clinical features: Diarrhoea +/– vomiting. Crampy abdominal pain (often seen with campylobacter), blood/mucus PR (salmonella, shigella, campylobacter). Prolonged diarrhoea with excessive flatus/eructation may suggest giardia. Profuse watery diarrhoea may suggest cholera. Complications: Dehydration, colitis, renal failure, HUS/TTP with E coli 0157 (verotoxin-producing).

INVESTIGATIONS

FBC, U&E, LFT, stool culture (MC&S, ova, cysts and parasites).

MANAGEMENT
Prevention eg cholera vaccination, hygiene. Hydration therapy (oral or IV if severe dehydration/comorbidity/extremes of age), antidiarrhoeal agents, empirical antibiotics (eg ciprofloxacin or azithromycin) if systemically unwell/severe illness/>48 hours. Metronidazole for giardiasis.

Trichomonas vaginalis
CLINICAL NOTES
See sexually transmitted infections and genital infections

Tricuspid regurgitation
See also
— Right heart failure

CLINICAL NOTES
Epidemiology: Trivial regurgitation common. Aetiology/risk factors: Functional (dilated right ventricle), pulmonary hypertension, carcinoid, congenital heart disease (eg Ebstein's anomaly), endocarditis, rheumatic heart disease, mitral valve disease. Clinical features: AF, JVP – large cv waves, pulsatile liver, pansystolic murmur LSE – loudest in held inspiration. Complications: Right heart failure, S3 hepatic congestion, ascites, peripheral oedema.

INVESTIGATIONS
ECG, chest X-ray, echocardiogram, cardiac catheterisation.

MANAGEMENT
Usually no action required. Diuretics, ACE inhibitors, manage AF, surgical treatment unusual, may be

DISEASES

performed if in conjunction with another valve repair, congenital heart disease, severe regurgitation. Treat underlying cause.

Tricuspid stenosis

CLINICAL NOTES

Epidemiology: F>M. Rare. Aetiology/risk factors: Rheumatic heart disease, carcinoid, infective endocarditis, SLE, endomyocardial fibrosis, congenital, Fabry disease. Clinical features: Breathlessness, fatigue, abdominal pain, (prominent a wave in JVP if in sinus rhythm), mid-diastolic murmur, split S1, ascites, hepatomegaly, pitting oedema. Complications: Syncope, AF.

INVESTIGATIONS

Chest X-ray –prominent right atrial contour. ECG – p-pulmonale. Echocardiogram – diseased tricuspid valve, dilated right atrium. Cardiac catheterisation, MRI.

MANAGEMENT

Diuretics, manage AF. Consider valvotomy, tricuspid valve replacement. Treat underlying cause.

Trigeminal neuralgia (tic douloureux)

CLINICAL NOTES

Epidemiology: F>M. >50 years. Aetiology/risk factors: Age, familial, DM, MS, syphilis, amyloid, sarcoid, nerve compression eg vascular aneurysm, tumour, vasculitis. Clinical features: Progressive short-lived severe shooting 'electric' facial pains, triggered by facial stimulation eg putting on make-up/shaving/brushing teeth. Phases may last days, weeks or months. In distribution of trigeminal nerve. Unilateral. Complications: Depression.

INVESTIGATIONS

MRI to exclude secondary causes.

MANAGEMENT

Anticonvulsants (eg carbamazepine, gabapentin), baclofen, alcohol/glycerol injections, microvascular decompression surgery (dividing blood vessels away from nerve), balloon compression, gamma knife radiosurgery, stereotactic radiofrequency thermal rhizotomy, partial sensory rhizotomy.

Trigger finger

CLINICAL NOTES

Epidemiology: Common. Aetiology/risk factors: Idiopathic, post-tendonitis, RA, amyloid, DM, renal dialysis. Clinical features: Difficulty straightening flexed finger, patient extends finger with force or by pulling on it. Click may be heard on straightening as obstruction released and finger straightens.

MANAGEMENT

Rest (may require splint), NSAIDs if tendonitis, corticosteroid injection, surgical release.

Tropical sprue

CLINICAL NOTES

Epidemiology: South-east Asia, Caribbean. Aetiology/risk factors: May be infective –incubation period up to 10 years. Clinical features: Acute and chronic forms. Diarrhoea, malabsorption, malnutrition, weight loss. Complications: Vitamin B_{12}, folate, iron deficiency, small bowel bacterial overgrowth.

INVESTIGATIONS

Tests to suggest malabsorption eg ↓Hb, vitamin B_{12}, folate, iron, ↓Ca^{2+}, ↓albumin. Small bowel biopsy. D-xylose absorption test.

MANAGEMENT

Fluid and electrolyte management, antibiotics may be useful depending on area of travel, nutritional and dietary support. Treat complications accordingly.

Trypanosomiasis

CLINICAL NOTES

Aetiology/risk factors: Parasitic (vector – tsetse fly). *Trypanosoma gambiense/rhodesiense* (African sleeping sickness, fever, headache, malaise, myalgia, lymphadenopathy, hepatosplenomegaly, myocarditis, arrhythmias, agitation, confusion, coma, death). *T cruzi* (Chagas' disease, fever, lymphadenopathy, hepatosplenomegaly, megaoesophagus, megacolon, cardiomyopathy, arrhythmias, eye involvement, cerebral disease).

INVESTIGATIONS

↑WCC, ↑ALT, identification of parasite in blood smears, CSF or lymph node aspirates, immunofluorescence, PCR.

MANAGEMENT

Suramin, melarsoprol, pentamidine, eflornithine. Treat complications accordingly.

Tuberculosis (pulmonary)

CLINICAL NOTES

Epidemiology: UK 2007, 8,417 cases. Aetiology/risk factors: Low income, immigrants, homelessness, immunodeficiency, alcohol abuse. Infected patients have 5-10% lifetime risk of active disease (5-10% annual risk if HIV +ve). London, non-UK born ethnic minorities. Increased risk of disease/dissemination with immunodeficiency. Clinical features: Primary TB: Often asymptomatic, mild cough, wheeze, erythema nodosum. Post-primary: Weight loss, fatigue, malaise, night sweats, cough, haemoptysis, lymphadenopathy. Complications: Pleural effusion, massive haemoptysis, aspergilloma, adenocarcinoma (cavity tumour), meningitis, miliary TB, distant spread; TB meningitis, bony, kidney, adrenals, bladder, skin infection, eye. Drug resistance (multidrug, extensively drug-resistant).

INVESTIGATIONS
FBC, atypical lymphocytes, ↑ACE. Chest X-ray (may be normal) sputum microscopy (three, including one early morning sample) and culture for six weeks, for acid-fast bacilli (AFBs); sputum nucleic acid amplification, pleural tap/biopsy, bronchoscopy/lavage, gastric washings. Morning urine for MSU. Sterile pyuria. Marrow, node, liver and skin biopsy. CSF microscopy/culture.

MANAGEMENT
Ensure drug adherence. Treat if symptomatic before culture results. Antituberculous therapy six months for pulmonary, one year for meningeal (isoniazid and rifampicin throughout treatment period with addition of pyrazinamide and ethambutol in first two months). Steroids used in meningeal disease. Monitor for drug side-effects. Vaccinate those at risk including babies. Screening at-risk groups including healthcare workers. Contact tracing.

Tuberous sclerosis

CLINICAL NOTES
Epidemiology: One in 5,000-10,000 newborns. Aetiology/risk factors: Autosomal dominant, 80% cases new mutation. Clinical features: Hamartomas (eyes, cardiac, kidneys, lungs, skin, bone), seizures, infantile spasms, autism, ↓IQ, hypertension, adenoma sebaceum (angiofibromata, from age four years, often butterfly distribution on face, nasolabial folds), shagreen patches (leathery plaques on back), ungual fibromas, hypopigmented macules, café au lait spots, gum hyperplasia. Complications: Renal cell carcinoma, cystic kidneys, cerebral astrocytomas, pneumothorax, cor pulmonale.

INVESTIGATIONS
CT/MRI brain (brain tubers), pulmonary CT, renal CT, echocardiogram.

MANAGEMENT
Counselling, genetic counselling, laser therapy, electrodessication, anticonvulsants, antihypertensives, oncological management.

Turner's syndrome

CLINICAL NOTES
Epidemiology: About one in 3,000 female births. Aetiology/risk factors: Genetic 45 X,0 or mosaicism (may present late eg with primary amenorrhoea, infertility). Clinical features: Amenorrhoea, primitive streak ovaries, wide-spaced nipples, short fourth metacarpals, low hairline, high-arched palate, otitis media, lymphoedema, osteoporosis, horseshoe kidneys; one in five have cardiac anomalies, commonly coarctation of the aorta. Epicanthic folds, ptosis, normal IQ, halo naevus. Complications: DM, Hashimoto's thyroiditis, keratoconus, infertility, hypertension.

INVESTIGATIONS
Amniocentesis/chorionic villus sampling, chromosome analysis, TFT, U&E, glucose, FSH, LH, oestrogen, ECG, DEXA, echocardiogram, renal USS.

MANAGEMENT
MDT approach, education, consider growth hormone, treat complications accordingly.

Tylosis

CLINICAL NOTES
Epidemiology: Rare. Aetiology/risk factors: Autosomal dominant. Clinical features: Palmoplantar hyperkeratosis, hyperhydrosis. Complications: Fissures, fungal infection, type A associated with oesophageal cancer.

INVESTIGATIONS
Genetic studies, regular endoscopy and biopsy.

MANAGEMENT
Chiropody, skin regimen, regular monitoring.

Typhoid (enteric) fever

CLINICAL NOTES
Epidemiology: Common in developing world/areas of poor sanitation. Aetiology/risk factors: Salmonella typhi. Faeco-oral transmission – contaminated water. Incubation up to three weeks. Clinical features: Fever, headache, malaise, constipation or later diarrhoea, cough, relative bradycardia, rose spots on trunk, splenomegaly. Complications: Meningoencephalitis, GI bleeding (intestinal haemorrhage, Peyer's patches), osteomyelitis (high risk if sickle cell disease), metastatic abscess, myocarditis, cholecystitis, renal involvement, chronic carrier, death.

INVESTIGATIONS
↓plts, ↑LFT, blood, stool and urine cultures, bone marrow sampling.

MANAGEMENT
Vaccination, rehydration, antibiotics eg ciprofloxacin, ceftriaxone.

Typhus

CLINICAL NOTES
Rickettsial infection (arthropod vector), number of different subtypes. Epidemiology: Asia, South America, Africa,

southern Europe. Aetiology/risk factors: Overcrowding, poverty. Incubation one to two weeks. *Endemic typhus (rickettsia prowazekii):* Fever, malaise, headache, photophobia, cough, rash (blanching, then purpuric, does not affect face), abdominal pain. *Murine typhus (rickettsia typhi):* Nausea, vomiting, diarrhoea, abdominal pain, cough, rash (may be blanching or petechial). Complications: Gangrene, renal failure, seizure, pneumonia and respiratory failure, cardiac failure, shock, death.

☾ INVESTIGATIONS
↓Hb, ↓plts, WCC, ↓eGFR, ↑ALT, serology, biopsy (and PCR), respiratory function tests, ECG, echocardiogram.

▯ MANAGEMENT
Preventive measures. Supportive, analgesia, doxycycline.

Ulcerative colitis

📖 CLINICAL NOTES
Epidemiology: Approximately up to 150 in 10^5 prevalence. Aetiology/risk factors: ↓in smokers, ↓in childhood/adolescent history of mesenteric adenitis or appendicitis. Clinical features: Affects rectum, colon and terminal ileum (backwash ileitis). Mucosal/submucosal inflammation, diarrhoea, blood and mucus PR, pallor, erythema nodosum, pyoderma gangrenosum, finger clubbing, ankle oedema, mouth ulcers. Complications: PBC, sclerosing cholangitis, chronic active hepatitis, toxic megacolon, carcinoma of colon.

☾ INVESTIGATIONS
↓Hb, ↑basophils, ↑ESR/CRP, U&E, ↓Mg^{2+}, ↑lipase, faecal calprolectin (correlates with disease activity), HLA-B27 (if associated arthritis). Barium studies, CT, USS, colonoscopy, endoscopy and biopsy, video capsule endoscopy (if no structure), white cell scans, abdominal X-ray if suspect toxic dilation, CT (if suspect abscess or perforation), MRI if anorectal sepsis.

▯ MANAGEMENT
Lifestyle/dietary advice, loperamide, codeine, 5-ASA drugs eg mesalazine (requires drug monitoring, causes reversible oligozoospermia), immunosuppressants, steroids (20-40mg per day for acute flare or use enemas, reduce dose once improving. If no improvement over four weeks, seek advice, consider steroid maintenance plus osteoporosis prophylaxis. Steroid-sparing agents (methotrexate not useful). Anti-TNF agents. Surgery. Regular follow-up. Treat complications accordingly. Urgent referral if toxic megacolon, severe pain/bleeding, generally unwell, accelerated weight loss, concern about cancer, complications eg iritis, abscess, fistulae.

Ulnar nerve palsy

📖 CLINICAL NOTES
Aetiology/risk factors: Nerve trauma (eg elbow/wrist fracture), nerve entrapment, distortion (eg OA), repetitive movement (eg carpenters), neuropathy (eg mononeuritis multiplex). Clinical features: Paraesthesia/numbness ulnar nerve distribution, hypothenar muscle wasting, wasting of first dorsal interosseous, wasting of intrinsic muscles of hand, claw hand if lesion is at wrist, high lesions also paralyse flexor digitorum profundus (hence less clawing), weak abduction and adduction of fingers, weak thumb adduction, weak flexion ring and little fingers.

☾ INVESTIGATIONS
Neuropathy screen, X-ray, MRI, nerve conduction studies.

▯ MANAGEMENT
Treat underlying cause; for entrapment, avoid ulnar nerve compression or irritation, splint, ulnar nerve decompression/transposition.

Umbilical granuloma

📖 CLINICAL NOTES
Epidemiology: Common. Clinical features: Red granulomatous non-healing umbilicus in neonates, may weep. Complications: Secondary bacterial infection.

☾ INVESTIGATIONS
Consider swab.

▯ MANAGEMENT
Treat associated infection, cauterise with silver nitrate.

Undescended testes (cryptorchidism)

📖 CLINICAL NOTES
Epidemiology: One in 50 live male births. Aetiology/risk factors: Family history, prematurity, maldescent, torsion in utero, testicular agenesis, hypospadias, associated with syndromes eg Prader-Willi, CAH, antenatal smoking/alcohol, gestational diabetes. Clinical features: Palpable and non-palpable – affects clinical management. Bilateral in one in four cases. Affects R>L side, may have coexistent hernia, may be non-palpable. *Bilateral non-palpable:* Consider diagnosis of prune belly syndrome (cryptorchidism, urological abnormalities and laxity of the abdominal muscles). Complications: Failure to repair increases risk of infertility and malignancy (up to x20 risk). Torsion. May be a presentation of a virilised female.

☾ INVESTIGATIONS
USS if within inguinal canal, MRI/laparoscopy (non-palpable testis), genetic testing.

▯ MANAGEMENT
Referral for specialist review at about six months of age

DISEASES

or earlier if bilateral or other associated genito-urological abnormalities. *Palpable testis:* HCG may be used to aid testicular descent, orchiolysis and orchidopexy (ideally performed by 18 months. *Non-palpable:* Surgical exploration, laparoscopic removal (if intra-abdominal >10 years of age), orchiolysis and orchidopexy.

Ureteral carcinoma

🗎 CLINICAL NOTES

Epidemiology: Rare. Clinical features: Frequency, dysuria, haematuria, hydronephrosis. Complications: Obstruction, metastases.

INVESTIGATIONS

IVU, retrograde pyelography, biopsy, staging scans.

MANAGEMENT

Stent, radical surgery +/– adjuvant radiotherapy or chemotherapy.

Urethral cancer

🗎 CLINICAL NOTES

Epidemiology: Rare, F>M. Aetiology/risk factors: Advancing age, chronic inflammation (eg recurrent UTI, STI), stricture. Clinical features: Most commonly SCC, but can also be transitional cell and adenocarcinoma. Split urinary stream, urinary frequency, haematuria, pain, offensive discharge, mass, lymphadenopathy. Complications: Fistula, outflow obstruction and urinary retention, metastases.

INVESTIGATIONS

Cystoscopy, urine cytology, biopsy, CT/MRI pelvis, staging scans.

MANAGEMENT

Laser, fulguration, surgery (including cysto-urethrectomy, urethroprostatecomy, penectomy, pelvic exenteration), adjuvant radiotherapy (external beam or brachytherapy), adjuvant chemotherapy.

Urinary incontinence

🗎 CLINICAL NOTES

Epidemiology: Common. Aetiology/risk factors: UTI, alcohol, caffeine, diuretics, BPH, prostate cancer, urological malignancy, interstitial cystitis, diabetes insipidus, DM, constipation, dementia, depression, schizophrenia, anxiety, MS, normal pressure hydrocephalus, developmental delay, NAI, chronic retention with overflow, uterine prolapse, overactive bladder, pelvic floor weakness, neurogenic bladder, seizures, cauda equina syndrome, chronic cough. Clinical features: Urge incontinence, stress incontinence, bed wetting, nocturia, lack of sensation, lack of self-esteem, low confidence.

INVESTIGATIONS

MSU, urine cytology, glucose, PSA, U&E, calcium, USS, urodynamics, cystoscopy, MRI brain/spinal cord.

MANAGEMENT

Treat underlying cause. Weight loss if high BMI, avoid caffeine. Psychological support, routine to void regularly, star charts/nocturnal alarms in children. Pelvic floor training, oxybutinin, solifenacin. Vaginal oestrogen if postmenopausal. Alpha-blockers/finasteride for BPH. Desmopressin for nocturia. Surgery for overactive bladder (eg botulinum toxin, sacral nerve stimulation), surgery for stress incontinence in women (eg vaginal tape procedures).

Urinary tract infection (adults)

🗎 CLINICAL NOTES

Epidemiology: Common. F>M. Aetiology/risk factors: Post-intercourse, postmenopause, calculi, anatomical defects (eg duplex kidneys, PCKD), immunodeficiency, poor hygiene, tumour, poor bladder emptying, bladder outflow obstruction, dehydration, urinary catheterisation. *E coli* is most common cause (80%), proteus and other urea splitting bacteria associated with renal stones. UTI (and asymptomatic bacteriuria) in pregnancy (risk due to obstruction, dilated ureters also increased risk of pyelonephritis and early labour. Clinical features: *Lower urinary tract*: Asymptomatic, dysuria frequency, urgency, suprapubic pain, malodorous urine, haematuria, acute confusion. *Upper urinary tract*: Fever, loin pain, nausea, vomiting. Complications: Antibiotic resistance, septic shock, renal failure, multi-organ failure, falls (elderly), acute confusion (elderly).

INVESTIGATIONS

Consider urinalysis (nitrites up to 60% sensitive, highly specific, leucocytes more sensitive than nitrites but less specific). MSU if treatment failure, severe infection, upper UTI, haematuria, men, comorbidity, acute confusion, catheterisation, recent hospitalisation. *Pregnancy:* send MSU with +ve dip even if asymptomatic. Consider STI screen. Imaging (USS/CT) – if proven UTI in men, concern about renal stone, recurrent UTIs in women, DM or immunodeficiency.

MANAGEMENT

Encourage hydration, urinary alkalinisation eg potassium citrate. Many infections might resolve without treatment. One in three women who have clinical symptoms of UTI have -ve culture but respond to antibiotics. First-line for lower UTI depends on local guidelines. *Non-pregnant:* Trimethoprim or nitrofurantoin (less effective with potassium citrate) for three days. *Pyelonephritis (non-pregnant):* Cephalosporins, broad-spectrum penicillins, quinolones. *UTI in pregnancy:* Cephalosporins and penicillins safe in pregnancy. *UTI in men:* Consider longer eg. 2 week course of quinolone eg ciprofloxacin. *Catheterised patients:* Only treat if symptomatic. Recurrent UTI (more than three per year) – women, cranberry juice, prophylaxis (post-coitally or at night); men, may be related to prostatism/residual volume, consider urology referral.

Urinary tract infection (children) [Ref22]

📋 CLINICAL NOTES
Epidemiology: Common. **Clinical features:** Fever, irritability, new onset nocturnal enuresis, abdominal pain, weight loss, vomiting, neonatal jaundice, haematuria, malodorous urine, frequency, dysuria. **Risk factors:** Outflow tract obstruction, previous UTI, anatomical defect or family history of defect eg vesico-ureteric reflux, constipation, spinal cord disease, abdominal mass, hypertension. **Complications:** Sepsis, renal scarring.

⚕ INVESTIGATIONS
Clean catch urine, urinalysis (nitrite +ve, suggestive of UTI, leucocyte +ve/nitrite -ve, may or may not be UTI). MSU (bacteriuria suggests UTI; pus cells without bacteriuria may be considered to have UTI if clinically likely). Imaging if less than six months of age: USS six weeks after treatment of infection. USS during infection if complicated eg non *E coli* (unless responds well to treatment), seriously ill, pyelonephritis, red flags, poor response to sensitive antibiotics. USS for recurrent UTI. DMSA and micturating cysto-urethrogram (MCUG) for recurrent or complicated or non *E coli* UTI. If aged six months to three years: USS for complicated infection (acutely unless well with non *E coli*), recurrent infection/DMSA for complicated or recurrent infection. If aged more than three years: USS for complicated infection (acutely unless clinically well with non *E coli*), recurrent UTI/DMSA for recurrent UTI.

🗓 MANAGEMENT
Refer if unwell/aged less than three months, antibiotics for seven to 10 days if upper UTI, three days if simple lower UTI, avoid prophylaxis after one UTI, avoid antibiotics in asymptomatic bacteriuria.

Urticaria and angioedema

📋 CLINICAL NOTES
Aetiology/risk factors: Idiopathic, allergic IgE type 1 hypersensitivity, immune complex mediated, C1 esterase inhibitor deficiency (hereditary angiodema), chronic urticaria (antibodies to mast cells). *Triggers:* Iatrogenic (eg opiates, NSAIDs, ACE inhibitors), skin trauma (pressure, cold, heat, sunlight, water, exercise, allergens). **Clinical features:** Wheals circumscribed by erythema (more than six weeks, chronic), angioedema, may last a few hours at a time, bronchospasm, tachycardia, hypotension. **Complications:** Cardiorespiratory collapse, anaphylaxis, death.

⚕ INVESTIGATIONS
Usually not required. FBC, ESR, thyroid antibodies, specific IgE, C4, biopsy.

🗓 MANAGEMENT
Avoid triggers, antihistamines, topical soothing agents eg calamine, oral steroids (short-term), leukotriene antagonists, immunosuppressants. *Anaphylaxis:* Oxygen, IM adrenaline (1:1000), IV hydrocortisone, IV chlorpheniramine, bronchodilators.

Uveitis

📋 CLINICAL NOTES
See *iritis*

Vaginal and vaginal wall prolapse

📋 CLINICAL NOTES
Epidemiology: 20-50% of parous women. **Aetiology/risk factors:** Advancing age, postmenopausal, multiparity, obesity, hysterectomy, chronic constipation, collagen disorders. **Clinical features:** Urethrocoele (urethral prolapse), cystocoele (bladder prolapse), rectocoele (rectal prolapse), enterocoele (Pouch of Douglas prolapse), uterine (first-, second and third-degree; procidentia – complete uterine descent). Dragging sensation, vaginal fullness, urinary incontinence, incomplete bladder emptying, UTI, faecal incontinence (vaginal digitation sometimes performed to empty bowels in rectocoele), dyspareunia, vaginal pain, back pain. **Complications:** Depression, bowel incarceration/obstruction (large enterocoele), cervical ulceration in procidentia.

⚕ INVESTIGATIONS
Usually clinical diagnosis. Imaging and urodynanics may be required.

🗓 MANAGEMENT
Pelvic floor exercises, PVC ring pessaries (eg shelf, ring) +/- HRT, (vaginal oestrogens), surgery (eg hysterectomy, anterior/posterior repair, sacrospinous fixation, paravaginal repair, uterosacral ligament plication, sacrocolpopexy).

Varicocoele

📋 CLINICAL NOTES
Epidemiology: Usually occurs in males after puberty. **Aetiology/risk factors:** Occasionally due to intra-abdominal malignancy eg renal. **Clinical features:** Left>>right side, asymptomatic, dull ache, scrotal mass like a bag of worms, more prominent on standing. *Red flags:* >40 years of age, acute, does not subside on lying flat, may be suggestive of renal tumour. **Complications:** Infertility, testicular atrophy, pain.

DISEASES

INVESTIGATIONS
USS, Doppler, abdominopelvic CT.

MANAGEMENT
Reassurance, scrotal support strap, consider varicocelectomy or embolisation.

Varicose veins

🗒 CLINICAL NOTES
Epidemiology: F>M. Aetiology/risk factors: Age, pregnancy, familial, obesity, occupational eg on feet, pelvic mass, DVT. Clinical features: Asymptomatic, pain (often aching), cramps, leg swelling, dilated tortuous veins. Examine distribution of long and short saphenous veins, groin for saphena varix (groin lump at junction of long saphenous and femoral veins, ↓on lying flat), check abdomen for mass. Complications: Bleeding, venous eczema/ulceration, scarring, oedema, lipodermatosclerosis, thrombophlebitis, haemorrhage.

INVESTIGATIONS
Hand-held Doppler, colour duplex ultrasound, ABPI to exclude coincidental arterial disease.

MANAGEMENT
Weight loss, avoid excessive standing. Compression hosiery, consider emollients and steroid ointments for eczema, analgesia, sclerotherapy, ligation, stripping, laser, radiofrequency ablation. Treat complications/underlying causes.

Vascular dementia

See also
— *Alzheimer's disease*

🗒 CLINICAL NOTES
Epidemiology: Prevalence 1-4% >in over-65s. Second most common dementia type. Aetiology/risk factors: CVD risk factors (hypertension, smoking, hypercholesterolaemia, DM), AF, severe hypotension, CVA, vasculitis, SLE, temporal arteritis. Clinical features: Stepwise deterioration in global cerebral functioning secondary to cerebral vascular insults, memory loss, mood changes, communication difficulty, visual difficulties eg agnosia, wandering, confusion, apraxia, urinary incontinence, poor organisation skills, may coexist with Alzheimer's dementia. Complications: Falls, environmental danger, aggression, disinhibition, violence, malnutrition, elder abuse.

INVESTIGATIONS
MMSE, score <25 suggestive of cognitive impairment, FBC, U&E, TFT, calcium, fasting lipids/glucose, ESR, ECG, CT/MRI brain, carotid dopplers, neuropsychology.

MANAGEMENT
Treat cardiovascular risk factors, exclude organic/functional causes for symptoms and other causes of dementia. Risk assessment (including driving, safety at home), memory clinics, family support, cholinesterase inhibitors, memantine. *Agitation:* Assess causes eg pain, environment. Treatment with light therapy, dance, music, pet therapy, multisensory stimulation. Only use antipsychotics at lowest effective dose for psychosis rather than for agitation (increased risk of CVA). Finasteride shown to reduce sexual disinhibition.

Vasomotor rhinitis

🗒 CLINICAL NOTES
As perennial rhinitis but no allergic trigger or eosinophilia in nasal discharge.

INVESTIGATIONS
Consider total IgE and FBC to exclude allergic component.

MANAGEMENT
Avoid triggers. Decongestants, steroid nasal sprays.

Ventricular ectopics (VE)

🗒 CLINICAL NOTES
Epidemiology: M>F, ↑with age/African-Americans. Aetiology/risk factors: Idiopathic, CHD, MI, hypertension, cardiomyopathy, myocarditis, MVP, digoxin toxicity, aminophylline, TCAs, caffeine, hypoxia, electrolyte imbalance, excess catecholamines, illicit drugs, alcohol, smoking, exercise, pregnancy, menstruation, menopause. Clinical features: Asymptomatic, presyncope, syncope, palpitations, thumps, missed beats, cannon wave on JVP, irregular pulse. Complications: None in young healthy individuals. Ventricular tachyarrhythmias particularly on background of cardiac disease.

INVESTIGATIONS
ECG – wide complex extra beat with compensatory pause, may also see bigeminy, trigeminy. Ambulatory ECG. K⁺, Ca²⁺, TFT. ETT – exercise-induced VEs suggestive of CHD. Echocardiogram. Angiography.

MANAGEMENT
Consider beta-blockers. Isolated ectopics (occurring at rest and in absence of symptoms, structural heart disease and underlying cause) usually require reassurance. Treat underlying cause. Refer for red flags – family history cardiomyopathy/sudden cardiac death, ectopics triggered by exertion, presyncope, syncope, evidence of structural heart disease, abnormal ECG eg Brugada syndrome, abnormal ambulatory ECG.

DISEASES

Ventricular septal defect (VSD)

📋 CLINICAL NOTES

Epidemiology: Most common isolated congenital lesion, about one in 500 births. Membranous type most common. Aetiology/risk factors: Isolated, may be part of complex, eg Fallot's tetralogy, or associated with other lesions eg PDA (10% cases), ASD or congenital conditions eg Down's syndrome. Acute VSD may be secondary to MI. Clinical features: Asymptomatic, failure to thrive, cardiac failure, recurrent chest infections, SOB, parasternal heave, thrill. Small lesions – harsh early ejection systolic murmur (defect closes during septal contraction hence small lesions may not lead to pansystolic murmur). Medium-sized lesions –pansystolic murmur. Very large defects may be silent (low pressure). Pulmonary outflow tract murmur. Complications: Ventricular failure, pulmonary hypertension, Eisenmenger's syndrome, endocarditis, ventricular aneurysm after closure.

☺ INVESTIGATIONS

ECG normal in small defects eg maladie de Roger, variable axis, RAD or LAD. Echocardiogram – membranous (infracristal, 80% cases), infundibular (supracristal, 8% cases, 30% Japanese population), just inferior to aortic/pulmonary valves, may be associated with AR, seen in Fallot's tetralogy. Posterior (inlet, 10% cases) closely related to pulmonary/aortic valves. Muscular types occur eg after MI (may have multiple defects, Swiss cheese type). Catheterisation – step-up in O_2 at level of defect.

🗄 MANAGEMENT

50% cases close spontaneously. Small membranous lesions may close spontaneously. Infundibular lesions do not close spontaneously. Surgical closure, pulmonary artery banding (to prevent pulmonary hypertension).

Ventricular tachycardia (VT) (non-sustained)

📋 CLINICAL NOTES

Non-sustained VT (Five or more beats/<30 seconds).

☺ INVESTIGATIONS

Ambulatory ECG.

🗄 MANAGEMENT

ICD especially if LV dysfunction, consider beta-blockers if symptomatic.

Ventricular tachycardia (VT) (sustained)

📋 CLINICAL NOTES

Sustained VT (>30 seconds). Aetiology/risk factors: MI, cardiac failure, trauma, shock, electrolyte/metabolic disturbance, hypoxia. Clinical features: Presyncope, syncope, chest pain, pulmonary oedema. Complications: VF, death.

☺ INVESTIGATIONS

ECG – may be difficult to distinguish VT from SVT with bundle branch block (BBB). Most wide complex tachycardias are VT.

🗄 MANAGEMENT

If haemodynamically unstable, immediate cardioversion/999. Shockable rhythm. Lidocaine/amiodarone IV if stable. Treat underlying cause. Long-term management: Beta-blockers. ICD. Note flecainide/sotalol may increase risk of death.

Vertigo

See also
 — Benign paroxysmal positional vertigo (BPPV)

📋 CLINICAL NOTES

Aetiology/risk factors: Vestibular: Benign paroxysmal positional vertigo (BPPV), sudden onset, 10-60 seconds, positional, eg turning in bed, horizontal non-sustained nystagmus triggered by Hallpike manoeuvre. Labyrinthitis: Acute vestibular neuritis, non-positional vertigo, unidirectional nystagmus, sustained, peaks within 24 hours, resolves over few days, may mimic cerebellar insult, head thrust test +ve. Ménière's disease. Suppurative ear disease. Brainstem/central: Migraine: Recurrent, non-persistent vertigo, headache.Cerebellar stroke, lateral medullary syndrome, MS, cerebellopontine angle tumour. Vertical nystagmus seen in cerebellar/brainstem insult. Vertigo with acute unliateral hearing loss: Ischaemia (labyrinth/brainstem). Vertigo with hearing loss: Cerebellopontine angle tumour, perilymphatic fistula.

☺ INVESTIGATIONS

Consider cerebral CT/MRI if concerned about cerebral insult or tumour.

🗄 MANAGEMENT

Refer if concerned about central lesions; red flags (occipital headache, vertical nystagmus, acute deafness, central neurological symptoms/signs eg diplopia, speech disturbance, facial weakness/numbness, long tract signs, ataxia, persistent vertigo with -ve head thrust test). BPPV: Epley, Semont or Brandt-Daroff manoeuvres, vestibular physiotherapy, antiemetics, surgery. Labyrinthitis: cinnarizine, prochlorperazine, consider short term benzodiazepines.

Vesico-ureteric reflux

📋 CLINICAL NOTES

Epidemiology: One in 100-200 live births. 40% resolve by two years. Aetiology/risk factors: Autosomal dominant. Clinical features: Asymptomatic, UTI. Complications: Reflux nephropathy (renal hypertension, proteinuria, CKD, renal stones), recurrent UTI, chronic pyelonephritis.

INVESTIGATIONS

May be identified antenatally, micturating cystogram, USS/DMSA to assess for renal scarring.

MANAGEMENT

Screen affected siblings, grades 1-3 resolve spontaneously, prophylactic antibiotics grade ≥2, surgery grades 4, 5. Control BP. Treat UTI promptly.

Vitamin deficiencies and excesses

CLINICAL NOTES

Vitamin A: Fat-soluble. Stored in liver. *Sources:* liver, dairy, fish oils. *Excess:* Teratogenic in pregnancy. Headache, nausea, vomiting, diplopia. *Deficiency:* Night blindness, dry eyes, thickened cornea, corneal ulceration, keratomalacia, conjunctival keratinisation, higher risk of vertical transmission of HIV. Vitamin B$_1$ (thiamine): Water-soluble. Stored in liver. *Sources:* Cereals, nuts, pork, beans. *Deficiency:* Beriberi (developing countries eg South Asia; dry type – neuropathy, leg weakness, paraesthesia, absent ankle jerks, Wernicke's encephalopathy, Korsakoff's psychosis; wet type, peripheral oedema, pleural effusion, ascites, cardiac failure). Alcohol-related (polyneuropathy, Wernicke's encephalopathy, Korsakoff's psychosis, beriberi). Vitamin B$_6$ (pyridoxine): Water-soluble. Deficiency normally drug related (eg isoniazid). Polyneuropathy. Vitamin B$_{12}$: Water-soluble. See *pernicious anaemia*. Vitamin C: Water-soluble. *Sources:* Fresh fruit and vegetables. *Deficiency (scurvy):* Weakness, myalgia, anaemia, poor wound healing, bruising, corkscrew hairs, perifollicular bleeding, bleeding gums. Vitamin D: Fat-soluble. See *rickets/osteomalacia.* Vitamin E: Fat-soluble. *Deficiency:* Rare, if on parenteral nutrition, abetalipoproteinaemia, acanthocytes on film. Vitamin K: Fat-soluble. Given IM or orally after birth. *Sources:* Dairy, green leafy vegetables, soya/rapeseed oil. *Deficiency:* Haemorrhage, ↑prothrombin time. Riboflavin (vitamin B$_2$): *Deficiency:* Does not occur in isolation. Glossitis, geographical tongue, angular cheilitis, conjunctivitis, seborrhoeic dermatitis. Niacin (B$_3$ nicotinic acid and nicotinamide): *sources:* Widespread. *Deficiency (pellagra):* Rare. Maize-only diets (eg Africa), Hartnup's disease, carcinoid, alcohol abuse, poor diet, isoniazid. Dementia, eczema, diarrhoea, absent ankle/ knee jerks with upgoing plantars.

Vitiligo

CLINICAL NOTES

Epidemiology: 1-2% of the population. M=F. Aetiology/ risk factors: Autoimmune, neuronal, genetic. Clinical features: Well demarcated hypopigmented lesions, non-inflammatory, associated with other autoimmune diseases. Complications: May cover >80% of body, low self-esteem, depression, stigma.

INVESTIGATIONS

Clinical diagnosis.

MANAGEMENT

Camouflage, sunscreen, topical steroid ointment, tacrolimus, azathioprine, phototherapy, depigmentation of normal skin (bleach, laser, cryotherapy), grafts, counselling.

Vitreous detachment

CLINICAL NOTES

Epidemiology: Common. Aetiology/risk factors: Age, iritis, surgery, trauma, myopia. Clinical features: Flashing lights, floaters, painless. Complications: Vitreous haemorrhage, retinal tear/ detachment (multiple floaters, visual disturbance).

MANAGEMENT

Refer to exclude retinal involvement/visual defect. *Retinal tear:* Laser to reduce risk of detachment.

Volvulus

CLINICAL NOTES

Epidemiology: About one in 500 live births. Aetiology/ risk factors: Congenital predisposition. Clinical features: Abdominal distension, bilious vomiting (including newborns/children), pain, malaise, PR bleeding, intermittent volvulus (change in bowel habit), tender abdominal mass. Complications: Complete bowel obstruction, shock, oedema, peritonitis, infarction, gangrene, sepsis, death.

INVESTIGATIONS

FBC, U&E, pH, crossmatch, abdominal X-ray, erect chest X-ray, contrast studies, USS, CT, diagnostic laparoscopy.

MANAGEMENT

Resuscitation, analgesia. Sigmoid volvulus, consider conservative approach; others, eg caecal, surgery +/– stoma.

Von Hippel-Lindau disease

CLINICAL NOTES

Inherited disorder causing multiple tumours, benign and malignant, in CNS and viscera. Epidemiology: Rare. Aetiology/risk factors: Autosomal dominant (tumour suppressor gene defect). Clinical features: Symptoms begin between 10 and 30 years of age. Brain/spinal cord haemangiomata. Retinal, liver and renal angiomata. Renal cell carcinoma (bilateral), endolymphatic sac tumours, phaeochromocytoma. Pancreas, liver, renal and epididymal cysts. Retinal detachment.

INVESTIGATIONS

USS, CT, MRI, 24-hour urine collection (urinary catecholamines), genetic testing.

MANAGEMENT
Genetic counselling, surgery, radiotherapy, laser therapy. Treat complications accordingly.

Von Willebrand's disease

CLINICAL NOTES
Epidemiology: Common. F>M. Aetiology/risk factors: Autosomal dominant, autosomal recessive, hypothyroidism, aortic stenosis, Wilms' tumour. Clinical features: Asymptomatic, purpura, epistaxis, bruising, menorrhagia, excessive wound bleeding, haemarthrosis.

INVESTIGATIONS
FBC, LFT, tests for activity and von Willebrand factor (vWF) levels; results depend on disease subtype. Factor VIII clotting activity, ristocetin-induced platelet aggregation, vWF antigen, bleeding time.

MANAGEMENT
No treatment may be required in mild forms, safety education, desmopressin, VIII-vWF complex (FFP or cryoprecipitate), may require recombinant VIII.

Vulval carcinoma

See also
— *Vulval intraepithelial neoplasia*

CLINICAL NOTES
Epidemiology: Increasing. Squamous (90%), basal cell, melanoma, adenocarcinoma. Two in three arise from lichen sclerosus, one in three from VIN. *Subtype 1:* Older women, non-smokers, non-HPV related, associated with lichen sclerosus/planus. *Subtype 2:* Younger women, HPV-related, smokers, immune paresis. Clinical features: Pruritus (45%), bleeding (14%), pain, burning, skin change, vulval lump, dysuria, dyspareunia.

INVESTIGATIONS
Biopsy, MRI.

MANAGEMENT
Wide local excision, vulvectomy, node dissection, pelvic exenteration, adjuvant radiotherapy, radical radiotherapy.

Vulval intraepithelial neoplasia (VIN)

See also
— *Vulval carcinoma*

CLINICAL NOTES
Premalignant lesion. *High grade:* Age 30s-40s, vulval carcinoma in situ, vulval atypia, bowenoid papulosis, Bowen's disease, erythroplasia of Queyrat. Associated with HPV 16, 18, immunodeficiency, CIN. *Differentiated:* High risk of progression to invasive disease, postmenopausal women, used to be called simplex type, associated with lichen sclerosus. Clinical features: Asymptomatic (50%), pruritus, burning, dyspareunia, PCB, IMB, red/brown/pink/whitish raised vulval leisons. Complications: SCC.

INVESTIGATIONS
Biopsy.

MANAGEMENT
HPV vaccination protective, excision, topical 5FU, imiquimod cream, laser ablation, monitoring.

Waardenburg syndrome

CLINICAL NOTES
Epidemiology: Rare genetic disorder. Various subtypes. Clinical features: Sensorineural deafness, white forelock, adjoining eyebrows, iris heterochromia, facial asymmetry, may be associated with Hirschsprung's disease. Complications: Cleft lip/palate.

MANAGEMENT
MDT approach. Genetic counselling.Treat complications accordingly.

Waldenström's macroglobulinaemia

CLINICAL NOTES
Epidemiology: Elderly. Clinical features: Lymphadenopathy, hepatosplenomegaly, headaches, malaise, night sweats, fever. Complications: Osteoporosis, hyperviscosity syndrome, haemolysis, haemorrhage, immunodeficiency.

INVESTIGATIONS
Anaemia, ↓plts, ↑ESR, IgM monoclonal gammopathy.

MANAGEMENT
Observation and monitoring, chemotherapy, plasmapheresis if hyperviscosity.

Wallenberg's syndrome

CLINICAL NOTES
See *lateral medullary syndrome*

Warts

CLINICAL NOTES
Epidemiology: 4% prevalence. Aetiology/risk factors: HPV direct contact/contaminated surfaces, immunosuppression, eczema. Clinical features: Painless or painful lesions. Common – roughened papules; plain – flat flesh-coloured/pigmented; plantar – verrucae, rough, black dots (thrombosed capillaries); filiform – finger-like growths. May occur in clusters. Complications: Some HPV strains, eg 16, 18, associated with cervical cancer; secondary infection.

MANAGEMENT

Two in three resolve in less than two years without treatment. Limit spread by covering. Salicylic acid (11% for all areas except face, 50% for feet, do not use if DM or PVD, two in three clear within two weeks). Cryotherapy (one to two treatments every three weeks, painful), occlusive dressing after softening with warm water soaks, file down twice a week, duct tape (six days at a time) to stimulate immune attack (may take two months to clear), pulsed dye laser, photodynamic therapy, podophyllin/podophyllotoxin/intralesional interferon for anogenital warts, formaldehyde if DM/PVD.

Weber's syndrome

See also
— *Cerebrovascular accident*

CLINICAL NOTES

Clinical features: Midbrain lesion (usually CVA). IIIrd nerve palsy and contralateral hemiplegia.

Wegener's granulomatosis

CLINICAL NOTES

Vasculitis. Can be life-threatening due to end organ damage. Epidemiology: Rare. Clinical features: Necrotising granulomas, epistaxes, haemoptysis, rhinitis, sinusitis, otitis media, oral ulceration, malaise, fatigue. Complications: Gum hypertrophy, glomerulonephritis, cranial nerve palsy, deafness, hypertension, saddle-nose deformity, pyoderma gangrenosum, eye (conjunctivitis, corneal ulceration, episcleritis, scleritis, orbital granulomas, uveitis, retinitis), death.

INVESTIGATIONS

FBC, U&E, cANCA (inactive disease, 63% sensitive, 99.5% specific; active disease, 91% sensitive, 99% specific; used for diagnosis and monitoring), pANCA. Urinalysis, chest X-ray.

MANAGEMENT

Systemic corticosteroids, cyclophosphamide, plasma exchange, long-term immunosuppression.

Weil's disease

CLINICAL NOTES

See *leptospirosis and Weil's disease*

Wernicke's encephalopathy

CLINICAL NOTES

Aetiology/risk factors: Thiamine (vitamin B$_1$) deficiency, alcohol withdrawal, hyperemesis, anorexia nervosa, pregnancy, pre-eclampsia, gastric cancer, dietary. Clinical features: Confusion, diplopia, falls, acute confusion, hypotension, hypothermia, nystagmus, VIth nerve palsy, conjugate gaze palsy, gait ataxia. Complications: Four in five develop Korsakoff's psychosis (severe memory loss, confabulation, retrograde amnesia).

INVESTIGATIONS

FBC, U&E, LFT, glucose, ↓serum thiamine, ↑pyruvate.

MANAGEMENT

Parenteral thiamine, treat alcohol withdrawal.

Whipple's disease

CLINICAL NOTES

Epidemiology: Rare. Aetiology/risk factors: *Tropheryma whippelii* infection, HLA-B27, M>F. Clinical features: Malapsorption, malnutrition, diarrhoea, arthritis, fever. Complications: Weight loss, cardiac involvement, GI haemorrhage, scurvy, ataxia.

INVESTIGATIONS

Tests to suggest malabsorption eg ↓Hb, ↓Ca^{2+}, ↓albumin. IgM against *T whippelii* PCR. Small bowel biopsy. D-xylose absorption test.

MANAGEMENT

Antibiotics, nutritional and dietary support. Treat complications accordingly.

Whooping cough (pertussis)

CLINICAL NOTES

Epidemiology: Reduction with immunisation as part of schedule. Aetiology/risk factors: *Bordetella pertussis*. Incubation seven to 10 days. Clinical features: Coryza and catarrh (highly infectious phase) followed by paroxysms of dry cough interspersed by an inspiratory whoop in younger children. Facial petechiae. Cough may last a few months. Complications: Subconjunctival haemorrhage, severe fatigue, meningitis, encephalitis, otitis media, hernia, rectal prolapse, anoxic seizure, pneumothorax, infantile death.

INVESTIGATIONS

Nasopharyngeal swab, serology.

MANAGEMENT

Macrolide eg erythromycin in early stages to reduce infectivity, admit young children (significant mortality risk especially aged less than six months), supportive, suction, O$_2$, hydration, systemic steroids if severe.

Williams syndrome

CLINICAL NOTES

Epidemiology: Rare. Aetiology/risk factors: Genetic, often sporadic. Clinical features: Clinodactyly, learning difficulties, pectus excavatum, flat nasal bridge, epicanthic folds, dental anomalies. Complications: Attention deficit, supravalvular aortic valve stenosis, pulmonary stenosis, pulmonary artery stenosis, hypercalcaemia, hypertension.

⚕ INVESTIGATIONS
Genetic studies, X-ray, echocardiography, cardiac catheterisation, Ca^{2+}.

⛉ MANAGEMENT
MDT approach, family support. Treat complications accordingly.

Wilms' tumour (nephroblastoma)

📖 CLINICAL NOTES
Epidemiology: Fifth most common childhood tumour; most common intra-abdominal tumour of childhood (20% all childhood malignancies), occurs mainly up to four years of age. Aetiology/risk factors: 1% familial, genetic (eg chromosome 13, trisomy 8 and 18), sporadic, may be part of a syndrome. Clinical features: Asymptomatic, fever, malaise, anorexia, fatigue, mass found on routine examination or by parents, abdominal pain/distension, haematuria (not common). Complications: Lymphadenopathy, encephalopathy, retinopathy, metastases (haematogenous metastases to bone, brain, liver, lung), bilateral tumours (associated with congenital anomalies), IVC obstruction, von Willebrand's disease.

⚕ INVESTIGATIONS
Urinalysis/microscopy (microscopic haematuria), consider urinary catecholamines to exclude neuro-blastoma. Chest X-ray, abdominal X-ray, IVP, USS (abdomen), CT (abdomen/pulmonary), MRI (abdomen), venography (for IVC obstruction), bone scan.

⛉ MANAGEMENT
Depending on stage, surgery (avoid renal biopsy), chemotherapy, radiotherapy. 90% survival.

Wilson's disease (hepatolenticular degeneration)

📖 CLINICAL NOTES
Excessive copper in tissues. Epidemiology: Rare. Aetiology/risk factors: Chromosome 13 mutation, autosomal recessive. Presents in teens. Clinical features and complications: Hepatitis, cirrhosis, chronic liver disease, hepatic failure, hepatocellular carcinoma, haemolysis, headaches, neuropsychiatric disease (tremor, ataxia, salivation, may mimic Parkinson's disease, spasticity, dystonia, seizures, affective disorders, psychosis, impulsivity), cardiomyopathy, cardiac

decompensation/failure, sunflower cataracts (slit lamp), Kayser-Fleischer rings, optic neuritis, Fanconi syndrome, nephrocalcinosis, arthritis, chondrocalcinosis, recurrent miscarriage, infertility, arthritis, fatal without treatment.

⚕ INVESTIGATIONS
↓Serum ceruloplasmin, LFT, ↑liver transaminases, ↑ALT, ↑urinary copper, liver biopsy.

⛉ MANAGEMENT
Family screening, avoid hepatic insults/copper-rich diet, copper chelation (penicillamine, zinc, dimercaprol), liver transplant, monitoring. Treat complications accordingly.

Wolff-Parkinson-White syndrome

📖 CLINICAL NOTES
Epidemiology: About 1.5 per 1,000 people. Aetiology/risk factors: Congenital accessory pathway (Bundle of Kent) causing pre-excitation of ventricles. Clinical feartures: Asymptomatic, palpitations, presyncope, syncope. Complications: AF, atrioventricular reentry tachycardia (AVRT) with rapid ventricular response, acute heart failure, shock.

⚕ INVESTIGATIONS
ECG – short PR interval (pre-excitation) with delta wave.LAD. Type A – upward deflection in V1; type B – downward deflection in V1. Ambulatory ECG (ventricular arrhythmia). Echocardiogram to look for congenital defects. Electrophysiological studies.

⛉ MANAGEMENT
Beta-blockade, sotalol, amiodarone, flecainide. Avoid AV blockade eg digoxin/verapamil (encourages conduction via accessory bundle). Ablation of accessory pathway, ICD device.

Xeroderma pigmentosum

📖 CLINICAL NOTES
Inability to repair DNA damage by UV light. Epidemiology: ↑in Japanese population. Aetiology/risk factors: Autosomal recessive. Clinical features: Dry skin, photosensitivity, sunburn, telangiectasia, CNS degeneration. Complications: Malignant melanoma, BCC, SCC.

⚕ INVESTIGATIONS
Skin biopsy with fibroblast culture, genetic testing, prenatal diagnosis available.

⛉ MANAGEMENT
UV protection, treat complications accordingly, genetic counselling.

Yaws

 CLINICAL NOTES

Aetiology/risk factors: Chronic *Treponema pallidum* infection, tropical areas. Clinical features: Incubation up to one month. Painless primary lesion (mother yaw) followed by development of further lesions. Bone pain and swelling. Complications: Scarring and deformity.

 INVESTIGATIONS

Dark field microscopy.

MANAGEMENT

Penicillin.

Yellow fever

CLINICAL NOTES

Acute viral haemorrhagic disease. Epidemiology: Africa, South America. Aetiology/risk factors: Viral, mosquito vector. Incubation three to six days. Clinical features: Fever, jaundice, sore throat, headache, nausea, vomiting, haemoptysis, myalgia. Complications: Haemorrhage, (toxic phase), renal failure, cardiac arrhythmia, pneumonia, confusion, seizure, coma, high mortality (20%).

INVESTIGATIONS

↓WCC, serology, clotting, ECG, chest X-ray.

MANAGEMENT

Vaccination (compulsory in some countries), no specific treatment available (previous infection confers lifelong immunity), supportive, treat complications accordingly.

Yellow nail syndrome

CLINICAL NOTES

Epidemiology: Rare. Aetiology/risk factors: Lymphatic hypoplasia. Clinical features: Thick yellow nails, onycholysis, swollen ankles, pleural effusion. Complications: Bronchiectasis, COPD, lung malignancy.

INVESTIGATIONS

Chest X-ray, pulmonary CT, lung function tests.

MANAGEMENT

No specific treatment. Treat complications accordingly.

Zollinger-Ellison syndrome

CLINICAL NOTES

Aetiology/risk factors: Gastrin-secreting tumour (may be malignant and multiple, most in pancreas), sporadic (most cases), MEN. Clinical features: Severe peptic ulcer disease, malabsorption, diarrhoea. Complications: Perforated viscus, GI haemorrhage.

INVESTIGATIONS

Gastrin (fasting), CT, somatostatin scintigraphy (non-specific).

MANAGEMENT

High-dose PPI, octreotide, chemotherapy, surgery may be required.

DISEASES

APPENDICES

CAGE QUESTIONNAIRE

This is best used in a clinical setting as part of a general clinical history taking, and may be phrased informally.

Have you ever felt you should **C**ut down on your drinking?

Have people **A**nnoyed you by criticising your drinking?

Have you ever felt bad or **G**uilty about your drinking?

Have you ever had a drink first thing in the morning to steady your nerves or to get rid of a hangover (**E**ye opener)?

Source: Ewing JA. Detecting alcoholism. The CAGE questionnaire. *JAMA*. 1984 Oct 12;252(14):1905-7. Copyright © 1984 American Medical Association. All rights reserved.

CHA$_2$DS$_2$-VASc SCORE

The 2009 Birmingham Schema Expressed as a Point-Based Scoring System, with the acronym CHA$_2$DS$_2$-VASc

RISK FACTOR	SCORE
Congestive heart failure/LV dysfunction	1 point
Hypertension	1 point
Age ≥ 75 years	2 points
Diabetes mellitus	1 point
Stroke/TIA/TE	2 points
Vascular disease (prior myocardial infarction, peripheral artery disease, or aortic plaque)	1 point
Age 65-74 years	1 point
Sex category (ie female gender)	1 point

Source: Reproduced with permission from the American College of Chest Physicians. Lip GY, Nieuwlaat R, Pisters R, Lane DA, Crijns HJ. Refining clinical risk stratification for predicting stroke and thromboembolism in atrial fibrillation using a novel risk factor-based approach: the euro heart survey on atrial fibrillation. *Chest*. 2010 Feb;137(2):263-72.

HAS-BLED BLEEDING RISK SCORE

Clinical characteristics composing the HAS-BLED Bleeding Risk Score

LETTER	CLINICAL CHARACTERISTIC	POINTS AWARDED
H	Hypertension	1
A	Abnormal renal and liver function (1 point each)	1 or 2
S	Stroke	1
B	Bleeding	1
L	Labile INRs	1
E	Elderly	1
D	Drugs or alcohol (1 point each)	1 or 2

HAS-BLED = Hypertension, Abnormal renal/liver function, Stroke, Bleeding history or predisposition, Labile INR, Elderly (>65 years), Drugs/alcohol concomitantly.

Source: Reproduced with permission from the American College of Chest Physicians. Pisters R, Lane DA, Nieuwlaat R, de Vos CB, Crijns HJ, Lip GY. A novel user-friendly score (HAS-BLED) to assess 1-year risk of major bleeding in patients with atrial fibrillation: the Euro Heart Survey. *Chest* 2010 Nov;138(5):1093-100.

MRC DYSPNOEA SCORE

1	Not troubled by breathlessness except on strenuous exercise.
2	Breathlessness when hurrying or walking up a slight incline.
3	Walks slower than contemporaries on level ground due to breathlessness/has to stop to catch breath when walking at own pace.
4	Stops for breath after walking about 100m/a few minutes on level ground.
5	Too breathless to leave home, or experiences breathlessness when dressing or undressing.

Source: Adapted from Fletcher CM, Elmes PC, Fairbairn MB et al. The significance of respiratory symptoms and the diagnosis of chronic bronchitis in a working population. *BMJ* 1959; 2:257-66.

SCOFF QUESTIONNAIRE

Do you make yourself **S**ick because you feel uncomfortably full?

Do you worry you have lost **C**ontrol over how much you eat?

Have you recently lost more than **O**ne stone in a 3 month period?

Do you believe yourself to be **F**at when others say you are too thin?

Would you say that **F**ood dominates your life?

One point for every "Yes"; a score of ≥2 indicates a likely case of anorexia nervosa or bulimia

Source: Reproduced with permission. Morgan JF, Reid F, Lacey JH. The SCOFF questionnaire: assessment of a new screening tool for eating disorders. *BMJ* 1999;319:1467 © BMJ Publishing Group Ltd.

MISSED PILL RULES FOR COMBINED ORAL CONTRACEPTIVES

If ONE pill has been missed
(48–72 hours since last pill in current packet or **24–48 hours late** starting first pill in new packet)

↓

Continuing contraceptive cover
- The missed pill should be taken as soon as it is remembered
- The remaining pills should be continued at the usual time

↓

Minimising the risk of pregnancy
Emergency contraception (EC) is not usually required but may need to be considered if pills have been missed earlier in the packet or in the last week of the previous packet

If TWO OR MORE pills have been missed
(>72 hours since last pill in current packet or **>48 hours late** starting first pill in new packet)

↓

Continuing contraceptive cover
- The most recent missed pill should be taken as soon as possible
- The remaining pills should be continued at the usual time
- Condoms should be used or sex avoided until seven consecutive active pills have been taken
  This advice may be overcautious in the second and third weeks, but the advice is a backup in the event that further pills are missed

↓

Minimising the risk of pregnancy

If pills are missed in the first week (Pills 1–7)	If pills are missed in the second week (Pills 8–14)	If pills are missed in the third week (Pills 15–21)
EC should be considered if unprotected sex occurred in the pill-free interval or in the first week of pill-taking	No indication for EC if the pills in the preceding 7 days have been taken consistently and correctly (assuming the pills thereafter are taken correctly and additional contraceptive precautions are used)	OMIT THE PILL-FREE INTERVAL by finishing the pills in the current pack (or discarding any placebo tablets) and starting a new pack the next day

The rules above do not include advice on Qlaira® (estradiol valerate/dienogest). Refer to the Qlaira SPC available at www.medicines.org.uk for guidance on the management of missed tablets.

Source: Faculty of Sexual and Reproductive Healthcare. FSRH Guidance (October 2011). Combined Hormonal Contraception. Clinical Effectiveness Unit. Copyright ©Faculty of Sexual and Reproductive Healthcare 2011

AGREED ADULT CLINICAL BIOCHEMISTRY REFERENCE INTERVALS

TEST NAME	UNITS	RANGE LOW	RANGE HIGH	COMMENTS
Sodium	mmol/L	133	146	
Potassium	mmol/L	3.5	5.3	
Urea	mmol/L	2.5	7.8	
Chloride	mmol/L	95	108	
Bicarbonate	mmol/L	22	29	
Phosphate	mmol/L	0.8	1.5	
Magnesium	mmol/L	0.7	1.0	
Albumin	g/L	35	50	
Total protein	g/L	60	80	
Osmolality	mmol/kg	275	295	
Alkaline phosphatase (ALP)	U/L	30	130	IFCC candidate method p-NPP using AMP buffer
Creatine kinase (CK)	U/L	40 25	320 (M) 200 (F)	Ranges are for white Caucasian only; other ethnic groups may have higher values
Bilirubin (total)	µmol/L		<21	
Adjusted calcium	mmol/L	2.2	2.6	Use adjustment equations normalised to mean calcium of 2.4 mmol/L
Urate	µmol/L	200 140	430 (M) 360 (F)	
Carbamazepine	mg/L	4	12	
Phenobarbitone	mg/L	10	40	
Phenytoin	mg/L	5	20	
Theophylline	mg/L	10	20	
Valproate	mg/L			No range should be quoted
Paracetamol	mg/L			No range should be quoted
Salicylate	mg/L			No range should be quoted
Methotrexate	µmol/L			No range should be quoted
Lithium	mmol/L	0.4	1.0	Complies with NPSA guidance

TEST NAME	UNITS	RANGE LOW	RANGE HIGH	COMMENTS
Digoxin	microgram/L	0.5	1.0	
Tacrolimus	µg/L			
250H vitamin D (including separately measured D2 & D3)	nmol/L			No ranges recommended
PTH	pmol/L			Method dependent
GNP/NTproBNP	ng/L			
Troponin I	ng/L			Method dependent
Troponin T	ng/L			
24 h urine calcium	mmol/24h	2.5	7.5	
24 h urine urate	mmol/24h	1.5	4.5	
24 h urine phosphate	mmol/24h	15	50	
24 h urine magnesium	mmol/24h	2.4	6.5	

Source: Reproduced with permission from Pathology Harmony Group, Clinical Biochemistry Outcomes, January 2011. Pathology Harmony is funded by the Department of Health. The group sees appropriate national implementation of agreed harmonisation as absolutely vital rather than implementation on regional level. www.pathologyharmony.co.uk

REFERENCE INTERVALS

AGREED PAEDIATRIC CLINICAL BIOCHEMISTRY REFERENCE INTERVALS

TEST NAME	AGE	UNITS	RANGE LOW	RANGE HIGH	COMMENTS
Sodium	No age-related differences	mmol/L	133	146	
Plasma potassium	Neonate	mmol/L	3.4	6.0	
	Infant	mmol/L	3.5	5.7	
	1-16 years	mmol/L	3.5	5.0	
Urea	Neonate	mmol/L	0.8	5.5	
	Infant	mmol/L	1.0	5.5	
	1-16 years	mmol/L	2.5	6.5	
Magnesium	Neonate	mmol/L	0.6	1.0	
	Infant - 16 years	mmol/L	0.7	1.0	
Plasma lactate	No age-related differences	mmol/L	0.6	2.5	Enzymatic method only
Bilirubin (total)	14 days - 16 years	µmol/L		<21	
Albumin	Neonate	g/L	30	45	
	Infant	g/L	30	45	
	1-16 years	g/L	30	50	
Calcium	Neonate	mmol/L	2.0	2.7	Actual not adjusted
	Infant - 16 years	mmol/L	2.2	2.7	
Phosphate	Neonate	mmol/L	1.3	2.6	
	Infant	mmol/L	1.3	2.4	
	1-16 years	mmol/L	0.9	1.8	
Alkaline phosphatase (ALP)	Neonate	U/L	70	380	p-NPP using AMP buffer
	Infant - 16 years	U/L	60	425	
Ammonia	Sick or premature	µmol/L		<150	Follow metbio. net guidance
	Neonate	µmol/L		<100	
	Infant - 16 years	µmol/L		<50	
Plasma bicarbonate	No age-related differences	mmol/L	19	28	

Definitions: Neonate <4 weeks; Infant 4 weeks – 1 year

Reproduced with permission from Pathology Harmony Group, Clinical Biochemistry Outcomes, January 2011. Pathology Harmony is funded by the Department of Health. The group sees appropriate national implementation of agreed harmonisation as absolutely vital rather than implementation on regional level. www.pathologyharmony.co.uk

2-1 HEART BLOCK

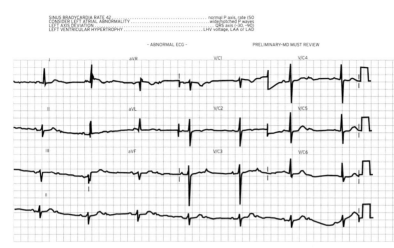

SINUS BRADYCARDIA RATE 42 .... normal P axis, rate (50
CONSIDER LEFT ATRIAL ABNORMALITY .... wide/notched P waves
LEFT AXIS DEVIATION .... QRS axis (-30, -90)
LEFT VENTRICULAR HYPERTROPHY .... LHV voltage, LAA or LAD

- ABNORMAL ECG -   PRELIMINARY-MD MUST REVIEW

25 mm/s   10 mm/mV   F – 0.05 Hz   - 150 Hz

25 mm/s

ANTEROSEPTAL STEMI

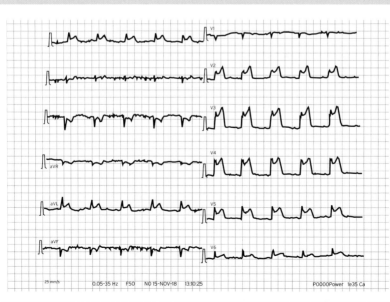

25 mm/s   0.05-35 Hz   F50   N0 15-NOV-18   13:10:25   P0000Power   1e35 Ca

COMPLETE HEART BLOCK

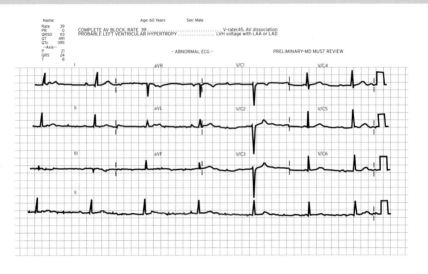

Name: Age: 60 Years   Sex: Male
Rate   39
PR   0   COMPLETE AV BLOCK, RATE 39 .... V-rate(45, AV dissociation
QRSD   113   PROBABLE LEFT VENTRICULAR HYPERTROPY .... LVH voltage with LAA or LAD
QT   491
QTc   395
--Axis--   - ABNORMAL ECG -   PRELIMINARY-MD MUST REVIEW
P   21
QRS   24
T   8

25 mm/s   10 mm/mV   F ~ 0.05 Hz   ~ 150 Hz

LEFT BUNDLE BRANCH BLOCK

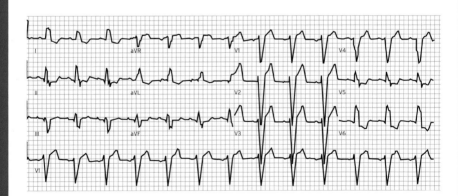

24 HOUR ECG RHYTHM OF A WOMAN WITH SICK SINUS SYNDROME WHO COLLAPSED AND NEEDED A PACEMAKER

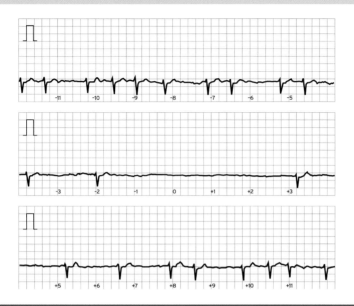

Q WAVES

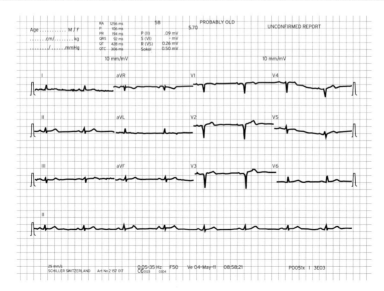

PACED ECGs

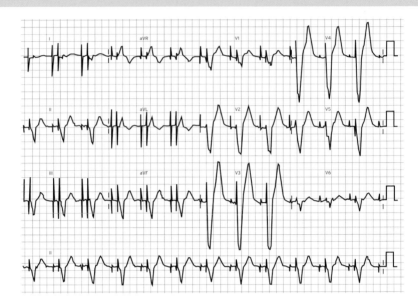

WOLFF-PARKINSON-WHITE SYNDROME

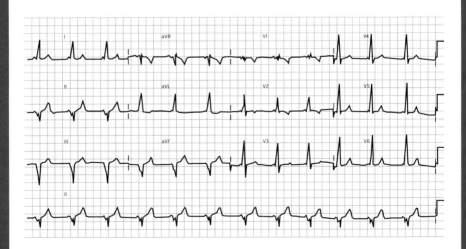

VENTRICULAR SEPTAL DEFECT

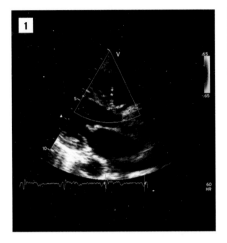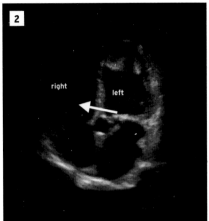

1. Colour Doppler showing a left-to-right shunt through an infracristal ventricular septal defect, parasternal long axis view
2. Inlet VSD in the apical four-chamber view

ATRIAL SEPTAL DEFECT

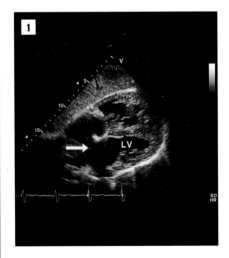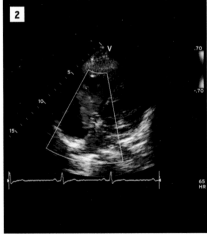

1. Secundum ASD with Eisenmenger's syndrome; arrow indicates location of defect
2. Colour flow mapping can be used to aid diagnosis and assess the size of the lesion in ASD

ECHOCARDIOLOGY AND LEFT VENTRICULAR FUNCTION

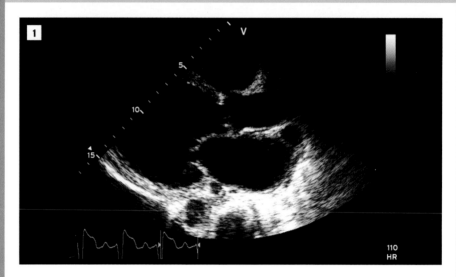

1. A dilated ventricle may indicate cardiomyopathy

MITRAL VALVE STENOSIS

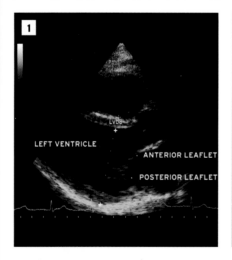
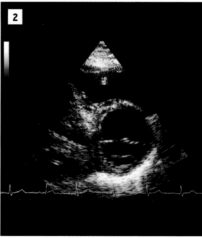

1. The anterior leaflet domes during diastole if restricted
2. Short axis view allows the valve area to be mapped

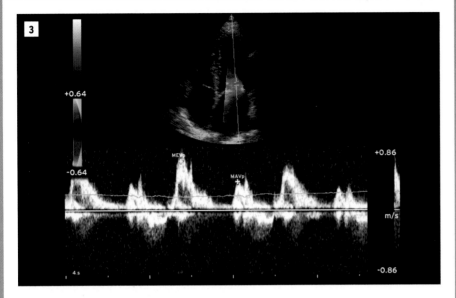

3. Doppler techniques allow the valve area to be calculated from the pressure half-time, indicating severity of mitral stenosis

MITRAL REGURGITATION SECONDARY TO ENDOCARDITIS

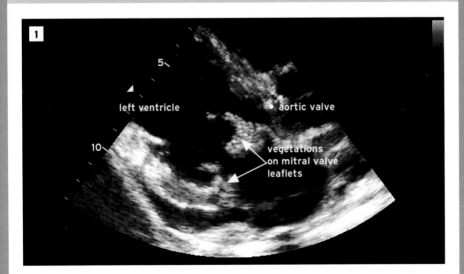

1. Mitral valve endocarditis in the parasternal long-axis view

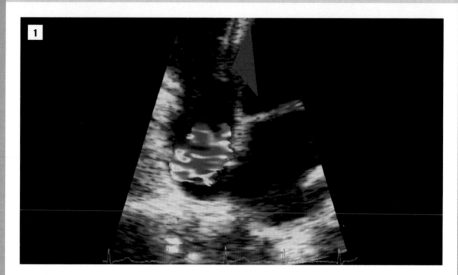

1. Tricuspid regurgitation, four-chamber view

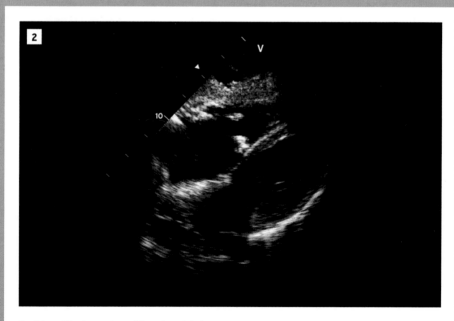

2. Triscupid valve endocarditis, subcostal view

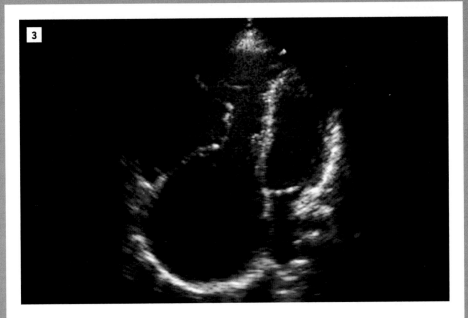

3. Ebstein's anomaly, four-chamber view

HEART FAILURE

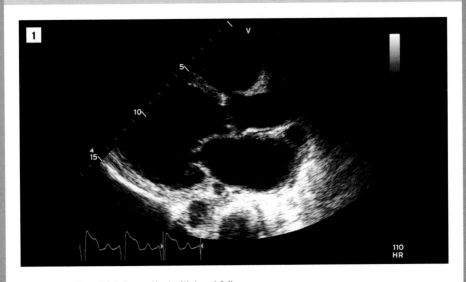

1. Dilated left ventricle in a patient with heart failure

ANTERIOR DERMATOME MAP OF THE BODY

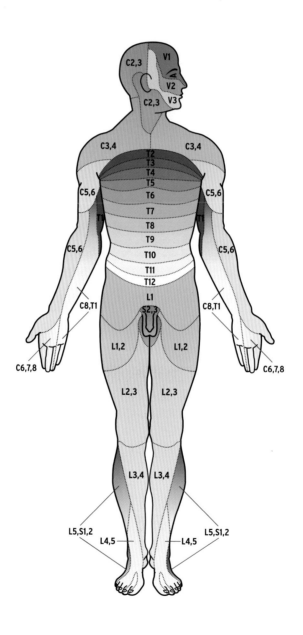

POSTERIOR DERMATOME MAP OF THE BODY

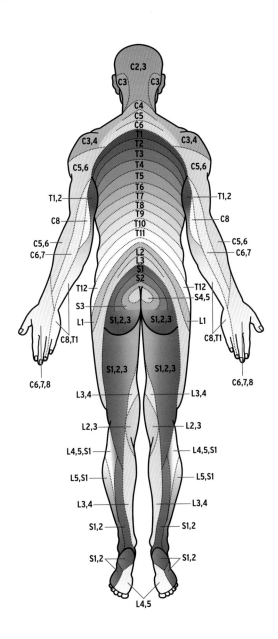

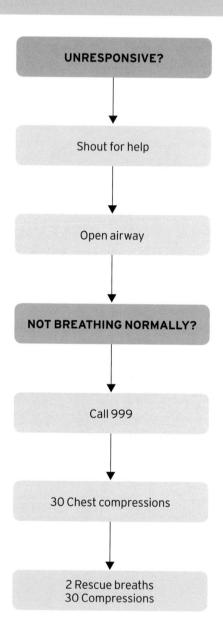

UNRESPONSIVE?

Shout for help

Open airway

NOT BREATHING NORMALLY?

Call 999

30 Chest compressions

2 Rescue breaths
30 Compressions

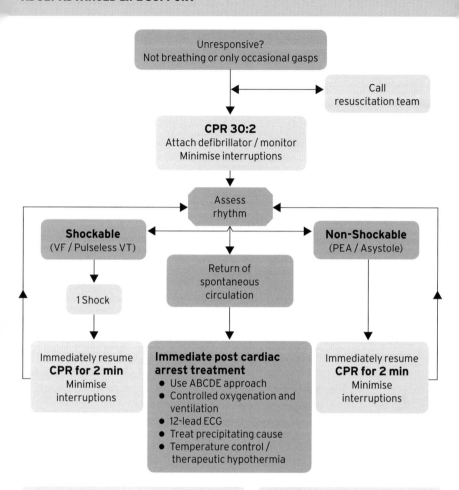

Source: Reproduced with the kind permission of the Resuscitation Council (UK)

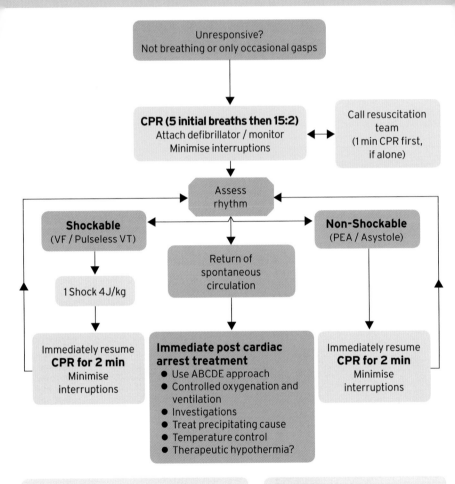

Unresponsive?
Not breathing or only occasional gasps

CPR (5 initial breaths then 15:2)
Attach defibrillator / monitor
Minimise interruptions

Call resuscitation team
(1 min CPR first, if alone)

Assess rhythm

Shockable
(VF / Pulseless VT)

Return of spontaneous circulation

Non-Shockable
(PEA / Asystole)

1 Shock 4J/kg

Immediately resume
CPR for 2 min
Minimise interruptions

Immediate post cardiac arrest treatment
- Use ABCDE approach
- Controlled oxygenation and ventilation
- Investigations
- Treat precipitating cause
- Temperature control
- Therapeutic hypothermia?

Immediately resume
CPR for 2 min
Minimise interruptions

During CPR
- Ensure high-quality CPR: rate, depth, recoil
- Plan actions before interrupting CPR
- Give oxygen
- Vascular access (intravenous, intraosseous)
- Give adrenaline every 3-5 min
- Consider advanced airway and capnography
- Continuous chest compressions when advanced airway in place
- Correct reversible causes

Reversible causes
- Hypoxia
- Hypovolaemia
- Hypo- / hyperkalaemia / metabolic
- Hypothermia
- Tension pneumothorax
- Toxins
- Tamponade – cardiac
- Thromboembolism

Source: Reproduced with the kind permission of the Resuscitation Council (UK)

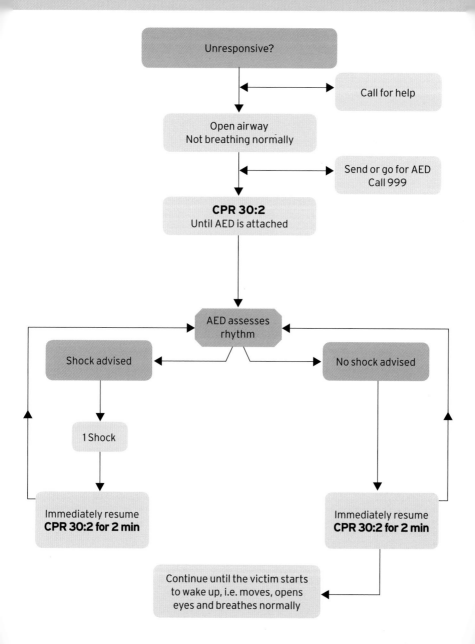

Source: Reproduced with the kind permission of the Resuscitation Council (UK)

Anaphylactic reaction?

↓

Airway, **B**reathing, **C**irculation, **D**isability, **E**xposure

↓

Diagnosis – look for:
- Acute onset of illness
- Life-threatening Airway and/or Breathing and/or Circulation problems[1]
- And usually skin changes

↓

- **Call for help**   • Lie patient flat   • Raise patient's legs

↓

Adrenaline[2]

↓

When skills and equipment available:

- Establish airway
- High flow oxygen
- IV fluid challenge[3]
- Chlorphenamine[4]
- Hydrocortisone[5]

Monitor:
- Pulse oximetry
- ECG
- Blood pressure

---

1 Life-threatening problems:
Airway: swelling, hoarseness, stridor
Breathing: rapid breathing, wheeze, fatigue, cyanosis, SpO_2 < 92%, confusion
Circulation: pale, clammy, low blood pressure, faintness, drowsy/coma

2 Adrenaline *(give IM unless experienced with IV adrenaline)*
IM doses of 1:1000 adrenaline (repeat after 5 min if no better)
- Adult: 500 microgram IM (0.5mL)
- Child more than 12 years: 500 microgram IM (0.5mL)
- Child 6-12 years: 300 microgram IM (0.3mL)
- Child less than 6 years: 150 microgram IM (0.15mL)

Adrenaline IV to be given only by experienced specialists Titrate:
Adults 50 microgram; Children 1 microgram/kg

3 IV fluid challenge:
Adult: 500-1000mL
Child: crystalloid 20mL/kg

Stop IV colloid if this might be the cause of anaphylaxis

	4 Chlorphenamine (IM or slow IV)	5 Hydrocortisone (IM or slow IV)
Adult or child more than 12 years	10mg	200mg
Child 6-12 years	5mg	100mg
Child 6 months to 6 years	2.5mg	50mg
Child less than 6 months	250 microgram/kg	25mg

Source: Reproduced with the kind permission of the Resuscitation Council (UK)

NATIONAL POISONS INFORMATION SERVICE

The four centres of the National Poisons Information Service (Birmingham, Cardiff, Edinburgh and Newcastle) provide a year-round, 24 hour information service for healthcare staff on the diagnosis, treatment and management of poisoning. The information is provided online (TOXBASE) and by telephone.

TOXBASE www.toxbase.org

Use as the primary source of information for the routine diagnosis, treatment and management of patients suffering from exposure to a wide range of substances and products. Information provided is sufficient to cope with most cases of poisoning.

TELEPHONE 0844 892 0111 (National Poisons Information Service)

Use for clinically or toxicologically complex cases that cannot be answered by TOXBASE.

REPUBLIC OF IRELAND 01809 2566 (National Poisons Information Centre)

Use for enquiries originating in the Republic of Ireland.

WHO PAIN LADDER FOR CANCER PAIN RELIEF

The WHO pain ladder is a framework for providing symptomatic pain relief. The three-step approach is inexpensive and 80-90% effective.

● **By mouth**
The oral route is preferred for all steps of the pain ladder

● **By the clock**
Cancer pain is continuous - analgesics should be given at regular intervals (every 3-6 hours), not on demand

● **Adjuvants**
To help calm fears and anxiety, adjuvant analgesics may be added at any step of the ladder

TREATMENT LADDER

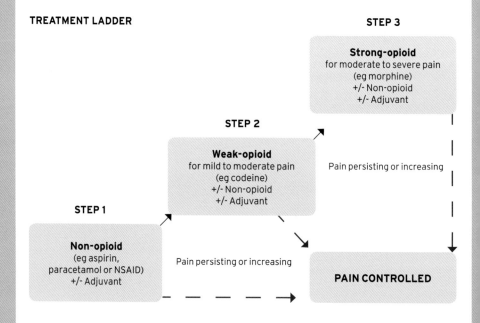

STEP 3

Strong-opioid
for moderate to severe pain
(eg morphine)
+/- Non-opioid
+/- Adjuvant

STEP 2

Weak-opioid
for mild to moderate pain
(eg codeine)
+/- Non-opioid
+/- Adjuvant

Pain persisting or increasing

STEP 1

Non-opioid
(eg aspirin,
paracetamol or NSAID)
+/- Adjuvant

Pain persisting or increasing

PAIN CONTROLLED

● The ladder has no 'top rung' as there is no maximum dose for strong opioids.
● If pain is still a problem with high doses of morphine (eg greater than 300mg every 24 hrs), or if there are severe side effects, reconsider the cause of pain (eg bone pain may be better helped by NSAIDs) and/or seek specialist advice.

Source: WHO Pain Relief Ladder for cancer relief pain - available at www.who.int

OPIOID ANALGESICS: APPROXIMATE POTENCY EQUIVALENCE WITH ORAL MORPHINE

Analgesic	Conversion ratio to oral morphine	Recommended dosing frequency	Available formulations
ORAL			
Codeine	0.1	4-hourly	Tabs, oral soln
Dihydrocodeine	0.1	4-6-hourly (or 12-hourly if SR tabs)	Tabs, SR tabs, oral soln
Hydromorphone	5-7.5	4-hourly (or 12-hourly if SR caps)	Caps, SR caps
Morphine	1	4-hourly (or 12-hourly or once daily for SR prep)	Tabs, SR tabs, SR caps, oral soln, granules for susp
Oxycodone	1.5-2	4-6-hourly (or 12-hourly if SR tabs)	Caps, SR tabs, oral soln
Pethidine	0.1	6-8-hourly	Tabs
Tramadol	0.1	4-hourly (or 12-hourly or once daily for SR preps)	Tabs, SR tabs, caps, SR caps, oral soln, orodispersible tabs, sol tabs
SUBLINGUAL			
Buprenorphine	80	6-8-hourly or PRN	Sublingual tabs
SUBCUTANEOUS			
Diamorphine	3	4-hourly	Inj
Morphine	2	4-hourly	Inj
Oxycodone	2	4-hourly	Inj
INTRAMUSCULAR			
Diamorphine	3	4-hourly	Inj
Morphine	2	4-hourly	Inj
TRANSDERMAL			
Refer to individual Summaries of Product Characteristics (SPCs)			

Multiply by the potency ratio to convert an opioid dose to the equivalent dose of oral morphine
eg, oral dihydrocodeine 30mg qds = 120mg/day; 120mg x 0.1 = 12mg oral morphine/day

Divide by the potency ratio to convert an oral morphine dose to the equivalent dose of another opioid
eg, oral morphine 30mg bd = 60mg/day; 60mg/2 = 30mg subcutaneous oxycodone/day

- The conversion ratios in the above table are approximate and are included to provide guidance only.
- Doses will need to be titrated up or down for individual patients.
- When converting at high doses (eg morphine or equivalent doses of ≥1g/24 hrs) it is recommended to use a lower than calculated dose (eg 1/3-1/2 lower) - PRN doses may be used to make up any deficit while titrating to a satisfactory dose of the new opioid.
- These ratios may differ from local formularies or guidance.

Approximate relative potencies taken from Twycross R, Wilcock A. Palliative Care Formulary.
www.palliativedrugs.com

1. European Heart Rhythm Association; European Association for Cardio-Thoracic Surgery, Camm AJ, Kirchhof P, Lip GY, et al. Guidelines for the management of atrial fibrillation: the Task Force for the Management of Atrial Fibrillation of the European Society of Cardiology (ESC). *Eur Heart J* 2010: 31: 2369-429.
2. NICE. Diagnosis and initial management of acute stroke and transient ischaemic attack (TIA). CG68. London, NICE, 2008. Available from: www.nice.org.uk/CG68.
3. The Renal Association. The UK CKD eGuide. Available from: www.renal.org/whatwedo/InformationResources/CKDeGUIDE.aspx (accessed 10 November 2011).
4. NICE. Early identification and management of chronic kidney disease in adults in primary and secondary care. CG73. London, NICE, 2008. Available from: www.nice.org.uk/Guidance/CG73.
5. NICE. Management of chronic obstructive pulmonary disease in adults in primary and secondary care (partial update). CG101. London, NICE, 2010. Available from: www.nice.org.uk/CG101.
6. Wells PS, Anderson DR, Bormanis J, et al. Value of assessment of pretest probability of deep-vein thrombosis in clinical management. *Lancet* 1997; 350: 1795-8.
7. NICE. Diagnosis and management of type 1 diabetes in children, young people and adults. CG15. London, NICE, 2004. Available from: www.nice.org.uk/CG15.
8. NICE. The management of type 2 diabetes. CG87. London, NICE, 2009. Available from: www.nice.org.uk/CG87
9. International Expert Committee. International Expert Committee report on the role of the A1C assay in the diagnosis of diabetes. *Diabetes Care* 2009; 32: 1327-34.
10. NICE. Clinical management of primary hypertension in adults. CG127. London, NICE, 2011. Available from: www.nice.org.uk/CG127
11. Baddour LM, Wilson WR, Bayer AS, et al. Infective endocarditis: diagnosis, antimicrobial therapy, and management of complications: a statement for healthcare professionals from the Committee on Rheumatic Fever, Endocarditis, and Kawasaki Disease, Council on Cardiovascular Disease in the Young, and the Councils on Clinical Cardiology, Stroke, and Cardiovascular Surgery and Anesthesia, American Heart Association: endorsed by the Infectious Diseases Society of America. *Circulation* 2005; 111: e394-434.
12. The Renal Association. Clinical guidelines on acute kidney injury. Available from: www.renal.org/Clinical/GuidelinesSection/AcuteKidneyInjury.aspx#downloads (accessed 10 November 2011)
13. NICE. Secondary prevention in primary and secondary care for patients following a myocardial infarction. CG48. London, NICE, 2007. Available from: www.nice.org.uk/CG48.
14. NICE. The early management of unstable angina and non-ST-segment-elevation myocardial infarction. CG94. London, NICE, 2010. Available from: www.nice.org.uk/CG94.
15. LeGall JR, Loirat P, Alperovitch A. APACHE II--a severity of disease classification system. *Crit Care Med* 1986; 14: 754-5.
16. Lim WS, Badouin SV, George RC, et al. BTS guidelines for the management of community acquired pneumonia in adults: update 2009. *Thorax* 2009; 64(Suppl III):iii1-55.
17. Rotterdam ESHRE/ASRM-Sponsored PCOS consensus workshop group. Revised 2003 consensus on diagnostic criteria and long-term health risks related to polycystic ovary syndrome (PCOS). *Hum Reprod* 2004; 19: 41-7.
18. Wells PS, Ginsberg JS, Anderson DR, et al. Use of a clinical model for safe management of patients with suspected pulmonary embolism. *Ann Intern Med* 1998; 129: 997-1005.
19. Guidelines for the diagnosis of rheumatic fever. Jones Criteria, 1992 update. Special Writing Group of the Committee on Rheumatic Fever, Endocarditis, and Kawasaki Disease of the Council on Cardiovascular Disease in the Young of the American Heart Association. *JAMA* 1992; 268: 2069-73.
20. Cooper RJ, Hoffman JR, Bartlett JG, et al. Principles of appropriate antibiotic use for acute pharyngitis in adults: background. *Ann Intern Med* 2001; 134: 509-17.
21. Johnston SC, Rothwell PM, Nguyen-Huynh MN, et al. Validation and refinement of scores to predict very early stroke risk after transient ischaemic attack. *Lancet* 2007; 369: 283-92.
22. NICE. Urinary tract infection in children: diagnosis, treatment and long-term management. CG54. London, NICE, 2007. Available from: www.nice.org.uk/CG54.